Social Problems

Social Problems

CRM/RANDOM HOUSE

Rodney Stark

University of Washington

with

Ronald L. Akers
University of Iowa

Robert C. Atchley
Miami University

James E. Blackwell
University of Massachusetts at Boston

Katharine Briar
Edmonds Community College

Scott Briar
University of Washington

Archie Brodsky
Boston, Massachusetts

Howard S. Erlanger
University of Wisconsin, Madison

Michael J. Hindelang
S.U.N.Y. at Albany

William Kornblum
C.U.N.Y. Graduate Center

Stanton Peele
Harvard University

Lynne Roberts
University of Washington

Marijean Suelzle
Northwestern University

R. Jay Turner
University of Western Ontario

Rita Roffers Weisbrod
University of Washington

Rolf Schulze, Graphics Advisor
San Diego State University

Brief biographies of the contributors and
attribution of their work in this text appear
on pages 466–468

Preface

Any new textbook ought to aim to overcome important inadequacies of other available books. In pursuit of a better social problems book, I began with several strong beliefs about current texts in sociology.

First, sociologists know much more than the texts we assign would make it appear. Sociology is not simply a rather unpleasant language. We have done much more than develop a special vocabulary. Our claim to student attention rests on our ability to explain (even if only partially) why certain important things happen in society.

Second, no school or brand of sociology has a corner on truth. Furthermore, the fact that sociologists are engaged in vigorous debates about how best to explain many social phenomena is not a shameful secret. These disputes reflect the most important work going on in sociology and reveal us at our best—as involved in an ongoing, relevant, human activity. Inviting students into our debates engages their interest and allows them to learn more of what we know.

Third, depth and clarity are not incompatible. A textbook does not have to be simple-minded in order to be clear and understandable. Important material does not have to be left out in order to have a book that students will enjoy and understand. Textbooks should be judged by the standards of fine journalism as well as those of scholarship—their task is to explain, clarify, and communicate the significant material.

Fourth, to be serious about communicating with students requires the use of every suitable means available. Good graphics are not decorations. Pictures, graphs, charts, and drawings can be used to open additional paths to understanding the subject matter. For example, a photograph can take a somewhat general discussion in the text and, by making the point personal and concrete, drive home the meaning. The graphics in this book offer a blend of design elements that invite and inform, provoke and personalize. Combined with the text, they create a unique and, I believe, effective invitation to investigate social problems.

Fifth, given the breadth of sociological interests, it is hard to think that one person could write a general social problems text that is current, comprehensive, or authoritative throughout. Even if one person could master all the specialities relevant to a social problems textbook, by the time he or she had completed the later chapters, the earlier ones would already be out of date. I believe it is safe to predict that many more texts in the future will be collaborative efforts.

Sixth, a good text must have a common voice and a consistent structure; it must be integrated yet flexible. To achieve the unity and still have the benefits of a collective effort, one person must take full responsibility for the final product. That was my role in this book.

Before its revision, my original blueprint for the book was reviewed by more than two dozen colleagues with experience teaching social problems in a variety of different kinds of schools. Qualified specialists were contacted to write draft chapters, and the chapter outlines were refined and expanded in consultation with each contributor. Through the process of writing, gathering advice (and encouragement) from reviewers, and rewriting, I developed the drafts into final chapters. I consulted with each contributor as revision after revision passed back and forth. In addition to frequent checks with the contributors, I had the benefit of reviews by a number of colleagues. John Clausen, Travis Hirschi, and Wilson Record reviewed the blueprint and each chapter in both its first draft and "nearly final" draft forms. Their criticisms and suggestions resulted in wholesale improvements in every part of the manuscript. Finally, James McMillin (California State College, Bakersfield) and Larry Frye (St. Petersburg Jr. College) read each chapter with a special eye for the student's perspective, and each contributed significantly to the logic and clarity of the final product. In consequence of all these efforts, I think we have produced a book that has all the benefits of using many specialists but in final form is tightly integrated and speaks to readers with one voice, which, for better or worse, is mine.

The major assumption guiding the book is that an adequate discussion of any given social problem has three fundamental elements. The analysis of each social problem is therefore done in three parts:

Part I, The Problem: to define and describe certain conditions and explain why they are regarded as a social problem. What are these conditions? To what extent do they exist? Where are they? Who is involved and who regards them as a problem?

Part II, Sources: to explain what is responsible for the problem. To the best of our knowledge, what causal factors are operating (or not operating)? What is required here is a very systematic examination of current explanations of the problem, including what we are pretty sure of, what is in dispute, and what remains a mystery. Because competing theories and explanations are directed at different aspects of a social problem, their mutual implications must be sorted out and explained. The search for explanations in each substantive chapter is therefore divided into five distinct levels of analysis, including the most micro and the most macro.

Part III, Responses: to explain what has been done about the problem and with what consequences. Have some responses made the problem worse (or caused other problems)? Which responses have been effective? What could be and is likely to be done? (Here it was vital to have the aid of specialists with intimate knowledge of current programs as well as the judgment to see past the fads of the moment and identify major trends.)

Throughout the book you will notice many charts designed to aid the student's understanding of the text. In addition, a concise chapter review concludes each chapter. An extensive glossary-index appears at the back of the book.

I recognize that our selection of the problems to be included in the text will not please everyone (nor can the discussions of any particular problem satisfy every taste). What we tried to do was to provide orderly, understandable, comprehensive, and authoritative treatment of those problems that presently hold the greatest public and scholarly attention. On these grounds, it seemed imperative to include a chapter on sex-based inequalities, for example, but not to devote a chapter to the youth movement, a topic that seems to have lost public attention since the late 1960s. For, as is pointed out in Chapter 1, social problems are defined by social processes, not by textbook writers or publishers.

Rod Stark
Seattle, Washington, 1974

Contents

Analyzing Social Problems

No one needs to take a sociology course to discover that the United States has serious social problems. Newspapers, magazines, television, and everyday experiences make all of us aware of crime, drug addiction, mental illness, poverty, racial conflict, and all the other problems included in this book. The aim here is to enlarge your understanding of social problems—to help you understand why these problems exist and what might be done to eliminate them or at least to make them less severe. This unit introduces the essential tools that social science uses to analyze specific social problems. Through social-science concepts, theories, and research, we seek the causes of and solutions to these problems.

Chapter 1 explains the social and political nature of social problems. It shows how perceptions of and responses to these problems depend on the particular society in which they arise. Social problems in the United States typically go through a series of stages, and at each stage they are shaped by the values, political conflicts, and governmental policies of American society.

Chapter 2 has two major goals. The first is to offer a concise introduction to the fundamental social-science concepts and theoretical premises on which all later discussions of social problems are based. It begins with basic concepts about human beings and small human groups and proceeds to a discussion of societies as systems. It explains major disputes and competing viewpoints and points out their relevance to understanding social problems. Its second goal is to use these basic concepts to examine the special features and problems of large-scale, modern, urban societies.

The difference between what "everybody knows" about social problems and what social scientists claim they know about them rests on research. Chapter 3 uses the detective-story approach to introduce you to the basic procedures of social-science research. It invites you to look over the shoulders of researchers as they conduct three major studies on juvenile delinquency. Each study uses a different method of research, and you will be able to see how different kinds of questions must be answered by different research methods. By knowing something about how actual research is done, you will be better able to evaluate the worth of the many research findings on which later chapters are based.

It is true that neither the ancient wisdoms nor the modern
sciences are complete in themselves. They do not stand alone. They call for
one another. Wisdom without science is unable to penetrate the full
sapiential meaning of the created and material cosmos. Science
without wisdom leaves man enslaved to a world of unrelated
objects in which there is no way of discovering (or
creating) order and deep significance in man's own
pointless existence.

Thomas Merton

Bruce M. Dean

1

Social Problems and Social Movements

All textbooks begin with a definition of their subject matter, but for a text devoted to social problems, a definition might seem unnecessary. Surely everyone knows what a social problem is—aren't social problems simply widespread conditions that have harmful consequences for society? Unfortunately, the issue is not that simple. To a considerable extent, social problems have to be discovered—perhaps even invented.

During the late nineteenth century, for example, many patent medicines for sale in this country contained narcotics, and many Americans were as dependent on drugs as today's drug addicts are. For a long time no one considered this state of affairs a problem. Even after many people thought of drug addiction as a problem, it was not yet a *social* problem. It did not become one until people who regarded drug addiction as harmful began to organize and agitate to do something about drug use.

WHAT ARE SOCIAL PROBLEMS?

A state of affairs (real or imaginary) becomes a social problem when a significant number of people or a number of powerful people define it as a problem. As we shall see, this is so whether or not people's perceptions of social conditions accurately reflect the facts. Furthermore, the mere existence of a seriously harmful condition in society does not constitute a *social* problem. People often ignore such conditions, at least for a long time.

In defining a social problem, we will consider the way groups of people perceive objective—factual, or real—conditions. In fact, one useful, recent definition identifies social problems as "the activities of groups making assertions of grievances and claims with respect to some putative [or alleged] conditions" (Kitsuse and Spector, 1973). This definition is based on people's activities and therefore makes no assumptions about the accuracy of their claims that a social problem exists.

SOCIAL CONDITIONS AND SOCIAL PROBLEMS

To focus on people's perceptions (their view of things) is to take a perspective that differs from the dominant social-science view of social problems, which has emphasized the study of objective—real or factual—conditions in society (Blumer, 1971). The emphasis on objective conditions is often useful. Indeed, it is an honorable tradition for social scientists to employ research to *create* social problems—that is, to take a leading role in asserting publicly that harmful conditions exist and need correcting. For example, a long series of detailed studies, in England and the United States, of the living and working conditions of the poor during the late nineteenth and early twentieth centuries played a central role in transforming poverty into a social problem and bringing about many legal reforms. The most famous and exhaustive study was conducted by the English merchant Charles Booth, who initially set out to demonstrate that socialist claims about poverty among workers were false. Finding instead that poverty was, in fact, widespread and extreme, he played a major role in sustaining the grievances of the poor and in obtaining new government policies (Gordon, 1973).

Nevertheless, the emphasis on studies of objective social conditions has tended to blur the important distinction between objective social conditions and social problems. Instead of emphasizing the fact that social conditions and social problems may be independent of each other, many social scientists pay attention to the differences among objective conditions themselves, between those that are *recognized* as problems and those that are not (Merton and Nisbet, 1971). To understand how and why social problems arise, it is important to understand that objective social conditions differ from people's perceptions of them and that there is no direct one-to-one relationship between such conditions and the presence or absence of claims that a social problem exists. Harmful social conditions do not always become the focus of group assertions that something is wrong and needs righting. And sometimes such assertions are made on the basis of a wholly inaccurate perception of objective conditions.

Most social problems, however, do have some basis in reality. Groups of people usually do not get upset over nothing or over mere imaginings (Becker, 1966). It is more likely, for example, that people would call narcotics use a social problem if the drugs did have some influence on the psycho-

logical states of individuals than if they did not. But there is no guarantee that social problems will either result from or reflect actual social conditions that exist.

We have already noted that people were aware of many of the properties of narcotics long before they called drug use a social problem. Similarly, racism existed for centuries before it was defined as a social problem. So did sexism. Indeed, as will be apparent throughout this book, social problems are born in conflict and controversy: They are preeminently political in nature. Typically, there is considerable resistance to the "discovery" of a social problem—the grievances and the demands for change by one social group typically impinge on the interests of other social groups who strenuously resist having some condition defined as a social problem, such as the group Booth represented when he undertook his research on the English poor to discredit radical claims that poverty was a problem.

Efforts to discredit a social problem may fail, but efforts to define some condition as a social problem may also fail. For example, efforts by many conservative religious groups to define contemporary American sexual standards as a social problem have not so far succeeded. Indeed, large numbers of Americans still refuse to acknowledge racism, sexism, pollution, and poverty as contemporary social problems. Thus, an objective condition in society may or may not become a social problem.

By the same token, a social problem may be created even though there are no objective conditions to support it. For example, during the 1930s, Adolf Hitler and his Nazi party rose to absolute power in Germany partly on the basis of claims that the presence of Jews in German society constituted a severe social problem. According to Hitler, the Jews were a subhuman species dedicated to perverting and subverting the German people and were the cause of widespread social harm through their secret manipulation of the economic system (the Jew as capitalist) as well as through their efforts to incite revolution among the workers (the Jew as communist). By the time the Nazi reign ended, its leaders had murdered 6 million Jews in an effort to solve this "pressing social problem."

Figure 1.1   Public perceptions of social problems are influenced by propaganda, and thus these problems often come and go quickly. During the 1950s, Senator Joseph McCarthy caused many Americans to believe that Communist infiltration of the government was a serious problem. The McCarthyism period (top) was followed by widespread apprehension about nuclear attack. Many Americans built home bomb shelters and schools held air-raid drills (bottom).

No informed, reasonable person today would agree with Hitler's view of Jews. Rather, we recognize the Nazi charges as an extraordinary instance of religious and ethnic prejudice. In fact, we now regard the anti-Semitism of the Nazis, not the behavior of the Jews, as the real social problem of that period.

Consider another example, which is taken up again in Chapter 4. Scientists now have evidence to argue against the classification of marijuana as a narcotic and against the popular belief that marijuana produces violent and dangerous mental states and leads to hard-drug use. However, certain groups are still successful in sustaining such beliefs and in defining marijuana use as a serious social problem requiring stiff legal penalties and vigorous government action.

We have emphasized the *independence of objective conditions and social definitions* not to suggest that social problems are usually capriciously or arbitrarily formulated but to alert you to the *process* through which social problems arise and are studied. The fact is that social scientists must give careful attention both to social problems as group activities and to the actual state of affairs in society. We must understand how a social problem does or does not come to be publicly defined as such and whether such a public definition accurately depicts reality.

The remainder of this chapter explains how social problems come into being. Later chapters pay close attention to the contrast between the public definition of how things are and what research shows or suggests about the way things really are.

SOCIAL PROBLEMS AS SOCIAL MOVEMENTS

In 1971, Herbert Blumer, one of the grand old men of sociology, published a stinging rebuke of the widespread tendency in social science to define social problems wholly in terms of objective social conditions. We have already discussed some reasons why such a practice may be unfruitful and may lead to confusion. In addition, Blumer demonstrated that despite the notion that social problems are rooted in "intrinsically harmful or malignant" objective conditions in society, sociologists usually fail to discover social problems in advance

5

of popular opinion. Instead, social-science recognition of social problems is continually "veering with the winds of public identification of social problems."

Illustrations are legion—I cite only a few of recent memory. Poverty was a conspicuous social problem for sociologists a half-century ago, only to practically disappear from the sociological scene [but not from society] in the 1940s and early 1950s, and then to reappear in our current time. Racial injustice and exploitation in our society were far greater in the 1920s and 1930s than they are today; yet the sociological concern they evoked was little until the chain of happenings following the Supreme Court decision on school desegregation and the riot in Watts. Environmental pollution and ecological destruction are social problems of very late vintage for sociologists although their presence and manifestation date back over many decades. (Blumer, 1971)

However, Blumer was not content merely to chastise his colleagues. He also offered a theoretical perspective for defining social problems: He argued that we must regard social problems as a manifestation of *collective behavior,* that is, as a group activity. More specifically, Blumer argued that social problems arise only through *social movements*—the activities of some social group to bring about or resist change in society. Social problems exist only when some social movement has succeeded in convincing itself and others that conditions are wrong and ought to be made right and that some plan of action ought to be formulated and implemented. Thus, social problems exist only when some social condition is selected, identified, and widely recognized by society as a problem.

It is this process, Blumer argues, that sociologists must examine and explain if they are to begin to see social problems coming rather than to trail along behind public opinion. However, the process through which social problems arise is very complex, for it

is a highly selective process, with many harmful social conditions and arrangements not even making a bid for attention and others falling by the wayside in what is frequently a fierce competitive struggle. Many push for societal recognition but only a few come out the end of the funnel. (Blumer, 1971)

Blumer provided only a bare sketch of the process through which social problems are generated

through social movements and enter into the political and social agenda of a society. But in 1973, Malcolm Spector and John I. Kitsuse took up this problem and developed a natural-history model for the analysis of social problems.

THE SOCIAL CAREER OF A SOCIAL PROBLEM

Spector and Kitsuse (1973) surveyed the history of a number of prominent social problems and found that there are a number of elements common to all. From these elements, they sketched four basic stages through which social problems pass. Their model does not explain the origins of social problems, but it does suggest the typical career of a social problem and the variety of social forces that come into play. A major reason why we have chosen to use Spector and Kitsuse's model in detail in this chapter is because it provides a systematic basis for understanding why it is so difficult to do something *effective* about social problems. When you have studied the institutional responses to particular problems treated in later chapters of this text, you will see that typically a variety of laws and massively expensive programs have been directed at every one of them. Yet the problems persist. Sometimes the laws and the programs have even made the problems worse. Throughout this book, many explanations are offered about why so many attempts to do good go wrong. But as will be made clear, many of the barriers to resolving social problems are inherent in the very processes through which social problems are socially defined and become the focus of public activity.

STAGE 1: AGITATION

By definition, social problems refer to the activities of a group claiming to have a grievance about some condition in society. Therefore, the process through which a social problem comes into being begins when some group of people discovers a grievance and begins to agitate on behalf of its claim. Initially, people in the group direct their activity toward two goals: (1) convincing others that the problem exists and (2) trying to initiate

THE NEW YORK TIMES, SUNDAY, JANUARY 15, 1967.

SAUL D. ALINSKY

A Professional Radical Rallies the Poor

By JOHN KIFNER

The New York Times (by George Tames)
FIGHTER: Saul Alinsky, a "Jewish Robin Hood," was preparing last week to organize the poor in Brooklyn, N. Y.

Like some wandering Jewish Robin Hood, Saul D. Alinsky, 57, has spent the last quarter-century merrily goading politicians, businessmen, religious figures, well-meaning liberals and other agents of the "Establishment" into paroxysms of wrath by his abrasive and successful methods of organizing the poor.

Last week, the man who describes himself as a "professional radical" was being attacked from two different directions. One attack came from antipoverty officials in the Fort Greene section of Brooklyn, where he had been hired by a group of clergymen as a once-a-month consultant to a nascent organization. The other attack came from Eastman-Kodak, the largest employer and dominant influence in Rochester, where his group is battling for implementation of a job-training agreement signed by a Kodak executive and then declared "unauthorized" and nonexistent by the company.

Sardonic, idealistic and profane, Mr. Alinsky appears to revel in such outrage. "You should have seen what they did to me in Oakland," he chortles. "The City Council passed a resolution to keep me out of town and introduced one to send 50 feet of rope and tell me to hang myself. I sent them a box of diapers."

The attacks often prove one of his major theses — that given the opportunity, the powers-that-be almost inevitably react with tactical blunders and so do much of his organizing for him.

Mr. Alinsky's philosophy and tactics are outlined in his 1947 book, "Reveille for Radicals," which begins with a Whitmanesque paen to American democracy. But he contends, democracy has evolved into the making of decisions on the basis of the interests and pressure of economic and political power blocs. The poor have no such power block, he argues, and are thus excluded from the democratic process and doomed to the scraps of the larger society.

Through his Chicago-based Industrial Areas Foundation, he contracts with representative local groups to build organizations of Negroes, slum dwellers or migrant laborers to compete in their own interests with established powers. The going rate for an Alinsky project is $50,000 a year, and he draws a $23,000-a-year salary from the nonprofit foundation.

Much of his business—he is currently operating in Buffalo, Rochester, Detroit and Kansas City—now comes from church groups, which does not inhibit him from taking delight in shocking clergymen by raising a glass in the Loyalist toast of the Spanish Civil War: "Death to our enemies."

Alinsky organizers filter through a slum seeking out existing organizations—ranging from those centered on churches to the more amorphous ones that cluster loosely in poolrooms and barbershops. Such organizations and their natural leaders are forged into a coalition, which after a period of two or three years is expected to develop its own leadership and financial independence.

The Alinsky groups' tactics are often designed to embarrass the "power structure" into living up to its own rules and rhetoric. But they draw a distinction between the marches of the civil rights movement, whose effects are sometimes transitory, and the creation of an organization which enables people to deal with their own problems.

Mr. Alinsky's groups have halted urban renewal plans that would have displaced the poor, developed job-training programs, won representation on decision-making bodies like school and antipoverty boards and forced city officials to deal with the problems of housing, police, sanitation and education. But their most important effect in the ghetto may be intangible: the replacement of alienation with participation.

Perhaps the most well-known of his groups is The Woodlawn Organization (TWO), now in its fourth year on Chicago's South Side. Through successful demonstrations against crooked merchants, rent strikes, picketing of slumlords in their homes in white suburbs and protests against inadequate schools, Mr. Alinsky welded a fragmented and apathetic slum into a formidable organization. It not only defeated the University of Chicago's urban renewal plan, but has become a major force in the city.

He has been denounced as a fomenter of "class conflict," but is currently packing college lecture halls from Berkeley to Smith, and—apparently briefly—in the Government's war on poverty, which he dismisses as a "prize piece of political pornography."

Mr. Alinsky was a consultant to the Federal pilot training program for organizers at Syracuse University. When the trainees began organizing Syracuse slum dwellers against city agencies, the Mayor was furious and funds were abruptly withdrawn. City boosters were glad to be rid of the bespectacled rebel, but are still smarting over his exit line.

"Hell," he growled when asked if he was sorry to be leaving, "have you ever been to Syracuse?"

Figure 1.2   The late Saul Alinsky was a successful moral crusader for the poor and other deprived groups. He taught disadvantaged groups to protest effectively on their own behalf through strong political organization.

Figure 1.3   Agitation draws public attention to the grievances of particular groups. The Detroit riots of 1967 and similar demonstrations by blacks in other cities helped raise public awareness of the problems of blacks but also created a certain amount of white "backlash."

action to improve conditions and to attack the alleged cause of the grievance.

It is not always the victims of the alleged problem who initiate this first stage. Alcoholics did not lead the battle for prohibition, nor have addicts led the campaign against drugs. Moral crusaders may act on behalf of victims and on behalf of what they regard as a better, more humane, more decent society. Or persons who have a direct personal stake in some state of affairs may raise the claim that it constitutes a social problem, as have women and racial minorities, such as blacks.

To a considerable extent, as Spector and Kitsuse (1973) point out, this initial stage is devoted to transforming "private troubles into public issues." However, not all, and perhaps very few, such attempts are successful. The complaining group may fail to enlist public support for a variety of reasons, including the following.

1. The group's claims may be too vague, incorrectly focused, or demonstrably false.

2. The group may be too insignificant and powerless to gain attention.

3. The group may adopt ineffective or even counterproductive strategies for pressing its claims.

4. The group may arouse opposition from other groups with conflicting values or competing interests and lose out in the ensuing competition for support.

To successfully create a social problem the complaining group must overcome or avoid each of these potential impediments. We now consider each in greater detail.

Claims

A group may experience some grievance or condition of deprivation in a variety of ways. As we pointed out, groups may correctly or incorrectly recognize what is bothering them. For example, Betty Friedan argued in *The Feminine Mystique* (1963) that for a long time suburban housewives experienced considerable unhappiness but incorrectly blamed themselves, their spouses, or their families for their pain, not the role of housewife itself. Something was wrong, but they could not figure out what it was. One must be able to identify a grievance before one can make claims that it

7

needs to be corrected. Furthermore, it is possible that groups may incorrectly diagnose the cause of the condition they oppose. For example, Hitler blamed the Jews for the economic troubles of Germans; many Americans blamed communists for the riots in black ghettos and on college campuses in the 1960s. The extent to which a group correctly identifies a troublesome condition and its cause will greatly influence the group's course of action and its consequences.

When people in a group are incorrect about what is bothering them or misunderstand the cause of a problem, they may still succeed in convincing others of their claim, but their success will be less likely. In principle, at least, their claims are subject to convincing disproof. For example, suppose that some ethnic or racial minority claimed that the courts needed massive reforms because they discriminate against that minority group. If it could be demonstrated that this group did not, in fact, receive discriminatory punishments for crimes and

that for the same crimes their sentences were the same as those given to others, then the fact that they had a disproportionate number of their members in prison would most likely be discounted as a grievance. Had the group instead argued that the misery of their living conditions caused too many of their young people to commit crimes and to end up in prison, they might still be ignored, but their grievance could not be dismissed as a false claim. Thus, if a group wrongly assesses their problem, they may attempt to place responsibility inaccurately and to call for irrelevant remedies. Indeed, when groups with vague and misdefined grievances succeed in generating a social problem, the results are frequently harmful—drug laws and programs that deepen the drug problem, criminal-justice systems that produce crime, mental hospitals that create insanity, or welfare systems that foster a new form of dependency. Conversely, when a group has a clear-cut sense of what is wrong and advocates specific action programs, it is

8

Figure 1.4 Groups with well-defined goals, numerical strength, financial backing, prestige, and other advantages are more likely to be successful in getting the public to recognize their grievances. The women's movement, for example, is well organized and has adopted broad-based goals that have won it much support over the last few years.

more likely to succeed in its efforts and to alleviate conditions. An example is how the legalization of abortion came about, which is taken up later.

Power

It seems obvious that the probability that some group will succeed in getting a sympathetic hearing for its grievances will partly depend on who its members are. Groups composed of the rich, groups that are very large, groups that are well organized, or groups accorded high social honor can make bigger waves than small, poor, disorganized, or stigmatized groups. For example, the women's movement has had rapid and widespread impact on American society in defining sex-based inequalities as a social problem (see Chapter 11). The gay liberation movement, on the other hand, with its much smaller base of potential members and the social stigma attached to its members, has had very limited success over approximately the same period of time.

A critical task faced by all social movements attempting to define a social problem is to build up sufficient strength. Typically, considerable effort is made in the beginning to enlist powerful supporters. For example, the civil rights movement relied heavily on the active support of influential white liberals until the black community could mobilize and organize a movement on its own. However, efforts designed to build the power of a movement also often serve to increase the extent of opposition.

Strategy

In the beginning, a major task in creating a social problem is to attract attention—to get society to listen. At any given moment, hundreds of groups with hundreds of messages are trying to get public attention. Most fail. Winning public attention has become a highly professional activity in American society. Groups that can afford to hire or that can recruit public-relations and advertising experts have a considerable advantage over other groups in getting a public hearing for their grievances. Regardless of the expertise available to them, all groups have a similar problem in strategy: to attract attention in a way that will not at the same time provoke outrage and opposition.

It is useful to think of social problems as efforts to change social *norms*. Norms are the socially accepted and enforced rules and expectations about which behavior in which circumstance is right or wrong, proper or improper. Norms imply what people should, ought to, or must do in certain situations. Inherent in social problems is the claim that some norm or set of norms is misguided, undesirable, dangerous, or even sinful. It is further claimed that in place of these norms a new or different norm or set of norms must be instituted.

A common initial strategy for groups seeking public attention is to publicly violate norms they object to and to act instead according to norms they advocate as superior. For example, Carrie Nation began chopping up saloons with her celebrated hatchet to demonstrate the prohibition movement's opposition to American norms governing social drinking. Similarly, on December 1, 1955, Rosa Parks, a black seamstress, sat down in the front of a city bus in Montgomery, Alabama, breaking the norm of segregated seating. Her action launched the famous black boycott of the buses that created a new era in the civil rights struggle and made Martin Luther King a national figure.

The strategic relevance of norm violation is that it attracts attention. Ordinarily, people conform to norms to avoid disapproval from others, or even to avoid punishment if breaking the norm carried severe sanctions. Potentially, norm violation is newsworthy—Walter Cronkite never reported how many women went to work wearing a brassiere, but he did give considerable coverage to a public burning of brassieres by a group of activist women in the news.

Although norm violation wins public attention, it may also offend the public. During the 1960s, campus demonstrations, strikes, and sit-ins attracted widespread publicity for students' opposition to the Vietnam War, but those activities impeded rather than speeded the development of antiwar sympathies (Mueller, 1973).

Furthermore, there is a danger that norm violation, once it is launched as a strategy for dramatizing and publicizing a social problem, has a tendency to get out of hand: groups may turn to more serious norm violations and therefore may provoke increased public hostility. Campus protests began

Figure 1.5   Some groups have used norm violations to draw public attention to their efforts to maintain their way of life. The Dukhobors, a Russian-Canadian religious and communal sect, has resisted government efforts to tax and school them. (Left) The Sons of Freedom, an extremist group of Dukhobors, protest materialism and government authority during a clothes-burning ceremony. They periodically strip naked and burn their clothing, their houses, and other belongings to show contempt for material goods.

with peaceful assemblies, turned to civil disobedience, and finally culminated in arson and bombings; the message was drowned out by the noise of the tactics and by the thunderous response of opponents.

Competition

Social problems involve the claim by some group that some unacceptable state of affairs must be changed. A social problem is therefore likely to be vigorously opposed by groups that hold contrary moral conceptions or that have a vested economic interest in the status quo. For example, the temperance movement met strong opposition from the liquor industry, whose livelihood was threatened by prohibition proposals, as well as from those who liked to drink and who denied that drinking was an immoral, sinful, or physically ruinous act. Similarly, demands for equality for women have not only run counter to government and industry's dependence on women for cheap clerical workers but have also challenged many men's and women's conceptions of femininity and proper female roles. For another example, the middle and upper classes perceive demands to reduce poverty as challenges to their own economic well-being and to their moral view that wealth is the legitimate reward for hard work, talent, far-sightedness, and other virtues.

Successfully raising a claim to a wide level of social acceptance means overcoming opposing claims. And the likelihood of success depends on three factors discussed previously: the relative power of proponents and their opponents; the clarity and accuracy of proponents' claims over those of opponents; and the adequacy of the adopted strategies and counterstrategies. In addition, the competition between proponents and opponents may, by itself, attract enough public attention to make a case that a social problem exists.

Consider the case of Ralph Nader and General Motors. Nader was an unknown young lawyer at the time he published his book *Unsafe at Any Speed* (1965), which alerted the public to the automobile industry's unconcern for safety in the design and construction of American automobiles. The book was a model of the kind of muckraking journalism that sometimes initiates the rise of a social problem; it presented clearly defined grievances and sharply focused explanations of who was to blame and why. Nader, however, was not the spokesman for any substantial group (car buyers are not organized), and he was limited to making promotional appearances and to giving testimony before congressional committees. His whole effort might have passed into history little noticed had it not been for the counterstrategy of General Motors. Instead of simply ignoring Nader,

General Motors panicked. The company sent private detectives out to shadow Nader and dig for dirt in his private life. The company even hired attractive women to try to proposition him. When these activities became public and General Motors executives had to admit their actions in congressional hearings, Nader became front-page news and his charges took on new weight. The public reasoned that his charges must be true and serious because General Motors had to resort to immoral tactics to oppose him. Thus, auto safety became an important social issue.

When a group reaches the point of successfully creating serious controversy and receives a considerable amount of public acceptance of its claims, the developing social problem typically undergoes a major transformation.

STAGE 2: LEGITIMATION AND CO-OPTATION

The natural history of a social problem changes in two important ways when major social institutions, usually government agencies, recognize the complaining group and begin to respond to the group's claims. First, the group (and its problem) receives *legitimation,* or official acknowledgment. The claimants, who may earlier have been regarded as peculiar, or even un-American, for speaking out strongly on a problem, are now treated as responsible and informed critics. For example, the public reputation of conservationists who vigorously warned throughout the 1960s that the nation was running out of energy greatly improved once the government admitted that an energy crisis had in fact occurred. Second, as government agencies enter the picture, they begin to take control of defining the problem and choosing its legitimate spokesmen. This process, a well-understood aspect of the behavior of large organizations, especially government bureaucracies, is called *co-optation.* Through co-optation, new interest or claimant groups are absorbed into the structure of an organization as a means of averting threats to the organization's stability (Selznick, 1966). The strategy is a "let's not try to lick them, let's get them to join us" principle. Often, opposition can be silenced or greatly reduced by putting the critics on the team, thus making them share the burden of

responsibility for decisions and increasing their stake in supporting the organization rather than opposing it. For example, during the campus protests of the 1960s, a major student demand was for some voice in campus decisions. Probably the majority of colleges and universities eventually responded by including student representatives on many important boards and committees. Yet, to anyone observing campuses today, it is obvious that including students in the decision making had vastly greater impact on quelling student protest than it did on changing the decision-making process. By absorbing students into the organization, the organization was not greatly changed. In fact, it became more stable by being exposed to less outside pressure. The student movement was thus co-opted.

As we shall see, Stage 2 may result in a solution to the social problem and thus mark the end of the process; more typically, the problem is merely changed and conflict over it renews.

11

Effects of Legitimation

Throughout Stage 1, a social problem ordinarily has only "unofficial" standing. The claimant group, although it may include high public officials in its ranks, is acting only in the capacity of private citizens in an effort to arouse public concern. But if the movement is successful, it eventually attracts, or even forces, official notice.

Initially, of course, such official notice may be quite hostile. During the late nineteenth and early twentieth centuries, official notice of workers' demands for the right to organize unions often took the form of police squads or soldiers sent to repress such activities. Similarly, early official notice of the civil rights movement often took the form of violent repression. Persons attempting to organize in black communities in the South were often murdered by segregationists (some of whom were law officers). Against the peaceful protest marchers, segregationists used firehoses, tear gas, dogs, and horse-mounted, club-flailing posses. Indeed, public revulsion to such scenes, which were shown on television, played a major part in winning support for the civil rights movement.

But when official recognition does take a more sympathetic initial form, or is made sympathetic

Life History of a Social Problem

Stage 1: Agitation
Victims of problem, interest group, or moral crusaders want public recognition of their problem.

Factors related to success of group:
1) Claims should be clear, concise, and correct in analysis of social problem and remedy.
2) Power of group is dependent on money, social status of members, knowledge, and organization and skills.
3) Strategy to win public attention and support through changing norms or violating existing norms without offending public.
4) Competition between groups with opposing views must be overcome through conflict, cooperation, or compromise.

Stage 2: Legitimation and Co-optation
Legitimation: Official acknowledgement of problem.
Co-optation: Official agencies define and take control of problem and choose "legitimate" spokespersons from groups making claims.

Effects of Legitimation: Appointment of government commission may mean that members of protest group become only witnesses or spokespersons—could spell end of group control.
Effects of Co-optation: Call on experts—government claims monopoly on understanding problem. Group may grow unexpectedly. Government often redefines problem and expands it.
Possible outcomes: Cooling out protesting group, dispelling claim, supporting claim, or righting grievance.

Stage 3: Bureaucratization and Reaction
Bureaucratic handling of problem not satisfactory to protest group—bureaucracy more interested in dealing with and processing complaints than in changing social conditions.

Fate of problem may rest on organizational features of government agency and its ability to deal with the bureaucracy.
Agency and bureaucracy may have interests at odds with those of protest group.

Stage 4: Reemergence of Movement
Rejection by protest group of official response (or lack of government action).
Development of new or alternative responses and institutions.

Emergence of new concerns and search for new institutions to press claims more effectively. Emergence of social reformers and private reformers.

Figure 1.6   A social problem is affected by the outcome of each stage it passes through in its career.

through continuing struggle, the protesting group and its claims will probably gain a higher standing than they had before.

Government is likely to take action beyond simple acknowledgment of a problem, however. A common initial response is to appoint a commission or committee to investigate the nature and the extent of the problem and to suggest corrective measures. At this point, a protest group may find itself transformed into spokesmen and expert witnesses, thus increasing its legitimate recognition. Spector and Kitsuse (1973) note that just as legitimation may be the claimants' "finest hour," legitimation may also "represent the beginning of the end of their control over the claims they raise." This is so even though group spokesmen get to air their views before committees, for "they are cast in the role of providing information rather than defining and negotiating the nature of the problem."

Effects of Co-optation

With the beginning of the official phase in the career of a social problem, the unofficial protest group is likely to be phased out of the operation. When government becomes officially involved in a problem, it usually calls on "experts" other than spokesmen for the protest group—including experts representing opposition groups. Indeed, government often quickly develops its own staff of experts and then claims monopoly on understanding the problem.

Furthermore, at this point the protest group may find itself with many unexpected "allies" and fellow complainants, often because the scope of the problem expands as others attempt to share in the group's initial success. Thus the civil rights movement became partly transformed into a poor people's movement that was expected to represent the interests of all poor people, not only of blacks. Subsequently, when radical groups argued that the problems of racism and poverty were inherent in the larger evil of capitalism, they applied considerable pressure on the civil rights and poor people's movement to become the vehicle for revolution.

The government may play a role in expanding the definition of the problem, but more often, it redefines the problem by narrowing the focus of the problem or diverting it. For example, the suf-

fragette movement at the turn of the century defined itself as a wide-ranging effort to overcome sex-based inequalities, but government succeeded in narrowing the issue to granting women the right to vote. Today, there are similar official pressures to narrow the focus of the women's liberation movement to the issue of job equality. Whatever else happens, official action usually quickly overshadows the unofficial group, at least temporarily. What becomes of the social problem at this point substantially depends on the outcome of official co-optation of the issue.

One outcome is that the government may cool out the protesting group by simply taking note of their grievances and promising to study them. As will be seen in later chapters, the mere appointment of a commission or investigating committee is often enough to satisfy public concern and to make the issue disappear from public view.

A second possibility is that the results of a government study will (correctly or incorrectly) dispell the claims of the protest group as unfounded. For example, in 1970, the President's Commission on Pornography reported that, contrary to the claims of those agitating for controls on the sexual content of books, magazines, and movies, there appeared to be no grounds for believing that exposure to pornographic material leads to sexual deviance or misconduct. (However, the Nixon Administration chose to ignore this finding.)

Even when government investigation supports the claims of the protest group, the problem may still go untended and the group's effort may dissipate. Many major recommendations by government commissions, from the United States Commission on Civil Rights to the National Advisory Commission on Civil Disorder, have gone unheeded by government. And after such recommendations have lingered for some time in the legislative or executive branches of government, the protesting groups may no longer be organized or interested in pushing for further action. Either way, it is clear that "commissions may be the burial ground of a great many social problems" (Spector and Kitsuse, 1973).

A fourth way that official action may end the career of a social problem is to remedy the grievances of the protesting group by effective action.

13

Righting grievances is most common when the protesting group's claims are sharply focused, when the remedy is clearly recognized and feasible, and when the only significant opposition is based on values and morality, not on economics.

An obvious example is the recent movement to legalize abortion. People had for some time regarded illegal abortion as a social problem, but efforts to prevent it (and thus end the death or serious injury of women) were unsuccessful. Then a combination of women's-rights and medical groups began to demand the legalization of abortion. Medical spokesmen argued that abortion is rightfully a medical decision to be made by a physician and his patient. Women's leaders argued that a woman has an unassailable right over her own body and ought to be able to choose whether or not to terminate pregnancy. At the same time, no significant groups in society had a stake either in a high birth rate or in providing expensive illegal abortions. On the contrary, the economic interests of the nation were widely regarded to lie in ending population growth. Furthermore, with modern medical techniques, a legal abortion is classified as minor surgery: both cheap and safe.

The only serious opposition to the legalization movement was on moral grounds. Some major religious bodies denounced abortion as murder. But even here, opposition was not unanimous, for many other religious bodies did not oppose the change—in fact, some actively supported it. With relative speed, in the 1960s states began to repeal or greatly liberalize laws against abortion. And within this climate of opinion, the Supreme Court completed the process in 1973 by declaring state laws against abortion unconstitutional, except in the case of the last three months of pregnancy and in the licensing of those permitted to perform the operation. Today there is no illegal-abortion social problem. And those who have made sporadic efforts to redefine legal abortion as a social problem have had no appreciable success so far.

It would be wrong, however, to assume that when government co-opts a social problem, it either solves or buries it. Both results are relatively uncommon. A more common outcome is for the government to create some institutionalized means of dealing with the problem or, at least, of dealing with complaints about the problem. Government either expands some existing institution and gives it new responsibilities (and money and staff), or it creates a new organization. Government thereby rapidly develops a vested interest in the problem and battles to maintain the budget, staff, and authority bound up with the problem. After making this investment, government has an interest in keeping the problem on the public agenda.

Government agencies and programs seem to take on a life of their own: After setting things in motion, the government finds it difficult to stop a line of action or to disband some agency. Thus, protest groups that have managed to get their problem translated into a government function have at least given some permanency to their quest for redress. But the question still remains whether redress will actually be forthcoming.

STAGE 3: BUREAUCRATIZATION AND REACTION

During the first two stages in the career of a social problem, attention is focused on claims that there is a problem. Stage 2 ends when the grievances of the protesting group have been turned into a government function. During Stage 3, the fate of a social problem hinges on organizational features of government agencies and on the ability of those groups affected by government action to deal with government bureaucracy.

Government Agencies

One critical issue is the organizational structure of government efforts to respond to a social problem. The responsibility may be turned over to an existing department or agency. In this instance, the problem may be a minor concern to the agency compared with its overall responsibilities and commitments. In fact, sometimes an agency made responsible for a problem may have significant vested interests that conflict with dealing with that particular social problem. Suppose that federal agencies responsible for procuring military equipment, low-cost housing, or federal highways are asked to enforce fair employment practices by requiring that contractors meet certain standards in employment of minority workers. Unless extraordinary pressure is put on such agencies, they are unlikely to see enforcement of fair employment practices as their primary mission. They are likely to take only minimal action on this problem and to continue to pursue their main goals—getting the houses, roads, and tanks built on schedule. Similarly, an agency may have a greater stake in the affairs of groups that would be threatened if a given social problem were solved. For example, the Department of Agriculture has, over time, developed strong ties to the agriculture industry. If this department were given charge of improving the lot of migrant farm workers, its response would most likely be judged inadequate by the workers and might, in fact, worsen their plight.

The effectiveness of government action is probably greater when a new agency is specifically created to deal with a given social problem. Even then, however, the agency may find its interests at odds with those of victims of the problem. Or it may be powerless to influence the behavior of other government agencies whose activities bear on the problem. Furthermore, a new agency may find its interests are best served not by relieving a problem but by maintaining the problem while monopolizing the means for dealing with it.

The failure of government programs to make headway against a problem does not usually mean that the program will be abandoned. Rather, such failure usually results in claims for more money and staff on the grounds that the problem has resisted previous, less costly programs. As Peter F. Drucker (1969) has noted, the federal payments to the big cities "have increased almost a hundredfold" during the past thirty years. Today there are "ten times as many government agencies concerned with city problems" as there were in 1939. Despite these massive increases in effort, the problems of the cities have got worse, not better.

Furthermore, because the careers of employees of a government agency are often dependent on the continuation and growth of that agency, a sudden solution to a given social problem might put them out of work. For example, when the dangers of wartime inflation ended following World War II, the many employees of the Office of Price Administration—those who monitored and set prices—faced unemployment. And when peace breaks out, military men face greatly diminished prospects for promotion. A particularly poignant example of the way success may threaten an organization comes from the private sector. The National Association for the March of Dimes was created during the 1930s to combat polio. It raised money through public fund-raising campaigns and used this money to aid victims of the crippling disease and to support medical research for a cure. Over the years a rather large organization was built up. Then one day, research sponsored by the March of Dimes produced the polio vaccine. Suddenly, an organization comprising a professional staff and a national network of volunteers had no reason for being and had to search frantically for new responsibilities—or go out of business. What finally emerged was the organization known today as the National Foundation, whose activities are directed toward the treatment and cure of birth defects. Such general goals are unlikely to be fully achieved, and thus the organization no longer faces the risk of being destroyed by success (Sills,1957).

By the same token, thousands of full-time employees at all levels of government have a personal stake in the continued existence of welfare programs, state mental-hospital programs, the prison system, and so on. If the problems of poverty, mental illness, or crime were to be solved, these employees would be left in the lurch. More important, new approaches to these problems may be equally threatening. For example, proposed alternatives to prisons and mental hospitals have aroused militant opposition from those who are dependent on existing institutions.

The point is that the interests of the bureaucracy often conflict with the interests of complainants. Those with a stake in a war on poverty may not have a stake in winning the war. Thus, a number of actions by a government agency concerning a particular social problem may have more to do with preserving the agency than with solving the problem. And the agency's policies may therefore move away from dealing with the problem to dealing with *complaints about the problem*.

Dealing with Complaints

It is not uncommon for agencies to treat protests as public-relations problems. The question becomes not "What can we do to cure the condition they

15

complain about?'' but ''How can we get them to stop complaining?'' As we have already seen, efforts to muffle protest can sometimes be accomplished simply by holding hearings or by appointing a commission to investigate the problem. By the time this process ends and no action results, the complaints may have blown over: The protesting group may have drifted apart in response to new concerns; a particular crisis that once gave urgency to the complaints may have subsided—for example, riots in the black ghettos—or public interest may simply have waned.

Even when the problem results in the creation of programs and agencies to deal with it, the public-relations view of the problem may predominate. For example, the creation of a consumer-affairs department may have only a cosmetic effect on business practices. The primary function of the department may be to deal with complaints in such a way as to minimize protest. It could be plausibly argued that a large number of government agencies—widely regarded as engaged in solving social problems—are primarily engaged in defuzing complaints.

Consider the police. Ostensibly, the police exist to enforce the law and fight crime. However, it is rare for the police to initiate any action on their own. Well over 90 percent of police activity is in response to citizen complaints. Furthermore, in only about one citizen call out of five do the police discover that any violation of the law (a crime) is involved. They therefore devote most of their time to dealing with a variety of complaints about noise, uncooperative landlords, angry spouses, lost keys, and stray animals. More important, in the overwhelming majority of crime complaints the police receive, they merely file a report and thereby often give victims the grounds for an insurance claim (Reiss, 1971). Thus, the typical police action in response to crime is to deal with a complaint, not with a crime. This is not to suggest that the police never make arrests or solve crimes but to point out that the major function of modern American police departments is taking complaints.

By the same token, it is possible to regard the present welfare system as an institution designed to channel and minimize complaints rather than overcome poverty and dependency. And many modern economists have pointed out that the welfare system—for all of the discontent about its huge costs—is a much cheaper way of dealing with poverty than would be programs aimed at eliminat-

16

ing poverty. The presence of the welfare bureaucracy prevents a crisis that would ensue over the distribution of wealth if people starved in the streets. By processing claims of poverty and disability, the welfare bureaucracy also impedes the ability of the poor to speak for themselves: As recipients of public charity, people on welfare appear as ungrateful persons when they complain about their plight. Indeed, many recipients are afraid to complain for fear of being found ineligible for subsequent support. The welfare system may have failed to cure the problems placed in its charge, but it has been fairly successful in minimizing complaints about these problems.

With all these difficulties, how can protesting groups deal with government agencies? Obviously, the more powerful the group, the more politically sophisticated it is—and the more clearly defined its goals, the better able it is to force the bureaucracy to be responsive to its claims. Thus, city services, such as street cleaning and repairing and garbage and snow removal, are excellent in wealthy neighborhoods.

When prominent business, labor, and church leaders became active in the civil rights movement in the early 1960s, they succeeded in getting major legislation enacted and vigorously enforced. The whole controversy over the impact of "special interests" on government policy and performance reflects the fact that some groups are much more effective than others in pressing their claims.

You will notice in the examples mentioned earlier that effective impact on government comes from powerful, nongovernmental, unofficial institutions and groups. The fate of claims concerning a social problem rests on the ability of complainants

Figure 1.7   One of the major functions of a government agency, or any bureaucracy, is to process complaints made by citizens. Although the government may create agencies to deal with social problems, the primary efforts of such agencies and bureaus seem to be directed toward minimizing protests about conditions rather than dealing with conditions themselves.

to continually monitor and renegotiate the thrust and character of government activities. A group gets this kind of power only by developing or maintaining the capacity to effectively pursue its interests. Frequently, protesting groups, although they have succeeded in getting their claims recognized and translated into policies and programs, lack the power, in terms of effective organization or sophistication, to deal with an operating bureaucracy. Often enough, the original protesting group will have declined in importance once the government begins to act. Then, if the complainants see that governmental actions are inappropriate, ineffective, or insincere, they must once again take up the task of mobilizing support and protesting the course of events. What happens next depends on how much success they have in accomplishing these tasks.

STAGE 4: REEMERGENCE OF THE MOVEMENT

Typically, the problem persists through the first three stages and finally becomes a captive of government agencies; government policies and programs then become the target of growing disillusion and discontent, which can take a number of different forms:

1. The original complainant group may reject the adequacy of governmental responses.

2. The original complainants may have been a group of moral crusaders who have been replaced, over time, by the actual victims (for example, poor people, black people, the elderly). Official action that satisfied the crusaders (civil rights laws or welfare programs, for example) might not satisfy the victims.

3. The activities and programs of the government may give rise to grievances by other groups who claim that the programs themselves constitute a social problem. (These new claims, such as those that occurred in reaction to antidrug laws and programs, antiabortion measures, and laws meant to "protect" women, will be taken up in later chapters.)

Whichever the case, in the fourth stage in the career of a typical social problem, we see a rekindling of concern about the social problem *and* opposition to existing programs and agencies that

17

deal with the problem. Furthermore, the reemergence of the movement usually involves not merely opposition to these programs but a search for new institutions.

Two different lines of development characterize this fourth stage. One line is toward the development of radically different institutions in the hope of finding *social*, or public, solutions that will benefit everyone. The second line is to withdraw from institutions altogether and seek *private*, limited solutions that benefit only group members. Although both alternatives turn away from the existing system, their implications for society are very different (Spector and Kitsuse, 1973).

Social Reformers

People who react to their disillusionment with existing programs by attempting to create new or different social institutions can be thought of as social reformers. Their aim is to restructure at least some aspect of society as a whole and to eliminate the problem from the whole of society. One example of this can be drawn from the free-school movement. There is widespread belief by many

groups in the United States that the public schools are failing in many ways: by stifling curiosity and intellectual growth in many students; by serving more as prisons than as schools; and by failing to compensate those from disadvantaged backgrounds. The free-school movement includes many people who want to transform the present school system. To the extent that they create a different kind of school system, their efforts will affect society as a whole.

Private Reformers

Members of another faction in the free-school movement show little or no interest in changing the existing school system. Instead, they have withdrawn from the public school system to institute "free schools" as an alternative educational system for themselves. In this way, they resemble upper-class Americans who have long used private schools to serve their children, middle-class Americans who have fled to suburban school districts to escape the severe problems of urban schools, and Southerners who have created private schools to avoid integration. These alternative institutions are

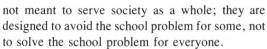

Figure 1.8   Attempts to deal with social problems may lead to social movements designed either to reform but retain the existing system or to create alternative systems. (Upper left) Ralph Nader has had good success in organizing consumers to effect needed reforms. (Lower left) "Free schools" and "free clinics" offer services not found in regular schools and clinics, and they often serve people who are not taken care of by tax-supported institutions. (Left center) Beef and other boycott movements put pressure on retailers to lower prices. All are attempts at reforming existing institutions. However, some groups have developed alternatives to existing institutions. (Far right) Black Muslims have created schools for their members' use only, and (above) many urbanites have moved to private developments like Lake Havasu City, Arizona.

not meant to serve society as a whole; they are designed to avoid the school problem for some, not to solve the school problem for everyone.

In similar fashion, the Black Muslims offer members some alternatives to living in a predominantly white society. Major civil rights organizations, on the other hand, desire to change race relations throughout American society. The consumer movement, led by such groups as Nader's Raiders, is attempting to create new institutions to change the conditions of American consumerism. Many consumer cooperatives, "food conspiracies," and similar organizations try to provide consumer benefits only for their members.

Attempts to create new social institutions or to radically reform old ones in order to deal more effectively with a social problem confront most of the same difficulties already outlined in this chapter. For example, plans must be effective, strategies must be suitable, and the group must muster sufficient power and overcome opposition. But beyond these problems, the movement will once again encounter the dangers of being co-opted by government agencies, repeating the cycle of be-

coming a government undertaking. Sometimes, of course, the movement succeeds in reshaping the goals and character of the co-opting government agency. On other occasions, co-optation greatly blunts the movement. Spector and Kitsuse (1973) offer a speculative example of how the free-school movement could be co-opted by the public system and thus tamed and changed:

Attempts to create alternative institutions outside the system may produce a new set of experts in the given field. They may be the leaders of various experiments in creating and running new kinds of institutions. Their experience may bring them credentials acceptable to establishment organizations, even though they are developed outside their jurisdiction. Successful and workable alternative institutions may stimulate the interest of the established institutions as they attempt to come up with answers to their critics. They may attempt to take over or to co-opt the alternatives developed and may make attractive offers to the leaders and experts of social problems groups.

For example, the government may invite leaders of the "free school" movement to participate in conferences, compile bibliographic references, accept grants to evaluate the alternative methods of education, *etc.* These invitations may serve the established system in a number of ways: it can drain off leadership from groups that threaten its institutional dominance; co-opt leadership into its structure, enabling it to claim the innovations as well as to control its effects on the system; insulate that leadership from the members of the group, thus discrediting it and reducing its future effectiveness in organizing social problems activities.

Spector and Kitsuse's four-stage natural history of the career of social problems makes it clear that social problems are preeminently a *political process* through which problems come to be publicly accepted as such and through which particular institutional responses to the problem are shaped and then reshaped.

Thus, crime does not become a social problem simply because there is a high crime rate or because the rate is rising (although attention to crime rates may stimulate the process). Crime is a social problem when there is widespread public concern about it. Furthermore, what will be done about the crime problem may or may not relate to the actual causes of crime (as social science understands these causes) or to effective crime-prevention programs. The actions taken on behalf of the crime problem depend very greatly on the political process—on whose interests are affected and how—and on the nature of the institutions developed to deal with the problem. In Chapter 6, we try to present the most accurate picture possible of the current state of crime in this country. We also attempt to present explanations of the causes of crime that social scientists regard as most probable. But to understand why the public is sometimes more concerned about crime than it is at other times and to evaluate and understand present programs that deal with crime, you will have to keep in mind the social and political nature of social problems.

THE DESIGN OF THE BOOK

To conclude this chapter, it will be helpful to know how the remainder of the book is organized.

The problems dealt with in Chapters 4 through 15 are those about which Americans are presently complaining the loudest and toward which government is directing its greatest efforts. It is the pub-

20

Figure 1.9   A social problem is based as much on widespread public concern as on objective indicators. Concern over crime, for example, may become contagious as more and more people buy such protective devices and services as (top) extra door locks; window grates; (bottom) car theft alarm systems; private guard services; and car-hood locks. Such responses may, in turn, affect crime rates by making it difficult for burglars to do their job.

lic, not social scientists, who determine what a social problem is. We include a chapter on sex-based inequalities (not found in most slightly older texts) because, very recently, women organized and succeeded in making their grievances a social problem. On the other hand, most slightly older texts devote a chapter to youth, particularly to student protest and the counterculture. This text does not because the youth movement of the 1960s has greatly subsided (partly because the young people born during the baby-boom, who kept up the movement, are no longer so youthful). To confirm our judgments about which problems to include, we examined recent public-opinion polls and conducted a large-scale poll of college social-problems instructors.

The remaining two chapters in this unit are devoted to the social-science tools used to analyze social problems. Chapter 2 reviews major social-science principles and concepts relevant to the study of social problems. The discussion is organized around three models. First, social problems involve the *actions of human beings*. To examine such matters as drug addiction, crime, or racism, we have to ask and answer questions about why people act in certain ways. Chapter 2 therefore begins with a discussion of concepts and principles vital for understanding human behavior.

A complete view of a problem such as drug addiction or racism cannot be gained simply from analyzing individual behavior. As subsequent chapters make clear, it is equally vital to understand the *workings of societies as systems*. To say that a person was born into poverty says more about the nature of the social system in which that person lives than it does about that individual's actions. Society is the stage on which individual action occurs—and the peculiarities of a particular stage greatly limit which actions can occur on it. Consequently, Chapter 2 offers a preliminary sociological look at societies as systems.

Finally, the problems taken up in this text are predominantly the problems of contemporary America. That means they are problems of special concern to (or even produced by) *large, urban, and industrial societies*. Chapter 2 concludes with a discussion of the special features of modern, highly developed, urban societies.

A major part of this text is based on the results of social-science research. If we want to know whether a particular anticrime program is effective, somebody has to do an appropriate study to find out. What you will learn from this book depends on what people have found out about a variety of topics. Whether what you learn from this book is correct and useful depends on whether the research was done well or poorly. Instead of trying to learn a series of standards against which to judge social-science research, it is more interesting (and therefore probably more effective) to discover research procedures in the context of actual research. Chapter 3 lets you look over the shoulder of social scientists as they conduct several major research studies. The accounts are informal and chosen for their interest as well as for their relevance. The purpose of the chapter is to let you see for yourself why specific research methods are chosen and what it is that social researchers actually do.

The remainder of the book is devoted to using the tools provided in Unit I to understand some of the most pressing social problems faced by our society. It seems useful to explain why the topics are taken up in the order in which they are presented. The governing principle is to aid your understanding of these matters.

As you will see, most social problems are interrelated. Sometimes, several problems have similar causes and need similar solutions. Often, one problem is a major cause of another. Consider drug addiction and crime. A large amount of the property crime in the United States is committed by drug addicts (Morris and Hawkins, 1970). Thus, much of the crime problem is in fact a drug problem. But it is also clear that a major part of the drug problem is a crime problem. Addicts do not rob and steal because they are drug-crazed criminals but because stealing is the only way they can get enough money to maintain their drug supply. Drugs are expensive because they are illegal, and because drugs are illegal, they also serve as a major source of income for organized crime—thus, in this way, too, drug laws increase crime. Organized crime, in turn, is a major source of police and political corruption. Obviously, decriminalizing drug addiction would have far-reaching effects on crime. But it might also have major effects on drug usage.

21

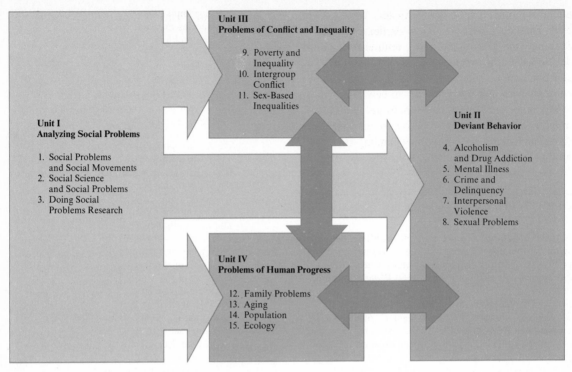

Figure 1.10   The analysis of social problems affects the so-cial problems covered in Units II, III, and IV. And because these problems are all interrelated, any given problem and its solution will affect other problems and their solutions.

Similarly, a close relationship holds between the ecological crisis and the rapid growth of the population. The fact that people are the major drain on natural resources and the environment is what makes a large population a problem. A major cause of rapid population growth has been the ability to greatly reduce death rates. Improved health can hardly be regarded as a bad thing, yet it has created considerable poverty in underdeveloped nations whose economic progress is being eaten up by population growth. Improved health has also made aging a much more intense problem. Never before have so many people lived so long. Conse-quently, never before has there been such a major problem of providing for the elderly.

It is virtually impossible even to discuss social problems one at a time—they are too intertwined. Furthermore, the interdependence of social prob-lems often limits how far we can go in completely solving any given problem. Sure-fire solutions for one problem may greatly increase the severity of

another. Prohibition of alcohol, for example, caused a staggering reduction in American con-sumption of alcohol and the amount of alcoholism, but it also created and sustained a gangster empire. Today, a similar empire flourishes on outlawed narcotics. Thus, all solutions must be studied in terms of their consequences *throughout* the society—even the best solutions will probably al-ways be trade-offs, with their benefits outweighing (but not eliminating) their social harm. And so it goes; social problems are not less complex than the societies they afflict, and ours is a very complex society.

In spite of these complexities, we must begin somewhere. We have chosen to begin with those problems that can be viewed *partly* as problems of individual deviance and to build up to problems that must be examined primarily at the level of how society operates as a system. However, be-cause societies are systems and because what hap-pens in one part of the system often has widespread effects in other parts, later chapters in the text often have occasion to return to earlier topics. For example, the chapter on aging returns to themes developed in the chapters on poverty, the family, and population; it develops them and traces their consequences and interrelations in new ways.

The purpose of this book is not to add more facts to your memory; it invites you to increase the scope and depth of your understanding of these problems that currently beset your life and time.

CHAPTER REVIEW

A social *condition* becomes a social *problem* when a significant number of people define it as one. This process of definition is political and involves various groups and power structures. Herbert Blumer suggests that it takes a *social movement* to define some condition as a social problem. In the model developed by Spector and Kitsuse, the "social career" of a social problem can be examined as a four-stage progression: (1) agitation, (2) legitimation and co-optation, (3) bureaucratization and reaction, and (4) reemergence.

Agitation marks the beginnings of a social problem, the earliest signs of discontent from a group of people. Their aims at this point are to eradicate the problem. The claims made by a group are important because those claims will be questioned by opposition groups first. If the groups have misperceived the actual condition or its causes, the "solution" to the problem could worsen rather than better the situation. At this stage, it is important to choose powerful allies and to adopt a strategy of change that will not alienate other powerful segments in the community. The claims, power, and strategies identified with a group will, in large part, determine the form of competition that will take place between that group and others seeking to maintain the status quo.

When powerful groups or government groups recognize the existence of a problem, they *legitimate* it. Legitimation gives status and credence to claims made in the early stage. The creation of a new government agency or committee to deal with the problem may result in *co-optation*, taking the problem out of the hands of the original complainants. Co-optation takes

power from the complainants, but the establishment of government agencies may serve the public by (1) taking action on the problem or (2) showing that the problem does not deserve public attention.

Once the problem is in the hands of an official agency or commission, the effects of *bureaucratization* can be seen. If it is turned over to an existing agency, the problem may not receive the attention it warrants. Not only may the new problem be viewed as relatively unimportant compared with the agency's existing duties, but it could also conflict with other interests of the same agency. The only alternative to this situation is to create a new agency or commission to deal specifically with that social problem. Although agency effectiveness will probably be greater in this case, the new agency or organization will have a vested interest in the continuation of the problem because the life of the agency—and the salaries of its personnel—depends on the problem.

The fourth stage of the social problem is the possible *reemergence* of the movement. Those who initiated the movement may claim that the official agencies have been ineffective in dealing with the problem. Or, it could be that the "moral crusaders" who adopted the problem are satisfied by government action but the original complainants are not. In this case, the original group might again agitate for change. Finally, although the original groups might be satisfied, the programs designed to alleviate some problems may have created new ones. Thus, the social problem may be rekindled and reformers seeking institutional or private reform may emerge—beginning the whole process anew.

SUGGESTED READINGS

Lipsky, Michael. *Protest in City Politics: Rent Strikes, Housing and the Power of the Poor.* Chicago: Rand McNally, 1970.

Olson, Mancur. *The Logic of Collective Action.* Cambridge, Mass.: Harvard University Press, 1965.

Platt, Anthony. *The Child Savers: The Invention of Delinquency.* Chicago: University of Chicago Press, 1969.

Selznick, Philip. *TVA and the Grass Roots.* Berkeley: University of California Press, 1966.

23

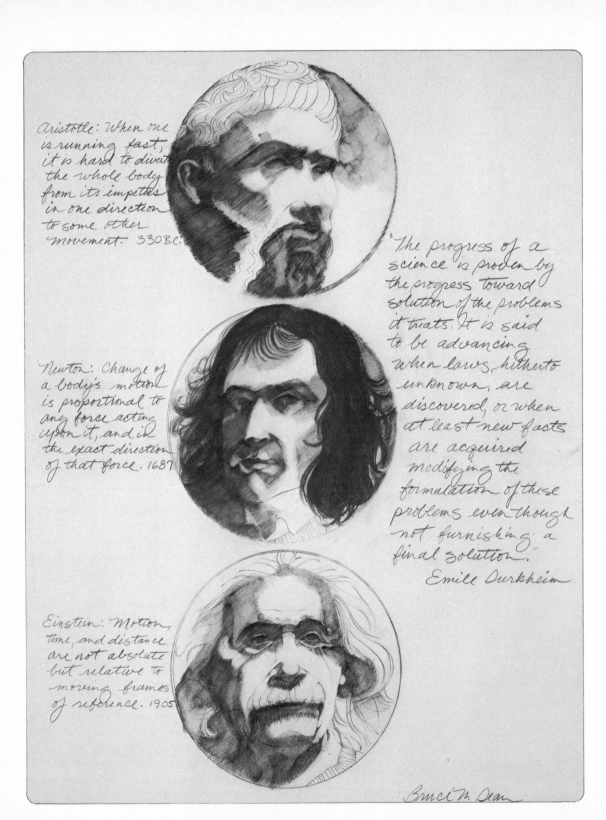

Aristotle: When one is running fast, it is hard to divert the whole body from its impetus in one direction to some other movement. 330 B.C.

Newton: Change of a body's motion is proportional to any force acting upon it, and in the exact direction of that force. 1687.

Einstein: Motion, time, and distance are not absolute but relative to moving frames of reference. 1905.

"The progress of a science is proven by the progress toward solution of the problems it treats. It is said to be advancing when laws, hitherto unknown, are discovered, or when at least new facts are acquired modifying the formulation of these problems even though not furnishing a final solution."

Emile Durkheim

Bruce M. Dean

2
Social Science and Social Problems

In the sense that human societies have always had suffering and inequity, social problems are as old as the human race. Yet, the idea of a social problem is relatively modern—because the idea that conditions can improve is modern. To regard a condition in society as a problem, then, is to suppose that something can be done about it. No matter how miserable they are, people will not try to improve their lot until they believe that change is possible. As long as they regard social arrangements as immutable—whether fixed by God or by the natural order of things—there is nothing to study and nothing to be done. For example, throughout most of human history, most people have been poor, but they have regarded poverty as a fixed fact of life.

Such fatalistic conceptions as "the poor are always with us" long prevented the recognition of social problems and the development of social science, both of which require us to assume that human behavior and the operation of societies are *caused* and that these causes can be *understood* and *manipulated.* Social science and the study of social problems, however, share more than the belief that human and social behavior are variable and understandable. They also share a motivation to cure social ills. Clearly, Karl Marx's lifetime work in economics and Sigmund Freud's in the human psyche were not done simply out of curiosity. Both theorists hoped to create a better world.

Both Marx and Freud were social scientists, and it is through social science that we seek the tools for dealing with social problems. The research you will encounter in this book was done mainly by psychologists, sociologists, anthropologists, political scientists, economists, and other social scientists. The theories that help explain the problems taken up in those chapters are also social-science theories.

All modern social science is built upon a few fundamental assumptions about the ways in which people and societies operate. We will identify and explain these assumptions here, and you will see in later chapters how they are part and parcel of theories that social scientists have applied to a variety of social problems. For this reason, this chapter offers a concise introduction (or review) of fundamental premises of social science. First, it discusses basic concepts and assumptions about human behavior. Then, it deals with conceptions of society. Finally, it discusses special features of modern society. These fundamental concepts and principles provide the unity of the rest of the book and, indeed, of the field of social problems.

HUMAN BEHAVIOR

The fundamental object of all social science is to understand human behavior. Whether it is the behavior of specific persons, the behavior of humans within groups, or even the behavior of millions of persons within a complex society, the fundamental questions ask why, and under which conditions, human beings act in certain ways. Therefore, all social-science theories, even those that try to explain the relations among major social institutions (between religion and politics, for example), depend on some set of assumptions about the nature of human beings.

Unit II examines a number of specific theories about human behavior in an attempt to explain, for example, why people become addicted, mentally ill, criminal, violent, or sexually deviant. But before you study that material, it will be helpful to review some of the basic elements of the social-science conception of what it means to be human; these elements underlie the specific theories.

THE HUMAN ANIMAL

All attempts to understand humanness must start at the beginning, with the fertilized human ovum and its genetic content, for much of what we are, and especially much of what we can become, is biologically fixed.

For a long time, social science paid little attention to biology because there had been too much reliance, during the late nineteenth century, on biological explanations of social behavior. Recently, however, the work of some biologists has been recognized as vital to a comprehensive social science. There are at least three major ways in which biology is critically important to the social-science understanding of human behavior. First, whatever else they may be, humans are biological organisms, and the particular kind of organism they are has major implications for social science. Second, many of these important biological characteristics are passed from one generation to the next through heredity. Finally, the line dividing humans and animals, once thought to be quite firm, has become

blurred as we have learned more from the study of animal behavior, or ethology.

Physiology and Behavior

The fact that we are flesh and blood has many implications for how we behave. A few examples will make clear how and why this is so. Consider the most obvious way in which our bodies determine our fate: we have two arms, not four; we have both eyes in front; we have vocal cords capable of producing complex sounds; and we have thumbs for grasping. All these physiological features narrow and define the range of potential human behavior. Similarly, the fact that the human infant is born helpless and is unable to survive alone for an extended period has profound implications. For one thing, the infant's prolonged period of dependency forces humans to be social animals, living together in fairly stable groupings and relationships. Furthermore, the fact that human females bear and nurse infants tended for centuries to restrict ''women's work'' to tasks that could be performed in proximity to dependent infants; ''men's work'' included tasks that put men at a distance from infants (D'Andrade, 1966). Similarly, the biological fact that human males are, on the average, considerably larger and stronger than

human females probably played a significant role in establishing patterns of male dominance (discussed further in Chapter 11). Today, these biological facts are much less important because infants may now be bottle-fed and because very little labor now depends on muscle power; however, patterns established for thousands of years have tended to persist.

Perhaps more surprisingly, research has found that even in our modern, highly automated society, physical size still influences a person's life chances. Taller men are more likely than shorter men to be hired into management positions and to be promoted (Deck, 1971). Indeed, taller women, more often than shorter women, get better jobs and marry men with better jobs (Tanner, 1970). In addition to size, researchers have begun to examine the social consequences of appearance. Glen Elder Jr. (1969) has shown that the better looking a woman is, the better her chances are of marrying a financially successful man. Karen Dion (1972) has found that adults treat homely and attractive children differently.

Genetics and Behavior

An important aspect of the biological features we have just discussed is that they are, to a consider-

27

Figure 2.1   The particular biological characteristics of the human animal impose limits on human behavior. We cannot fly in our natural state, and we would have difficulty outrunning most large mammals—even though 1936 Olympic gold medal winner Jesse Owens once beat a race horse and buggy with driver in the 100 yard dash.

Figure 2.2   The chimpanzee has been a favorite laboratory subject because chimps and humans share many abilities. Social scientists have been able to teach chimpanzees to communicate with sign language.

able extent, genetically determined. Tall people are more likely than short people to have tall offspring. The same holds true for physical attractiveness and intelligence. Indeed, inheritance influences even physical maturity and sexual maturity—children of parents who were early maturers are also likely to be early maturers. Genetic inheritance, however, does not guarantee any of these characteristics, for environmental factors can considerably suppress genetic potential. Poor nutrition, illness, or other deprivations can keep people from growing up to be as large, as intelligent, or as attractive as they might otherwise be. But genetic factors do serve as limits beyond which environmental factors cannot influence the outcome. No amount of good nutrition can cause individuals to grow taller than their genetic potential would permit.

A major technique for assessing the role of heredity has been to compare various traits of identical twins who have been raised in different homes. Because identical twins are genetically the same, comparisons of them shed light on the extent to which a trait, such as intelligence or schizophrenia, is determined by heredity or by environmental differences.

In this way, the study of genetics becomes of major importance to social science. Social factors can only partly account for many socially important human variations; therefore, to know the extent of social causes, it is necessary to first find out how important a part genetic causes play. For example, if intelligence differences are of major importance in determining economic success, and if it is the case that, to some degree, inequalities in intelligence are caused by genetic variations, then there is a limit to the extent to which such environmental influences as schools and other educational programs can compensate for these underlying differences. In fact, if it proved possible to wipe out all social causes of intellectual differences, we would be faced with a situation in which all intellectual differences would be wholly genetic in origin. At present, it is not clear to what degree intelligence stems from inheritance and to what degree from social conditions. Although no expert on the subject denies that there is an important genetic component to intelligence, there is no basis for

28

Figure 2.3 Socialization is the process of becoming human, of becoming a social being. It means learning many things that distinguish us from the newborn and naked infant, from other animals, and from each other. It includes, among many other skills, learning how to dress for the specific occasion.

attributing racial differences in IQ scores to genetics or heredity.

Animal and Human Behavior

For a long time, it was believed that humans were extremely different from all other animals and that the study of animals could shed little light on human behavior. For one thing, only humans were thought to have speech. For another, only humans were thought to have technology—the capacity to alter materials to make tools, weapons, and the like. More careful observation of animals, especially primates, has now shaken our sense of uniqueness. Recently, researchers have had considerable success in teaching chimpanzees to communicate by using the sign language developed for the deaf (Fleming, 1974). Others have been trying to decipher the languagelike sounds made by dolphins (Lilly, 1969). Furthermore, researchers have observed animals making and employing tools and passing on this ability to other animals (Mazer and Robertson, 1972).

Perhaps even more important is the knowledge that many animals do not behave entirely by *instinct,* that is, by inherited patterns of behavior, such as the ability of spiders to spin webs. Instincts are not learned but are genetically determined, automatic responses to the environment. We now know that much of the behavior of many animal species is not of this automatic kind but is learned from other animals. Thus, a competent adult lion or gorilla has had to learn how to behave appropriately—to stalk game or to build a sleeping nest in the trees.

For all these reasons, we now realize that much can be learned about human behavior from ethology. Studies of the effects of isolation on infant monkeys, for example, have told us much about the proper development of human babies.

BECOMING HUMAN: SOCIALIZATION

Every so often, the media report tragic cases of children who have been locked away in attics or closets and who have been raised in virtual solitary confinement by deranged parents or guardians. When found, such children appear to be extremely mentally defective—they cannot speak and usually they are not even toilet trained. These *feral* children—the word literally means wild, or untamed—have had only their genetic resources to draw on in order to become human. Not one of these children has ever become normal, but those who lived long enough have shown considerable ability to learn. Their condition was caused by being cheated and deprived of the opportunity to *learn to be human.*

Like lions and gorillas, human infants must learn a great deal; otherwise, they will be human in physical form only. The process through which this learning occurs is *socialization.* When an individual has become adequately human, we say he or she has been properly *socialized*—made social. Humanity is a social product. We learn who and what we are and become what we are through interaction with others. Children locked away in attics do not become human; they remain, at most, potentially human.

Adequate socialization requires a high level of human stimulation of the newborn infant and continual interaction with others—parents, siblings, playmates, teachers, and the like. Learning to act and react in the ways that other people call normal requires a great deal of experience, a fact that we recognize when we excuse inappropriate behavior in small children, who are "too little to know better."

In many ways, socialization is a self-evident phenomenon. Virtually everyone recognizes that it goes on. Yet, we must also recognize that it is a chancy process. At many points along the way, something can go wrong and persons can be missocialized. It is not necessary to completely isolate an infant in order to harm it. Simply placing it in an orphanage may be enough to impede normal development considerably (Dennis, 1938; 1960). Even being born into a large family may cause a child to miss out on the needed amount of attention and stimulation (Clausen, 1966b). Studies indicate that setbacks in early childhood *may* be permanent, or at least very difficult to make up. Thus, compensatory programs in the schools may come too late to help some disadvantaged children reclaim their full potential.

The most comprehensive data on the effects of deprivation during infancy and early childhood

29

come from the work of Harry Harlow, who has conducted a series of experiments with rhesus monkeys. In one classic experiment, Harry and Margaret Harlow (1965) raised three groups of infant monkeys: some wholly in isolation, some isolated with their mothers, and some isolated with several other infant monkeys. The wholly isolated monkeys grew up to be very abnormal. When later put in contact with other monkeys, they made extremely poor adjustments to the group; they tended to cower in corners and failed to learn to engage in sexual behavior. But a startling result was that those monkeys raised in isolation with their mothers were nearly as abnormal in later life as the completely isolated monkeys; they, too, failed to adjust to social contact with other monkeys. Those raised as a group without mothers made better adjustments but did not become normal. Probably the most important conclusion from Harlow's research on monkeys is that the effects of isolation are at least partly irreversible. Although the Harlows' monkeys made some progress when finally admitted to a normal social environment, they remained markedly maladjusted, even after long periods of social contact.

If the essence of humanness is to be social, it is also to be continually responsive to the expectations of those around us; in fact, the socialization process never ends. Throughout life, we are placed in new circumstances that require us to learn new ways of behaving—we take a new job, get married, become parents, move, retire, and so on—all of which require us to become someone new. Consequently, human beings are always vulnerable to being poorly socialized and are therefore vulnerable to learning inappropriate behavior.

Because socialization can, and so often does, go wrong, it is a major focus of social science. As will be evident in subsequent chapters, socialization is the key *process* linking a variety of social factors.

30

Figure 2.4   The socialization process is extremely important in learning to become a socially functioning human being. When the socialization process is altered with young monkeys in the laboratory, as was done by Harlow in his experiments (below), the monkeys fail to grow up normally. Harlow substituted wire and terry-cloth "mothers" for normal maternal nurturance. The young monkeys reacted better to the terry-cloth than to the wire "mothers," but even those with terry-cloth surrogates suffered a permanent loss of social adjustment. Total isolation is even more damaging. (Right) A still from the film The Wild Child, *which documents Jean Itard's efforts to civilize and educate Victor, a feral child. It has been conjectured that everyone begins life much like Victor, but, unlike Victor, other people are successfully socialized and educated.*

For example, when social scientists argue that having delinquent friends is a major cause of delinquency, what they are asserting is that such friends influence socialization—that they teach people to behave in delinquent ways.

THE HUMAN ACTOR

The fundamental outcome of socialization is the ability to play social *roles*. A role is a *set of expectations* applied to a particular social position. These expectations define how any particular person holding the position is supposed to act. Put another way, they are a set of *norms* about what a person should and should not do when holding a particular position in society. Positions to which roles, or a set of expectations, are attached are countless. All of us occupy many such positions: student, son or daughter, friend, employee, policeman, nun, landlord, spouse. For each of these positions there is a role—those around you expect you to behave in certain ways if you are to be regarded as playing the role properly. Being judged a normal, competent, mature person depends on having learned to play assigned roles properly. A disruptive student, alcoholic father, negligent mother, or brutal friend is not fulfilling his or her role.

Socialization teaches us to play our roles successfully. Furthermore, it is through learning and playing social roles that we develop our conceptions of self—our identities. If you were to take a sheet of paper and begin to write down a list of brief answers to the question "Who am I?" you would find that most of your answers would relate to social roles. For example, you might write "eighteen years old," "a student," "a liberal," "a sister," "an American." Each of these positions implies a social role. Eighteen-year-olds are expected to act differently from sixteen-year-olds or from twenty-one-year-olds. Students are expected to act differently from professors or salesmen, and so on. Each of us probably has a unique total set of roles. And this set of roles incorporates us into social life and defines who we are.

The process through which humans acquire identities, self-conceptions, or personalities has long been a major preoccupation of social scientists. Although many theoretical traditions have conflicting descriptions of this process, all agree that it is a *social* process and that it has to do with learning to play social roles. Sigmund Freud, for example, focused on the parent-child relationship. Other theorists have emphasized relations with peers. Both Charles Horton Cooley and George Herbert Mead, founders of the symbolic-interactionist school of social psychology, emphasized that we develop our sense of self by learning to see ourselves from the outside, as others see us. Through experience in playing several different roles, we learn to *take the roles of others* and, from this vantage point, learn to act toward ourselves as others would act toward us. Through this process, we learn to shape our behavior to fit others' expectations of us. Over time, we form some consistent view of ourselves.

Not all humans learn to take the roles of others well—many seem to badly misperceive how others see them and to act selfishly, insensitively, or in other inappropriate ways. Furthermore, many people learn through this process to view themselves as unpopular, inarticulate, incompetent, stupid, or otherwise inferior. As already pointed out, the socialization process is both fragile and variable. Some of us learn to play our roles well, others to perform them poorly. Thus, some of us form favorable conceptions of ourselves, and some of us are damaged along the way and are inadequately or inappropriately socialized.

To talk of roles and self-conceptions is to use language characteristic of sociologists, but these sociological concepts are wholly compatible with psychological conceptions of personality. The self can be called the *personality* if one means the relatively enduring modes of thinking, feeling, responding, and behaving that people retain in different situations and in different roles. Despite the fact that we have a fairly consistent set of expectations about how all persons in any given position should behave, we recognize that people will differ in how they actually behave. For example, some people show considerable anxiety about the adequacy of their behavior in whichever role they are playing—at work they seek constant reassurance that they are doing an adequate job, and at home they seek reassurance that they are good spouses or

31

responsible parents. Thus, a person's behavior represents a blend of role performance and personality. But it is important to recognize that social scientists do not see the personality as something passed out to each person at birth along with hair color and sex. Personalities are the result of the socialization process—we learn to be who we become. Attempts to explain personality or to change personality "defects" therefore focus on the relationship between the individual and his or her social situation.

THE HUMAN GROUP

It is obvious that roles are social. Because roles exist only in relationship to other roles and depend on a shared consensus about how they ought to be performed, roles are properties of groups. It is the group that both socializes us into roles and defines what the roles are. Furthermore, groups are collections of roles. Thus, without roles there is no group; without groups there are no roles. The role of father, for example, is meaningless outside the context of a group called the family. You cannot say what expectations you have about fathers without saying how someone in that role should relate to others in the roles of mother and child.

Not every bunch of people who happen to be in the same place at the same time is a group. People waiting to cross a street or passengers in an airplane are not groups, they are *aggregates* or *collectivities*. Social scientists restrict the use of the word group to describe *a collection of people who are involved in some organized and recurrent pattern of interactions*. A group consists of some recognized set of roles and norms. Furthermore, groups are oriented toward some set of goals, whether these involve winning a battle or enjoying friendship and play. Because of shared goals and recurrent interaction among members, groups give rise to a sense of solidarity among participants. As a result, groups have at least a vague notion of the boundary that distinguishes members from nonmembers. To be a group, a collection of people must perceive that they share a collective existence and common purposes.

Social scientists have found it useful to distinguish among several varieties of groups. Most important is the distinction between *primary* and *secondary groups* and *reference groups*.

Primary and Secondary Groups

The terms primary group and secondary group take into account that groups differ in the degree of intimacy among members and in the degree to which members stake their identities in groups. *Primary* groups play a major role in socialization. They are characterized by intimate relations among members and by a strong sense of group membership. As Charles Horton Cooley (1909) put it, when persons find it natural to refer to a group as "we," they are probably describing a primary group. Typical examples of primary groups are families, street gangs, play groups, some social clubs, and villages. Primary groups are the usual scene of our "private lives," and because of our intimacy with and our long exposure to them, they serve as primary sources of identity.

Secondary groups are characterized by less personal relationships among members and demand only a limited part of our loyalties and feelings. In secondary groups, relationships are based more on calculation and utility than on sentiment. We tend to take part in such groups because of what they *do* for us, not because of what they *mean* to us. Typical examples are work groups, civic organizations, and college classes that never gather except for their specific function.

Reference Groups

The concept of *reference* group has become extremely useful in analyzing social behavior. This concept has much in common with the notion of the primary group, but it is also importantly different. Many primary groups are also reference groups, but not all are; secondary groups can also serve as reference groups.

Quite simply, reference groups are those groups to which people refer in order to make comparative self-judgments. Individuals evaluate themselves according to the standards and values of their reference groups, and they orient their behavior, either positively or negatively, toward these groups. Thus, people take from their reference groups a set of values, standards of behavior, and even, in some cases, a certain self-image (Shibutani, 1955).

Sometimes people have negative as well as positive reference groups. Various activities may be disdained because they are associated with a group that the individual holds in contempt. Young people, for example, may avoid certain activities because their parents engage in them.

Conformity to Group Norms

You have already encountered the concept of norms in Chapter 1. Norms are simply the rules defining what is required or acceptable behavior in certain situations. Norms, like roles, are the property of groups. They are the agreed-on rules of the group, and the group is the source of enforcement of these rules. A major part of socialization in both childhood and adulthood, as people move from one group to another, is learning what the rules are and conforming to them. Groups have consider-

able power to make members conform to the norms—from withholding approval to beating up, banishing, or otherwise severely punishing those who transgress.

Social scientists have conducted many experiments to demonstrate the power of groups to enforce conformity. Perhaps the most famous of these is the Asch experiment, named after the social psychologist who first conducted it, Solomon Asch (1952). Asch usually uses a group of seven people. He explains that he is conducting research on visual perceptions and wants each person in the group to judge the length of lines in a series of comparisons. He then displays two large white cards, like the ones shown in Figure 2.5 On one card is a single vertical line. He asks the people to determine which of three obviously different lines on the second card is the same length as the single

Figure 2.5 (Right) *In a series of experiments, Solomon Asch asked people in a group to say which comparison line matched the standard line. It often turned out that an individual would eventually agree with the group even though that meant giving an obviously wrong answer.* (Bottom) *This ability of a group to exert pressure is well illustrated in the film* Twelve Angry Men, *in which a group of jurors finally manages to influence a holdout to change his verdict to "not guilty."*

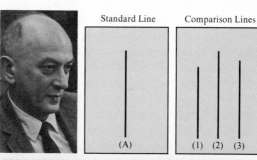

33

line. In the beginning, every member of the group answers correctly—it is a very easy task. But after a few trials, the first five people suddenly pick a line that is obviously incorrect. The sixth person sometimes gazes at them with amazement and then gives the right answer. But the seventh person, agreeing with the first five people, picks an obvious error. This pattern continues. The sixth person becomes anxious. In more than a third of the trials, the sixth person soon begins to go along with the group, no matter how obviously wrong the group's judgment is. The fact is, of course, that the sixth person is the subject of the experiment; the others are all confederates of Professor Asch.

Asch's experiment demonstrates that even in a group of seven strangers gathered for a simple experiment, group pressure is so powerful that many people will conform. Some subjects even reported that they had decided there was something seriously wrong with their vision or that their position in the room must have caused them to misperceive. They simply could not hold out against the group despite what their eyes were telling them.

An individual is even more likely to conform when faced with a more ambiguous judgment or with pressure from primary or reference groups that wield greater control because the individual attaches more importance to them. Humans are social beings. Our identity and behavior are substantially determined by the groups in which we live during our lives.

Ranking Within Groups

Groups are made up of roles, but no group is made up of only one role. Instead, even the simplest groups are internally differentiated—there are always several different positions in a group; therefore, there are always several roles within any group. Furthermore, the roles within a group are not only different but also unequal in power and influence, creating in all groups some degree of ranking of members.

The more complex the group and its tasks, the more highly defined and specialized are the roles and the more likely is the internal ranking of the group to be explicitly acknowledged. But even short-lived and simple groups created in the laboratory quickly develop a dominance structure. If a

number of strangers are brought together and are given a task to perform, someone begins to take charge almost immediately.

DEVIANCE AND ITS CAUSES

We have stressed the power of groups to socialize people by inducing them to conform, to observe the norms, and to fulfill their roles. The socialization power of groups, however, is limited. Although most people conform most of the time, not everyone does all of the time. Failure to conform is *deviant behavior*. Deviance may consist of minor violations of norms or role performance that may be overlooked, but sometimes other group members take deviance seriously and punish the deviant or try to prevent a recurrence of the behavior.

Ordinarily, social scientists pay little attention to minor acts of deviance. They are primarily interested in acts regarded as serious transgressions. They have focused on explaining why serious acts of deviance occur—crime, delinquency, alcoholism, drug addiction, assault, childbeating, prostitution, rape, and the various bizarre behaviors associated with mental illness. These acts are judged important because they violate norms sufficiently to "exceed the tolerance limit of the community" (Clinard, 1968). Put another way, social scientists choose deviant acts to study on the basis of two criteria: (1) the acts must be of major importance to a great number of people in the society, as demonstrated by (2) the existence of formal activities or agencies specifically meant to stymie such acts. Social science tries to explain deviance that has been defined as a *social problem*. Thus, the acts in question are frequently not simply deviant but are against the law. Society has decided it cannot or will not tolerate such behavior and turns to social scientists for aid in finding ways to prevent it.

In fashioning answers to why deviance occurs, social science explicitly or implicitly invokes the basic model of human behavior outlined earlier. Many researchers have inquired into the role of biology in various forms of deviance. For example, there is growing evidence that human biochemistry somehow plays a significant role in mental illness (see Chapter 5). Even greater effort has gone into exploring the influence of personality factors on deviance. For example, is alcoholism a response to the unmet, excessive dependency needs that are characteristic of some personalities? Socialization and the impact of the immediate social situation—primary and reference groups, for example—on personality development or directly on deviant behavior is a major area of inquiry. How does socialization break down and produce a dependent personality? How does socialization fail to produce humans who behave appropriately? Are people socialized into engaging in deviant behavior? Social scientists also direct considerable attention to understanding the structure and operation of groups in relation to deviance. Do the unequal rankings in groups create pressures that cause some members to deviate? Do defects in group mechanisms for punishing deviance or rewarding conformity produce deviance? To what extent is deviance the result of conformity to the norms of deviant groups? As will be clarified toward the end of this chapter and demonstrated in detail in Units II, III, and IV, these and related questions form the fundamental outline of all comprehensive efforts to answer why deviance occurs.

SOCIETIES

Not all social problems involve deviance. For example, poverty is not typically caused by failure to conform to the norms of the group. Furthermore, problems that do primarily involve deviance cannot be wholly understood by analyzing human behavior. It is important to recognize that even if we can fully explain, for example, why certain Americans become drug addicts and others do not, we still face unanswered questions about drug addiction: Why is drug use more widespread in the United States than in some other countries? Why are drugs and addicts dealt with as they are in the United States? Why are drugs regarded as a social problem here? Many of the social factors that influence individual behavior (outlined earlier) also need explaining. For example, if deviance is conformity to the norms of a deviant group, what accounts for the existence of such groups in society?

In order to ask or to answer such questions, we must raise our sights from human behavior to a higher level of analysis—the structure and operation of societies—for social scientists must work on two different levels of analysis. Much of their study is directed toward understanding the behavior of individuals or of relatively small groups. Study at this level is often called *micro* analysis because it is close to the individual (think of microscope). But a considerable amount of social-science study asks how society as a whole operates. Here, social scientists adopt a very broad perspective in which the individual recedes to a dot and very large features of society come into view. Study at this level is called *macro* analysis. Attempts to fashion complete answers to what causes a given social problem always involve both micro and macro considerations.

The preceding section clarified some fundamental premises about human behavior that underlie specific social-science theories. By the same token, macro theories about the operation of societies flow from a number of fundamental assumptions about the nature of societies.

35

SOCIETY AND CULTURE

The starting point for all macro social analysis is understanding the distinction between two fundamental sociological concepts: society and culture. Sociologists often use the term society synonymously with the term nation. Most nations are societies if we mean by society *an aggregate of people who are united by social relationships and who are relatively self-sufficient and self-sustaining, who live in a definite physical location, and who have so existed for a relatively long time.* Obviously, the state of Nevada is not a society. Although Nevadans are united by social relationships, they are not very self-sufficient, for they are economically, militarily, and politically dependent on other states and on the federal government. A nation, too, may not be a society. Internal divisions may exist, even to the point of armed conflict, as in the American Civil War period and in Northern Ireland today; a nation, then, may house two or more societies. By the same token, although a map of a given area may show a number of nations, the area may represent only one society; for example, a map of the Middle East shows many small Arab nations, but their consensus on political aims and their frequent talks of merger suggest that they may not be separate societies. This matter can only be clarified by understanding the connection between societies and cultures.

Sometimes people migrate from one society to another. Between 1820 and 1970, more than 45 million people left their homelands to become Americans. For some of these immigrants, this move presented few problems. For example, groups such as the English and the Scots found it very easy to adjust to life in America. Others, such as the Scandinavians and the Germans, found the change somewhat more difficult. They had to learn to speak English, and they found American customs slightly more alien than did the English and the Scots. But, beginning about 1880 and continuing until after World War I, groups of immigrants arrived in America who found life here extremely different. These newcomers were mainly Catholics and Jews, who were unaccustomed to living in a predominantly Protestant society such as the United States. Many of them came from societies much less technologically advanced than the United States. They came mainly from nations with repressive political regimes, so they had no experience with democratic politics and no basis for taking individual liberties for granted. In short, immigrants to the United States confronted an entirely new way of life.

The point to be made is that differences among societies stem from the fact that *all societies possess a culture.* Society refers to a relatively self-sufficient group of people bonded in time and space by social relationships. *Culture is their way of life.* The classic definition of culture, offered in 1871 by the anthropologist Edward B. Tylor, is still used by social scientists:

Culture . . . is that complex whole which includes knowledge, belief, art, morals, law, custom, and any other capabilities and habits acquired by man as a member of society.

If society is often synonymous with nation, culture is often synonymous with civilization. Culture is that complex pattern of living that humans have evolved. Culture is learned. And the process of socialization is the process of passing on the culture of a group to the next generation. The roles,

36

Figure 2.6   *The human species is biologically the same from country to country, but human customs and modes of dress vary greatly. (Top) In keeping with Moslem culture and religion, Moroccan women wear traditional Arab attire that is designed to cover the face and body. The Russian fashion model (below) and the American beauty contestants (bottom) both wear clothes that emphasize facial and body features. The difference betweeen Soviet and American fashions is less pronounced than that between modern and premodern styles of dress. However, the understated Soviet style of dress contrasts sharply with the American emphasis on glamour in women's clothing.*

norms, traditions, knowledge, technology, beliefs, and values of a group constitute its culture. Obviously, culture and society are interdependent. Without culture there is no society; culture exists only as an aspect of society.

The late waves of immigrants to the United States found even greater problems of adjustment than earlier immigrants had because they came from societies whose cultures were at considerable variance with the dominant culture of the United States. Indeed, most of these immigrant groups never did fully embrace that American culture or completely renounce their previous cultural patterns. We are not interested here in examining the process of *assimilation*—how people exchange one culture for another. Rather, we merely wish to point out that given a great influx of persons, some of whom retained significant portions of their original culture, the United States became a *culturally plural society.* To some extent, several cultures flourish side by side within American society.

In order to deal conceptually with such a situation, social scientists have developed the idea of *subcultures.* A subculture is a culture within a culture—a group that has developed or maintained its own distinctive set of beliefs, morals, customs, and the like. These beliefs may be at variance with those of the larger society, or they may be at variance with those of other subcultures, or both. Groups that have maintained a distinctive ethnic identity in the United States—for example, Jews, Italians, and Spanish-speaking groups—can be regarded as subcultures. By the same token, other groups may have developed into subcultures. Social scientists describe some economic classes in terms of subcultures, or they speak about criminal, delinquent, drug-using, or homosexual subcultures; they see such groups as maintaining norms at considerable variance with the norms of the rest of American society. *Subcultural conflict* within American society plays a major role in the analysis of social problems.

SOCIETIES AS SYSTEMS

The most fundamental premise social scientists make in studying society is that societies are not simply accidental collections of people and cul-

ture. As the sociologist Pitirim Sorokin was fond of pointing out, societies are not garbage dumps; they are not made up of elements that have accidentally come together and get united only by being in the same place at the same time. Social scientists work from the assumption that societies are *systems.* This idea has three important elements: (1) that society consists of a number of "parts"; (2) that these parts are interdependent, so that changes in one part will produce changes in at least one other part; and (3) that there will be a tendency for these parts to maintain some degree of equilibrium, balance, or steadiness in their relationships throughout the system.

Parts of Society

When one considers the whole of the population and the culture, it is obvious that even the simplest society consists of innumerable parts. Social scientists have focused their attention on a few main parts or sectors of societies.

Institutions

Foremost among the parts of societies are *social institutions.* Looking around the social landscape, social scientists recognize that social roles, groups, and activities are not randomly scattered. They tend, instead, to be clustered into identifiable groupings. Social scientists also notice that these groupings tend to be organized around dealing with or solving some fundamental requirement for the maintenance of human societies. For example, all societies have a cluster of roles, groups, and activities devoted to reproduction of the species. This cluster they identify as a social institution called the family. We may define all social institutions as *relatively permanent patterns of specialized roles, groups, procedures, and activities through which fundamental social functions are performed.* Through economic institutions, for example, the society produces and distributes valued goods and services. Through its political institutions, a society coordinates and organizes its activities, especially those involving goals, and makes decisions about goals and means. Societies also need to maintain some degree of commitment of members to the society. Religious institutions perform this function by integrating societies, legitimating existing social arrangements, providing a sacred sense to social norms and values, and giving members of society a shared set of solutions to questions of ultimate meaning.

All societies display some semblance of these basic institutions. A society without an economy is an obvious absurdity. However, the complexity and distinctiveness of institutions differ greatly from one society to another. In primitive societies, for example, there is little specialization and the line separating political, religious, and family activities is somewhat hazy; for example, the political leader may also be the religious leader. However, as societies become more culturally complex, specialization increases and it becomes fairly easy to pick out institutional sectors.

Classes

A second vital way in which social science conceives of a society in terms of parts is to focus on the division of its population into classes. The idea of *class* is fundamentally based on economic inequality, but, as will be clear throughout this book, there are many different consequences and correlates of class divisions. For example, one fundamental and far-reaching research question has prompted hundreds of studies: To what extent do classes within a society exhibit the same or different cultures?

People have observed and have written about classes as far back as our records go. The first important modern effort to systematically define social class was made in the nineteenth century by Karl Marx. Because Marx wrote a great deal over a long period of time and addressed so many complex matters, he tended to use the concept of class in a number of different ways. However, the definition of class he used most often, and for which he is famous, is *a group of people who share a common relationship to the means of production:* factories, machines, land, raw materials. In Marx's view, there were only two basic relationships to the means of production: either you owned the means of production or you had to sell your labor power to those who did own them. Thus, Marx focused on two classes in capitalist societies: owners and workers, or as he called them, the *bourgeoisie* and the *proletariat.* Furthermore,

Marx insisted that a group sharing a common relationship to the means of production could only be considered a true class if its members possessed *class consciousness,* or a realization of their common position in the organization of production, of their common interests, and of their common antagonism toward the other major class.

For Marx, the fundamental feature of class was economic; that is, people's position in the economic order played the major role in fixing their place in society—their prestige, their political power, and even their family life.

Max Weber elaborated on Marx's view, placing less emphasis on economic factors. Weber saw social stratification as based on three principal factors. He argued that these three factors varied somewhat independently and that their interplay had to be understood in order to fully comprehend social stratification. First, Weber identified the *economic order,* which he defined in a way similar to Marx's concept of class. The economic order was based on a person's economic life chances or opportunities. The second factor that he saw in stratification was the *social order,* by which Weber meant the distribution of social honor, prestige, and deference in society. The third factor was the *political order,* by which Weber characterized the distribution of power in society.

Contemporary social scientists employ both Weber's and Marx's conceptions of class. The important point is that, however defined, classes can be taken as distinctive parts of a society and as such they are parts of a *system.*

Interdependence

Simply to view societies as having distinctive parts is not sufficient to call societies systems; one must also view the parts as *interdependent.* This premise is central to macro social science. From it flow the assumptions that changes in one part of society will produce changes in other parts, because the various parts of society as a system depend on one another. The idea of a system includes the idea of interactions and feedback among the units or parts. Marx, for example, argued that if one could detect substantial changes going on in economic institutions and especially in the class structure of a society, one would be certain to find effects of this change showing up in other institutions such as religion, the family, or politics.

Social scientists do not take this premise for granted. They recognize that societies may vary considerably in the degree to which parts are interdependent. Some societies may be highly integrated systems in which the parts are very interdependent; others may have a rather low degree of interdependence among parts. Furthermore, not every part may depend on every other part. It is quite conceivable that substantial changes could go on in one part with the effects showing up in only a few other parts. Seeking the nature and degree of these linkages is a major activity that social scientists engage in.

The idea that societies are systems is relatively new. Indeed, older texts in sociology and anthropology had to devote considerable space to convincing unbelieving readers that societies were systems. Today we are believers, for recent developments in our society have made it obvious how immensely interrelated and complex a system it is. We have discovered that the old saw "as useless as spitting in the ocean" is false. When enough people "spit in the ocean," or dump sewage into it, or spill oil into it, the ocean gets polluted. We have discovered that the earth is a delicate ecological system. Similarly, we now see how interconnected our social life is. A shortage of gasoline begins as an inconvenience, then causes a slowdown in the economy, alters leisure behavior, causes political turmoil, and ultimately may end up influencing family relations and the birth rate and who knows what else. Most people now recognize that virtually every substantial social action and decision sets off ripples in far places in the system.

Equilibrium

The interdependence among parts of the social system inevitably limits the degree to which any given part may change. The result of this mutually limiting relationship is a tendency for the various parts to establish a certain degree of balance, or *equilibrium*—a steady state within which all the parts are aligned within the limits imposed by their connections with other system parts. This state may undergo constant change and readjustment and may best be conceived of as a moving equilibrium in which parts are constantly shifting to realign themselves but in which there are limits on the degree to which any part may change.

When such limits are exceeded, the system will begin to pull apart. For example, if economic changes produced a situation in which the rich had *all* the valued goods and services available in the society, the poor would either die or have to desert the society. But if the work of the poor is necessary to the well-being of the rich, such a development would destroy both rich and poor and thus the whole society. Similarly, religious prohibitions of sexual behavior can never go so far as to bar all sexual relations without destroying the society. More to the point, religious standards that govern sex and that also prohibit birth control will face strong opposition from the family and the economy if the prohibition places too great a burden on these institutions. Such prohibitions have been substantially ignored by many Catholic families in the United States.

A major consideration in system equilibrium is what Alvin W. Gouldner (1959) calls the *principle of functional reciprocity,* or mutual influence. The proposition is that the interdependence among parts of a social system constitutes mutual interchange—the parts not only influence one another but *reciprocally contribute* to the operation and persistence of one another. The economy makes family life possible by providing the necessary food, clothing, and shelter. The family, in turn, contributes the personnel needed to keep the economy operating. The reciprocity need not be wholly symmetrical. For example, if Part A contributes to Part B, Part B need not contribute to Part A. It may contribute to Part C, which contributes to Part D, which contributes to Part A.

It is very important to understand that both interdependence and equilibrium are tendencies only. Different systems vary. *Systems can become misaligned; they can malfunction.* When crises result, they are often resolved by a major reorganization of the society. But sometimes systems collapse. History is littered with the rubble of societies that fell apart.

Most social scientists regard societies as systems. However, they disagree vigorously about which aspects or parts of society play the most important role in determining the operation of the system. These disagreements come into sharpest focus when efforts are made to understand how social problems arise in a society or to understand what should be done to the system to eliminate social problems. We will now discuss these differing perspectives on the operation of societies.

SOCIAL DISORGANIZATION AND FUNCTIONALISM

For the past three or four decades, a dominant theoretical view in social science, especially in sociology and anthropology, has been *functionalism*. The logical form of functionalist analysis was adapted from the biological sciences. Functionalist analysis searches for the particular functions of some feature of society. What is that feature contributing to other features? When one wants to understand why some structure or process occurs in society, one examines how it contributes to or is sustained by its relationships with other parts of the system. For example, in a classic functional analysis, Robert K. Merton (1949b) tried to understand why political machines existed for a long period in American history even though they ran counter to democratic norms and values and often violated the law. Assuming society to be a system, Merton looked to see what political machines did and attempted to demonstrate that the machines made positive contributions to needs of other parts of society that were not being adequately met in other ways. Merton discovered that political machines served several functions: they centralized political power to meet the various demands of a variety of community subgroups; they gave lower-class groups personal assistance in the form of jobs, legal aid, foodbaskets, and so forth; they offered channels for upward social mobility for disadvantaged groups, especially poorer ethnic groups; and they offered protection for illegal services (such as gambling) that many members of the public desired. In short, Merton argued that in their day, political machines offered more means for resolving urban political tensions and social needs than did the available alternative political institutions.

Functional analysis seeks *to explain social phe-* *nomena on the basis of their consequences (functions) for other parts of the system*. It does not follow, however, that whatever one finds in society must be having "good" consequences. Functionalists are quite aware that the systems can get out of kilter and that societies can become so misaligned that they break down. This is precisely the notion that underlies the functionalist analysis of social problems. Social problems, in the functionalist view, reflect failures or breakdowns in the social system. Functionalists use the term *dysfunction* to refer to instances in which one part of society is having negative effects on the other parts and thus on the operation of the system as a whole. Functionalists would say that religious conflicts within a society are dysfunctional for political stability and that in modern times rapid population growth is certainly dysfunctional for economic development.

In the functionalist view, *social problems reflect social disorganization:* something is going wrong within the system; it is not working as well as it could be, or should be; it is becoming disorganized. Merton (1971) put it this way:

Social disorganization refers to inadequacies or failures in a social system . . . such that the collective purposes and individual objectives of its members are less fully realized than they could be in an alternative workable system.

Social disorganization is the result of "multiple social dysfunctions" (Merton, 1971). The functionalist view therefore stresses *objective* conditions as the cause of social problems. Something is wrong with the social system, and as Merton (1971) points out, any claim that a social problem exists "amounts to a *technical judgment about the workings of a social system.*"

This view of what causes social problems clearly indicates where their solution is to be found. Actions must be directed toward overcoming the disorganized features of a society. The dysfunctions must be reduced or eliminated and must be replaced with social arrangements without harmful effects or with less severe effects.

Functionalism and Conservatism

It is often charged that functionalist conceptions of social problems are fundamentally conservative;

that is, they take for granted that a society ought to be preserved, and they regard social problems as symptoms of social disorganization, not as symptoms of an intrinsically wicked society. Radical critics sometimes claim that functionalist views incline toward regarding social unrest as a problem to be resolved by reform, not as the harbinger of a needed social revolution. The very tensions that functionalists would seek to relieve are the forces vital for producing the revolution: consequently, say the critics, functionalists are antirevolutionaries. Certainly, many functionalists do believe in reform rather than in revolution. But reformism is not a necessary consequence of the functionalist perspective. To notice that a society is becoming increasingly disorganized is not necessarily to want to act to preserve it. Functionalism need not imply approval of tyrants or approval of a society based on terror.

As we shall see, the fundamental sticking point between functionalists and those committed to radical views stems from a tendency of functionalists to emphasize the functioning of systems as a whole. They consider their view both realistic and fair because it focuses on the way social arrangements affect all parts of society—all classes, for example. Radicals, however, respond that the functionalists' view inevitably makes them settle for compromise solutions. The debate ultimately turns on judgments about whether a given society ought to be repaired or whether it ought to be discarded entirely because it is so flawed. Those holding the latter view must regard any proposal for reform as compromise.

Social Change

Social disorganization requires an explanation. How does it happen? What makes social systems get out of whack? The answer offered by functionalists is *social change*. Changes occur in systems from two sources. Factors outside the system may cause it to undergo changes. Contact with a more advanced society may introduce rapid technological changes; war usually produces rapid change; famines or droughts cause changes. Changes can also be produced internally. A new invention may lead to rapid changes in industry, which in turn may touch off changes in other parts of the system.

Changes within the family may increase fertility and thus have considerable impact on the economy and on politics. Whatever the source of change, functionalists regard change as the source of social disorganization. This may occur in several ways.

Changes may make it possible to overcome some state of affairs that previously had to be endured. For example, medical discoveries may make it possible to eliminate a dread disease. But until this discovery has been applied to the problem—made accessible to everyone—there will be growing tension between what could be and what is. Application of the new treatment may be delayed, however, because it may require major changes in the economy, in medical practice, in family relations, in religion, or even in the laws of a society.

Change can also cause new problems to arise or minor problems to worsen. For example, at the very time when changes in the structure of American families made them less able to care for the elderly, changes in life expectancy caused an immense increase in the proportion of elderly persons in our society (see Chapter 14). These changes have produced a crisis within our social system. Throughout this book we will be examining how the rapid change that characterizes modern industrial societies causes them chronic problems of social disorganization.

CONFLICT APPROACHES

As was made clear in Chapter 1, social problems always involve judgments by some group in society that something is wrong and needs righting. Merton partly acknowledged this fact in his definition of social disorganization (cited earlier) when he said that the "collective purposes and individual objectives" of a society's members were "less fully realized than they could be." Nevertheless, functionalists like Merton most often emphasize objective flaws in the operation of the social system, not people's perceptions of them, as the cause of social problems.

Two competing views of social problems put greater stress on people's interests and values as the root of social problems than functionalists do. According to these views, not only are value judg-

41

ments inevitably the basis for declaring that something is or is not a social problem but conflicting value judgments play a major role in causing social problems and in preventing their cure. One of these viewpoints, the *value-conflict* approach, takes value conflicts for granted and focuses on the extent and consequences of these conflicts. The second position focuses on the causes of value conflicts as the fundamental source of social problems. Social theorists of the second position attribute social problems to fundamental inequalities built into the social system and to the *class conflicts* that result.

The Value-Conflict Approach

Proponents of the value-conflict approach to social problems make several points. They argue that it is only on the basis of values that people are able to define some state of affairs as undesirable. *Values* are evaluative standards of what is desirable.

If norms are described as prescribed ways of behaving, then a value can be defined as a preference for some state of being. . . . Values underlie norms in the sense that they sum up what makes the norm . . . a proper and good way of behaving. (Glock and Stark, 1965)

A norm may prescribe, for example, that citizens ought to vote in an election. The value of democracy justifies this norm as vital to the maintenance of democratic government. Values such as human dignity, the right of individual liberty, and equality before the law have played a major role in the judgment that racism, sexism, and poverty are wrong. It is on the basis of values that people have a standard against which to judge some state of affairs in the society as harmful, sinful, criminal, or otherwise unacceptable. Some societies find capital punishment repugnant. Others take it for granted as in accord with their conception of justice. What can be defined as a social problem depends upon the values of a society.

But, as many proponents of the value-conflict approach point out, it is often the case that the values (and norms) of a society are inconsistent. There may be a tension or conflict among the values themselves. For example, values of individual liberty and of national security are always in conflict in any society. It is clear that maximizing national security usually curtails individual liberty;

42

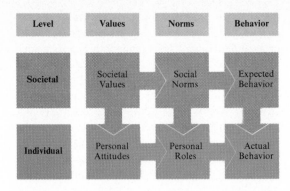

Level	Values	Norms	Behavior
Societal	Societal Values	Social Norms	Expected Behavior
Individual	Personal Attitudes	Personal Roles	Actual Behavior

Figure 2.7 (Above) *Societal values are transmitted to the individual through the process of socialization, but this process does not always work as expected, nor are all individuals willing or able to think and act according to the same set of norms and expectations. Thus, deviance may result and individual behavior may differ from societal expectations. Moreover, societal values themselves may conflict, and individuals may disagree about which values ought to prevail. For the man in the picture below, values of patriotism are sacred.*

in war time, the liberty of those drafted into the army is greatly curtailed. It is also clear that maximizing individual liberty might make a society unable to compel its citizens to make the self-sacrifices necessary to thwart external enemies.

In consequence, values that are somewhat at cross-purposes may be a cause of a social problem (Waller, 1936; Fuller and Myers, 1941). For example, Americans value romantic love, and marriages are arranged not by the parents but by the couple themselves, on the basis of mutual attraction. This value, however, appears to conflict with values concerning the sanctity of marriage and the maintenance of the family, for romantic attraction often proves fragile and, when it breaks down, may prompt extramarital affairs and divorce. Similarly, the value Americans place on individualism seems to be in conflict with the value of cooperation—the good of the individual often conflicts with the good of the community. Indeed, Alexis de Tocqueville, a French aristocrat who, during the nineteenth century, was one of the most astute observers of the American way of life, felt that the value of social equality stifled the social conscience of Americans as well as their sense of community.

Aristocracy links everybody, from peasant to king, in one long chain. Democracy breaks the chain and frees each link. As social equality spreads, there are more and more people who, though neither rich nor powerful enough to have much hold over others, have gained or kept enough wealth and enough understanding to look after their own needs. Such folk owe no man anything and hardly expect anything from anybody. They form the habit of thinking of themselves in isolation and imagining that their whole destiny is in their own hands. Thus, not only does democracy make men forget their ancestors, it also clouds their view of their descendants, and isolates them from their contemporaries. Each man is forever thrown back on himself alone, and there is a danger that he may be shut up in the solitude of his heart. (Tocqueville, 1835)

If value conflicts can cause social problems, they can also keep them alive. As Willard Waller (1936) pointed out, "social problems are not solved because people do not want to solve them." He argued that the solution to a given problem often threatens other strongly held social values and thus effectively bars action. Writing in the 1930s, he pointed out that the problem of venereal disease could not be dealt with at that time, not because medical means were lacking but because a campaign to cure venereal disease was regarded as dangerous to values regarding sexual chastity. A more current example can be found in recent proposals to deal with poverty by guaranteeing an annual income through which persons with incomes below the minimum, whether they worked or not, would be subsidized by public funds. Such a proposal arouses fear and challenges cherished values: Would a guaranteed income undercut individual initiative? Would it be fair if some people lived at the expense of those who worked hard? Would it enlarge government control of the individual? Would it overtax the economy and lead to economic stagnation and to the decline of the whole nation?

Given the conception of society as a system in which the parts are interrelated in complicated ways, it is not idle to wonder what the system-wide consequences of any given change may be. Because the many parts of society are strongly related to a multiciplicity of values, it can readily be seen that disputes over how to deal with any given social problem will inevitably invoke debates and controversy about values.

There is another way in which social problems are related to value conflicts. The previous discussion assumed that although the values of a society may be contradictory, there is some general consensus among members on what the values are. But, as was pointed out in the discussion of culture and society earlier in this chapter, this is not always or necessarily the case. Various groups in society vigorously disagree over which values ought to prevail. Efforts to establish some condition as a social problem may therefore involve conflicts over values. Furthermore, proposals about what ought to be done about a social problem may revolve around disagreements over values. The movement to legalize abortion, for example, raised several issues: People on the one side spoke of values of individual autonomy, values about sexuality as separable from procreation, values of a way of life that would result from a lower birth rate, and the like. People on the other side voiced values about religious obligations, about the sanctity of all human life, and about chastity.

43

Because values inevitably have a semisacred quality—they are our ideals about what ought to be—conflicts among them are not easily settled. Antiabortion forces have not accepted their defeat and still strive to reassert the older values. Similarly, groups such as the Women's Christian Temperance Union have not accepted the repeal of the prohibition of alcoholic beverages and continue to work on against demon rum.

A number of features of American society foster different value systems for different groups. For one thing, the United States is made up of many ethnic and religious groups who still retain some degree of commitment to their traditional cultures. Cultural differences are always a source of value conflict. Birth control and abortion issues have invoked Protestant and Catholic value conflicts. Another source of value conflict has been regional differences. Many issues involve value conflicts between rural and urban groups. Others have brought the differences between Northern and Southern values into play. But perhaps the source of value conflicts given most attention is social-class differences.

The Class-Conflict Approach

Contemporary class-conflict theories of social problems utilize many of the assumptions of functionalist theories. However, instead of examining how some social arrangement affects the social system as a whole, conflict theorists tend to concentrate on the ways in which a society is organized to serve the interests of the few at the expense of the many. From this basic difference in outlook flow a number of disagreements between functionalist and conflict interpretations.

Class Interest and Power

The main difference between conflict theory and ordinary functionalism lies in their answers to the question "Functional for whom?" Often, functionalists answer "Functional for the society as a whole." They stress *the links among all parts of society* and use the state of the social system as a whole as their basis for assessing the costs and benefits of problems and policies. But most conflict theorists follow Karl Marx and answer "Functional for the ruling class." They stress the

way in which particular social arrangements— especially economic arrangements—serve *particular groups within societies at the expense of other groups.* They use class interests rather than the whole society as the basis for assessing costs and benefits. Often, they argue that it is meaningless to speak of the interests of society as a whole, for society (at least under capitalism) is composed of classes whose interests are inevitably and ceaselessly in opposition.

Thus, conflict theorists argue that the working class (the proletariat) is exploited by the owners and bosses (the bourgeoisie) and that the two groups cannot have common interests. Furthermore, the social system is inevitably designed to give maximum advantage to the most powerful groups in society. Indeed, the values of a society are those of the powerful, not those of the population as a whole. As Marx wrote in *The Communist Manifesto* in 1848, "The ruling ideas of any age are the ideas of its ruling class." The reasoning he used is that the more powerful a social class, the more impact it has on how a society operates, and the powerful inevitably use their power to shape society to their own interests. In this view, social problems exist because they benefit the most powerful members of society.

Class Struggle and Revolution

Conflict received careful attention from Marx in his concept of *class struggle,* but it is interesting to note that, in other respects, Marx was an early and special kind of functionalist (Stinchcombe, 1968). Marx clearly assumed that societies are systems and that change in one aspect of society affects many other aspects of society. Similarly, Marx explained the origins and persistence of particular social structures and activities on the basis of their consequences. Furthermore, Marx was a perceptive detector of dysfunctions, which he characterized as "contradictions." He argued that the fundamental design of capitalist societies was flawed and that the parts could never achieve a state of equilibrium because of contradictions among them. The long-term effect of these contradictions would be the steady increase of social disorganization and of social problems, culminating in the final crisis: the revolution that would sweep away the old system and create a new one free of such internal contradictions.

Predictions of revolution follow from the assumptions of conflict theorists. Although they deny common interests among social classes, they tend to assume a much *tighter interdependence* among the parts of a social system than do functionalists. Thus, they argue against the possibility of reform. Like Marx, they frequently argue that the whole society must be overhauled in order to alter certain offending aspects of it (Nisbet, 1971). They reason that because the whole of society is set up to benefit the powerful, it is wholly in need of change. And they argue that substantial change can be accomplished only if power is seized from the ruling classes.

Reform

Conflict theorists are not wholly consistent in their denial that reforms are feasible. They do seem to believe that if reforms succeed, they will succeed only for the ruling class, whose interests lie in staving off revolution; they have long opposed reforms as serving the interests of the bourgeoisie. Few conflict theorists would hold up any existing socialist state as a good model of a post-revolutionary society; in fact, it must be pointed out that problems of individual deviance seem equally widespread in socialist and capitalist societies. Furthermore, exploitation of workers and attendant problems such as poverty and racism are demonstrably much less severe in Western nations today than they were 100 years ago when Marx denied the possibility of reform.

Clearly, class conflict does play a major role in social problems. If conflict theorists have tended to overlook the extent of common interests among social classes within a society, functionalists have tended to overemphasize these matters and to gloss over the deep divisions in class interests. As will be seen repeatedly in subsequent chapters, government usually deals more vigorously with problems that affect the middle and upper classes than with problems that only affect less powerful groups.

A comprehensive understanding of how our society operates requires a blending of both points of view. If we want to know why a situation in society is the way it is, we must follow the functional-

ists' advice and seek the consequences of that situation for other parts of the system. But we must also follow the conflict theorists' advice to determine how that situation serves the interests of groups with the most power to shape policies.

A THEORETICAL OUTLINE

We have reviewed the basic concepts and premises that social scientists use to assess social problems. First, we looked at basic aspects of individual human behavior and the individual's immediate social situation. Then we took up macro questions about the nature and operation of societies as systems and different approaches to social problems at the system level. These fundamental principles are applied and utilized by the various theories about particular social problems discussed in Units II, III, and IV. Before moving on, we will sum up where we have been. A *comprehensive* explanation of any given social problem must draw on *all* the material covered so far. Put another way, social problems must be considered in terms of a series of levels of analysis, beginning with biology and ending with the way society operates at the macro system level.

It may be useful to consider the levels of social-science analysis as a ladder (see Figure 2.8). At the most micro level are questions about human physiology; at the most macro level are questions about societies as whole systems. What is important to recognize is that these levels of analysis are nested within one another much like a set of progressively larger boxes that may be placed one over another. Each level of analysis permits certain questions to be asked that could not be asked at any lower level of analysis. Indeed, each higher level can ask questions about the causes of certain features of the questions raised at the lower level. For example, the psychological level of analysis permits questions about how aspects of individual personalities interact with and influence physiological aspects of individuals. Similarly, the social-psychological level of analysis is appropriate for asking how the group—the immediate social setting—influences personality as well as individual behavior. The middle-range sociological level of analysis permits questions about why and how internal processes

45

Figure 2.8   Levels of Analysis and Issues Appropriate to Each Level.

Levels	Levels	Appropriate Questions
MICRO LEVEL 	Physiological (the human animal)	To what extent is any particular behavior produced by such physiological factors as hormones, bodily characteristics, biochemical reactions, and the like? Are such factors hereditary?
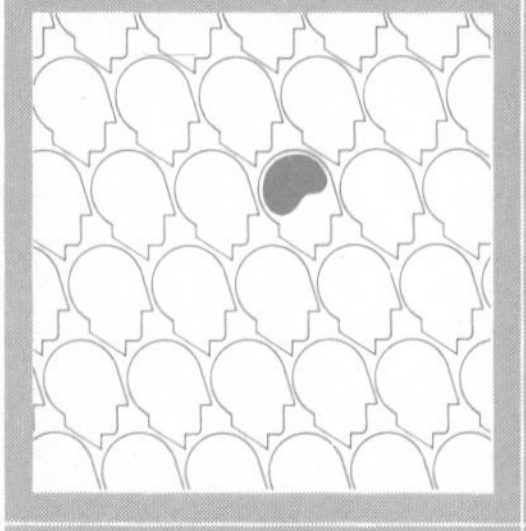	Psychological (the human actor)	Do enduring cognitive or emotional characteristics (personalities) of individuals play an important role in producing the behavior? Are these unusual characteristics?
	Social Psychological (the human group)	How and to what extent are particular personality features shaped by interpersonal relations and the immediate social situation? How is behavior shaped by these same features of social life?
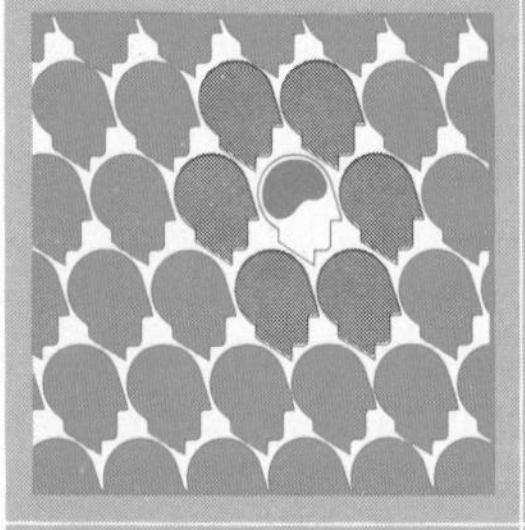	Sociological: 1. Middle-range (processes *within* a social system)	How and to what extent does the general social environment in which people find themselves vary? How do these variations influence psychological and social-psychological factors? How do these variations affect behavior?
MACRO LEVEL 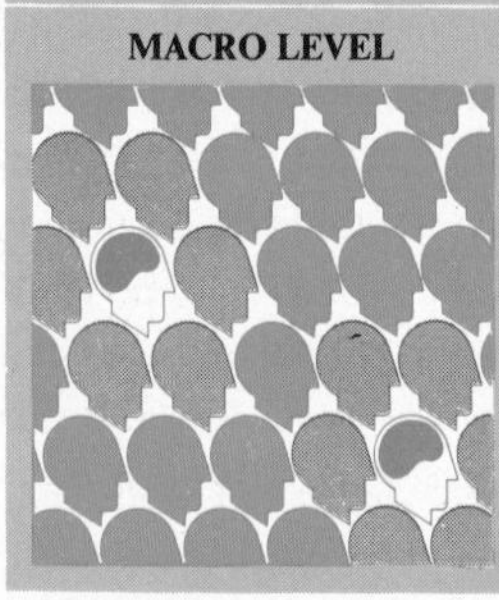	2. Societal (comparisons *across* systems; the operation of the system as a whole)	Why do societies differ in certain ways? To what extent do cultural, technological, and institutional differences between societies influence social problems? How do changes within the system create or reduce social problems?

46

within a social system influence the immediate social situation of the individual. Questions about why societies differ and the impact of the total social system on all lower levels of analysis must be raised at the societal level of analysis.

Study of Figure 2.8 will show you how the material presented so far in this chapter fits together. And it will prepare you for the figures displayed in the chapters in Units II and III. (Unit IV utilizes a different approach.) Those figures, however, focus on specific social problems and thus outline the specific questions about the problem to be considered at each level of analysis. In context, you should find these figures useful roadmaps to the discussions of what causes certain social problems.

SOCIAL PROBLEMS AND COMPLEX INDUSTRIAL SOCIETIES

To conclude this chapter, we will briefly explore the special features of the complex, industrial society—the kind of society in which we live. As will be clear throughout this book, the kinds of social problems we face (and how we can best deal with them) are substantially determined by the features of such societies.

First, many long-standing social conditions have been *recognized* as social problems only in societies equipped to alter these conditions. Only industrial societies, for example, have been able to do without child labor and therefore have had the luxury of asking whether children *should* work. Such societies have had the technology to greatly eliminate infant mortality; therefore, only such societies can charge that when one nation's mortality rate remains noticeably higher than others' (as ours does above that of most European nations), this reflects shocking social negligence.

Second, some problems have been *created* (or worsened) by the development of industrial societies. Problems such as environmental destruction and old age are the direct consequences of a highly technological society capable of ravaging nature and of enabling a substantial number of persons to survive to an old age.

Finally, most of the problems taken up in this book are overwhelmingly *urban,* or city, prob-

lems. As we shall see, urbanism and industrialization are inextricably linked.

For all these reasons, an understanding of complex, urban, industrial societies is fundamental to understanding American social problems. The most important thing to recognize about advanced modern nations is that they are essentially new things under the sun—we are living in the first few decades during which highly industrialized and highly urbanized societies have existed. Humans have had little more than two generations of experience with them. Consequently, we are only just beginning to grasp some fundamental understanding of the problems and character of such societies.

PROBLEMS OF SCALE

Perhaps the most staggering difference between modern times and all previous human experience is one of scale. Never before have societies, nations, cities, or organizations been nearly so large as they are today. Because most of us have grown up since the virtual quantum jump in the scale of social life that occurred during the late nineteenth and early twentieth centuries, we tend to take such size for granted and to read it back into history. But many of our present problems stem from this immense shift in scale and from the fact that we have so little understanding of how to deal with it.

Consider the following examples of the enormous change in scale:

In 1776, at the start of the American Revolution, there were only about 3 million Americans. Perhaps more surprisingly, Great Britain, that awesome world power across the Atlantic against whom we pitted our puny forces, had only 6 million citizens—today, everyone on both sides of the Revolutionary War could be housed in the New York City area.

When George Washington took office as first President of the United States, he personally attested to the "fitness of character" of all employees of the federal government. There were fewer than 700 of them. Today, *excluding* the members of the armed forces, there are approximately 3 million federal employees (and another 10 million state-governmet and local-government employees).

47

Until recent times, cities have been the size of what we today consider modest-sized towns. When Queen Elizabeth reigned during the Golden Age of English sea power, there were only 152,000 inhabitants of London. Paris, at the time of the French Revolution, had only 600,000 people. At the time of the American Civil War, Abraham Lincoln tried to see all the citizens who called at the White House, and cows grazed in Brooklyn.

The growth of populations, cities, and government has been matched by the growth of large organizations. Until very recently, industry typically comprised many small firms competing for markets. Today, industry is the affair of giants. In 1919 more than 315 independent firms in the United States manufactured automobiles. Today there are only four automobile manufacturers. One of them, General Motors, employs nearly 800,000 people—a work force larger than the able-bodied adult American population in 1776. In fact, the 500 largest corporations in the United States account for 65 percent of the sales of all our industrial production and employ 76 percent of all our industrial workers.

As the scale of modern societies expanded, there came a point when the change was no longer a matter of degree but of *kind*. For one thing, a whole new technology of management had to be invented to grapple with monitoring and managing systems of present-day size. Gone are the days when the person officially in charge could personally oversee operations of such huge organizations. An early sign of this trouble appeared at the beginning of the nineteenth century, when even such a genius as Napoleon found that military operations approaching modern scale were simply beyond his ability to direct personally. Since Napoleon stood on a hilltop and watched his Grand Army slip from his command, management science and organizational analysis have become central concerns because they deal with vital new questions: How can systems beyond the grasp of any individual be managed? How do (and should) organizations of this immense scale operate?

Modern communications inventions have made it possible to coordinate such enormous organizations—to the extent that they can be coordinated at all. Radios or field telephones would

have given Napoleon a chance to continue personal command a while longer. But as we shall see, even he would have had to soon surrender his power to staffs and committees. Furthermore, in many ways, modern communications have increased the problem of scale by making systems more integrated and their parts more interdependent—and thus of larger functional scale than before.

Consider America in the 1890s. It had a population of almost 63 million, a huge number by the standard of national populations 100 years earlier. It was spread over roughly the same area as today, yet in many ways, America as a nation was something of a fiction then. Most people did not experience life as national; they oriented their lives to their immediate community, and few of them traveled beyond the surrounding district. The larger society impinged little on local communities. News was late in arriving. Furthermore, local communities differed greatly in customs, speech, politics, fashions, and the like.

Modern communications have changed all that. Every night, in every community in the nation, citizens see the same news reports and watch the same television shows. Fads and fashions that used to take months or years to spread across the land now take only days to penetrate every corner of the country. Marshall McLuhan has argued that instant communications have turned the world into a "global village." Whether or not the conception of a single village can be applied to the world, it seems an apt description of the impact of mass communications in the United States. We have been shifting our sense of community from our local surroundings to the nation as a whole. It is hardly surprising that the patriarch of this new national village—the most known and trusted figure among us—is CBS anchorman Walter Cronkite. The decline of localism and regionalism has meant that the nation is becoming the primary social and political system. This further compounds the problem of scale.

One of the more obvious problems stemming from the development of huge organizations and institutions is the loss of personal relations and individuality. Unlike the small retail merchant, large corporations are incapable of knowing their customers and of dealing with their individual needs. (Ironically, computers offer the only means for "personalizing" relations between individuals and huge organizations; properly programmed, a computer can remember and respond to huge numbers of us.) And unlike small employers, huge corporations are not able to deal personally with their employees.

A second problem has been inefficiency and bureaucracy. Having had so little experience with huge organizations, we have been overloaded with problems of keeping track of what is going on, which has sometimes meant putting more effort into knowing what we are doing than into doing something. As later chapters will point out, many government agencies spend a great deal of time and money keeping track of what they are up to. Yet, frequently, they have simply lost sight of what is going on, which results in waste, duplicated effort, and negligence. Perhaps the most important consequences of the new problems of scale are the increasing specialization of organizational roles and the increasing diffusion of authority.

Specialization

Human societies have always been characterized by a division of labor—not all members of a group perform identical tasks. In simple, preliterate groups, work was divided according to age and sex differences—there was men's work, women's work, and children's work. As societies grew and became more technologically complex, the division of labor became increasingly more complex. Members concentrated their efforts along particular lines, such as farming, leather tanning, or weapon making.

Modern societies are marked by an immensely complex division of labor. Work has been broken down into highly specialized tasks, and most jobs require special training. Advanced technology accounts for part of specialization, but part is a consequence of scale. When dealing with a large work force, it is more efficient to have people specialize in a few tasks than to have them moving from task to task. In small work groups, people can keep track of one another and of what tasks need to be accomplished next. In very large-scale organizations, however, members can glimpse only a small part of the whole operation and cannot function

effectively without direction. Indeed, unless people are assigned specific tasks, it is impossible to supervise them or to know who is responsible for what or even to keep the system going.

Specialization is so great in this country today that the United States Department of Labor lists 21,741 distinct occupations. That is but an indication, for within any of these occupations people are often assigned different specific tasks. For example, an airplane manufacturer, such as Boeing, employs many design engineers. But some of these engineers have never worked on any part of an airplane other than the wings. Others have worked only on tails. Thus, one group of engineers engaged in designing airplanes may have very little understanding of what another group does.

Such specialization is necessary in large-scale, complex organizations. But specialization also creates new problems. It requires an immense number of managers and record keepers to coordinate the activities of such a vast collection of specialists. Moreover, specialization has necessitated a considerable diffusion of authority downward through large-scale organizations.

Diffusion of Authority

In his book *The New Industrial State* (1967), John Kenneth Galbraith pointed out that specialized knowledge and assignments have become so great in modern organizations that it would take a formidable genius to command all the knowledge and skill required to deal with even a few of the ordinary decisions that must be made daily. Responsibility has therefore passed to groups composed of various specialists—indeed, as Galbraith put it, one could do worse than to think of modern organizations as composed of a "hierarchy of committees." Decisions tend to flow upward from these committees, and the man at the top lacks the special knowledge and skills to challenge those decisions. Galbraith (1967) recalled that during his days in charge of the Office of Price Administration during World War II, he was nearly helpless to alter decisions fixing particular prices when these decisions came to him "after an extensive exercise in group decision-making in which lawyers, economists, accountants, men knowledgeable of the product and industry, and specialists in

49

public righteousness had all participated.'' To challenge such a decision, he would have needed a similar committee to guide him. He concluded: ''To have responsibility for all of the prices in the United States was awesome; to discover how slight was one's power in the face of group decision-making was sobering.''

Galbraith correctly saw that under present conditions of organizational specialization and complexity, power inevitably passes into the hands of a great many subordinate specialists, into the hands of the *technostructure*. Decisions in the modern organization are shaped by the technostructure, and thus the power of those at the top is greatly reduced, which is precisely what President John Kennedy meant when in response to various proposals he would say, ''I agree but I don't know whether the government will agree.''

If the diffusion of authority means that modern organizations are more democratic because a larger proportion of people share the power to make decisions, it also means that decisions are harder to make than they used to be and that a great many groups with narrow vested interests within any organization have considerable veto power. It is important to keep this widespread veto power in mind when considering the ways in which governmental and private organizations in the United States have responded to social problems. The fact that new people with new ideas are put in charge of the government or of some large organization does not necessarily mean that what goes on will significantly change. Unless people can sell their ideas to the technostructure, things are likely to continue as they did before.

PROBLEMS OF URBANIZATION

Until very recently, nearly all human beings lived on farms or in small villages. In 1790, only 5 percent of Americans lived in cities of more than 2,500 inhabitants. Even 100 years ago, there were no predominantly urban societies. At the beginning of this century, Great Britain had reached the point at which it could be called urbanized. Since then, the rush to the city has resulted in all advanced industrial nations becoming urban societies. More than half of Americans today live in cities, and most of them live in very large metropolitan areas. Fewer than 5 percent of Americans now live on farms.

Why did people rush to the city? What causes urbanization? First, changes in the technology of farming made large cities possible. In earlier times, the overwhelming majority of citizens had to farm in order to raise enough food for the society. The surplus from the farms was sufficient only to support a small proportion of the population in cities. Today, only a small proportion of the population needs to farm in order to feed the rest. Second, industrialization made urbanization *necessary*. To industrialize, societies must free a major portion of their labor force from farming and make them available to supply the work force for factories and offices. Furthermore, industrial labor must be concentrated close to the plants and industries. Industrialization requires urban living. Thus technological changes in farming forced people out of the countryside while technological changes in urban industry drew them to the city. And the cities created new kinds of problems.

Alienation

Compared with farming hamlets and small towns, cities are huge and necessarily complicated systems. Because of their scale, cities pose problems of impersonality and ''strangerhood.'' In small towns, people can deal with one another on personal terms and assess one another on the basis of friendship or at least acquaintanceship. The masses of persons in cities make wide acquaintanceship impossible. We have had to learn haltingly how to deal with one another as strangers (Lofland, 1973). We must constantly confront others without any direct knowledge of their intentions.

It is often pointed out that the lower crime and delinquency rates of rural areas may not reflect fewer acts in violation of the law. Instead, they may reflect the greater capacity of highly personal systems to solve such matters through informal means. Consider a group of young males creating a disturbance on a street. If the disturbance occurs in a small town, chances are that the youths are known to people living along the street and that the offended citizens can settle the problem on their own by telling the group to shut up and move on or

Figure 2.9   Yosemite Park. In 1930 the national parks had 3 million visitor days a year (one person staying twelve hours) out of a population of 122 million. By 1960, this rose to 79 million visitor days from a population of 179 million. In 1968 there were 157 million visitor days in the parks from a population of 200 million.

perhaps by a call to the parents of the boys. Even if the police are called, they may be able to settle the problem informally because they know the boys and their true degree of threat to the community. If the boys creating the disturbance are strangers, however, the citizens cannot estimate their likely reaction to being told to shut up. Nor do the police know whether these are a gang of "toughs" or a bunch of "good" kids being rowdy. Among strangers, there is often more recourse to impersonal standards of judgment.

Similarly, communities of strangers have fewer informal resources for dealing with human problems. Small-town teachers know the families of their students. They have less need for specialists, such as social workers or educational counselors, to take over problem children. Small-town merchants know when a family is only temporarily short of money, so they can more readily risk extending credit to tide the family over. But in cities the informal networks for assisting people during times of trouble or need are unable to form. In cities personal troubles become social problems and require the creation of special organizations and occupations.

Density

The sheer human density of cities creates special problems. As Chapter 15 points out, cities tax the ecological system because they expell such concentrated amounts of waste products into the air and water. Density also results in congestion; streets and sidewalks are clogged because so many people must get from place to place at the same time. Furthermore, the density produced by the concentration of people in urban areas puts a severe strain on outside recreation and wilderness facilities. Going out to hike or camp is an urban activity—farmers have never shown much interest in getting closer to nature than they ordinarily are. For the most part, urbanites trying to get closer to nature are limited to natural areas near cities. Thus, Yosemite National Park, only a day's drive from San Francisco and Los Angeles, is literally breaking down under the masses who crowd in trying to get away from it all.

An additional source of urban problems is that large cities have more or less just happened. No one planned on cities of the present size, and even those who anticipated them knew little about how to best design and organize them. Consequently, many of our cities have sprawled over an immense area, and their growth was based on the private automobiles that moved people from homes in the suburbs to factories and offices at the center. But we now find that center-city streets and parking cannot handle the number of cars going in and out each day. Nor can the air surrounding cities sustain the pollution from automobile exhaust.

It is probably no surprise that our first attempts to design such huge cities were less than successful—first attempts at difficult new problems are usually not very successful. We are left with worsening crises caused by the misdesign and malfunction of our cities and with an increasing need to devote massive amounts of resources to remodeling and rebuilding cities. Worse yet, we have no certain basis for fashioning a new model city. We had thousands of years to develop an agrarian life style suitable for human needs—but we will perhaps have only decades in which to learn about urban life. There are too many of us, and our lives depend too much on industry and technology for a return to rural life to be a possible alternative.

PROBLEMS OF COMPLEX TECHNOLOGY

We have already discussed how modern societies have resulted in major changes in the kinds of work people do. The vast majority of workers no longer farm for a living. Furthermore, work has become extremely specialized within modern societies. But we are now in the midst of perhaps an even more remarkable change in the nature of work. With industrialization, the initial shift in the work force was from farm labor to industrial labor, from the field to the factory. More recently, the major shift has been from the factory to the office.

Increasingly, work is shifting from manual labor to mental labor. As Peter F. Drucker (1969) has put it, we are shifting from an economy based on industry to one based on knowledge. It is not simply that work is becoming more specialized but that *more and more people are becoming specialists in technology and information*. In 1900, just

over 17 percent of the American work force was employed in white-collar occupations. By 1960, 42 percent of the labor force held white-collar jobs, and white-collar workers outnumbered manual workers, who made up only 37.5 percent of the labor force (the remainder farmed or were in service occupations). By 1980, it is estimated that about 51 percent of employed persons will be in white-collar jobs. Of these, about a third will be in professional and upper-technical occupations.

White-collar workers, especially those employed in technical and professional occupations, earn their living not by manipulating objects but by manipulating information and ideas. The manipulaton of objects is rapidly being automated, and human resources are being diverted to knowledge work. By the late 1970s, the knowledge sector of the economy is expected to account for half of the national economy—half of the dollars earned will come from the production and distribution of ideas and information (Drucker, 1969).

A knowledge-based economy presupposes a large labor pool of persons highly skilled in acquiring and applying new knowledge. The growth of mass education in this country (52 percent of eighteen-year-olds now begin college) permitted the shift to a knowledge economy. And the development of an increasingly complex technology both permitted and necessitated the growth of a knowledge economy.

Although this shift has meant great increases in the earning power of most Americans and has greatly reduced the proportion forced to do hard physical labor or boring assembly-line tasks, it has had severe consequences for other groups in our society. Not all Americans have been prepared for knowledge jobs; indeed, many have not been prepared for skilled industrial tasks. Thus, each day it becomes less possible to use those potential members of the labor force who lack skills. The trap of poverty and unemployment is daily closing more tightly on groups such as the rural poor, disadvantaged racial and ethnic minorities, and anyone who is qualified only for unskilled, manual work. The gap between the skills they have to offer and the openings in the job market is rapidly increasing. Table 2.1 shows the job qualifications of unemployed persons in New York City's black community in 1966 and the distribution of job openings expected to occur over the next decade. The plight of the unemployed and the small chance most have of getting jobs is obvious. More than 52 percent are qualified only for laboring jobs, but less than 1 percent of the expected job openings will be for laborers. About two-thirds of the expected job openings are for white-collar workers, but only about 14 percent of unemployed blacks are qualified to obtain such jobs. The days are over when a person without training or skills could at least expect to be able to sell his muscle power on the labor market; to make the point, in November 1970, more than 3,000 men applied for thirty-two openings for street sweepers in San Francisco. Only about 2 percent of the energy used to do work in the United States today comes from human muscle power (Lenski, 1966). Technology has been a mixed blessing. It has made the lives of the majority of persons far easier and more interesting, but it threatens to reduce the lives of others to poverty.

Table 2.1   Skills Gap in the New York City Ghetto

SKILL LEVEL	QUALIFIED UNEMPLOYED BLACKS 1966	ESTIMATED JOB OPENINGS 1965–1975
White-Collar	13.6%	65.7%
Craftsmen	2.8%	7.4%
Operatives	14.7%	7.7%
Service	16.6%	18.6%
Laborers and Others	52.3%	0.6%

Source: Adapted from "Poverty and Economic Development in New York City" (First National City Bank, December, 1968), p. 12.

A fundamental feature of our rapidly increasing technology has been increased control over our physical environment. With this control comes a new problem of the impact of humans on the environment (see Chapter 15). The simple fact that humans now *can* move mountains raises the problem of which mountains to move where and which mountains to leave alone. We now recognize that resources are not infinite and that we must establish priorities for their use. We must learn how to deal with these questions because turning back to a less technological society is out of the question. We will not solve the population problem by withdrawing public health technology and letting the death rate rise. We will not resolve technological unemployment by discarding bulldozers in favor

of gangs of laborers who work with picks and shovels.

An unanticipated consequence of our technological capacity probably has been to encourage unrealistic expectations about what can be accomplished and how quickly. Repeatedly, one hears people say, "Well, if we can go to the moon, why can't we lick poverty," or remake the cities, or cure crime, or whatever social problem is on their minds at the moment. The fact is that going to the moon was not a feat that taxed our technology. It merely required effective organization of existing engineering technology; no new breakthroughs were required. Compared with most social problems that beset us, going to the moon was a relatively minor problem. For one thing, the solar system is a predictable system; we have no trouble predicting exactly where the moon will be at any given moment. But we do not yet have the technical capacity to predict exactly where the economy or other major sectors of society will "be" at any particular time. Social engineering is much more complicated than the engineering required for space travel.

To the extent that people do not recognize the greater complexity of social engineering, they undergo unnecessary frustration. Many people think that we could solve social problems easily if only we had the will to do so. By the same token, many lose heart too quickly when programs such as the war on poverty fail to achieve quick success. But perhaps the greatest problem is a tendency for everyone to be his or her own expert on many social problems.

SOCIAL SCIENCE AND COMMON SENSE

It is obvious to nearly everyone that it takes experts to build a moon rocket. No politician, newspaper editor, or community organization submitted original blueprints for rocket engines or command modules. But a problem for social science is that everyone is somewhat familiar with its special subject matter—people. Most of us see our first algebraic equation or our first chemical reaction in a classroom. But we have all been participating in human society all our lives. Thus, we all do know something about social science, but this familiarity

Figure 2.10   *Many aspects of American culture and society are reflected in systems and behavior related to driving and the automobile, which provides us with a common theme in these photographs illustrating some fundamental social-science concepts and assumptions.*

Human behavior and socialization: Picture 1 shows that human beings share a common biological heritage with other animals; like chimpanzees, we are biological organisms and can be studied as such. The line separating the human animal from other species is sometimes very fine, as is demonstrated in the case of the chimpanzee who was given a traffic ticket for driving on a Florida highway. Many animals are capable of learning complex forms of behavior, including driving a car. It is not

clear to what degree behavior, such as aggression (Picture 2), is biologically determined. Picture 3 illustrates one of the ways in which young people are socialized into our car culture.

Groups: Pictures 4 and 5 show a primary group—a nuclear family, with kids, pet, and parents all packed for a trip in their station wagon—and a secondary group—school children with their bus. Picture 6 shows a reference group, a gathering of sports-car-club members with their cars.

Norms, roles, and deviant behavior: In picture 7, British drivers take for granted the norm of driving on the left-hand side of the road. The process of ranking within a group is found among the members of a race-car-pit crew (Picture 8), where different roles and tasks are associated with higher or lower

54

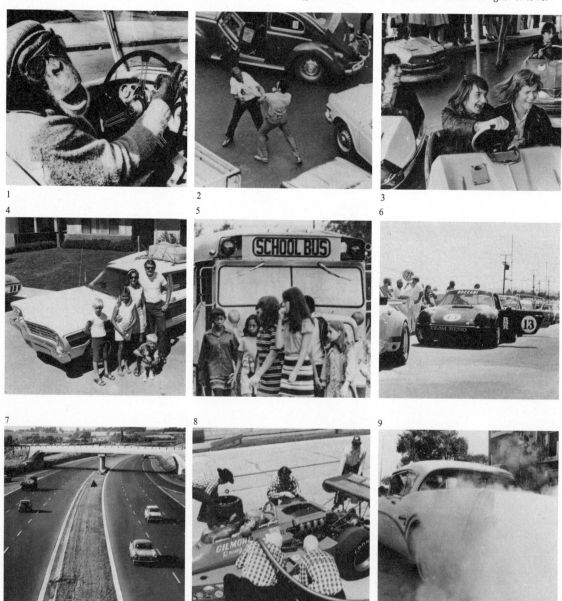

status and rank. Just as in other spheres of society, deviance is also found in the car culture. The smoking exhaust of the car shown in Picture 9 marks its owner as a polluter who deviates from norms governing the individual's responsibility to help clean up the environment.

Levels of analysis: In Picture 10, we move to the level of a macro analysis of society via aerial photography of a highway system. The emphasis is on major patterns; the next picture (11) represents a middle-level view of our car culture, showing groups of cars on a highway interchange; Picture 12 represents the micro level of social analysis, focusing on an individual driver.

Societies as systems: Societies can be seen as systems, just as highway networks are systems, sometimes controlled from a computer-assisted center as in Picture 13. Just like other institutions, traffic systems may become misaligned, (14).

Urbanization: Anyone who must regularly fight rush-hour traffic on urban highways can well appreciate the problems of scale and growth. The construction of additional roads merely seems to provide more space for more cars (15). The increase in urbanization and scale has also produced increased specialization (16). Some of the problems of urbanization, scale, and growth may be alleviated through the kind of social engineering and transportation planning exemplified by the Bay Area Rapid Transit (BART) system of the San Francisco area (17). Finally, a sign advertising auto insurance along with motor tune-ups (18) shows the interrelatedness of systems.

10

11

12

55

13   14   15

16   17   18

too often encourages people to act as their own social scientist.

Although some social scientists may be called on to advise on the creation of a new drug program or a new prison system, they typically play only a limited role in these matters. They are never told by the Congress, "Here is the money. Do what has to be done." Instead, social scientists usually only evaluate the effectiveness of programs they had little role in designing and virtually no role in operating. As will be clear in subsequent chapters, such programs are often designed in ways that violate well-established research findings. It has been demonstrated, for example, that the amount of police patrolling has no impact on the crime rate and that delinquency-prevention programs do not prevent delinquency (see Chapter 3). This knowledge has so far had no restraining influence: Police patrol efforts have been massively increased in order to stem the rising crime rate; each year the failure of delinquency-prevention programs to deflect the delinquency rate is somehow taken as proof that more money needs to be spent on such programs.

Here is the root of the problem: Most people in our society have not yet learned to question their commonsense beliefs about social life. Most of us recognize that the evidence of our senses is not a trustworthy guide in the realm of physical science—the sun does not go around the earth; heavier objects do not fall faster than lighter ones; the earth is not flat. But we still place unjustified faith in our commonsense notions about society, even when these notions are demonstrably false.

Did you know that interpersonal violence is *not* more common among poor people than among middle- and upper-class persons? Or that truly believing that God punishes sins has *no* restraining influence on juvenile delinquency? Or that the world population explosion was *not* caused by a rise in the birth rate? Or that the stresses of modern living have *not* caused an increase in mental illness? These and many other facts are demonstrated and explained in subsequent chapters. Unfortunately, wrong views still frequently shape our laws, policies, and social programs. It is little wonder that they often worsen the conditions they were meant to improve.

What to do? Clearly the answer is *not* to resign our responsibilities by turning our lives over to social-science experts. Many of the most fundamental questions have to do with values, with how we want the world to be, not with technical judgments. These are matters that require political resolution. What is needed is a clearer understanding of what is and what is not a matter for social scientists to decide.

Physicists were asked to build an atomic bomb; they were not asked whether a bomb should be built or used, but only whether it could be. Engineers are not asked whether a bridge or a moon rocket should be built—they are consulted about feasibility. In similar fashion, whether to try to eliminate poverty is a political decision. Social scientists, therefore, cannot make the decision, but they should have maximum influence on the nuts and bolts of designing any feasible program. Furthermore, it should be accepted as inevitable that plans will have to be altered on the basis of early results. Many early rockets never got off the ground. Much was learned from these failures. Social engineering, too, ought to be permitted to learn from failures. At present, one failure often means the end of efforts to correct a social problem. Or, worse yet, nothing changes after a failure, and we continue the same old program. This is like building the same defective rocket again and again without consulting engineers.

A primary purpose of this book is to help you learn to question your commonsense understanding of society and to begin to think about appropriate ways to utilize social-science knowledge in political decision making. Indeed, the society in which we live is increasingly becoming a society in which the fundamental questions have to do with the creation of knowledge and with its appropriate use.

CHAPTER REVIEW

To study social problems, we must begin by examining the individual and the determinants of his or her behavior. Biological make-up plays an important role because it sets *limits* on behavior and ability. To a large extent, biological characteristics are passed on by heredity. The *socialization* process, or "humanizing'' process, is what forms the biological human into a social one. This process is continual throughout life and shapes our responses to the social needs of others. We learn to define the *roles,* or sets of expectations, within given social positions. To a great extent, a person's social self, or *self-concept,* is defined through interactions with, and observations of, others.

When people come together in some goal-oriented behavior, they have formed a group. Some groups reflect strong, intimate relations among members and are called *primary* groups. In *secondary* groups, a greater distance is maintained among members, and relations tend to be based more on practical matters. Groups serve many functions for a society, not the least of which is to give people some kind of reference point from which to evaluate their own behavior. A group that serves this purpose is called a *reference group* and may be primary or secondary. In any group, members tend to be differentiated according to their power and influence, but all groups define certain *norms* (or rules about expected behavior) for their members and punish or pressure those who deviate from group norms. Chronic deviations from societal norms often cause the formation of agencies to prevent or punish deviance. Serious and common forms of deviance are often defined as social problems.

One can discuss the causes of social problems on several levels of analysis—from the lowest level (the individual or small group) to the highest (society as a whole). Some analytical positions and some forms of deviance lend themselves rather well to a discussion of individual behavior (for example, sexual deviance), whereas other positions and problems seem to demand a broader analysis that takes account of aspects of society as a whole (for example, poverty and old age).

Societies form the context within which social problems occur. The larger social context comprises a number of interdependent parts seeking to maintain an *equilibrium,* or balance. Important parts of societies are *institutions* and *classes.*

From the view of society as a system, social problems can be regarded in several ways. *Functionalists* try to analyze how each act contributes to the smooth running of the social system. They believe that social problems develop when the society becomes *disorganized* and that problems can be remedied by changing the part of the system that is *dysfunctional;* it is usually not necessary, they say, to change the whole system. *Conflict theorists* (whether focusing on *value conflict* or *class conflict*) claim that social problems arise from a flaw in the system and can be remedied only by overhauling the entire system.

The social problems that concern us most today are primarily ones that have arisen in highly *industrialized, urban* societies, societies in which people have become alienated from their fellow human beings and in which technology has contributed to a belief that any problem can be conquered. In one sense, this belief itself represents a problem because many social conditions will take much time and effort to change. In another sense, this hope and belief that conditions *can* be changed is necessary for a social problem to be so defined—and for action to be taken. Without this hope, we would not strive to change society.

SUGGESTED READINGS

Bell, Daniel. *The Coming of Post-Industrial Society: A Venture in Social Forecasting.* New York: Basic Books, 1973.

Clinard, Marshall B. *Sociology of Deviant Behavior.* New York: Holt, Rinehart and Winston, 1968.

Goffman, Erving. *Presentation of Self in Everyday Life.* Garden City, N.Y.: Doubleday, 1959.

Lofland, Lyn H. *A World of Strangers.* New York: Basic Books, 1973.

Mazer, Allan, and Leon S. Robertson. *Biology and Social Behavior.* New York: Free Press, 1972.

Putney, Snell. *The Conquest of Society.* Belmont, Calif.: Wadsworth, 1972.

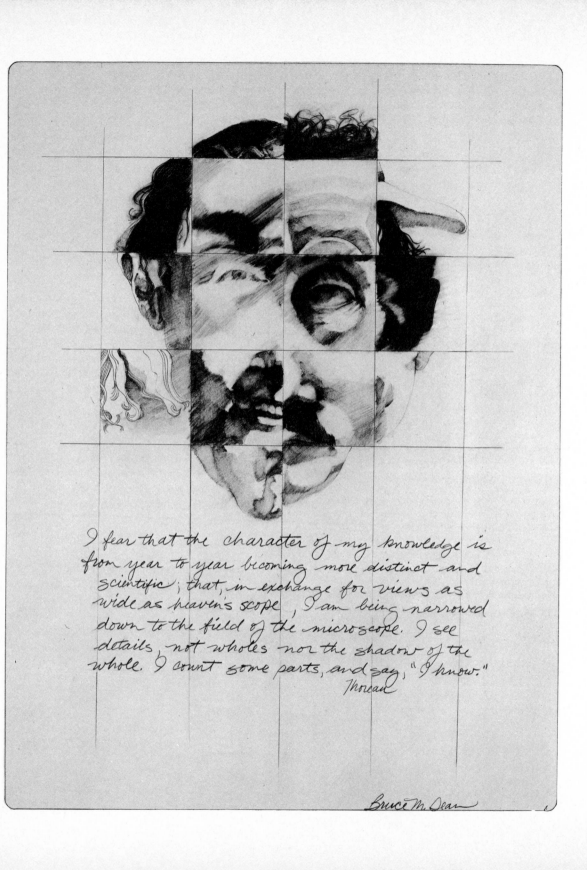

I fear that the character of my knowledge is from year to year becoming more distinct and scientific; that, in exchange for views as wide as heaven's scope, I am being narrowed down to the field of the microscope. I see details, not wholes nor the shadow of the whole. I count some parts, and say, "I know."

Thoreau

Bruce M. Dean

3
Doing Social Problems Research

This year approximately one out of every twenty urban Americans between the ages of ten and eighteen will appear in juvenile court charged with breaking the law. Yet these cases represent only the tip of the iceberg. Only a small proportion of criminal acts by young people ever become known to the police, and of these, only a much smaller proportion lead to arrest. Juvenile crime is a major fact of American life.

For decades, social scientists have tried to understand juvenile delinquency. What causes young people to commit crimes? What is the best way to deal with young offenders? Does sending them to reform school make them more likely or less likely to commit future crimes? To what extent do treatment programs, such as probation and counseling, or prevention programs, such as neighborhood youth activities, reduce juvenile crime?

Discussion or reflection cannot settle such questions. We require facts. For example, either young people who take part in a delinquency-prevention program have a lower rate of delinquent behavior than young people not in the program, or they do not. To assemble and analyze appropriate facts is to do research.

It is through research that persons who study social problems qualify to be called social *scientists.* Science consists of testing theories against appropriate and carefully gathered data, or evidence. Put another way, if a particular theory leads to the prediction that poverty causes young people to commit crimes, research is required to see whether the prediction is accurate. Someone must go out and collect data on the economic background of some appropriate group of young people and determine who among them has committed juvenile crimes. Then researchers must make comparisons to see whether young people from lower-income homes are more likely to have committed crimes than young people from higher-income homes. (They are not.) Scientists conduct research in different ways and use specific methods for specific kinds of questions.

This chapter uses the subject of delinquency to provide examples of how social scientists conduct research. (Delinquency as a social problem is more comprehensively treated in Chapter 6.) This chapter offers a behind-the-scenes view of several research methods directed at various central questions about delinquency. The purpose is to let you look over the shoulders of social scientists as they go about their business: doing research on a major social problem.

The accounts are informal for two reasons: to let you see for yourself how research is done and to let you see that social researchers are not some strange and special breed of people. Like the rest of us, they are sometimes lazy, they blunder, they have good and bad luck, and they frequently have to compromise between practical demands and ideal research designs. The goal of the chapter is to help you understand basic research and analysis procedures. Instead of taking up these procedures as textbook principles, we let them emerge as tools that people who encounter real research use.

GETTING BUSTED: PARTICIPANT OBSERVATION

60

Social scientists have developed a number of research methods. The method chosen depends on a particular researcher's skills and personality; some researchers relate well to people, others relate better to computers. In the final analysis, the nature of the problem determines the research method. Some questions are best answered by careful analysis of documents, such as court cases involving teenagers. Some are best answered by interviewing a randomly selected sample of persons. Other problems lend themselves to experimentation. However, certain kinds of questions are best answered by going out and actually observing what people do in real-life situations.

A number of questions about delinquency seem to require direct observation. For example, if we wanted to understand the extent to which delinquent acts are committed because of encouragement from other juveniles—who perhaps egg on a friend to steal something—we could gather accounts from young people who have been apprehended, but we could not be sure of their stories unless we, too, had been on the scene.

The fact that self-reports may not be accurate has long prompted sociologists to use the method of *participant observation* in studying delinquency. The social scientist witnesses the events he or she is attempting to study and carefully and systematically records these observations. Social scientists using this method usually have long-term interaction with the people they are studying.

LIMITS OF THE METHOD

Participant observation has obvious limitations. For one thing, the presence of observers can always change the behavior of those they observe. People who know that you are watching them are likely to behave differently in order to impress or deceive you. For example, teenage boys might commit more delinquent acts in order to show how tough they are, or they might decrease their delinquency in order to appear in a better light. For these reasons, participant observation with any given group of people may require an observer with very special characteristics. Someone who wanted to observe (unnoticed) some boys hanging around a pool hall would have to be young enough and have the appropriate social style to not appear as an outsider. This criterion would eliminate most social scientists as suitable observers.

Moral Problems

Important moral problems also beset the observer. If the behavior they are studying is illegal, observers may find themselves in the position of

Figure 3.1   One of the problems faced by participant observation is that the social scientist's presence affects the social process he is studying. Would the Ghanaians shown at top with Michael Lowy interact as naturally in his presence as they would without him? The participant observer usually tries to become fully immersed in the interactions of the group he is studying. Fitting into the situation under study solves some problems of participant observation, but it raises other important questions, especially those involving invasion of privacy and such questions of ethics as whether or not the researcher should intervene to prevent law violations.

being accessories to a crime. At what point, if any, must the observer drop the role of participant in response to conscience? Suppose, for example, you are a social scientist observing a youth gang that is planning to hold up a store. If you do nothing and the robbery goes off as scheduled, you have become an accessory to a serious felony. If, on the other hand, you tip off the police, you may abort your study. The gang may end up in jail, making further observation impossible and irrelevant. Or you may blow your relationship of trust with the group. Could you try to talk the gang out of the holdup? If you did, your intervention would significantly change the phenomenon you are trying to observe. Conclusions about what goes on in the real world are suspect when the observer importantly acts as an influence on what goes on.

In actual practice, observers have chosen each of the previously mentioned strategies. Others faced with such moral dilemmas have simply halted their observations and gone elsewhere. It is not clear what to do in such circumstances.

Practical Problems

Participant observation of delinquency has always faced an additional important problem: who to observe and where. Obviously, a person can only be in one place at any given moment and can carefully watch only a small number of people present in any given place. But experts in the field know that

delinquency is a relatively infrequent act, even among the most delinquent teenagers—no one goes around breaking the law most of the time, or at least not for very long. More typically, teenagers only occasionally commit illegal acts. Thus, an observer may have to watch some young people for an extremely long time to be able to observe even one instance of delinquency. In fact, observers may never see a significant delinquent act—either because they are absent when it happens or because no delinquent act is committed. Such a possibility is too bleak to encourage social scientists to invest months of their lives in observation. Typically, observers have tried to guarantee success by concentrating on youth gangs already known to engage in delinquency.

In opting to observe such gangs, social scientists have had to ignore the majority of delinquent acts and youths who commit delinquent acts. The fact is well established that delinquent gangs are responsible for very few of the total of delinquent acts, and very few teenagers belong to groups even faintly resembling a delinquent gang (Hirschi, 1969). Furthermore, there is every reason to believe that gang delinquency is quite different from ordinary delinquency. In consequence, detailed social-science accounts of the way gangs sustain themselves through group pressure and group norms favoring delinquency may not help us understand nongang delinquency and the vast major-

61

ity of delinquents. In offering explanations of how gangs recruit members and socialize them into a stable delinquent group role, social-science observers have left us to wonder how "normal" young people who are not socialized in a delinquent role and who do not regard themselves as delinquents come to commit such acts.

Therefore, it can be seen that a practical problem—trying to be in the right place at the right time—makes it difficult to simply go out into the real world and observe the way the immediate social situation generates delinquent behavior. The decision to observe delinquent gangs may make being in the right place at the right time more likely, but it also allows practical considerations to delimit the original question and forces the researcher to settle for data on a rare species of delinquency. The original question has instead become the responsibility of survey researchers who, in turn, have had to trade the potential accuracy of direct observation for the broader applicability of findings based on large samples of teenagers who report their illegal actions, the behavior of their friends, and so on. However, not all questions about delinquency have proved impractical for participant-observation studies.

ENCOUNTERS BETWEEN POLICE AND JUVENILES

In the early 1960s, two social scientists at the University of California, Berkeley—Irvin Piliavin and Scott Briar (1964)—became convinced that one important determinant of delinquency would be found in encounters between the police and juveniles. They were well aware that the police have considerable freedom in deciding what to do with juveniles in trouble. They arrest some young offenders and refer their cases to the court and probation system. They send others on their way after chewing them out, and the encounter does not result in an official record of a juvenile offense.

Piliavin and Briar knew that police decisions were not random and that the police considered such factors as the seriousness of the offense and the juvenile's record of previous offenses. Nevertheless, they suspected that the wide discretion afforded the police and certain features of the encounter situation itself, including the nature of the interaction between the police and juveniles, must influence police decisions on whom they let go and whom they arrest. Piliavin and Briar also wanted to find out what criteria the police use, because they knew that police decisions are a major factor in determining delinquency rates. If the police are influenced by personal biases—for example, racism—then statistics showing that blacks are more likely than whites to be delinquents may reflect differences in the behavior of policemen rather than trends in the behavior of young people.

For this reason, Piliavin and Briar decided to observe a number of encounters between policemen and juvenile suspects. But where does one go in order to see such encounters? Clearly, it would be futile to trail after some ordinary group of teenagers in the hope that the police would show up. Equally clearly, Piliavin and Briar did not want to focus on some delinquent gang. They wanted to know how the police operated with the average, not the unusual, delinquent. Their solution was to observe the police and to take careful notes on all their encounters with juveniles.

Cruising in the Patrol Car

Piliavin and Briar first secured official permission to regularly accompany officers of the juvenile bureau of a large West Coast police department. Approximately thirty officers served in this bureau during the observation period, and the researchers made sure that they observed each officer. In all, the two social scientists spent nine months riding in police cruisers with two-man teams of juvenile officers (each observer with a different team). Although they took care to observe the teams during all work shifts every day of the week, they spent most of the time cruising on evenings and weekends—the busiest periods.

Although the observers arranged their schedules to increase the likelihood of seeing police-juvenile encounters, during nine months of concentrated effort they saw only seventy-six encounters. (This gives strong testimony to the futility of trying to conduct such a study by focusing on juveniles.) In ten of these encounters, the police let youths go so quickly that Piliavin and Briar saw no reason to include these cases in their primary analysis.

Figure 3.2   Police reaction toward juveniles is influenced by a number of factors. The demeanor of the person apprehended may be the primary factor, especially when records of previous police encounters or arrests are unavailable. However, new electronic devices are now available to the police (computer terminals in patrol cars, which link the cop on the beat with record-keeping centers). They provide almost instant information about each person stopped.

You might wonder what the police assigned to the juvenile bureau were doing during this nine-month period if they had only seventy-six encounters with juveniles.   For one thing, they cruised assigned beats and essentially functioned as routine patrol officers; occasionally, they arrested adults for some offense. Most of the time, as with all policemen assigned to drive beats, they just rode around and frequently stopped for coffee. As all studies of policing report, it is mostly a boring, uneventful job (Reiss, 1971). Piliavin and Briar were trapped night after night in the backseat of a patrol car with little or nothing to do to pass the time, and they recall their months of observation as mainly a period of enforced boredom.

Encountering Juveniles

Nevertheless, their patience was rewarded. In time, they assembled enough data on juvenile-police encounters to shed light on the decision-making process.

In every encounter, the police had several options. They could simply let the juvenile offenders go, or they could let them go after giving them an informal reprimand. They could also take them to the police station and do one of three things: give them an official reprimand and release them to a parent or guardian; cite them to appear in juvenile court; or arrest them and have them held in juvenile hall. The last two options placed the eventual disposition of the case in the hands of the courts.

Piliavin and Briar found, somewhat to their surprise, that the police were reluctant to take official action against youths, partly because they tried to avoid stigmatizing the youths with an official police record and partly because they lacked confidence in the effectiveness of correctional agencies and programs to achieve rehabilitation. The police believed that the juvenile-justice and correctional processes were simply punishment, not treatment. Therefore, unless they confronted a juvenile they believed to be a serious and chronic offender, they were inclined toward leniency.

Factors in Decision Making

The fundamental problem the police had to resolve was to assess the juvenile offender's character. Should this offender be turned over for punishment

63

or let go—is this a "bad" kid or simply an ordinary kid who has done something bad?

Character

According to Piliavin and Briar's observations, the police usually found little difficulty in assessing the character of offenders "who had committed serious crimes such as robbery, homicide, aggravated assault, grand theft, auto theft, rape, and arson." The magnitude of such offenses confirmed their conclusion that the offender was a confirmed delinquent. However, even in a few instances involving serious offenses such as burglary and auto theft, the police let the juvenile go without court action. Furthermore, in over 90 percent of the cases, the infraction was minor and therefore did not help the police in assessing character.

A second major consideration in police decisions was the youth's record of previous offenses. The police ordinarily use a record as grounds for judging the youth to be of "bad" character and thus not an appropriate candidate for leniency. However, at the time they had to make a decision, the police usually had no information about a juvenile's past record, or lack of one, unless one of the officers had had previous contact with the youth. (Juvenile records were not then maintained in such a fashion that the police could call in and obtain information on records.)

Lacking such information and nearly always being confronted with juveniles whose offense was too minor to use as a gauge of character, the police mainly used cues that "emerged from the interaction between the officer and the youth—cues from which the officer inferred the youth's character."

Demeanor

The most important of these cues was demeanor—how the youth behaved during the encounter with the police. The critical element was how cooperative or uncooperative the youth was in dealing with the officers. As Piliavin and Briar (1964) reported:

The cues used by police to assess demeanor were fairly simple. Juveniles who were contrite about their infractions, respectful to officers, and fearful of the sanctions that might be employed against them tended to be

viewed by patrolmen as basically law-abiding or at least "salvageable." For these youths it was usually assumed that informal or formal reprimand would suffice to guarantee their future conformity. In contrast, youthful offenders who were fractious, obdurate, or who appeared nonchalant in their encounters with patrolmen were likely to be viewed as "would-be tough guys" or "punks" who fully deserved the most severe sanction: arrest.

To check these conclusions, Piliavin and Briar wanted to compare the police dispositions of cases in which juveniles had been cooperative with those in which they had been uncooperative. To prevent their own knowledge of how cases had been dealt with from influencing their judgments, Piliavin and Briar submitted their field notes, minus information on police actions, to a disinterested third person to classify. This independent classification is the basis for the data shown in Table 3.1. It is

Table 3.1   How Demeanor Affects Police Treatment of Juveniles

SEVERITY OF POLICE DISPOSITION	YOUTH'S DEMEANOR		
	Cooperative	Uncooperative	Total
Arrest (most severe)	2	14	16
Citation or official reprimand	4	5	9
Informal reprimand	15	1	16
Admonish and release (least severe)	24	1	25
Total	45	21	66

Source: Adapted from Irvin Piliavin and Scott Briar, "Police Encounters with Juveniles" (*American Journal of Sociology*, 70, 1964), p. 210.

easy to see that youths who cooperated with the police were likely to be treated leniently, to get off with only an admonishment or an informal reprimand—thirty-nine out of forty-five were treated leniently. But youths who were uncooperative, who were defiant or unrepentant, rarely received lenient treatment: two-thirds of them were arrested. These data powerfully confirmed Piliavin and Briar's hypothesis that demeanor determines police decisions about leniency.

Race and Demeanor

Piliavin and Briar also noticed that race seemed to play an important role in shaping the interaction between the police and juveniles. They believed their observations justified a conclusion that the police usually used race as a cue to character and behaved toward black juveniles in ways that made this a *self-fulfilling* cue.

First of all, they reported that of the ten juveniles inappropriately stopped and immediately dismissed by the police during the observation period (and dropped from the primary analysis), seven were black, but only a third of the youths police stopped for actual infractions were black. Thus, the proportion of encounters with blacks was high relative to the proportion who seemed to be guilty of wrongdoing. (Blacks made up 23 percent of the population of the city.) The police tended to be unduly suspicious of blacks. In one instance, after the officers stopped and questioned a black youth walking down the street and then let him go, they explained that they had been suspicious because "he was a Negro wearing dark glasses at midnight." In addition, eighteen out of twenty-seven officers interviewed openly admitted a dislike for

Figure 3.3 This copy of a worksheet used by Piliavin and Briar in their study of police encounters with juveniles shows which kinds of data were collected and how such data can be used in social research. Piliavin and Briar asked a noninvolved third person to judge the data independently in order to test their hypothesis that race and demeanor affect police decisions.

R. T. Aug '63

Police Encounters with Juveniles

Date	Time of Day	No. of Juv.	Sex	Race	Age	Probation	Priors	Offence	Situation	How Encountered	Demeanor	Resolution
June 28	night	3	M	W	16(?)	Unk	Unk	loitering	street	uniformed policeman	polite	Told to leave
July 2	day	2	F	N	14	Unk	Yes	purse snatch	school	report	indignant indolent	* Arrest
..			F	N	13	Unk	Unk	..	..	..	?	?
..	..	1	M	N	15(?)	Unk	Unk	Assault	school	Informer	aggrieved	Absolved
..	..	3	M	N	17(?)	Unk	Unk	loitering	street	Ecological	Hostile insolent	Told to leave
..	..	1	F	N	15	Unk	Unk	purse snatch	home	informer	self-possessed	* ?
3rd	night	1	M	W	16(?)	Unk	Yes	pinball	bowling alley	committing offense	polite	R. and R. (?)
..	..	1	M	W	?	Unk	Unk	..	..	..	cool	legit
	..	5-6	M	W or Asiatic	16-17(?)	Unk	Unk	..	..	..	polite	informal rep
..	..	2	M		14-18	Unk	Unk	loitering	..	time	polite	talk
4	..	3	M	N	14(?)	Unk	Unk	suspicious circ.	street	behavior	flat	talk
5	..	2	F	W	17	No	Unk	Possession of alcohol (?)	car	Beat man	ironical-hostile	* Arrest
			F	W	17	No	Unk	..	car	..	Frightened hostile	* citation
9	day	1	M	Mx	15(?)	?	Yes(?)	assault	home	report	aggressive	informal rep.
..	..	1	M	W	17	?	?	disturbance	home	report	apathetic nervous	talk
.		1	M	Mx	17	No	Yes	Run away	home	report		unfounded
13	night	1	M	W	13(?)	No	?	vagrancy	street	ecological	mild polite	R. and R. (?)
..	..	1	M	W	17(?)	No	?	pinball	bowling alley	committing offense	polite	R and R (?) (citizenship class)
24	night	1	M	W	13	no	Yes	incorrigible	home	report	truculent	R. and R.
	..	1	M	Mx	15	Yes	Yes	run away	friend's house	report	resigned	arrest
25	..	1	M	W	11	No	?	Breaking bottles	street	committing offense	polite	informal rep
..	..	2	M	W	17	No	Yes	loitering	street	ecological	polite	F.I. card
			M	W	18	?	?	loitering	street	..	polite	..
27	night	1	M	W	16	?	?	failure to appear	home	report	polite	arrest on warrant
	..	3	M	W	15 ?	?	?	loitering	parking lot	ecological	polite	talk
			F	W	15 ?	?	?	..	..	..	..	..

65

blacks. They reported that blacks were more likely to commit crimes, to give officers a "hard time," and to show no remorse over their actions.

Piliavin and Briar argued that police attitudes lead to a process by which black delinquents are "manufactured." First, because of their belief that blacks are more likely than whites to be criminal, these officers did more patrolling in black neighborhoods than in white ones. Furthermore, the officers were much more likely to accost black youths simply because their skin color identified them to the police as potential troublemakers.

Because they are more likely to experience police investigation, even when innocent of wrongdoing, black youths are more likely than white youths to develop hostility toward the police. Furthermore, overexperience with police questioning reduces the importance of such encounters in the eyes of black youths; they begin to see them as routine. Both of these responses—hostility and unconcern—are the precise cues that the police use to judge character, to identify the serious delinquent. And so begins a vicious circle: The police become less lenient and thereby produce statistics showing that blacks are more likely than whites to have official records of delinquent behavior. And these statistics further reinforce the police in their belief that blacks are lawless.

Piliavin and Briar concluded that the police used their discretion to be lenient or tough on the basis of their perceptions of the offender. When the offense was petty—as was nearly always the case—they relied on demeanor and, indirectly, on race to make their decision. The police decision determines who will and who will not have a juvenile record; clearly, those who are cooperative and white are less likely to get their infractions recorded. Thus, if "nice" boys do not have records, it does not mean that they do not break rules.

ASSESSING THE STUDY

One problem with these findings is that the study was limited to one police department and to relatively few cases. The researchers have no way of showing that these findings can be generalized to other departments. But an even stronger objection can be raised against the findings.

It is logically possible that although police relied on race as a cue to character because they held racist views, race may have operated nonetheless as an accurate cue to delinquency. The distinction is subtle but significant. The police may, in fact, have accurately picked out the most serious delinquents—the chronic offenders—even though they misunderstood *why* race might be a valid cue. It is possible that the pressures of racism itself and ghetto existence serve to push a disproportionate number of black youths into delinquency. If so, then although the police are wrong in their understanding of the link between race and criminality, they may be accurate in regarding race as a cue to who is more seriously delinquent.

It is not our intention to assert that the above is true, but only to point out that it *could be* true. And we are not outlining this point to argue against Piliavin and Briar's premise that the police manufacture black delinquency rates but simply to clarify what additional evidence would be needed to make their argument more persuasive. We do this to demonstrate that one kind of research method more readily produces some kinds of evidence; other kinds of evidence require different methods of research.

Recall that neither the observers nor the police actually knew the past behavior of youths suspected of petty offenses. Piliavin and Briar's data simply cannot resolve whether race is a valid cue or whether the police manufacture black delinquency rates. To do that, different data are required. One would first need to know the actual delinquent behavior of representative samples of black and white youths. Then one would need to determine whether or not blacks are more likely than whites to acquire police records when both have committed the same offense. If so, then Piliavin and Briar are probably correct in asserting that the police manufacture black delinquency rates. The final research study reported in this chapter brings precisely the needed data to bear on this question.

To conclude this discussion, let us reconsider what Piliavin and Briar did. As participant observers, their behavior differed significantly from everyday association with other people—for example, from what you do when you are with friends or in class. First, they systematically re-corded all their observations as they occurred. They made efforts to pick out and note specific kinds of information—for example, the race of juveniles, the offense for which they were suspect, what they did and said, and what the police did and said. Furthermore, they took some pains not to delude themselves into believing what they wanted to believe. For example, they arranged to have an unbiased party—someone not associated with the study and unaware of their views—classify the youths as cooperative or uncooperative. It is pre-cisely this care given to accuracy and to eliminat-ing bias that qualifies social science as a science and makes it different from our commonsense un-derstanding of social life.

DELINQUENCY TREATMENT: THE CAMBRIDGE-SOMERVILLE EXPERIMENT

As far back as written records go, human societies have distinguished between children and adults when punishing criminal acts (Sanders, 1970). Fur-thermore, child lawbreakers have always called forth strong social impulses to attempt their reform before it is too late. Common sense tells us that if only someone had intervened during the childhood years of adult criminals, had set them on the right path early on, much human suffering could have been spared.

All present-day probation and counseling pro-grams for juvenile delinquents—juvenile homes and treatment centers, juvenile courts, and neigh-borhood delinquency-prevention programs—are motivated by this urge to save the young. But nag-ging questions have persisted. Which, if any, of these methods of dealing with delinquency is actu-ally effective? And if the methods are not effec-tive, what should be done?

Clear-cut answers to these questions require elaborate social experimentation. As we shall see, experimental programs may take a great deal of money and time, raise painful moral decisions, and bring disappointments to those who devote signif-icant parts of their lives to making these programs work. Finally, simply to arrive at a clear answer in

no way guarantees that social policies and prac-tices will take such answers into account. The rea-son for choosing as an example a study that began in 1937 and ended in 1945 (even though the findings were intensively analyzed and reanalyzed for an additional twelve years) is to let you ex-amine the process by which governmental and pri-vate policy makers and programs have held out against research evidence that refutes the basic premise on which they are operating.

In 1935, Richard Clarke Cabot, a distinguished and wealthy New England physician and social philosopher, decided to do something about juve-nile delinquency. He believed that delinquency could be deflected early in life if only the child could form a close and friendly relationship with an adult able to enrich his life and give him effec-tive guidance. He decided to create a program to try out his notions and to assess their effectiveness.

There was nothing particularly novel about Cabot's views. They reflected the views prevalent among the leading experts on child welfare at that time and, indeed, remain the dominant views to-day. What was indeed novel was Cabot's willingness—and financial ability—to conduct a large-scale social experiment to find out whether a program conceived and carried out under optimum conditions could, in fact, save young people from delinquency.

Cabot launched his project in 1937. He selected two highly industrialized, economically depressed cities that were near Boston—Cambridge and Somerville—as the sites for the experiment. Next, he hired a staff and set to work, and they selected 650 boys from Somerville and Cambridge for study. The boys' average age was eleven, still young enough, in Cabot's judgment, to respond to efforts to keep them from becoming delinquents.

THE EXPERIMENTAL DESIGN

Cabot wanted to know if participating in his delin-quency-prevention program actually prevented de-linquency. He therefore could not let all 650 boys participate. If he had, how could he have deter-mined whether the proportion who committed de-linquent acts was lower (or even higher) than it would have been if they had not participated? He could not. There would be no standard against which to compare the boys in his program.

Therefore, Cabot decided to split the boys into two groups. Half were recruited into the program; the other half were not. Later, records of program boys could be compared with those of nonprogram boys to see which group was less delinquent.

By May 1939, he had split the boys into two equal groups of 325, and the staff went to work to recruit those chosen for treatment into the program. When the counselors visited the boys' homes to recruit them, the parents often suspected them of being door-to-door salesmen, but they responded very favorably to the project once it had been explained to them. And well they might, for during the depths of the Depression, these poor families were offered a chance for their sons to receive free medical and dental care, special tutoring on their school work, interesting field trips, stays at summer camps, and other advantages far beyond what their families could afford. In fact, the counselors also helped the families secure welfare aid and other benefits. Overall, the project was designed to resemble the very best efforts made by progressive probation officers, family welfare agencies, and private groups such as the Big Brother Association. Each boy would have a personal counselor doing his best to help him cope with the world.

Sad to say, Dr. Cabot died of a heart attack in 1939 at the commencement of his project. But the project did continue, first under the direction of P. Sidney de Q Cabot, later under Edwin Powers. World War II soon brought difficulties: Many of the original male counselors were replaced, often with women, so few boys had the same counselor throughout their participation in the program. Tire and gasoline shortages made transportation difficult for the counselors and cut down field trips. And by the project's end in December 1945, many of the boys had entered military service.

Despite these limitations, the project was carried out. If the actual program was not as elaborate as Cabot's vision, it nonetheless equaled or surpassed government and private delinquency-treatment programs in actual operation both then and now. As William and Joan McCord (1959) put it in their volume reanalyzing data from the project,

the staff could look back with satisfaction at their record. A very large number of children had received social aid and some individual counseling averaging close to five years per boy. Furthermore, careful records had been kept. Thus, the Cambridge-Somerville project ... stands as a unique event in the battle against delinquency.

But what did the project actually accomplish? *It demonstrated that its efforts to deflect delinquency were futile.* Few sets of data in the history of social research have been analyzed so many times, so many different ways, and by so many different researchers; yet no significant differences have been found between boys in the program and those denied access to the program. In fact, about 40 percent of the boys in the program and those left out of the program were subsequently *convicted* of a criminal offense. Furthermore, boys in the program were convicted of approximately the same number of offenses as boys who were left out of the program.

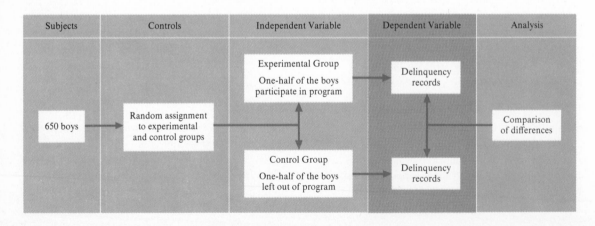

At the time the original findings were reported, it was suggested that a "latent effect" might show up—that boys in the treatment program might turn out to be more stable adults and thus less apt to commit criminal offenses later on. But a follow-up study found that adult convictions for crimes were equally common among those who had been in the program and those who had not. Indeed, the only significant difference found was that those in the program, for some reason, were significantly more likely than those not in the program to be convicted of traffic violations as adults (McCord and McCord, 1959).

Having now gained a general picture of the Cambridge-Somerville experiment and its results, we can re-examine it in a more analytic fashion. Present are all the critical elements of a proper experimental design. Figure 3.4 displays these elements, and the following discussion explains each one of them.

The Independent Variable

All experiments include at least one independent variable over which the experimenter has control. It is called *independent* because it is the factor that is thought to be the cause of something else. It is called a *variable* because this factor takes more than one value: if the independent variable were electric current, for example, it would be necessary for the experimenter to at least be able to switch it off and on.

In the Cambridge-Somerville experiment, the independent variable was the delinquency-prevention treatment program. The experimenters

were able to *manipulate,* or control, it—they could decide which boys did or did not get included in the program. Boys who were assigned to be recruited into the program made up the *experimental* group; they were to receive the experimental treatment. The other half of the boys were not recruited into the program. They made up the *control* group; they were the standard against which the experimental group was evaluated.

The Dependent Variable

The dependent variable is the factor that you expect the independent variable to affect—this factor is believed to be *dependent* on the independent variable. If your expectations are correct, you will find that changes in the independent variable are followed by changes in the dependent variable.

In this study, delinquency was the dependent variable, and it was defined and measured in a number of ways. The chief criterion was conviction for a criminal offense. Three years after the treatment program ended, official police and court records for all 650 boys making up the original group were secured. As we have already reported, this study found that the independent variable had *failed* to produce any changes in the dependent variable. Boys in the program were as likely as those denied participation to have been convicted. It is clear that the program had no impact on delinquency whatsoever.

Controls

Experiments are designed to rule out the possibility that some factor other than the independent vari-

Figure 3.4 (Left) *The experimental design used in the Cambridge–Somerville delinquency-treatment program. Randomly assigning boys to be included or excluded from the program ruled out differences between the groups. If boys who participated in the program had been less likely to commit offenses than boys ignored by the program, there would have been substantial grounds to believe that the program was effective.*

Figure 3.5 Scientific research that treats human beings like laboratory animals goes against all moral values. (Right) *A newspaper account of an experiment conducted forty years ago in which human subjects were denied medical treatment for syphilis in order to obtain a control group for experimental purposes. Many of the subjects later died.*

THE NEW YORK TIMES,   MARCH 29, 1973

SYPHILIS EXPERIMENT TERMED UNJUSTIFIED

WASHINGTON, March 28 (AP)—A Government panel concluded today that a Federal syphilis experiment involving Alabama black men was not justified.

But the committee decided to note in its final report the context of the times 40 years ago when the study was begun and to suggest there may have been an initial scientific validity to the study.

The panel recommended that Congress establish a permanent board to regulate "at least all federally supported research involving human subjects."

In the United States Public Health Service experiment, called the Tuskegee Study, more than 430 Macon County, Ala., black men were not treated for their syphilis so doctors could study what eventual damage the untreated disease did to the human body.

At least 28 and possibly as many as 107 of the men died as a direct result of untreated syphilis.

able (and simple chance) could cause changes in the dependent variable. The experimenter uses *randomization* in assigning subjects to the experimental or control groups in order to rule out other possible causes. Whether a boy was recruited into the program or left out was determined randomly, in this case, by flipping a coin to decide what happened to each boy. If the experimenters had not used randomization to select boys for each group, they could not have been sure that unconscious biases or other unforseeable factors were not operating to make differences between boys included and excluded from the program. For example, "good boys" might have been disproportionately selected for treatment over boys who seemed dubious delinquency risks. Eventual differences in delinquency between the two groups might then have been a result of initial selection rather than of the treatment program. In fact, any group of 650 boys includes a great many differences: some are bigger, some are tougher, some are smarter, some are better looking, some get along better with their families, some do better in school, some are more religious. In an experiment it is important to equalize *all* such differences between the experimental and the control groups. The only way they should differ is in exposure or nonexposure to the treatment program. When assignment to the experimental or the control group is decided randomly, boys selected for study in both groups ought to be the same in all ways.

Statistical Analysis

Once an experiment is complete, the first step is to compare the experimental group with the control group on the dependent variable. If both score equally on the dependent variable, it is evident that the independent variable has failed to produce the expected effects. The experimenter must reject as false all predictions that the independent variable utilized in the experiment is a cause of the dependent variable. In the present instance, the results cause us to reject Cabot's hopes to create an enlightened program that could deflect boys from delinquency. Had the comparison of the experimental group and control group revealed a difference—with program boys less likely to commit crimes—then Cabot's expectations would

have been borne out, provided that a second step in analyzing all these experimental results had been taken successfully.

We have pointed out that randomization is used to ensure that experimental and control groups are the same in all respects save receiving or not receiving the experimental treatment. But randomization does *not absolutely guarantee* that both groups will be the same in all respects. Instead, it simply makes it possible to compute the *mathematical odds* that any difference in the dependent variable found between the two groups is the result of the independent variable or the result of other differences between the two groups that occurred by *chance* during the random assignment.

The odds against such chance-produced findings in an experiment depend on two factors: the size of the experimental and control groups and the size of the difference found in the dependent variable. The larger the difference is, the less likely it could be produced by chance. The larger the experimental and control groups are, the smaller the difference required to discount chance findings. Obviously, the greater the number of times you flip a coin, the *closer* you will come to flipping heads exactly 50 percent of the time. It is equally obvious that small differences in the dependent variable are more likely to be the result of mere chance than are very large differences.

The usual way to compute these odds is to apply a *test of statistical significance.* As a rule of thumb, experimenters usually require that the odds be at least 20 to 1 against chance findings before they call the results statistically significant or put any trust in them. There was no need to worry about statistical significance in the Cambridge-Somerville experiment because no differences were found between boys in the experimental and control groups on such crucial matters as subsequent criminal convictions. When a difference *is* found, the next step is to turn to significance tests to compute the probability that the difference is the result of chance. You will recall that a difference did turn up in one comparison in the McCords' follow-up study (1959)—boys in the experimental group were more likely than those in the control group to have been convicted of a traffic offense after reaching adulthood. But this difference was in the wrong direction to offer any support for the program's effectiveness.

However, this finding does raise the question of significance. As is shown in Table 3.2, 16 percent of the boys who participated in the delinquency-prevention program had been convicted of traffic offenses, but only 10 percent of the boys excluded from the program had a record of such a conviction

Table 3.2   Differences in Traffic-Crime Convictions After Age 21

GROUP	PERCENT CONVICTED	
Experimental	16	
Control	10	$p < .05$

Source: Adapted from William McCord and Joan McCord, *Origins of Crime: A New Evaluation of the Cambridge-Somerville Youth Study* (New York: Columbia University Press, 1959).

after age twenty-one. What is the probability that this represents a real difference between the two groups rather than simply a chance fluctuation? As is shown in the table, the odds are more than 20 to 1 that a finding this large could not occur purely by chance. Thus, if this study were repeated twenty times and if there were no real difference in the traffic behavior of the experimental and control groups, one would expect to find a difference of this size only *once* through chance. This is what is indicated by $p < .05$ in the table. The probability (p) that these findings are a result of chance is less than ($<$) 5 chances in 100 (.05), or 1 chance in 20.

Replication

A final guard against incorrectly accepting findings that are merely the result of chance or incorrectly rejecting real differences as mere chance is *replication*. To replicate a study means to repeat it—in this case, to select a new group of boys, subject the experimental group to a delinquency-prevention program, and then compare their eventual delinquency with that of boys in the control group. The odds of getting a difference resulting from chance twice in a row are relatively low. Furthermore, replication is an excellent way to determine whether findings based on one population in a certain place at a certain time can be generalized to another population in a different place at a different time.

Different researchers, in the United States and abroad, have replicated the basic Cambridge-Somerville experiment many times (Empey and Lubeck, 1971). When the fundamental features of experimental controls have been observed, the results have matched those of the original study. Nothing that we presently do to reform delinquents or prevent youths from becoming delinquents has had any significant effect. This fact confirms the views held by the juvenile officers studied by Piliavin and Briar. Recall that they were inclined to be lenient with youthful offenders, feeling that official programs had no influence on reform.

SOCIAL APPLICATIONS

Despite the results of the Cambridge-Somerville experiment and later replications, we still deal with delinquency in the very same way that Cabot did—unsuccessfully. Indeed, researchers have so often replicated this study and reanalyzed the original data precisely because so few of them can accept its findings as accurate.

When the initial analysis of the data failed to reveal any worthwhile consequences of the program, immediate efforts were undertaken to dig deeper into the data. Edwin Powers, the director of the Cambridge-Somerville study, and Helen Witmer, his associate, tried in many ways to show that their years of effort had not been wasted. They examined a number of psychological tests and measures of school adjustment for the experimental and control groups and found no differences between the two groups. Still, they could not accept the findings, and Dr. Witmer decided to pursue the study. Her first step was to discard the control group. Then she did a case-by-case study of experimental cases. Only this, she wrote, could

> satisfy the clinical worker, who, by the nature of his task, has little interest in averages. What such a person wants to know is whether there were any cases—even if only a few—in which the introduction of the new factor tipped the balance in a boy's favor. (Powers and Witmer, 1951)

On the basis of her own private reading of the files, she concluded there was evidence that fifty-one of the boys in the project had "clearly benefited" from their involvement in the delinquency-prevention program. But if so many boys benefited, why did the experimental group not show a noticeably lower crime rate than the control group? What was helping the boys excluded from the program, for they did equally well? Only the experiment itself can shed light on this question, not selected instances from the experimental group.

Dr. Witmer's efforts to find hidden evidence of success reveal a fundamental problem in social research. A staff of counselors gave a considerable proportion of their lives to attempt to help Cambridge and Somerville children keep out of trouble. In order to function, they had to believe in what they were doing. All across the country, social workers, probation officers, youth workers, and the like were similarly giving themselves to work in which they believed. How does one get such people to accept as true the shattering word that they are wasting their time? How does one tell them that kids will do just as well or as badly when left alone? More important, many of these people earn their living by running programs and agencies in the youth-reform and delinquency-prevention business. They have devoted time and effort to getting trained and sometimes even to getting licensed to follow these occupations. When social researchers come along and tell them to close up shop and find a new line of work, they are hardly going to be receptive to the news.

Social scientists know—having tested the proposition frequently—that present delinquency programs do not help the problem, but the delinquency-treatment business has grown larger with each passing year. Those engaged in the business are able to admit only part of the truth—they know that they do not help most youths, but, like Dr. Witmer, they say that the many failures are redeemed by those whom they are able to help.

As part of the follow-up to the study, the Cambridge-Somerville staff asked former participants if they felt they had benefited from the program. One young man wrote a glowing testimonial about how much his counselor had helped him:

He told me what to do—what's right and wrong—*not to fool around with girls.* It gives a boy a good feeling to have an older person outside the family to tell you what's right and wrong—someone to take an interest in you. (Powers and Witmer, 1951)

Several years later this young man began serving a five-year sentence for a serious sex offense (McCord and McCord, 1959).

In 1955, William and Joan McCord again took up the Cambridge-Somerville study. Their goal was to see whether the treatment might finally show some effects ten years after the program had ended. They found no effects (McCord and McCord, 1959).

A fundamental reason for the failure of delinquency-prevention programs lies in their fundamental assumptions about the *causes* of delinquency. They appear to be based on the notion that delinquency is primarily a lower-class phenomenon and, more specifically, a product of the values dominant in lower-class families and neighborhoods, of poor advice on getting ahead in life, of the lack of high aspirations for success, and of ignorance of the consequences of crime. Programs are therefore aimed at providing delinquents with an inspirational model—a counselor who espouses middle-class values, who tries to overcome the poor examples and poor advice given by lower-class parents and friends, who points out the lifelong consequences of a criminal record, and who encourages youngsters to aspire to success.

The problem is simply that the initial premises are false: The lower classes espouse the same values and conceive of right and wrong and lawful and unlawful in the same way as other social classes. Lower-class youths are about as likely as middle-class youths to have high aspirations. And the poor are as much, if not more, aware of the consequences of criminal convictions as any other class. Moreover, if social class is related to delinquent behavior at all, the relationship is, at best, trivial and inconsistent. Present programs fail in large measure because they attempt to treat factors that are not, and never were, the real causes of delinquency. In addition, as is taken up in Chapter 6, research indicates that the factors that do cause delinquency are difficult to treat through practical programs (Hirschi, 1969).

Evidence on all these matters came to light in the study that follows. Many earlier studies had found similar results, but the one we shall discuss is the most comprehensive, carefully integrated, and best executed survey research on delinquency produced to date.

THE RICHMOND
YOUTH STUDY: SURVEY RESEARCH

In the spring of 1965, Travis Hirschi and the staff from the Survey Research Center at the University of California, Berkeley, administered a lengthy questionnaire to several thousand students, randomly selected from among the more than 17,000 junior-high-school and high-school students in the public school system of Richmond, California. The purpose of the study was to find out what causes juvenile delinquency.

They spent more than a year designing and pretesting the questionnaire. Such caution is necessary partly because large-scale *survey research*, the method employed in this study, is expensive. If researchers ask the wrong questions, phrase them badly, or forget to ask something important, they may have wasted a large amount of the time and money allotted for the research. It simply costs too much to go back and ask questions again.

THE SCOPE OF THE METHOD

In spite of these pressures, survey research is the only reliable procedure to follow to acquire certain kinds of information. If you want to know the *distribution* of some trait in a *population*—for example, delinquent behavior or religious beliefs—no other method suffices. If it did, nobody would pay the Gallup or Harris polling organizations tens of thousands of dollars to conduct a survey. Piliavin and Briar could not reckon what proportion of boys commit delinquent acts simply by riding around with the police—the police only encounter a small proportion of boys, even of boys who commit crimes. Indeed, simply by observing the police, Piliavin and Briar could not determine what proportion of boys at some time or other have run-ins with the police. To determine these proportions, one must examine the whole population of teenage boys, or a *representative sample* of them,

and compute the percentage who have been picked up by the police, have committed a delinquent act, and so on.

By the same token, a search for the causes of delinquency does not lend itself to the experimental method. In order to find out what causes delinquency, social scientists could not take a group of children and try to manipulate thier lives so that some would become delinquents; that would be both immoral and impractical. Furthermore, few of the independent variables in such a study could be created or manipulated experimentally. You cannot take people and re-create some of them as students and others as school dropouts. Nor could you raise some young people in close-knit families and deprive others of affection in a laboratory. These restrictions apply to most phenomena social scientists want to study, so researchers are forced to take people as they are and try to determine why they are that way. Clearly, the staff in the Cambridge-Somerville experiment could not study *why* 40 percent of the boys in their study became delinquents; they could only try to assess whether or not their prevention program made boys less likely to become delinquents. To show that aspects of young people's backgrounds and social circumstances relate to delinquency requires the kind of systematic data available only through a survey.

Hirschi's research design was guided by his intentions to test predictions about delinquency that follow from three competing theoretical traditions: strain, cultural, and social control. These theories, which we spell out in detail in Chapter 4 and utilize throughout Unit II, can largely be ignored here. The point to be made here is that because Hirschi was testing particular theories, he had some clear notion of which data were relevant to his needs. You cannot gather all possible information about a sample of young people. Having a theory and knowing which arguments you plan to test clarifies what you need to know and ask.

MEASURING DELINQUENCY

One cannot explain delinquency without first measuring it. On what grounds are teenagers to be classified as more or less delinquent? It is well

73

known that most delinquent acts are not detected; therefore, when you measure delinquency on the basis of official court and police records, you have several possible sources of substantial error. First of all, you may end up explaining not who *commits* delinquent acts but who *gets caught* for committing delinquent acts. Suppose out of 100 boys, 80 at one time or another steal an item worth more than $50 from a store. Suppose that only 5 of them are caught by the police. Assume also that you have IQ scores on all 100 boys. By comparing the IQs of the 5 caught by the police with the IQs of the other 95 without police records, you find that the 5 are not nearly as intelligent as the other 95. Not knowing that the uncaught group contains 75 undetected thieves, you might erroneously conclude that low intelligence causes boys to steal. But the truth might be that low intelligence is not related to stealing at all but only to getting caught.

Hirschi's strategy for measuring delinquency was to ask all teenagers in his sample to respond to six questions that would reveal commission of delinquent acts. The questions measure petty and grand larceny, auto theft, vandalism, and battery. The more frequently respondents reported committing these acts and the more of them they committed, the higher the respondents scored on delinquency. Eventually, Hirschi created a three-point measure of self-reported delinquency: those who had in the past year committed *none* of these acts, those who had committed *one* of them, and those who had committed *two or more*.

Record of Gallup Poll Accuracy

Year	Gallup Final Survey (percent)	Election Result (percent)	Error (percent)
1952	Eisenhower 51.0	55.4 Eisenhower	-4.4
1956	Eisenhower 59.5	57.8 Eisenhower	+1.7
1960	Kennedy 51.0	50.1 Kennedy	+0.9
1964	Johnson 64.0	61.3 Johnson	+2.7
1968	Nixon 43.0	43.5 Nixon	-0.5
1972	Nixon 62.0	61.8 Nixon	+0.2

(American Institute of Public Opinion.)

Figure 3.6   The Gallup poll has been very accurate in predicting the outcome of presidential elections since 1952. This accuracy is due to interviewing a random sample of the public. Slight error occurs because people say they will vote but do not and because the last poll is taken more than a week before people actually vote.

In addition to using this self-report measure of delinquency, Hirschi had his staff check the official police records for all boys in the sample and record all the official offenses for the past two years. (Most delinquency studies focus on boys only because boys are so much more likely than girls to commit delinquent acts. Hirschi included girls in his original sample but dropped them from subsequent analysis.) Hirschi was now in a position to conduct a parallel analysis of delinquency using both self-report and official delinquency measures. (The sources of error in each measure are discussed in Chapter 6.)

DATA ON RACE AND DELINQUENCY

After all the questionnaires had been punched on IBM cards and fed into a computer, one of the first questions that Hirschi put to his data was the issue raised by Piliavin and Briar about police reactions to racial differences in juvenile offenders. Not only was this question an important one, but Hirschi's interest in it was heightened even further because Piliavin and Briar shared an office across the hall from his in the Survey Research Center (despite its name, a good many observational studies as well as surveys have been done under the center).

The first thing Hirschi wanted to know was whether black and white teenagers differ in their involvement in delinquency. His first step was to divide his sample into whites and blacks. The result is shown in Example A.

Example A

WHITE	BLACK
1303 youths	828 youths

The next step was to see how each group was distributed on the *dependent variable,* delinquency. Initially he used self-reported delinquency as his dependent variable. The results are displayed in Example B.

Hirschi then compared blacks and whites to see which group was more likely to report committing delinquent acts. Looking at the raw numbers in Example B, it would be very hard to make such a judgment. Although it is true that the largest number (247) of boys who admitted to two or more

Example B

NUMBER OF DELINQUENT ACTS	WHITE	BLACK
None	730	422
One	326	207
Two or more	247	199
Total	1,303 youths	828 youths

delinquent acts during the year were white, they were also the largest group (730) who had committed no offenses during the year. The statistics reflect the fact that there are considerably more whites than blacks in the sample (and in the city of Richmond).

Percentage Conversions

When groups contain different numbers of people, they are hard to compare. The solution to this problem is to convert the raw numbers into percentages, which take account of size differences and make direct comparisons easy. You divide 730 by 1303 to get the percentage of white boys who denied committing any delinquent acts: 56 percent. Similarly, you divide 422 by 828 to get the percentage of blacks who denied committing any delinquent acts: 51 percent. The results of this division are shown in Example C.

Example C

NUMBER OF DELINQUENT ACTS	WHITE	BLACK
None	56%	51%
One	25%	25%
Two or more	19%	24%
Total	100%	100%

Reading across the table, you can see that there are only modest differences between blacks and whites in the proportions reporting delinquent behavior. Of whites, 56 percent denied any delinquent acts; of blacks, 51 percent. Exactly the same proportion (25 percent) of whites and blacks reported committing one delinquent act. Finally, looking across the bottom row in the table, you see that l9 percent of the whites and 24 percent of the blacks said that they had committed two or more such acts. Hirschi concluded that blacks were only slightly more likely than whites to have committed delinquent acts.

He next looked at responses to a question asking "Have you ever been picked up by the police?" Again he created a percentage table so that he could compare black and white teenage boys. Here he found a slightly larger, but still modest, difference: 65 percent of whites and 57 percent of blacks said they had *not* been picked up by the police. Finally, Hirschi turned to his official measure of delinquency based on police and court records. Here he found a very substantial difference: 81 percent of the white boys had *no record* of delinquency, but only 57 percent of the black boys had *no record*. These findings strongly implied that Piliavin and Briar were right—the police were responding differentially to black and white teenagers. Whites were only slightly less likely to admit offenses and nearly as likely as blacks to have been picked up by the police, but they were *much less* likely to have acquired an official record despite these similarities.

To make these differences clear, Hirschi computed a new table, as shown in Example D. First, he selected *only* those boys who admitted they had been picked up by the police. Then, he separated them into blacks and whites. Finally, he computed the proportions of each group who had an official record of delinquency. As can be seen, the majority of whites who have been picked up by the police (55 percent) have no official record. In contrast, the overwhelming majority of blacks who have been picked up by the police (76 percent) do have an official record. These findings strongly suggest that when whites encounter the police, they are usually able to get off without a record. When blacks encounter the police, they typically do not get off without a record.

Example D

OFFICIAL RECORD	BOYS WHO ADMITTED BEING PICKED UP BY POLICE	
	White	Black
Yes	45%	76%
No	55%	24%
Total	100%	100%

Although these findings offered confirmation of Piliavin and Briar's perceptions of how the police operate, the analysis can hardly stop here. Recall that in the Cambridge-Somerville experiment, boys were randomly assigned to the experimental and control groups. Randomization permitted control of all of the other possible causes of differences—besides differences created by chance—between those who participated in the program and those who did not. It established (within known probabilities) that both groups would be equal in terms of such factors as family background, attitudes, size, and all other potential sources of bias.

In experiments, the analysis of findings is complete when the initial comparison between groups has been made. The investigator then uses a simple statistical method to determine whether the size of the relationship found—for example, the differences between the proportions of blacks and whites who have been both picked up and have been given official records—is great enough to make it extremely unlikely to have been caused merely by chance. If the difference is significant, the experimenter then publishes his findings with considerable confidence that they are accurate.

Spuriousness

When survey research is the method used, one is not able to rule out other differences through random assignment. There is no way to randomly assign people to be black or white. Thus, black and white youths in Hirschi's study differ in many ways besides race. There is always the possibility that some of these other factors are responsible for the finding and that race has nothing to do with it.

This problem, over which most survey analysts lose sleep, is called *spuriousness*. When it can be demonstrated, in this example, that something other than race caused the differences in the proportions of official delinquency records, then it can be said that the relationship between race and record is spurious—there is no causal relationship between race and record.

There is nothing mysterious about the idea of spuriousness. It is part of ordinary common sense, and most of us use it all the time. For example, it is the case that the more fire trucks present at a fire the greater damage the fire will do. Suppose someone told you that this proves that fire trucks cause fire damage. You would rightfully laugh out loud. It is obvious that both the number of trucks present

Figure 3.7   Manhattan. Suppose that we want to find out about the distribution of some trait in the population of New York City—for example, how people are going to vote in an upcoming election. If we were to ask each person in the city how he or she planned to vote, we would obviously have an accurate preview. But that would mean interviewing millions of people, a prohibitively expensive and time-consuming task. So, instead, we interview only some of the citizens of New York on the assumption that those whose opinions we obtain will be representative of the whole population. When findings based on a sample closely resemble findings based on the whole population, representativeness has been achieved. But how do we find a representative sample? We might decide to stand on a street corner and interview passersby, but there are thousands of street corners in New York, and the people found on one corner are often very different from those found on another. For example, those who pass by a corner in Times Square (1) are likely to be quite different from those who might be found outside a sidewalk cafe in the east Eighties (2) or passing in front of the Regency Hotel (3). Certainly, any of the people found at any of the first three locations are different from those we would interview if we stood on a corner in Chinatown (4) or in the Bowery (5) or on Wall Street (6 and 7). Indeed, Pictures 6 and 7 indicate that the day one chooses could make a drastic difference—the few persons to be found on Wall Street on a Sunday morning are likely to be quite different from those who crowd the area in the middle of a weekday. Clearly, standing on a corner, any corner, would not provide a representative selection of New Yorkers.

Social scientists obtain an accurate sample of a population by selecting the sample randomly. Their procedures assure that every person in New York has an equal chance of being selected. When that is the case and when a sufficient number of people are included in the sample, the sample will automatically include the right proportions of the many different kinds of people who make up New York City. However, random samples are not chosen from streetcorners. Instead, a typical sampling design begins by using the U.S. Census to determine the number of people who live on each block in a city. Blocks are then randomly selected, with each block being given chances for selection equal to its number of residents. At that point, a preliminary survey is conducted of selected blocks in order to create lists of all persons living on each sample block. From these lists, individuals are randomly selected to be interviewed. The result is a sample that very accurately represents the whole population of the city. Oddly enough, the accuracy of the sample depends in part on how large it is, but not on its size in relation to the population being sampled. Thus, a sample of 1,500 persons (a typical sample size) chosen from the entire United States population gives as good an estimate of the national scene as a sample of 1,500 chosen from New York City does of the population of that city. That is why nationwide polls interview no more people than do polls of a particular city.

at a fire and the amount of damage done is caused by the size of the fire. Big fires draw more fire trucks and cause more damage than small fires do.

Or consider another example. Suppose someone told you that on the average, whites have larger bank accounts than blacks have, and they also said that this showed that race differences cause differences in willingness to save money. You would undoubtedly dismiss such a claim as foolish because you would immediately see that the difference in the average size of bank accounts simply reflects the fact that the average income of blacks is lower than that of whites. We do not expect poor people to have as much money in the bank as rich people have, so willingness to save and race have nothing to do with the size of bank accounts, although race may have much to do with being poor.

In similar fashion, something other than race could be producing differences in the rate at which blacks and whites picked up by the police get official records. Indeed, many sociologists might suggest that the police are responding to social class, not racial differences. The argument could go as follows: The police believe that offenses committed by juveniles who come from lower-class homes more urgently require official action than do offenses committed by juveniles from middle- and upper-class homes. Therefore, it is not on racial grounds but on class grounds that the police discriminate.

How does one test such arguments? Social scientists use *statistical controls* to test for spuriousness. They try to remove the effect of factors that might be producing a spurious relationship. The principle involved is very simple: In the present example, Hirschi would simply compare the relationship between race and having an official record separately for boys of differing social-class backgrounds. For the sake of simplicity, let us suppose that it would be sufficient to divide boys who had been picked up by the police into two groups: those whose fathers were employed in blue-collar occupations and those whose fathers held white-collar jobs. Classifying boys by their fathers' occupations would create two tables out of the data in Example D—one for sons of blue-collar fathers, the other for sons of white-collar fathers.

Table 3.3 is a *hypothetical* illustration showing

Figure 3.8   *In 1936, the* Literary Digest *conducted a massive poll to predict the outcome of that year's presidential election. Nearly 2.5 million American voters returned postcards indicating their choice. On the basis of these returns, the magazine predicted an overwhelming victory for the Republican candidate, Alf Landon. If you have never heard of him, that is because his opponent, Franklin Delano Roosevelt, was reelected to a second term by one of the greatest landslides in American political history. The* Literary Digest *became the object of nationwide ridicule and soon went out of business. Their error was that the large number of postcards they had received were not based on a random sample of the population. The Digest relied on telephone-book listings for their sample at a time when only well-to-do people had phones. The postcards they received therefore represented a narrow, Republican selection of Americans. That same year, George Gallup accurately predicted the vote from interviews with only about 1,500 people. But his sample was properly selected and thus representative.*

Figure 3.9   *The uses and limitations of the three types of sociological research strategies discussed in the text: participant observation, experiment, and survey research. No single method is adequate by itself to answer all sociological questions. You may find it helpful to refer to this table as you read about various studies in subsequent chapters.*

78

QUESTIONS	PARTICIPANT OBSERVATION	EXPERIMENT	SURVEY RESEARCH
Typical Cost	Inexpensive (but much research time required)	Depends on equipment used, size of staff, and duration; can be very inexpensive but is occasionally very costly	Depends on sample size and whether questionnaire or interview is used (interview is generally more costly)
Size of sample or group or number of subjects	Usually small	Limited by funds and time—usually small	Depends on size of population, funds, and time—can be very large
Type of interaction with subjects of study	Face to face—formal or informal	Face to face—formal or informal	If questionnaire used, indirect (by mail); if interview used, face to face but formal
Type of problem	Theory and variables generated in process of research—not controlled by researcher	Theory and variables known in advance and controlled by researcher	Theory and variables known in advance but not controlled by researcher
Can the independent variable be manipulated by the researcher? (Can events be timed?)	No	Yes	No
How are the variables controlled?	Through testing and revision of the theory	By random assignment to experiment and control groups	Through statistical analysis
Can the results be generalized to a larger population?	Yes (only if groups have been selected randomly)	No (except when random sample is used)	Yes (by random selection of cases)
Must the theory based on research findings be predictive?	Yes	Yes	Yes
Can it be used to find out the distribution of a variable (for example, age) in a population	No	No	Yes
Where does the research take place?	In the field: In limited area	In the lab or in the field	In the field: In extended area or several areas
Criteria for selection of groups, subjects, or cases	Nature of the study, availability	Convenience	Random sample from the population

what would happen if social class, not race, were in fact the real cause of the differences that were found in official records.

Assume that simply by separating boys into two groups on the basis of their fathers' occupations, everyone in each group is now of the same social class. If *within* each occupation in the table, social class no longer varies, the social class differences have been controlled. If uncontrolled class differences had been the source of the original differences in official records between whites and blacks, then when social class is controlled, the original relationship ought to *disappear*. In other words, blacks and whites from equal family backgrounds ought to be equally likely to have official records if the argument being tested is true.

Notice that this is what has happened in the hypothetical table (Table 3.3). Among boys whose fathers have blue-collar occupations, 90 percent of

Table 3.3 Percentage of Boys with Records by Race and Fathers' Occupation

OFFICIAL RECORD	BLUE COLLAR		WHITE COLLAR	
	Black	White	Black	White
Yes	90	90	20	20
No	10	10	80	80
Total	100	100	100	100

both blacks and whites have official records. Among boys with white-collar fathers, only 20 percent of both blacks and whites have official records. Race makes no difference when class is controlled. If Hirschi had controlled for social class with these results, he would have had to reject the notion that the police respond differently to white and black juveniles. The apparent racial differences would simply have to be judged as an accident of the fact that blacks and whites differ in their social class, and we would have to say the original relationship between race and police records was spurious.

These results did *not* appear when Hirschi controlled for social class. Instead, he found that differences between blacks and whites remained little changed within each class. Regardless of class, the police seemed to single out blacks for official action. This finding increased Hirschi's confidence that his survey supported Piliavin and Briar's observations. He gained further confidence when other control variables, such as neighborhood, also failed to wipe out racial differences. This procedure is followed in all nonexperimental statistical analyses. Because differences cannot be removed through randomization, the analyst tries to exclude likely sources of spuriousness by systematically holding each possible source constant, as was shown in the hypothetical table. This procedure lacks the finality of experimental methods because possible sources of spuriousness are never exhausted, but it is the only possible way to study social phenomena that cannot be manipulated by experimental controls.

Hirschi went on to examine the effects of a great many factors on delinquency. Many of his findings were summarized in the criticism of current delinquency-prevention programs earlier in this chapter. Others are reported in Chapter 6.

The method of analysis we have just examined is not limited to survey-research studies. It is the method used on *all* numerical data other than that obtained from an experiment. For example, a great many social scientists spend their time analyzing data from the U. S. Census. As you will see in Chapter 14, census data are vital for computing such things as birth and death rates. In Chapters 6 and 7 you will encounter many efforts to determine causes of crime and interpersonal violence based on official police data as well as on surveys of victims and offenders. Whatever the source of nonexperimental numerical data, the question of spuriousness is always an urgent concern. Thus,

in analyzing their data, social scientists always observe the same logical procedures that we have examined in order to control for possible sources of spuriousness.

The purpose of this chapter has been to give you some insight into how research is done. As is evident, methods must be matched to what you want to find out. When you want to investigate particular social processes, such as interaction between the police and juveniles, the best method is to go out and see what is going on. When you are interested in causation and are able to manipulate the variable in which you are interested, such as who receives a particular form of help or counseling, the experiment is much to be preferred because its findings are unlikely to be spurious. When you want to know how some trait is distributed in a population and how one such trait is related to another, the appropriate method is to select a representative sample and use interviewers or a questionnaire to collect the data. All of these methods have provided fundamental evidence on social problems that are treated throughout the remainder of this text.

CHAPTER REVIEW

To gather and analyze *facts* and to test *theories* is to do research. *Systematic* research is what distinguishes the findings of social science from commonsense knowledge. The kinds of questions asked in large part determine the *kind* of research that will be done.

If one wants to study the *process* by which something takes place, the best approach would be to watch it occur without influencing it in any way. This, essentially, is *participant observation*. Because social scientists do not want to have any effect on the actions of people in a group they are observing, they will often try to pass as members of the group. In this way, a researcher can observe and *systematically* record all the actions of the group being studied. The Piliavin and Briar study provides a good example of participant observation. The researchers wanted to find out how the police react in encounters with juveniles. Accordingly, they chose to ride in patrol cars on regular police patrols and to record police-juvenile encounters. From many observations, they found that the character, demeanor, and race of juveniles in large part determined the outcome of the encounters that juveniles had with police.

Asking what *causes* some phenomenon is a different

kind of question, and it requires a different research method. If you were interested in reforming juvenile delinquents (as Cabot was), you would want to compare the results of different treatment programs. *Experimental* research is possible when you can manipulate some condition and observe and compare the results. You manipulate the *variable* (or condition that is capable of changing) that you believe to be causing a certain outcome; that variable is the *independent* variable. What is being caused is called the *dependent* variable; it is dependent on the variations in the independent variable. In an experimental situation, to rule out the possibility that some other factor is affecting the dependent variable, you assign people randomly to either the *experimental group* (where, for example, they receive a certain treatment) or to the *control group* (where no treatment is given). It is then possible to compare outcomes in the control group and the experimental group to see whether the kind of treatment used (the independent variable) made any difference between the groups on the dependent variable. In the Cambridge-Somerville experiment, the researchers treated half of their sample of delinquents with counseling and similar therapy. The other half received no treatment at all. Later delinquency records (the dependent variable) were then compared to find out whether the treatment had affected delinquency rates. Unfortunately, the treatment had no effect whatsoever—there was no difference between the two groups. Had a relationship appeared, the researchers would have applied a test of *statistical significance.* They would have statistically determined the likelihood of getting that kind of an outcome just by chance. If the likelihood was small, they would be fairly sure that the result had been caused by their treatment, not by chance. Even when an experiment "fails," social scientists have gained knowledge. In the Cambridge-Somerville study, they found that the factors being "treated" in the experiment in all likelihood were not the ones causing the delinquency.

Still another kind of question may emerge when studying a social problem such as juvenile delinquency: You may wish to know the *distribution* of certain behaviors or characteristics in the population—for example, how many juveniles have committed delinquent acts. That was one of Hirschi's questions when he studied young people in his Richmond youth study. He wanted to know about delinquency among *all* high school juveniles—not just ones that had been caught. He therefore chose the *survey* technique, in which a representative sample of the population he wanted to study answered a questionnaire about their own behavior. In analyzing the data, Hirschi also faced the risk that some uncontrolled factor other than his independent variable was causing changes in the dependent variable. To guard against this effect—called *spuriousness*—he examined the relationship between, for example, race and delinquency within all categories of a third variable, social class. Thus, he was able to *control* and evaluate the effect of that third variable. As a result of his study, Hirschi found that blacks were only slightly more likely to be delinquent than whites but that blacks were overrepresented in the *official* statistics. This finding, which supported the Piliavin and Briar study, would not have been possible without survey research.

SUGGESTED READINGS

Babbie, Earl R. *Survey Research Methods.* Belmont, Calif.: Wadsworth, 1972.

Lofland, John. *Analyzing Social Settings.* Belmont, Calif.: Wadsworth, 1971.

Tanur, Judith, and ASA-NCTM Joint Committee on Statistics (eds.). *Statistics: A Guide to the Unknown.* San Francisco: Holden-Day, 1972.

Webb, Eugene J., *et al. Unobtrusive Measures: Nonreactive Research in the Social Sciences.* Chicago: Rand McNally, 1966.

Zeisel, Hans. *Say It with Figures.* Rev. ed. New York: Harper & Row, 1968.

Deviant Behavior

The problems included in this unit have a number of features in common. First, each involves overt individual actions. *Unlike poverty or racial discrimination, which are typically done to* people regardless of their own actions, crime and violence are committed *by* people. *No one can be an addict without taking drugs or become a burglar without stealing something. Second, all the individual actions* deviate *from or violate social norms. In fact, most of the deviant acts examined in this unit are* against the law. *Third, responses to these acts have been similar. Treatment of these social problems is usually either (1) legal punishment in the form of fines, probation, and imprisonment or (2) treatment in the form of therapy designed to change or reform the individual so that he or she will cease committing these deviant acts.*

Perhaps the most important common feature of the problems in this unit is that many of the same social-science theories have been used to explain why they occur. For example, many of the theories of mental illness are also applied to alcoholism, drug addiction, violent behavior, and sexual deviance. Indeed, many of the problems taken up in this unit are often claimed to cause one another.

Thus, some social scientists argue that most deviant behavior is the result of mental illness. Much crime is blamed on drug use. Much interpersonal violence is attributed to intoxication.

For all these reasons, grouping these problems in a single unit makes it easier for you to apply what you learn in one chapter to each of the others. However, each chapter has been designed so that the chapters can be read in any order in which they are assigned, with one possible exception. Chapter 4 introduces and outlines many theories that are reapplied in later chapters. Therefore, you might find it helpful to read at least Part II of Chapter 4 before you turn to other chapters. Or you may find it helpful to turn back to Chapter 4 should you have questions about the discussion of a particular theory in any later chapter.

Can a man take fire in his bosom
and his clothes not
be burned?
Can one go on
hot coals and his
feet not be burned?
Proverbs 6:27,28

4
Alcoholism
and
Drug Addiction

The main difference between alcoholism and drug addiction—that liquor is legal and narcotics are not—has enormous implications for the analysis of these two social problems: Buying "hard" drugs is illegal, the drugs are very expensive, and drug treatment programs are frequently at odds with laws and law enforcement.

Nevertheless, drug addiction and alcoholism have much in common. Both alcohol and narcotics raise questions about addiction—about physical dependency, bodily cravings, and biochemical "hooks"; people regard both substances as potentially destructive to body and mind, as turning their victims into "dope fiends," "junkies," "lushes," or "drunks." Furthermore, similar theories are offered to explain addiction and alcoholism, and similar treatment programs are applied to both. For all these reasons, we have combined alcoholism and drug addiction in a single chapter. Indeed, the fact that the two are presently treated differently under the law is a major reason to consider them together. It provides an opportunity to make illuminating comparisons. For example, present attempts to deal with drugs through prohibition can be compared with previous experiences with the prohibition of alcohol. By the same token, the study of how the legalization of alcohol affected the extent of alcoholism can offer a preview of what might happen if drugs were legalized.

As with all subsequent chapters, the problem of drinking and addiction will be broken down into three major parts. Part I will define the problem and describe the extent and social location of alcoholism and drug addiction. Part II will outline the causes of the problem: Why do people become alcoholics or addicts? Part III will examine the ways in which our society has responded to the problem: What policies and programs have government and private groups directed toward the problem? What is the effect of these responses? Finally, we will assess future trends.

PART I: THE PROBLEM
ALCOHOLISM AND DRUG ADDICTION

Two developments have contributed to the breakdown of old beliefs and have stimulated new ways of thinking about drugs and their consequences. First, increased drug use by the youth culture since the mid-1960s has focused both scientific attention and public concern on drugs like marijuana and LSD (lysergic acid diethylamide), which most people regard as nonaddictive. Second, as we shall see later in this chapter, we now have a growing body of evidence showing that even hard drug use does not always lead to addiction. These two developments make us somewhat cautious in dealing with the issue of addiction and in choosing terms to describe it.

This chapter will point out some of the fallacies in traditional views of addiction, and it will focus not only on what alcohol and drugs do to people but also on what people—both individually and culturally—*think* alcohol and drugs do, that is, on how people define drugs and their effects.

DRUG USE IN AMERICAN SOCIETY

86

Different people make different assumptions about the underlying meaning and causes of addiction, so let us start with what we clearly know from direct observation about addiction and drug use in American society. First, researchers estimate that 80 million Americans drink alcohol and that 6 million of these are alcoholics; 75 to 80 million smoke cigarettes; 6 to 12 million smoke marijuana; 20 to 25 million take sedatives; and countless persons indulge in coffee, tea, tranquilizers, amphetamines, cocaine, glue sniffing, and so forth (Fort, 1969). All these substances are *psychoactive* drugs, which means they have some fairly *rapid, noticeable effect on the user's mind and emotions.*

Effects of Psychoactive Drugs

If you take vitamin C every morning in the belief that it will maintain you in good health, you are not using a psychoactive drug; vitamins do not make you feel different immediately after taking them. On the other hand, if you drink a cup of coffee every morning, anticipating an immediate burst of energy or thinking it will make you feel ''right,'' you *are* using a psychoactive drug. You feel coffee's effects as soon as the caffeine stimulates your nervous system. It is generally agreed that psychoactive drugs do affect the nervous system, even

Figure 4.1   Public concern about drugs has sometimes led to misleading news reports. An example is the 1968 story about six college students allegedly blinded by looking into the sun for several hours after having taken LSD. The story, later exposed as a hoax, was widely circulated.

Figure 4.2   Drug use in America is widespread. The advertisement below draws attention to one city's effort to solve the drug problem through extensive community involvement.

though individual and cultural responses to them may differ when conditions differ.

Types of Psychoactive Drugs

Psychoactive drugs are usually divided into three major categories: stimulants, depressants, and hallucinogens. Stimulants activate the central nervous system, increasing alertness and, depending on the dose, energizing and exciting the user. Natural stimulants include cocaine, caffeine (in coffee, tea, and cola), and nicotine (in tobacco). Amphetamines (collectively known as ''speed'') are synthetic stimulants. Depressants calm people by slowing down the functioning of the nervous system. Among the drugs classified as depressants are the opiates, or narcotics—opium, heroin, morphine—and the sedatives, including natural sedatives, artificial sedatives, or barbiturates, and the more recently synthesized milder tranquilizers. Even between such basic categories as depressant and stimulant, the boundary is not always clear. Many drinkers consider alcohol a stimulant, but pharmacologists label it a depressant because, by depressing the brain's inhibitory centers, it liberates impulses. For example, some people cry forlornly when they drink; others laugh foolishly; some get violent. The next day, they say, ''But I was not myself.''

Classifying the *hallucinogens,* such as marijuana and LSD, is more difficult. Hallucinogens can cause disorganized thoughts and distorted perceptions. For example, marijuana tends to first stimulate then to depress the user; it is sometimes considered a sedative as well as an hallucinogen. The stronger hallucinogens—LSD, mescaline, psilocybin—do not fit into either the stimulant or depressant category because their effects are altogether different. Categories of psychoactive drugs, however, are merely suggestive, not definitive. As we shall see in Part II, different people in different social settings will have different experiences from the same psychoactive substances. We can say only that the effects of drugs offer a clue about what people want from a drug.

Indicators of Addiction

At present, there is a growing belief that the American population's vast involvement with psychoactive drugs, including cigarettes and medically prescribed tranquilizers, is a serious social problem (Lennard *et al.,* 1971). People seem to believe that there is something basically unsound in the need to modify one's consciousness artificially. Everyone agrees that heroin is harmful, but different groups within the larger society typically isolate one particular form of drug use as an area of social concern. They often fail to realize that various forms of psychoactive drug use are *interrelated.*

Before we can establish that they are interrelated, we have to study the popular conceptions of addiction and the effects of drugs. To say people are *addicted* (a term commonly used) to a drug is to imply that they cannot control their own lives or determine their own priorities and that their dependency obliterates other interests and pursuits and leads to antisocial behavior. Most observers consider tolerance and withdrawal the behavioral indicators of addiction.

Tolerance is the tendency for users to become increasingly accustomed to a drug, with the result that they require larger and larger doses to get the effect they seek from it. Tolerance is commonly observed in alcoholics and heroin addicts, but it seems to operate the same way in the cigarette smoker who builds up to a three-pack-a-day habit or the coffee drinker who requires five or six cups just to get started in the morning. Many marijuana users report a *reverse tolerance effect* (Jones and Stone, 1970) whereby smaller doses—in some cases, just its taste and smell—can set off the feelings and behavior associated with the drug in the experienced user. Nevertheless, the fact that many experienced marijuana smokers seem able to function better when they are high suggests that marijuana use does produce a tolerance effect in its customary sense (Weil *et al.,* 1968).

When an addict cannot obtain a certain drug, he goes through a traumatic process of readjustment called *withdrawal.* Symptoms of withdrawal from heroin resemble an attack of the flu and may include sweating, shivering, vomiting, diarrhea, fever, sleeplessness, and alternate periods of frantic activity and total lethargy. The self-reports of addicts also convey a sense of their intensely felt malaise—a terrible yet indefinable feeling of ill-being. Again, symptoms comparable to these can

87

be observed in the less severe agonies of someone breaking a cigarette or coffee habit. When the syndicated newspaper columnist Joseph Alsop mentioned in his column that ex-smokers often have trouble concentrating without cigarettes, he received a flood of replies from readers who agreed that this was so (see also Brecher *et al.*, 1972).

Another indicator of addiction, which is more behavioral, is the addict's desperate single-minded *craving* for and pursuit of the drug when withdrawal distress occurs. When any motivation toward a single object becomes this strong, the intensity of other motivations decreases and the person may lose all other interests.

HISTORICAL AND CULTURAL VARIATIONS

So that we may better understand the role of drugs in addiction, let us look at the usage patterns of two of the best-known psychoactive drugs. We will try to avoid what Erich Goode (1972) calls the "chemicalistic fallacy": the assumption that a given drug has an invariable chemical effect on everyone who takes it. We shall see instead that variations in use and response occur with any drug in different cultures and at different times and that chemistry can be a secondary factor in a drug's action. At the same time, the properties of a drug are a good starting point for studying the significance that people have attached to different drugs.

Once we know how a drug tends to affect the nervous system, we can trace the ways in which different cultural and personal frameworks may modify this effect.

Alcohol

Richard Blum uses alcohol to illustrate the way properties of a drug combine or *interact* with the social and psychological characteristics of the user to determine that drug's ultimate effect (Blum *et al.*, 1969). Different drinkers, or the same drinkers on different occasions, show a range of emotions and desires—including rage, aggression, sexuality, verbal self-expression, love, conviviality, nostalgia, sadness, grandiosity, and self-pity.

Blum draws a major distinction between two contexts of alcohol use: where drinking is integrated into the life of a culture and where it is disruptive to the culture (Blum *et al.*, 1969). For example, drinking is integrated into the Italian culture. Traditionally, Italians have thought of wine as a healthful drink and have not ascribed the psychological potency to it that Americans have. As one might expect, Italian-Americans now become alcoholics more frequently than do Italians in Italy but less frequently than do other Americans. Blum's study shows that drinking has an addictive potential when people *think of it* as dangerously powerful and see it as an individual, private activity rather than as part of everyday life in society.

Figure 4.3   (Right) *Before their prohibition, opiates were easily obtained in over-the-counter products such as aspirin and cough medicine. After the turn of the century, however, public opinion took a firm line against opiate use. Public attitudes about alcohol have wavered but have always been more favorable, even during periods of prohibition, when alcohol was available in speakeasies (far right). Prohibition of alcohol resulted in a decrease in the number of users for a while, but the proportion of opiate users has not diminished as a result of prohibition; in fact, it has increased.*

88

A Drug Addict
I had not taken a bath in a year nor changed my clothes or removed them except to stick a needle every hour in the fibrous grey wooden flesh of terminal addiction. I never cleaned or dusted the room. Empty ampule boxes and garbage piled to the ceiling. Light and water long since turned off for non-payment. I did absolutely nothing. I could look at the end of my shoe for eight hours. I was only roused to action when the hourglass of junk ran out. If a friend came to visit—and they rarely did since who or what was left to visit—I sat there not caring that he had entered my field of vision—a grey screen always blanker and fainter—and not caring when he walked out of it. If he had died on the spot I would have sat there looking at my shoe waiting to go through his pockets.
Quote is from William S. Burroughs, who was a drug addict for fifteen years.
—William S. Burroughs, *Naked Lunch* (New York: Grove Press, 1959), p. xli.

Alcoholism that leads to self-destructive or antisocial behavior occurs in cultures or subcultures that have no prescribed social pattern of drinking. Such cultures consider drinking an individual pursuit and associate it to some degree with pleasure seeking or escapism. Among these cultures are those in which alcohol has been recently introduced, in which newly imposed legal controls have replaced traditional social regulations, and in which one social group has used alcohol to keep another group in subjection. The American Indians offer an example. The widespread alcoholism among American Indians occurred because their culture was disrupted and alcohol was introduced, both at the same time (Blum *et al.*, 1969).

Reviewing the history of alcoholism in America, Blum notes that drinking was moderate and universally accepted in the colonial era. By the middle of the nineteenth century, however, both heavy drinking and total abstinence became more common. Blum relates this change to the growing division of American society into two opposing forces: (1) the large cities and the frontier, both of which encouraged individual deviance and (2) the American heartland, which tried to impose a puritan notion of sin on the nation. Abraham Myerson (1940), using the term *social ambivalence* to describe the effect of these two forces, argues that the conflict between these extremes of asceticism (self-denial) and hedonism (pleasure seeking) has

made it hard for Americans (and groups like the Irish) to develop such moderate attitudes toward drinking as the Italians have taken.

In any case, nineteenth-century Americans showed considerable indecision over what to do about alcohol: Three separate waves of state prohibition laws were passed and then repealed—the first in the 1850s, the second in the 1880s, and the third in the 1910s; the third wave culminated in the ratification of the Eighteenth Amendment in 1919 (repealed in 1933). Those dates are also very important in the history of opium use in America.

Opium and the Opiates

In Asia, opiate addiction first took on the dimensions it has for us today, and the first recorded instance of opium prohibition was in China in 1729. The contrast between China's and India's uses of opium illustrates Blum's cross-cultural model. People in India have stably integrated opium into their culture and employed it moderately and nonhabitually, even in the twentieth century. People in China, however, were introduced to opium by Arab traders who brought it from India—but in China there was no established cultural place for it. In this outside imposition of a drug on a culture, we can see a parallel to the crippling of the American Indians with alcohol. The result in China was the spawning of millions of opium smokers, ranging from moderate users

89

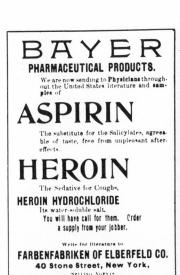

(generally the well-to-do) to large numbers of addicts who came to the fore by the middle of the nineteenth century (Blum *et al.,* 1969).

During the 1850s Chinese laborers on the west coast introduced opium in noticeable quantities, and other historical events, especially the Civil War, converged to lay the groundwork for the opium problem in the United States.

Remember that the 1850s saw an intensification of efforts to control drinking in America. We recall this fact for two reasons: First, it shows that American society had reached a stage of susceptibility to addictive drug use. Second, with prohibition laws making liquor harder to obtain in many states, individuals who had fixed patterns of drug dependence were looking for a substitute. In fact, former heavy drinkers were switching to opium, and the habit was spreading quickly from soldiers wounded in the Civil War to their families (Kolb, 1958). At this time, too, bottlers of popular patent medicines began to use opium as an active ingredient. Yet even by this time, people had developed no clear conception of addiction.

The two decades between 1890 and 1909 saw a dramatic increase in the amount of opium imported into the United States—greater, for example, than the amounts imported during the Civil War (Clausen, 1966a). The increase coincided with the discovery in 1898 of heroin (diacetylmorphine), produced by binding morphine to acetic acid.

With opium now available in a convenient powdered (and much more powerful) form, it became more widely used and the public therefore took more notice of it. In the first two decades of this century, physicians began to speak of addiction as a disease. In this period, organized medicine and pharmacy stopped classifying opiate addiction with habituation to tobacco, alcohol, and caffeine and assigned it a significance of its own (Isbell, 1958; Sonnedecker, 1958). Once this distinction was made, public policy took a definite line—without the wavering shown in the case of alcohol.

Later in this chapter we will go into legal restrictions on the opiates and examine the way the social definitions of the addiction problem have helped to create the problem itself. For now, we can note that America's small-town, puritan values were triumphant; there was to be no repeal of opiate prohi-

bition. When Americans defined opiate use as outside the limits of normal behavior, the stage was set for its association with crime and degeneracy.

PAST AND PRESENT USAGE PATTERNS

Having seen something of the broad range of psychoactive drug use—the forms it takes and the issues it raises—let us now take a closer look at the two drugs thought to constitute a serious addiction problem in the United States, opium and alcohol. We want to see which population groups use them most, what the total number of users is estimated to be, and how these patterns have changed.

Changes in Opium Use

One major change in opium use has been in the form of the drug that is taken: People have smoked or have eaten opium throughout recorded history; nineteenth-century Americans drank it in patent-medicine compounds or injected it in the form of morphine; since the turn of the century, it has appeared primarily in the form of heroin. With the shift to heroin use, a change has also occurred in the social characteristics of the users. Summarizing the data presented in many different sources (O'Donnell, 1969; Clausen, 1966a; Meyer, 1952), we find the following trends for this century.

1. A decrease in the average age of users.
2. A decline in the proportion of female users from a majority to a minority.
3. An increasing concentration of users in urban areas.
4. A decline in the average socioeconomic status of users.
5. An increase in the proportion of users from ethnic, religious, and racial minority groups.

Clearly, opiate users were once respected citizens but are now social outcasts. We will see how and why the status of users changed when we discuss the role of institutions in creating the addiction problem in America. We should be cautious, however, about accepting the stereotype of the ghetto heroin addict. Irving Lukoff's (1972) study of heroin users in Brooklyn ghettos offers a surprising finding: Not only are there more of these

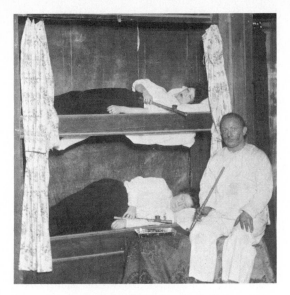

Figure 4.4   An opium parlor in New York City's Chinatown. The form of opium used and the social characteristics of users have changed over the past century. Before heroin use became popular, many users smoked opium, and a large proportion of these users were women.

Figure 4.5   Since vigorous antidrug programs were instituted in the late 1960s, drug addiction in the United States has continued to increase. Heroin addiction declined slightly in 1970—apparently because some heroin addicts turned to other narcotic drugs, the use of which rose sharply between 1969 and 1970. In 1971, the number of heroin addicts shot up again, and use of other narcotic drugs fell back.
(U.S. Bureau of Narcotics and Dangerous Drugs.)

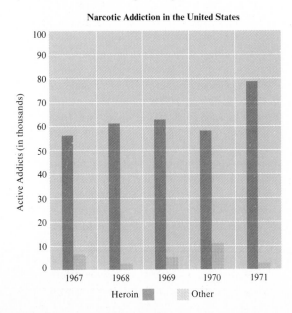

Narcotic Addiction in the United States

users than we previously supposed but they are better educated and have more money than the criminal addict we usually visualize. It seems reasonable to suspect that, like visible alcoholics, the most visible heroin users are those least able to support their habit and to keep it under control.

When we turn to the question of how many opiate users there are—and have been—we find that the best estimates give us a very different picture from the one painted by antidrug propagandists over the years. These estimates suggest that the population of users in America remained relatively constant at 100,000 for about half a century—from 1914, when an addict could still get a doctor's prescription for an opiate or could purchase it directly from a druggist, through 1924, when the Narcotics Bureau was whipping up a public crusade with images of millions of addicts stalking the streets of the nation's cities, to 1964, when the Bureau's enforcement policies had been in effect for decades (Clausen, 1966a). Since the early 1960s, the number of users has multiplied several times. Current estimates vary, but they generally place the number at several hundred thousand. Finally, we should bear in mind that although the user population is and was considerably lower than the popular estimate, it is still a hundred times that of any other Western country.

91

Changes in Alcohol Use

Alcohol has been a more constant feature of human experience than opium has. In America, its use has always been accorded respectability within large sectors of the population, even when it was outlawed. Excessive drinking, severely frowned upon as it is, does not as readily inspire fear, loathing, and ostracism as does the slightest involvement with heroin. Thus, we would not expect to find such extreme variations in people's drinking patterns—either over time or among different groups—as we do in heroin-usage patterns. For the country as a whole, change has been more gradual with alcohol use, and the differences in usage patterns are of degree, not of kind.

Recent surveys (Cahalan and Cisin, 1968; NIMH, 1967) show that approximately 68 percent of all American adults drink alcohol at least occasionally; the rates for men and women are 77 percent and 60 percent, respectively. Alcoholics are thought to constitute 6 to 10 percent of this total drinking population. One estimate (Efron, Keller, and Gurioli, 1972) places the number of alcoholics at 5,400,000. If numbers alone were the criterion, alcoholism would be considered ten or twenty times more serious a social problem in the United States than heroin addiction. The drinking population has remained fairly stable over the years, with a gradual increase in percentages—from 60 percent in 1943 to 70 percent in 1965 (Mann, 1970). Gallup polls show self-reported drinking increasing from 55 percent in 1958 to 65 percent in 1966 (Cahalan and Cisin, 1968). This increase seems to have come almost entirely from a rise in the proportion of women drinkers, for men continue to drink at the same rate (Cahalan and Cisin, 1968; NIMH, 1967).

The rate of increase for alcoholism during the same period seems to have been somewhat sharper. Marty Mann (1970), using Elvin Jellinek's formula for estimating the incidence of alcoholism from deaths caused by cirrhosis of the liver, comes up with figures of 3 million alcoholics in 1943, 5 million in 1956, and 6.5 million in 1965. The figures indicate that the percentage of the total American population who were alcoholics rose from 2.2 percent in 1943 to 3.35 percent in 1965.

Where are all these alcoholics to be found? Like the stereotype of heroin users, the popular stereotype of the alcoholic as a skid row bum does not match the facts: Fewer than half of the skid row derelicts in Chicago and New York are alcoholics (NIMH, 1967). Statistics presented by the Department of Health, Education and Welfare (NIMH, 1967), as well as later studies (Rubington, 1972), indicate that 70 percent of the alcoholics in America are respectable individuals who contain their habit within an orderly life. Earl Rubington, in his study *The Hidden Alcoholic* (1972), finds that our distorted image of the alcoholic comes partly from the greater visibility of the lower-status alcoholic and partly from our hesitation to label a higher-status problem drinker as an alcoholic.

Research shows that the drinking patterns of some groups have changed but that patterns of other groups have held constant. Three decades ago, John Dollard (1945) found that the middle

class drank less than any other socioeconomic group—a reflection of the role of the middle class as the main exponents of traditional American values. Antisocial and aggressive behavior while drinking was primarily a lower-class problem; such behavior was largely suppressed within the upper class. But Robin Room (1972) has shown that the relationship between social class and drinking patterns is not so clear-cut today. In particular, there has been an upsurge in middle-class drinking, which David Pittman (1967) attributes to a rejection of small-town abstinence in favor of a liberated cosmopolitanism. This rise in middle-class involvement with alcohol, along with the greater proportion of women drinkers, stands out as a major contributing factor to the overall increase in the drinking rate.

The fact that drinking also varies among ethnic and religious groups in America is consistent with a theory we reviewed earlier: that drinking becomes a social problem only when it is not integrated with a group's cultural life. The Jews, for example, for whom drinking is part of numerous religious rituals, show a very high percentage of drinkers but a very low percentage of alcoholics. But these relationships, too, are changing as such groups are influenced by the larger social environment. Italian-Americans, coming from a culture with a stable and well-integrated approach to drinking, are showing an *increasing* rate of deviant drinking. Irish-Americans, starting out with cultural ambivalence toward alcohol and with an ingrained pattern of deviant drinking, are showing a *decrease* in the rate of alcoholism (NIMH, 1967). Thus, the mixed culture of America seems to be exerting a leveling effect on its ethnic groups, even though these groups still retain some of their original habits and traditions. One relationship that continues to hold true is the one between drinking and age. Drinking (NIMH, 1967) and drinking-related problems (Cahalan, 1969) decline with increasing age for both men and women.

Turning to the youth culture, we find that the adoption of marijuana and other drugs does not seem to have caused a decline in drinking by young people. Alcohol has remained the most universally used psychoactive drug (leaving aside cigarettes and coffee) among college students (Groves *et al.,* 1970) and high-school students (Johnston, 1973). Now that marijuana use is being assimilated into the more moderate, less deviant life styles of the 1970s, alcohol has become an accepted feature of the youth culture, both in conjunction with and as a substitute for other drugs—and probably with the approval of parents who would rather see their children drinking than taking LSD.

One intriguing variable that appears to determine rates of alcohol and drug use is the size of the potential user's population group. Surveys have shown that the proportion of drinkers is higher among residents of larger communities (NIMH, 1967), a fact that probably has to do with characteristics of large cities other than their size—for example, pace of life, overcrowding, unassimilated minorities, and slums. A better index of the effect of size emerges from Lloyd Johnston's (1973) study of drug use among high-school students. It shows that the per capita use of illicit drugs (marijuana and hallucinogens) increases with the number of students attending a school. This is not simply because large schools tend to be in large cities. Per capita use of illicit drugs is high in large rural schools, too. In the laboratory, Cedric W. M. Wilson (1969) has observed that alcohol consumption in rats varies with the number of rats kept in one cage. One of his findings was that only the rats kept in the larger groups increased their alcohol consumption as time went on. Clearly, the relationship between group size and psychoactive-drug use merits further investigaton.

We have examined several factors that determine which psychoactive drugs people will use and how they will use them. We have seen that drug use relates not simply to the properties of available drugs but also to cultural, historical, and social factors.

PART II: SOURCES
ALCOHOLISM AND DRUG ADDICTION

Now we must ask the central question about alcoholics and drug addicts: Why do they do it? All our concern, pity, outrage, anguish, and remorse over addiction, as well as all our efforts to cope with drug addicts and alcoholics, comes back to

this question. Without a good idea of why they do it, how can we know what to do? Indeed, as this chapter attempts to make clear, incorrect answers to this question often lead to laws and treatment strategies that actually make the problems worse.

Social scientists are in a position to provide a general outline of the answer. In this chapter, we shall see that research has established several factors that do influence drug addiction and alcoholism. And it is evident that an adequate answer to this question must include a number of causes. Like virtually all other forms of human behavior, drug taking and excessive drinking have no single cause; rather, a great many causes interact to produce the behavior, and although one set of causes may be producing addiction in some people, another set may be producing addiction in others.

It is also evident that the causes of drug addiction and alcoholism must be sought at a number of *levels* of analysis. Both micro and macro levels of causation must be unraveled and combined. For example, to discover why people become alcoholics or drug addicts, it is necessary to begin by exploring the fundamental physiological effects of drugs and alcohol. Yet, factors other than human physiology must be involved: Not everyone who drinks or takes drugs becomes hooked; of those who do become hooked, some are able to quit and others are not. It is therefore necessary to examine the role of individual psychological differences in addressing the question of why people become addicted.

Furthermore, factors outside the individual play an important role in drug addiction and alcoholism, so an individual's family, work, and friendship patterns must be taken into account. However, the chain of causation continues beyond a person's immediate social situation. No explanation is adequate or complete unless it takes into account the functioning of society as a whole. We have already seen that cultural values and definitions greatly influence alcohol and drug usage. For example, in societies that define liquor as a beverage rather than as an intoxicant, alcoholism is relatively infrequent. Furthermore, such factors as the nature and extent of economic and social inequalities or the speed, direction, and uniformity of social change can play a major role in determining

93

who and how many become alcoholics or drug addicts. Finally, how the society deals with alcohol and drug use plays a major role in answering the question of why people become addicted.

The distinct levels of analysis and the major questions that must be assessed at each level are depicted in Figure 4.7 The specific content of the questions reflects our interest in why drug addiction and alcoholism occur. However, the general outline applies to all five problems discussed in this unit. Furthermore, many of the theories introduced in the following pages will reappear and be reapplied in later chapters. Your efforts to understand the theories taken up here will be well spent and justified when you read subsequent chapters.

PHYSIOLOGICAL SOURCES

Public concern about alcohol and drugs focuses on how these chemical substances affect the human body. Before we can sensibly raise social and psychological questions about drug addiction and alcoholism, we must try to determine the extent and nature of these physiological effects.

The man in the street's notion of drug addiction is this: that sufficient dosages of an opiate will invariably and permanently addict anyone, irrespective of his or her personality or situation. Alcoholism is also frequently seen in a physiological light, although a greater familiarity with liquor rules out the wilder myths that circulate about opium—for example, that a single dose leads to a lifetime of enslavement. These myths, and the physiological explanations on which they are based, were widely accepted in the 1910s and 1920s. Since that time, scientific research on addiction and on related questions has challenged these myths. We will review some of the key developments in the growth of scientific enlightenment about the complexity of drugs and their effects. The research presented in this section will show that the physiological effects of drugs are relative, not fixed.

The Placebo Effect

One line of research with important implications for the relativity of psychoactive drug action is the

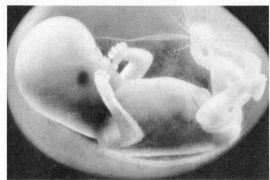

THIS JUNKIE HAS A FIFTY DOLLAR A DAY HABIT.

He won't be born for 6 months. He weighs one thirteenth of an ounce and is less than an inch long.

And he's as much of a junkie as someone who's 35 years old and shoots into the vein of his leg.

Tonight, Geraldo Rivera will take a close hard look at the junkie population of New York that hasn't even been born yet. Last year alone, 1,500 mothers with a monkey on their back gave birth to babies with a monkey on theirs.

Sometimes, if the mother goes through withdrawal while she's pregnant, the baby never gets born. He goes through cold turkey, too. And in the process will simply kick himself to death.

The program is an Eyewitness News

Special called "The Littlest Junkie." And it not only explores the problem with agonizing honesty.

But it sets forth what's being done, what should be done before it's too late. And what a pregnant mother can do if she's not only eating for two, but shooting for two.

So watch tonight and see what the 70's have done to the miracle of childbirth.

⑦ TONIGHT 7:30
THE LITTLEST JUNKIE
With Eyewitness News
Correspondent, Geraldo Rivera.

Figure 4.6   The effects of drugs are greatly influenced by personality and social factors. However, there is a physiological basis for heroin addiction. The physiological factor is the only element in the newborn baby who has been addicted while in the mother's womb.

Figure 4.7   Levels of Analysis and Issues Appropriate to Each Level. This summary chart does not cover all the points raised in the chapter. Use it only to review what you have read. Page numbers are given for the full important discussion of any topic.

study of the *placebo effect*. Such research has shown that the way people react to a drug is determined not only by what the drug *is* but also by what the drug *is presented as being*. It is well known that many physicians often prescribe placebos—substances that have no physical effects—for overanxious patients who want to feel that they are being treated for some genuine physical ailment.

An important early study of morphine and the placebo effect was conducted by Louis Lasagna, Frederick Mosteller, John M. von Felsinger, and Henry K. Beecher (1954). In this experiment,

Levels	Appropriate Questions	A Partial Synopsis of Present Conclusions
Physiological	Do drugs and alcohol create a physical dependency? Do people really get "hooked" so that they physically suffer without alcohol or drugs?	The best evidence is that they do. However, psychological and social factors affect the extent and nature of "being hooked." (pp. 93–101)
	Can people control their use of narcotics?	Through controlled use, apparently some people are able to lead normal lives while using these drugs. (pp. 98–100)
	Do all people experience similar physical sensations from alcohol or from a specific drug?	Not all. For example, mental set and surroundings greatly influence the sensations people experience. (pp. 94–98)
Psychological	Do differences in psychological make-up (personality) influence who does and who does not become an alcoholic or drug addict?	There is evidence that being excessively dependent and insecure can contribute to drug and alcohol use. However, many people with traits associated with alcoholism and drug addiction do not drink or take drugs; many addicts and alcoholics seem devoid of these traits. (pp. 102–105)
	Can addiction and alcoholism be the result of conditioned learning?	The pleasurable sensations produced by alcohol and drugs can reinforce their use. But since many people are exposed to these reinforcements without becoming drug addicts or alcoholics, conditioning is at best only a partial cause. (pp. 101–102)
Social-Psychological	Does being socially labeled an alcoholic or drug addict lock people into such behavior?	It may. However, many people eventually "mature out" of drug addiction and alcoholism, and labeling theory tells us nothing about why people begin to drink or use drugs. (pp. 105–108)
	Do people learn to be alcoholics and drug addicts through interaction with others?	Social learning undoubtedly plays a role in these forms of deviance. It may account for people's relapse into drug or alcohol use once they return to the social setting in which they originally learned to use drugs and alcohol and to enjoy their effects. However, many who are exposed to the same social settings do not become drug addicts or alcoholics. (pp. 105–108)
Sociological: Middle Range	Does frustration from not being able to achieve socially accepted goals cause alcoholism and drug addiction (strain theory)?	Perhaps some people turn to alcohol and drugs to ease their pains in life. Yet most people who seem to suffer such frustrations do not become drug addicts or alcoholics, while many quite successful people do. (pp. 108–109)
	Are drug addiction and alcoholism simply conformity to the norms of a subculture that encourages such behavior?	Although many subcultures encourage drinking, none define alcoholism as normal. However, certain subcultures may encourage drug addiction. (pp. 109–110)
	Does having little to gain from conformity and little to lose from deviance account for much alcoholism and drug addiction (control theory)?	This explanation fits many of the known facts. People with little to lose—because they lack close ties to others, or have poor jobs, or have low self-esteem—seem especially prone to deviant behavior. (pp. 110–113)
Societal	Why do some persons in society have less to lose by alcoholism and drug addiction than do others?	Because not all are equally rewarded for conformity. Many bases for inequality are taken up in Unit III. (pp. 112–113)
	Are some cultures more able than others to deal with alcohol and drugs?	Yes. Cultural patterns can enable most members to control their use of these substances. For example, Italian cultural traditions result in low rates of alcoholism although alcohol use is considered normal. Similarly, for centuries opiates have been widely used in India with little addiction. (pp. 88–92)

95

Name	Slang Name	Typical Single Adult Dose	Duration of Action (hours)	How Taken	Legitimate Medical Uses (present and projected)	Psychological Dependence Potential	Tolerance Potential
Alcohol Whisky, gin, beer, wine	Booze Hooch	1½ oz. gin or whisky. 12 oz. beer	2–4	Swallowed	Rare; sometimes used as a sedative	High	Yes
Caffeine Coffee, tea, Coca-Cola, No-Doz, APC	Java	1–2 cups 1 bottle 5 mg.	2–4	Swallowed	Mild stimulant; treatment of some forms of coma	Moderate	Yes
Nicotine (and coal tar) Cigarettes, cigars	Fag	1–2 cigarettes	1–2	Smoked	None	High	Yes
Sedatives Barbiturates Nembutal Seconal Phenobarbital Doriden Chloral hydrate Miltown, Equanil (meprobamate)	Yellow jackets Red devils Phennies Goofers	50–100 mg. 500 mg. 500 mg. 400 mg.	4	Swallowed	Treatment of insomnia and tension; induction of anesthesia	High	Yes
Stimulants Amphetamines Benzedrine Methedrine Dexedrine Cocaine	Bennies Crystal, speed Dexies Coke, snow	2.5–5.0 mg. Variable	4	Swallowed or injected Sniffed or injected	Treatment of obesity, narcolepsy, fatigue, depression Anesthesia of the eye and throat	High	Yes
Tranquilizers Librium Phenothiazines Thorazine Compazine Stelazine Reserpine	Downers	5–10 mg. 10–25 mg. 10 mg. 2 mg. 1 mg.	4–6	Swallowed	Treatment of anxiety, tension, alcoholism, neurosis, psychosis, psychosomatic disorders, and vomiting	Minimal	No

morphine and a placebo were administered under similar conditions to hospitalized patients suffering postoperative pain. The patients always thought they were getting morphine, but the doctors who gave the injections were not told which substance was which; that way there could be no subtle, unintended communication from doctor to patient. Two important findings emerged. First, between 30 and 40 percent of the patients were as satisfied with the placebo as they were with the morphine. Second, the morphine itself was ineffective in relieving pain about 20 percent of the time for those patients who responded to the placebo at least once and about 40 percent of the time for those who never responded to the placebo. In other words, a substantial minority of the patients responded to *anything* as having an analgesic effect, and another substantial minority responded to *nothing*.

Studies of Mental Set and Surroundings

Two social psychologists, Stanley Schachter and Jerome Singer, published a study in 1962 that revealed the influence not only of a person's expectations about a drug but also of the social setting in which the drug is taken.

Two groups of subjects were injected with epinephrine (adrenalin), a stimulant normally secreted by the adrenal gland during moments of

Physical Dependence Potential	Overall Abuse Potential	Reasons for Use	Typical Short-term Effects*	Typical Long-term Effects	Form of Legal Regulation† and Control
Yes	High	To relax; to escape from tensions, problems, and inhibitions; to get "high"	CNS depressant; relaxation; sometimes euphoria; drowsiness; impaired judgment, reaction time, coordination, and emotional control; frequent aggressive behavior and driving accidents	Possible obesity with chronic excessive use; irreversible damage to brain and liver, addiction with severe withdrawal illness (DT's); habituation	Available and advertised without limitation in many forms, with only minimal regulation by age (21 or 18), hours of sale, location, taxation, ban on bootlegging, and driving laws; some "black market" for those under age and those evading taxes; minimal penalties
No	None	For a "pickup" or stimulation	CNS stimulant; increased alertness	Sometimes insomnia or restlessness; habituation	Available and advertised without limit, with no regulation for children or adults
No	Moderate	For a "pickup" or stimulation	CNS stimulant; relaxation (or distraction) from the process of smoking	Lung (and other) cancer, heart, and blood vessel disease, cough, etc.; habituation	Available and advertised without limit, with only minimal regulation by age, taxation, and labeling of packages
Yes	High	To relax or sleep; to get "high"	CNS depressants; sleep induction; sometimes euphoria; drowsiness; impaired judgment, reaction time, coordination, and emotional control; relief of anxiety-tension	Irritability, weight loss, addiction with severe withdrawal illness (like DTs); habituation, addiction	Available in large amounts by ordinary medical prescription, which can be repeatedly refilled or can be obtained from more than one physician; widely advertised and "detailed" to M.D.s and pharmacists; other manufacture, sale, or possession prohibited under federal drug abuse and similar state (dangerous) drug laws; moderate penalties; widespread illicit traffic
No	High	For stimulation and relief of fatigue; to get "high"	CNS stimulants; increased alertness, loss of appetite, insomnia, often euphoria	Restlessness; irritability, weight loss, toxic psychosis (mainly paranoid); habituation; extreme irritability, toxic psychosis	Amphetamines, same as sedatives above; cocaine, same as narcotics below
No	Minimal	Medical (including psychiatric) treatment of anxiety or tension states, alcoholism, psychoses, and other disorders	Selective CNS depressants; relief of anxiety-tension; suppression of hallucinations or delusions, improved functioning	Sometimes drowsiness, dryness of mouth, blurring of vision, skin rash, tremor; occasionally jaundice, agranulocytosis	Same as sedatives above, except not usually included under the special federal or state drug laws; negligible illicit traffic

97

*Figure 4.8   This chart (continued on the following two pages) summarizes available information about many commonly used psychoactive drugs.   * The effects of these drugs depend on their purity, the amount used, the frequency of use, the time interval since ingestion, whether there is food in the stomach, whether different drugs are combined, and most important, the personality of the individual taking the drugs and the context in which they are taken.*

(Adapted from J. Fort, M.D., *The Pleasure Seekers*, Indianapolis: Bobbs-Merrill, 1969, pp. 236-243.)

stress. The researchers told both groups that they were receiving an "experimental vitamin" but told only one group about the actual energizing effect the injection would have, describing it as a "side effect" of the vitamin. After the injection, each subject was left in the company of a stooge (a paid assistant acting under the experimenters' instructions). Half the subjects in each group had a happy, euphoric stooge, the other half an angry one. The subjects who were informed that the injection would arouse them acted without regard for the stooge's cues, but those who were not informed adopted the stooge's mood—whichever that was! Presumably, the stooge's behavior provided a

Name	Slang Name	Typical Single Adult Dose	Duration of Action (hours)	How Taken	Legitimate Medical Uses (present and projected)	Psychological Dependence Potential	Tolerance Potential
Cannabis (marijuana) THC (tetra-hydrocannabinol)	Pot, grass, tea, weed, stuff	Variable— 1 cigarette or 1 drink or cake (India)	4	Smoked Swallowed	Treatment of depression, tension, loss of appetite, sexual maladjustment, and narcotic addiction	Moderate	No
Narcotics (opiates, analgesics) Opium Heroin Morphine Codeine Percodan Demerol Cough syrups	Op Horse, H	10-12 "pipes" (Asia) Variable—bag or paper with 5-10 percent heroin 15 mg. 30 mg. 1 tablet 50-100 mg. 2-4 oz. (for euphoria)	4	Smoked Injected Swallowed	Treatment of severe pain, diarrhea, and cough	High	Yes
Hallucinogens LSD Psilocybin Mescaline (peyote) DMT (dimethyl-tryptamine)	Acid, sugar Cactus	150 micrograms 25 mg. 350 mg. 25 mg.	12 6 12	Swallowed Chewed Injected	Experimental study of mind and brain function; enhancement of creativity and problem solving; treatment of alcoholism, mental illness, and the dying person	Minimal	Yes (rare)
Antidepressants Ritaline Dibenzapines (Tofranil, Elavil) MAO inhibitors (Nardil, Parnate)	Uppers	10 mg. .25 mg., 10 mg. 15 mg., 10 mg.	4–6	Swallowed	Treatment of moderate to severe depression	Minimal	No
Miscellaneous Glue Gasoline Amyl nitrite Antihistamines Nutmeg Nonprescription "sedatives"		Variable 1-2 ampules 25-50 mg. Variable	2	Inhaled Swallowed	None except for antihistamines used for allergy and amyl nitrite for some episodes of fainting	Minimal to moderate	?

model that permitted subjects both to act out and to account for the arousal they were feeling. The experiment demonstrated that people are extremely susceptible to social influence when they have no explanation for the way they feel. It also demonstrated that the way people behave and the emotions they act out while on a drug depend both on what they think the drug does and on what is going on around them at the time.

Controlled Drug Use

The investigation of the role of situational and social factors in people's reactions to drugs led to a reexamination of the supposedly inevitable, universal addiction process with narcotics. In the early 1960s, Charles Winick conducted two studies indicating other usage patterns were possible.

Winick's first study (1961) looked at physicians, a group long known for its large proportion of narcotics users. Some physicians are susceptible to taking some drugs—usually morphine or Demerol (meperidine), a synthetic narcotic—because they normally have unsupervised access to them and the strain of their professional lives invites a desire for the calming sensation of narcotics.

Winick discovered a group of stably functioning doctors who were successfully practicing medicine after (or in some cases during) a period of regular drug use. Very few of these doctors had voluntarily sought treatment, and the majority of doctors

Physical Dependence Potential	Overall Abuse Potential	Reasons for Use	Typical Short-term Effects*	Typical Long-term Effects	Form of Legal Regulation and Control
No	Moderate	To get "high"; as an escape; to relax	Relaxation, euphoria, increased appetite, some alteration of time perception, possible impairment of judgment and coordination; (probable CNS depressant)	Usually none	Unavailable (although permissible) for ordinary medical prescription; possession, sale, and cultivation prohibited by state and federal narcotic or marijuana laws; moderate to severe penalties; widespread illicit traffic
Yes	High	To get "high"; as an escape; to avoid withdrawal symptoms	CNS depressants; sedation, euphoria, relief of pain, impaired intellectual functioning and coordination	Constipation, loss of appetite and weight, temporary impotence or sterility; habituation, addiction with unpleasant and painful withdrawal illness	Available (except heroin) by special (narcotics) medical prescriptions; some available by ordinary prescription or over-the-counter; other manufacture, sale, or possession prohibited under state and federal narcotics laws; severe penalties; extensive illicit traffic
No	Moderate	Curiosity created by recent widespread publicity; seeking for meaning and consciousness expansion	Production of visual imagery, increased sensory awareness, anxiety, nausea, impaired coordination; sometimes consciousness expansion	Usually none; sometimes precipitates or intensifies an already existing psychosis; more commonly can produce a panic reaction when person is improperly prepared	Available only to a few medical researchers (or to members of the Native American Church); other manufacture, sale, or possession prohibited by state dangerous drug or federal drug abuse laws; moderate penalties; extensive illicit traffic
No	Minimal	Medical (including psychiatric) treatment of depression	Relief of depression; stimulation	Basically the same as tranquilizers above	Same as tranquilizers above
No	Moderate	Curiosity; to get "high"	When used for mind alteration, generally produces a "high" (euphoria) with impaired coordination and judgment	Variable—some substances can seriously damage liver or kidney	Generally easily available; some require prescriptions; in several states glue banned for those under 21

99

who were caught by others were *not* reported for inadequate job performance; they were turned in by nurses, wives, pharmacists, federal narcotics agents, or others who uncovered evidence of their illegal drug use. But as far as anyone could see, they were carrying out not only a normal but a highly demanding daily routine while using narcotics. Only rarely did their drug dependence get out of hand. These privileged, highly controlled users demonstrated that where the usual cycle of limited availability, inflated prices, and poverty and crime is absent, narcotics can be taken regularly as part of a productive life.

Winick's second study (1962), which focused on the predominantly lower-class heroin addicts registered by the Federal Bureau of Narcotics, challenged the standard notion of addiction as a permanent disability. The Bureau places registered addicts on an inactive list when there is no record of their having been involved with narcotics for five years—and because of the risks involved in obtaining heroin on the street, it is practically impossible for a known user to maintain a drug habit for five years without getting caught. Using this list, Winick calculated that a quarter of the addicts (most of whom started on drugs in their teens) became inactive by the age of twenty-six, half by thirty, and three-quarters by thirty-six.

This regular pattern of outgrowing a heroin habit is called *maturing out*. On the basis of the age ranges in which people begin and abandon addiction, Winick speculates that addiction is a temporary reaction to the challenges of late adolescence and early adulthood, a detour taken from adult responsibility. Maturing out may occur when addicts overcome their fears, when they find a substitute dependency, or when they comfortably settle into another deviant life style (like that of criminal or prisoner) and no longer have to fill adult roles.

The concepts of controlled use and maturing out are more commonly accepted for alcohol use than for opiate use. D. L. Davies (1969) defines *normal drinking* as the kind of nondependent, socially appropriate drinking that most drinkers engage in and defines *controlled drinking*, or stabilized addiction, as the use of small, regular daily doses of alcohol in the context of a normal, productive life. Controlled drinking is a mild form of alcoholism that entails dependency and withdrawal distress but not tolerance (dosages are not increased); it is similar to the controlled narcotic dependency Winick observed in some doctors. The evidence about the decreasing use of alcohol and rates of alcoholism that occur with age suggests that maturing out applies to alcohol as well as to narcotics. Another little-known fact about kicking the drinking habit appears in a study of hospitalized alcoholics who later resumed drinking. A majority of these were able to become normal drinkers, and a smaller number were able to become controlled drinkers (Davies, Shepherd, and Myers, 1956).

The Range of Usage Patterns

Winick's suggestive studies of alternative patterns of drug use, together with the growing literature on the way setting and expectations influence drug effects, led to two important studies in 1964 that conclusively demonstrated how wide a range of usage patterns there is for opiate users. One of these was *The Road to H* (Chein *et al.*, 1964), an exhaustive investigation of heroin use among adolescent delinquents in New York City. Isidor Chein and his co-workers confessed that they had begun this project with the usual preconceptions about addiction, but their observations changed their outlook considerably. When they found that many of the street users they studied were getting doses of heroin too weak to have any physical

impact, they concluded that it was the ritual of obtaining and administering the drug that bound the users to the drug and to each other.

Meanwhile, Norman Zinberg and David Lewis (1964) were discovering what they called a spectrum, or continuum, of narcotic use on the basis of an in-depth study of 200 users. Zinberg and Lewis roughly divided their subjects into six groups: those who

1. rarely used opiates but adopted superficial features of the addict's life style.

2. were addicted to the injection procedure, or ritual, rather than to the drug.

3. were addicted to a person associated with drug use rather than to the drug.

4. were depressed and self-destructive and took the drug only to relieve the pain of living.

5. used opiates regularly without developing tolerance or disrupting their lives (for example, doctors).

6. showed the classical addiction syndrome—tolerance, withdrawal, compulsion, and craving.

Of these groups, only the last fits the popular description of the addict, and the subjects falling into this category were a minority of the total sample.

More recently, Dr. Zinberg studied 100 hospital patients who, for at least ten days, required doses of morphine in stronger concentrations than addicts get on the street (*Boston Globe*, February 6, 1973). Once they were taken off the drug, only one patient felt any craving, and that was in response to actual physical pain. Zinberg's research with medical patients shows that withdrawal distress is not an invariable physiological experience.

The Functional Equivalence of Addictive Drugs

We have seen that the *same* drug, taken under a variety of conditions, can have many *different* effects. Equally important to changing concepts of addiction has been the observation that *different* drugs can have the *same* effect when the user comes to them with the same needs. Drugs as chemically dissimilar as alcohol, the opiates, and the barbiturates all appear to create physical dependence. What is more, we do not know how they do so, despite all the research that has gone into the physiology of addiction. Summarizing the state of this research in a leading pharmacological textbook, Jerome H. Jaffe (1970b) concludes, "At present, the mechanisms by which the opioids exert their effects remain unknown." Similarly, Maurice .H. Seevers and Gerald A. Deneau (1963) characterize the literature on physical dependence as being descriptive rather than explanatory.

Because their knowledge of how addictive drugs work is in such an uncertain state, researchers are now focusing on similarities in the observed effects that various drugs produce in the user rather than on the different chemical composition of various drugs. At the crux of this distinction are questions about two important features of some psychoactive substances—cross-dependence and cross-tolerance. When one drug can be used to suppress withdrawal symptoms in someone who is habituated to another drug, the two drugs are said to be *cross-dependent*. When a person habituated to one drug requires a larger dose of a second drug than a novice user normally requires to feel an effect from that drug, the two drugs are said to be *cross-tolerant*. Alcohol and the barbiturates are recognized to be cross-tolerant and cross-dependent.

Current Trends in Research

Pending some major clarification of the concepts of cross-dependence and cross-tolerance—which is not likely in the near future—theory and research on addiction are moving toward less emphasis on the chemcial properties of different drugs and the physiological attributes of addiction. William D. M. Paton (Steinberg, 1969) summarizes these developments as follows: There is

1. less emphasis on the withdrawal syndrome as a defining attribute of addiction and more emphasis on the positive, subjective rewards a user obtains from a drug.

2. less emphasis on the opiates exclusively and more emphasis on the range of drugs that cause dependence.

3. greater recognition of cultural differences in patterns of drug use.

Researchers, then, are shifting from a purely medical and physiological to a sociological and psychological approach, from the study of drugs to the study of the people who use them. They are thinking of dependence in terms of the positive experi-ence the drug provides for the user. Depressant drugs, including narcotics, sedatives, and alcohol, can give certain people some very desirable sensations—calmness, relaxation, relief from anxiety and pain, forgetfulness, a sense that things are right with the world. We are beginning to see addiction less as a bodily adaptation to a chemical and more as a progressive inability to face life without the presence of these reassuring sensations.

PSYCHOLOGICAL THEORIES

Clearly, physiological explanations of dependency, or being hooked, cannot adequately account for why people become addicted. In the first place, such discussions are after the fact—people have to use liquor or drugs for a considerable period of time before the question of physical dependency can even arise. So we must first ask, Why do people begin to use drugs? In the second place, the research cited in the previous section shows that even after someone is addicted, the subjective experience of drug dependency itself is probably as much a matter of cultural and psychological conditioning (and personal needs) as chemical reactions.

Finally, if physiological explanations do not account for the addict's behavior *before* and *during* a period of drug dependency, they likewise do not account for the tendency to relapse *after* dependency has been terminated. Many existing programs guide the addict through the withdrawal period in such a way as to bring to an end the state of active dependency. Once an alcoholic has undergone detoxification treatment or a drug addict has undergone withdrawal, the resumption of drinking or drug taking becomes more clearly a deliberate act. Indeed, because ex-addicts and ex-alcoholics so often relapse, we must focus on the basic experience of contentment or completeness that they are missing when they do not indulge. The question, Why do they relapse? boils down to the same thing as the earlier questions, Why do they begin? and Why do they continue?

To offer some answers, psychologists have turned their attention to a revised question: What do they get out of it? Two major lines of work have grown out of this tradition. One of these is reinforcement theory, which examines drug and alcohol use in terms of habits and how they are learned and maintained. The other is personality theory, which examines how liquor and drugs satisfy certain psychological needs or compensate for certain psychological shortcomings.

Reinforcement Theory

Considerable research on drug addiction and alcoholism has been done with animals, many of which—including monkeys, pigs, and dogs—turn into drunks or addicts when alcohol or drugs are regularly available to them. This has led a number of investigators, most notably Abraham Wikler (1961, 1970), to conceive of drug addiction and alcoholism in terms of simple *conditioned learning.* It is an axiom of behavioral psychology that organisms will repeat actions that are *reinforced,* that is, associated with pleasure or with the avoidance of pain. Through this process, they learn to engage in certain kinds of behavior and learn not to engage in other kinds. To some extent, drugs and alcohol are directly rewarding. People and many animals quickly come to experience the effects of drugs and liquor as pleasurable. Furthermore, people and animals quickly learn that taking the drug or consuming alcohol brings relief from withdrawal symptoms.

A major reinforcement theory of drug taking has been proposed by Alfred Lindesmith, a sociologist. Lindesmith (1968) argued that people become conditioned drug users and thus addicts by learning consciously to associate withdrawal pains with abstinence from the drug and to associate taking the drug with relief from such pain. Beyond the kind of learning Lindesmith talks about, it is also clear that alcoholics and drug addicts learn to associate taking liquor and drugs with many other environmental stimuli, in much the same way that people come to associate drinking a first cup of morning coffee with opening the morning paper and to associate smoking their first cigarette with finishing their first cup of coffee. In order to change such habits, it is necessary to break down these stimulus chains that serve to reinforce the undesired behavior (Goldberg, 1970). Understanding that habits result from reinforced behavior is the principle behind two new related therapies being used with

alcoholics and drug addicts.

Behavior modification therapy attempts to find ways to reinforce (reward) new behavior patterns, such as avoiding drugs or alcohol. Behavior therapists attempt to help the individual find new ways to respond to situations that previously prompted drinking or drug taking and reward these desirable new responses.

One way to make people stop taking drugs or drinking is to make them feel an aversion for drugs or alcohol, to make these substances seem disagreeable or offensive. *Aversive therapy* attempts to associate discomfort and unpleasantness with drinking and drug taking. Alcoholics may be given drugs that cause them to become violently nauseated when they drink; the treatment may be continued even to the point at which seeing a bottle causes unpleasant feelings. Similarly, drugs and alcohol may be paired with an unpleasant stimulus, such as an electric shock, in an effort to condition an aversion reaction to drinking or drug taking. Both techniques have shown some promise in treating alcoholics and drug addicts.

Although reinforcement theories have considerable merit, they suffer from incompleteness. They tell us nothing about *why* some people become alcoholics or drug addicts and others do not. Furthermore, reinforcement theories depend too heavily on the notion of a universal, physiologically determined withdrawal experience.

Personality Theories

Most people do not become alcoholics or drug addicts. To explain this fact, psychologists have long concentrated on finding distinctive personality traits that might be associated with becoming an alcoholic or a drug addict. Over time, a fairly elaborate personality profile of alcoholics and drug addicts has been built up. A major element is what is loosely characterized as a *dependent* personality. People with dependent personalities require unusual amounts of emotional support and attention from those around them. In a manner of speaking, they have not matured and still have the childish needs to be pampered and looked after by others. Alcohol or drugs are used as a substitute for affection, as a way of attracting attention and getting even with those who fail to produce this attention,

Figure 4.9   Alcoholism is an example of a complex behavior that can develop through social learning. Drinking behavior can be reinforced and therefore strengthened by the pleasant effects of the alcohol itself and by reduction of anxiety and inhibitions. Conditioning techniques, such as those used at Patton State Hospital in California, have been successful in the treatment of alcoholism. The Patton staff sets up an actual bar. Under these familiar conditions, alcoholic patients are permitted to drink until they collapse. The sequence of events is videotaped and later played back to the patients. The purpose is to lead patients to associate their drinking behavior with the physical sensations of nausea and collapse as well as with the auditory and visual feedback of themselves as sick and intoxicated—both of which they usually find aversive.

and as self-punishment for feeling hostile and inadequate (Knight, 1937).

Robert Freed Bales (1962) applied some elements of the dependent-personality concept in his well-known analysis of alcoholism among Irish males. In Ireland, many people never marry and many others are unable to marry until middle age. Sons frequently cannot afford to support a family until their parents die or manage to retire, and many adult Irish males, years after physical maturity, have the social status of boys; indeed, many remain boys for life, living at home and remaining economically dependent. The severe sexual standards also restrict all sexual relations to marriage. Bales argued that Irish culture supports drinking by males as a relatively safe outlet for their hostility, which results from their enforced dependency (particularly mother-son dependency), their sexual deprivation, and their uncertainty about the future. Immigration to America sustained the drinking culture of Irish males, who again found themselves on the bottom of the economic ladder and who were further stigmatized as Catholics in a Protestant culture.

In his major study of heroin addiction, Isidor Chein (Chein, 1969; Chein *et al.*, 1964) found that several personality traits were associated with addiction. These included passivity, defensiveness, low self-esteem, little ability for self-direction, distrust of other people, need for predictable gratifications, and exploitation of others for gratification. Chein's findings, along with the research showing that drug users are likely to have been trained into accepting and exploiting a dependent "sick" role at home (Blum *et al.*, 1969), are broadly consistent with the dependency model of alcoholism and with Winick's explanation of heroin addiction as a detour to avoid maturity. The findings suggest that the person predisposed to addiction is one who has not resolved childhood conflicts. Chein further theorizes that the rituals associated with heroin use have a powerful appeal for the person who is not psychologically prepared to accept an adult role or who has not been trained by society to fill such a role. Such rituals—making connections, raising money, avoiding arrest, and preparing and administering the injection—give addicts a feeling of activity and a full life, a feeling they have not been

103

permitted to gain through a capacity to live in normal society.

With alcoholism, David McClelland and his co-workers (1972) have challenged the dependency theory of addiction. They argue instead that drinking is an expression of a person's need for power. They distinguish between needs for *social power*—needs to deal successfully with groups of people—and needs for *personal power*—needs to dominate others individually. From the perspective of this theory, people drink to resolve conflicts arising from having needs for power that cannot be gratified in socially acceptable ways. For the light drinker, an occasional drink gives a pleasurable feeling of enhanced social power. The heavy drinker, or alcoholic, engages in habitual, excessive drinking because he possesses a high need for personal power together with a relative lack of inhibition. His heavy drinking enables him both to fantasize about personal power and to act out some variety of it.

104   McClelland uses several methods to demonstrate the association between drinking and thoughts of power. For example, he and his co-workers analyze the power imagery of Thematic Apperception Test responses (stories people make up about ambiguous scenes, pictures that one can interpret several ways). People are asked to take the test before and after drinking. The researchers also compare the power imagery in the folk tales of different cultures. Their theory is therefore both psychological and cultural, assessing individual differences within a culture as well as variations among cultures. McClelland feels that this theory is better equipped than the dependency theory to explain such phenomena as light drinking (which has not been shown to gratify dependency needs), greater drinking by men than by women, and the low rate of alcoholism among Jewish males, who have high needs for maternal nurturance (dependence) but at the same time are made to feel secure about their status as men (adequate feelings of social power). But McClelland and his co-workers also recommend testing rival theories by comparing results achieved by treatment centers deliberately set up to satisfy dependency needs of alcoholics with those set up to satisfy their power needs.

Figure 4.10   *Like original objects of addiction, harmless substitutes will be used repeatedly and under similar circumstances. Actor Telly Savalas, who was trying to quit smoking shortly after the television show "Kojak" began, substitutes lollipops for cigarettes.*

Drawing from both the dependency and power theories of addiction, Stanton Peele (1975) has analyzed the dynamics of the addict's personality in a historical and cultural framework. According to his analysis, certain kinds of people can be addicted to anything, whether that thing is a drug, a role in society, or a relationship with a lover. Peele's theory begins with the concept of the *weakened self*—a condition wherein the person lacks a sense of power to accomplish things and is unable to deal with the world—and traces from this inner condition a need to form a dependency relationship with some external prop or support. The object of the addiction is something that can be used repeatedly and helps to insulate the addict from novel or threatening experiences. In this view, addiction is a response to fear, whether actual or anticipated. Peele's analysis traces the addict's pervasive fear and insecurity to the conditions of modern life—in particular, the forms of social organization in which we participate. Thus, his theory can serve to introduce the next level of analysis we will be considering—the social-psychological level.

SOCIAL-PSYCHOLOGICAL THEORIES

By themselves, psychological theories of deviant behavior, including theories of alcoholism and drug addiction, are incomplete in two fundamental ways. First, even if psychologists could isolate some set of personality traits exclusive to alcoholics or drug addicts, their theory could not tell us *why certain people develop or fail to develop such traits*—it could only tell us what would become of these people if they did develop such traits. Second, they cannot say why it is that this syndrome leads to drugs or drink rather than to some other behavior, such as suicide, compulsive television viewing, or thumb sucking. They cannot explain why people choose liquor or drugs because objects of addiction are *cultural,* not psychological, artifacts. Surely there have been and could be societies that do not have these substances. In such societies, no personality syndromes tailored for alcoholism or drug addiction will ever produce alcoholics or drug addicts. (Indeed, this is the logic behind prohibition and efforts to enforce drug

laws. The logic is not faulty even though efforts to achieve prohibition have failed.) In addition to the failure to explain why certain people do or do not become addicted to certain substances, psychologists have not been able to identify a set of personality traits exclusive to drug addicts or alcoholics. Many people with similar personality profiles do not turn to drink or drugs. For all these reasons, our search for an explanation must move on to a further level of analysis, beyond individuals to their social and cultural environment.

Labeling Theory

A prominent line of thought in sociology and social psychology today begins by denying that deviance is primarily found in the acts of persons identified as deviant. Instead, this line of thought considers deviance to be in the eyes of the beholders—in the way people evaluate the acts of a particular person. Howard S. Becker, a major proponent of this point of view, put the argument this way:

> Social groups create deviance by making rules whose infraction constitutes deviance, and by applying those rules to particular people and labeling them as outsiders. . . . The deviant is one to whom that label has been successfully applied; deviant behavior is behavior that people so label. (Becker, 1963)

Similarly, Kai T. Erickson (1964) argues:

> Deviance is not a property *inherent in* certain forms of behavior; it is a property *conferred upon* these forms by audiences which directly or indirectly witness them. The critical variable in the study of deviance, then, is the social audience rather than the individual actor, since it is the audience which eventually determines whether or not any episode of behavior . . . is labeled deviant.

Chapter 1 argued that social problems are what people say they are. Similarly, *labeling* theorists argue that deviance is what people say it is. However, most labeling theorists do not follow the advice given in Chapter 1: that to understand a social problem, we must examine both the social claims that a problem exists and the objective conditions that may or may not warrant such claims. Most labeling theorists simply dismiss the act alleged to be deviant and focus on explaining why it is that some group defines some particular act as deviant.

Labeling theory begins with the fundamental social-science premise that our identities (personalities) are socially constructed—we come to see ourselves as others see us, to respond on the basis of how we are responded to. Thus, if someone is labeled by others as bad, weird, a criminal, a drunk, a dope fiend, or a lunatic, the label may become a self-fulfilling prophecy and may lead that person to satisfy these expectations. Thus, someone who is developing a slight drinking problem or who is experimenting with drugs may be pushed further into becoming an alcoholic or drug addict by being treated like one by others. Labeling may also greatly impede efforts by alcoholics or addicts to reform. As we shall see in subsequent chapters, labeling theories have been useful in explaining mental illness and sexual deviance.

A shortcoming of labeling theory is its inability to explain why people *first* engage in the kind of behavior that gets them socially labeled as deviants. Although the theory can outline a process by which a person who drinks may become an alcoholic under pressure of being labeled an alcoholic or by which a youthful offender may become a chronic delinquent through being labeled a delinquent by the police and the courts, the theory cannot explain why a person began to drink or why the youth committed the *initial* illegal act that got him arrested. A competing social-psychological theory has taken this question as its primary focus.

Differential Association and Social Learning

In the 1920s, the American criminologist Edwin H. Sutherland first proposed a rigorous *differential-association* theory of deviance. He began with the premise that all human behavior, whether piano playing, safecracking, or taking drugs, is learned through socialization. Whether what an individual learns to do conforms to or violates social norms depends on who is doing the teaching or socializing. Fundamentally, Sutherland's argument comes down to attributing deviant behavior to keeping bad company. People learn to be drug addicts, alcoholics, or car thieves by keeping company with others who engage in or admire such behavior. The theory is called differential association because it attributes differences in behavior to differences in the groups people associate with (Sutherland, 1947).

Figure 4.11 *Differential-association theory explains differences in behavior by looking at differences in the groups people associate with. Alcoholics Anonymous provides a supportive group environment for people who, in another setting, might begin drinking again. Support is given formally through lecture sessions* (top) *and informally through group interaction* (above).

Howard S. Becker (1963) used a differential-association approach in a classic study of marijuana smoking. He pointed out that people are introduced to marijuana smoking through their friends. In fact, people usually rely on their friends and do not buy their own supply of the drug until they have become relatively experienced marijuana smokers. Furthermore, people usually *learn to detect and enjoy* the effects of marijuana from their friends. As Becker pointed out:

The novice does not ordinarily get high the first time he smokes marihuana, and several attempts are usually necessary to induce this state. . . . If nothing happens, it is manifestly impossible for the user to develop a conception of the drug as an object which can be used for pleasure. . . . The ability to get high and to enjoy getting high are mainly socially determined. (Becker, 1963)

It is widely held in the drug culture that people who say they cannot get high have been improperly instructed in how to smoke grass and that people who say they did not enjoy their high did not smoke with persons they liked or trusted. Research by Erich Goode (1969) has further confirmed the social nature of marijuana use. Persons without friends who use the drug have little opportunity either to obtain the drug or to learn to like it.

These same principles clearly apply to the use of narcotics and alcohol. Few people have taken up drinking entirely on their own; they at least started out as social drinkers. Indeed, most people have to learn to enjoy the effects of alcohol—to experience the high as pleasant rather than as a loss of full faculties and to learn to pace their consumption to maintain the high without becoming nauseated. Indeed, most people even have to learn to like the taste of alcoholic beverages. Thus, novices and very occasional drinkers typically prefer mixed drinks that cover up the taste of the liquor.

Introduction to narcotics is similarly social. Novices have no source of supply but friends. They must learn the proper preparation and administration of the drug, including the use of a hypodermic syringe. Furthermore, beginners must learn to select a proper dose of the drug and to define the drug's effects as pleasurable. In Chein's study, over two-thirds of those who enjoyed their first use of heroin continued to use the drug. But many first-time users did not enjoy it; in fact, many had an unpleasant first experience. Of these, about three out of five did not experiment further with the drug (Chein *et al.*, 1964). Through social support, however, about two persons out of five eventually learned to use and enjoy heroin despite an aversive first encounter.

Recently, Sutherland's differential-association theory has been formulated anew on the basis of *social-learning* theory (Akers, 1973; Burgess and Akers, 1966). Social-learning theory is an expansion of reinforcement theory, which we have already discussed. Reinforcement theory merely assumes that addiction and alcoholism are instances of simple conditioned learning. Social learning

goes on to examine the *social sources* of the reinforcers that operate in the learning process. Sutherland's differential association is incorporated to account for the sources of reinforcement: "bad" company reinforces drug taking or drinking; "good" company does not reinforce such behavior. For example, a college freshman may be initiated into drinking and intoxication by fraternity brothers who praise his ability to consume large amounts of alcohol and who reward him for regular appearances at the group's favorite tavern; they thereby establish him in a pattern of heavy and frequent drinking. What the social learners add to Sutherland's theory is a specific set of learning principles through which the social situation shapes a person's behavior. The underlying learning proposition is that deviant behavior, such as drinking or drug taking, will be committed if, under similar circumstances in the past, it has been rewarded (reinforced) more frequently and consistently than conforming behavior (Akers, 1973).

Both labeling theory and the combination of differential-association and learning theory have considerable capacity for explaining the relapse of persons into drugs or alcohol following treatment. Both street junkies and the square world seem to believe the adage "Once a junkie, always a junkie." Upon release from treatment, addicts do not really expect to remain clean. Others around them, especially the police, do not accept them as cured. Instead, people with such attitudes treat addicts suspiciously—continuing to label them at least as probable addicts—and therefore fail to reward any attempts they do make to remain drug free (Ray, 1964); people impose similar judgment on alcoholics. To make matters worse, most alcoholics and drug addicts return to the same social setting in which they first acquired their drinking or drug-taking habits, so that the same system of social reinforcers that supported their past behavior supports a resumption of that behavior. It is not surprising that a large majority relapse. In contrast, people typically view the physician addict or the middle-class addict who returns from drug withdrawal as one who has been ill and is now cured; relapse in these groups is lower (Akers, 1973).

The general thrust of personality theories is compatible with both of these social-psychological perspectives on drugs and alcohol. Not all people who try drugs in a socially supportive setting become drug addicts or alcoholics. However, those who do find psychoactive drugs satisfy intensely felt psychological needs—for example, through providing a substitute for unmet dependency feelings or for unfilled power needs—may well be the people most susceptible to social reinforcers and to developing drug and alcohol problems.

Both labeling and differential-association theories credit the individual's social environment with a powerful role in causing deviant drug-taking and drinking behavior. But these social-learning theories are relatively silent about what causes *variations* in the social environment. Why do only some people have friends who drink, shoot heroin, or smoke marijuana and who are willing to introduce them into and to reinforce them for similar behavior? Why are some people labeled deviants while others are not? This question leads us again to a higher level of analysis.

SOCIOLOGICAL THEORIES: MIDDLE RANGE

Contemporary middle-range sociological theories of deviance are of three general kinds or varieties: *strain* theories, *subcultural-deviance* theories, and *social-control* theories (Hirschi, 1969). The three fundamentally disagree in their answers to three questions about human nature and society:

1. Is there a general consensus among members of society about norms—about what is and is not acceptable or required behavior in certain situations?

2. Is the sanctioning system of society—the system through which adherence to norms is rewarded and violation of norms is punished—uniform? Is everyone equally likely to be punished or rewarded?

3. Are human beings fundamentally moral—does the process of socialization create people who desire to conform?

The fact that these three theories disagree does not necessarily mean that there are correct and incorrect answers to the questions. As we shall see, by applying these theories to a variety of social problems, a given theory will prove more useful in accounting for some kinds of deviance but less useful in accounting for others. The contribution of each must be understood.

Strain Theories

Strain theories can also be called motivational theories because they focus on the forces that drive people to commit deviant acts (and are particularly compatible with personality theories of deviance). The foremost strain theorist in contemporary sociology is Robert K. Merton, and his classic paper "Social Structure and Anomie" (1938) remains the most concise statement of strain theory.

Strain theories begin with the premise that humans are fundamentally moral because they *internalize the norms of their society* or group and want to obey the rules; that is, through the process of socialization, people develop a *conscience*. The argument is that human beings are profoundly sensitive to the expectations of others, and because others expect us to conform, we can only deviate at great psychic cost, or strain. In addition, strain theories assume that members of a society largely agree about what the norms are.

Having argued that people are fundamentally moral and are in agreement on the nature of morality, strain theorists meet an extremely difficult problem: What causes people to deviate? Strain theories argue that intense pressures must be put on individuals to cause them to deviate.

According to Merton, the source of this pressure is the discrepancy between goals and means: People are uniformly committed to the *goals* society tells them to desire, but they encounter unequal access to the *means* socially defined as legitimate for achieving these goals. Many people in society are thus subject to intense frustration of their socially legitimate desires, for example, to be successful, popular, and happy. By being born poor, black, homely, unintelligent, sickly, or otherwise disadvantaged, many people are severely handicapped in the race toward the goals society tells them they ought to value and pursue. Because of this frustration in finding access to legitimate means for achieving goals, people sometimes turn to illegitimate means to achieve them and thus violate norms (deviate).

Merton argued that people are of four basic types because they have four fundamental options in life: (1) They can accept both the goals of society and the means defined as legitimate. He calls this type of person a *conformist.* (2) A person can accept the goals and reject legitimate means. Merton calls this type the *innovator.* (3) People can also be driven to reject the goals of society. When such persons nonetheless continue to adhere to legitimate means, Merton calls such behavior *ritualistic.* (4) A person may eventually reject both the goals and the means advocated by society and be classified as a *retreatist* by Merton.

Our concern here is with the retreatist type because Merton classified alcoholics and addicts as having withdrawn from both the legitimate goals and the means of their society. Such people are literally social dropouts. As Merton (1938) says:

Defeatism, quietism and resignation are manifested in escape mechanisms which ultimately lead the individual to "escape" from the requirements of the society. . . . The conflict [between internalized commitment to society's goals and approved means for achieving the goals, on the one hand, and failure to achieve these goals, on

the other] is resolved by eliminating *both* . . . the goals and means. The escape is complete, the conflict is eliminated and the individual is asocialized.

In Merton's view, the process creates dependent personalities and causes people to turn away from life to the substitute comforts of drugs and alcohol.

In support of this line of analysis is the fact that alcoholism and drug addiction are concentrated among groups most deprived of access to legitimate means for achieving socially approved goals—poor people and minority groups. However, strain theory seems inappropriate for accounting for the alcoholism or drug addiction of persons who appear to have all the advantages. The rich and successful are hardly immune to alcoholism and drug taking. Furthermore, some critics have pointed out that strain theory may rely too much on the idea that frustration will result in deviance. Most people who are frustrated, in terms of Merton's goals-means typology, do *not* take to drink or to drugs or to any other form of deviance (Hirschi, 1969). Their seeming capacity to ignore strains is an embarrassment to the theory.

109

Subcultural Theories

Like strain theories *subcultural* theories of deviance begin with the assumption that human beings are fundamentally moral. But they go even further. They essentially *deny that persons are capable of deviant behavior.* How, then, can they account for the great numbers of acts that appear to deviate from, or to violate, social norms? They begin by denying that members of society agree about norms. Instead, they say that different groups within society are socialized into *different sets* of norms and that deviance is simply a judgment imposed by an outside group. Thus, what may appear to be deviant behavior is really conformity to a set of norms espoused by one group but rejected by another. Everyone conforms, but some kinds of conformity are frowned on and labeled as deviant by outsiders. When the outside group is more powerful, the behavior will be socially defined as deviant and perhaps punished.

This perspective agrees with the two social-psychological theories considered earlier. With labeling theory, this viewpoint agrees that deviance is in the eye of the beholder; with differential-

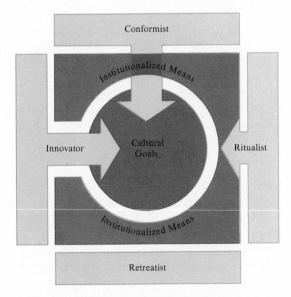

Figure 4.12   Strain theorists assume that because most people are in agreement about the goals *of success, they will not deviate from norms unless they experience great strain in achieving those goals. The source of strain is unequal access to the* means *of achieving goals. Such strain may become so great that people* retreat *from society altogether, abandoning both its goals and means and turning instead to alcohol, drugs, or some other object of addiction.*

association theory, that behavior is a product of the social environment and that people conform according to which behavior is reinforced. Thus, subcultural-deviance theories assume that when we isolate and examine a particular social environment, we see norms uniformly sanctioned within it. It is only when we look at society as a whole that discrepancies occur: Some behavior appears to be deviant, and the sanctioning system appears to be inconsistent.

The argument of subcultural theories is that society is not made up of a single uniform culture (a single set of norms, for example) but instead is a mosaic of different subcultures. In recognizing the existence of these subcultures, one sees that there is no deviance, only conflict among subcultures over which behavior shall be permitted.

Subcultural-deviance theory can be summed up as ''different strokes for different folks.'' It is popular at present and is at the heart of many intense political disputes in the United States. When we hear that the poor or minority groups are being inappropriately judged against white middle-class standards, we are hearing an application of subcultural-deviance theory. When young people claim adults are hypocritical to ban marijuana in a society where alcohol drinking is legal, and when adults denounce marijuana as a more dangerous substance than alcohol, two subcultures are fighting over whose norms shall prevail. When homosexuals demand liberation and claim their sexual inclinations are as normal as those of heterosexuals, this too is an application of the theory.

The problem with the theory has been its failure to demonstrate clearly that major types of deviant behavior do represent conformity to the norms of some distinctive subculture. For example, rather than defend their behavior, most delinquents accept and support the norms governing honest behavior (Hirschi, 1969). Admissions of·guilt feelings over wrong behavior are inconsistent with subcultural-deviance conceptions. And although it is true that many homosexuals participate in a supportive subculture, it is unclear whether the subculture produces homosexuality or whether people primarily enter this subculture *after* having become homosexuals. If the latter is true, their initial homosexual behavior represented deviance from the

larger culture, not conformity to the subculture.

It is certainly doubtful that subcultural theories can account for any appreciable proportion of alcoholism. There may be social settings in which chronic intoxication could be regarded as conforming to cultural norms—those of skid row, for example. But the overwhelming majority of alcoholics are members of groups that frown on alcoholism even though they permit drinking.

There is somewhat better support for a subcultural view of drug addiction. It cannot be argued that more than a small majority of people, even in the most drug-ridden slum neighborhoods, actually take drugs or approve of drug use (Burnham and Burnham, 1970). But, as Richard Blum (1967) has pointed out, in such neighborhoods there are enough people who do advocate the use of drugs, and these people set an example for young people who are already potential drug users because of their personality traits or family background. Furthermore, because drugs are illegal, to sustain a narcotics habit, a person almost has to join an underground culture of pushers and users—indeed, an underground of criminals—because of the necessity of committing crimes in order to raise money for drugs. Addicts' commitment to drugs may indeed cause them to reject a variety of social norms and to regard themselves as conforming to the norms of their own society. This may be a major impediment to curing addicts. On the other hand, alcoholics are about equally likely as drug addicts to relapse, and they are not doing so for the sake of conforming to an alcoholic subculture.

Control Theories

Control theories turn the traditional ''why do they do it'' question around so that it reads ''why don't they do it?'' They take deviance for granted and consider instead why people *do* conform.

Control theorists reach this position by rejecting all assumptions that humans are fundamentally moral. Examining Merton's goals-means typology, control theorists ask why most people do not become innovators and adopt illegitimate means, for this approach appears to be the quickest and easiest strategy for getting ahead (Nye, 1958). By removing the moral barrier against deviance, control theories are freed from the need to make assumptions, such as those in strain theory, about people's motivation to deviate. Unlike the subcultural theorists, they need not argue that many different sets of norms flourish side by side in society. Instead, they argue that there are important variations in the *control*, or sanctioning, system of society—some people are rewarded more for conformity and punished more for deviance than are some other people. Conformity occurs only when people have more to lose than to gain by deviance. *Deviance occurs when people have little to gain from conformity and much to gain or little to lose from deviance.*

Along with strain theories, control theories of deviance argue that access to the good things in life is unequally distributed among individuals and groups in society. Poor people, minority groups, the uneducated, and the disadvantaged simply have less chance to succeed. But instead of arguing, as do strain theorists, that lack of access to the good things in life causes intense frustration and drives people to use illegitimate means (to deviate), control theorists argue that inequality makes some people more *free* to act in deviant ways.

The reasoning behind this idea is that the more opportunities people have (or believe they have) to achieve desirable goals through conventional means, the more those people have to *lose* by engaging in deviant behavior. The rising executive has a great deal to lose by being detected in petty theft or in excessive drinking. The outstanding high-school student risks a promising future by engaging in acts of juvenile crime or by being busted for drugs. But for many people, the cost of deviance is relatively low. The student who is at the bottom of the class is not risking much through truancy. A person qualified only for unskilled jobs does not risk blowing a career by being drunk.

Thus, reason control theorists, some persons in society are relatively free to deviate, and because people are not intrinsically moral, they are quite likely to do so. Along with the songwriter Kris Kristofferson, control theorists would argue for the notion that "freedom's just another word for nothin' left to lose."

Control theory combines nicely with social-learning theory in that it, too, assumes that people are differentially rewarded for conformity and de-

viance. It does not fit well with differential-association theories or with subcultural theories, however. Control theorists argue that it is not so much the case that bad company reinforces and produces deviance as that "birds of a feather flock together." People with similar life chances tend to associate; thus, people with little going for them will both associate and deviate. As control theory would predict, deviance is powerfully related to how high a stake one has in conformity (Hirschi, 1969). The data in Table 4.1 show that the higher the expectations a high-school boy has about his future educational achievements, the less likely he is to drink alcohol.

Table 4.1   Percent Who Drink by Expected Education

EXPECTED AMOUNT OF HIGHER EDUCATION	PERCENT WHO DRINK ALCOHOL
College Graduation	16
Some College	33
Less Than College	37

Source: Adapted from Travis Hirschi, *Causes of Delinquency* (Berkeley and Los Angeles, University of California Press, 1969) p. 165.

It has been pointed out that theories of subcultural deviance have some applicability to drug addiction. But it must also be reported that the drug culture is markedly short on self-esteem. Even in groups receptive to experimentation with drugs, addiction is often frowned on (Chein *et al.*, 1964). Irving Spergel (1966) found in his research that among delinquent boys,

The status of drug addict was neither desirable nor acceptable to either addicts or non-addicts. Much effort was exercised to conceal the fact of addiction, which was commonly recognized as indicative of personal weakness and failure.

Control theories are perhaps the oldest of the three sociological approaches to deviance. They were eclipsed by strain and subcultural theories, but lately they have made a strong comeback because of research results such as those we have just mentioned for delinquency. In addition, control theories also solve some of the problems associated with the other two kinds of theories. Control theory takes the position that deviance is prevented by any number of *bonds* between the individual and conventional society—bonds that would be jeopardized by deviance. Among these are not only economic rewards and opportunities but significant interpersonal relations, such as those with parents, friends, teachers, coaches, spouses, children, steady dates, and the like, that would be threatened by deviant behavior; in fact, finding a girl friend often ends a boy's delinquency record, and finding a boyfriend has caused some teenage prostitutes to quit. People from all classes have such bonds. Control theory can therefore account for the fact that some economically advantaged persons deviate as well as for the fact that most economically disadvantaged persons do not deviate. Strain theory cannot explain these facts.

By the same token, unlike subcultural theories, control theories are not embarrassed by deviance that is not rooted in conformity to the norms of some significant subculture. Thus, guilt-ridden criminals, vandalism by "good" boys, homosexual acts by people who are usually heterosexual, or secret drinking by elderly spinsters present no explanatory difficulties to control theory, but such examples sharply contradict subcultural theories.

Control theories also fit well with personality theories of drug addiction and alcoholism. People with little to lose are likely to manifest personality traits such as dependency or the need for power. For example, psychologists might say a person with a dependent personality drinks because he feels no one is giving him adequate ego support. The control theorist is likely to examine that individual's social relations and say that, in fact, no one much cares about him and that he therefore has little to lose—and the satisfactions of alcohol to gain—by drinking. Obviously, the same agreement could be reached about drug addicts. Perhaps the main value of live-in therapeutic communities in aiding alcoholics and drug addicts is that they help foster interpersonal commitments that become "something to lose" by a return to liquor or drugs.

It is clear that strain, subcultural, and control theories leave a number of questions unanswered; at the very least, they leave a certain number of their own key elements unexplained. Thus, both strain and control theories assume that inequalities exist in the sanctioning system of society. Some people are more rewarded than others for conformity, according to both theories. Control theories also argue that some are less punished than others for deviance. Neither theory is able to tell us

112

Figure 4.13   Legal sanctions against trafficking in or possessing drugs vary from country to country. While possession of a small amount of marijuana may be nothing more than a misdemeanor in Ann Arbor, Michigan, some foreign countries sanction even minor infractions of their drug laws severely.

anything about why the sanctioning system works the way it does and how it might vary over time or from one society to another. Similarly, subcultural theories cannot tell us how conflicting subcultures develop and are maintained in societies or why some groups are more powerful in determining which norms will be enforced. Why is liquor legal but drugs illegal in the United States? Why are they defined as social problems? Why are the problems dealt with as they are? All three theories remain mute on these matters.

SOCIETAL THEORIES

Questions like the preceding ones can only be examined by considering the basic operations of societies as total systems. We now consider these matters in a brief and preliminary way. The discussion will make clear why extended analysis at the societal level is best postponed until later on in the book.

It is obvious that to explain the present legal status of drugs and alcohol would require a detailed account of the social and political processes by which public policies and laws were established and changed. Similarly, to explain why drugs and alcohol are currently considered social problems would require an analysis of the rise, career, and fate of social movements that defined them as social problems. Some of this material is presented earlier in this chapter; much of it is presented in Chapter 9.

Economic differences, the primary focus of Chapter 9, play a major causative role in drug and alcohol problems. The poor are disproportionately afflicted with drunkenness and addiction (as both strain and control theories can predict). But drug addiction and alcoholism are not merely consequences of poverty; to some extent they sometimes cause poverty—alcoholics and drug addicts often become unemployable. This kind of two-way connection is hardly limited to poverty and drugs and alcohol. Family disorganization, racism, aging, mental illness, crime, violence, and sexual deviance may also reduce people's stake in conformity (control theories) or may subject them to intense frustrations (strain theories) and thus produce addiction or alcoholism. For example, the frustra-

tions encountered by blacks, divorcees, or ex-convicts could easily lead to alcoholism or drug addiction. Similarly, drug addiction and alcoholism may play a significant role in breaking up marriages, causing emotional problems, motivating crime and violence, facilitating acts of sexual deviance, or making old age a particularly unpleasant experience.

It is at the societal level that one can view the complex interconnections among social problems, for it is from this vantage point that the workings of the system as a whole can be seen. But how can these connections be adequately discussed when only drug and alcohol use have been discussed in detail? They cannot. Therefore, these matters receive more extended coverage in later chapters in this unit. However, primary attention is paid to them in Units III and IV where problems at the societal level are taken up.

PART III: RESPONSES ALCOHOLISM AND DRUG ADDICTION

113

An adequate discussion of addiction has to include the social and institutional patterns that, to some extent, create addiction and determine which forms it will take. We have already seen how drug use and alcohol use are shaped by societies' responses to and definitions of these substances. We will now consider how the policies of government agencies and important private agencies shape the addiction problem in societies. First we shall briefly recount the way American society responded over time to heroin and formulated the concept of addiction. Then we will consider the British response to heroin in an effort to show how the United States might have responded (and how it could yet respond) differently. The rest of the chapter will focus on present efforts by government and by private self-help organizations to deal with the drug and alcohol problem.

THE AMERICAN APPROACH: THE MANUFACTURE OF ADDICTION

As we saw in Part I of this chapter, many Americans in the late nineteenth century were developing what might be called an opiate habit, yet people did not regard usage as a social or medical problem at that time. It was in the early twentieth century that drug addiction came to mean something distinct from—and much more dangerous than—a cigarette or even an alcohol habit. It was at this time, too, that drug addiction actually began to have more serious consequences, disturbing the lives of many it touched.

It is not easy to judge the extent to which the formal labeling of addiction was merely an acknowledgment of a state of affairs that was coming into being anyway and the extent to which it led people to anticipate a problem that had not been there before. It is undeniable that the actions taken against heroin and its users by government and private institutions in the decades after 1914 had a profound impact on all that followed, determining not only who became an addict but how the addict (and his countrymen) conceptualized the problem.

The Bureaucratic Reaction

The Harrison Act of 1914, which restricted possession of opiates to certain registered individuals, immediately cut off users' independent sources of supply but left open the question of whether they could still obtain a drug through a doctor's prescription. Some historians feel that the intent of the Act was merely to make the distribution of opiates an orderly process supervised by such responsible parties as physicians (Clausen, 1966a). But some prosecutors at the time thought otherwise and began proceedings against doctors who prescribed opiates for people who had a habit. A few of these doctors were guilty of flagrant abuses, and some were convicted. The Supreme Court sustained these convictions, and the majority of the Justices interpreted the Harrison Act as prohibiting the prescription of opiates. In 1925, the Court unanimously reversed its position, but by then a pattern of law enforcement had been established and public opinion had been conditioned to accept narcotics regulation as a legal, not a medical, question.

Because the Harrison Act was a revenue act, its enforcement came under the domain of the Narcotics Bureau of the Treasury Department. As time went on, the Bureau expanded its scope, gaining power and congressional support as it grew from a

114

tax-collection agency to a moral scourge (King, 1957). The change was a predictable instance of bureaucratic empire building; the agency was simply overstating the importance of its function. But it is worth noting that these enforcement efforts, including the prosecution of physicians, were supported from the beginning by the American Medical Association—the A.M.A. (Kolb, 1958). Leading members of the medical profession joined the movement to take responsibility for narcotics control away from the individual physician and hand it over to the police.

The Narcotics Bureau and the A.M.A. together nurtured public attitudes of intense fear and loathing toward opiates through a propaganda campaign that exaggerated the seriousness of the drug problem. False reports of a vast increase in opiate use were circulated, even though the number of addicts was, if anything, declining because of the severe restrictions on the drug (Clausen, 1966a; Kolb, 1958). Official propaganda also fanned the public's contempt for opiate users by condemning them as degenerates and criminals. As a result, opiates could be taken only in secrecy, and the use of such drugs could no longer be reconciled with middle-class respectability. Users risked being consigned to the lower ranks of society, and the new users would come mainly from these ranks.

In the aftermath of the crackdown on physicians, public-health clinics were set up in various cities for the benefit of long-time addicts whose supply was now cut off. This was America's only experience with heroin maintenance, and it was to be short-lived. The clinics could not survive in the climate of opinion created by the Narcotics Bureau. By the time the last clinic closed in 1923, the addict and the public were burdened with repressive attitudes and erroneous ideas about addiction that are only now beginning to be challenged.

Lasting Consequences

The results of official narcotics policy can be summarized as follows:

1. Harmful and severe punishment of the addict, with an emphasis on imprisonment rather than rehabilitation.

2. Pressure on the addict to turn to crime because prohibition so inflates the price of drugs.

3. Public stigmatization (and self-stigmatization) of the addict.

4. Exaggeration of the potency of the drugs, including such myths that trying a drug once will cause addiction, that the drug produces incredibly pleasurable physical sensations, and that the drug does irreversible damage to the body.

5. Application of these beliefs and policies to other drugs such as marijuana and LSD.

In assessing these social and psychological consequences of the heroin orthodoxy, Stanton Peele (1975) emphasizes the way drug users' lives are affected by their beliefs about drugs and addiction. Believing that the drug is all-powerful and that they themselves are too weak to oppose it, users anticipate and then accept the first mild indicators of withdrawal distress as signs of the inevitable process of becoming heroin addicts. Addiction, then, is a process of *self-labeling.*

Other researchers, such as Lawrence Geiger, have concerned themselves with the extent of the public's misconceptions about drugs and drug users. Geiger (1971) reports the results of a national poll on marijuana, which showed, even as late as the 1960s, that 81 percent of the adult population believed that marijuana is addictive and that comparable majorities accepted many of the old myths about marijuana that were originally circulated about heroin—that it changes the user's personality, is dangerous to health, leads to crime and violence, and so forth.

Side Effects of Prohibition

The parallels between the prohibition of alcohol and that of drugs are striking. First, prohibition of alcohol had some of the effects intended by those who supported the ban: Drinking in America did, in fact, decline far below preprohibition levels. Indeed, it took until the last few years for per capita alcohol consumption to reach the level of the days before passage of the Eighteenth Amendment.

Similarly, without prohibition, drug use probably would be much more widespread than it is today. It is clear, however, that prohibition of drugs has not stamped out the drug problem any more than prohibition of alcohol stamped out drinking. The pusher is not hard to find; neither was the bootlegger during the 1920s. When a sig-

nificant number of people desire drugs or alcohol, and when these substances are illegal, there are immense profits to be made through illegal sales. Indeed, these profits are so great that they readily serve to corrupt those in charge of enforcing prohibition. Like the bootleggers half a century ago, present-day pushers cannot be eliminated, for they can pay a high price for protection.

What are the primary social costs of these experiments with prohibition? The prohibition of liquor not only failed to dry up the flow of alcohol but also created and bankrolled gangster empires. The legendary gang bosses of the 1920s, such as Al Capone, were fundamentally beer barons—they grew immensely powerful through their control of bootleg liquor. This side effect of prohibition led many to doubt whether society could afford to continue such a costly policy.

The prohibition of drugs has created a worse situation. Not only does the sale of outlawed narcotics finance the empires of organized crime but the high cost of illegal drugs has turned thousands of drug addicts into criminals. Estimates vary greatly, but all experts agree that drug addicts trying to feed their habits, which can cost as much as several hundred dollars a day, account for a staggering amount of crime. Crime may or may not pay, but it *always* costs.

A major stimulus for reconsidering our policies on drugs stems from a growing concern that the crime produced by prohibition is simply too expensive. A recent study argues that the legal suppression of narcotics has been a disaster:

It has resulted in an extreme rise in the serious crime rate, thus endangering the life and property of everyone instead of merely endangering the health of a few. (Stark, 1972)

We therefore need to consider alternatives to the present prohibition policy.

THE BRITISH APPROACH: HEROIN MAINTENANCE

The American response to heroin addiction has been one of prohibition and punishment. It is now becoming clear that this response rests on a false conception of addiction, has destructive consequences for the people it seeks to save, and generates the very conditions it seeks to eliminate. See-

115

ing the tremendous human waste this cycle entails, many Americans have begun to look favorably upon the way the British deal with heroin users. Edwin Schur (1962) writes sympathetically about the British approach, which, until recently, kept the total number of known addicts in the country in the hundreds. Doctors in Britain have been allowed to prescribe opiates as part of a gradual withdrawal cure or to prescribe them indefinitely for addicts who upon withdrawal lose the capacity to live productive lives (some do lead productive lives while using stable doses of the drug). The practice of maintaining an addict on a regular minimum dose of heroin, without any attempt made at reduction, is called *heroin maintenance.*

According to Schur, the difference between the British and American orientations lies in the greater control that the medical profession has retained in dealing with the problem in Britain. On occasion, the profession has successfully resisted government efforts to institute a more restrictive policy. The consensus of British doctors is that there is only a 15 to 20 percent rate of lasting cures from withdrawal treatments (a figure probably very close to the American rate). Maintenance treatment is therefore the rule, even though each case is evaluated to determine whether a gradual withdrawal program is feasible.

Schur observed a situation in Britain in the early 1960s that more closely resembled the United States of 1900 than the United States of today. In the 1960s, most addicts in Britain were over thirty, and a slight majority were female. One-fourth of the addicts were involved directly or indirectly with the medical profession, and the remainder were *not* predominantly lower class. There was no geographic concentration of addicts, no connection between addiction and crime, practically no addict subculture, little tendency for addicts to spread the habit, and only a small black market in heroin. Although addiction in Britain was associated with poor job and marital adjustment, it was not clear which was the cause and which was the effect. The British did not consider heroin addiction a major social problem.

In the decade since Schur's book came out, the Western world has felt increasing social strains, and the narcotics situation in Britain, too, has be-

come somewhat worse (Jaffe, 1970a). After a few doctors gave some patients the opportunity to sell the drug by prescribing more than the patients needed, the number of registered addicts increased (to 3,000 in 1971) and the beginnings of a youthful heroin subculture emerged. In response to these developments, the British government has reduced the number of doctors authorized to prescribe for addicts and has increased supervision of distribution. But the underlying principles of the British policy remain unchanged.

Noting that the growth of the heroin problem in the United States has been so much more pronounced than Britain's over the same period of time, observers have been moved to urge the adoption of the British model. The practical and moral feasibility of heroin maintenance has become a focus of controversy; both sides have used as evidence the only previous American experiment with maintenance clinics, in the years before 1923. Opponents of maintenance cite the failure of these clinics, but proponents argue that the clinics failed only because of specific abuses and inefficiencies and the hostile climate of opinion at the time. The issue is a complex and explosive one.

Can heroin maintenance be introduced in a country that has been conditioned to regard the drug as dirty and sinful and that *already* has a large population of street addicts? Some critics fear that new users will more willingly pick up the habit on the street once they know that they can continue their supply at a clinic (Markham, 1972). Others raise a more fundamental objection: that heroin maintenance, although it is more humane than the present policy, makes an addict permanently drug dependent and does not attack the individual and cultural problems of reliance on the power of drugs (Lennard *et al.,* 1972). This objection has considerable validity. But given the social costs of the present policy, most informed observers favor some degree of decriminalization of narcotics together with greater leeway for medical personnel to treat narcotics users.

METHODS OF TREATMENT

In the absence of heroin maintenance, hospitals and other agencies in the United States employ several techniques for reducing or eliminating an addict's dependence on drugs. There are also many treatments for alcoholism. These treatments are usually given in conjunction with counseling or job training aimed at helping the drug addicts or alcoholics restructure their lives.

Detoxification

Detoxification is the elimination of active dependence on a drug through a program of supervised gradual withdrawal. Progressively decreasing doses of the drug or of a cross-dependent drug are administered to patients over a period of days or weeks to bring down their tolerance level and finally to enable them to readjust to a drug-free state without severe withdrawal symptoms. Morphine was originally used as the withdrawal agent, but it has now been supplanted by methadone, a synthetic narcotic that is cross-dependent with the opiates and that produces a similar, though less euphoric, effect.

Detoxification is the first step in any drug rehabilitation program. By itself, it accomplishes little because it does not treat the conditions underlying the patient's drug problem; people are likely to go back to the drug for the same reasons that led them to take it in the first place. The memory, or image, of their positive experiences with the drug can cause them to crave it even after they are physically withdrawn. For a long time, narcotics addicts have come, voluntarily and involuntarily, to the United States Public Health Service Hospital at Lexington, Kentucky, for detoxification. Follow-up studies of some of these treated addicts have shown that over 90 percent relapse or have some criminal problem within a year after discharge (Vaillant, 1966). Such results indicate the need for a thorough therapeutic program to supplement detoxification.

Methadone Maintenance

Many addicts for whom detoxification does not have lasting results prefer methadone maintenance. Resorting to a maintenance program means conceding that the addict is so habituated to drugs, whether physiologically or psychologically, that he or she cannot or will not live without them. Methadone is legally used as a substitute for heroin

because addiction to methadone is considered less dangerous and more easily managed than heroin addiction. Unlike heroin, methadone does not lose its effect when taken orally, and using it in fruit juice eliminates injection—a major social ritual of addiction. Even when injected, it produces less of a "rush" than heroin, does not make the user as drowsy, and, perhaps most important, takes longer to wear off. It has to be administered only once a day or every two days, instead of three or four times a day. For these reasons, methadone fits better into an orderly, controlled, productive life style than does heroin, and patients need not be hospitalized to be treated. It also produces "blockading"—so high a level of tolerance for narcotics that the addict cannot obtain a noticeable effect from any but a prohibitively large dose of illicit heroin.

Methadone maintenance is popular with addicts, many of whom shy away from the rigors of self-denial or the total group involvement of a residential therapeutic community. At the Boston City Drug Program, patients have their choice of treatment and choose methadone most frequently. People also make the greatest claims of success for methadone maintenance. An evaluation of the methadone program at the Beth Israel Medical Center in New York City between 1964 and 1969 revealed that 81 percent of all patients orginally admitted remained under treatment. Compared with those who left treatment, those who stayed rarely returned to regular heroin use; they had a higher rate of employment (it rose from 26 percent on admission to 74 percent after four years); and they had a lower arrest rate (Glasscote *et al.*, 1972). The statistics indicate that methadone maintenance can have encouraging results in helping addicts live orderly, law-abiding lives.

Nonetheless, one has to consider some serious objections raised against methadone maintenance. For one thing, it cannot satisfy addicts who are drawn to the excitement of street life; these addicts will continue to seek illicit heroin even though its physiological impact will not be any greater than methadone's. Some critics have charged that experimental methadone programs have shown good success rates not because of the drug's properties but because of the personal attention given to addicts in such programs. They note that larger programs, like the Veterans Administration clinics, have proved less manageable (Malcolm, 1972; Markham, 1972).

Furthermore, one has to challenge the logic of treating one form of addiction with another. Like heroin maintenance, reliance on methadone not only does not solve the problems of self-esteem and personal adequacy that lead an individual into addiction in the first place but also may foster a view of new drugs as cure-alls for other complex social problems (Lennard *et al.*, 1972). If methadone maintenance does work at all, it seems that its main advantage over heroin maintenance is its legality in the United States.

Blocking Agents and Aversive Therapy

A blocking agent, or antagonist, is a drug that works against another drug. When an alcohol antagonist such as disulfiram is administered regularly to patients, they cannot drink alcohol without experiencing nausea, vomiting, flushing, palpitations, and other unpleasant sensations. In *aversive therapy*, a drug that by itself produces nausea and vomiting (emetine or apomorphine) is administered along with alcohol so that the alcoholic will learn to associate liquor with the disagreeable effects of the emetic. (We noted in Part II of this chapter that aversive therapy is based on conditioning, or learning, theory.) These techniques are employed more commonly for alcoholism than for narcotics addiction, although narcotics antagonists, such as cyclazocine and naloxone, are now in experimental use (Jaffe, 1970b). It is unlikely that such treatments will achieve widespread use: They do not get to the root of the addict's problem; an addict whose drug is blocked can simply switch to another drug—for example, a barbiturate—that does not react to the antagonist.

118

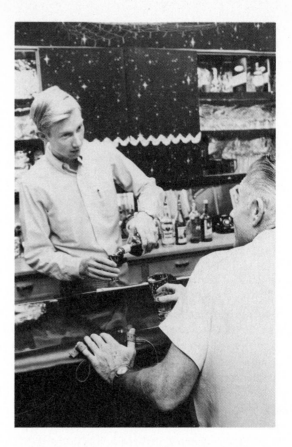

Figure 4.14 *Aversive therapy attempts to link unpleasant sensations, such as electric shock* (above) *or nauseating drugs, with the undesired behavior.* (Below) *A client in a Schick Center antismoking program sees himself as a smoker.*

TREATMENT CENTERS AND COMMUNITIES

The growing recognition of the need for a comprehensive, successful approach to drug rehabilitation has led to the establishment of a variety of treatment centers and therapeutic communities for addicts. These centers may be governmental or private, residential or outpatient, medically super-

vised or run by addicts themselves. They work from widely differing philosophies and emphasize different forms of treatment. Peer-group communities such as Synanon and Daytop Village create some pressure for change by encouraging self-understanding and emotional development through group interaction. These communities and other treatment centers face a serious retention problem (Glasscote *et al.*, 1972). Impatience, lack of concerted effort, resistance to discipline, and the temptation of quicker and easier solutions on the outside cause more than half of the patients to drop out of many programs. Still, for a small number of addicts, these programs offer the only hope—and sometimes the realization—of a new life.

Alcoholics Anonymous

Because alcoholism does not usually mean expulsion from normal society—as long as alcoholics can keep roofs over their heads—there has been no large movement to establish residential alcoholism-treatment communities. Alcoholics do not have the threat of incarceration to drive them to treatment centers, and they often get by with support from family and friends. Alcoholics Anonymous (AA), the most widely known organization for treating alcoholics, is a world-wide, nonresidential voluntary association having a single aim—to help its members stay sober through mutual support. It achieves this aim very effectively for a large number of people through a combination of group interaction and religious principles.

All members of Alcoholics Anonymous are on equal terms; it is a cooperative group with no leaders. Therapy takes the form of meetings, with open discussions for all members and more formal sessions in which speakers give inspirational accounts of their troubles with alcohol and of their redemption through AA. At the meetings, members have a chance to relate to people with the same problem in an atmosphere of mutual respect and candor. AA does not generally attempt any major restructuring of its members' lives and concentrates instead on conventional outlets such as hobbies and social activities. A beneficial psychological impact, especially on one's self-esteem, comes from participation in this kind of nurturant social setting (Maxwell, 1967). Applying the power-drive theory

of alcoholism (discussed in Part II of this chapter), McClelland and his co-workers (1972) consider two of AA's traditional techniques to be very sound—the effort to derive strength from outside oneself through faith in God and the socializing of one's need for power through the opportunity to help others. On the other hand, the AA group itself may become a substitute prop in life, one that prevents attempts at successful resolution of problems external to it, such as problems in the alcoholic's family environment.

Daytop Village

A therapy program for addiction reflects beliefs about what addiction is. For example, the Connecticut state program for drug treatment reflects the assumption that drug use is a fruitless but nonetheless real attempt to cope with the problems of life. Therefore, the addict is respectfully treated as an adult who has learned the wrong habits of adaptation and who must go through a long period (two to four years) of relearning in order to be cured. This program accepts the personality structure of the individuals it deals with.

At Daytop Village, on the other hand, the addict is seen as immature, lacking in self-confidence, and unable to handle stress. Daytop Village residential communities in New York State therefore try to destroy the personality structure that has resulted in addiction because they see it as false and harmful (Glasscote *et al.*, 1972). The first step in the program is to break down what is considered an unhealthy self-image; only after addicts change their views of themselves can they admit their immaturity to themselves and to others.

Daytop is a peer-group community staffed largely by ex-addicts. It offers no gradual withdrawal or maintenance schedule and encourages the prospective residents to go through detoxification elsewhere. If addicts experience withdrawal after arriving at Daytop, they are shown no special consideration and are not excused from work. In fact, at Daytop communities one finds less severe forms of withdrawal symptoms than in jails and other environments that expect and accept these symptoms (Zinberg and Robertson, 1972).

Once the new residents accept the community's authority, they go through a maturation process in

119

which they take on progressively more responsible jobs and enjoy greater privileges. They are expected to model themselves after residents who have achieved a more advanced position than their own, and if they misbehave, they are punished with humiliating tasks and with loss of privileges. Their development is monitored through intensive group therapy sessions. Finally, when they have shown sufficient maturity and have developed plans for living on the outside, they are considered prepared to reenter society—where they will not find the cooperative values and closely knit community support of Daytop. Despite its high dropout rate (about 50 percent), Daytop achieves good results: 90 percent of the graduates and 50 percent of those who stay in treatment for six months remain drug free (Glasscote *et al.*, 1972).

The Workshop

From what we have studied in this chapter about the psychology and sociology of addiction, we might design an ideal treatment program with the following aims.

1. To provide peer-group support and psychotherapy to help patients examine their individual problems and what has caused them.

2. To help patients gain self-confidence and a positive self-image and to provide them with skills to deal with the outside world.

3. To keep from reinforcing the patterns of addiction—to avoid substituting addiction to one drug for addiction to another and to avoid transferring a person's dependency on drugs to a dependency on a particular group or interpersonal situation.

One program that follows these aims to a remarkable degree is The Workshop, a nonresidential center in the Roxbury ghetto area of Boston. It provides a simulated eight-hour work setting for ten to twenty patients at a time. Operating in conjunction with other treatment centers in the Boston area, The Workshop takes patients who are stabilized on methadone or who have gone through detoxification elsewhere and attempts to give them new skills for dealing more successfully with society and its institutions. The program assumes that these patients are unable to hold jobs because they lack psychological strength, not because of an un-

controlled drug problem. It builds up a person's self-image by giving the kind of detailed feedback on performance that real-life work settings do not offer. Patients work together on an assembly line, learning to cooperate and handle job pressures, while counselors structure the work so that the patients can watch their own abilities developing.

The Workshop believes that a job is essential to a person's sense of a complete life as well as to full participation in life and that work is therefore a person's chief bulwark against the hopelessness that leads to addiction. The program does not permit patients to remain for much more than a month and does not employ rehabilitated patients permanently—to do so would prevent them from participating fully in life in the outside world. In this way, people do not have time to develop a substitute dependency on the program, and they concentrate on preparing themselves to deal with reality. The Workshop is not a complete program, focusing as it does on only one aspect of rehabilitation. But its approach to that one aspect seems to be a good model of how addicts—treated as real people with longstanding problems—can be helped to make their own successful and fulfilling relationships with the world.

CHAPTER REVIEW

Both drug and alcohol abuse are potentially destructive to the human mind and body, yet the problems created by each have been different because alcohol use has been legal while most drug use has not. Both alcohol and drugs are *psychoactive;* that is, they have a pronounced effect on the nervous system. In recent years there has been a growing belief that addiction to psychoactive drugs, which is characterized by *dependency, tolerance, withdrawal,* and *craving,* is a social problem.

Whether alcohol or drug use becomes a social problem depends on whether it is integrated into the culture. For example, when drinking patterns are well defined, as they are in Jewish cultures, alcoholism rates are low; when they are not, as in Native American cultures, rates are high. The same patterns characterize opium use. In India, it was well integrated into the culture and was not socially disruptive, whereas in China, the reverse was true. The *cultural definition* of alcohol or drug use in combination with the *psychological characteristics* of the user determines whether or not it becomes a "social problem."

Less emphasis has been placed on the physiological sources of addiction in recent years since the *placebo effect* and the importance of mental set and surroundings have been documented. Such variations in addiction patterns as *controlled* drug use by physicians have also focused research attention more on the users and their environments rather than on chemical properties of drugs.

The psychological theories of alcoholism and drug addiction ask what addicts "get out of it." *Reinforcement theories* say that pleasure (relief from withdrawal symptoms) acts to reinforce drug use. Therapy would therefore involve punishing drug use (*aversive therapy*) or rewarding new desired behavior (*behavior modification*). Reinforcement theories, however, do not explain why some people become addicted and others do not. *Personality theories* try to answer this question by defining certain traits, such as dependence or the need for power or security, that make people susceptible to addiction.

Social psychological theories focus attention less on the individual and more on the interaction between the person and society. *Labeling theory,* for example, assumes that individual identities are socially constructed and that people's expectations of a person will help shape his or her behavior. This makes reform very difficult for someone defined as a "drunk" or a "dope fiend." This theoretical perspective, however, does not explain why people engage in drug or alcohol use in the first place. *Differential association* and *social-learning theories* answer this in part by claiming that a person's associates introduce him or her to drugs or alcohol. The friendship group not only introduces the new behavior (for example, becoming a marijuana smoker) but rewards it by approval as well.

Middle-range sociological theories try to explain why some groups deviate more than others. *Strain theories* say that there is a discrepancy between the goals of society and the means available to people to achieve these goals, so people without the means have to deviate. When people reject both the goals and the means of society they "retreat" into alcoholism or drug addiction. *Subcultural theories* claim that what is judged as deviant in one subculture is merely conformity to the norms of a different one. This has some merit for explaining drug use but has little merit for explaining alcohol use. *Control theories,* however, address a totally different issue by asking why people conform rather than why they deviate. Social bonds are stakes in conformity; they include interpersonal relations as well as economic interests. People without stakes have nothing to lose, so they will deviate.

Societal responses to drug and alcohol addiction have varied. In America, the bureaucratic and legal control of drugs has contributed to punitive treatment of addicts and an exaggeration of the power of drugs. Furthermore, people have become criminals in order to support their habits. In Britain, by contrast, control of drug use has remained in medical hands. Heroin maintenance controls the addict's habit and eliminates the need for crime. Thus the British have not considered addiction as a serious social problem.

Treatment programs in America have responded to addicts in different ways. Many facilities detoxify the person without examining the *causes* of addiction. *Methadone maintenance* eliminates much of the ritual attached to heroin addiction, but it, too, does not examine or attempt to change the conditions that led to addiction. *Blockading agents* and aversive therapy are used more often with alcoholism than with drug addiction.

Many programs try to give addicts and alcoholics emotional support; some focus on work and skills. Alcoholics Anonymous is a nonresidential group giving mutual personal support to alcoholics who join voluntarily. Daytop Village is a residential community for drug addicts that works to break down immature self-concepts and replace them with mature ones. Other communities, such as The Workshop focus on developing skills and generally offering the addicts an opportunity to gain the self-confidence needed to survive without drugs in society. Each of these approaches to treating the alcoholic or drug addict reflects an emphasis on different aspects of addiction in much the same way that the theories of addiction explained its different aspects. Similarly, addicts themselves have different needs, and therefore society requires different kinds of treatment programs.

121

SUGGESTED READINGS

Blum, Richard H., *et al. Drugs I: Society and Drugs.* San Francisco: Jossey-Bass, 1969.

Lennard, Henry, *et al. Mystification and Drug Misuse.* San Francisco: Jossey-Bass, 1971.

McClelland, David, *et al. The Drinking Man.* New York: Free Press, 1972.

Peele, Stanton. *Love and Addiction.* New York: Taplinger, 1975.

Pittman, David J. (ed.). *Alcoholism.* New York: Harper & Row, 1967.

Hamlet: Ay, marry, why was he sent into England?
First clown: Why because he was mad; he shall recover
his wits there; or if he do not, 'tis no great
matter there.

Hamlet: Why?
First clown: 'Twill not be seen in him there: there the
men are as mad as he.

William Shakespeare

5
Mental Illness

All societies have had to deal with people who show symptoms of madness or severe mental illness. Such symptoms vary widely. People may use speech that is out of keeping, muddled, or senseless. Or they may engage in violent or self-destructive behavior. Some may hallucinate or see things that do not really exist. Others may withdraw into states of extreme depression or unresponsiveness. All societies, too, have taken some notice of less pronounced symptoms of emotional discomfort—anxieties, excessive fears, unhappiness, and the like. Although mental illness exists everywhere, societies have interpreted it and treated it in incredibly different ways. Our own society uses several methods to treat the mentally ill. Some persons receive drugs. Some undergo psychotherapy. Others are committed to mental hospitals or treated through surgery. A few are even exorcised to drive out evil spirits.

A wide range of disturbances have been labeled "mental illness" in our society. Indeed, in all modern societies, medical and social scientists disagree about what mental illness is, what causes it, and what cures it. This chapter cannot resolve the present confusion. But it can clarify the disputes and provide a reasonable guide to what is known, what is only suspected, and what is still unknown about mental illness. How is it defined? How widespread is it? What factors probably play a part in causing it, and what factors do not? What treatment strategies seem at least promising?

PART I: THE PROBLEM MENTAL ILLNESS

The symptoms of mental illness and the proportion of people who display those symptoms have been remarkably similar from one society and era to another. However, societies have differed greatly in their reactions to madness. Some societies have interpreted madness as a sign of special magical or religious powers. The ancient Greeks, for example, went for prophecies to the famous priestesses at Delphi, who were probably severely mentally ill (Zilboorg and Henry, 1941). In other societies, the mentally ill have been banished, tortured, or slain because they were thought to be evil or possessed by the Devil. Still other societies have pitied the mentally ill, and some have tried to cure them.

HISTORICAL APPROACHES

Ancient societies commonly regarded mental illness as a result of possession by devils or evil spirits. The sacred Hindu texts of India, for example, classified a number of forms of mental illness according to the demon that was thought to cause each (Ullmann and Krasner, 1969).

The ancient Greeks were among the first to define madness in medical terms and to attempt to treat it. Hippocrates, who is honored as the father of medicine, did not believe that mental illness had supernatural causes. He saw mental illness as stemming from natural causes such as physical disorders, conflicts within the personality, and external social pressures. Hippocrates' views prevailed throughout the Greek and Roman periods. As a result, the mentally ill often were treated with sympathy and kindness. Physicians advised people to rest, to avoid excitement, and to seek a secure and comfortable environment.

During the Middle Ages, much of the knowledge gained by the Greek and Roman civilizations was lost. Ignorance and superstition reigned. Demonic views of mental illness replaced the belief that madness had natural causes. Treatment therefore took the form of driving out the evil spirits through exorcism. Flogging, starvation, immersion in hot water, and burning were justified as

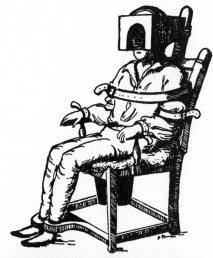

124

Figure 5.1   An important step in treatment of the mentally ill came when Phillippe Pinel persuaded officials to unchain some of the inmates of various asylums, such as the one at Salpêtrière (bottom right). Somewhat later, American physicians began to try new treatment methods. (Right) A "tranquilizing chair" used to restrain unmanageable patients. (Below) A more humane treatment method developed in the late nineteenth century involved the use of a primitive headphone set, phonograph (then recently invented), and projector designed to put the patient to sleep.

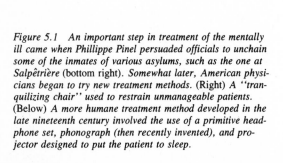

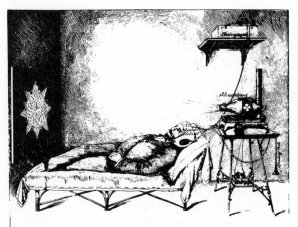

DR CORNING'S METHOD OF TREATMENT WITH MUSICAL VIBRATIONS AND MOVING SLIDES.

ways to make the body inhospitable for the Devil. Hundreds of thousands of the mentally ill were tortured or put to death as witches or as devils in disguise.

Slowly, Western civilization rediscovered the learning of Greece and Rome. With the rebirth of science and philosophy, the notion that mad people were only sick people became popular again. In 1547, the monastery of St. Mary of Bethlehem in London was converted into a hospital for the insane. (People shortened the name to "bedlam," which became a common word for insane asylum.) Later, hospitals for the insane were founded in Mexico (1565), Paris (1641), and Moscow (1765).

These new institutions were an immense improvement over earlier practices. Yet conditions inside them more closely resembled prisons or zoos than hospitals. Inmates lived in filth and hunger. Many were kept in chains. Members of the public bought tickets to view the antics of the "lunatics."

In 1793, a French physician, Phillippe Pinel, finally convinced officials to let him unchain some of the inmates in the asylum at Bicêtre Hospital in Paris. He gave these patients rooms and permitted them to walk around the hospital grounds. As a result, many recovered and were released. Encouraged by this success, Pinel wanted to unchain all his patients. The President of France, looking at 300 inmates screaming and rattling their chains, said to Pinel, "Are you mad yourself that you want to unchain these animals?" But Pinel prevailed, and the reforms he made have influenced the treatment of the mentally ill to the present time.

However, the triumph of more humane treatment methods has not made the problem less serious. Approximately one out of every twelve persons born in the United States will at some point in his or her life be committed to a mental institution (Clausen, 1971). At any given time, millions of Americans are thought to be psychologically disturbed. Even though the problem has been studied intensively over the last century, we are not yet even sure what "mental illness" or "mental health" entails. As Marie Jahoda (1953) put it, "Apart from extremes, there is no general agreement of the types of behavior which it is reasonable to call 'sick.' " Indeed, as we shall see, some

social scientists argue that no one should be called "sick." They say that it is the concept of mental illness itself (not the "sick" person) that is out of touch with reality. Thus, we must look at the ways mental illness has been defined.

DEFINING MENTAL ILLNESS

Mental health and mental illness are defined in many ways. But most definitions are variations of a few basic approaches. As we examine these approaches, it will become clear why proposals for dealing with mental illness, as well as theories of the causes of mental illness, often differ so greatly and raise so many debates. How one defines mental illness often determines what conclusions one can draw about it.

The Statistical Approach

One way to define mental illness is to use a simple majority-rule notion of the terms *normal* and *abnormal*. Normal traits, or characteristics, are those present in most people. Abnormal ones are those absent in most people. This view prompts researchers to measure the distribution of psychological traits among people to see which are normal and which are abnormal. Then they use these *statistical measurements* as an objective standard against which to assess the normality of any particular individual.

By itself, however, the statistical approach will not provide a standard of mental health because it will not tell whether a trait found in only a few people is desirable or undesirable. The measurement of intelligence, or IQ, offers a clear example of the problem. On simple statistical grounds, normal intelligence means an IQ between 85 and 115. Two-thirds of the population falls between these two scores. Obviously, then, it is abnormal to have an IQ of 130 or of 70. But we do not consider the high and the low scorers as equally in need of treatment (presuming that IQ could be changed by treatment). Thus, in order to interpret the meaning of statistical normality, we have to use nonstatistical criteria, such as values. We have to determine what is desirable. However, it is important that we take statistical normality into account when we define mental health. Otherwise, we could end up in

125

the absurd position of defining "normal" in a way that would classify the majority of people as abnormal (Buss, 1966).

The Clinical Approach

The *clinical* view of mental illness comes from the practice of physical medicine. Clinicians define normality as the absence of disease, and abnormality as the presence of certain symptoms of disease. This view also prevails among psychiatrists (Offer and Sabshin, 1966). With respect to the *origins* or sources of disorder, the clinical approach is said to use a *disease model.* In terms of treatment, the clinical approach is called the *medical model.* And even though there are several variations of the disease or medical model (Buss, 1966), they share the following assumptions:

1. Mental disorder (disease) is caused by *inner* dysfunction.

2. Symptoms of the disease are only *external* manifestations of the dysfunction.

3. Therapy, to be effective, must uncover and treat the inner disorder whether its source is physiological or psychological.

The disease model does not necessarily, or even usually, imply biological causes. Some of those who use the model believe that in the future physiological or biochemical origins will be found for most disorders (Rimland, 1969). But most people who take the clinical approach think that environmental factors such as a person's social experiences are important sources of most types of mental disorder. Thus, whatever the shortcomings of the clinical approach, they do not stem from a failure to consider factors outside the individual. The problem is that the clinical approach, although it depends on symptoms of abnormality to identify mental illness, cannot, in and of itself, say which symptoms are abnormal.

Values and Practical Criteria

It is widely recognized that the standards of normality and abnormality used in clinical practice are based on the norms, values, and aspirations of the larger society. Two basic themes are involved, and these should be kept in mind: what is desirable *for* people and what is wanted *from* people.

THE SAN DIEGO UNION   Thursday, June 27, 1974

SOVIET EX-GENERAL FREED FROM ASYLUM

MOSCOW (AP) — An outspoken Soviet civil rights advocate, former Maj. Gen. Pyotr Grigorenko, returned home yesterday from an insane asylum after a total of five years in prisons and mental institutions.

Grigorenko's release came on the eve of President Nixon's arrival in Moscow, but it had been expected for some time and there was no indication the move was timed to coincide with the presidental visit.

Soviet security police have detained more than two dozen Jewish activists in what dissidents say is an attempt to prevent embarrassing demonstrations during the Nixon visit.

The 67-year-old ex-general, who has suffered several heart attacks, arrived at his Moscow apartment and said: "I'd like to thank all those people who helped secure my release and helped prolong my life."

Figure 5.2   Mental hospitals have often been used to stifle political dissent, as the above example makes clear. However, in both East and West, other institutions such as prisons and work camps have also been used to restrain political dissent.

Figure 5.3   Definitions of mental illness and mental health depend to a large extent on our social values. If we were to assume that the extreme left or dark side of the continuum below represents severe mental illness and the right or light side represents perfect mental health, it becomes possible to visualize that most people fall somewhere between those two extremes. Many people experience occasional mental problems such as a mild depression or nervousness, anxiety, phobias, or the like. They are neither very ill nor very healthy; they are somewhere in the gray area between these two extremes. The distance from either extreme would depend on the values of the person who judges.

Judgments of normality may take the point of view of the individual and try to say which standards best define a worthwhile human existence. For example, there is wide agreement that each of us ought to find a reasonable amount of happiness in our lives. We ought to find sources of personal satisfaction, to have friends, to love and be loved, and to be able to cope with life. And we ought to be free from undue pain, fear, anxiety, confusion, and emotional or bodily distress.

Judgments of normality may also take the point of view of the group. We desire others to fulfill certain expectations—to perform their roles well, obey certain norms, and behave in predictable and appropriate ways. The two themes—happiness for the person and desirable behavior from the person—may mingle. For example, we may find that a person is totally gripped by depression and seems unable to meet such minimal expectations as eating or going to the toilet. In that case, we would conclude that the condition is unacceptable both for that individual and from the view of others.

Erich Fromm (1941) has summed up this dual standard of normality:

The terms normal or healthy can be defined in two ways. Firstly, from the standpoint of a functioning society, one can call a person normal or healthy if he is able to fulfill the social role he is to take in that given society. . . . Secondly, from the standpoint of the individual, we look upon health or normalcy as the optimum growth and happiness of the individual.

Generally speaking, three practical criteria are used to assess mental illness: (1) severe emotional discomfort; (2) bizarre behavior; and (3) social disability—the inability to perform ordinary activities adequately. As Arnold Buss (1966) noted, these criteria "are difficult to quantify and depend in part on social context, but they constitute the clinical bases for labeling the individual as psychologically abnormal." It is not always easy to say just when these criteria apply. For example, some professionals in mental health argue that marriage problems, juvenile delinquency, drug addiction, and sexual deviance are proof of mental illness. Others denounce such views. Over the past few decades, some people have tried to define mental illness so as to include many forms of deviant behavior. But these efforts are now being criticized,

both from within clinical circles and from outside the profession. For example, the American Psychiatric Association in 1974 removed homosexuality from its list of mental disorders, although some psychiatrists strongly opposed this move.

What conflicts like these make clear is that all judgments of abnormality are based on social values—on what we want life to be like. To the extent that members of a society disagree on what is desirable, they will also disagree on how to define "normal." Therefore, any discussion of mental illness has to be very clear about the value assumptions being used. Mental-health professions in particular need to look at the values they are using when they express their views (Cumming, 1968; Smith, 1961). Bringing such assumptions to light should become a conscious part of assessing research, treatment, and theory.

CATEGORIES OF MENTAL ILLNESS

Volumes have been devoted to outlining the types of mental disorders recognized by psychiatry. In order to understand mental illness as a social problem, however, we need to consider only a few general types of disorder.

A major distinction is drawn between disorders known to be related to diseased or damaged brain tissue (brain damage, tumors, birth defects, and the like) and those for which no clear organic or physical cause has been shown. Problems that are not organic are called *functional* or *psychogenic* disorders. This means that the condition is thought to be caused by psychological or social factors. There is evidence that physiological and genetic factors may also play a role in some functional disorders. At present, however, social factors seem to play the clearest role in affecting these disorders. Four major functional disorders need to be distinguished: neuroses, psychoses, psychosomatic disorders, and personality disorders.

Neuroses

Neuroses typically involve two of the three practical criteria we have mentioned, discomfort and some disability. A neurotic symptom, according to Buss (1966), "is an observed reaction or complaint that does not constitute a clean break with reality.'' The major symptoms include anxiety or depression or both. Neurotics frequently report experiences of worry, pain, recurrent thoughts, phobias (excessive fears), and the inability to concentrate. People under stress report similar symptoms, but these tend to go away when the stressful situation is over. Thus, anxiety is a symptom of neurosis only if it persists or keeps coming back over a long period of time and recurs even when there is no stressful circumstance to cause it. Neurotics are usually able to get by—to hold jobs and fill roles in society—but their lives are fraught with worry, anxiety, and fear.

Psychoses

Psychoses involve more serious deviant symptoms. Psychotics have a very hard time evaluating and relating to external reality. Their bizarre acts seem to be responses that are out of keeping with circumstances in the real world. Psychiatry recognizes two broad categories of psychosis: *schizophrenia* and the *affective disorders*.

Schizophrenia

Contrary to popular belief, schizophrenia does not mean ''split personality.'' Such cases are called multiple personality and are quite rare in medical history. The schizophrenic has one personality, and it is ''split'' only in the sense that feeling and thought are not integrated. Unfortunately, it is easier to specify what schizophrenia is not than to describe what it is.

There is much disagreement on just what schizophrenia is and who is schizophrenic (Mosher and Feinsilver, 1970). But there seems to be a consensus on the types of symptoms that are present in the disorder: (1) There are disturbances in the thought process and thought content—loose association, flight of ideas, and fragmented and senseless speech. (2) Schizophrenics show many problems in perceiving and in interpreting reality—hallucinations and delusions. (3) They have trouble in interpersonal relationships—social withdrawal and isolation.

The *incidence* (rate at which new cases occur) of schizophrenia is not high. However, compared with other types of disorder, this disorder contributes very strongly to mental illness as a social

128

Figure 5.4 *Many types of mental illness also affect the body. In catatonic schizophrenia, the person may assume a strained posture and maintain it for a long time. The body is generally quite malleable and if, for example, an arm is extended, the limb remains in that position for a long period of time, a condition known as waxy flexibility.*

A Schizophrenic

When the illness finally hit me with all its force, I spent months of living hell in Toronto before my mother realized that something was wrong and flew down to take me home and put me in a hospital. During those months my mind convinced me completely of intense feelings of other people toward me—feelings of love, hate, indifference, spite, friendship. These certainties were groundless and led me into dreadful relationships with people. My physical health was low and I worked fitfully at a job which left nothing but an irritating sense of failure. My sick leave piled up until I was going to have practically no pay cheque. I could eat and sleep very little because of voices telling me I mustn't. I was "forced" by voices to walk miles and miles about the city until my feet were blistered and bleeding, and then I was persuaded to do an increasing number of senseless things. Still no let-up in the vicious thoughts that tortured my imagination. Visual and tactile hallucinations came to enliven the auditory ones. Though I fought the idea of hospital restrictions desperately, I experienced a sense of relief as well, knowing that I might be afforded some protection from the nameless threats outside in the world.

Quote from Norma MacDonald, who was hospitalized for ten months with schizophrenia.

—Norma MacDonald, ''Living with Schizophrenia'' (*Canadian Medical Association Journal*, vol. 82, January 23, 1960), pp. 218–221, 678–681. Reprinted by permission of the *Canadian Medical Association Journal*, in Bert Kaplan (ed.), *The Inner World of Mental Illness* (New York: Harper & Row, 1964), pp. 174–175.

**Most Frequently Diagnosed Conditions by
Type of Facility and Sex, United States, 1970**

Facility	Men	Percentage of Admissions		Women
State and County Mental Hospitals	Alcohol Disorders	32.1	37.7	Schizophrenia
	Schizophrenia	24.0	16.9	Depressive Disorders
	Personality Disorders	6.3	10.6	*Organic Brain Syndromes
Private Mental Hospitals	Depressive Disorders	31.3	45.2	Depressive Disorders
	Schizophrenia	20.2	22.6	Schizophrenia
	Alcohol Disorders	16.8	6.6	Other Neuroses
General Hospital Inpatient Unit	Depressive Disorders	23.6	40.1	Depressive Disorders
	Alcohol Disorders	22.3	15.1	Schizophrenia
	Schizophrenia	14.0	13.6	Other Neuroses
Community Mental Health Center	Schizophrenia	14.6	20.7	Depressive Disorders
	Transient Situational Personality Disorders	13.5	15.6	Schizophrenia
	Personality Disorders	13.3	13.5	Transient Situational Personality Disorders
Outpatient Clinics	Transient Situational Personality Disorders	15.7	14.9	Depressive Disorders
	Personality Disorders	12.5	14.2	Transient Situational Personality Disorders
	Schizophrenia	11.4	13.2	Schizophrenia

*Excluding alcohol and drug abuse.

Figure 5.5 The above chart summarizes the data for the major mental disorders and treatment facilities by sex. It has been conjectured that women not only have different mental health problems than men, but also different means of coping with these problems.

(National Institute of Mental Health, 1973.)

problem in the United States. This is so because schizophrenia tends to be a condition that is chronic—people tend to suffer repeated episodes of illness—and because so many schizophrenics are found in mental hospitals. About one-fourth of all persons under the age of forty who are admitted to mental hospitals in the United States are diagnosed as schizophrenic. At any given time, schizophrenics take up half the beds in the nation's mental hospitals.

In their recent report on schizophrenia, Loren Mosher and David Feinsilver (1970) pointed out there was a 30 percent decrease in the number of hospitalized schizophrenics between 1953 and 1968. But there was also a corresponding increase in the admission rate. It is likely that patients were staying in the hospital for shorter periods but were more frequently admitted. As a result,

In 1968 alone, there were more than 320,000 episodes of illness diagnosed as schizophrenia in the United States. The cost of schizophrenia . . . is . . . estimated at 14 billion dollars annually. This figure represents the indirect as well as the direct costs being borne by society for the two to three million living Americans carrying this diagnosis. (Mosher and Feinsilver, 1970)

Schizophrenia, then, is a significant social problem in its own right.

Affective Psychoses

Affective psychoses are marked by disturbances (usually extremes) of mood or feeling. Included are *manic-depressive psychosis* and *involutional melancholia.* The second of these disorders is characterized by a depression similar to that shown by persons regarded as manic-depressive. The difference is that it occurs during the involutional period (the change of life, in the case of women).

Most episodes of manic-depressive reactions occur at particular periods in one's life. They more often happen in middle life but sometimes occur in young adulthood. Classic symptoms are violent swings from mania, or extreme happiness, to extreme depression. But mania is rare. Many cases are diagnosed simply as psychotic depression.

Mental illness diagnoses are somewhat unreliable partly because there is too much overlap in the sets of symptoms that are thought to characterize different types of disorder. A clear example is seen

129

in the way clinicians disagree on just where schizophrenia ends and affective psychosis begins. There had been apparent differences between England and the United States in the incidence of schizophrenia and affective psychoses. But a study found that there really were no differences. Different diagnostic methods in the two countries accounted for the apparent differences. American psychiatrists, it turned out, tended to diagnose schizophrenia whenever they observed some disorganization of thought. They did so even when the patient also showed marked mood disturbance. British psychiatrists, on the other hand, tended to diagnose affective disorder whenever they observed marked mood disturbance. And they did so whether or not thought disorder was also present. When standard interview techniques and criteria were used, the differences just about disappeared (Zubin *et al.,* 1969).

Psychosomatic and Personality Disorders

130 *Psychosomatic disorders* are physical symptoms of illness that cannot be explained by biological or medical causes. Instead, the illness seems to be the result of psychological stress. Psychosomatic disorders are of special interest to the social scientist, for these disorders are thought to arise as a result of stress that is associated with the demands of social roles. For example, a person who hates his or her job, or one who is torn between wanting a divorce and a concern over what the divorce will do to the children, may develop symptoms of illness (Leighton *et al.,* 1964). The person may feel physical pain when there is no physical ailment. Evidence suggests that psychosomatic disorders may be the most common expression of emotional disorder in the general population.

Personality disorders are fundamentally problems of conduct. The diagnosis refers to behavior that goes against the rules and values of society. Included as subcategories are alcoholism and drug addiction, sexual deviations, certain instances of delinquency or crime, and psychopathy (antisocial behavior). In the diagnosis of personality disorder, one looks for an element of bizarreness, an absence of guilt, and an inability to inhibit forbidden responses. To an extent, then, this category represents the opposite of neurotic disorder. Neurotics

are overcontrolling, inhibited, and guilt-ridden. But people with personality disorders are impetuous, unrepentant, and unable to control their actions by themselves.

Because personality disorders often involve conduct that society does not approve of, people are often tempted to use this category as an explanation of criminal or other deviant behavior. But, as we see throughout these chapters on deviant behavior, it may be wrong to say that mental illness causes deviant behavior. It is not even correct to say that deviant acts are irrational. A deviant act may be very rational—from another point of view. For example, one need not be mentally unbalanced or incapable of feeling guilt in order to rob a bank, take drugs, or beat up a neighbor. Furthermore, the behavior that one explains in terms of a personality disorder may simply be behavior that a particular individual has learned. It may not be caused by underlying psychological problems at all.

MEASURING MENTAL ILLNESS

Thus far we have reviewed general definitions of mental illness and its typical varieties. However, researchers have had to devise ways to define mental illness in order to measure the extent of the problem and to answer such questions as "Who are the mentally ill?" and "What social characteristics are associated with mental illness?"

At least five distinct ways of defining mental illness have been used in research: psychiatric treatment, psychiatric diagnosis, subjective unhappiness, social maladjustment, and objective psychological inventories (tests). We will assess the merits of each definition from the standpoint of how each affects the validity of research that has been based on it.

Psychiatric Treatment

The most common way of identifying the mentally ill in research studies is to compare persons undergoing *treatment* for mental illness with the general population. At first glance, this technique seems reliable. However, it has serious defects. First, it assumes that everyone who is mentally ill is undergoing some sort of treatment at any given

Figure 5.6   Three cards similar to those used in the Thematic Apperception Test (TAT). The scenes depicted in the drawings permit a variety of interpretations, and the person taking the test is therefore assumed to project his or her own needs, wishes, defenses, and other personality factors into the story. One problem with analyzing the responses to the TAT cards is that the story a person tells might occur to him or her because of some incident that recently happened rather than because of a basic attitude about life that the person holds.

moment. But the limited number of treatment personnel doubtlessly sets a limit on the number of people who can be counted. Second, studies using this measure have typically considered only hospitalized patients. Thus, they miss all those being treated by private therapists or through outpatient clinics (where patients receive treatment but live at home). Even when these other treatment facilities are taken into account, there is another problem to consider. Various segments of the population differ in their degree of access to outpatient facilities and in their willingness to seek psychiatric treatment. These differences would bias findings by underestimating the amount of mental illness and by giving a distorted view of who is mentally ill (Scott, 1958b).

To minimize these biases, some investigators have tried to include all mental-health treatment facilities, whether public or private, hospitals or outpatient clinics, that are located within the particular area being studied (Jaco, 1960; Hollingshead and Redlich, 1958; Faris and Dunham, 1939). Furthermore, some counties have made research easier in recent years by keeping one central file for all of the diagnosed cases of mental illness (Gardner *et al.*, 1963). But such files record only officially diagnosed cases. Indeed, official statistics on psychiatric treatment tell us more about the access to and use of mental health facilities than they do about the real incidence of mental illness (Scott, 1958b; Clausen and Kohn, 1954). Thus, many critics dismiss measures based on psychiatric treatment as "grossly inadequate" (Dohrenwend and Dohrenwend, 1969).

Others strongly disagree. They grant that psychiatric treatment may be a poor measure of less severe forms of mental illness such as neurotic anxiety. But they agree that it is accurate in the case of severe psychoses such as schizophrenia. Both Ørnulv Ødegaard (1961) and Henry Dunham (1965) believe that sooner or later nearly all cases of schizophrenia come to the attention of treatment agencies. However, evidence to settle this dispute is not yet available.

Psychiatric Diagnosis

A second research approach for defining and measuring disorder uses *psychiatrists* to rate the mental health of persons selected in a sample of the population. Typically, researchers interview each person in the sample. Then they give these interviews to psychiatrists to rate on the basis of the symptoms or level of mental illness shown by each interviewee. In this way, the mental health of a representative sample of the entire population to be studied can be rated.

This approach overcomes the limits of the psychiatric-treatment approach. The trouble with this method is that it assumes psychiatric judgments of mental health are correct. Studies have shown, however, that agreement on diagnosis is notoriously low. It is low not only for community samples but even for hospitalized populations, where one would expect more consistent diagnoses because the symptoms are more severe (Conover, 1972; Mechanic, 1970). In their analysis of community studies, Bruce and Barbara Dohrenwend (1969) found an absurdly wide range of estimates of the percentage of people who have mental disorders. They concluded that psychiatrists have a hard time agreeing on how much disease is present in any given individual and how much needs to be present before the individual can be regarded as mentally ill. A study of diagnoses reported to the Monroe County (New York) Psychiatric Case Register showed schizophrenia to be the most reliably diagnosed of all disorders except organic brain disorder. Seventy percent of all patients first diagnosed as schizophrenic received the same diagnosis on the subsequent contact (Babigian *et al.*, 1965). This level of consistency is suspect, however, because first and second diagnoses are not always made independently. For example, psychiatrists' knowledge of a previous diagnosis of schizophrenia has been shown to bias their judgments (Turner, 1972).

Unhappiness

The third approach to measuring mental disorder is *subjective unhappiness*. Individual subjects answer a series of questions about themselves. From their answers, studies have tried to determine the relationship between happiness and factors often associated with mental health. In *Americans View Their Mental Health* (Gurin, Veroff, and Feld, 1960), a strong relationship was found to exist

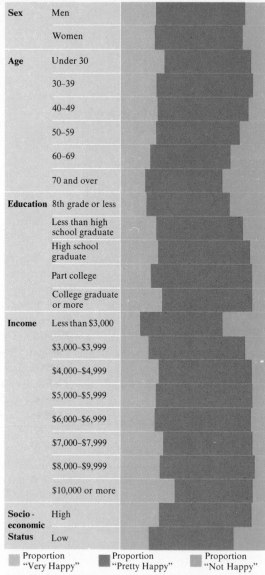

Relative Happiness in the United States by Selected Characteristics

Proportion "Very Happy" Proportion "Pretty Happy" Proportion "Not Happy"

Respondents were divided into two social classes. "High" consists of people who have at least two of the following attributes: Family income of $5,000 or more, high school graduate or more, and white-collar occupation. "Low" consists of those with none or only one of the above attributes.

Figure 5.7 Happiness increases with more education, more money, and higher socioeconomic status. However, women are somewhat less happy than men, and happiness decreases for both sexes with advancing age.
(From N. Bradburn and D. Caplovitz, 1965.)

between worrying and self-reports of happiness or unhappiness. Herbert Goldings (1954) also observed a significant correlation between neurosis and unhappiness. Other studies also have shown a negative relationship between happiness and neurosis (Wilson,1967; Davis,1965; Hartmann,1934).

It is hardly surprising, of course, that happiness should correlate with measures of personal adjustment. But the degree to which it can be said to fit the concept of general mental health depends, as we have noted, on social values and the view of mental health that one holds. In a study of self-reports of happiness, Norman Bradburn and David Caplovitz (1965) proposed that happiness has been and can be used to mean the same thing as mental health. They have defended their use of self-reports of happiness by arguing that "there is no evidence that self-reports are any less (or for that matter more) valid than expert ratings or psychological tests for rating people on a mental health dimension."

The problem with the happiness definition, as Jahoda (1953) has noted, is that it does not take a person's environment into account. But environments vary greatly and are likely to make a considerable difference. In some settings a person would almost have to be "crazy" to be happy. For example, parents of a child with cancer may be extremely unhappy—but not mentally ill. Another problem with this approach is that it neglects two of the three practical criteria of mental illness, bizarreness and disability. The level of a person's happiness seems to be a necessary—but not a sufficient—measure of mental health.

Social Maladjustment

Social maladjustment, or deviance from the norms of society, has been used to define mental illness in a variety of studies. It has often been used in studies of the effects of interpersonal processes. Its main advantage is that it forces us to consider the norms and expectations of the social system in which the individual takes part and interacts. The basic sociological premise is that behavior cannot be understood independently of the social context in which it occurs.

Despite its advantages, this definition leads to two major problems. First, different social struc-

tures have different norms and personal frames of reference associated with them. These variations make it nearly impossible to make definitions that are "mutually consistent" (Scott, 1958a). Second, because these personal frames of reference differ, some behavior will be labeled deviant when, by any other criterion, it would be considered normal. Other behavior, which by all other criteria would indicate disorder, will not be labeled deviant.

Objective Psychological Inventories

The final research approach used to define and measure abnormality is psychological testing. Tests are called *psychological inventories.* These inventories measure disorder with a high degree of reliability; that is, they tend to provide the same assessments each time a test is administered. However, reliability does not guarantee a valid assessment. For the content of items in a test obviously depends on the test developer's particular views about abnormality. So once again we confront value assumptions. Even if all other problems were resolved, we would still have the problem of the criteria that we have used to define abnormality before we even begin to test for it.

Our review of major research definitions shows that all of them are somehow limited. And so long as the way we define mental health and mental illness is ambiguous and inconsistent, our research, planning, and clinical practice will have limited effectiveness.

133

HOW MUCH MENTAL ILLNESS?

Keeping in mind the problems of definition just discussed, we now attempt to answer the question: How much mental illness is there in the United States? Answering this question is the task of a specialized branch of public health called *epidemiology.* It is the study of the frequency and distribution of a disease within a geographic area or within a specific population.

Epidemiological studies of any disease employ two basic measures: incidence and prevalence. *Incidence* refers to the number of new cases occurring in a defined population group over a certain interval of time (usually one year). The *incidence rate* is the proportion of the total population under study that these new cases represent. *Prevalence* refers to the total number of cases existing within a defined population group at a specific point in time or over a specified interval of time. The *prevalence rate* is the proportion of the total population under study that these cases represent.

An additional distinction must be made between *treated rates* and *true rates*. True rates represent efforts to count *all* instances of disorder, whether treated or not. We will treat only prevalence rates here because estimates of incidence are not available and their use raises problems that are beyond the scope of this chapter.

Treated Prevalence

From 1955 to 1972 there was a 50 percent decrease in the number of residents in this country's mental hospital system (Brown, 1973). The number fell from a peak of 558,992 in 1955 to 275,955 in 1972. While this dramatic change is highly encouraging, it cannot be said to signal a real decline in the mental-health problem in the United States. It only reflects major changes in the places and programs where patients receive treatment. In 1955, 77 percent of all cases were inpatient, while in 1971 inpatient treatment accounted for only 43 percent of all cases. By 1973, there were "as many patients being treated in community programs as in state programs" (Brown, 1973).

Even though the number of hospitalized patients has decreased, the number of people who undergo treatment has increased. New programs for the treatment of the mentally ill have been possible because the number of mental-health professionals has quadrupled over the past twenty-five years. As Bertram Brown (1973) reported,

our estimate is that in 1946 less than one million people had a contact with a mental health professional in hospital, clinic, or office. By mid or late fifties this number had doubled, and by 1971 this had doubled again to four million people; approximately two percent of the population received some form of psychiatric or mental health care every year, and the number and percentage are continuing to rise.

A further indication of the rate of this rise is provided by a comparison of this 2 percent figure with data from the same source for 1966. During that year, there were 2,687,424 patient-care epi-

134

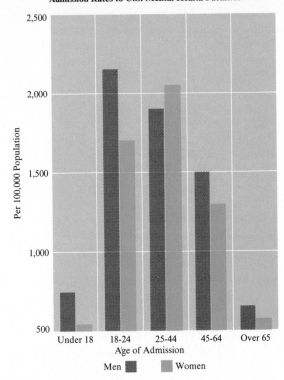

Admission Rates to U.S. Mental Health Facilities

Figure 5.8   In 1971, there were over 2.5 million admissions to various mental-health facilities, a rate of 1,239 per 100,000 population. Of these, 38 percent occurred in the twenty-five to fourty-four age group, and 22 percent occurred in the forty-five to sixty-four age group. Males accounted for 52 percent of the admissions. The male rate exceeded the female rate in every age group except the twenty-five to forty-four age group.

(Adapted from National Institute of Mental Health, 1973.)

sodes involving approximately 2,392,761 separate individuals. Thus, about 1.2 percent of the total population received care in some psychiatric facility (Kramer, 1969). In just five years, the increase in treated prevalence involved 0.8 percent of the total population. The 2 percent figure for treated prevalence, then, is likely to be a low estimate.

True Prevalence

We have already described the problems of using "being in treatment" to define mental illness. Because of such problems, there have been at least forty-four separate attempts to count untreated as well as treated cases. The most thorough analyses of these studies have been made by Dohrenwend and Dohrenwend (1965, 1969, 1970). Among their observations are these:

1. That for all forms of disorder lumped together, reported annual prevalence rates ranged from less than 1 percent to 64 percent.

2. That this extremely wide range in reported rates could not be explained on such grounds as geographical area, the rural-urban distinction, or differences in age or sex.

3. That contrasting ideas of what constitutes a psychiatric case explained the greater part of the variance.

4. That the median rate reported by studies published in 1950 or later was more than seven times greater than that for studies published earlier and that this difference more likely reflected a broader definition of disorder than of any real change in prevalence.

It is, of course, difficult from such data to estimate true prevalence with any confidence. Perhaps the best estimate is the median value of 15.6 percent reported by Dohrenwend and Dohrenwend (1969) for studies published since 1950. If we were to accept this figure, we could conclude that the extent of mental illness is more than seven times greater than the 2 percent figure suggested by treated prevalence.

WHO ARE THE MENTALLY ILL?

Studies of mental illness have tried to say how the mentally ill differ from the general population. The aim is to identify which, if any, groups in society are especially prone to (or immune from) mental illness. An answer to this question would give clues about what may cause mental illness. Perhaps the major finding is that *all groups, regardless of age, race, religion, social class, occupation, or geographic location, are struck by mental illness.* However, two groups in society are especially likely to turn up among the mentally ill: the unmarried and the poor.

Marital Status

No matter how mental health is measured, studies find a lower rate of mental illness among married people than among people unmarried (Sherman *et al.*, 1964; Turner *et al.*, 1970). And mental illness is highest among those who have been married but who no longer are—the widowed, the separated, and the divorced. It is lower among those who have never been married.

Social scientists do not question the validity of these correlations, but they do argue about cause and effect. Some believe that being unmarried is a cause of mental illness. Others think that mental illness is a cause of being unmarried. The latter position is called the *selection* interpretation. People who take this view argue that the personal inadequacies of those who are later diagnosed as mentally ill cause them not to be selected for marriage, or, if they do marry, cause them to be divorced. The *social causation* interpretation takes the opposite view. It says that being unmarried puts people under stress (lack of sympathetic understanding, for example). And such stress makes it more likely that they will become mentally ill. Furthermore, those who support this interpretation argue that marriage also gives some protection against treatment or hospitalization for married people who do become mentally ill; married people have families to care for them until they recover. We shall consider this dispute again when we take up theories of mental illness.

Social Class

Perhaps the best known and most important finding about mental illness is that it falls quite disproportionately upon the poor. However, class is related only to some, not all, specific forms of mental illness. It has been found to be strongly

135

related to mental illness in general (when all forms and types of symptoms are lumped together). And class is related to schizophrenia but not to any specific category other than schizophrenia (Dohrenwend and Dohrenwend, 1969).

The highest rate of disorder occurs at the lowest social-class level. However, the relationship varies with city size (Kohn, 1968; Clausen and Kohn, 1959). In very large cities, the lower the social-class position, the higher is the rate of disorder. But this relationship holds only for people in large cities, not for persons in small cities or towns.

It is important to understand that *this body of data implies neither that most disordered people are lower class, nor that most lower-class people can be regarded as disordered.* We can only say that there is significantly more disorder in the lowest class than could be expected by chance alone.

As with marital status, there has been strenuous debate over *selection* and *social causation* in interpreting these findings. The social-causation argument is that the hardships of low social class cause some persons to become mentally ill. The selection argument is that mental illness causes people to be economically unsuccessful. We assess this argument in the next part of this chapter.

PART II: SOURCES MENTAL ILLNESS

An understanding of what causes mental illness is needed not simply to know how to cure this age-old affliction but also to know how to *prevent* it. It would be invaluable to know how to effectively treat mental illness. But until we know how to prevent it, there will be an unending supply of new afflicted patients to be treated, and considerable human suffering will persist.

Mental illness probably has received more attention from social scientists than any other single social problem. A massive body of research and theory is devoted to understanding this problem. Furthermore, a great deal of work has been concentrated at each level of analysis used in this unit. No thorough explanation of the causes of mental illness is yet available. But it seems clear that any future explanation will have to deal with the whole

Cause and Effect Theories of Mental Illness

Social Causation	Selection

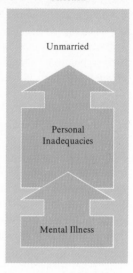

Figure 5.9 (Above) *Does the stress of being unmarried cause mental illness? Or does being mentally ill cause people not to be selected for marriage? Social scientists who see stress as a major cause of mental illness argue that various social factors, including being poor, unmarried, or unemployed, produce stress and thus mental illness. Other social scientists see mental illness, however caused, as the major reason for personal inadequacies and social problems. They favor selection over social causation as an explanation of individual and social problems.*

range of questions raised by these different levels of analysis. Put another way, it seems certain that mental illness has no single cause but is the result of a complex set of causes. These range from the biological functioning of the human body to the workings of society as a system.

Some social scientists argue that stress may be the underlying cause of both biochemical abnormalities and mental illness. Others suggest that stress may trigger abnormal biochemical processes and that these in turn cause mental illness. In either case, stress—environmental conditions that cause anxiety, fear, frustration, and tension—is seen as a major factor in mental illness. As we will see later, stress is of great importance in theories linking social class to mental illness.

Given the great number of theories on the causes of mental illness, we must limit ourselves to outlining some of the most prominent and promising work that is now available. We make no pretense of doing justice to the full complexity of any of these theories. We can, however, offer a general understanding of what each theory means.

PHYSIOLOGICAL SOURCES

It is obvious that profound mental changes can be produced by injury, physical disease, aging, and nutritional deficiencies. The question before us, however, is whether severe functional disorders such as schizophrenia can be explained, in whole or in part, by physiological or biochemical abnormalities. We must also ask what role genetic factors play.

Chemotherapy and Model Psychoses

Psychiatrists have found that certain drugs are effective in helping people with certain forms of disorder. For example, chlorpromazine usually reduces the disturbed behavior of a schizophrenic person, and lithium sometimes reduces the severity of depression. But the fact that drugs are effective in treating certain psychological disorders does not mean that chemical factors necessarily cause these disorders. Nevertheless, *chemotherapy,* or the use of drugs to treat disorder, has led many researchers to conclude that mental disorder could have a biochemical basis.

Researchers note, however, that the biochemistry of human beings is extremely complex and that our understanding of it is far from complete.

The medical and life histories, and even the diets, of psychiatric patients are very different from those of ordinary people. Most hospitalized schizophrenics, for example, eat an institutional diet, smoke incessantly, get little exercise, and have long histories of chemotherapy. Any of these factors can alter a person's biochemistry. Moreover, as D. Rosenthal and S. S. Kety (1968) have pointed out, the extreme emotional and physical stresses associated with being mentally ill can also cause changes in biochemical functioning. When the researcher finds peculiarities in the body chemistry of disturbed persons, he must find ways to determine whether these peculiarities are related to the causes of the disorder or whether they are the effects of the person's emotional state or the situation he or she is living in. Researchers have not yet been able to produce convincing evidence that people with certain mental disorders have unique biochemical substances that cause the disorder. However, much research continues in this area.

In addition to studying effects of drugs on certain symptoms of disorder, researchers have looked at drugs that create *model psychoses,* or artificial disorders. According to Solomon Snyder in *Madness and the Brain* (1974):

The idea is simple and can be approached in . . . two straightforward ways. If the symptoms produced by drugs like LSD resemble those of schizophrenia closely and meaningfully, then all we need do is to find out just how LSD does its thing within the brain, and we have for ourselves a reasonable guess as to what might be the malfunction in schizophrenia. The second approach holds that the bodies of schizophrenics might produce a toxic substance which resembles psychedelic agents.

Snyder warned, however, that many drugs, in large enough doses, can create model psychoses, replete with hallucinations and delusions. He also noted that there are many differences between schizophrenia and typical psychedelic experiences. So we cannot put much faith in the LSD experience as a model of schizophrenia.

A better model psychosis for schizophrenia is produced by cocaine and the amphetamines (speed). The two drugs, although chemically dif-

137

ferent, "share the ability to produce psychoses which are very much like paranoid schizophrenia" (Snyder, 1974). In paranoid schizophrenia, hallucinations are usually auditory—the patient hears voices. Prolonged, heavy doses of speed in many cases produce the same kinds of hallucinations. In fact, patients with amphetamine psychosis are often misdiagnosed as schizophrenics when they are first hospitalized.

Unlike people tripped out on LSD, "amphetamine psychotics are clinically indistinguishable from acute paranoid schizophrenics" (Snyder, 1974). Furthermore, amphetamine psychosis responds to treatment with the same drugs (the phenothiazines) that are used to treat symptoms of schizophrenia. Doses of amphetamine, moreover, make schizophrenics worse, whereas doses of LSD do not. LSD merely makes schizophrenics experience a different set of sensations, feelings, and thoughts—ones that the schizophrenic can distinguish from his or her familiar experiences and feelings (Feinberg, 1962). For all of these reasons, the speed-induced psychosis is receiving more research. However, this psychosis is a model only for paranoid schizophrenia, not for other types.

Genetic Factors

Many persons suspect that biochemical sources of serious mental illness may be inherited. Whether or not this proves to be the case, the evidence is overwhelming that genetic factors play an important role in mental illness, especially in schizophrenia. Many studies have tried to determine the extent to which relatives of persons treated for schizophrenia also display schizophrenia. Thus, studies have found that about 10 percent of children with one schizophrenic parent and nearly half of those with two schizophrenic parents develop schizophrenia.

Perhaps the most widely known study of this type is the study of identical (single-egg) twins by Franz Kallmann (1938). He observed that in 86 percent of the cases in which one twin was schizophrenic the other also exhibited the disorder. This 86 percent figure is still widely quoted even though a number of later studies, using more rigorous methods, have shown that the true rate is probably less than 40 percent. The main point is that as

long as the rate for identical twins is less than 100 percent, we can be certain that nongenetic factors must play an important role in determining who becomes schizophrenic and who does not (Rosenthal, 1970).

The effort to separate hereditary from environmental factors has also involved the study of adopted children whose mothers were schizophrenic. These studies provide strong support for the idea that genetic factors contribute to schizophrenia (Rosenthal and Kety, 1968; Heston, 1966). Not even these studies, however, have provided clear evidence about the relative strengths of heredity and environment. Nor have they been able to show just what it is that is inherited. It could be a specific vulnerability to schizophrenia, a more general vulnerability to mental disorder, or even a type of personality structure (Kohn, 1972). What these studies do show, beyond any reasonable doubt, is that some genetic mechanism must be involved. However, it is also clear that genetic inheritance does not guarantee that a person will become mentally ill.

PSYCHOLOGICAL SOURCES

Why do some individuals fall prey to emotional problems while others, who face similar circumstances or have similar genetic make-up, do not? Theorists often turn to studies of personality to answer this question. Indeed, the view is widely held that whatever else mental health or mental illness may be, it surely involves personality factors. There are literally dozens of personality theories, but we will consider here only two. We will examine *psychoanalytic theory*. We will also consider its chief alternative among psychological explanations, *learning theory*.

Psychoanalytic Theory

Sigmund Freud is the father of *psychoanalysis* and *psychoanalytic theory*. His basic view of psychodynamic functioning remains influential today. In simplified form, his view is that the personality develops largely by building up compensating devices. Individuals are born with a certain set of drives, and they acquire others. The individual is acted upon by internal and external forces. These

138

forces produce tensions and conflicts and make the individual act in order to get release from tension. Psychoanalytic theory sees behavior as beginning with force and ending with the dissipation of force. New forces always follow. And these must be discharged through tension-reducing processes. The goal of human activity is thus seen as *homeostasis,* or equilibrium.

Freud developed a model of personality structure to explain the internal pressures that affect behavior. He likened the mind to an iceberg with the smaller portion, showing above the water line, representing the region of *consciousness*. He saw the larger mass, hidden from sight, as representing the *unconscious*. In his model there are three systems: *id, ego,* and *superego*.

The *id* is the original system of personality. It encompasses everything that is present at birth, including needs, impulses, and cravings. It is the pool of all psychic energy and provides the substance out of which the other systems later become differentiated. This psychic energy (*libido*), largely sexual and aggressive in nature, provides the force or power by which the total personality, including the ego and superego, works. The id itself operates in accordance with a kind of homeostatic mechanism called the ''pleasure principle''; its total aim is to avoid pain and to obtain pleasure.

The *superego* is pictured in psychoanalytic theory as the opposite of the id and as similarly irrational and single-minded. The superego substitutes self-control for parental control. It consists of introjected (internalized) parental attitudes and social values. The superego is said to strive for perfection largely by censoring id impulses.

The *ego* is the dimension of personality structure that is oriented toward the real world and carries out the organism's necessary transactions with the outside environment. It controls the gateways to action and determines whether and when id impulses will be expressed. In performing this function, the ego must synthesize the often conflicting demands of the id, the superego, and the external world. According to psychoanalytic theory, these conflicts underlie all symptoms of mental disorder. Symptoms are always expressions of some degree of failure on the part of the ego to accomplish its synthesizing, or integrating, function.

It can be seen that this model is directly analogous to the disease model described in Part I. Symptoms are but superficial signs of unresolved inner psychic conflicts. Specific symptoms give clues to the underlying conflicts of the inner person. And, as in the medical model, the only way to intervene is to discover and treat the internal source of the symptoms. In this case, it is through painstaking psychoanalysis in which inner psychic conflicts are brought to the surface and are resolved by a strengthened ego.

It is important to realize that despite its concern with intrapsychic conflicts, psychoanalytic theory represents a completely environmental approach. The critical factor is the individual's developmental history. This depends on the training conditions provided by parents and significant others as the child passes through a fixed sequence of psychosexual stages during the early years of life. Each stage influences the personality in general. And adults with mental disorders presumably show symptoms that indicate which stage or stages produced particular conflicts that the individual was unable to resolve.

In his biography of Freud, Ernest Jones (1953) pointed out that Freud's choice of language reflected the prevailing thought of his time, especially in physical science and economics. The model of economic distribution, based on the economics of scarcity, is basic to Freud's theory. He constantly referred to the economy of personality. Basic to his thinking was the libido-fund concept, which is analogous to the wage-fund theory. According to this concept, a limited amount of psychic energy (or money) is available. It can be redistributed. And obstacles to its proper distribution can be removed, but it cannot be enhanced or enriched. The implication of this concept is that love of, or devotion to, other persons or one's work or duty is possible only to the extent that the self is not threatened. For when the self is in danger, energy must be taken away from external objects and directed internally. Effective transactions with the environment depend, then, on the ego's well-being.

Many of Freud's opponents have criticized specific elements of his theory. But they have not denied that his model accurately handles many aspects of personality development and functioning.

139

A more general criticism is that while homeostatic principles are important, they are not sufficient to explain why disorder occurs. Recent years also have brought an increasing disenchantment with psychoanalysis as a form of treatment, along with increased attention to ego functions (such as social skills) as central factors in the treatment process.

Learning Theory

We have seen that all disease models of mental disorder, including psychoanalytic theory, locate the "real" ailment or malady deep within the individual. Treatment is directed toward this internal source with the expectation that the disappearance of symptoms will follow. In Freudian theory, even though the ultimate causes of the disorder might be social experiences, the problem nevertheless establishes itself in the personality. Symptoms therefore point to inner causes and call for treatment of the inner conflict. There are, however, alternatives to this idea, and learning theory is a major one.

Unlike psychoanalytic theory, which attempts to explain all normal and abnormal behavior in terms of a single model of psychodynamic development, learning theory has no all-inclusive explanatory model. Therapists or clinicians who base their practice on learning theory try instead to discover how each patient has acquired inappropriate behavior and which factors in the environment are currently maintaining it. They work with the hypothesis that abnormal behavior is learned in the same way as all other behavior: through classical (Pavlovian) conditioning or operant (Skinnerian) conditioning.

Classical conditioning is a learning procedure in which a stimulus (such as food) that normally evokes a given response (such as salivating) is repeatedly presented with a neutral stimulus (such as a flashing light) that does not usually evoke the response. Eventually the neutral stimulus, when presented by itself will evoke the response. J. B. Watson and R. Rayner's experimental demonstration (1968) of how a person learns maladaptive behavior through classical conditioning is the case of "Little Albert." Little Albert was a nine-month-old child who learned a phobia (irrational fear) of furry objects of all sorts. He had no fear of rats until the experimenters began to pair a loud noise with each presentation of a white rat. Soon the sight of the rat without the frightening noise was enough to cause a fear reaction in Albert. This fear rapidly generalized to all sorts of other furry objects such as rabbits and fur pieces even though no noise had been paired with them.

Operant conditioning is a learning procedure in which spontaneous behavior is reinforced. The probability that a person will emit a certain behavior is determined by the consequence (usually a reward or punishment) that immediately follows it; a behavior that is rewarded will probably be re-

peated. The person with a disorder is seen as differing from other people because he or she has either learned inappropriate or maladaptive behaviors or has failed to learn the adaptive behaviors that most people acquire. Operant learning theorists assume that people learn maladaptive behaviors because their social or physical environment in some way reinforces or rewards these behaviors. For example, a child who hates going to school might develop imaginary illnesses or might learn to behave in ways that cause the school to repeatedly suspend him. Either of these ploys would be reinforced by the consequence: he is allowed to stay away from school.

The various learning-theory explanations share a number of assumptions and concepts.

Learning theorists believe, for example, that a given disturbance can result from one or more aspects of the person's learning history. Clinicians keep an open mind when they consider a person with a specific problem; that is, they assume that there are many possible explanations for it. When they see that a person has more than one symptom—for example, a woman has both a fear of driving and an acute fear of heights (acrophobia)—clinicians assume that these two symptoms may have different origins. Similarly, when they encounter two different people with identical disorders, they assume that the problem may be rooted in very different histories or se-

quences of learning. The only similarity that they always assume is that the disorders reflect the learning of inapproporiate responses.

Learning theorists also view the make-up of psychological disorder as nothing more than a series of maladaptive behaviors. Unlike psychoanalytic theory, which views symptoms of disorder as symbolic expressions of inner conflicts, the learning-theory view postulates no such underlying process.

For adherents to the learning model, the symptom *is* the disorder, and to get rid of the symptom through "unlearning" or counterlearning is to get rid of the disorder. Those persons holding the psychoanalytic position, on the other hand, argue that treating symptoms without getting at their internal source will only lead to the appearance of new symptoms—a view that appears to be unsupported by research evidence presently available.

Like psychoanalytic theory, learning theory gives a major role to conflict and sees symptoms as compromises in relation to conflict. The conflict, however, is not intrapsychic but is that between competing or incompatible *responses*. Symptoms are compromises in that they represent tension-reducing but unhealthy, or maladaptive, responses. It is a major axiom of learning theory that nonreinforced responses will not long continue. Persisting symptoms, therefore, must be getting rewarded somehow, probably through some degree of tension reduction.

141

Figure 5.10 Learning theorists assume that all human behavior, including phobias, is learned and can be unlearned through conditioning techniques such as desensitization. (Left) A woman undergoes desensitization to overcome her fear of snakes. Through a series of stages, she learns to relax in the presence of the feared object. First, she simply observes the snake in the hands of the attendant, who is on the other side of a screen. Relaxing while seeing another person handling the snake helps decrease her fear. She gradually gets closer to the snake until she is able to touch it without fear.

Figure 5.11 (Right) When the American public discovered that vice-presidential candidate Thomas Eagleton had undergone psychiatric treatment on several occasions, many changed their favorable impressions of him to negative ones. Eagleton's consequent removal from the 1972 Democratic ticket was an example of the labeling of persons with a history of mental illness. The stigma associated with mental illness prevented others from treating Eagleton as "normal."

Learning principles are probably the most firmly established principles in psychology, and their use in various types of behavior therapy has resulted in remarkable success in treating some disorders. Nevertheless, a note of caution is required. To show that a symptom can be "unlearned" is not the same thing as proving that the symptom was learned to begin with—just as the fact that certain drugs can relieve symptoms cannot be taken as evidence that the symptom was initially caused by biochemical disturbance.

SOCIAL-PSYCHOLOGICAL THEORIES

We have seen that different individuals respond differently to the same drugs, the same parents, the same environments. Obviously, the variable of personality has something to do with these differences. Beyond personality factors, it is clear that social experiences and processes play an important role. Such higher-level forces affect the onset, course, and duration of all behavior, including behavior that we consider disordered or mentally ill. Of the many social-psychological hypotheses that have been offered to explain disorders, we will consider only labeling theory and its corollary hypothesis concerning residual deviance.

The Manufacture of Madness

Labeling theory is widely applicable to the study of deviance, focusing as it does on the context in which the behavior occurs and the social processes by which a person comes to be regarded as deviant.

As Stephan Spitzer and Norman Denzin (1968) observed, mental illness, examined from the labeling perspective,

is not a consequence of any intrinsic feature or features which characterize the mentally ill. Rather, mental illness is the by-product of the evaluation and labeling by certain persons of certain kinds of behavior. More specifically, mental illness is not a function of the content of an individual's acts (his symptomatology), but is, instead, defined by the reactions to his acts and the categorizations of them by those with whom he is associated.

Thus, mental disorder is taken to refer not to any state or condition of an individual at all, or even to his or her deviant behavior, but simply to the occupancy of a social role that is *ascribed* by other persons rather than *achieved* by the individual.

Clearly, labeling theory stands in direct opposition to virtually all major psychiatric and psychological formulations. Rather than locating the source deep within the individual, or even on the surface in terms of conflicting learned responses, labeling theorists fix the critical issues entirely outside of the individuals involved and describe them wholly in terms of an external social context.

Residual Deviance

Perhaps the most explicit application of labeling theory to the problem of mental disorder is that provided by Thomas Scheff (1963, 1966). He noted that all societies tend to categorize and label norm violations as crime, sin, stupidity, and the like. "After exhausting these categories, however, there is always a residue of the most diverse kinds of violations, for which the culture provides no explicit label" (Scheff, 1963). He grouped such norm violations under the category of *residual deviance* and suggested that most psychiatric symptoms fall into this category.

According to Scheff, labeling provides the major explanation for severe and persistent mental disorder and, therefore, for the existence of mental disorder as a significant social problem. Scheff recognized that genetic, physiological, and environmental stress factors may play a role in the origins of residual deviance. However, he viewed symptoms such as hallucinations, depression, compulsions, and withdrawal as very common phenomena that we all experience at one time or another. From this perspective, the causes of such behavior or experiences are of no real consequence or interest.

Scheff recognized that the true prevalence of mental disorder is much higher than the number of treated cases. A related assumption, which also seems well documented, is that most of the grossly deviant behavior that remains untreated does not tend to be viewed either by deviants or by those around them as indicative of, or relevant to, the issue of mental illness. This process of inattention or rationalization is called *denial.*

Scheff proposed that when deviant behavior is denied or ignored, it tends to be temporary. That is, if no one pays any attention to such behavior, it soon tends to go away. The trouble is, according to Scheff, that residual deviance is often not ignored. Instead, it is labeled as mental illness. This begins a process that results in making the temporary residual deviance relatively persistent—instead of going away, it becomes fixed.

But how does the labeled deviant know how to play the role of "mentally ill" that other persons have assigned? As Scheff (1966) put it:

Role imagery of insanity is learned early in childhood and is reaffirmed in social interaction. In a crisis, when the deviance of an individual becomes a public issue, the traditional stereotype of insanity becomes the guiding imagery for action, both for those reacting to the deviant and, at times, for the deviant himself. When societal agents and persons around the deviant react to him uniformly in terms of the traditional stereotypes of insanity, his amorphous and unstructured rule-breaking tends to crystallize in conformity to these expectations, thus becoming similar to the behavior of other deviants classified as mentally ill, and stable over time. The process of becoming uniform and stable is completed when the traditional imagery becomes part of the deviant's orientation for guiding his own behavior.

Scheff's premise also has implications for the interpretation of relationships such as that between social class and mental disorder.

From this point of view, social position matters not because of its role in producing the initially deviant behavior but because it affects other people's perceptions of and reactions to that behavior. The class-schizophrenia relationship [is seen as documenting] the discriminatory readiness of many people to see signs of mental disorder in lower-class behavior. (Kohn, 1972)

Few social scientists would deny that the labeling process can have important and unfortunate consequences in certain situations and for certain individuals. It is considerably more difficult, however, to accept the proposition that labeling is the single most important cause of, or explanation for, mental disorder. There is just too much contrary evidence, as we have noted in discussing physiological and psychological sources. There are clearly many instances of severe disorder that persist, despite "denial" that there is anything wrong with the person. There are also many instances in which disorder proves short-lived and the victim recovers quickly, even after having gone through the full labeling process. In addition, the fact that psychoses such as schizophrenia and manic-depressive

reactions are found in all known societies suggests that purely cultural factors, such as those involved in labeling, cannot play the major role. To sum up, labeling theories of mental illness promise to explain a great deal, but they have received little supporting evidence (Gove, 1970a, 1970b; Gove and Howell, 1974).

SOCIOLOGICAL THEORIES: MIDDLE RANGE

The previous chapter on drugs and alcohol introduced three major midrange theories of deviant behavior: strain, subcultural, and social-control theories. These theoretical positions not only conflict with one another but also differ in their applicability to different forms of deviant behavior, including mental illness.

Subcultural and social-control theories display little power in dealing with mental illness. While it is certainly the case that a person from one culture might think the behavior of persons in some other culture is bizarre and incomprehensible, no one seriously argues that a significant number of the mentally ill in our society are people who are merely conforming to the norms of some deviant subculture. There is no subculture in which the behavior associated with schizophrenia, for example, is regarded as normal. By the same token, it is probably true that persons with little to lose by acting in an odd way are more likely to do so than are persons with much to lose—as control theory would predict. But again, no one would seriously argue that people behave like schizophrenics or manic-depressives simply because they are relatively free to do so. (Nevertheless, control theory does offer an alternative explanation of psychopathic personalities, as is taken up in Part II of Chapter 6.)

However, strain theory attempts to speak to the causes of mental illness. In terms of Merton's types (see Chapter 4), the mentally ill represent the *retreatist* response to the frustrations of failing to achieve socially valued goals, such as success. The retreatist withdraws from the game of life, abandoning both the goals and the legitimate means for attaining goals.

A major conclusion to be drawn from strain theory is that the frustrations of lower-class life will manifest themselves in mental illness: The poor ought to be more prone to mental illness than the

143

rich. Earlier in this chapter we noted that this is indeed the case, particularly for schizophrenia, but the meaning of this fact is subject to considerable debate. Strain theory argues further that if low economic position causes mental illness, persons diagnosed as schizophrenic should also have been born disproportionately into lower-class families rather than becoming poor later in life. On the other hand, if mental illness is related to social class because of selection—because persons have certain traits (disorders) that will make them unsuccessful—the parents of schizophrenics ought to show the same range of economic positions as the general population.

Several recent studies suggest that at best strain theory can apply only to some of the mental illness found in the lower classes. The data show that although schizophrenia is concentrated in the lowest economic groups, fathers of schizophrenics held occupational positions distributed much like those of the general population (Turner and Wagenfeld, 1967; Dunham, 1965; Goldberg and Morrison, 1963). Thus it appears that *selection* is at work—that characteristics of those prone to develop schizophrenia tend to cause their low social position. A second problem for strain theorists is that they generally argue that it is the high amount of stress lower-class persons experience in life that causes their mental illness. If this is so and if we separate people who have faced severe stress from those who have not, we ought to find social class is no longer related to mental illness in either group. But this is not the case. Research has shown that when stress is controlled, the relationship between social class and mental illness is still observable (Langner and Michael, 1963). Thus, Melvin Kohn (1968) concluded that the relationship between mental illness and social class cannot be explained wholly by the fact that lower-class people experience greater stress.

However, more recent work on the connection or the relation between social class and mental illness—especially schizophrenia—does offer some degree of support for strain theory. If schizophrenics are found disproportionately among the poor, even though their parents are not, then it is obvious that many of the mentally ill have been *downwardly mobile*—have dropped to a social po-

144

Figure 5.12   Levels of Analysis and Issues Appropriate to Each Level. This summary chart does not cover all the important points raised in the chapter. Use it only to review what you have read. Page numbers are given for the full discussion of any topic.

sition lower than that of their parents. Research has demonstrated that men diagnosed as schizophrenics are both more often and more extremely downwardly mobile (relative to their fathers) than are members of the general population (Turner, 1968). This does not mean that the majority of lower-class schizophrenics are downwardly mobile. It does mean, however, that the susceptibility of the lower classes to mental illness has been exaggerated by failure to recognize the influx of persons from higher classes who are prone to mental illness.

The downward mobility of persons prone to schizophrenia can also be interpreted so that it applies to another problem besetting strain theories of deviant behavior. Strain theories have trouble with deviant behavior exhibited by middle-class and upper-class persons since such people should not be frustrated. Thus, strain theory appears to have no explanation for mental illness found outside the lower class. But the data show that it is not only among lower-class schizophrenics that one finds persons who have fallen from higher economic positions. In fact, many schizophrenics in higher economic groups have also fallen there from an even higher family background. Thus, downward mobility is associated with mental illness among well-to-do persons as well as with mental illness among persons who are poor.

It can be argued that the downward mobility of schizophrenics simply reflects selection, not social causation. Those characteristics associated with a vulnerability to mental illness—genetic defects, personality conflicts, strange habits, and the like—may be the primary causes of the marked loss of class position by schizophrenics. Yet, another interpretation is possible. It seems likely that low social position is much more painful for those who did not expect it—who grew up in more affluent surroundings and did not expect to descend the economic ladder. If this painful experi-

Levels	Appropriate Questions	A Partial Synopsis of Present Conclusions
Physiological	Is there a relationship between body chemistry and mental illness?	Yes. Drugs have proved effective in treating some forms of mental illness. Drugs have also been found to produce model psychoses—reactions and sensations similar to certain psychoses; such as paranoid schizophrenia. But it has not been demonstrated that psychosis is caused by abnormalities of body chemistry. (pp. 137–138)
	Can mental illness be inherited?	Studies of identical twins indicate there is an important genetic factor in schizophrenia. The offspring of schizophrenic parents have a much higher risk of schizophrenia than do children of nonschizophrenic parents. (p. 138)
Psychological	Does psychoanalytic theory regard behavior disorders as the result (as the symptoms) of intense inner conflicts?	Yes. Psychoanalytic theory employs a disease model and sees the disturbed behavior of the mentally ill as symptoms of unresolved conflicts or imbalances in the personality system. It argues that if one set of symptoms is suppressed, others will appear unless the basic inner conflicts are isolated and resolved. (pp. 138–140)
	Does learning theory regard the symptoms as the problem?	Yes. The effort is to determine how the inappropriate behavior of the mentally ill is learned and sustained and to alter behavior accordingly. (pp. 140–142)
Social-Psychological	Does labeling theory deny that mental illness is located in the individual?	Some labeling theorists argue that society in effect picks some people and calls them mentally ill without justification. (pp. 142–143)
	If mental illness is caused by labeling, why do some people appear to be so seriously ill?	Labeling theorists argue that once people are so labeled, they perform the role of the psychotic or lunatic. (pp. 142–143).
	How does labeling theory propose to "treat" mental illness?	Essentially by ignoring it. If we ignore the alleged symptoms of mental illness, the person will not be stabilized into the role. However, the theory cannot account for cases in which symptoms worsen even though other people ignore them, or for cases in which people recover in spite of their label. (pp. 142–143)
Sociological: Middle Range	Is social class related to mental illness?	Yes. The lower a person's income, education, or occupational status, the more likely it is that he or she will be diagnosed as mentally ill. (pp. 143–146)
	Does social class cause mental illness?	Sometimes it seems to (social causation), but it also seems to be the case that mental illness causes low social class (selection). Many lower class persons who are mentally ill have been downwardly mobile. (pp. 144–146)
Societal	Have the stresses of life in modern, industrial societies produced an increase in mental illness?	Apparently not. Studies have not found differences between rural and urban populations. (pp. 146–147)
	Is mental illness related to capitalism?	Some radical therapists claim that those diagnosed as mentally ill are the truly sane members of society and that the capitalist system is what has gone mad. Such claims cannot deal with the heritability of mental illness or with the fact that it seems to be equally common in all known societies, including socialist societies. (pp. 147–149)

145

ence does play a role, strain theory may apply. Moving severely downward, rather than simply remaining in a lower economic position, would supply the needed degree of intense frustration assumed as a social cause of mental illness.

At present, the question of selection versus social causation cannot be settled. Indeed, as Melvin Kohn (1968) has pointed out, both play a role in schizophrenia: "There is evidence both for the proposition that lower-class origins are conducive to schizophrenia and for the proposition that most lower-class schizophrenics come from higher socioeconomic origins." Little wonder, then, that social scientists have debated this issue for so long.

SOCIETAL SOURCES

We now consider several major arguments that mental illness is not so much an individual affair as it is a product of a "sick" society. First, we consider the notion that mental illness is associated with the abnormal stresses imposed on human beings by the complexities of modern life. Then we deal with arguments that mental illness is a manifestation of a repressive society and that radical political change is the only suitable therapy. Finally, we examine a current theory that attempts to

combine physiological, psychological, and sociological factors to account for mental illness.

Madness and Modern Life

A great many people are convinced that there is something fundamentally unnatural about life in modern urban societies. As proof that life has become too stressful, they contrast the complexity, the hectic pace, the impersonality, and the speed of contemporary social change to the tranquillity of simpler times. The great increase in mental health practitioners and the expansion of facilities are often taken as proof that modernization has been purchased at a great psychic price—that, in effect, increasing numbers of persons are breaking down under the stresses generated by society.

Obviously, many people do think that life used to be better than it is today; there is considerable nostalgia for the close interpersonal relations and the "timeless" customs of rural life. Many critics point out, however, that these notions of the past are badly biased. They omit the human suffering, the grinding labor, the uncontrollable diseases that killed as many as half of all the children born, the ignorance, and the bitter feuds of former days. But regardless of how one feels about the past, it is certain that life is now very different from the way

it used to be. Have these changes included an increase in mental illness?

What evidence there is suggests that mental illness is not more common in modern urban life than it was in simpler settings. A number of studies have failed to find any difference in the mental health of urban and rural populations (Dohrenwend and Dohrenwend, 1969). Of course, it could be argued that even rural life has become hectic and stressful in our society. Thus, scholars have searched for better evidence.

One important finding concerns the Hutterites. These people have rejected modern ways of living and have successfully maintained isolated farming communities in various parts of the United States and Canada. Tightly knit family life goes on in these communities much as it did several centuries ago. The Hutterites do not have electricity or machines, and they adhere strictly to old-fashioned customs and dress. For a long time it was thought that they also were virtually immune to mental illness. However, studies have shown that rates of severe mental disorders are about the same among the Hutterites as among other Americans. The difference is that the Hutterites rarely seek treatment for their mentally ill members but instead care for them at home. Thus they do not become recorded

cases of mental illness (Eaton and Weil, 1955), but being sheltered from modern life does not seem to offer them any protection against mental illness.

Perhaps the best known study of the impact of modernization on mental illness was based on records of admissions to mental hospitals in Massachusetts from 1840 to 1940. The data revealed that there was no increase in hospitalization for psychosis during this 100 years of rapid change from traditional rural to modern urban life (Goldhamer and Marshall, 1953).

Upon reflection, it does not seem surprising that the evidence does not link mental illness with modern urban life. It is obvious that mental illness is not a new phenomenon; something in human existence was causing many of us to go mad long before there were freeways or two-martini lunches.

Oppression and Mental Illness

One of the more fashionable and vocal groups in the mental-health field today is gathered under the banner of radical therapy. These therapists combine aspects of labeling theory with Marxist political doctrines and consider mental illness as a mere symptom of an oppressive and inhumane society. Indeed, the most famous of the radical therapists, R. D. Laing, contends that the mentally ill, par-

147

Figure 5.13   The stress associated with modern, urban life (right) does not produce more mental illness than was the case in earlier times. Life in the past was not without problems and stress. However, there was one important difference—in the premodern period, those judged to be mentally ill or deviant, like the older man exposing himself (left), were rarely institutionalized; they usually were taken care of by their family and relatives.

ticularly schizophrenics, are possibly the only truly sane individuals in a society that has gone mad. Laing has suggested that schizophrenics are an emotional elite who have explored aspects of their inner space that others fear to enter.

For most radical therapists, it follows that if the mad are sane and the sane mad, the hope of the future lies with the mad. Through them, political revolution will create a society that will not label the oppressed as mentally ill. Such a society they conceive of in Marxist terms. Thus, radical therapists propose that they "treat" mental illness by

organizing a community to *seize* control of the way it's run; . . . rooting out our own chauvinism and mercilessly exposing it in others; focusing on the social dimensions of oppression and not on "intrapsychic" depression, fear, anger, and so on; organizing against the war, against polluting industries, against racist practice; developing a political therapy center for young people. (Agel, 1971)

One can find such goals wholly appealing and still doubt that radical therapy offers a solution to the problem of mental illness. There is no basis for believing that emptying the mental hospitals and sending the inmates out to man the barricades and overthrow the existing society will make such persons less prone to disordered thought processes, uncontrollable depressions, or delusions and hallucinations. Furthermore, to credit persons afflicted with such symptoms as being the truly sane is to assert that the inability to cope with reality—for example, the inability to locate and utilize bathrooms—is a desirable human condition. It is one thing to assert that people sometimes flee from reality because they find it unbearable; it is quite something else to glorify that flight.

Furthermore, the position of radical therapists is challenged by what facts are available. For one thing, it cannot deal with evidence that the psychoses, especially schizophrenia, are to some extent hereditary and have a physiological component. For another, radical therapy ignores the fact that mental illness apparently has been about equally common in all known human societies and eras. If the radical therapists are right, surely some societies, somewhere, have been less oppressive and less given to the manufacture of madness than oth-

148

ers. Yet they cannot point to a society where mental illness was or is less common. Indeed, assuming that the Marxist position is right, mental illness should have declined in societies that have undergone a socialist revolution. But there is no evidence that such a decline has occurred.

Although most social scientists have rejected the radical-therapy position as simply irrelevant to the facts about mental illness, many are inclined to support a more modest version of the role of social inequalities in producing mental illness. We have already seen in this chapter that the lower a person's economic position in society, the greater is the likelihood of mental illness. There has recently been a considerable amount of work done to isolate which conditions of being poor may contribute to mental illness.

Blaming the Victim

William Ryan (1969, 1971) noted that studies of class-related factors have focused on class differences in status or prestige. These include such status elements as life style, values, and child-rearing practices. According to Ryan (1969), when one seeks explanations from this limited perspective, one omits consideration of two other elements that determine social stratification—power and class (money). This omission results in

blaming the victim . . . an intellectual process whereby a social problem is analyzed in such a way that the causation is found to be in the qualities and characteristics of the victim rather than in any deficiencies or structural defects in his environment. (Ryan, 1969)

Ryan did not question either the honesty or motives of most social scientists whom he would classify as victim blamers, but he saw their concept as defending the status quo, however inadvertently. Locating the defects within the characteristics of the lower-class population leaves the operating social system itself unchallenged. By contrast, interpreting social class in terms of money and power suggests the need for their redistribution and, therefore, for change in the social order.

Although Ryan believes that a solution to the problem of mental illness, like solutions to other social problems, lies in significant social change, he nevertheless appears to accept the fact that lower-class life has personally damaging consequences. For example, he argues that self-esteem is not only an important element in mental health but is an essential requirement for the very survival of the human animal. He notes that

powerlessness is a major characteristic of low income neighborhoods and of the residents of these neighborhoods, which in turn leads to significantly lowered self-esteem in such populations and significantly higher levels of emotional disorder and other forms of social pathology. (Ryan, 1969)

Ryan rejected the notion that powerlessness, and hence low self-esteem, can be corrected by individual therapies. Only power can cure the sense of powerlessness. Preventive action, therefore, requires social change: the redistribution of power.

Social Class and Conformity

Melvin Kohn (1969) reported a relationship between social class and conformity. He combined this relationship with the factors of stress and heredity to form one coherent interpretation of schizophrenia and the class-schizophrenia relationship (Kohn, 1972). In general, his proposal was that the conditions of life experienced by lower-class people—if combined with both high levels of stress and genetic vulnerability—contribute to schizophrenia.

Kohn's (1969) research suggested that lower-class men are likely to value conformity to external authority and to perceive such conformity as the only option allowed by either the outside world or by their own capacities. He argued that

the lower a man's social-class position, the more likely is his orientational system to be marked by a rigidly conservative view of man and his social institutions, fearfulness and distrust, and a fatalistic belief that one is at the mercy of forces and people beyond one's control, often, beyond one's understanding. (Kohn, 1972)

From this and other evidence, Kohn saw practical implications that are subtantially in accord with those expressed by Ryan and others:

the most efficacious way to alleviate the burdens of lower social-class position is not by therapy, resocialization, or other efforts to teach middle-class values and orientation, but by changing the social conditions to which lower-class people are subject. (Kohn, 1972)

Can such changes ever be accomplished? As we consider in detail in Chapter 9, the answer depends on whether the action required is to improve the conditions of the lower class or to eliminate inequalities in power, prestige, and income among all members of society. As will be made clear, much can be done to eliminate poverty in the sense of actual suffering for want of food, clothing, shelter, and opportunity. But there is considerable doubt that a society can be created in which everyone is equal. It appears that inequalities in power, for example, are inherent in the very structure of societies; not only do Marxist principles fail to eliminate social inequalities, but such inequalities probably cannot be eliminated under any form of social organization. Thus, whether social change can help eliminate mental illness seems to depend on how extensive such a change would need to be.

Finally, as pointed out earlier in this chapter, the notion that societal factors play a major role in mental illness may not even be correct. It may be that psychosis, if not neurosis, is a disease in the same sense that diabetes and cancer are. If so, the cure will not be found in changing society.

149

PART III: RESPONSES
MENTAL ILLNESS

Historically, responses to people with strange or disordered behavior have varied. Treatment has often been either brutal or indifferent but has sometimes been humane (Rosen, 1968; Alexander and Selesnick, 1966). For about two centuries, the main way of dealing with the seriously disordered has been confinement in an insane asylum, or what in more recent times has come to be called a mental hospital.

THE COMMUNITY APPROACH

Over the past two decades, however, radical changes have occurred in philosophy as well as in treatment approaches. An important change was the development of drugs that made it possible to treat seriously disordered persons in the community rather than in hospital wards. Nyla Cole and her colleagues (1962) summed up the philosophy behind the community approach: "If the patient's usual milieu is disrupted as little as possible, his degree of recovery will be enhanced."

Because of drug therapy and the emphasis on community care, hospitalization of the mentally disordered is now more often a matter of months or even weeks than of one or more years. Howard Freeman and Ozzie Simmons (1963) pointed out that care of the discharged patient is now the biggest problem to deal with.

Other significant developments that have contributed to the trend toward community treatment include the following:

1. The recognition that there are a great many "disordered" but untreated individuals in the community.

2. Acceptance of the fact that among the disordered, whether diagnosed or undiagnosed, treated or untreated, the disadvantaged are disproportionally represented.

3. Evidence that, despite their obviously greater need, lower-class people had been receiving few of the mental health services available.

4. Evidence that the more severely disordered patients received the least favored forms of treatment.

Victor Sanua (1966) has pointed out that education, financial status, race, geography, and socioeconomic status are important factors. They may determine such matters as being accepted for treatment, the type of treatment received, and the likelihood of seeking help in the first place.

People have tried to explain away the fact that so few severely disordered, lower-class patients receive outpatient services in individual therapy (even with free or low-cost clinics). But their explanations seem to contradict the facts. They say, for example, that lower-class patients would be unlikely to profit from such treatment because they are thought to have communication problems and low motivation. Yet, problems of attentiveness and communication are, by definition, associated with psychotic disorder. In spite of this, treatment programs often require that patients be adequately "motivated" and "able to communicate." So lower-class patients often do not get into therapy

Figure 5.14   Nine out of ten patients in mental hospitals are housed in institutions financed and administered by state or county governments. More often than not, these institutions lack sufficient space, personnel, and funds and have ineffective programs. They tend to prolong hospitalization by fostering dependence and docility. Research has shown that mentally disturbed people generally benefit greatly when they are actively involved in work and when they have frequent contact with therapists and other patients.

programs. And research has shown that these same characteristics that lower-class people are thought to have make psychotherapists reject certain patients as untreatable (Cole *et al.*, 1962).

In relation to social class, a study in the 1950s reported that ''the higher an individual's social class position, the more likely he was to be accepted for treatment, to be treated by highly trained personnel, and to be treated intensively over a long period'' (Myers and Schaffer, 1954). The same relationship between treatment and social class was found in a ten-year follow-up study of the same population (Myers and Bean, 1968; Bean *et al.*, 1964). In this later study, when only the schizophrenic subjects were considered, the relationship still held. Eight times as many upper-class patients as lower-class patients were receiving outpatient care at the end of the ten-year period. Similarly, in a study of a representative sample of schizophrenic males, Gary Labreche and his co-workers (1969) observed that the same class differences applied to the use of outpatient services. These class differences held true even for

treatment of severe mental disorder.

It seems clear that professionals (at least through the early 1960s) often determined who received what kind of treatment. However, Robert Rieff (1967), among others, has argued that the current philosophy of mental health programs may be alien to members of the lower classes. Thus, even if they were accepted for treatment, lower-class people might be less likely to seek help from or tolerate these programs.

The issue with respect to the seriously disordered has been most aptly described by Ryan (1969). On the basis of his experience with the Boston Mental Health Survey, conducted between 1960 and 1962, he noted that people with hard-core disorders, such as schizophrenia and affective psychosis, make up

only a small minority of the many millions of persons who are ordinarily caught up in the broad net of mental health problems as they are usually defined. . . . They ordinarily appear in very small numbers in the offices of psychiatrists in private practice; they are relatively scarce in low-fee psychiatric clinics. When they appear

151

in these settings, they are often not able to thread their way through the fine holes of the intake screen. The only kind of mental health facility in which they appear in substantial numbers is the public mental hospital.

SERVICES AND GOALS

The factors and developments we have just reviewed are among many that contributed to the shift toward a community approach. This shift was reflected to a degree in the Joint Commission on Mental Health Report of 1961 and was formalized in the Community Mental Health Center Act of 1963. In passing this legislation, Congress provided the basis for a network of community mental health centers throughout the country. The regulations made the centers offer five essential services. Five additional services that would make the program "complete" were recommended.

Required Services

1. *inpatient care* for people who need intensive care or treatment around the clock;
2. *outpatient care* for adults, children and families;
3. *emergency care* on a twenty-four hour basis;
4. *partial hospitalization:* at least day care and treatment for patients able to return home

evenings and weekends; perhaps also night care for patients able to work but needing limited support or lacking suitable home arrangements;

5. *consultation and education* to community agencies and professional personnel;

Recommended Services

6. *diagnostic service;*
7. *rehabilitation service,* including both social and vocational rehabilitation;
8. *precare and aftercare,* including screening of patients prior to hospital admission and home visiting or halfway houses after hospitalization;
9. *training* for all types of mental health personnel;
10. *research and evaluation* concerning the effectiveness of programs and the problems of mental illness and its treatment. (Smith and Hobbs, 1966)

In general, the goals of the community mental health movement are many. One is to provide alternatives to the mental hospital and to hospitalization. Another is to offer a range of services to people who previously had been denied them. Another goal is to intervene with as little disruption as possible to a person's everyday life. In addition, there was, and remains, the hope of changing aspects of the social environment to im-

prove the overall mental health of the population being served. For example, the community programs would support other community efforts to improve living conditions. These efforts might be toward better housing, safer neighborhoods, better recreational facilities, and the like.

It is difficult at this time to evaluate the community mental health approach and the extent to which its goals are being reached. The evidence suggests that considerable progress has been made. It is clear that the development of a network of centers is proceeding rapidly. More than 2,000 partial or complete community mental health centers are now in operation.

With the shift from hospitalization and inpatient care toward community hospitals, it is easier for patients to have shorter stays and to maintain their family and neighborhood ties. In 1966, the number of first admissions for mental disorder to community hospitals exceeded for the first time the number of such admissions to state mental hospitals. In 1973, community programs had the same number of patients as state programs.

It seems obvious that the greater emphasis on community-based treatment programs and outpatient care represents considerable progress toward the goal of keeping patients within their own communities. Community programs seem to be meeting their goals: fewer patients are falling through the cracks in the treatment process. Fewer are being hospitalized. And the disadvantaged groups who most need services are receiving them.

Despite these positive signs, it would be premature to make even a qualified claim of success in meeting the goals of the Community Mental Health Act. We must ask, for example, whether the thousands of patients who have been released from state mental hospitals are really any better off and receiving any better care than they had earlier. It is clear that community mental health centers are providing more and better services. But we do not yet have convincing evidence on how effective these treatment programs are and whether they really meet the mental health needs of the communities they serve.

The most difficult goal of the community mental health movement lies ahead. It is to build programs to *improve mental health* and *prevent mental disorder*. So far, most centers are so burdened with meeting treatment demands that they have little time or money left over for their broader goals. And it is not at all clear what prevention programs

Figure 5.15 (left) *A Los Angeles crisis center where trained volunteers are available to receive calls twenty-four hours a day. This telephone emergency service, or hotline, eliminates both the long delays and the necessity for dealing with authorities—situations that so often frighten people away from seeking help. Crisis-center workers have a chart that helps them identify drugs that have been taken by a caller who has overdosed or is on a bad trip.*

Figure 5.16 Alternatives to traditional treatment methods include informal group therapy sessions like the one pictured at right. Group therapy uses various techniques, including physical contact among the participants to promote trust. Groups typically include a leader who participates as a group member and does not interfere unless the group or some of its members require help and direction.

should be like. For effective prevention requires knowledge of causes. And, as we saw in Part II of this chapter, our knowledge of the cause or causes of mental disorder is in its infancy.

What information there is points toward poverty and factors that go along with it as possibly significant. Elaine Cumming (1972) has argued that social inequalities also "cause physical illness and mental retardation and are associated with crime, delinquency, despair, suicide, and numbers of other unwanted effects, and always have been." In her view, "the moral and social problems that afflict our society should be attacked because they are insupportable, not because they cause mental illness, which has not been demonstrated." Research into the causes of mental disorder probably will continue to show that social inequalities play an important role. A discussion of these inequalities and their solution—and whether a solution is possible—is the subject matter of Chapter 9.

154   CHAPTER REVIEW

The symptoms of mental illness have remained fairly constant across time and cultures, but definitions and explanations of those symptoms have varied greatly. In ancient societies, and in the Middle Ages, bizarre behavior was attributed to the influence of devils and evil spirits. In more recent times, societies have followed the Greek example of treating symptoms as indicative of a disease caused by physical, emotional, or social pressures. It has been difficult to define what mental illness is, however. Some claim that mental illness is anything that differs from the norm (but this does not tell us whether normative behavior is "rational" or not). The clinical approach defines the symptoms of mental illness as external manifestations of inner dysfunctions. This does not tell us which symptoms are abnormal, however. It is only when the values of the society are considered that abnormality can be defined. In the United States there has been a tendency to define "abnormality" in terms of the amount of a person's discomfort, bizarre behavior, or inability to function socially.

There are many kinds of mental illness. Probably the least serious kind is *neurosis*, which involves anxiety, depression, and limited social disability. Neurotics do not make a clear break with reality and are usually able to keep functioning in society. Psychotic individuals, however, are unable to cope with life; they may experience one of several forms of *schizophrenia*, severe disturbance in thought processes and

interpersonal relations, or one of the *affective psychoses*, severe disturbance of mood and feeling. *Psychosomatic disorders* are physical symptoms caused by stress, while *personality disorders* involve problems such as alcoholism and violent or antisocial behavior. It is important to remember, however, that there is often much disagreement in diagnosing forms of mental illness because of the overlap in symptoms.

Various methods of measuring mental illness have been used, from comparing hospital records of psychiatric treatment to surveying the general population and having psychiatrists make diagnoses on the basis of interviews. Whether the criteria used are classic symptoms, general "unhappiness," or simply deviation from the "norm," these methods of measuring mental disorder do not usually take into account environmental factors such as the subculture to which the person belongs. The number of patients hospitalized has decreased, but the number of people receiving outpatient treatment has increased. The mentally ill are more likely than the average person to be unmarried or poor, but social scientists are not at all sure of the causal connection between mental illness and marital or economic status. They do not know which causes which.

Some kinds of mental illness, especially schizophrenia, seem to have a genetic origin. Other possible physiological bases for mental illness have been suggested through research with drugs that seem to produce certain psychotic symptoms. *Psychoanalytic theory*, founded through the work of Freud, attributes most mental illness to a faulty development of the individual and to the inner personality conflicts that result. Treatment based on this theory has not been very successful, though. *Learning theorists*, on the other hand, claim that "abnormal" behavior patterns are learned through conditioning in the same way as "normal" ones are. Treatment using this theory has been more successful, but it is important to remember that this does not confirm the theory that learning is the *cause* of mental illness.

Social-psychological theories focus on society's responses to bizarre behavior. Scheff claims that mental illness is a label attached to deviance that cannot otherwise be easily categorized and that when the label is ignored, the "abnormal" behavior disappears by itself. Critics, however, claim that this position fails to account for recovery of the labeled person or for the severe psychoses that exist across cultures, regardless of a society's response.

The only middle-range sociological theory that contributes much to the study of mental illness is *strain theory*, which describes it as a "retreat" from the frustration of lower-class status and of downward mobility of some of the middle class. Critics of this point of view claim that downward mobility does not cause mental illness. Their research has shown instead that mental illness is a cause of downward mobility. In examining possible societal sources of mental illness, some theorists have claimed that urbanization has contributed to mental illness, but this idea has not been substantiated. Others have called for a redistribution of power and the eradication of the inequality that leads disproportionate numbers of the lower classes to become mentally ill.

The traditional response to mental illness has been to confine the patient, but recent approaches have focused on the community. The Community Mental Health Act of 1963 established many community mental-health centers to provide services to the poor and alternatives to institutionalization. The goal is to disrupt or change the person's social environment as little as possible. If these centers are able to accomplish their goals, agencies may approach the more complicated goal of *preventing* mental illness.

SUGGESTED READINGS

Goffman, E. *Asylums*. New York: Doubleday, 1961.

Kohn, Melvin L. *Class and Conformity: A Study in Values*. Homewood, Ill.: Dorsey Press, 1969.

Mechanic, David. *Mental Health and Social Policy*. Englewood Cliffs, N.J.: Prentice-Hall, 1969.

Ryan, William (ed.). *Distress in the City*. Cleveland: Case Western Reserve University Press, 1969.

Szasz, T. "The Myth of Mental Illness," *American Psychologist*, 15 (1960) 113–118.

Rule a nation with justice. Wage war with surprise moves.
Become master of the universe without striving. How do I
know that this is so? Because of this. The more laws and
restrictions there are, the poorer people become. The sharper men's
weapons, the more trouble in the land. The more ingenious
and clear men are, the more strange things happen. The
more rules and regulations, the more thieves and robbers.
  Therefore, the sage says: I take no action and the people
are reformed. I enjoy peace and people become honest.
I do nothing and people become rich. I have no
desires and people return to the good and simple life.
                                        Lao Tsu

Bruce M. Dean

6

Crime
and
Delinquency

All human groups maintain some set of norms—rules about what members are expected to do and not to do under certain circumstances. All groups impose considerable pressure on members to conform to the norms. And although such group pressure is effective enough to make most people conform most of the time, no one has ever found a group so effective that everyone obeyed its norms all of the time. Deviance is also a universal feature of groups.

Groups consider some forms of deviance relatively harmless and therefore make little effort to punish some instances of norm violation. They take other forms of deviance extremely seriously. Indeed, nearly all human groups have regarded some norm violations as so serious that they have made death the appropriate punishment.

As human societies became more complex, the enforcement of norms shifted from informal to formal procedures. Certain norms were enacted into legal codes, and the state assumed responsibility for determining guilt and assigning punishments. Thus, the concept of deviance applies to all norm violations, but crime applies only to deviance that is prohibited by law.

PART I: THE PROBLEM
CRIME AND DELINQUENCY

In Western societies, the criminal law slowly emerged from the practice of private vengeance. A doctrine developed that injury to an individual was not a private concern but a public one because such actions were harmful to the community as a whole. Thus, the right of vengeance was taken out of the hands of the injured parties (or their family) and was assumed by the state (Quinney, 1969; Clark and Marshall, 1967). The modern state provides for the protection of its citizens by the enactment and enforcement of laws.

THE FOCUS OF CRIME

Because crime is whatever the law prohibits, it is clear that crime is rooted in politics. What is and is not lawful in any society is the result of political decisions. As we point out later, functionalists and conflict theorists disagree vigorously on which criteria societies use when they define legality and enact criminal laws.

The fact that there are variations in legal definitions makes it evident that crime is a *relative* concept. Some actions that are against the law in one society are legal in another. Among Eskimos, for example, killing the elderly used to be customary (Cavan and Cavan, 1968); in the United States it is murder. Similarly, what is legal or illegal changes over time within the same society. Abortion used to be a serious criminal offense. Narcotics use was legal until recent times—Coca-Cola contained cocaine until 1903. Because legal definitions change, crime changes. Thus, all discussions of crime depend on what is against the law at the time and place in question.

Nevertheless, certain actions—murder, rape, robbery, and burglary—are classified as criminal in virtually all societies that have laws. Descriptions of acts that fit each of these crimes may differ from society to society, but societies seem to agree on general categories of crime.

158

Our discussion of crime will focus on the laws of the United States. We will concentrate on serious offenses that are least subject to differences in legal definition over time and from place to place. Crimes that take the form of interpersonal violence seem importantly different from crimes against property. For example, the motives for beating a wife or child, for knifing a drinking companion, or for picking a fistfight with a neighbor seem significantly different from those involved in stealing and robbing for material gain. Similarly, sex crimes—rape, child molesting, and the like—and vice crimes, such as prostitution—are also importantly different from property crimes. We discuss crimes of violence, sex crimes, and prostitution in later chapters. Vice crimes other than prostitution are dealt with only in passing. In part, this omission reflects the lack of widespread concern about vice these days. Many former vice crimes have recently been legalized—for example, abortion, and in many states, gambling. Others that remain prohibited are rarely subject to legal penalties—homosexuality, for example.

Our coverage of white-collar crimes, such as embezzlement, stock swindles, and consumer

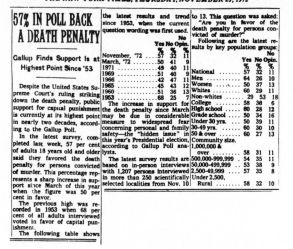

Figure 6.1 *Crime is a relative concept—so are our definitions of what constitutes proper punishment. Changing attitudes toward crime and the treatment of offenders are reflected in public opinion polls on the death penalty for murder (reported in a 1972 Gallup poll). A shift in public attitudes may also lead to changes in the law through legislative or judicial action.*

Figure 6.2 *Adults and juveniles differ in their involvement in various violations of the law. Some offenses, of course, apply only to juveniles, for example, running away from home or being on the streets after the curfew hour. But for other offenses, age limits do not apply. Vandalism is primarily committed by juveniles; larceny is primarily an adult offense.*
(Adapted from Uniform Crime Reports, 1972.)

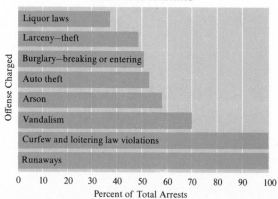

fraud is limited. But we discuss white-collar crime briefly in Part II and include an article that assesses possible bias in the way the courts deal with white-collar crime, using the Watergate sentences as a case study. Most varieties of white-collar crime are better understood in terms of the operation of the economy, the government, corporate power, and the structure of the legal system than they are in terms of individual deviance. With white-collar offenders, it is not so much the question of why they do it as why they are permitted or even encouraged to do it. If the odds are very good that one can successfully sell millions in fraudulent or forged stock to major financial institutions, it is likely that people will do so. And it is not hard to understand why people abscond to Latin America with embezzled millions (and why they cease doing so when new extradition treaties destroy these safe havens). It is less obvious why someone would try to earn a living by sticking up small grocery stores. Such actions do force us to theorize about individual human behavior.

Our primary focus here is on what the police commonly call "street crime" (although much of it does not actually happen in the streets). Our concern is to describe and explain common crimes against persons and property. However, juvenile crime is necessarily defined more broadly.

THE IDEA OF DELINQUENCY

No society judges crime only on the basis of the act committed. Societies have invariably recognized that some people are less responsible than others for their actions. Indeed, laws typically specify which people are not to be held responsible for violations, and most legal codes include some conception of diminished responsibility—that the action of "naturall fooles, or other persons that bee non compos mentis," or not of sound mind, should not be judged in the same way as the actions of normal persons (Sanders, 1970).

All legal codes that survive in the historical record make *age* a critical determinant of criminal responsibility. The age of responsibility varies from code to code—from as low as seven to as high as twenty-one—but all codes treat children more leniently than adults. In earlier times, the law took age into account by authorizing a softer penalty or simply by excluding children from the application of some law; one seventeenth-century English criminal code says, "it is not Burglary in an Infant of fourteene years of age" (Sanders, 1970). More recently, the legal system has taken a much more active course in dealing with juvenile offenses. Since the turn of the century, we have redefined juvenile delinquency.

Changes in the way our society conceived of and dealt with youthful offenders occurred in response to a social movement. It began when a group of Americans organized themselves to agitate for the rescue and reform of "wayward youth." This group, which successfully defined juvenile delinquency as a social problem, had no youthful offenders in its ranks, however. Its members were predominantly upper-middle-class feminist reformers. In his recent study of this historical movement, Anthony Platt (1969) calls them "the child savers." Child saving was the moral justification they used to appeal for the creation of special new judicial and correctional institutions for dealing with troublesome young people.

These reformers thought that poor home conditions and the evils of urban slums propelled youth into trouble and eventually into a life of crime; however, they viewed adolescent crime as a temporary and reversible manifestation of the deplorable social conditions to which youth were exposed. The implication for action was clear to the child savers: As Charles Cooley observed, "When an individual actually enters upon a criminal career, let us try to catch him at a tender age, and subject him to rational social discipline" (Platt, 1969).

The child savers lobbied for and ultimately helped pass the Juvenile Court Act of 1899, which established in Illinois the first official juvenile court in this country; in less than two decades, all but three states had followed suit. As a result of the proliferation of juvenile courts, proceedings involving juveniles were conducted differently from proceedings involving adults: Juvenile-court proceedings were informal, and the court could use wide discretion in deciding how to resolve the problems of juveniles so that they might enter the mainstream of society.

159

It followed from the child savers' philosophy that the problem must be nipped in the bud: The earliest indications that a youth was being attracted to the "evils" of urban life required remedial action. Thus, many reforms imposed sanctions on conduct unbecoming to youth and disqualified them from adult privileges. Reform efforts were aimed largely at strictly supervising children's leisure and recreational activities. Activities of youth that came under the purview of the juvenile courts included not only behavior that would be criminal if committed by adults but also behavior that would be a violation of the law only when committed by juveniles, for example, breaking curfews, being truant, drinking, or frequenting billiard parlors and bars (Platt, 1969). These acts were prohibited and came under the jurisdiction of the juvenile court because they were viewed as "predelinquent" behavior that might lead to serious criminal violations if no action were taken.

According to the Illinois Juvenile Court Act of 1899, "the words delinquent child shall include any child under the age of 16 years who violates any law of this State or any city or village ordinance." However, by 1905, the Act had been amended to read:

The words delinquent child shall include any male child under the age of seventeen years or any female child under the age of eighteen years who violates any law of this State or any city or village ordinance; or who is incorrigible; or who knowingly associates with thieves, vicious or immoral persons; or who, without just cause and without the consent of its parents or custodian, absents itself from its home or place of abode, or who is growing up in idleness or crime; or who knowingly frequents a house of ill-repute; or who knowingly frequents any policy shop or place where any gaming device is operated; or who frequents any saloon or dram shop where intoxicating liquors are sold; or who patronizes or visits any public pool room or bucket shop; or who wanders about the streets in the night time without being on any lawful business or occupation; or who habitually wanders about any railroad yards or tracks or jumps or attempts to jump onto any moving train; or enters any car or engine without lawful authority; or who habitually uses vile, obscene, vulgar, profane or indecent language; or who is guilty of immoral conduct in any public place or about any school house. Any child committing any of the acts herein mentioned shall be deemed a delinquent child and shall be proceeded against as such in the manner herinafter provided.

In Anthony Platt's view, the juvenile-court movement focused attention on, and thereby "invented," new categories of youthful deviance. In this instance, behavior that was once informally handled—or even ignored—came under the control of government agencies (Platt, 1969). The wide range of behavior that has come to be considered delinquent may help to explain why one

out of every six American males will be referred to a juvenile court before he reaches his eighteenth birthday (President's Commission on Law Enforcement and the Administration of Justice, 1967b). If there is more juvenile crime today than there used to be, it may be because we now count more acts as offenses. It is in this sense that Platt speaks of the "invention" of delinquency, and it is also in this sense that delinquency is a new social phenomenon.

COUNTING CRIMES

Crime and delinquency are defined as acts prohibited by law. The definition is clear: every time a car is stolen, a drugstore is held up, or a woman's purse is snatched, a crime has been committed. The total of such acts in a given year is the amount of crime that occurred that year. However, in order to make comparisons, one needs to know the amount of crime in relation to population size. When the number of crimes is divided by the population size, the result is a *crime rate*. (The result is ordinarily multiplied by 100,000 to avoid working with very small decimals, and thus we speak of crime rates per 100,000 persons in the population. At the end of 1972, for example, it was computed that 8.9 homicides had occurred that year for every 100,000 Americans.)

Crime rates are fundamental to all discussions of crime in society: Is crime increasing or decreasing? What are the effects of various laws or programs on reducing crime? What kinds of crimes are occurring how often? Few questions taken up in this book match these in terms of the extent of public anxiety, conflict, political exploitation, and pontification that they have produced during the past decade. People on all sides fear to walk the streets; home-security appliances have enjoyed a bonanza market; politicians promise law and order; and prophets proclaim the doom of a society overwhelmed by criminality.

Despite this immense concern, the shocking fact is that crime statistics are inaccurate and unreliable. Thus it is often difficult to make more than an educated guess about the kind and amount of crime that occurs today and about whether the amount represents an increase or a decrease from that of previous years. We will discuss the four main sources of statistics about crime in America and point out the more important defects in each. Only then can we undertake cautious conclusions about the nature and extent of American crime.

Official Crime Statistics

The most publicized and detailed crime statistics in the United States are those gathered from official law enforcement agencies and collated and pub-

161

Figure 6.3   Juvenile mischief, which may be tolerated and handled informally by adults in rural communities, often results in formal police action, a juvenile arrest record, and criminal labeling in large urban centers. Even using water from a fire hydrant to cool off during the heat of a big-city summer may result in police action. And boys breaking windows in a slum clearance project would surely be labeled and treated as vandals by the police in any large city. The inability of the police in urban areas to treat juveniles informally may contribute to the rising rate of juvenile delinquency and crime.

lished by the FBI as the *Uniform Crime Reports* (UCR). Local police agencies send to the FBI monthly and annual summary reports on crimes in their jurisdiction; these provide the basis for the UCR statistics. These reports include data on the number of offenses discovered by or reported to these law enforcement agencies. There are seven categories of offenses:

1. Murder and nonnegligent homicide (all willful homicides as distinguished from deaths caused by negligence).
2. Forcible rape (including assault to rape and attempted rape).
3. Robbery (stealing or taking anything of value by force or threat of force).
4. Aggravated assault (assault with intent to kill or to do great bodily harm).
5. Burglary (breaking or unlawful entry into a structure with the intent to commit a felony or theft—includes attempts).
6. Larceny over $50 (theft of items of more than $50 in value without force, threat of force, or fraud; excludes embezzlement and forgery).
7. Auto theft (stealing or driving away in a vehicle without lawful consent).

The FBI calls the first four offenses on the list *violent crimes* because each has a component of violence or threat of violence. The last three offenses are called *property offenses*. The seven offenses are collectively called *index offenses*.

Newspaper stories that report higher or lower crime rates for your city, for your state, or for the nation are based on changes in the UCR index of offenses. Sad to say, the statistics that inform such stories may not accurately reflect what is really going on.

One source of inconsistency is local authorities, whose participation is voluntary. In 1972, police agencies that had jurisdiction over about 7 percent of the population did not cooperate. The proportion giving reports varies from year to year, with obvious consequences for comparing one year with another (Kelley, 1972). A second problem is that local authorities differ considerably in the way they classify offenses. For example, some reporting agencies would classify as robbery an incident in which a school child forced a classmate to surrender his lunch money; other agencies would not. A third source of error is primitive and inaccurate record keeping and reports that reflect a lot of guessing and faking. For example, several years ago a major West Coast city police department reported—allegedly from the same set of records—more crime to the state than to the FBI. An additional problem stems from the fact that the local law enforcement agencies frequently intentionally overreport or underreport crime, sometimes by changing the basis for classifying crimes and sometimes by falsifying the reports. Local pressures may make it expedient for the police or city hall to show by lower crime rates that they are winning the battle to control crime, or by higher crime rates that police need increased budgets or salaries. One clue to such goings-on is when claims of a significant change in the crime rate rest wholly on shifts in burglary and larceny—offenses most easily manipulated—and the change is not reflected in the homicide rate (the presence of, and the need for, a corpse makes this a difficult category of crime to juggle or falsify). Auto theft is also more difficult for the police to manipulate because the insurance companies are able to independently check on this offense and the companies keep thorough records.

An additional serious defect in the UCR statistics is that the FBI index offenses exclude a number of types of serious crime. For example, the index does not include consumer fraud or most kinds of corporate and white-collar crimes. The kid who steals a bike worth more than $50 becomes a larceny statistic; the banker who embezzles $10 million does not. The index offenses also exlude trafficking in drugs, polluting the environment, violating civil rights statutes, fixing prize fights, running a gambling syndicate, running a house of prostitution, and molesting children.

But even if defects in the statistics and their classification were corrected immediately, official crime statistics would still be unreliable indicators of the actual levels of crime in the nation. Even perfect statistics would only tell us the number and kinds of *offenses known to the police.* An immense proportion of actual crimes never become known to the police, for some crimes are never discovered. When a gangland figure drops out of sight, the police may suspect that he has been fitted with cement overshoes and dumped in the river, but unless the body floats up or is otherwise discovered, no homicide will be recorded. Even when crimes are discovered, a great many of them are never reported to the police. For example, more than a third of all robberies and more than two-fifths of all burglaries are never reported.

Victimization Statistics

Through research, we know that an immense amount of crime goes unreported to the police. A few years ago, social scientists decided that it would be worthwhile to try to estimate the extent of crime by consulting *victims* rather than officials. Survey interviewers went to 10,000 homes making up a representative sample of the American population to interview people about crimes committed against them and to members of their family. Interviewers asked them about being burglarized, about being assaulted, about having cars stolen, and so forth—until they had covered a lengthy list of crimes that paralleled the UCR offense index (Ennis, 1967).

Later, we present a picture of crime in America based on victimization survey data. However, we must point out here that these data, too, are misleading. A study conducted by Albert J. Reiss Jr. (1967) determined that because of faulty recall or because of hesitance, a significant number of persons *underreport* the extent of their victimization even to survey interviewers. Reiss selected persons who had several months prior to being interviewed reported to the police that they had been victims of a crime. When interviewed, 20 percent failed to recall, or at least to mention, the incident they had reported. In another study, Anthony G. Turner (1972) discovered an additional source of error in victim surveys. Some respondents tend to telescope time when recalling victimization; that is, some victims who were asked to report on any incidents that had occurred in the past year reported on incidents that had occurred before that time. Telescoping falsely inflates victimization statistics, whereas failure to recall or mention incidents falsely deflates statistics. We are unable to judge whether the one cancels out the other, leaving us with quite accurate estimates, or whether the

estimates that surveys provide are somewhat too high or too low.

Self-Reported Crime

A third basis for estimating crime is to ask people to admit through questionnaires or interviews any criminal acts they have committed. Austin L. Porterfield, in 1946, and James S. Wallerstein and Clement J. Wyle, in 1947, pioneered this approach. Their studies found that persons were willing to admit a considerable amount of criminal activity, the majority of which had never led to their detection or arrest. These studies, too, indicate that official crime statistics greatly underestimate the amount of crime in society.

A number of means have been used to determine whether people will be truthful in self-reports. One of the first studies (Clark and Tifft, 1966) utilized a lie detector (polygraph) to reinterview college students who had just filled out a self-report questionnaire about their illegal activities. They found that 81.5 percent of the individual answers were truthful. Deviant sexual activities were considerably underreported, and fistfighting was considerably overreported. In general, the findings indicated that self-reported data on many standard categories of crime were accurate.

A second study (Gold, 1970) also found self-reported statistics to be relatively accurate. First, the interviewers selected groups of students who were friends and asked them about their own illegal activities and those of others in the group. They then compared every individual's report with reports made about him by his friends. The comparisons revealed that only 17 percent of the individuals failed to reveal an illegal act that several friends had disclosed.

A final way to test the accuracy of self-reports is to compare them with the official records. Travis Hirschi's study (1969), found in Chapter 3, used this procedure. Few of the boys in his sample who had police records denied having them. Similarly, Robert Hardt and George Bodine (1965) found that 95 percent of their respondents told the truth when they claimed to have no police records.

A major shortcoming of self-report measures and of studies to validate them is that they have been used almost exclusively with adolescents. It

163

is possible that young people are more truthful than adults would be when faced with requests to report their illegal behavior.

Public Perceptions of Crime

A final source of data on crime is public opinion. Pollsters, such as Gallup and Harris, frequently ask randomly chosen samples of the American public what they believe about crime, how much they worry about it, what they think ought to be done about it, and so on. Polling people who get their opinions from what they read or hear about official statistics does not tell us much about the actual level of crime in the nation. However, public opinion about whether crime is increasing or decreasing can be a vital source of information on crime *as a social problem.*

What the public believes, whether accurate or not, greatly shapes policies and determines which programs are possible. Furthermore, what the public believes frequently causes them to respond in ways that affect the crime rate. Thus, if the public believes there is a crime wave, they may alter their behavior in ways that influence the incidence of crime. For example, assaults and muggings necessarily decrease if everyone (out of fear of attack) stays off the streets (of course, this might cause an increase in family fights). Or public beliefs about some action may cause its legal prohibition and thereby may increase crime by increasing those acts that will be counted as crimes. Marijuana smoking is an obvious example.

Similarly, crime could easily be decreased if public opinion led to the revoking of many criminal laws. Norval Morris and Gordon Hawkins (1970) have demonstrated that we could make a major cut in the present crime rate simply by treating most vice and "victimless" crimes, such as drunkenness, as noncriminal problems. Furthermore, decriminalizing drug addiction would make drugs easier to obtain and would end a substantial amount of burglary and theft because addicts would no longer be forced to steal. Thus, what the public thinks has considerable impact on crime and on crime rates.

Keeping in mind all the sources of error in various kinds of crime statistics, we now attempt some provisional answers to the questions: How much

164

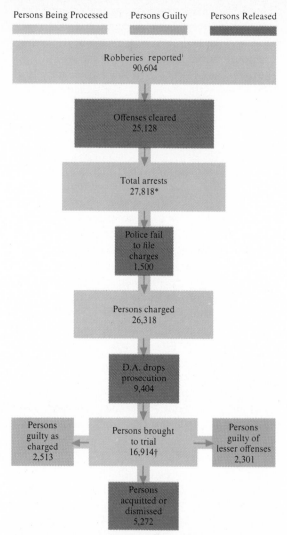

Persons Being Processed   Persons Guilty   Persons Released

Robberies reported[1]
90,604

Offenses cleared
25,128

Total arrests
27,818*

Police fail to file charges
1,500

Persons charged
26,318

D.A. drops prosecution
9,404

Persons guilty as charged
2,513

Persons brought to trial
16,914†

Persons guilty of lesser offenses
2,301

Persons acquitted or dismissed
5,272

[1]2,567 cities; 1972 estimated population 50,966,000
*There is a discrepancy in this number because some offenses resulted in more than one arrest and some offenders arrested committed more than one offense.
†Of persons brought to trial, 6,828 were referred to juvenile court.

Figure 6.4   Because many crimes are never solved, many offenders go unpunished. Even when people are arrested for a crime, they are unlikely to spend time in jail. A sample of burglary cases committed in 1972 reveals the process from offense to jail. Many arrests are dropped by the police for lack of evidence. The prosecutor drops many more for lack of a good case to take to trial. Many persons brought to trial are found "not guilty." And of those finally convicted of burglary, a significant, but unknown, number are not sent to jail but are instead fined or put on probation. Thus, perhaps no more than one out of every twenty-seven persons arrested for burglary in this sample actually went to jail.
(Adapted from Uniform Crime Reports, 1972.)

crime is there? Who commits it? Who are the victims? Is the level of crime changing?

CRIME IN THE UNITED STATES: OFFICIAL RATES

In 1972, the FBI reported 5.9 million index criminal offenses known to the police in the United States that year. Of these, about 5.1 million were *property* crimes—burglary, larceny (over $50), and auto theft. Of the slightly more than 800,000 *violent* crimes, approximately 19,000 were homicides, 46,000 were forcible rapes, 375,000 were robberies, and 389,000 were aggravated assaults.

As noted earlier, by dividing these numbers by the number of persons in the population and then multiplying by 100,000, we can produce crime rates. Such rates permit us to compare one city with another, despite the fact that one may be larger than the other and thus have a larger total number of offenses. We can also use these rates to compare crime in different years, despite the fact that the population has grown considerably between the years in question. Examining such rates—and remembering that the official statistics are unreliable—we can see certain patterns emerge.

For one thing, the crime rate is strongly influenced by city size. In 1972, cities with populations in excess of a quarter million had a violent-offenses rate of 998.6 per 100,000 (that is, there were 998.6 known violent index offenses for every 100,000 people living in large cities), whereas the comparable rate in the rural areas was 128.2 per 100,000. The same year, cities whose populations were over a quarter million had a property-offenses rate of 3,949.3 per 100,000, whereas the comparable rate in rural areas was 1,026.1 per 100,000. These figures underscore the extent to which the crime problem is an urban problem. The risk of being a victim of violent crime in large cities is more than eight times the risk in rural areas, and the risk of being a victim of property crime in large cities is nearly four times the risk in rural areas.

Table 6.1 shows the recent trends in known offenses. The upper half of the figure gives the *number* of known offenses for each category from 1960 through 1972; the lower half of the table gives the

rate per 100,000 for known offenses for each category for the same period. The last row of the table reports the percent increase in the rate per 100,000 for each offense over the 1960 to 1972 period. For example, in 1960, the rate per 100,000 for homicide was 5.0, whereas in 1972 the rate was 8.9—an increase of 78 percent ($3.9 \div 5.0 = .78$). The table shows that the rates for both violent and property crimes increased about 150 percent from 1960 to 1972; of the individual offenses, larceny and robbery show the greatest rate increase and homicide and aggravated assault show the smallest rate increase from 1960 to 1972. It is interesting to observe from Table 6.1 that after many years of generally increasing rates of known offenses, between 1971 and 1972 the rates for robbery, burglary, larceny, and auto theft decreased. It is too early to tell whether this shift represents a temporary lapse or the beginning of a long-term downward trend. Certainly, in comparison with previous year-to-year changes, these recent statistics are encouraging.

As noted at the outset of this discussion, one cannot make firm statements about the level of offenses being committed on the basis of offenses reported in the UCR. Perhaps the difficulty that affects the data most is that, over time, victim *reporting behavior* may change substantially. Thus, if robbery victims in 1972 were more likely to report these victimizations than were robbery victims in 1960, the UCR could show a substantial increase in robbery offenses known to the police, but there would be no actual increase in robberies committed. The UCR data cannot address this problem directly; however, some inferences may be in order.

Some offenses are better reported to the police than others. Homicide is well reported; auto theft, primarily because of insurance regulations, is consistently reported to the police. Thus, it is likely that increases in the rates of these two offenses (homicide, 78 percent and auto theft, 133 percent) reflect *real* increases in offenses committed. On the other hand, some of the increase in the rate of rape from 1960 to 1972 *may* reflect increased reporting behavior, which could have resulted from changing social attitudes (see Chapter 8). For offenses such as robbery and larceny, it is difficult to

Table 6.1   Index Offenses Known, United States, 1960–1972

YEAR AND POPULATION[1]	TOTAL CRIME INDEX	VIOLENT CRIME[2]	PROPERTY CRIME[2]	HOMICIDE	FORCIBLE RAPE	ROBBERY
		Number of Offenses				
1960—179,323,175	2,019,600	285,980	1,733,600	9,030	17,030	107,340
1965—193,818,000	2,937,400	384,020	2,553,400	9,880	23,200	138,040
1970—203,184,772	5,581,200	732,940	4,848,300	15,860	37,650	348,240
1971—206,256,000	5,995,200	810,020	5,185,200	17,630	41,890	385,910
1972—208,232,000	5,891,900	828,150	5,063,800	18,520	46,430	374,560
		Rate per 100,000 Inhabitants				
1960	1,126.2	159.5	966.7	5.0	9.5	59.9
1965	1,515.5	198.1	1,317.4	5.1	12.0	71.2
1970	2,746.9	360.7	2,386.1	7.8	18.5	171.4
1971	2,906.7	392.7	2,514.0	8.5	20.3	187.1
1972	2,829.5	397.7	2,431.8	8.9	22.3	179.9
Percent increase						
1960–1972	+151.2	+149.3	+151.6	+78.0	+134.7	+200.3

[1]Population is Bureau of the Census provisional estimates as of July 1, except April 1, 1960 and 1970 census.
[2]Violent crime is offenses of homicide, forcible rape, robbery, and aggravated assault. Property crime is offenses of burglary, larceny $50 and over, and auto theft.
Source: Adapted from Uniform Crime Reports, *Crime in the United States* (Washington: U.S. Government Printing Office, 1972).

166

imagine that the whole rate increase (more than 200 percent) could be accounted for by changes in victim reporting or by other extraneous changes.

Delinquency Cases

Official records regarding the extent of juvenile delinquency in the United States are found primarily in records of the juvenile courts, but there is no uniform, nationwide reporting program for these courts. Therefore, in order to estimate the number of delinquency cases that the courts process, the Department of Health, Education and Welfare (HEW) collects data from a sample of courts from which national estimates are made (U.S. Department of Health, Education, and Welfare, 1970). These data indicate that in 1970 more than one million delinquency cases were processed in juvenile courts in the United States. According to the HEW report, the rate of delinquency cases processed in the United States has risen steadily: For youths aged ten to seventeen, there were 1,980 cases per 100,000 in 1957; 2,360 cases per 100, 000 in 1965; and 3,230 cases per 100,000 in 1970. In 1970, juvenile courts serving urban areas processed 5,190 cases per 100,000 youths. The comparable rates for semi-urban courts and rural courts were 4,350 and 1,830, respectively. These juve-

nile court data attest to the fact that the delinquency problem is disproportionately urban. Regrettably, the nature of the juvenile cases processed is not reported by HEW. However, by examining data on characteristics of arrested persons—both adults and juveniles—some inferences can be drawn about the nature of the offenses for which juveniles are sent to juvenile court.

Who Is Arrested?

Just as nationwide information on known offenses is compiled by the FBI and reported annually in the UCR, so, too, is information on arrests. In 1972, arrest information was reported to the FBI by police agencies that had jurisdictions over a little more than three-fourths of the American population. In 1972, there were 5.9 million known index offenses, but only 1.7 million arrests made in the nation for index offenses. Many factors affect the likelihood that an offense will result in an arrest: the nature of the offense, whether there were witnesses, whether clues were left by the offender, the quality of the police investigation conducted, and so on. Perhaps most closely tied to the likelihood of arrest is the type of offense committed; for example, in 1972, four out of five murders and seven out of ten aggravated assaults were resolved by

Table 6.1 Index Offenses Known, United States, 1960–1972 (continued)

YEAR AND POPULATION[1]	TOTAL CRIME INDEX	AGGRAVATED ASSAULT	BURGLARY	AUTO THEFT	LARCENY $50 AND OVER
		Number of Offenses			
1960—179,323,175	2,019,600	152,580	900,400	325,900	507,300
1965—193,818,000	2,937,400	212,900	1,266,000	493,400	794,000
1970—203,184,772	5,581,200	331,190	2,176,600	921,900	1,749,800
1971—206,256,000	5,995,200	364,600	2,368,400	941,600	1,875,200
1972—208,232,000	5,891,900	388,650	2,345,000	881,000	1,837,800
		Rate per 100,000 Inhabitants			
1960	1,126.2	85.1	502.1	181.7	282.9
1965	1,515.5	109.8	653.2	254.6	409.7
1970	2,746.9	163.0	1,071.2	453.7	861.2
1971	2,906.7	176.8	1,148.3	456.5	909.2
1972	2,829.5	186.6	1,126.1	423.1	882.6
Percent increase					
1960–1972	+151.2	+119.3	+124.3	+132.9	+212.0

[1]Population is Bureau of the Census provisional estimates as of July 1, except April 1, 1960 and 1970 census.
Source: Adapted from Uniform Crime Reports, *Crime in the United States* (Washington: U.S. Government Printing Office, 1972).

arrest, but less than one out of five larcenies and auto thefts were so resolved. The offenses most often resulting in arrest are face-to-face violent offenses: The victim, of course, observes the offender in these crimes—in fact, the victim and offender in violent offenses are often acquainted. In 1972, one-quarter of the murders and the majority of the aggravated assaults were committed by one family member against another (Kelley, 1972); in many of the remaining murders and aggravated assaults, the victim and the offender were often friends or at least acquaintances.

In examining data on characteristics of arrested persons, it is important to bear in mind that those arrested for a particular type of offense, especially property offenses, are only a sample of offenders, for many elude arrest. It may well be that arrested offenders have different characteristics from those of offenders not arrested. Many people who are arrested are ultimately acquitted, have the charges against them dropped, or are convicted of a less serious offense; unfortunately, no nationwide data on convictions exist. The arrest data are the only data currently available that can give us an indication of the characteristics of apprehended offenders. In 1972, nearly all those arrested for rape, robbery, burglary, and auto theft were males. Of those arrested for larceny, three out of ten were female; of those arrested for murder and aggravated assault, about one out of six were female.

The data show that arrestees tend to be relatively young. More than half of those arrested for property offenses are under eighteen years of age; more than four out of five of those arrested for these property offenses are under twenty-five years of age. The data with respect to the age of arrestees can be misleading if one fails to take into account the proportion of the United States population that is under twenty-five years of age. The 1970 census shows that about 46 percent of the population in the United States was under twenty-five years of age. Thus, the proportions of those arrested for murder and aggravated assault who were under twenty-five (44 percent and 47 percent, respectively) were about equal to their representation in the population. The proportions of those arrested for the remaining offenses were substantially larger than their representation. Children under thirteen years of age account for 26 percent of the population at large, but they account for only about 3 percent of all arrests; thus, arrests of those in the fourteen to twenty-four-year-old age group for all index offenses are proportionately greater than their representation in the population.

167

The data also show that racial characteristics of arrestees vary markedly by offense. Only about one-third of those arrested for property offenses were nonwhite, but more than three out of five of those arrested for murder and robbery and about half of those arrested for rape and aggravated assault were nonwhite. The UCR arrest data covered only about 75 percent of the United States population in 1972, so it is very difficult to estimate the proportions of whites and nonwhites included in the areas covered; it is probable, however, that these areas are disproportionately urban. In 1970, 15 percent of those in urban areas were nonwhite. If this figure is taken as an estimate of the proportion of nonwhites in the areas served by the police agencies who report arrest data to the FBI for the UCR, then nonwhites are disproportionately represented among the arrestees for all the index offenses—especially robbery, murder, and rape.

A word of caution: These are arrest data only. As such, they are measures of police activity and may or may not reflect offender behavior; that is, police may respond in different ways during encounters with different kinds of offenders. For all these reasons, arrest data must be viewed cautiously, and any interpretation of the figures must consider the possibility that several factors operate to produce and alter these statistics.

Crime Rates Based on Victim Reports

We have already discussed the way interviews with a sample of the population may be used as a basis for estimating crime rates. The results of a survey can easily be projected for the nation as a whole and then used to construct crime rates per 100,000 people. In this way, data for the seven UCR index offense categories were collected from 10,000 families in the 1967 survey (Ennis, 1967). To no one's surprise, the results showed that there was substantially more serious crime committed in the United States than the UCR statistics showed—overall, the victim survey uncovered about twice as much crime than FBI statistics revealed. For example, whereas the UCR larceny rate per 100,000 was 267.4, it was 360.8 according to the victim survey.

In spite of the fact that the victim survey showed higher rates, the two sources of data agreed closely in some respects. Both sources of information showed that Northeastern, North Central, and Southern states had similar rates of index offenses but that Western states had a considerably higher rate of index offenses; in addition, just as it was pointed out earlier that the UCR showed a much higher rate of violent offenses in metropolitan areas than in rural areas, so did the victim survey. Finally, both the UCR and the victim survey indicate that about five out of six index offenses are property offenses.

Who Are the Victims?

One of the most important aspects of the victim-survey technique is that it provides information about the characteristics of victims—an important area that is virtually ignored by the UCR. Generally speaking, victims of index crimes are more often male, nonwhite, and from lower socioeconomic groups; for the crimes of aggravated assault, robbery, and rape, the victims are more likely to fall between the ages of twenty and twenty-nine. So victims of crimes have some of the characteristics of those arrested for crimes.

Table 6.2   Victim Survey Rates of Index Offenses Against the Person and Against Property, per 100,000 Population by Income and Race, United States, 1965–1966

TYPE OF CRIME	INCOME UNDER $6,000		INCOME $6,000 OR MORE	
	White	Black	White	Black
Against Person	402	748	244	262
Against Property	1,829	1,927	1,765	3,024

Source: Adapted from Philip H. Ennis, *Criminal Victimization in the United States,* Field Surveys II, A Report of a National Survey, President's Commission on Law Enforcement and Administration of Justice (Washington: U.S. Government Printing Office, 1967), p. 32.

Table 6.2 presents victim survey rates of crimes against the person (the same as violent crimes) and crimes against property per 100,000 population in various race and income categories. In the lower-income category, blacks are substantially more likely than whites to have been victims of crimes against the person and slightly more likely than whites to have been victims of crimes against property. In the higher-income group, blacks were slightly more likely to have been victims of crimes against the person and substantially more likely to have been victims of crimes against property.

Regardless of race, those in the lower-income group were more likely to have been victims than those in the higher-income group, with one dramatic exception—blacks in the higher-income group had a higher property-crime victimization rate than any other group. This exception may well reflect the fact that racially segregated housing, more often the rule than the exception in the United States, produces neighborhoods in which only blacks—but black residents with varying incomes—live. In such a situation, it seems likely that the relatively small number of well-to-do residents of the neighborhood would be the targets for crimes against property.

As we have noted, males are generally more often victims of index crimes than females are. However, when race is taken into account, some exceptions emerge. Among whites, males are more than twice as likely as females to be robbed and four times as likely as females to suffer aggravated assaults; however, black females more often than black males are victims of robberies and aggravated assaults.

Victims of offenses against the person are likely to be relatively young. For example, the robbery and aggravated assault rates for females in the age group of twenty to twenty-nine are substantially higher than for females in any other age group. Males in this age group are more than twice as likely to suffer assault and are 20 percent more likely to be victims of robbery than are males in any other age group.

When the race of the offender was known to the victim—probably most often in face-to-face offenses—both the victim and the offender were generally of the same race. When the victim was white, 88 percent of the offenders whose race was known were identified as white; when the victim was nonwhite, 81 percent of the offenders were identified as nonwhite.

There are considerable grounds for being suspicious of arrest statistics that show a substantial overrepresentation of blacks. Racial differences in arrest rates can readily be manufactured by police actions. Indeed, police action appears to play a big role in the racial differences in official juvenile

records. Whatever racial differences in adult arrest statistics mean, one thing seems certain: the image of black criminals preying upon whites is simply false. Most crime is *intra*racial not *inter*racial; it occurs within rather than between races. And blacks are more likely than whites to be victims of crimes. Indeed, upper-income blacks are almost twice as likely as upper-income whites to suffer property crimes.

SELF-REPORTS

Self-reports of criminal behavior have proved relatively truthful, but most of the self-report data have been limited to the behavior of juveniles. Despite this limit, the findings have turned out to be quite informative.

Self-report studies generally show a high level of reported involvement in illegal behavior, even among samples of high-school students (Empey and Erickson, 1966; Dentler and Monroe, 1961). Lamar Empey and Maynard Erickson found that their respondents reported "violations running into the thousands" (1966). Although many of these activities were not serious, some of them—such as theft, assault, and use of drugs—would have resulted in police and court action if they had been detected. However, over 90 percent of illegal acts reported by juveniles go undetected by the police (Gold, 1970; Empey and Erickson, 1966). The relatively high level of reported illegal behavior among juveniles holds not only for samples drawn from rural, suburban, and urban areas in the United States (Clark and Wenninger, 1962; Dentler and Monroe, 1961) but also for samples drawn from Canada (Vaz, 1967), Oslo and Helsinki (Anttik and Jaakkola, 1966), Stockholm (Elmhorn, 1965), and London (Belson, 1969).

Sex and Age

Although males report engaging in illegal behavior substantially more frequently than females do, the *pattern* of illegal behavior that males and females report engaging in is similar; that is, males and females most frequently engage in the same illegal acts (Hindelang, 1971; Gold, 1970). The belief that adolescent females engage primarily in sex delinquency and running away and not in theft,

169

property destruction, fighting, and drug use appears unfounded.

Many researchers have found a small relationship between age and the extent of reported delinquency. Travis Hirschi (1969) and John Clark and Eugene Wenninger (1962) found that delinquency tends to increase during adolescence until it peaks at fourteen or fifteen years of age; after that, it declines. Martin Gold (1970), on the other hand, found that delinquency continues to increase through later adolescence. These inconsistencies among studies are of minor importance, however. We may not be sure exactly when delinquency begins to drop off, but we do know that eventually it drops off very greatly. Only a small minority of those who commit juvenile offenses continue to be offenders during their adult years.

Class

Many researchers have used self-report studies to examine the relationship between social class and delinquency. Some results have shown no relationship (Dentler and Monroe, 1961; Short and Nye, 1957). Others have found a very slight tendency for those from well-to-do homes to engage in less delinquency (Gold, 1970; Hirschi, 1969). Others have found this upper-class group to be slightly more delinquency prone (Williams and Gold, 1972; Voss, 1966). The best interpretation of these research findings is that there is either no relationship between social class and delinquency or a very slight and inconsistent one. We return to this question later and attempt to assess its theoretical implications.

PUBLIC ATTITUDES TOWARD CRIME

Public perceptions of the extent of the crime problem—although they may be very inaccurate indicators of the actual amount of crime—may be quite useful in our understanding of the nature and the effects of the crime problem.

In 1965, a national sample of respondents were asked, "Is there any place around here—that is, within a mile—where you would be afraid to walk alone at night?" To this question, 17 percent of the men and 49 percent of the women replied yes. In 1972, 20 percent of the men and 58 percent of the

women said yes to the same question. In 1972, twice as many people age fifty and over (49 percent) as people age eighteen to twenty (24 percent) were fearful. Twice as many people with incomes under $3,000 (58 percent) as people with incomes over $15,000 (28 percent) were fearful. And twice as many urban dwellers (53 percent) as rural dwellers (24 percent) were fearful (Gallup, 1972).

In the period from 1965 to 1972, the rate of index crime increased 90 percent, yet fear of walking alone at night in the streets near one's own neighborhood increased only slightly, perhaps because people believed that the crime problem was really a problem in other people's neighborhoods. The available data suggest that nonwhites, those with lower incomes, females, urban residents, and older people have greater apprehensions about being victimized.

A national survey in 1966 (Ennis, 1967) asked whether respondents were concerned about having their houses broken into. In this study, 11 percent of the white males, 22 percent of the nonwhite males, 14 percent of the white females, and 25 percent of the nonwhite females answered that they were very concerned. The same subjects were asked how likely they thought it was "that a person will be robbed or attacked around here." One out of five white males and females and two out of five nonwhite males and females thought it likely. The fact that blacks are more likely than whites to be victims of both violent crimes and property crimes seems to be reflected in their generally higher levels of apprehensiveness about being crime victims.

Throughout the late 1960s, crime was very much on the public mind and was given very high priority when national samples were interviewed about the most pressing political issues facing the nation. After 1972, however, the Watergate scandals and economic troubles—inflation and the energy crisis—began to take center stage. The public did not become less anxious about crime but people simply became even more worried about other economic problems. Sales of handguns, locks, burglar alarms, and guard dogs remained, and still remain, at high levels—presumably a reflection of the public's ongoing concern about the high incidence of crime.

Figure 6.5   One indicator of the degree of public concern about the prevalence of crime in any given area is the number of warning signs one sees posted. Warnings may also affect crime rates. For example, there will be fewer muggings if people no longer walk alone in areas where crimes have been frequent.

We can draw a number of possible conclusions from the data we have presented. Despite defects in the data, it seems almost certain that crime has risen appreciably in the United States during the past ten years. Furthermore, the official statistics on which we base our national concern about rising crime greatly underestimate the extent of the problem. Data collected from crime victims and self-reports of criminal actions suggest that there is much more crime than is ever reported. Furthermore, the level of crime in the nation is high enough to make many Americans afraid to walk the streets and anxious about the safety of their homes. One consequence of these public fears has been massive purchases of handguns. More firearms have resulted in a higher homicide rate as well as in more deaths through accidental gunshot wounds. Finally, all these statistics refer only to street crimes. Organized crime, corporate and white-collar crime, crimes of discrimination, and vice crimes are in addition to the types of crime we have discussed.

171

Clearly, some politicians and pundits have played on and exploited public fears about crime for personal or partisan reasons, but that does not mean that the problem does not exist. However, by itself, concern may do more harm than good—by flooding the nation with handguns, for example. Concern must be matched with realistic and effective policies. But to make effective policies requires an understanding of why crime occurs.

PART II: SOURCES
CRIME AND DELINQUENCY

Theories of crime and policies for dealing with criminals are as old as recorded history. Indeed, the Book of Ezekiel reported a crime wave in 600 B.C. and regarded crime, even then, as an urban problem—"the city is full of violence" (7:23). Three hundred years later, Aristotle argued that crime results from too much affluence, not from economic deprivation (*Politics*, 322 B.C.). Throughout history, people have looked for the causes of crime. The Roman historian Livy blamed irrationality. Others blamed greed and lust. Napoleon blamed religion. Countless church leaders have blamed godlessness. However, until relatively modern times, little effort was made to test any of these ideas. Before the development of social science, few people related criminal behavior to social influences—most made asssertions about character, or the lack of it, in individuals.

THE CLASSICAL AND POSITIVE SCHOOLS

Crime is one of the oldest acknowledged social problems and one of the very earliest to stimulate systematic social-science inquiry. Two important schools of criminological thought developed in Europe during the eighteenth and nineteenth centuries, and their views continue to influence conceptions of crime.

The Classical School

172

Modern criminology began in a book originally published anonymously in 1764 in Italy. The author, Cesare Beccaria, feared that the radical reforms he recommended in his book, *Of Crimes and Punishments,* would cause him political trouble. Although he granted that society had the right to punish those who violate its laws, he insisted on the guarantee of certain safeguards: Offenses and their punishments must be written out in advance; restrictions on individual freedom (laws) should be as few as possible; and punishments imposed by the state should correspond in severity to the offense committed.

The central premise of Beccaria's work was a conception of human beings as rational and as free to choose how to act. However, he also argued that society can influence individual actions by threatening to punish certain kinds of behavior. It followed that if the costs of the punishment outweigh the pleasure or benefits gained by violation of the law and if one is certain to be punished, then one will obey the law. This position is fundamental to what came to be called the *Classical School* in criminology. It has much in common with social-learning and social-control theories of deviance.

Perhaps the major figure in the Classical School was Jeremy Bentham, an English philosopher, social reformer, and eccentric. Bentham is famous for his moral calculus. He proposed that decisions about whether to commit a certain act should be based on the consequences of the act, which are

Figure 6.6   Levels of Analysis and Issues Appropriate to Each Level. This summary chart does not cover all the important points raised in the chapter. Use it only to review what you have read. Page numbers are given for the full discussion of any topic.

determined on a "pleasure-pain" scale. One adds up the pleasures in one column and the pains in another and then compares the columns. Presumably, one refrains from an action whose painful consequences outweigh its pleasurable ones. Bentham argued that criminals would conform if they were taught to use his methods, for they would see that crime does not pay—the sum of pains will be greater than the sum of pleasures. In 1778, in pursuit of his aims, he made an important recommendation to the government: to keep careful statistics on criminal activities in order to provide lawmakers with information on fluctuations in crime rates, so that they could intelligently determine punishments for various crimes. Bentham argued that when certain crimes are increasing, one can conclude that the punishments attached to them are not sufficiently severe and should be made more severe until such crimes decrease.

Governments did begin to collect statistics on crime, and by the early nineteenth century, France and other European nations began to publish their crime statistics. Soon, early social scientists began to analyze these data (Guerry, 1860; Quetelet, 1842). These analyses revealed regularities and showed that crime was predictable over time and related to such factors as age, sex, race, education, urbanization, and season of the year. These regularities made it seem unlikely that crime could be conceived of as stemming from purely individual sources; instead it seemed that "social facts" beyond the control of the individual were at work in generating crime. People do not pick their own age, sex, or race; nor do they make the seasons change or, by themselves, create cities.

These early statistical findings had a profound influence on thinking about crime. Focus shifted from a concern with criminals and punishments to the general causes of crime, a concern that remains central today. However, the first consequence of crime statistics was in conjunction with the concurrent revolution in biology and gave rise to a new school in criminological thought.

Levels	Appropriate Questions	A Partial Synopsis of Present Conclusions
Physiological	Is IQ related to crime and delinquency?	Yes, but there are many possible interpretations of this relationship. The fact that prison populations have a lower average IQ than nonprison populations may mean only that low IQ is related to getting caught, not to committing crimes. Self-report data, however, show that juveniles with lower IQs are more likely to commit delinquent acts, which may indicate either that low intelligence causes delinquency or that delinquency results from other social factors related to low intelligence. (pp. 174–175)
	Is cortical inhibition (the insensitivity of some brains to stimulation) related to crime?	Perhaps. More research is needed at the physiological level. (p. 175)
Psychological	Does psychosis cause criminal behavior?	In rare instances it may, but persons convicted of crimes show no greater incidence of psychosis than does the general population. (pp. 175–176)
	Are most career criminal offenders psychopaths—unable to feel guilt?	No. Unless psychopathy is defined as criminal behavior. (pp. 176–177)
Social-Psychological	Does the labeling process—officially identifying someone as a criminal or a delinquent—cause subsequent law violation?	In some cases. Labeling may expose an individual to other lawbreakers and to more sophisticated criminal techniques. It may also cause an individual to be shunned by society. But labeling theory cannot account for the fact that most juveniles labeled as delinquents eventually cease committing delinquent acts. (pp.177–179)
	Does "keeping bad company" contribute to crime and delinquency?	Apparently not for those with a high stake in conformity. But for those with a low stake in conformity, it seems to increase law violations. (pp. 179–180)
	Does reinforcement influence crime and delinquency?	Probably. Stealing is directly rewarded by possession of the stolen items and, in the absence of punishments, is likely to be repeated. (pp.179–180)
Sociological:Middle Range	Are the frustrations assumed by strain theories important causes of crime and delinquency?	Probably not. Most "frustrated" people do not commit crimes. Most crimes lack sufficient pay-off to solve frustration. Yet, many who would appear not to be frustrated do commit crimes. (p. 180)
	Does a significant amount of crime and delinquency actually reflect conformity to the norms of some subcultural group?	Some probably does (organized crime, for example). Most probably does not. (pp. 180–181)
	Does the absence of strong bonds between the individual and society influence law violations (control theory)?	Those with relatively little to lose are prone to commit illegal acts, whereas those with strong attachments, high commitment, and extensive involvements (who thus have much to lose) are unlikely to commit illegal acts. (pp. 181–184)
Societal	Does low social class play a role in criminal activities?	Among adults, yes. Among juveniles, family social position seems to have no relationship to delinquency, but their own position in teenage society does. (pp. 184–185)
	Does the criminal justice system discriminate against those with the least power?	Yes, in many ways. However, since discrimination against the powerless is general throughout society (see Unit III) it is often hard to know whether the criminal justice system is discriminating or whether it is merely confirming earlier discrimination. (pp. 186–190)

173

The Positive School

Crime statistics demonstrated that certain groups of people in society were especially likely to commit crimes—particularly males with little education or income. Furthermore, the statistics made clear that some significant proportion of those who engage in criminal behavior do so persistently. Their lives are a recurrent pattern of crime and punishment. At this same time, Charles Darwin's monumental work in biology—set forth in *On the Origin of Species* (1859) and *The Descent of Man* (1871)—created widespread support for biological determinism. Social scientists of the period readily accepted the notion that humans evolved from lower animal species, and thus they sought to account for human behavior primarily through genetic explanations.

In this intellectual climate, Cesare Lombroso, an Italian physician, published his epoch-making work *Criminal Man* in 1876. In this and subsequent publications, Lombroso and his followers (who came to be called the *Positive School*) put forth the notion that about one-third of all people engaging in criminal activity were "born criminals." Although born criminals were a numerical minority, they engaged in the most persistent and vicious crimes (Lombroso-Ferrero, 1911).

The positivists argued that born criminals were throwbacks to their more primitive ancestors. Applying the ideas of Darwinian biology, positivists saw born criminals as less evolved and more primitive than normal men. Born criminals had visible stigmata, such as abnormalities of the skull, overdeveloped jaws, flat noses, large ears, excessively long arms, high cheek bones, and other apelike traits. Lombroso and his followers did not ignore the importance of the environment as a factor influencing behavior, but in the case of born criminals, they judged the impact of the environment to be minimal; little could be done to change born criminals or prevent their crimes. Lombroso believed that because born criminals were not able to help themselves, they ought to be treated humanely—locked away in a decent environment in order to protect society.

Lombroso was an advocate of the scientific method. He studied prison populations and came to his conclusions on the basis of what he judged to be appropriate empirical evidence. Because Lombroso's work was empirical—not simply based on his opinions—it provided a model by which it was to be disproved. Later empirical studies showed him to be wrong. We now know that his evidence was badly selected and that criminals do not possess primitive physical traits.

Although the specific components of the original Positive School have been substantially discarded, the concern to explore the role of human genetics and physiology in causing crime remains a modern research activity. Furthermore, modern criminology remains committed to the scientific method and in this way also follows in the Positive School tradition. By the same token, as we have mentioned, elements of the Classical School are readily found in modern theories of criminal behavior which have to meet the test of agreement with the crime rates that we have described.

CRIME AND PHYSIOLOGY

Lombroso's theory of the born criminal was both physiological and genetic. Although his theory did not stand the test of time, social scientists trying to account for crime are still interested in aspects of the human animal.

Intelligence

From Lombroso's time to the present, it has been recognized that persons serving time in prison are, on the average, less intelligent than the general population (Tappan, 1960). Such evidence fails to establish, however, that persons with less intelligence are more likely to *commit* crimes than are persons with higher intelligence. Because less intelligent people could simply be more likely to get caught, comparing convicts with nonconvicts cannot resolve this matter.

The only reasonable way to explore the relationship between intelligence and criminal behavior is to use data based on self-reported criminal actions. Unfortunately, as we pointed out earlier, self-report techniques have been mainly limited to studies of adolescents. Consequently, we do not know the role of intelligence in adult criminal behavior. But we do know that intelligence, measured by a variety of tests, is negatively related to juvenile delinquency. For example, Hirschi (1969) found that boys with high IQs were much less likely to report committing delinquent acts or to have police records than were boys with low IQs—and the relationship held for both black and white boys in his sample. These findings are subject to interpretation by a number of sociological and social-psychological theories. Looked at purely in physiological terms, it is possible to argue that some delinquent behavior (and presumably some adult criminal behavior as well) results from a lack of good sense. It can be argued that some people break the law because they lack the mental capacity to apply Bentham's moral calculus and correctly compute the benefits of breaking the law against the costs of detection.

It should also be pointed out that intelligence is only partly a physiological phenomenon. Studies have established that inheritance plays a significant role in determining individual intelligence. However, environmental factors such as poor nutrition, lack of early stimulation, and poor education also play important roles. Thus, some portion of the relationship between IQ and delinquency reflects social, not genetic, factors. Perhaps only intelligence differences caused by social factors relate to delinquency. However, Hirschi found that even among white boys from upper-income homes, who enjoy positive environments, lack of intelligence was related to delinquency.

Cortical Inhibition

Another way in which the physiology of the human brain may be implicated in crime is suggested by the work of the British psychologist Hans Eysenck (1964). He argued that some individuals have brains that become insensitive to stimulation. Specifically, some people's brains very rapidly build up *cortical inhibitions*—a kind of fatigue that results from stimulation. People who are insensitive to stimulation will not take readily to conditioning (whether by reward or punishment). Therefore, they will be poorly socialized.

This fact has obvious implications for social-learning theories. If humans are socialized to conform because others reward them for obeying the norms, persons who condition poorly will be less

completely socialized than persons who condition, or respond to rewards, easily. Thus, Eysenck argues for a genetic factor that seems to shield some persons from full socialization—including the development of "conscience." Such people will become bored more rapidly and are perhaps genetically driven to become thrill seekers in their need for greater stimulation. These people are more likely to run afoul of the law—especially in light of their inability to be adequately socialized and to learn to conform to group norms.

As with many physiological analyses of human behavior, the data we have considered leave many questions unanswered. Clearly, not all persons with low intelligence commit crimes; some highly intelligent persons commit them. Similarly, rapid development of cortical inhibitions may make persons more subject to boredom, but not all bored people seek out illegal sources of stimulation. For all their possible importance in unraveling the causes of crime, physiological factors provide only incomplete answers.

175

PSYCHOLOGICAL SOURCES OF CRIME

Frequently, people who are accused of serious crimes—especially of serious violent crimes such as murder or rape—plead "not guilty by reason of insanity." Thus, the law recognizes that mentally unbalanced persons should not be held accountable for their actions. This view reflects a long and intimate relationship between psychiatry and the courts. The courts call on psychiatrists to determine when insanity pleas are justified. And psychiatrists and psychologists have long been assigned a leading role in efforts to reform those convicted of criminal offenses.

The underlying assumption in this link between the law and psychiatry is that the psychological make-up of individuals plays a major role in determining whether they commit crimes. Not all social scientists find this assumption convincing. Although most of them readily accept the idea that insanity pleas are sometimes justified—that, for example, a person may commit murder because of psychotic compulsions—most are uncomfortable with the idea that most crimes reflect personality disorders. As we shall see, psychological explanations of criminal behavior are too often circular; that is, they use definitions as explanations. For example, people who define criminal behavior as a psychological problem are begging the question, or using circular reasoning, if they take the fact that someone commits a crime as evidence that he or she has a personality disorder and that the disorder caused the criminal behavior.

Psychosis

Severe mental illness—*psychosis*—is most frequently alleged in sensational crimes—mass murder, for example. In fact, people have a tendency to assume that anyone who commits an especially horrible crime must be insane. Why else would someone go on a murder spree, randomly killing total strangers? We may accept the idea that such crimes typically involve psychosis, but we know little about the general role of psychosis in crime. Such crimes are sensational because they rarely happen. What about more usual varieties of crime?

176   Studies have shown that only a tiny proportion of persons sentenced to prison can be diagnosed as psychotic. Findings indicate that not more than 5 percent (and in many studies less than 1 percent) of persons were psychotic at the time of their admission to prison (Sutherland and Cressey, 1970). And these percentages nearly match the estimates of the rate of psychosis for the general population, which indicates that convicted criminals are not disproportionately psychotic. Furthermore, many of those diagnosed as psychotic upon arrest were in fact alcoholics temporarily undergoing the DTs (delirium tremens).

Furthermore, the fact that a person convicted of a crime is diagnosed as psychotic does not necessarily mean that his or her psychosis *caused* the criminal behavior. Daniel Silverman (1943, 1946) found in a study of psychotic and nonpsychotic federal prisoners that the two groups had remarkably similar social backgrounds. But psychotic prisoners had very different social backgrounds from psychotic persons not in prison. These findings suggest that the social factors that produced crime among nonpsychotics also produced it among psychotics and that their mental illness is therefore *incidental* to their lawbreaking. This conclusion is further backed up by studies showing

that the overwhelming majority of psychotics do not commit crimes (Dunham, 1939; Erickson, 1938). From these findings, we can only conclude that psychosis plays, at most, an extremely minor role in causing crime.

Psychopathy

The major focus of psychological analysis of criminal behavior has been on the psychopath. As William and Joan McCord (1956) put it:

Psychopathy, possibly more than any other mental disorder, threatens the safety, the serenity, and the security of American life. From the ranks of the psychopaths come political demagogues, the most violent criminals, the riot leaders, sexual misfits, and drug addicts.

An immense amount of writing and research by psychiatrists and psychologists has been devoted to understanding the psychopathic personality and giving a detailed portrait of the psychopath. But just what is a psychopath? In general, the psychopath is described as "an asocial, aggressive, highly impulsive person, who feels little or no guilt and is unable to form lasting bonds of affection with other human beings" (McCord and McCord, 1956). An additional trait frequently attributed to psychopaths is that they are able to appear very charming and normal, and thus it often comes as a shock when they later commit crimes.

Although psychological researchers find strong correlations between psychopathy and criminal behavior, the use of this category of disorder involves the same kind of circular reasoning that we noted earlier. Typically, the term psychopath is used to *explain* the same behavior that was initially used to *define* the concept.

To apply the category of psychopathy as a cause of crime is tantamount to looking around the world and saying, "There are a lot of criminals out there. If they were sufficiently conscience-ridden, they probably wouldn't commit crimes; therefore, there must be a lot of conscienceless people in the world. I shall call such people psychopaths. I have now explained crime—crime is committed by psychopaths. That is, crime is committed by criminals." Such circular explanations will not do.

Even when the concept of psychopathy has been used more carefully, it has not borne much fruit.

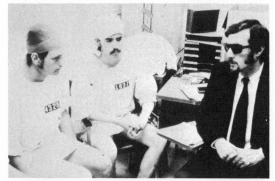

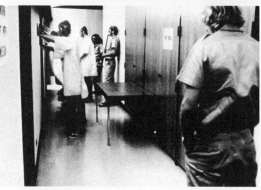

Figure 6.7   Philip Zimbardo conducted a mock prison experiment that demonstrated some consequences of role playing, labeling, and depersonalization in institutional settings (Haney, Banks, and Zimbardo, 1973). These photographs, taken during the experiment, show the aggressive and sometimes sadistic manner assumed by "guards" and the passive, self-demeaning behavior exhibited by "prisoners." The simulation used college students who were randomly assigned to "prisoner" or "guard" roles. It had to be terminated after several ays due to severe psychological and physical reactions exhibited by many of the "prisoners."

Studies have failed to find that persons diagnosed as psychopaths differ significantly in personality traits from persons not diagnosed as psychopaths (Sutherland and Cressey, 1970).

In addition to psychosis and psychopathy, many other personality traits have been studied as potential sources of crime and delinquency. On the whole, efforts to establish that categories of abnormality are sources of crime have been relatively unsuccessful (Waldo and Dinitz, 1967). As self-report studies have shown, most people have committed delinquent or criminal acts sometime during their lives. If this is so, it is futile to try to find an explanation of widespread behavior based on an alleged psychological abnormality, for, by definition, "abnormal" means "uncommon." It is true that the average person commits fewer criminal acts than the average person sent to prison. It is possible that some abnormal personality trait could account for this greater frequency of criminality. So far, such a syndrome has not been found.

To sum up, the concepts of psychosis and psychopathy have been of little use in explaining crime. They endure because of their inherent circularity. When we learn that people have committed acts that seem senseless and irrational to us, we conclude that they must be crazy. But, as we shall see, what is crazy to us might not appear so crazy to someone else. Social circumstances are powerful determinants of what is and what is not considered irrational.

177

SOCIAL-PSYCHOLOGICAL THEORIES

We now move beyond the individual to examine how elements in the immediate social environment influence criminal behavior.

Labeling Theory

A major strength of labeling theory is its insight that deviant behavior can be created. It says, in effect, that if you give a dog a bad name, it is likely to be a badly behaved dog. Labeling theory cannot tell us why persons first commit acts that cause them to be labeled as criminals or delinquents. The theory says only that once labeling occurs, there are four ways in which it will increase the likelihood of future deviant behavior.

First, people labeled as criminals or delinquents may find that the social stigma of the label limits their associations. They may be forced to associate with others who are similarly stigmatized. At this point, labeling theory joins differential-association theory to argue that by being with others who are labeled as lawbreakers, persons may find themselves in a social setting that encourages future violations. For example, by being labeled as a lawbreaker and getting locked up in a jail or prison, a person is often instructed by other inmates in future criminal activities.

Second, labeling can increase deviance by increasing surveillance. Police, parents, associates, and teachers may keep a much closer watch on the behavior of people labeled as criminal or delinquent, and such persons are therefore much more likely to be detected in offenses than are persons not so labeled. For example, when certain kinds of crimes have occurred, the police often check out persons with a previous record of such offenses.

Third, people may come to accept their label and thus to see themselves as "bad" or criminal and act accordingly. Or labeled persons may simply find they have less to lose from future transgressions because they see that they have already lost their reputations.

Finally, labeling theory provides a mechanism for class-conflict theories of crime. As we shall see, such theories set down the conditions under which persons will or will not be labeled as criminals or delinquents, regardless of their actions.

The labeling perspective is most useful in connection with other theories of crime and delinquency. However, it should be pointed out that the evidence in support of labeling is quite mixed. Simply to be labeled as an offender seems to have, at most, a very weak effect on subsequent criminal behavior. Most adolescents who are officially labeled as delinquents do not go on to a life of crime. Indeed, most adolescents discontinue their delinquency around age sixteen (Hirschi, 1969). Similarly, it is very rare for either juveniles or adults who are apprehended for shoplifting to ever be apprehended a second time for that offense (Cohen and Stark, 1974). Furthermore, data on federal prisoners diagnosed as psychopaths show that they are heavily overconcentrated in the

178

White Policeman

. . . I'd rather work in a black neighborhood. They need me more than the white. White neighborhoods are not as involved in actual crime, the dirtiness, as they are in poor neighborhoods. I don't mean blacks alone. There are Southern whites that come up here, they live in jungles. So do the Puerto Ricans.

You can go into an atmosphere of doctors and lawyers and educators and get a point across verbally. They understand. You can also work on the South or West Side (black neighborhoods), where you can talk your fool head off and get nothing. They don't understand this nicety-type guy. So you walk with a big stick. Like the adage of a mule: He's a very intelligent animal, but in order to get his attention you have to hit him on the head with a stick. Same thing applies on the street.

The radicals and the black militants, they're the dangers. They could be standing here on the street corner selling this Black Panther thing. . . . I look at them and I laugh. I'd like to break his neck. But I'm a policeman, a professional.

Black Policeman

They're [policemen] sure the person who has stolen a car is probably driving, the person who is transporting stolen merchandise is in a vehicle, the person selling dope has it in his car. In their minds, the average black person driving down the street falls into one of these categories. (Laughs.) . . . Black folks don't have a voice to complain. . . .

The young black is the big police hang-up because his tolerance of police brutality has grown short. They say, "The new niggers don't respect us any more the way the old niggers used to. We used to holler at 'em and shout at 'em and kick 'em and they went along with it." Young niggers ain't going along with it and that's what bugs them more than anything in the world. . . .

There are more cops in the black community than in the white. . . . The crime rate's highest in this area because we're underprotected. We've got more and more policemen here, yet the crime rate rises. Evidently something's wrong.

A large amount of young white officers are gung ho. It's an opportunity to make a lot of arrests, make money, and do a lot of other things. In their opinion, black people are all criminals, no morals, dirty and nasty. So the black people don't cooperate with the police and they have good cause not to. On the other hand, they're begging for more police service. They're overpatrolled and underprotected.

"White Policeman" and "Black Policeman" quotes are from two Chicago policemen.
—Studs Terkel, *Working* (New York: Pantheon Books, 1974): "White Policeman" from pp. 130–133; "Black Policeman" from pp. 137–141.

twenty to twenty-nine age group (Cason and Pescor, 1946a; 1946b), which suggests that such persons cease to be psychopathic after age thirty or cease to commit federal crimes after age thirty.

All these findings contradict the position that persons labeled as criminal or delinquent will tend to increase their deviance or, at least, be increasingly detected in deviance. Nevertheless, labeling theory can point to the high recidivism rates for adults convicted of serious crimes (excluding white-collar crimes and murder, which are rarely repeated). The question is, did they repeat the crime because they were labeled as criminals or because of other factors? Labeling can at best provide only a partial account of criminal and delinquent behavior.

Differential Association and Social Learning

According to differential-association and social-learning theories, criminal and delinquent behavior, like all behavior, is learned—we learn to repeat behavior that is rewarded. Crime and delinquency are learned by exposure to social groups that reward (teach) such behavior. Briefly put, learning theory thus describes the mechanism by which keeping bad company results in bad behavior.

It is clear that learning plays an important role. Many kinds of crime require considerable technique. For example, in order to be more than a petty burglar, one must learn a good deal about locks and alarm systems—indeed, a whole repertory of entry techniques must be mastered. In addition, burglars must learn which things are worth taking, so they may have to learn about art, antiques, and other valuables. Finally, they must learn where and how to sell what they steal. Obviously, many kinds of crime require instruction from others who have mastered the trade. Thus, we can be fairly sure that a good burglar, safecracker, forger, or hold-up man has a record of criminal associations. However, it is not clear that such associations turned him into a lawbreaker in the first place. It may be that such associations turned a petty or unexperienced criminal into a more skilled and serious offender only *after* the individual had already committed a first offense. Indeed, it is widely believed that much, if not most, tutoring in crime occurs in jail and in prison.

If so, then keeping company with other criminals will change an offender but will not create one.

It has been pointed out that most juvenile delinquents cease their illegal activities whether or not they are caught. But we must now point out that it is also true that most adult offenders have a prior record of juvenile crime; however, a much smaller proportion of the population commits adult offenses than commits juvenile offenses. Thus, the fundamental question about adult crime may be what sustains and modifies such behavior, not what initiates a pattern of offenses. And we may have to examine the causes of juvenile delinquency to find the *starting point* of criminal careers. We have already seen that the differential-association, social-learning perspective can explain how adult crime is sustained and professionalized. But to what extent can it explain delinquency?

The evidence is quite mixed. Hirschi (1969) found that boys whose friends were delinquents were more likely to report committing delinquent acts than boys whose friends were not delinquents. Were boys delinquents because they had delinquent friends, or did they have delinquent friends just because they were themselves delinquents? Hirschi concluded both patterns occur, but he emphasized the latter one. He found that boys who were doing well in school, who liked their parents, and who had high aspirations for future success were little influenced by delinquent friends; in fact, they usually had no delinquent friends. However, successful youths who did have delinquent friends were not much more likely to commit delinquent acts than those who did not. But boys who did badly in school, who were not attached to their parents, and who had low aspirations *were* influenced by delinquent friends. Hirschi concluded that having delinquent friends was more a result of delinquent behavior than a cause of it. Similarly, Diana Gray reported that teenage prostitutes, contrary to widespread belief, typically experiment with prostitution prior to any exposure to the subculture of prostitutes and pimps.

Although these data raise serious questions about the importance of differential association as a cause of delinquency, they do not necessarily challenge the social-learning aspect of this theoretical position. *People can learn criminal or delin-*

quent behavior through being rewarded more for such behavior than for conformity, even though they do not rely on a delinquent or criminal group for such rewards. In the absence of punishments, or when punishments are seldom and not severe, property crime is always rewarding. And nonconformity may be directly rewarding. Illegal acts may offer thrills and excitement, and status as a "bad kid" may bring attention from nondelinquents. For example, teenage girls who experiment with prostitution have already discovered that promiscuity attracts more attention than conventional behavior does, and they are initially socialized into prostitution by males who approach them as potential clients rather than by other women who are already prostitutes (Gray, 1973). Thus, conventional groups have the capacity to serve as the source of reinforcements for deviant behavior.

We need not demonstrate that delinquents are immersed in a delinquent group in order to argue that their delinquency is learned. The material and emotional rewards of law violation and the capacity of conventional groups to reward some members more for deviance than for conformity may suffice as a mechanism for the social learning of delinquency. Yet, it is obvious that only some persons are differentially rewarded for deviance (or less rewarded for conformity).

180

SOCIOLOGICAL THEORIES: MIDDLE RANGE

Why do some people have delinquent or criminal associates while others do not? Why are some people apparently immune to the effects of delinquent or criminal friends? How do we account for the fact that some persons appear not to be burdened by guilt or prevented by conscience from committing crimes? Is there a social explanation for the phenomenon that psychologists call psychopathy? Once again we move to a higher analytic level and apply strain, subcultural, and social-control theories to answer these questions.

Strain Theories

Strain theories of crime and delinquency argue that social inequalities drive persons to commit crimes despite the bonds of conscience. People commit crimes in order to get rewards they cannot obtain through legitimate means. The image of the delinquent or criminal is a person torn between guilt and desire, with desire winning out when the person is sufficiently deprived of desired goals.

Robert Merton's innovator category (see Chapter 4) is meant to apply to some criminals and delinquents. The innovator accepts the goals society defines as desirable but lacks access to the means society defines as legitimate for attaining these goals. Faced with intense frustration, the individual innovates—engages in illegitimate methods for attaining goals.

Strain theory runs into trouble because its concepts rely too heavily on people's frustration. The majority of those who, according to the theory, would seem to be subject to frustration are not particularly likely to be delinquent during youth and are not implicated in crimes as adults.

A different kind of problem with strain theory is that the deviant behavior that it predicts would, in most cases, not relieve the intense frustration that people are supposed to be feeling. Most delinquent crime is petty and in no way puts poor kids on the same material footing as rich kids. Although adult crime sometimes pays, for most criminals it usually pays very poorly. The average hold-up man could do better at an unskilled labor job.

Finally, the theory, being fundamentally economic, is unable to account for crime and delinquency committed by those who would seem not to suffer from frustration in the form strain theory describes. Why do middle- and upper-class young people break the law? Why do the well-to-do shoplift? We must seek answers from other theories.

Subcultural Theory

Subcultural theory also assumes that persons are bound by conscience, but it adopts an extreme form of differential association to define the particular elements of conscience that are dictated by the group or subculture. All people are conformists, from this view, but conformity to the norms of one group may represent deviance from the norms of another. Along with labeling theory, subcultural explanations of deviance assume that deviance is in the eyes of the beholder, not in the actions of those labeled as deviant.

According to subcultural theories, crime and delinquency represent conformity to subcultural norms that the rest of society has defined as criminal. We would expect, then, to find delinquency predominantly the product of delinquent subcultures and crime to be mainly the work of members of a subculture whose norms have been labeled as criminal. From this view, delinquents and criminals would not feel remorse, because they are conforming to the dictates of their consciences—they are behaving in the way their group has taught them to behave.

It is true that some crime is sustained by deviant subcultures. Certainly, a criminal subculture exists to some extent where the best safe-cracker, the slickest con man, the cleverest forger, or the toughest mob enforcer is held up as a desirable model. It is also true, as we note in the next section, that powerful elements in society sometimes outlaw behavior that some subcultural group considers acceptable—for example, polygamy among the Mormons, gambling among the urban poor, and norms of personal and family vengeance among the Appalachian mountain folk. Most delinquents and most criminals, however, seem to subscribe to the same set of norms as those who judge their acts to be criminal; that is, most crime is not sustained by the norms of some distinctive subcultural group. So subcultural-deviance theories cannot explain most crime and delinquency.

Control Theory

At present, *control* theory seems to fit the facts of crime and delinquency better than strain and cultural or subcultural theories do. Control theory does not assume that people are intrinsically moral or bound by conscience. Instead, it assumes that deviance is to be expected when people have little to lose by such behavior and that society is structured in such a way that some people have much and some have little to lose by deviant behavior.

The crucial element in control theory is that the source of morality and the pressures for conformity are in the *bond* between the individual and society. Individuals will conform to society's norms to the extent that the bond between them and society is strong. When the bond between the individual and society weakens, the likelihood of norm violation

increases. But what is this bond? According to Hirschi (1969), it has at least three elements: attachment, commitment, and involvement.

Attachment

According to Hirschi, *attachment* is the primary element in control theory. Attachment is the bond of affection between an individual and other conventional persons—the degree of attachment is how much the person cares about others (and is cared about by them) and how much the person values others' feelings, opinions, and expectations. An individual who is strongly attached to others is likely to consider how his or her behavior will affect others and their attitudes, including their attitudes toward that individual. Unattached people lack such interpersonal stakes in conformity and have only themselves to think about.

Research shows that attachment is a powerful inhibitor of crime and delinquency. The more young people are attached to their parents, peers, or teachers, the less likely they are to commit delinquent acts (Hirschi, 1969). Furthermore, the concept of attachment overcomes many problems that plague other theoretical positions. For example, strain and labeling theorists are embarrassed by the fact that delinquency begins to decline in later adolescence. Control theory, however, emphasizes the fact that adolescence is a time when many young people reshape their attachments. The parent-child relationship, for example, frequently undergoes considerable stress before being re-established as an adult relationship. During the period when parent-child attachments are weakened, delinquency reaches its highest point. Similarly, the fact that boys frequently stop being delinquent when they establish romantic relations with girls gives support to the concept of attachment. The lack of any important relationship between social-class background and delinquency presents no great problem for control theory because attachment is common in all classes.

In addition, the concept of attachment has fewer logical pitfalls than that of psychopathy. Control theorists locate "conscience" in the *bonds of attachment,* not in the individual personality. Feelings of guilt arise, then, from our fears of disappointing or offending those to whom we are

181

attached. To conceive of conscience as some kind of personality feature inside the individual creates problems. Recall that persons diagnosed as psychopaths were disproportionately between the ages of twenty and twenty-nine. If we conceive of psychopathy as a feature of the personality, we must assume that people somehow recover as they get older. When we place conscience in the bonds of attachment, however, we need only recognize that younger people tend to be less attached—for example, the young are more often single and childless—than older people. Similarly, it is well known that persons are more likely to commit deviant acts following a divorce but that they tend to conform again after remarriage. Must we argue that they somehow lost their conscience when they got divorced and then found it after remarriage? A more satisfying account is that changes in their deviance correspond to changes in their attachment. For control theorists, attachment is the counterpart of what psychologists mean by such terms as conscience or superego, but it is essentially social, arising from and changing with the relationships among people.

Commitment

If attachment is the counterpart of conscience, *commitment* is the counterpart of common sense.

Commitment is one's stake in conformity. The more time and energy an individual invests in conventional activities (getting an education, building up a business, establishing a reputation for honesty and trustworthiness), the greater will be his or her stake in conformity to the norms. Thus, commitment serves as a bond between the individual and social norms and represents *what the person has to lose* through deviant actions. As Hirschi (1969) pointed out:

> To the person committed to conventional lines of action, risking one to ten years in prison for a ten-dollar holdup is stupidity, because to the committed person the costs and risks obviously exceed ten dollars in value. . . . In . . . control theory, it can be and is generally assumed that the decision to commit a criminal act may well be rationally determined—that the actor's decision was not irrational given the risks and costs he faces.

The concept of commitment is strongly supported by data on delinquency. The more energy students have invested in school performance and the more they hold high educational and occupational aspirations, the less likely they will be to risk their position by committing delinquent acts. By the same token, most adult crimes are committed by those with little stake in conventional forms of activity—street crime is overwhelmingly committed by persons with little to lose and for whom

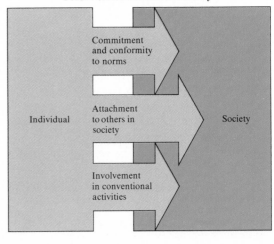

Bonds Between Individual and Society

Individual

Commitment and conformity to norms

Attachment to others in society

Involvement in conventional activities

Society

the fruits of crime at least seem to be worth the risks involved. Similarly, relatively successful and committed adults rationally assess costs and benefits when they commit crimes. They have much to lose and therefore usually commit only white-collar crimes that offer large gains. It would be irrational for a banker to stick up a liquor store, but it would not be so irrational for him to embezzle a million dollars.

Oddly enough religious beliefs and church participation do not serve as effective commitments. Despite the fact that judges sometimes sentence teenagers to a period of church attendance, religiousness is not a restraint on delinquent behavior. For example, research has shown that young people who believe that God sees and punishes sin (and who presumably might think they have something important to lose by sinning) are no less likely to commit delinquent acts than are young people who do not believe in a God who judges. Attendance at church and Sunday school, moreover, does not have any effect on delinquent behavior (Hirschi and Stark, 1969).

Involvement

A third aspect of the bond between the individual and society is well expressed by the saying "the Devil finds work for idle hands." Persons who are busy doing conventional things have less time and energy to devote to deviance than people who are idle. As Hirschi (1969) put it: "Many persons undoubtedly owe a life of virtue to a lack of opportunity to do otherwise. Time and energy are inherently limited." It is obvious that attachment and commitment play a major role in determining *involvement.* People with families, people who work hard in school, or people who are busy establishing themselves in a career have much less opportunity to be deviant than persons without such attachments and commitments.

Table 6.3   Relationship Between Delinquent Acts and Riding Around in a Car

HOURS YOUTHS SPENT RIDING AROUND	PERCENT WHO COMMITTED DELINQUENT ACTS
None	28
Less than one	35
One to two	44
Three to four	53
Five or more	59

Source: Adapted from Travis Hirschi, *Causes of Delinquency* (Berkeley, University of California Press, 1969), p. 194.

Hirschi's data on delinquency revealed that the more spare time young people had, the higher was their delinquency rate. In Table 6.3, for example, if we assume that persons who spend considerable time just "riding around in a car" have more spare

Figure 6.8 (Far left) *Irene Pappas, playing the role of a young widow in the movie* Zorba the Greek, *is shown just prior to being stoned by a group of village women who resented her unconventional behavior and her violation of the norms of her community. Control theorists see such nonconformity as arising from a breakdown in the bond between the individual and society.*

Figure 6.9 (Left) *A depiction of the three elements that, according to control theory, bond the individual to society.*

Figure 6.10 The cheating scandal engaged in by some Boy Scout leaders is an example not only of a form of white-collar crime (at stake were substantial federal subsidies to the Boy Scouts of America, based on membership figures) but also of the rationality implied in control theory. Some leaders apparently assessed the costs and benefits of padding the Boy Scout rolls and decided that getting federal grants was worth the risk of losing their position.

Saturday, June 15, 1974   THE SAN DIEGO UNION

ROSTERS PADDED
Cheating Laid To Scout Aides

SACRAMENTO (AP) — Seven professional Boy Scout leaders in nine counties in California and Nevada were fired in late 1971 and early 1972 for padding membership rolls and other abuses, says a Scout executive.

Falsification of local membership rolls was revealed after the national head of the Boy Scouts admitted earlier this week that such cheating had occurred in several areas of the country.

Calvin Wheelock, executive officer of the Golden Empire Council of the Boy Scouts of America, said the seven had been trying to improve their standing with the organization.

"The seven professionals tried to advance themselves, partly by registering boys who were no longer or never active in the scouting program," Wheelock said yesterday.

183

time than those who do not, we can see that spare time is strongly related to delinquency. Of those who spent no time riding around, 28 percent had committed one or more delinquent acts in the past year, whereas of those who spent five or more hours a week riding around, 59 percent had committed one or more delinquent acts. Similar findings were obtained when young people were classified according to how frequently they reported finding themselves with "nothing to do." Time spent on homework or spent talking with friends was also related to delinquency—more time spent on these activities meant less delinquency.

Control Theory and Delinquency Treatment

In Chapter 3, we saw that delinquency-prevention programs have been failures. In light of what we now know about causes of delinquency, why did the Cambridge-Somerville experiment fail?

Many of the ideas behind the experiment are consistent with control theory, but others are not. First, Dr. Cabot, who initiated the program, seemed to have recognized the importance of attachment. His solution was to try to provide the boys in the program with sympathetic adult counselors who would become their friends. Had this occurred, bonds of attachment might have formed to make the program a success. The problem is that no delinquency-prevention program, including Cabot's, can afford enough counselors to create strong bonds of attachment for program boys. To be effective, especially with boys who have no other attachments, a counselor would have to be able to work with the boys every day. There simply is not enough money to hire counselors with small enough caseloads. And even if counselors could spend sufficient time with them, it is not certain that they would succeed in forging close friendships with most boys, especially with boys having trouble forming attachments elsewhere.

Second, delinquency-prevention programs are not designed to build commitments. One does not risk being eligible to join a delinquency-prevention program by committing delinquent acts—more likely the reverse is true. Furthermore, these programs offer few inroads to the world of achievement. You do not build up an academic record or a career in a delinquency-prevention program. Per-

haps the most that such programs are able to offer is some involvement in conventional activities that give teenagers less time to get into trouble. Such programs, nevertheless, have only a small effect on the lives of their participants, who continue to spend most of their time at home, at school, or in hangouts with their friends.

The key to conformity lies in attachment—to parents and relatives in the home and to teachers and friends in the school—for it builds a stake in conformity. At present, we have found no effective way to intervene in the family and to compensate those persons who are failing to build attachments or commitments.

SOCIETAL THEORIES OF CRIME AND DELINQUENCY

Societal-level discussions focus on two related arguments about causes of crime and delinquency. Both are put forward by conflict theorists. First, they argue that crime and delinquency are the inevitable by-products of a society that is inherently unequal. Poverty and inequality drive people into crime and, indeed, some crimes can be seen as primitive forms of rebellion and revolution. Second, they argue that the laws of our society are laws that favor the interests of the ruling class. What is and what is not defined as criminal is thus rooted in social inequalities, and in this sense, those in prison are political prisoners. Functionalists at least partly reject both arguments. We shall consider each.

A CLASS ANALYSIS OF CRIME AND DELINQUENCY

It is well established that crime among adults is quite strongly related to social class. Persons charged with crimes are disproportionately from the least-educated, lowest-income groups in society. To that extent, the basis for a class analysis of crime exists. But what about delinquency? Haven't studies uniformly found social class to be either not related or only trivially related to delinquency? They have. However, there is at least one basis for a class analysis of delinquency; it rests on a different definition of social class.

Figure 6.11   Conflict theorists argue that crime and delinquency result from social inequalities. Poverty and the unequal access to opportunity are seen as the cause of much "conventional" crime and delinquency. (Above) The activities of the Symbionese Liberation Army (SLA), including the kidnapping and conversion of Patricia Hearst, can be seen either as examples of crime or as political activity rooted in social inequality. (Right) The Berrigan brothers, both Catholic priests, have engaged in a variety of illegal activities, including the burning of draft-board records removed from the Cantonville, Maryland, draft-board offices. While the government considered such actions criminal, the Berrigan brothers and their supporters view these actions primarily as a legitimate form of political protest.

Social scientists, both conflict theorists and functionalists, long thought that class—usually measured by father's occupation and income—had a direct effect on delinquency. They were wrong. When family-class position was the measure, or defining feature, of class, the relationship failed to hold true. However, when a young person's *social rank within the adolescent society* of schoolmates and peers is the measure, class is found to influence delinquency.

Academic achievement, high educational and occupational aspirations, popularity, and achievements in sports or other extracurricular activities are all negatively related to delinquent behavior. Although young people's status in high school is weakly related to their family position, their high-school status is strongly related to the status posi-

tion they will hold as adults. Thus, if we ignore family status and look only at the status position of young people within their own adolescent society, we find that class, defined in this way, is a strong predictor of delinquency and that unsuccessful youths are likely to become delinquents, regardless of how well off their family may be. As control theory would postulate, youths at the bottom of the school pecking order (and who are likely to be on the bottom of the economic order as adults) have little to lose by delinquency and correspondingly have little to gain from conformity. The fact that those with lower status are more likely to be delinquent also fits the idea of conflict theory that crime and delinquency result from social inequalities.

Let us assume that conflict theorists are correct and that social inequalities are a major cause of crime and delinquency. Does the solution to the crime and delinquency problem then require the elimination of social inequalities? And *can* social inequalities be eliminated? A substantial portion of Chapter 9 is devoted to this question. At this point, we can only point out that no one has ever seen a society without substantial inequalities in wealth, power, and prestige among its members. And no one has ever seen a society without crime. It seems likely that class differences account for a major amount of crime and delinquency, but it is vital to keep two qualifications in mind: (1) poor people are not the *only* people to commit crimes, and (2) only *some* poor people *do* commit crimes.

A CLASS ANALYSIS OF LAW AND JUSTICE

There is now widespread agreement among social scientists that laws tend to be somewhat biased against the least powerful groups and persons in a society because power plays an important role in structuring the legal system. Perhaps the best way to approach this topic is to examine the operation of the legal system and then to examine the extent to which class interests (as opposed to the common interests of all citizens) have an influence on what is legal or illegal.

186

Liberty and Justice for Whom?

In both the criminal and civil jurisdictions of the legal system, the poor get less justice than the rich. Much of civil law is designed to benefit the "haves" over the "have-nots." A recent presidential commission on credit reported that widely used sales contracts and court procedures for legal bill collection victimize the poor because they are designed to mislead the debtor and to maximize the advantages of the creditor over the debtor. In addition, most legal defenses against fraud or against other damages suffered by the poor at the hands of merchants, employers, or landlords are rarely utilized by the poor; they typically lack the knowledge of their rights or the money to hire lawyers to protect their interest. Thus, they are disadvantaged both in defending themselves against the law and in using the law to protect themselves.

The poor and powerless are also denied equality under the criminal law. Many commissions and

Figure 6.12 Social scientists agree that the poor get less justice. The rich and the powerful not only create the law but use it more effectively because they can afford better and more influential lawyers when they need them. Even if convicted, the rich often get off with a fine while the poor go to jail.

investigations have reported that law enforcement is much less adequate in poor than in wealthy neighborhoods. The police simply do not respond as urgently or give the same quality of patrol in poor sections of town.

When the poor are accused under criminal law, they once again find themselves treated unequally; they lack the resources to obtain the quality of legal aid available to the middle and upper classes. All criminal defendants are entitled to legal counsel, but court-appointed lawyers or public defenders are not drawn from among the ranks of the most skilled criminal lawyers. Furthermore, those defending the poor have neither the money for private investigators nor the time to prepare their cases carefully—advantages normally available to high-priced defense attorneys. As a result, the poor are poorly defended and more often convicted.

But inequality does not stop there. The poor are apt to receive longer and more severe sentences than are middle- and upper-class people convicted of the same or even more serious offenses. Thus, in May 1972, in the same courthouse, a man who stole $15 from the post office was sentenced to six months in jail, whereas a bank employee who embezzled a grand total of $150,000 was put on probation (Oelsner, 1972).

Even when the rich and the poor receive identical sentences, inequities frequently result. For example, a $50 fine for speeding simply does not represent the same loss for a person earning $50,000 a year and a person earning $3,000 a year. A day at any local traffic court will show many cases in which offenders do not even appear because they could afford to post bond and then to forfeit it as their fine. Meanwhile, others receive jail sentences to work off fines they cannot pay—ten days in jail is hardly equivalent to a $100 fine. American justice may be among the fairest in the world—but it is not blind to wealth and power.

Power and Legality

Perhaps the most fundamental charge that class analysis can make against the legal system is that the rich and powerful create the laws, and as a result, many criminal statutes apply to acts that only poor people commit. As the French novelist Anatole France (1922) pointed out, "The law, in its majestic equality, forbids all men to sleep under bridges, to beg in the streets, and to steal bread—the rich as well as the poor."

Furthermore, the historical record is filled with examples of the way powerful groups in societies have utilized the laws to increase or protect their privileged position. William Chambliss (1964) has traced the evolution of vagrancy laws from their origin in England in 1349. He argues that vagrancy laws were used primarily to control labor and to protect the property of the rich. After the Black Death killed about half the English population during the 1340s, there was a severe shortage of labor. Chambliss argues that the vagrancy law—which prohibited alms giving as well as idleness by those of able body—had "one express purpose: to force laborers . . . to accept employment at a low wage in order to insure the landowner an adequate supply of labor at a price he could afford to pay."

As the labor force grew and there was no longer a shortage of workers, the vagrancy laws went unenforced. They were rewritten and once more enforced in the fifteenth century during the rise of commerce. Merchants traveling the highways began to complain vigorously about bandits who robbed them of the goods they were transporting. The vagrancy laws then prohibited "any ruffian [who] shall wander, loiter, or idle use themselves" from traveling on the highways. The English vagrancy and poor laws were instituted by the early American colonists to drive persons without visible means of support out of town. Chambliss argues that the history of vagrancy laws shows how extensively the legal system is used by the powerful to exploit the powerless.

Indeed, some conflict theorists argue that the major feature of our present legal system is the exploitation and repression of workers and disadvantaged minority groups. Functionalists accept the charge that the laws do reflect various powerful interests, but they argue that many criminal statutes also reflect the interests of society as a whole and rest on a consensus among all sectors of the population.

White-Collar and Street Crime

The focus of this dispute is on the difference in the severity of penalties attached to "white-collar"

187

White-Collar Crime—Justice or Injustice?

Opportunity is an essential element in all crimes. It is differential opportunity that distinguishes white-collar crime from street crime. Street crime is democratic. In principle, at least, everyone has the opportunity to rob a bank or break into a house. But the opportunity to commit white-collar crimes is restricted to a few. For example, only those in positions of financial trust have the opportunity to embezzle funds. Indeed, white-collar crime took its name from the fact that only persons in higher-status

occupations—where white collars are traditionally worn to work—*can* commit these illegal acts. White-collar crimes are thus exclusively *class* crimes. Their uniqueness has made them an object of considerable debate about the fundamental fairness of the criminal justice system in dealing with them.

Recently, the Watergate case has intensified the debate over whether the penalties attached to white-collar crimes are equitable or whether they reflect bias in favor of the high-status law violator. The fol-

lowing excerpts from a *Los Angeles Times* article surveying this debate lay out the central issues and the opposing positions. You will see that persuasive arguments can be made for both sides and that the position one takes depends on the priority one gives to each of several competing values. Furthermore, these issues transcend this particular group of men who violated the trust of their high offices. Thus, although every story from the daily press quickly becomes dated, the dispute retains its relevance.

Legal Scholars Wage Debate on Sentencing

by David Shaw
Times Staff Writer

"... To make the punishment fit the crime."
—*The Mikado, Gilbert & Sullivan*

[*At the time this story appeared, more than 30 persons had pled guilty to or had been convicted of offenses stemming from the Watergate scandals. Many had not yet been sentenced. But those who had been sentenced rarely received more than a year in jail. These light sentences*] *aroused a fire storm of controversy in the nation's legal community.*

There are many who contend the sentences . . . have been shockingly and disgracefully lenient. There are others, however, who say the sentences have been not only appropriate but, in a few instances, perhaps even a bit too harsh.

The battle lines in this con-

troversy have not been drawn along predictable partisan or ideological lines.

A. L. Wirin, for example, chief counsel to the American Civil Liberties Union for 42 years, is a longtime, outspoken foe of President Nixon. . . . But Wirin thinks most of the 16 Watergate defendants sentenced to date have been dealt with too harshly by the courts.

"The ACLU wants to discourage violations of the law, especially violations by men of power in high places," Wirin says, "but prison sentences won't accomplish that. Prison just isn't the kind of institution that these wily, ambitious, amoral, self-serving Pres-

ident's men will get any benefit from—not for themselves nor for society."

On the other hand, Atty. Gen. William B. Saxbe—a Republican and a Nixon appointee—said last month:

"It is hardly reassuring when one man goes to prison for years for theft while another man involved in a conspiracy to steal our freedoms is in and out of jail in the wink of an eye. . . . Criminal violations cannot be tolerated on the part of anyone. . . ."

Stripped to its essentials, the controversy over sentencing in the Watergate cases is a controversy over the specific purposes of sen-

tencing in any criminal prosecution. These purposes are many:
—Punishment.
—Rehabilitation.
—Retribution by society.
—Isolation.
—Deterrence of the individual offender.
—Deterrence of potential future offenders.
—Reaffirmation of society's values and standards.

It is generally agreed that several of these are irrelevant in Watergate—and maybe no longer appropriate in any cases in a civilized society. . . .

[The desire for punishment and] traditional societal vengeance—an eye for an eye— is for barbarians and animals, not for modern man, most progressive penologists agree.

Rehabilitation, isolation and primary deterrence are not applicable in the Watergate cases:
—Rehabilitation is for offenders who need academic or vocational education. That clearly is unnecessary for the Watergate defendants—most of whom are lawyers, and all of whom, it is generally conceded, will resume productive lives once they're out of prison.
—Isolation is for violent criminals. The Watergate defendants—despite the enormity of their offenses—have not been charged with any violent crimes.
—Primary deterrence is for criminals who might have the opportunity or inclination, or both, to be repeat offenders. It is unlikely that any of the Watergate figures will ever have the opportunity to do that, whatever their individual and collective inclination.

That leaves deterrence of potential future offenders and a reaffirmation of society's values and standards—and it is over those two intertwined points that the Watergate sentencing controversy

swirls most vigorously.

Those who argue that the sentences meted out thus far have been reasonably appropriate generally advance what might best be termed the "fall-from-grace" theory.

As put forth by Earl Johnson . . . former Justice Department prosecutor . . . this theory holds:

"All of these men have already been . . . stripped of their power and influence and their status and good name. Some of them may lose their license to practice law. All of them will be stigmatized for life. That is not only sufficient punishment for the individuals involved, it's also more than enough to deter future presidential advisers and others in similarly high places from doing the same thing."

Many lawyers and legal scholars interviewed by The Times . . . disagreed. . . . [According to one,] "Precisely because these men in Watergate have been the recipients of so many gifts from society—and precisely because they have been given and have violated a high public trust—they must be held accountable and severely punished for their crimes. . . ."

Critics of the Watergate sentences maintain that lenient treatment of these offenders will lead to a general erosion of respect for the system of criminal justice in America. . . . [One claimed]

"The public concept of our system of justice is important. We can't let people think the rich and powerful get off easy. You tell some kid in the ghetto that disgrace and humiliation are enough punishment, and he'll say, . . . 'If it was me, they'd throw my [expletive deleted] in jail.' . . ."

But all the Watergate figures are first-time offenders. A first offender in a street crime will generally get off without any jail time at all. It might be his third offense before he actually has to go to jail for longer than six months.

Of the 16 sentenced Watergate defendants, however, 15 have been sent to prison. . . .

Lawyers and law school professors who think these sentences too light say the Watergate defendants cannot be treated as typical first offenders. . . . Most lawyers and legal scholars interviewed by The Times agreed that some jail time was necessary for all Watergate figures—"as a symbol that not even the rich and powerful go unpunished," said one law professor. . . .

Hopefully, most legal experts agree, the disparities of the Watergate sentences will focus public attention on . . . [needed reforms. One] much needed reform, it is generally agreed, is the development of realistic alternatives of imprisonment and fines. Prison sentences generally are too long, it is felt, and they serve no useful purpose except for the most violent and incorrigible criminals.

In the Watergate cases, long jail sentences seem particularly inappropriate. Big fines would not help either, since the general public would probably assume the men could either pay the fines themselves or get help from Republican fund-raisers.

"What we need," says Thomas S. Jackson, former president of the Washington, D.C., Bar Assn., "is a whole new range of criminal sanctions. Maybe you can make a guy work free for a government agency or take away his tax shelters and driver's license or make him donate his time to collecting things for the Goodwill. . . . We need some way of dealing with certain kinds of criminals, like those involved in Watergate, where neither jail nor fines accomplish what society wants."

It is time, most experts agree, to abandon the Mikado's admonition "to make the punishment fit the crime," and, instead, make the punishment fit the criminal.

189

crimes as opposed to "street crimes." It is the case that the average white-collar crime does not result in as serious a sentence as the average street crime.

Conflict theorists argue that this inequity occurs because of class biases in the law. The upper classes are more likely to be charged with white-collar crimes than with street crimes. Thus, it is in their interest to have light sentences attached to such white-collar offenses as embezzlement, forgery, fraud, tax evasion, and other various violations of laws governing business and finance. Street crime, on the other hand, represents a threat to the life and property of the rich and may even reflect a rejection by the lower classes of the present system of social inequalities. Thus, it is argued, the law is constructed to bear down hard on the lower classes.

Functionalists admit there is some truth to this argument, but they consider it exaggerated. They point out that street crime is at least as much a burden on the poor as it is on the rich—indeed, lower-income people are more likely to be victims of crimes than are upper-income people. They argue that all classes in society demand tough laws against murder, rape, robbery, burglary, and other street crimes. Even if the poor are more likely to commit such crimes, they say, the laws prohibiting such crimes do not reflect narrow class interests.

But then why are white-collar crimes not severely punished? Functionalists offer several reasons. For one thing, white-collar crimes typically do not victimize an individual; instead they have impersonal victims such as the company, the government, the bank, the investment community, or the public in general. Functionalists point out that vice crimes, such as gambling or prostitution, which are also victimless crimes, are not severely punished either, although they are lower-class crimes. A recent study (Rossi *et al.*, 1974) found that there is overwhelming consensus among Americans of all classes and races about what are and are not serious crimes. Crimes of violence are judged most serious and property crimes against individuals are next most seriously regarded. White-collar offenses were not rated as very serious crimes.

A second reason for lighter punishments stems not from the law—because many white-collar crimes carry stiff maximum penalties—but from

differences in persons convicted of white-collar and street crimes. The legal system is designed to consider the character of offenders in determining sentences. When the offense is very unlikely to be repeated and when the offender seems in little need of reform, sentences are often light. It happens to be the case that those convicted of white-collar crimes typically do not have prior criminal records and do not tend to commit subsequent offenses. Consequently, they frequently receive suspended sentences or probation or, if sent to prison, serve relatively short terms. But it is also the case that those convicted of street crimes are quite likely to have prior convictions for such crimes and are quite likely to commit such crimes in the future, so they receive stiffer sentences.

Perhaps the best conclusion to draw from this dispute is that class interests do shape the laws of a society but that the various classes do not always have antagonistic interests. Rich and poor murder victims are equally dead. And the law in that regard tries to protect the interests of all classes.

PART III: RESPONSES CRIME AND DELINQUENCY

Ways of handling offenders are based on assumptions about the nature of crime and criminals. In the United States today, imprisonment is one societal response to criminality. Many people do not realize that it is a relatively new phenomenon.

TREATMENT OF THE CRIMINAL

David Rothman, in his *The Discovery of the Asylum* (1971), observes that institutions to deal with deviants did not begin to become popular until the Jacksonian era in the early nineteenth century. He notes that

Americans in the colonial period . . . fined or whipped criminals or put them in the stocks or, if the crime was serious enough, hung them; they did not conceive of imprisoning them for specific periods of time.

Retribution and Deterrence

Concepts of crime and punishment changed over time. The criminal law, as we have noted earlier in this chapter, replaced the earlier practice of private vengeance in retaliation for a wrong suffered. The punishments that the criminal law provided, however, did not do much more than take the right to execute vengeance from the individual who was wronged and give it to the state. The well-known principle of lex talionis—an eye for an eye—was widely practiced in many cultures. Under this system, murderers were typically killed, those who mutilated others were mutilated themselves, and so on. In addition to the punishments of death and mutilation, Richard Korn and Lloyd McCorkle (1959) point out that the Code of Hammurabi provided for punishments of branding and banishment as well. Other punishments such as flogging (used as recently as 1952 in Delaware) and the stocks were commonly used in the American colonial period (Barnes and Teeters, 1959). One punishment popular in England and France was the transportation of convicts to penal colonies. For a time, England transported some of its convicts to penal colonies in America; later, Australia became the major dumping ground for Britain's convicts.

Such punishments were primarily *retributive*. The premise of the retributive view is that it is right for the wicked to be punished. There are two major versions of the retributive position. The first rests on the idea that revenge for a wrongful act is an appropriate societal response; the second rests on the notion that only by suffering can the criminal atone for his offense. Both versions espouse the same principle: the criminal is punished because he has committed an offense (Packer, 1968).

Recall Cesare Beccaria and Jeremy Bentham, who agreed that the punishment inflicted should fit the crime committed. An important premise of their position was that crime could be prevented or deterred by the proper application of punishments. Deterrence operates on two levels: First, *general deterrence* is achieved because the population at large is discouraged from committing crimes out of fear of punishment; second, *special deterrence* is achieved because the individual offender who suffers punishment will be discouraged from committing future crimes (Middendorff, 1968).

Rehabilitation

The severe and cruel punishments of retribution ran against the humanitarian grain of the Quakers who inhabited Pennsylvania. In the latter seventeenth century, the Quaker Assembly decreed that imprisonment should replace all existing punishments for serious crime, except capital punishment for homicide. In the early nineteenth century, Pennsylvania built two penitentiaries (places for "penitence"). Under a system of completely separate confinement, each prisoner had his own individual cell and exercise yard in which he spent the entire duration of his sentence without ever coming into contact with other inmates (Korn and McCorkle, 1959).

Separate confinement served several purposes: it prevented inmates from influencing each other; it provided them a good deal of time to contemplate their deeds and become penitent; and it gave them ample time, space, and tools to work hard at and become proficient in such occupations as shoemaking, weaving, and tailoring. Although inmates were not permitted to see or communicate with each other, personal friends and members of the Philadelphia Society for Alleviating the Miseries of Public Prisons could visit them.

These new methods for the *rehabilitation* of criminals were consistent with the views of the members of the Quaker Society of Friends that all people, including criminals, had a share of the divine "inner light" that could be nurtured with appropriate treatment (Lewis, 1965). To this end, members of the Philadelphia Society supplied bibles, religious counsel, and instruction to the inmates (McKelvey, 1936).

The Pennsylvania system, although duplicated in New Jersey, did not come to be widely adopted in the United States. Other states recognized the merits of prohibiting the inmates from associating with each other, but there was concern that prolonged periods of isolation could have catastrophic psychological consequences. Perhaps a greater concern was that the Pennsylvania system, because of its individualization of work and exercise space, was likely to be more expensive.

In order to solve the problem of prisoner association, an institution built in Auburn, New York in 1823 tried a new method. The Auburn system permitted the prisoners to work in a common area but forbade them to speak or gesture to each other at any time—they could not even look

191

at each other. To keep inmates from having their eyes meet, prison personnel saw that they walked with eyes downcast and forced them to march with their hands on the shoulders of the men in front of them and with a heavy shortened gait known as the lock step. In order to enforce the rule of silence, Auburn's first warden imposed a harsh system of discipline and repression (Korn and McCorkle, 1959).

Most states subsequently chose the Auburn system over the Pennsylvania system. The remnants of the repression of these early prison methods can be found in many prisons today. For example, in a 1971 United States District Court decision, Federal Judge Robert Merhige Jr. enjoined the Virginia State Department of Welfare and its Division of Corrections from

1. Imposing a diet of bread and water on any inmate for any infraction of prison rules.
2. Using chains, handcuffs, hand-restraining tape or tear gas "except when necessary or required to protect a person from imminent physical harm or to prevent escape or serious injury to property."
3. Using physical force against an inmate as punishment.
4. Placing more than one inmate in a solitary confinement area—Virginia's solitary cells are 6 1/2 by 10 feet—"except in an emergency."
5. Interfering with or imposing punishment for efforts by inmates to file court documents, to have confidential communications with lawyers (even when confined to solitary), and to write legislative or other government officials (Landman v. Peyton, Civil No. 170-69-R, U.S. Dist. Ct. E.D.Va. Oct. 31, 1971).

FAILURES OF CONTEMPORARY RESPONSES

In the United States, especially during the past quarter century, rehabilitation has been the predominant aim of imprisonment. Grand speeches have been made about rehabilitation, but few would be willing to defend the record of prisons as effectively pursuing this aim.

Rehabilitation or Custody?

A study reported by the President's Commission on Law Enforcement and the Administration of Justice (1967a) revealed that less than 7 percent of

192

Comparison of Model and Traditional Prisons

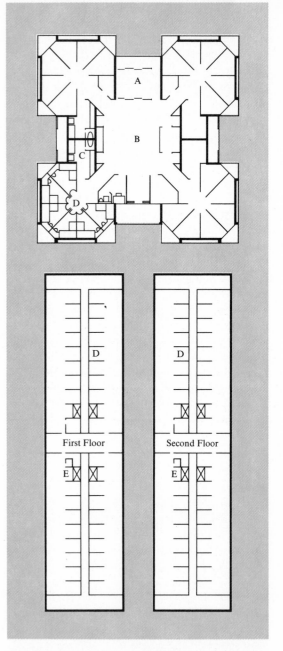

Figure 6.13   Prisons have generally failed to rehabilitate their inmates. In fact, many believe that time spent in prison is more likely to encourage future criminal behavior than to prevent it. One reason is the dehumanizing conditions of life in most prisons. Prisoners isolated from one another in cells lined up like animal cages along stark corridors do not become more attached to others. Today, social scientists collaborating with architects are suggesting drastic changes in

the physical design of prisons. The new design (top left) *is meant to break up the isolating long corridors and encourage maximum interaction among inmates and staff. The aim is resocialization of prisoners through the development of a community.*

correctional employees in state institutions have treatment of inmates as their main responsibility; this study found that there was 1 custodial staff member for every 7 inmates, but only 1 professional staff member (psychologist, social workers, or counselor) for every 179 inmates. These figures strongly suggest that prison administrators themselves view custody, rather than rehabilitation, as their most pressing responsibility; it should not be surprising that inmates leaving institutions have generally not been rehabilitated at all.

A recent study of male felons confined in California state prisons, for example, revealed that nearly nine out of ten of these inmates had previously served sentences in a reformatory, jail, or prison (California Department of Corrections, 1967). There is ample reason to believe that rather than rehabilitating offenders, our prisons, as they are now operating, may actually be debilitating offenders. Unfortunately, the mere custody of prisoners (let alone treatment) is very expensive. In 1971, local, state, and federal governments spent $2.3 billion for correctional activities (Law Enforcement Assistance Administration, 1973a).

In a frank recognition of the gap between rhetoric and practice in correctional institutions, the National Advisory Commission on Criminal Justice Standards and Goals (Law Enforcement Assistance Administration, 1973b) made recommendations.

Each correctional agency should immediately develop and implement policies, procedures, and practices to fulfill the right of offenders to rehabilitation programs. A rehabilitative purpose is or ought to be implicit in every sentence of an offender unless ordered otherwise by the sentencing court. A correctional authority should have the affirmative and enforceable duty to provide programs appropriate to the purpose for which a person was sentenced. Where such programs are absent, the correctional authority should (1) establish or provide access to such programs or (2) inform the sentencing court of its inability to comply with the purpose for which sentence was imposed.

The rehabilitative approach that is being stressed in these Standards and Goals, although apparently humanitarian, may ultimately cheat the offender.

Procedural Injustices

Looking closely at this approach, we see that "treatment" or rehabilitation may actually subject

193

the offender to a more substantial deprivation of his or her liberties—*with fewer procedural safeguards*—than would pure punishment. If the offender is viewed as being in need of help, he or she may, in fact, be held until rehabilitated. Furthermore, in the process of determining whether offenders need help and, if so, what kind of help, the courts may deny offenders some of the rights that they would be guaranteed if they were simply being punished (Kittrie, 1971).

Juveniles have suffered such procedural injustices. Recall that Platt observed, in connection with the rise of the child-saving movement, that the reformers supporting the establishment of juvenile courts were interested in rescuing children from seduction into a life of crime. Because delinquent juveniles were viewed as being in need of help—and this was the aim of the court's intervention—many of the procedural safeguards guaranteed to adults were viewed as unnecessary encumbrances and were denied to juveniles. After all, each party to the proceeding had the best interests of the child uppermost in mind. Thus, over the years, proceedings in the juvenile court became informal and therefore lacked most of the safeguards guaranteed to adults.

In a landmark decision, the United States Supreme Court affirmed that juveniles should be guaranteed many of the protections afforded adults [*In re Gault*, 387, U.S. 1 (1967)]. In that case, the appellant, Gerald Gault, fifteen years of age, had been committed to a state industrial school (for making a lewd phone call) until the age of twenty-one "unless sooner discharged by due process of law." As a juvenile, Gault had been denied notice of the charges against him, the right to counsel, the right to confront and cross-examine witnesses, the protection against self-incrimination, the right to a transcript of the proceedings, and the right to appeal to a higher court. In the Gault decision, the Supreme Court took a rather dim view of these circumstances, which had become common practice in juvenile courts, and instituted an era of greater formality in juvenile proceedings that afforded juveniles some of the basic safeguards guaranteed to adult defendants.

If Gerald Gault had been an adult who was being *punished* for making a lewd phone call rather than a juvenile who was being helped by the court, he would have had certain rights that he was actually denied, and if found guilty, he probably would have been sentenced to confinement for a shorter period of time. The court noted that an adult in Gerald Gault's position would only have had to pay a fine. The experience of juveniles offers a warning that the rehabilitative ideal leaves a great deal of room for unanticipated abuses.

COMMUNITY CORRECTIONS

From the time that prisons became widespread, some of their negative consequences have been recognized. Prisons are not only expensive but, as we have noted, serve as classrooms for learning techniques of criminal trades and for making new criminal associations. It is not surprising, therefore, that very early in the history of prisons, attempts were made to divert convicted offenders from correctional institutions. During the past decade, this trend has been accelerated as attempts have been made to *reintegrate* the offender into the community.

At the end of 1970, there were approximately 200,000 inmates in state and federal prisons in the United States (Federal Bureau of Prisons, 1970). In addition, another 70,000 inmates were serving sentences in county and local jails in the United Staes (Law Enforcement Assistance Administration, 1971). The primary distinction between prisons and jails is that prisons generally hold inmates serving longer sentences. Typically, jails are operated by county and local governments, whereas prisons are operated by state governments; jails also hold persons awaiting trial, awaiting arraignment, and awaiting other legal actions (however, none of these persons are included in the 70,000 figure). Because data regarding those held in jails are not available, our discussion applies only to state and federal prison inmates.

In 1970, the rate of incarcerated offenders in state and federal institutions in the United States was 96.7 per 100,000 civilian population; in 1939—the first year for which comparable data are available—the incarceration rate per 100,000 was 137.1. During World War II, this rate dropped sharply but began to rise slowly during the late

194

Figure 6.14   Although many prison authorities pay lip service to the goal of rehabilitation and correction, few prison systems manage to achieve this goal. Limitations of money, time, and staff condemn many prisoners to mere custodial care and monotonous activities, such as hoeing and other work-gang labor.

1940s and the 1950s; in 1961, the rate was higher than it had been in nearly two decades (120.8 per 100,000), but since 1961 it has steadily declined (Federal Bureau of Prisons, 1970).

Despite a continually increasing arrest rate in the United States during the past decade, the incarceration rate has gradually decreased. The decrease reflects, in part, greater use of community supervision—probation, parole, and referral to noncorrectional agencies.

Probation

Probation is a sentence to community supervision; it usually imposes conditions on the probationer, including periodic meetings with a probation officer. Modern probation practices are said to date back to the efforts of a Boston bootmaker who, of his own initiative, began to bail defendants out of jail in Boston's lower courts in the mid-nineteenth century. Shortly after the turn of the century, the use of probation began to accelerate, partly as a result of the juvenile-court movement, for putting juveniles on probation seemed a good way to supervise their behavior without exposing them to the harsh life of institutions. By 1925, every state provided for the probation of juveniles, but not until 1956 was this the case for adults (President's Commission on Law Enforcement and the Administration of Justice, 1967a).

Conditions of probation often include the probationer's promise to obey all laws; to maintain steady employment; to support his family; to avoid criminal associates; not to drink to excess or enter bars or taverns; and to obtain approval before marrying, moving, driving, incurring debt, or traveling. In some jurisdictions, probationers must agree to let field agents search them and their premises at any time; narcotics users must agree further to submit to medical tests for drug usage (Remington *et al.*, 1969). In addition, probationers are required to meet with their probation officers at specified intervals, depending on the individual probationer and the officer's work load.

Parole

Parole involves conditional release from a correctional institution and from community supervision after the prisoner has served a portion of his or her

sentence (American Correctional Association, 1966). The parolee's release and continued freedom in the community depend on conformity to the conditions of parole. Parole differs from probation in that it always applies to offenders who have served a portion of their prison sentences.

The decision to release prisoners on parole is usually made by a paroling authority—appointed by the governor—with the recommendation of the institution in which the inmate was held (O'Leary and Nuffield, 1972). The conditions of parole are often similar to those of probation. Violation of these conditions during the term of probation or parole can result in imprisonment for the remainder of the sentence.

About two-thirds of those under correctional supervision are serving supervised terms in the community as probationers or parolees. Perhaps one reason for the fact that community supervision is gaining in popularity is the rapidly rising dollar cost of imprisonment. The President's Commission reported that in 1965 the average annual cost per institutionalized adult felon in the United States was about $2,000, but the average annual cost per adult felon under community supervision was only one-tenth that amount. In order to encourage probation instead of prison, the State of California, in its probation-subsidy program, actually pays counties for handling offenders through probation programs and *not* sending them to state prisons. A county using its state subsidy can therefore offer offenders on probation better supervision and services (Vorenberg and Vorenberg, 1973).

Unfortunately, we do not have data that would show, in terms of subsequent arrests, the effectiveness of community supervision over imprisonment. However, the *Uniform Parole Reports*, maintained by the National Council on Crime and Delinquency, do provide some nationwide information on the proportion of parolees who have their parole revoked. Of 22,000 parolees released from institutions in 1968, about one-third had their parole revoked within two years; of the 7,800 paroles revoked, 1,500 of the parolees had run away, 3,100 had violated conditions of parole, and the remainder had committed new offenses (National Council on Crime and Delinquency, 1972). Surprisingly, those incarcerated for homicide had the best parole performance (one-fifth were revoked), while those who had been incarcerated for vehicle theft, forgery, or passing bad checks had the worst performance (almost one-half).

On the basis of recent trends, it seems clear that community supervision will be used more and more, partly because of the rising costs of keeping people in prisons and jails and partly because community supervision promises to help reintegrate the offender into the community.

Future Prospects

During the past few years, there has been greater and greater emphasis in the criminal justice field on diverting individuals away from the criminal justice system. The National Advisory Commission on Criminal Justice Standards and Goals (Law Enforcement Assistance Administration, 1973b) has concluded:

A number of factors justify noncriminal treatment, counseling, or restitution programs. The existing system has failed to achieve reformation in any large number of cases; it is discriminatory in nature; and it is costly in relation to outcomes. Personal values, costs, and humanitarian interests also contribute to the arguments for diversion.

If other social agencies or community resources can provide services that will alleviate the problems at hand, these other mechanisms should be used in lieu of the criminal justice system. This philosophy of *diversion* from the criminal justice system has been widely used with juveniles. In Massachusetts, the Youth Services Commissioner, Jerome Miller, recently closed the public juvenile institutions and diverted about 700 youths to a variety of community programs. Youth Services Bureaus are beginning to spring up in several states in order to handle the minor misconduct of juveniles outside of the court and within the community. These bureaus provide and coordinate programs aimed at making social services available to youths who in earlier times would have been processed by the juvenile justice system (Harlow, 1970).

Diversion from the criminal justice system has also been used in varying degrees with adult misdemeanants, alcoholic offenders, and narcotics of-

fenders. One theme underlying the recent upsurge in diversion programs is that, in the United States, we tend to overcriminalize certain behaviors in our attempt to control them. Diversion is one attempt to decriminalize some behaviors by reducing the emphasis on the use of the criminal justice system as a response to some categories of deviant behavior. Just as the emphasis on rehabilitation can have unanticipated negative consequences, so, too, can the emphasis on diversion. For example, diversion programs could actually result in a net increase in the number of people being handled by the system. Thus, rather than being sent home, a minor juvenile may be referred for informal counseling or to another social agency. It is difficult to tell whether the final effects of diversion efforts will be positive or negative. Although it is too new to assess adequately, the diversion trend is certain to continue as we move away from the custodial model of imprisonment.

RADICAL NONINTERVENTION

Recently it has been argued that in the case of juvenile delinquency, even the programs that divert offenders to community supervision, such as probation, may be out of keeping with the actual problem. Recently, Edwin M. Schur (1973) has suggested that the best response to delinquency is to use *radical nonintervention*—simply put, to "leave the kids alone wherever possible." Obviously, young people who are a real threat to the safety of others may have to be isolated from society. But most other youths, Schur argues, would probably be better off if courts and juvenile authorities intervened as little as possible.

Schur bases his judgments on a number of the facts about delinquency. First, present programs apparently have not been helpful in reforming delinquents. Indeed, there is some evidence that incarceration in a detention center or juvenile hall may actually turn young people into more serious offenders because they are likely to improve their criminal skills through contact with other offenders. Second, the overwhelming majority of juvenile offenders do not go on to a life of crime. They cease committing offenses as they reach their late teens. Present programs of dealing with juveniles seem pointless; they have not been helpful and may in fact be harmful and they are expensive to operate. Thus, Schur would probably praise the police officers who let most juvenile offenders go with a scolding (see Piliavin and Briar's study in Chapter 3). Indeed, he would probably urge them to use this procedure even more frequently.

Schur is well aware that much juvenile crime is associated with particular neighborhoods and with particular segments of the youth population—for example, with youths who, regardless of family background, have low status in teenage society. He therefore argues that efforts should be aimed at young people collectively, not individually. He suggests that the way to deal with a teenage gang is not through individual juvenile charges and counseling but collectively and out in the streets. Furthermore, instead of interpreting such a wide range of youthful behavior as predelinquent, we should ''err'' in the opposite direction by learning to tolerate a very wide range of youthful behavior.

This last point touches on a discussion in Chapter 2. We pointed out there that people in small towns are able to tolerate or deal informally with a lot of disruptive adolescent behavior because they know the teenagers involved and what they are likely to do. In cities, however, people often make such behavior a police matter because the youths are strangers to the complainants. Consequently, small towns tolerate a great deal more rowdy or disruptive behavior and even petty vandalism in the belief that it is normal for young people to go through a period of wildness or mischief making. In the vast majority of cases, this judgment is confirmed. Most ''wild'' teenagers eventually settle down to be dependable adults. Thus, official delinquency statistics may give a false impression that small towns are more tranquil than the cities. It may be that small towns have just as high a rate of unlawful acts by young people as cities but that fewer of these acts are regarded (and thus recorded) as delinquency.

However it seems doubtful that small towns also underrecord adult crimes to the extent that they underrecord juvenile offenses. Hence, their relatively low adult crime rate may reflect the fact that they have responded to juvenile delinquency with radical nonintervention all along. Put another way,

small towns may have less adult crime because radical nonintervention works. There is only one way to find out if this is so—to adopt the radical-nonintervention delinquency strategy in big cities and see if adult crime rates eventually fall. Because the present delinquency programs seem ineffective, it would appear that the cities have little to lose by trying radical nonintervention. Even if this strategy failed, the cities at least would have saved money they would have spent on present programs. Since before the turn of the century we have been trying to save the children. We could hardly do worse by leaving them alone.

CHAPTER REVIEW

The age of offenders often determines whether or not a society will define offenders' acts as criminal and also determines societal response to acts defined as criminal. Before societal reaction can be studied, however, the *extent* of crime needs to be measured.

The Uniform Crime Reports, or *official statistics,* measure certain ''index offenses'' for the government. However, they tend to be unreliable because they include only offenses reported to the police, and much crime is unreported. Local departments also use inconsistent classification schemes and often keep inaccurate records. *Victimization studies,* which question victims of crimes, may also produce somewhat inaccurate estimates of the extent of crime because of respondents' faulty recall and tendency to ''telescope'' time in reporting crimes. *Self-report studies,* although they are valid, have been used only with adolescents and are therefore of little value in estimating adult crime.

Both official crime rates and self-report studies indicate that most urban crime is committed by young, nonwhite males. It is also apparent that most delinquents mature out of their illegal behavior patterns. Public perceptions of crime are important when studying the social problem of crime because they shape policies by influencing legislators, law-enforcement people, and citizens. And if people behave differently because of their perceptions—for example, by staying off the streets at night—their behavior can affect crime rates.

Theories about why people commit crimes have changed over time and have reflected prevailing views about human nature and human behavior. The *classical* theorists, including Beccaria and Bentham, considered humans to be rational beings who would weigh the consequences of their acts. They would therefore refrain from committing crimes if society made the punishments for crimes sufficiently severe. Bentham's suggestion to gather data on crimes eventually led many *positivists* to discover regularities among the *kinds* of people who committed crimes. During this period, Lombroso and others adopted Darwinian theory and tried to identify born criminals, evolutionary "throwbacks" who had criminal tendencies. The more extreme theories were later rejected, but they spawned further research that, for a time, indicated that criminals had lower intelligence or suffered from physiological disorders of the brain. Lower intelligence is related to juvenile delinquency, but this relationship reflects environmental factors, such as poor education and nutrition, as well as genetic factors.

Psychological theories of crime tend to be circular in their arguments (they use definitions for explanations). For example, they say that psychosis or psychopathy causes people to commit sensational, aggressive acts, but they use these same acts to define these mental disorders and to identify the people who are psychotic or psychopathic.

Social-psychological and sociological theories seem to be more useful lower-level theories for understanding criminal and delinquent behavior. The *labeling* process helps create deviance in people who are labeled criminal. Such labeling increases police surveillance over people, limits their associations, and causes them to accept the label and act accordingly. Labeling theory also relates to class-conflict theories of crime by describing how people's social class may cause them to be labeled as deviant. However, labeling theory fails to explain why people first commit deviant acts. *Differential association* and *social-learning* theories claim that crime and delinquency are learned and rewarded through participation in groups. These theories have greatest relevance to the ways in which minor offenders learn how to commit more difficult and serious offenses. However, many people who commit delinquent or criminal acts do not seem to have done so because their friends encouraged such behavior. *Strain* theories take up this problem by explaining that frustration in achieving legitimate goals leads to the use of illegitimate methods. Yet most people who would seem to be frustrated do not violate laws, and many who do violate laws do not seem to be frustrated. *Subcultural* theories claim that deviance is really conformity to subcultural norms. However, many criminals and delinquents continue to subscribe mainly to conventional norms, so it is not clear that their deviance reflects conformity to subcultural norms. *Control* theory says that deviance occurs because the deviant has weak bonds of attachment, com-

mitment, and involvement with society. When such bonds are strong, they give people a stake in conformity to societal norms. Considerable evidence supports this view.

Societal theories of criminality tend to focus on the distribution of *power* in the society. Power (generally economic) can shape crime rates by determining where law enforcement will take place, who can afford competent legal aid, and how the heavier prison sentences are distributed. Furthermore, *class conflict* theorists claim that the legal system is essentially created by and for the wealthy. *Functionalists* say that inequalities in the criminal justice system do not reflect only class interests. They say that people of all classes, not just the wealthy, think that street crime is more serious than white-collar crime and that the sentences received by white-collar criminals are therefore not lighter merely because the criminals have class advantages, such as the money to get better lawyers.

Responses to crime and delinquency have ranged from *retribution* and *deterrence* to attempts at rehabilitation. Official custody is expensive and has largely failed to rehabilitate criminals. More and more emphasis is being put on *community* supervision through *parole* or *probation*, and efforts are being made to reintegrate the offender into society. The newest trends also call for diversion of alcoholics and drug addicts from correctional systems to community programs. Efforts to reform delinquents have been unsuccessful, so the idea of radical nonintervention—interfering as little as possible with youths—is likely to become more popular in the future.

199

SUGGESTED READINGS

Hirschi, Travis. *Causes of Delinquency.* Berkeley: University of California Press, 1969.

Kelley, Clarence. *Crime in the United States, 1975: Uniform Crime Reports.* Washington, D.C.: U.S. Government Printing Office, 1975.

Matza, David. *Delinquency and Drift.* New York: Wiley, 1964.

Quinney, Richard (ed.). *Crime and Justice in Society.* Boston: Little, Brown, 1969.

Sutherland, Edwin H., and Donald R. Cressey. *Principles of Criminology.* 7th ed. New York: Lippincott, 1970.

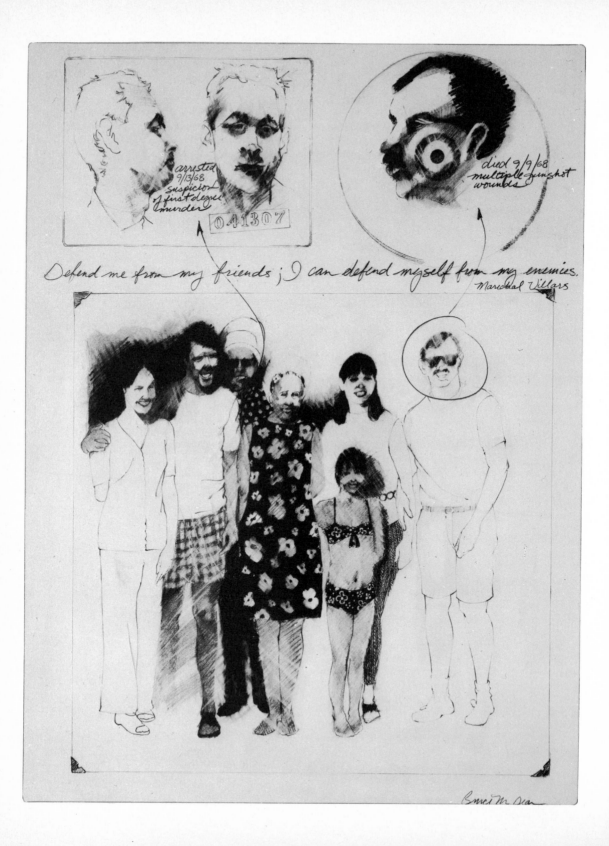

7

Interpersonal Violence

This chapter is about violence. It is not about metaphors of violence, as when we protest the violence done to our ideals and hopes. Nor is it about psychic scars or emotional hurts. This chapter is about a kick in the stomach, a knife in the chest, a shot in the head. It is about battered infants, about beaten-up old women and men, about murdered spouses, and about barroom fights. It is about America today.

How violent a nation are we? Who are the violent among us? Who are the victims? What are the causes of violence? What, if anything, can we do about violence?

Interpersonal violence is *the exertion of physical force by a person in order to injure or abuse the body of another person when such action violates prevailing social norms or laws.* This definition excludes instances of self-defense or other lawful violent actions, even though such actions may be in response to violence or threats of violence by others. A policeman shooting or clubbing someone in order to protect himself or others does not fit our definition of violence. But when the police shoot people needlessly (illegally), their behavior constitutes violence. By the same token, the violence that occurs during times of war is excluded from our definition of interpersonal violence, but war crimes are not excluded.

PART I: THE PROBLEM
INTERPERSONAL VIOLENCE

Although interpersonal violence, by this definition, is another category of crime and delinquency, we are treating it in a separate chapter for several reasons. First, much of the present public concern about violence is distinct from concern about crime. For example, there is considerable debate about the impact of violence depicted in movies and on television but little debate about the depiction of crime per se. Furthermore, the widespread public reluctance to walk the streets at night is not based nearly so much on fears of being robbed as it is on fears of being hurt. Second, social scientists find the distinction between violence and other kinds of crime necessary for purposes of explanation. The causes of violence and the causes of other kinds of crime, such as property crime, seem to be significantly different.

CRIMES OF VIOLENCE

Crimes of violence and property crimes differ in a number of important ways (Clinard and Quinney, 1973). For one thing, the economic motive is typically lacking in crimes of violence. Burglars hope to benefit at least economically from their crimes, but monetary rewards rarely play any part in fist-fighting, wife beating, child battering, and rape. People support themselves with property crime, but few make a career out of interpersonal violence. In fact, the term *career* offender is virtually restricted to property offenders. Those who repeat crimes of violence are usually identified as *chronic* offenders, but the recidivism rate (offenders committing another offense) is lower among those convicted of crimes of violence than among those convicted of property crimes.

202

Another way in which crimes of violence differ from other kinds of crime is in the offender-victim relationship. As is discussed at length later in this chapter, a sizable proportion of crimes of violence are committed against victims who know or are even related to the offender—more than half of the female murder victims are slain by a member of their own family. So violence is often a family affair. It is often characterized by an interpersonal dynamic that is lacking in the case of thieves and their victims. These differences let us treat separately property crimes and crimes of violence.

Before going further, however, we must ask more specifically what is meant by violence. How violent is violent? Recent public discussions of violence in our society have tended to blur this question and people often disagree about what is violent. Some consider shouting and making obscene gestures as acts of violence. Others doubt that it is violent for a man to slap his wife as long as he does not strike her with a closed fist. Obviously, these are matters of individual judgment. Throughout this chapter, we shall identify the specific acts of violence on which any given study or discussion is based. You can (and should) judge for yourself the relative seriousness of these acts.

In this section, we assess the extent and nature

of violent acts in the United States. The data available for this task come from the same sources we used in Chapter 6. All the defects of these statistics must be kept in mind. The Uniform Crime Reports (UCR), which are the *official* statistics, considerably *underestimate* what is actually occurring. Only crimes reported to the police and reported by them in turn to the FBI show up in these data. The nationwide *victimization* study (Ennis, 1967), discussed at length in Chapter 6, and other similar studies probably give more accurate estimates of the extent of violence. However, victimization data present a special difficulty in this chapter. Many crimes of violence, such as murder and rape, are relatively rare events, compared with burglary and robbery. Thus, sample surveys turn up so few cases that the data on these crimes are virtually meaningless. For example, the largest victimization study was based on nearly 33,000 interviews, but it uncovered only one report of murder and thirteen reports of rape (Ennis, 1967). Because the one murder occurred in the South, a projection of regional murder rates from this study would lead to the absurd conclusion that all murders occur in the South. We will also consider *self-reports* of violent actions in this chapter. But recall from Chapter 6 that one self-report study (Clark and Tifft, 1966) determined that college students *overreport* their involvement in fistfights. Whether this finding applies to the general population as well is unknown. These defects in the data must be taken into account in the following discussions.

HOW MUCH VIOLENCE DO AMERICANS COMMIT?

Because it is not clear what behavior to classify as violent, it is impossible to compute some overall violence rate. All that can be said about how much violence there is in the United States is that certain acts of violence occur with a particular frequency. In this section, we assemble data from the official statistics, victimization surveys, and self-report studies to try to estimate how frequently certain kinds of serious acts of violence occur.

Murder and Assault with a Deadly Weapon

As has been mentioned in previous chapters, the homicide rate is probably the most accurate of all the UCR official statistics. During 1972, nearly 9 (8.9) out of every 100,000 Americans were homicide victims, which means that 19,000 Americans a year are being killed by their fellow human beings. This figure for one year is more than half the number of American military losses for the entire Korean War and is considerably higher than our military losses in our worst year in Vietnam. Indeed, it is equal to the total number of U.S. Marines killed during the whole of World War II.

These figures report only "successful" homicides. Just as the wounded far outnumber the dead in war, the rate of attempted homicides is much higher than the homicide rate. The majority of homicides were the result of gunshot wounds, for gunshot wounds are much more likely to be fatal than are attacks with knives, clubs, or fists.

Homicide rates are based on incidents in a given year, but people run a lifelong risk of becoming a victim of homicide or attempted homicide. If we assume a life span of seventy years and a homicide rate of 9 out of 100,000 per year, the average American from birth to age seventy has 630 chances out of 100,000 (or about 1 out of 166) of becoming a homicide statistic. Arnold Barnett has estimated that American males born in 1974 stand a 3 percent chance of being murdered during their lifetime. That percentage is higher than the combat death rate of American servicemen in World War II (Barnett *et al.*, 1974).

In 1968, the Harris Poll conducted a national survey for the National Commission on Causes and Prevention of Violence, which President Lyndon Johnson established in the wake of the assassinations of Robert F. Kennedy and Martin Luther King. A representative sample of the adult American population was selected, and 1,176 persons were interviewed. These data provide estimates on how many Americans have had encounters involving dangerous weapons (Stark and McEvoy, 1970). A substantial number of American adults have been involved in knife and gun incidents (military combat experiences excluded). One out of every twelve reported they had, as adults, been threatened or actually cut with a knife. One out of every seventeen said they had been threatened with guns or had been actually shot at. Furthermore, one adult out of every seventeen admitted having

used a gun or a knife against another person. Little wonder that one American becomes a homicide victim every twenty-eight minutes.

Assault

Official statistics on assault include attacks with deadly weapons and attacks with fists and feet. In 1972, the assault rate was 186.6 per 100,000 persons; 389,000 assaults were reported to the police. Surveys of victims, however, indicate that assault is perhaps twice as high as official statistics indicate. The large-scale study of victims conducted in 1965 (Ennis, 1967) indicates 218 assaults per 100,000 persons during that year, whereas the official rate for 1965 was only 109.8 per 100,000.

Such rates suggest that a very substantial number of Americans engage in or are victims of assaults. This indication is confirmed by the Harris Poll data (Stark and McEvoy, 1970). Among adults, about one out of eight say they have punched or beaten another person or have been punched or beaten. Among men, the proportion is one out of five. In addition, about one out of five adults admits to having slapped or kicked another person. (Childhood incidents and those that occur in sports or military service are excluded from these statistics.)

As will be discussed later, a substantial proportion of assaults occur within the family, especially between husbands and wives. The Harris Poll found that about one out of five American adults could imagine a situation in which they would approve of husbands and wives slapping each other in the face (Stark and McEvoy, 1970).

Battered Children

Recently, there has been considerable public concern about the "battered-child syndrome," about infants and young children who are beaten savagely—sometimes to death. As a result, every state except Hawaii has passed laws requiring physicians and others who encounter evidence of child abuse to report it.

How common a problem is child abuse? UCR statistics do not have a separate category for battered children—some incidents show up as homicide, some as assault. A recent study by David Gil (1970) attempted to determine the incidence of se-

203

vere child abuse. Gil and his staff screened all reports for the years 1967 and 1968 and discarded 40 percent of them as unfounded and trivial. Using the remaining reports, Gil estimated that during these two years there were about 9 such incidents per 100,000 children under age eighteen. However, more than half of these incidents involved only minor injuries to the child. Thus, Gil concluded that the battered child is a relatively rare phenomenon. The seriousness of this crime and the shock and outrage people feel whenever they encounter a report of a battered child, much more than the frequency of this form of violence, are the cause of the present efforts directed to prevent it.

Keep in mind that this discussion has been about the severe mistreatment of children. Spanking is another matter. Eighty-four percent of American adults report they have at some time spanked a child (78 percent of men and 90 percent of women). Furthermore, 93 percent of all Americans recall being spanked from time to time as children. However, 92 percent of Americans would *not* approve of ''a parent beating his or her child'' (Stark and McEvoy, 1970).

Although most serious kinds of violence occur much less frequently than do property crimes in the United States, acts of serious violence, taken together, cannot be considered rare. Most of us have at least seen a serious fistfight—and chances are someone we know has been or will become a homicide victim.

IS VIOLENCE INCREASING?

It is very difficult to estimate whether or to what extent the incidence of violent acts has been changing in America. For one thing, we must rely mainly on official statistics; victimization and self report studies are all too recent to provide data on trends. Worse yet, even the official statistics do not go back very far (and the basis of the statistics has changed over time).

Historical research for the Violence Commission suggests that there was considerably more violence in the United States during the nineteenth century than there has been during the twentieth century (Graham and Gurr, 1969). This change, although we lack solid data to confirm it, does

agree with modern statistics showing that the violent-crime rate is much lower in advanced industrial nations than in underdeveloped nations. Another indication of declining violence in America since the last century comes from a study of police deaths. The rate at which police officers are killed in the line of duty has dropped each decade since the turn of the century (Stark, 1972).

Even if the long-term trend has been a decline in violence, it seems that during the last decade there has been a rise in violence. The Violence Commission has examined UCR statistics back to 1933, the earliest date for which usable national records exist. These statistics show that crimes of violence (homicide, rape, robbery, and assault) declined during the 1930s, rose after World War II, stayed fairly steady during the late 1940s and 1950s, and then climbed sharply from the mid-1960s on. Some of this increase is undoubtedly due to better police record keeping and reporting. Some probably reflects changes in the criteria used by the police for classifying offenses. And some may be the result of increased public reporting of crime. It seems implausible, however, given the magnitude of the increases, that there has been no corresponding actual increase in the rate at which these crimes have been occurring.

IS AMERICA A VIOLENT NATION?

We now compare levels of violence in the United States with those experienced in other nations in order to determine whether the United States has a disproportionate amount of violence or whether violence is common in all human societies. International comparisons are difficult to make because, once again, only official statistics are available. Variations in the quality of record keeping and the basis for classifying crimes differ greatly from one country to another. By restricting ourselves to homicide rates, we minimize these problems.

Figure 7.1 shows that the homicide rate in the United States is very much higher than in other developed nations. For example, the homicide rate in 1966 was 6 per 100,000 in the United States. Across the border in Canada it was only 1.3 per 100,000. In England and Wales the homicide rate in 1966 was 0.7—miniscule in comparison to the

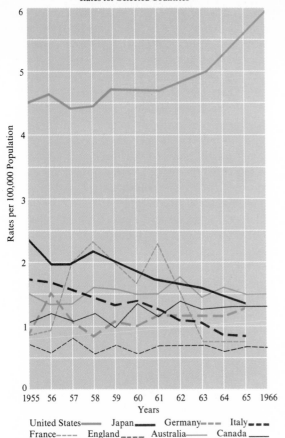

Variations in Reported Homicide Rates for Selected Countries

Rates per 100,000 Population

Years

United States——— Japan——— Germany——— Italy———
France———— England———— Australia——— Canada———

Figure 7.1 (Above) *Our relatively high homicide rate is partly due to the large number of "gun murders" in the United States. Such murders are less frequent in other industrialized countries, such as West Germany, England, and Japan, that control the sale and use of firearms.*
(Adapted from United Nations *Demographic Yearbooks*, 1955-1967.)

Figure 7.2 (Below) *Homicide rates are higher in larger cities. These differences have increased since 1962.*
(Adapted from United Crime Reports, 1968.)

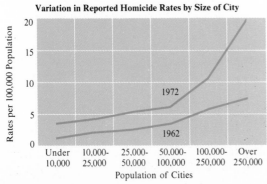

Variation in Reported Homicide Rates by Size of City

Rates per 100,000 Population

1972

1962

Under 10,000 10,000-25,000 25,000-50,000 50,000-100,000 100,000-250,000 Over 250,000

Population of Cities

American figure. In fact, there are more homicides each year in the city of Philadelphia (population 2 million) than in all of Great Britain (population 54 million). Similarly, nations such as Japan, Germany, France, Italy, and Australia have homicide rates many times lower than ours.

To find homicide rates as high or higher than ours, we must look at the impoverished, underdeveloped nations. However, even many of these countries have rates much lower than ours: Ceylon with 2.2 per 100,000; the Philippines with 2.1; Mozambique with 2.6. Others have much higher rates, especially Latin American countries: the homicide rate is 21.3 in Columbia, 29.3 in Nicaragua, and 18.9 in Mexico. (Many experts believe that the homicide rates in underdeveloped nations are seriously underreported.)

The answer to the question of whether America is a violent nation thus depends on which society we choose for purposes of comparison. Compared with nations that most closely resemble us economically and culturally, we are an extremely homicide-prone nation. Compared with many underdeveloped nations, we appear in a much better light. However, these data tell us only about homicide. We cannot be sure that comparisons for assault, rape, or other acts of violence would tell the same story. Indeed, in Part III of this chapter, we attempt to demonstrate that the main cause of the high homicide rate in this country is the extraordinary prevalence of privately owned firearms. If this is so, then other nations may have lower homicide rates because they have fewer guns, not because their citizens are less violent.

205

WHERE DOES AMERICAN VIOLENCE OCCUR?

So far, we have discussed violence in America. We will now look inside the national statistics to see if violence is especially a city problem and if there are important regional differences.

Cities

Official statistics on violence make it clear that the problem is overwhelmingly concentrated in major urban areas. The larger cities have higher official rates for violent crimes. For example, in 1972, as shown in Figure 7.2, the homicide rate for cities with more than a quarter million inhabitants stood at 19.7 per 100,000, or more than twice the national rate. For cities having fewer than 10,000 inhabitants, the homicide rate was only 3.8 per 100,000. Differences of similar magnitude apply for other violent crimes (see Chapter 6).

Victimization surveys and self-report studies also find that violence is heavily concentrated in the cities. Indeed, Figure 7.2 tends to minimize this fact. When we examine the homicide rates for the very large cities, some truly frightening facts emerge. For example, Detroit, once known as the "Motor Capital," is now called the "Murder Capital" of the nation by the press. In 1973 the homicide rate in Detroit was 49.4 per 100,000, or one murder a year for every 1,806 residents. Based on a seventy-year life span, the approximate odds against being murdered in Detroit are only 26 to 1. In second place is Cleveland with a rate of 36.8, in third place, Washington with 36.5, then St. Louis with 36.3, and New Orleans with 33.7. Contrary to popular belief, New York has a relatively low rate of 20.7, well below the rates of such cities as Denver and Portland, which have reputations for being safer cities to live in.

A massive victimization survey released by the Law Enforcement Assistance Administration in 1974 confirmed these variations among thirteen major cities. The study again showed that crimes of violence are extremely underreported to the police, and thus the official statistics (aside from homicide figures) greatly minimize the incidence of violence. The study also found that underreporting varied greatly from one city to another. These findings are summarized in Figure 7.3. Column 1 shows the ratio of unreported to reported crime. Crime reporting is highest in Newark, where there were only 1.4 crimes of violence found in victim surveys for every violent crime reported to the police. Reporting is worst in Philadelphia, where the victim survey found 5.1 violent crimes for every one reported to the police. Based on these victimization data, violent crimes (in this case, rape, robbery, and assault) were most frequent in Detroit (6,800 such crimes per 100,000 residents per year) and were least often committed in the city of New York (3,600 per 100,000).

Crime in the large cities has been increasing each year. For example, between 1966 and 1972 the national homicide rate increased by 60 percent. But in cities of over a quarter million the rate increased by 100 percent during the same period.

Geographic Regions

For decades, the South has had the reputation of being a region of violence, and this view is supported by official statistics. For years, the Southern homicide rate was about twice that of the rest

Ratio of unreported to reported crimes	Cities	Total crimes of violence per 100,000 residents per year
2.7 to 1	Detroit	6800
2.9 to 1	Denver	6700
5.1 to 1	Philadelphia	6300
2.6 to 1	Portland, Ore.	5900
2.2 to 1	Baltimore	5600
2.8 to 1	Chicago	5600
2.4 to 1	Cleveland	5400
2.9 to 1	Los Angeles	5300
2.3 to 1	Atlanta	4800
2.6 to 1	Dallas	4300
1.4 to 1	Newark	4200
1.5 to 1	St. Louis	4200
2.1 to 1	New York	3600

of the nation. However, recent increases in homicide in the rest of the nation have begun to close the gap; in 1972, there were 12.6 homicides per 100,000 in the South, compared with 7.3 outside the South. Assault rates have similarly distinguished the South from the rest of the nation.

Other data suggest, however, that this view of a violence-ridden South may be mistaken. Victimization data show that the South has a considerably *lower* incidence of assault than other regions and less than half the assault rate of the West (Ennis, 1967). Self-report data also fail to single out the South (Stark and McEvoy, 1970). The South had the least amount of self-reported punching and beating of and by other persons; Southerners report the same amount of experience with knifing and shooting as persons living elsewhere in the nation. Indeed, if there are any meaningful regional differences in the self-report data, they indicate that the West (primarily California) has slightly more violence that other regions.

It is unclear why the official statistics show a higher rate of violence than do victimization and self-report data in the South. It may be that crimes of violence are more often reported to the police in the South and thus inflate official comparisons. But this could hardly be the case with homicide. Rodney Stark and James McEvoy (1970) have speculated that ''it may be that the South's surface

pattern of gentility suppresses many violent urges—so that there is less violence generally, but when it erupts it does so with greater passion and more deadly results.'' It is also the case that gun ownership is higher in the South, so attempts at murder may be more successful in the South than they are in other parts of the country.

WHO ARE THE VIOLENT AMERICANS?

Because questions about the characteristics of persons most likely to commit acts of violence are so vital to explanations of violence, the bulk of this discussion is deferred to Part II. Here we offer but a brief profile.

Official statistics indicate that young people under twenty-five are most likely to be arrested for acts of violence, but self-report data offer only weak confirmation that young people are more violence prone. Not surprisingly, however, self-reports of men over forty-five indicate considerably less willingness to personally engage in physical violence than do self-reports of younger men.

Both official and self-report statistics show a very marked sex difference. Women are much less likely than men to be arrested for violent acts or to report having engaged in them.

Official statistics indicate a very high over-involvement of blacks and other disadvantaged

207

Figure 7.3   (Far left) Contrary to the popular stereotype of New York as a violence-ridden city, the violent-crime rate shows New York to be a less violent place to live than Detroit. The ratio of unreported to reported crimes may vary by city, but victimization data have shown that in every case there are fewer violent crimes reported than committed. (Law Enforcement Assistance Administration.)

Figure 7.4   (Left) Bullet holes made by police firearms during a raid on a house occupied by members of the Black Panther organization. Fred Hampton, a Black Panther, died in his bedroom during the raid by the Chicago police in December 1969.

Homicide in the Home
Most homicide victims are killed at home. Where in the home the killing occurs is closely related to the sex of the victim. The bedroom is the most dangerous room in the house, and nearly a fifth of all homicides happen there. The bedroom is especially dangerous for females. Although more males than females are killed in the bedroom, that is because men are much more likely than women to be killed. But of women homicide victims, more than a third die in the bedroom (while only 14 percent of male victims succumb there).

The kitchen is the dangerous place for men. While men rarely kill women in the kitchen, nearly one out of three female killers strikes in the kitchen (and their victim is nearly always a man). The usual murder weapon in kitchen killings is a butcher knife. Elsewhere in the home guns are the usual weapons. These patterns suggest that homicide is typically an angry, impulsive act, committed with a weapon conveniently at hand and in the room where the conflict breaks out.
—Adapted from Marvin E. Wolfgang, ''Who Kills Whom'' (*Psychology Today*, vol. 3, October 1969), pp. 54–56, 72–75.

groups in crimes of violence. These statistics may well reflect differences in police surveillance (recall Chapter 3), in whom the police arrest and whom they let go, and in which violent acts are and are not reported to the police. Self-report data do *not* reveal important interracial differences in committing violent acts.

As with race, the official statistics of income level suggest a considerable overrepresentation of persons with low incomes and little education, whereas self-report data do not.

WHO ARE THE VICTIMS?

Perhaps the most surprising thing anyone can learn about violence in America is that the profile of the victim of violence is virtually identical to the profile of the violent offender. It seems to be true, as the Bible says, that ''As ye sow, so shall ye reap.'' Studies of violence have therefore focused on the *relationship* between offenders and victims.

In a now classic study, Marvin Wolfgang (1958) analyzed the police files on homocides committed in Philadelphia from 1948 to 1952 and concluded that ''criminal homicide is probably the most personalized crime of our society.'' Wolfgang found, for example, that only about 15 percent of 550 solved homicides were committed by a total stranger. A study based on a random sample of arrest and offense reports from seventeen major cities in 1967 confirmed these findings (Mulvihill and Tumin, 1969). The study found that the victim and aggressor were known to have had no prior relationship in only about 18 percent of the murders in the seventeen cities. (In another 21 percent of the cases, the relationship was unknown; in these cases there was probably no close prior relationship between offender and victim, although they were not necessarily strangers.)

The closeness of the victim-offender relationship varies considerably by race and sex. Figure 7.5 shows, for example, that at least 64 percent of white females and 67 percent of black females were murdered by a primary-group member. For men, however, the pattern is very different. For this analysis, the researchers did not subdivide the nonprimary group category into acquaintances and strangers; therefore, the variation by race and sex

Victim-Offender Relationship

Percent of Blacks   Percent of Whites

60 50 40 30 20 10 0   0 10 20 30 40 50 60

Killed by spouse

Killed by other family member

Killed by other primary group member

Killed by nonprimary group member

Killer unknown

■ Female   Male ■

Figure 7.5 (Top) *The majority of female murder victims are killed by persons they knew well.*
(Adapted from Task Force Victim-Offender Survey.)

Figure 7.6 (Below) *Unlike violence among humans, fighting among animals within the same species rarely results in death. One of these fighting hippos will give up, and the fight will stop before either suffers serious injury.*

in murder by strangers cannot be determined. However, because there is frequently a relatively close relationship between victim and offender, contrary to popular opinion, most murders are *intra*racial rather than *inter*racial; that is, they occur within the same race, not between races. In about 90 percent of the murders involving blacks *or* whites, the victim and the offender were of the same race. Of the remainder, 6 percent involved a black killing a white, and 4 percent involved a white killing a black.

The close prior association of many victims and offenders in homicide and aggravated assault suggests the possibility that many of these crimes may grow out of interpersonal struggle or conflict rather than out of any one-sided action by the offender. Marvin Wolfgang and Franco Ferracuti suggest, for example, that in many homicides, "chance, prowess, or possession of a particular weapon dictates the identity of the slayer and of the slain" (1967). In his study of homicides in Philadelphia, Wolfgang (1958) estimated that in about 25 percent of the cases the victim was the first to use physical force against his or her slayer. In the Seventeen Cities Survey, 22 percent of all homicides were thought to have involved victim precipitation (Mulvihill and Tumin, 1969). In many cases, the events leading to a homicide cannot be discovered. When these mysterious cases are left out, the proportion of victim precipitated homicide increases to 40 percent. In other words, the homicide victims themselves apparently "started the fight" or at least had antagonized the offender at an earlier time. The Seventeen Cities Survey found that victim precipitation—which even includes being the first to use insinuating language—was a weaker factor in cases of aggravated assault.

PART II: SOURCES
INTERPERSONAL VIOLENCE

Keeping in mind the shortcomings of the data, we have now reviewed the essential facts on violence in our society. But the facts never speak for themselves. There are many plausible accounts to offer. We now turn to the task of sorting through the many explanations offered for violence and dis-

covering which ones the facts make unlikely and which ones seem to make sense.

PHYSIOLOGICAL SOURCES OF VIOLENCE

For centuries, there has been heated debate over the fundamental nature of human beings. Are we driven by dark and destructive instincts, as Hobbes and Freud argued, or is our basic nature peaceful, as Locke and Rousseau believed? And if there is a fundamental human nature, why are some people violent and others not?

It was very fashionable during the late nineteenth century to attribute basic human nature (whether violent or gentle) to instinct—to assume that at bottom our nature is biologically determined in the same way that spiders are born with the ability to spin webs. For most of the twentieth century, instinct theory of this kind has been in disrepute. Lately, however, it has been greatly revived in a series of popular books, particularly Konrad Lorenz's *On Aggression* (1966) and Robert Ardrey's *African Genesis* (1961) and *The Territorial Imperative* (1966).

Because these interpretations of violent behavior that are based on instinct have received such widespread publicity, we shall deal with them here. Indeed, if they are correct, our examination of the causes of violence can be very brief: We can simply conclude that violence is a fundamental and unalterable part of the human genetic inheritance. Fortunately, it appears that "human nature" is neither so simple nor so hopeless. After discussing instinct theories of violence, we will briefly examine other physiological factors that may influence violent behavior.

The Murderous Animal

Konrad Lorenz is a world famous observer of animal behavior, and he won the Nobel Prize for his studies of the greylag goose. His observations, especially of birds, lead him to conclude that animals have a basic aggressive instinct that serves to space animals apart (so that they do not compete so directly for food) and to establish a hierarchy necessary for orderly social life and for defense against other animal species. But, in addition, he argues that most species capable of killing one

209

another have developed inhibitions against carrying aggression to the point of killing. For example, various animals have noncombative controls over territory and have rituals, such as songs, to avoid fighting. If fights do develop, an animal may make appeasement gestures, such as offering a vulnerable part of its body to the aggressor.

The most widely cited part of Lorenz's work, and by far the most controversial, is his argument that only pride and arrogance prevent our applying these observations to the study of human behavior. Lorenz argues that humans failed to develop the natural inhibitors to aggression because they were not strong enough to kill each other. With the development of weaponry, however, inhibitors were needed, and customs (social inhibitors) had to be developed to control aggression. Lorenz holds that the aggressive drive cannot be bottled up. Other animals express this drive in *gestures* such as threat behavior or even in mating rituals. Humans, too, need socially acceptable outlets, and competitive sports are important in this regard.

Robert Ardrey is another widely read author writing in the same tradition as Lorenz. In 1955, he learned of the discovery in Southern Africa of the skull of the earliest human prototype. Examinations of injuries to this skull raised the possibility that the development of weapons preceded much of the development of the human brain. Some scientists accept this hypothesis, but it is still very much in dispute.

Since he learned of the skull, Ardrey has devoted his time to the study of the instinctual nature of aggression. He has drawn on the work of scientists who accept the thesis that weapons came first and that the brain developed to serve a violent life style. He therefore argues that the potential for rational social control is limited and that "rational" ideas developed in the political arena will not be as effective in the control of aggression as will the insights gained from the study of animals. Drawing on a wide variety of studies of animal societies, including Lorenz's, he concludes that one of the most effective of these mechanisms of control is territoriality, which he seems to identify with private property and nationalism.

The instinct theories of Lorenz and Ardrey have been severely criticized on a number of grounds

210

(Montagu, 1973). First, both theories underestimate the extent to which animal behavior is learned rather than inborn. Second, one cannot generalize from birds to human beings without explaining why differences between the two are unimportant. As Leonard Berkowitz (1973) put it, "for Lorenz, man is remarkably similar to the Greylag goose." Clearly, humans and higher primates lack certain instinctive traits present in geese. A goose raised in isolation, for example, is perfectly capable of mating when given the opportunity, but as Chapter 2 pointed out, monkeys raised in isolation are unable to engage in sex. Indeed, Chapter 8 shows that a major problem exists in our society today because people lack the means to learn appropriate sexual behavior. If humans and primates have to learn sexual behavior but geese do not, who is to say that humans have instinctual aggressiveness simply because research shows that geese do?

Finally, a serious problem arises when we take up the question of variations in violent behavior. An instinct is present in all normal members of a given species. But what social scientists want to know about human aggression is why some people are violent and aggressive and others are not. Instinct theory cannot address that question. At best, instinct theory can argue that there is a certain underlying energy or potential present in all humans and that under some circumstances this energy is "discharged" in the form of aggressiveness. But this tells us very little, for our concern must be with the circumstances under which such discharges occur.

Genes and Hormones

Several years ago, considerable publicity was given to what seemed to be a major breakthrough in finding a physiological basis for violence. Geneticists discovered the existence of XYY human males. Normal males have an X chromosome (from their mother) and a Y chromosome (from their father); when two X chromosomes (one from each parent) combine, the offspring is female. But a small number of males in fact have one X and *two* Y chromosomes. The consequence of this accident is an increase in their amount of male hormones. XYY males tend to be taller than average and to have exaggerated secondary sex characteristics, such as a heavy beard and a deep voice. Early studies suggested that XYY males were overrepresented in the prison populations. There was considerable speculation that a by-product of excessive male characteristics would be a tendency toward violent and aggressive behavior. This line of research failed to be fruitful. Subsequent studies of prison populations have failed to show a disproportionate number of XYY inmates. Additional studies have been unable to demonstrate that XYY males have any unusual tendencies toward aggressiveness (Hook, 1973).

Additional research has focused on brain damage and on the role of the hypothalamus and related organs at the base of the brain in causing violent behavior. Researchers are able to cause outbursts of violent and aggressive behavior in animals such as cats and monkeys by stimulating the hypothalamus. Others have implicated certain kinds of brain damage in violent behavior. It is as yet too early to tell where this research will lead. At present, we simply do not know the extent to which physiological factors, such as the ones we have discussed, are involved in violent behavior.

PSYCHOLOGICAL SOURCES OF VIOLENCE

Two dominant themes characterize psychological writing on interpersonal violence. The first tends to emphasize the individual's loss of control over behavior, often in response to stressful situations. The second examines the role of learning, especially of imitative behavior. Obviously the two ideas are not incompatible. The first emphasizes the motives for violence; the second tries to explain how an individual, once motivated, has these particular behavioral patterns available.

Loss of Control

It seems appropriate here to relate our discussion of violence to problems taken up in earlier chapters. It is well known that alcohol lowers inhibitions, and people therefore do things while intoxicated that they would not do when sober. It should be no surprise that studies have found an important link between alcohol and violence. In his study of homicides, Wolfgang (1958) found that in 64 per-

cent of the cases, either the victim, the offender, or both had significant amounts of alcohol in their blood. And it is no coincidence that assaults, homicides, and family fights most commonly occur in the evenings and on weekends when the largest number of persons are intoxicated. While we do not know they are related, it is the case that the rise in alcohol consumption since World War II parallels the rise in violent crimes. On the other hand, research has not shown that narcotics directly influence violence. People high on drugs tend to be passive rather than aggressive or violent. Narcotics use probably produces violence mainly as a by-product to the crimes addicts commit in order to finance their habits. Mental illness could also produce—or, indeed, represent—a lack of control over violent impulses. However, as we pointed out in Chapter 6, the role of mental illness in crime, including crimes of violence, seems to be limited.

The major psychological theory that tries to explain loss of control is *frustration-aggression* theory. The fundamental premise, given its classic statement in 1939 by John Dollard and his associates at Yale, is that aggressive behavior (of which violence is one form) occurs when some activity is interrupted or prevented—when a person is frustrated or when his or her efforts to obtain some goal are thwarted. The theory does not assume that frustration lowers a person's inhibitions but rather that frustration builds up to the point that it overcomes any inhibitions that a person might have against aggressive behavior.

For more than three decades, psychologists have recognized that many qualifications must be added to this theory, and they have been testing and refining it (Berkowitz, 1969). For one thing, frustration does not *always* lead to aggression. For another, aggression can occur in the *absence* of frustration, for example, out of boredom. Furthermore, many factors may operate to increase or decrease the likelihood that frustration will result in aggression. For example, aggression is more likely to occur if the cause of the frustration is not explained or understood. For example, students are often willing to wade through boring material if they are shown why it will be useful to them, but they are likely to throw the book at the wall if they are simply told they must read it. Aggression is

211

less likely to follow frustration if aggression in the past has proved unsuccessful; for example, the small boy soon stops hitting bigger and stronger boys who frustrate him. Aggression is also less likely to follow frustration if a nonaggressive response has proved effective in the past; for example, a child has learned that crying, not hitting, will get him the candy his mother had originally refused him. It is evident that frustration-aggression is greatly influenced by *learning*.

Learning Theories of Violence

Aggressive and violent behavior is learned; that is, if people are reinforced (rewarded) for aggression they tend to repeat it. It seems to be a fact of social life that some amount of aggressive behavior is rewarded beginning in early childhood. For example, children increase their aggressive behavior in nursery school, for they quickly find that aggression is rewarded—others yield them toys, a place in the game, and other things they want in response to the use of force. Passive children entering nursery school are initially the victims of aggression. But eventually they fight back and are reinforced for doing so (Patterson *et al.*, 1967). A great many studies have found that aggressive behavior among children can be increased or decreased by controlling whether or not such behavior is rewarded (Zigler and Child, 1973).

Perhaps even more significant is the work by Bandura and Walters (1959, 1963), which shows that children often learn aggressive behavior with-

Figure 7.7 (Above and top right) *Aggressive behavior among children is learned early from peers or adult models and may be reinforced and rewarded by toy weapons or by adult and peer approval. Aggressive behavior may also result from frustration. (Bottom right) A fight breaks out between a frustrated soccer fan and a player during a game in Mexico City.*

out being reinforced. This learning is called *modeling,* or copying someone else's (the model's) behavior. In a great variety of experiments, Bandura and Walters have let children observe a model (usually an adult) engaging in a number of aggressive acts, such as hitting a large rubber doll or pounding on furniture. Children who have observed the aggressive behavior tend to imitate it in their play, while children who have not observed the model are less apt to pound on dolls or perform other imitative acts.

These findings have been the major basis for present concern over aggressiveness and violence on television and in the movies, especially in children's cartoon shows. Because children in experiments do tend to model, or imitate, aggressive

behavior even when they are not reinforced for doing so, it is argued that they undoubtedly learn a great deal of aggressive and even violent behavior from exposure to the mass media. There is a considerable campaign going on to minimize the violence and aggression in children's programing and in the mass media generally. Because such claims have been raised so vigorously, it is worthwhile to assess them.

Mass Media Violence

A number of studies have attempted to determine whether exposure to aggressive and violent behavior via the mass media causes people to subsequently behave in aggressive or violent ways. Much of this work was summed up in a report

213

issued by the Surgeon General's Scientific Advisory Committee on Television and Social Behavior in 1972. Unfortunately, the findings are contradictory, and it is difficult to say whether or not media violence produces violent behavior. Clearly, the overwhelming majority of children can distinguish between reality and make-believe. They know they cannot jump off a two-hundred-foot cliff just because cartoon characters do so. They can even distinguish between reality and make-believe violence to human beings in television dramas. Children's ability to discriminate between fantasy and reality has considerable bearing on many of the modeling experiments. The aggressive behavior observed in most of those studies was make-believe aggression. Children were not shown one person hitting another person but only a person hitting the Bobo doll (a large rubber doll that bounces back when hit) or some other inanimate object. Similarly, the aggressive behavior the children engaged in after observing the model also involved play with inanimate objects. The studies did not find that watching a model strike a big rubber doll led children to strike one another. We are probably not concerned about children whacking away at their dolls so long as it does not carry over into their interpersonal behavior.

Unfortunately, it is difficult to tell from existing studies whether or not such behavior does carry over. Several studies suggest that only some (perhaps very few) children are influenced by media violence. It appears that children with a prior history of exceptionally aggressive behavior are more likely than others to be prompted by mass media exposure to act aggressively. Of course, many factors cause such children to behave aggressively. Indeed, it is possible that it is not media violence that causes them to react but simply that any stimulus that excites them (including comedy as well as violence) may set them off. Other data suggest that boys may be more influenced than girls by media violence.

Other scholars, especially Seymour Feshbach and Robert Singer (1971), challenge the idea that exposure to media violence stimulates aggressive behavior in young viewers. They argue that watching mass media violence often has a cathartic effect—that pent-up frustrations are harmlessly and vicariously released in this way. Indeed, one study recently found that some children showed an increase in prosocial rather than antisocial behavior after viewing violence on television (Surgeon General's Scientific Advisory Committee on Television and Social Behavior, 1972). Perhaps the best conclusion we can draw is that media violence may have a slightly harmful effect on some children or some effect on a very few children, but it does not seem to be a major stimulus to aggressive and violent behavior in our society. That should not be a surprise, for violent behavior, unlike television, is hardly a twentieth-century invention.

SOCIAL-PSYCHOLOGICAL SOURCES OF VIOLENCE: SOCIALIZATION

Our discussion of the impact of mass media violence on children leads us to inquire into childhood socialization. Many believe that the tendency to react in violent ways is instilled in childhood. In this section, we discuss the role of socialization of the young in violent behavior.

What difference does it make how parents deal with their child's aggressive behavior toward others? It seems almost self-evident that mothers (or whoever is raising a child) can play a major role in discouraging or reinforcing aggressive behavior. (However, we have seen that what seems self-evident is not always true.)

One of the major studies done on childhood socialization is known as the Six Cultures Study. Mothers and children were carefully studied in six Western and non-Western societies: a village caste group in northern India, an American community in New England, an Indian village in Mexico, a Gusii village in Kenya, a barrio in northern Luzon, Philippine Islands, and a village on Okinawa. The researchers tried to make sure that communities were selected so that families in any given society were economically and culturally similar. A team of researchers went to each community and intensively observed behavior.

One major focus of the study was how parents dealt with their children's aggressive behavior and the effects of these parental practices on the child's subsequent behavior (Minturn and Lambert, 1964). The research showed that there was considerable variation in child-rearing practices *within* each culture. Although differences across the six cultures were considerable, in each community there were mothers whose child-rearing methods were more like those predominant in another culture than those predominant in their own culture.

The research revealed that mothers in the Indian village in Mexico were *most* likely to punish their children for aggressive behavior toward other children. The American mothers in the New England town were *least* likely to punish aggressive behavior. The study also found that when relatives lived nearby (sharing a central courtyard, for example), rules against children's fighting were strictest. Within each culture they found that the more children there were in a family, the more likely parents were to punish fighting. Apparently, fighting within families is more disruptive than fighting among unrelated children.

But the important question is, Did the punishment of aggressive behavior influence the way the children acted? Surprisingly, the answer is no. In all six cultures, children who were punished for aggressive behavior against other children were no more or less likely to be aggressive in the future than children whose aggressive behavior went ignored by their mothers. Similarly, whether or not a mother punished aggressive behavior directed toward her by the child had no effect on future aggressive behavior by the child (Minturn and Lambert, 1964). These findings are in accord with recent studies that show virtually no relationship between being subjected to punitive treatment as a child and engaging in acts of violence as an adult (Yarrow *et al.*, 1968).

Nevertheless, the levels of aggressive behavior by children differed considerably across the six cultures. Whether or not Mexican mothers punished aggression (as they tended to do) had no effect on their children's behavior. Yet their children exhibited less aggressiveness overall than did the New England children. Why? The answer seeems to lie in the peer group and in the values of the larger culture.

The study showed that the most lively children—those who display the highest rates of interaction with others—appear to conform most closely to the norms of their particular culture re-

gardless of how their mothers deal with them. Thus, the most lively children in the Mexican village were less likely than others to be aggressive with other children. The most lively kids in the New England town were more likely than others to be aggressive. How does this happen? Minturn and Lambert drew upon social-learning theory to explain this fact. Through observation of adult behavior, children learn what kind of behavior is valued, and they model or imitate that behavior in their interaction with one another. Thus, it is the positive or negative response of other children to a child's aggressive behavior that shapes that child's behavior. The lively children, because they do more interacting, receive more feedback or reinforcement from other children. Thus, the livelier the child, the faster his or her behavior is shaped to meet the standards of the group. The conclusion is that children are more influenced by the society's norms governing violence than they are by the rules and regulations enforced by their parents.

This is simply to say that childhood socialization is primarily a learning process. Through interaction with our environment, especially our human environment, we learn to be human—including the capacity for acting aggressively.

However, assuming that violence is the product of social learning, why is it that some people learn to behave violently and others do not? Indeed, why do only a few people seem to be reinforced for using their fists, feet, knives, and guns on others? The conventional answer to that question is *differential association*. Some people are surrounded by others who reinforce them for violent behavior, but most people are not. Differential association raises the question of why some people have associates who reinforce them for violent behavior. And that question takes us to a higher level of analysis.

215

SOCIOLOGICAL EXPLANATIONS OF VIOLENCE: MIDDLE RANGE

Is there something about larger social structures, processes, and institutions that causes some people to be violent? As we shall see, recent efforts to explain violence have concentrated on this question. Unfortunately, much of what we thought we knew has, during the past several years, turned out to be wrong. For reasons that will be apparent, we turn most of our attention to subcultural explanations; however, we will also summarize the contributions of strain and social-control theory.

Violent Subcultures

Perhaps the best-known theory of violence is the *subcultural* theory. It combines the insights of social-learning and differential-association theories to explain why some people learn to behave violently. It assumes that in the larger society there are certain social groups in which violent behavior reflects conformity to group norms. Subcultural theory has long been used to explain the behavior of juvenile gangs. Wolfgang (1958), however, applied the theory more generally to violence, using his study of victims and offenders in homicides.

Wolfgang and his colleague Ferracuti expanded their application of the theory in 1967, arguing that violent subcultures have two main characteristics: First, compared with other groups, people in such subcultures have a lower threshold of insult—they are "thin-skinned." Members of violent subcultures regard certain situations—that other groups would find trivial—as serious challenges to their integrity. Second, the norms of such subcultures require violent responses to such challenges: "Quick resort to physical combat as a measure of daring, courage, or defense of status appears to be

a cultural expression" (Wolfgang and Ferracuti, 1967).

Toughness, "machismo," and the ready use of violence are said to be highly admired traits in such a subculture. Persons who have these traits are claimed to be cultural heroes, as in the song lyrics "Bad, bad LeRoy Brown, baddest man in the whole damn town."

Accordingly, Wolfgang and Ferracuti saw violence as rooted in conformity to the violent norms of some subcultures in our society. In support of their views, they cited official statistics. The highest official rates for violent crime are found among blacks, poor people, males, and young adults. This theory certainly seemed plausible. It fit not only official statistics but also commonsense observations: Everybody knew that middle- and upper-class persons are less likely to vent their rage in physical ways; that the wives of the poor get beaten up; and that nonwhite minorities are especially burdened with violence. And everybody knew that to reduce violence, ways must be found to reduce the adherence to norms of prowess, manliness, and toughness prevalent in these subcultures.

But it seems that everybody did not really know at all. Victimization and self-report studies completed in the last several years contradict official statistics and show that the subcultural theory of violence fails in a number of ways. First, most

216

persons of all races and economic classes oppose violence. In fact, black and low-income parents are more opposed to fistfights among teenage boys than are white and middle-class parents. Toughness and other components of "machismo" are not the ideal among poor people, young people, males, nonwhites, or any combination of these groups (Erlanger, 1974; Ball-Rokeach, 1973). Second, there is no evidence that people who behave in violent ways have positive attitudes toward violence (Ball-Rokeach, 1973). Third, and most important, violent behavior does not seem to be related to race or social class.

The subcultural theory of violence is inadequate even though it does reflect the official statistics. Data that show blacks and poor people no more violence prone than white and middle-class people directly contradict police statistics that show blacks and poor Americans more likely to commit homicides and assaults and to have violent family fights. Leaving homicide for discussion below, the reason for the differences between official and self-report statistics seems to lie in differential visibility. The affairs of the poor, including their arguments and fights are more likely to come to the attention of the police. Middle-class people have many better alternatives than calling the police. For example, a middle-class wife whose husband beats her can turn to a marriage counselor, a psy-

chiatrist, or even a divorce lawyer rather than call the police. The poor more often have only the police to call and therefore more often become official statistics. Furthermore, Stark and McEvoy (1970) point out:

lower-class people are denied privacy for their quarrels: neighborhood bars, sidewalks, and crowded, thin-walled apartments afford little isolation. The privacy of the middle-class life-style preserves an illusion of greater domestic tranquility; but it is, apparently, only an illusion.

Faced with the collapse of what had seemed to be a powerful theory, social scientists recently began to reexamine the violent-subculture position from its earliest roots: observational studies of juvenile gangs. A rereading of these studies suggests that the conclusions drawn were incorrect.

First, the original studies had reported fluid and short-term gang membership for most members (Short and Strodtbeck, 1965; Matza, 1964; Yablonsky, 1962). That is, observations showed that the typical juvenile gang lacks sufficient structure and bonds among members to serve as a true subculture. Second, the evidence suggested that most of the aggressive acts observed were of low intensity, and nearly as many acts were directed to control and suppress physical aggression as to demonstrate toughness (Miller *et al.*, 1961). This does

217

Figure 7.8   The Young Lords, a militant Puerto Rican group, parading in New York City. Social scientists have recently reexamined widespread beliefs about violent gangs and violent subcultures. They discovered that such groups, for all the image of "toughness" they may project, are not unusually prone to violent behavior.

Figure 7.9   Middle-class violence is more common than most people suspect. The film Who's Afraid of Virginia Wolfe? *portrays one night in the lives of two couples. Edward Albee's play won wide acclaim because it so poignantly exposed the inner conflicts and violent eruptions of marriages that appear to be "normal."*

not mean that there are no tough, violence-prone gangs—indeed, one defect of observational studies is that the most violent gangs have disproportionately been the ones studied—nor does it mean that such gangs are not concentrated in poor and minority neighborhoods. However, the facts are that only a small minority of youths in such neighborhoods belong to such gangs, that the gangs are much less violent than assumed, that the gang members often act to enforce norms against violence, and that the gangs do not reflect adherence to violent norms by poor people or minorities.

Interestingly enough, the three most famous observational studies made of American slum communities—Whyte's *Street Corner Society* (1955), Liebow's *Talley's Corner* (1967), and Suttles' *Social Order of the Slum* (1968)—make little or no mention of violence. These upper-middle-class white observers with Ph.D.s did not seem to find the slums of the cities they studied (Boston, Washington, and Chicago, respectively) notably violent, even though they lived in these slums for extended periods. Liebow, for example, reports that a concern for masculinity and protecting one's dignity are central elements of street-corner groups of black males in Washington, D.C., but he notes that the assumed emphasis on violence is absent.

Explanations of Extreme Violence

We must remember that Wolfgang's initial formulation of the violent-subculture theory was based on homicide data. Given the serious nature of homicide, there is no reason to question the accuracy of police statistics or to doubt that homicide is extremely concentrated among the very poorest groups in our society, white and nonwhite. Extreme acts of violence, such as homicide, at-

tempted homicide, and very serious assault, might reflect the existence of a violent subculture, even though less extreme acts of violence do not, for less extreme acts are about equally common in all groups in society. However, there is another way to explain the high incidence of extreme violence among the poorest groups without using notions about violent subcultures. We shall call this explanation the *misfit* theory. It challenges conventional beliefs about both *violence* and *social class*. It argues two points: (1) that violent acts differ not merely in degree of seriousness but in kind and (2) that some members of the very poorest groups in the society are not part of the class system at all (Erlanger, 1971). We shall see how this theory combines these two concepts about violence.

Violence: Degrees or Kinds?

Social-science studies have usually conceived of violence as a matter of degree, as a shading from minor to extreme acts. This conception is depicted in Figure 7.10. At the far left, we see acts of symbolic and verbal violence—for example, when people shout threats of violence. Moving right, we see more physically harmful acts—for example, slapping, hitting, beating. At the far right, violence has reached the point where death may result. According to this view, violence is a process that tends to escalate from less serious to more serious acts, and people differ in their willingness to let this process begin.

The strength of this conception of violence as a process is that it can account for the fact that people who commit the most extreme acts of violence have typically engaged in all the lesser forms of violence as well. Its weakness is that it ignores the fact that most people have engaged in the least serious acts of violence but very *few*

SO YOU SEE, DEAR
BERNARD, WHILE I
THINK YOU'RE
SWEET AND
KIND AND
GOOD - I
CAN NEVER
LOVE YOU.

BERNARD
YOU HIT ME.

YES I DID!
WANT TO SEE
ME DO IT
AGAIN?

BUT BERNARD
THAT'S SO
UNLIKE YOU.
YOU'RE NOT
VIOLENT!

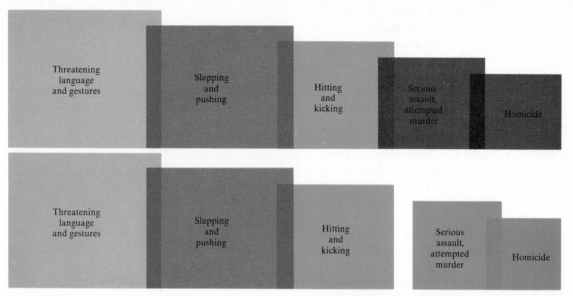

Figure 7.10 (Above) *All types of violence may initially appear to be of a kind, differing only in degree. However, in trying to account for homicide and serious physical assault, it makes more sense to classify these extreme acts as a separate category of behavior.*

> **A Killer**
> *In my lifetime I have murdered 21 human beings, I have committed thousands of burglaries, robberies, larcenies, arsons and last but not least I have committed sodomy on more than 1,000 male human beings. For all of these things I am not the least bit sorry. I have no conscience so that does not worry me. I don't believe in man, God nor Devil. I hate the whole damned human race including myself.*
> Quote is from Carl Panzram, who was executed on September 5, 1930, at the U.S. Penitentiary, Leavenworth, Kansas, for murder.
> —Thomas E. Gaddis and James O. Long, *Killer: A Journal of Murder* (New York: Macmillan, 1970), p. 12.

people have committed extreme acts such as severe assault, attempted homicide, or homicide.

To account for the fact that so few of us ever engage in such acts, we require a different conception of violence. A more adequate view sees acts of extreme violence as not merely more serious than lesser forms but as altogether *different kinds* of acts. This view is also depicted in Figure 7.10.

Killing your wife, for example, is not simply more serious than slapping her; killing is altogether different from slapping. Similarly, beating an infant nearly to death is not just an uncontrolled instance of spanking; spanking and beating are different kinds of acts. They probably stem from different motives. Moreover, people who spank children are probably different from those who batter children.

How do these people differ? To answer that question we shall consider the class system.

Class Boundaries

The subculture of violence theory sees acts of extreme violence as being concentrated in the lower reaches of the *class system.* It is among the very poor and deprived members of society that norms of violence are thought to justify homicide and other extreme acts. But, as we point out in detail in Chapter 9, many social analysts, including Marx, have long argued that at the very bottom of society are persons who cannot meaningfully be assigned any class position. Some people are not simply members of the most deprived class but are fundamentally *outside organized society* and the class system. They bear the marks of *outcasts.* Their lives are chaotic and deviant in many ways: They lack stable interpersonal relationships. They are chronically unemployed. They show high rates of alcoholism, divorce, illegitimacy, mental illness, and criminality. In a sense, they are the casualties of society—the misfits, the damned.

We have already seen that when we think of *violence* as simply a matter of degree and when we think of *social class* as including all members of society, then we are led to an inadequate theory of violence. For it would logically follow from this theory and from the concentration of extreme acts of violence among the most deprived members of society that the severity of violent behavior engaged in would gradually *decline* as one moves upward through the class structure. But we have already seen that this is not the case. Persons who are part of normal society, that is, part of the social-class system, (and who are likely to be located and interviewed in survey studies) display *no* variations in violent behavior on the basis of their social class. For example, college graduates are no less likely than those who do not finish high school to be involved in fistfights. This strongly suggests that extreme violence is different from less serious forms and that persons who commit extreme acts are not simply clustered on the lowest rung of the class system but are *outside* that system. There is recent evidence that this is in fact the case.

The study of homicides in seventeen major American cities in 1967, which we previously re-

ferred to (Mulvihill and Tumin, 1969), attempted to assemble data on the occupations of persons arrested for homicide. The researchers found that in most cases where occupation could be determined, the person held a manual or other low-status job. However, even more important was that in 63 percent of the cases the occupation was recorded as "unknown." This was because so large a proportion of homicide suspects *had no definite occupation and held no job* at the time. By the same token, data on males arrested for battering children reveal that a very high proportion of them are chronically unemployed.

According to the misfit theory of extreme violence, these data indicate that people who commit acts such as homicide are usually not part of the class structure and that their acts are different from the more ordinary kinds of violence that some members of all classes engage in. Chapter 9 explains who these outcast members of society are, what their lives are like, and how people end up in such circumstances.

It might be argued that the outcasts and underdogs themselves constitute a violent subculture. But, as we shall see, it seems more plausible to explain their behavior on the basis of psychological variables in conjunction with strain theories and control theories.

Strain Theories

Strain theories of violence represent a loose adaptation of frustration-aggression theories. The social source of frustration is the strain that results from the lack of legitimate means to achieve success. As we have seen, strain theories usually assume a strong relationship between social class and the phenomenon to be explained. Strain theorists have considerable difficulty with the lack of a relationship between violent behavior and social class (except in the special and limited sense of extreme violence among social outcasts). Indeed, not even among outcast members of our society—those subject to severe strain—is violent behavior common. Although homicide, assault, and the like are concentrated among social outcasts, these acts remain relatively uncommon events in this group.

The best known strain theory of violence makes some effort to overcome the difficulty of establish-

Figure 7.11   Various theories may be advanced to explain the causes of homicide. However, no matter which theory may best fit, the availability of inexpensive handguns, so-called "Saturday-night specials," in the United States has added significantly to our comparatively high rate of homicide. People who commit multiple murders, such as Richard Speck (above left), *who killed eight student nurses in Chicago, and Howard Unruh* (above right), *who slew thirteen people in Camden, New Jersey, seem to have little trouble finding lethal weapons.*

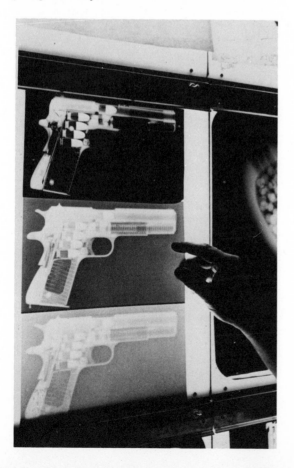

ing a connection between violence and social class. Andrew Henry and James Short, in their classic study *Suicide and Homicide* (1954), distinguished two patterns of strain and attempted to relate the patterns to fluctuations in the business cycle. First, they argued that in their interpersonal relationships, poor and working-class persons are subject to "external restraints." They are often required to conform to the demands of others, such as their employers, and to highly structured work situations. In contrast, upper-middle-class and upper-class persons have much more personal control over what they do. Henry and Short argue that such persons develop "internal restraints"; they must rely on themselves rather than on others to control what they do. Henry and Short hypothesized that these different kinds of restraint lead to different responses to frustration. When a person subject to external restraint is frustrated, he or she will turn aggression outward, as in homicide. When a person subject to internal restraint is frustrated, he or she will turn aggression inward, as in suicide. Using this theory, they predict that during periods of prosperity, low-status persons suffer the greatest frustration because they fail to achieve the economic rewards that seem plentiful. Thus, homicide should rise in times of prosperity and should fall with recessions. But during hard times it is the high-status people who are most frustrated because they are experiencing unexpected failure (while low-status people have the comfort of company in their misery). Thus, during economic recessions and depressions, the suicide rate should rise as high-status people turn their frustration inward.

Examinations of overall fluctuations in the homicide and suicide rates in response to the business cycle tend to support the Henry and Short hypothesis. However, more detailed study of the rates shows considerable ambiguity. Suicide and homicide rates for groups presumably differing in their degree of internal and external restraint (blacks and whites and males and females, for example) do not behave as predicted. Furthermore, the concepts of internal and external restraint are vague, and Henry and Short did not offer any direct evidence that groups actually differ in these ways. Finally, the theory cannot deal with lower-

221

class suicide or upper-class homicide. Other strain formulations run into similar difficulties.

Control Theories

You will recall from previous chapters (especially Chapter 6) that, unlike subcultural and strain theories, *control theory* does not require a strong correlation between social class and deviant behavior.

Control theory locates "conscience" or restraint in the bonds between the individual and society, primarily in the bonds between the individual and other persons. Most people, regardless of their economic situation, have significant bonds to others. Poor children are about as likely as rich children to love their parents and to have close friends; in terms of intimate relationships, they have just as much to lose by committing acts of deviance. Thus, it should be no surprise to find that interpersonal violence is not related to social class. So far, there is little direct evidence to show that at each class level it is persons without normal bonds to others who are the most prone to violence. However, Travis Hirschi (1969) found that lack of attachments to parents, teachers, and friends was strongly related to assaultive behavior among teenage boys of all class backgrounds.

But perhaps the strongest present evidence for control theory is that extreme acts of violence are heavily concentrated among persons who are virtually social outcasts and among whom other kinds of stigmatizing deviance is also most widespread. Persons who are without occupations, who are alcoholics, who are mentally ill, or who bear the stigma of ex-convict are loose social atoms—to an unusual degree they lack close ties to friends and family. This does not mean that such people do not marry or associate with others. It means that they remain somewhat *estranged from others,* even *within* these relationships.

Even inside prisons, violent behavior is heavily concentrated among convicts called "outlaws" by other prisoners. Such people fail to find a social niche within the prison. Indeed, their violence both causes their isolation and permits it to continue. Isolation can motivate violent behavior because such behavior is the only effective way to force others to respond to one's existence.

In this way, control theory complements psy-

Figure 7.12   Levels of Analysis and Issues Appropriate to Each Level. This summary chart does not cover all the important points raised in the chapter. Use it only to review what you have read. Page numbers are given for the full discussion of any topic.

chological and learning theories of violence. A lack of bonds can both cause and be caused by a defective self-conception or personality. People who are unable to restrain their selfish impulses or to sustain affectionate relations with others are free to use violence and may feel driven to use it because of their inability to influence others in conventional ways. As we shall see in Chapter 8, rapists often seem to be attempting to use rape as a way to establish a conventional relationship with women. Indeed, assault and even homicide can be regarded as efforts to deal with others when conventional means fail or are inadequate.

Control theory makes sense of the fact that violence does not occur primarily between strangers but is concentrated within family, marital, and friendship networks. In this sense, violence typically reflects *a defect in or a pathology of relationships.* Akers (1973) argues that what we frequently call "senseless violence" depends on one's point of view. When a man says he beat his wife to death in an effort to make her love him, we think he is irrational, but such action may have seemed rational to him. He was trying the only means that seemed available to establish a marital relationship, which is widely judged as desirable.

SOCIETAL CAUSES OF VIOLENCE

So far in this section, we have asked why certain people are violent. But the question of why violence, especially homicide, is so much more common in the United States than in other advanced nations is still unanswered. How is our society different from others?

What is it about American society that produces interpersonal violence? In this section we consider a number of aspects of our society that have been blamed for violence. The reader is warned that many commonly made accusations about the causes of American violence are spurious.

Levels	Appropriate Questions	A Partial Synopsis of Present Conclusions
Physiological	Is human violence instinctual?	Instinct theories cannot explain variations in violent behavior—why some people are given to violent behavior while most are not. (pp. 209–210)
	Does the presence of an extra male chromosome (XYY) result in violence-prone males?	Apparently it does not. (pp. 210–211)
Psychological	Does loss of inhibitions through intoxication produce violence?	It often does in our society. For example, a high proportion of murders are committed under the influence of alcohol. (p. 211)
	Does frustration-aggression explain violent behavior?	Only to a limited extent. (pp. 211–212)
	Is violent behavior learned?	Probably, both through simple reinforcement and through modeling. (pp. 212–213)
	Does exposure to violence in the mass media lead people to behave in violent ways?	The findings are mixed. Such exposure may have a small effect on some children or even a strong effect on a very few children, but it is probably at most a very minor cause of violent behavior. (pp. 213–214)
Social-Psychological	Do parents' child-rearing practices influence their children's use of violence?	Probably very little. For example, punishment seems to have little or no effect on future aggressive behavior. (pp. 214–215)
	Does exposure to others who admire or reinforce violent behavior increase one's use of violence?	Apparently so. Children's behavior seems to be shaped by interaction with peers and by the values of the larger culture. (pp. 214–215)
Sociological: Middle Range	Is violence substantially concentrated in violent subcultures?	In general, it is not. (pp. 216–218)
	Do acts of violence differ only in their degree of seriousness?	No. Acts of extreme violence—homicide, attempted homicide, and child battering—seem altogether different from less extreme acts. (pp. 218–220)
	Are acts of extreme violence related to social class?	Some usually unemployed people who chronically commit deviant acts are essentially outside the class system. Extreme violence is concentrated among these outcasts. (p. 220)
	Does control theory account for many of the facts about violent behavior?	Yes, by emphasizing the deviant person's lack of bonds to society and by locating the source of the problem in unsuccessful relationships with others. (p. 222)
Societal	Does American violence stem from the survival of a "frontier spirit"?	No. Australia and Canada ought then also to have high homicide rates, but they do not. (pp. 222–224)
	Does the relative neglect of poverty in America play a role in causing extreme violence?	Probably. Compared with the poor in many other advanced industrial nations, the American poor are worse off, both relatively and absolutely. This means that a higher proportion of Americans (than Norwegians, for example) fall outside the class structure. (pp. 224–225)
	Does the prevalence of guns account for the abnormally high American homicide rate?	Yes. Guns are much more often fatal than are knives, fists, and other weapons used in homicide attempts. Most homicides in America involve guns. (pp. 225–226)

223

The Frontier Spirit

Much has been made of the effect of the rowdy and violent history of the American frontier in establishing a national character that emphasizes individualism and a quick resort to violence. Cultural traits developed in the early and lawless days of westward settlement are thought to live on today in a "gunfighter" mentality (Graham and Gurr, 1969). Chapter 9 makes the point that American values of individualism and self-reliance do considerably shape our perceptions of and responses to a great many social problems, especially to poverty. But it is doubtful that a lingering frontier spirit can account for violence in America.

For one thing, data reported earlier in this chapter indicate that Americans do not generally approve of violent behavior and that there do not seem to be subcultures that sustain violent norms. And even when confronted with a hypothetical situation—"the government starts arresting and shooting large numbers of innocent people including members of your own family"—the majority of Americans said they would not put up violent resistance (Stark and McEvoy, 1970). This attitude hardly reflects the spirit of the Old West.

A second argument against the theory is that the United States is not the only advanced nation that has had a frontier tradition. Australia was initially settled mainly by convicts transported there against their will. And today its frontier is still expanding. Yet Australia has a very low homicide rate (see Figure 7.1). Canada was also settled by immigrants and still has a rough and rugged frontier. But Canada also has a very low homicide rate. If our frontier experience was a cause of our present violent behavior, one would expect Canada and Australia also to have more homicide than European nations. But they do not. But why, then, does the United States have an unusually high homicide rate? There seem to be at least two likely answers.

Deprivation and Homicide

We have already discussed how acts of extreme violence are concentrated among outcasts. Al-

though the great majority of Americans enjoy more affluence than people in any other society, Americans are also more negligent of the poor than are most other advanced societies. In comparison with the poor in such industrialized nations as Norway, Sweden, England, and France, our poor are poorer and suffer greater physical and mental deprivation and social stigmatization. The reasons for this difference are discussed in Chapter 9. What is important for our present concern with extreme violence is that, compared with other advanced nations, a larger proportion of poor Americans probably fall into the outcast group. Consequently, the proportion of our population with a somewhat high potential for extreme violence is probably greater than the proportion in other industrial nations. Our homicide rate is closer to that found in underdeveloped nations because a segment of our population is living a life more typical of underdeveloped than developed nations.

However, this answer is only a partial one. For the fact is that all economic groups in America

Figure 7.13   Even though the majority of homicides in the United States are committed with firearms, particularly handguns, there is a lot of public resistance to gun control on the part of various organized groups and gun lobbies. The effort to register and control firearms has largely failed, and dealers and sellers of handguns and other firearms are common throughout the United States.

have a high homicide rate in comparison with other industrial nations.

Firearms and Homicide

One way in which the United States is strikingly different from other developed nations is that in no other developed nation are firearms so common. It is estimated there are well over 100 million firearms in the hands of private citizens in the United States. Furthermore, the sales of guns have been rising for the past decade, and the proportion of homes in which there are guns has been increasing rapidly. During this same period, the homicide rate has also increased rapidly. In other developed nations with lower homicide rates, firearms are rare and subject to strict registration and licensing.

Handguns (pistols and revolvers) are particularly an American problem. Presently, Americans are accumulating handguns at an enormously high rate. In fact, the rate has been estimated by the Department of the Treasury to be more than 1.8 million weapons a year. Furthermore the nation's private arsenal of handguns alone has been estimated to be in excess of 30 million (Newton and Zimring, 1969).

The majority of homicides in the United States are the result of firearms, especially handguns. Several recent government commissions have attributed our high homicide rate to the mass possession of firearms, and they are probably right. First, many attempted homicides probably would not take place if a gun were not readily at hand. Guns permit attacks when other weapons, such as knives, clubs, or even bare hands would be physically or psychologically impossible to use. Guns are nearly instantaneous in their effectiveness. A shot fired in anger can be conclusive, whereas other, less immediate means permit second thoughts. Indeed, many homicides with a gun are virtual accidents, in that the person did not intend to pull the trigger. So high a proportion of homicides with a gun occur in the heat of passion (often during a family fight) that it seems unlikely that a homicide would occur if the individual had to wait to secure an effective weapon. Frequently, studies show, the gun was *used* because it was *there*.

A second reason why guns greatly increase the homicide rate is that they are so deadly. If all

225

present homicide attempts took place with a less deadly weapon (and many would not occur if only weapons other than a gun were available), the homicide rate would fall drastically. The fact is that when a gun is used, the fatality rate is five times higher than when any other weapon is employed (Newton and Zimring, 1969). Thus, even if the number of *attempted homicides* were not reduced by the removal of guns from society, the *homicide rate* might fall by as much as five-sixths if guns were removed.

People in other industrialized nations also fly into rages and attack one another; however, because they lack guns, their acts usually add to the assault, not to the homicide, rate. Thus, in Tokyo, Japan, a city of 11 million where it is illegal to own, possess, or manufacture handguns, there was only one handgun homicide in 1971. During the same year Los Angeles County, with a population of about 7 million, reported 308 handgun homicides (National Advisory Commission on Criminal Justice Standards and Goals, 1973). It is not the tradition of the frontier that accounts for American homicide—it is the tradition of gun ownership.

As we pointed out earlier, gun ownership has been rapidly increasing in the United States. Ironically, people are buying guns in response to fears of crime and violence; most handguns are bought for individual and home protection. Unfortunately, the self-protective feature of gun ownership is illusory. Guns much more often end up being used to commit homicides than to defend home and family. Indeed, a survey of Detroit revealed that more people were killed in household handgun *accidents* in one year than were killed by home burglars and robbers in four-and-a-half years (Newton and Zimring, 1969). Antigun control groups proclaim, ''When guns are outlawed, only outlaws will have guns.'' They fail to see that if in fact only outlaws did have guns, many fewer people would be getting killed in our society.

The Founding Fathers guaranteed Americans the constitutional right to bear arms. They gave this right to all Americans because the European practice of restricting the right to bear arms to the upper classes was undemocratic. It gave the upper classes a monopoly on the means of force and the power to repress challenges to the system. But in the context of the modern state and modern weapons of war, the pistol in the bedroom drawer can hardly help prevent the state from repressing people. The Founding Fathers' ideal was to have a militia or armed citizenry rather than a professional army. They did not contemplate citizens' private abuse or use of guns.

So long as Americans continue to live with guns, they will continue to die by them at an appalling rate. In Part III, we will consider why efforts to control guns have not been too successful in the United States. Looking over Part II, one can see that social scientists seem to know a lot more about what does not cause violence than about what does cause it. It is important to get rid of falsehoods about what causes violence, but it is frustrating not to be able to say more about what causes it. Frankly, we do not know more.

PART III: RESPONSES INTERPERSONAL VIOLENCE

Because interpersonal violence has been dealt with as a crime in our society, everything taken up in Chapter 6 concerning the deterrence and rehabilitation aspects of the criminal justice system—their successes and failures—also applies to violence.

Our society has shown little response to violence apart from treating it as a crime. Admittedly, there is an ongoing campaign to cut down on the violence depicted in the mass media, especially in children's shows. In fact, new guidelines have been adopted by the television networks and substantial changes have been made in children's programing. But, as reported earlier, it is not clear that such changes bear on the causes of interpersonal violence. Indeed, a major reason no more has been done to counteract violence is that we know so little about what its causes are.

One apparent cause of violence is extreme poverty and deprivation—the existence of a substantial number of persons who have virtually been discarded by society. Clearly, a campaign to reduce violence would have to find means to ''reattach'' such persons to the social and moral order. This problem is the primary focus of Chapter 9. Here, we consider two specific proposals for dealing with violence. First, we examine the question of gun control. Second, we focus on a major scene of interpersonal violence—the family—and consider ways of dealing with family violence.

GUN CONTROL

The failure of national, state, and local governments to enact strict gun-control legislation offers considerable insight into the American political process. For decades a dedicated minority has had its will over an apathetic majority. What does the majority believe?

Back in 1938, the Gallup Poll first asked the American public its views on gun control. They found that 84 percent believed "all owners of pistols and revolvers should be required to register with the Government." In 1959, Gallup found that 75 percent of Americans (and 65 percent of gun owners) believed no one should be permitted to buy a gun without a police permit. In the aftermath of the political assassinations of the 1960s, public support for tough gun regulations continued to run very high (Gallup, 1972). In fact, no poll conducted in the United States has ever found that more than a third of those polled opposed tough gun controls (Erskine, 1972).

Over the past decade, a number of federal gun regulations have been introduced in Congress. Yet, as this book goes to press, we are without any substantial controls. Indeed, any citizen willing to pay a $250 tax to the government may legally own a machine gun in operating condition. How can such a state of affairs continue?

The fact is that while the overwhelming majority of Americans advocate strict regulation of firearms, few are very concerned about doing so. In contrast, a vigorous antiregulation lobby, led by the American Rifle Association, has vigilantly and vigorously compaigned against passage of gun control legislation. Many congressmen have explained in private that voting to control guns would earn them very few votes but would certainly lose them a substantial number of votes from the anticontrol minority. Those in favor of gun control have failed to mobilize public concern.

Until recently, the group with the greatest potential power to bring about gun control and seemingly with the greatest stake in doing so—the American police—has remained either silent on the issue or has in fact opposed gun legislation. Presumably, the police are the group most informed about the devastating role that firearms play in homicide and in gun-related crimes such as robbery. Furthermore, handguns in private hands kill many police officers each year. Yet the police have continued to oppose gun regulation, partly because of their generally conservative political outlook and partly because substantial numbers of them belong to antiregulation groups such as the American Rifle Association.

It was therefore a considerable break with the past when the National Advisory Commission on Criminal Justice Standards and Goals—a commission dominated by police and law enforcement officials—took a vigorous stand in demanding strict gun controls in their 1973 report. Specifically, the commission recommended the absolute prohibition of hand guns. Manufacture and sale of handguns should be terminated, the commission wrote, and existing handguns should be confiscated by the government. Only collectors items, modified to be inoperable, should be permitted to remain in private hands. Rifles and other "long" guns would be left in private hands, according to the commission proposal, for these rarely figure in crimes of violence.

Unfortunately, the commission's report was released by the Justice Department during one of the many Watergate crises, so it received little publicity. But if the report does signal a change in the police position on the control of handguns, strict regulation may soon come to pass.

FAMILY VIOLENCE AND THE POLICE

One of the most frequent types of calls to the police reports a family disturbance or, as the police call it, a "family beef." Several studies reveal that such calls outnumber the total of all other police calls combined, including calls concerning burglars, prowlers, and robbers (Reiss, 1971; Wilson, 1968; Cumming, Cumming, and Edell, 1964). For the policeman on patrol, the family beef is the most common, and most dreaded, assignment. Again and again the police enter people's homes to face emotion-charged situations. The police dislike encounters with fighting family members because they have such limited resources for dealing with them. Officially, just about all they can do is arrest the offending party or parties. But typically, that is unwise. Often, other family members refuse to press charges. Furthermore, arrest usually solves nothing and might even cause greater family conflict later. Typically, the police try to cool the situation down—to separate the conflicting parties and talk them out of further conflict. But, as the police often complain, they are not trained therapists and furthermore are not equipped to follow up on the problems of families in crises. Their follow-up usually takes the form of repeatedly being called to settle the most acute incidents of chronically troubled families. They are able to halt a specific wife-beating incident, for example, but they can rarely solve the underlying problems.

Some recent experimental programs have attempted to train policemen for dealing with family conflicts. For example, in 1967 New York City developed a Family Crisis Intervention Unit in a West Harlem precinct. Police in this unit also perform normal duties, but they have had special training by psychologists for dealing with family fights. When they encounter a family beef, they "avoid unnecessary shows of force, deescalate anger through informality, concede a man's masculinity, listen and discuss with sympathy the arguments of both sides, and suggest alternative solutions" (Mulvihill and Tumin, 1969). The Task Force on Violent Crime reports that this program has proved very effective. Over the first fifteen months and 1,000 calls, there were no accusations of police brutality, none of the citizens involved committed homicide or suicide, and no patrolman was injured (family beefs are a frequent source of police injuries, for participants sometimes turn on the police for intervening).

Nevertheless, this program and others like it has not found universal favor among policemen. Many argue that they did not join the force to become family therapists and that, even after training, they do not have much faith in their own capacities to deal with such problems. Furthermore, even police trained in therapy are restricted to dealing with the problem on the scene, not on a continuing basis.

Urbanization has caused a breakdown of informal, self-help networks for dealing with private troubles. Consequently, such problems must now be dealt with through formal public agencies. The police have been forced into filling this need mainly because they are at hand and are the only easily accessible, twenty-four-hour-a-day public trouble-shooters. So it is not surprising that approximately eight out of ten calls to the police involve noncriminal matters (Reiss, 1971). Recently, many commentators have questioned the use of the police in this capacity. They suggest taking the police out of the business of dealing with family crises, "disturbed" people, or alcoholics and creating instead a new type of public servant: a mobile, on-call, public-service officer. Service officers would be prepared to bring the resources of present public agencies (welfare, health, psychiatric, and the like) to bear on problems now fleetingly and ineffectively dealt with by the police. Emergency calls would not simply be dealt with on the spot but would entail a program of continuing aid.

Could such programs reduce violence? Possibly. Recall that earlier in this chapter, self-report data indicated that middle-class and upper-class Americans were about as likely as the poor to have engaged in and experienced violence. However, it was pointed out that middle- and upper-class violence, particularly family altercations, were much less likely to become police problems. There is also evidence that interpersonal violence among employed people, regardless of their income, is much less likely to result in homicide. And people who have the money and the awareness to take their personal troubles to psychiatrists, family counselors, or divorce lawyers seem much more likely to weather family conflict before tragedy occurs. Creation of a public-service corps to replace the police in this function might provide the same results for those presently lacking these private resources.

CHAPTER REVIEW

Interpersonal violence differs from other crimes in the level of public concern that it raises, in the motives that seem to cause it, and in the theories used to explain it. Interpersonal violence is less well reported than property crime, so official statistics tend to underestimate the extent of it in society. The peculiar victim-offender relationship that characterizes interpersonal violence probably explains why it is underreported. Because the victim and offender often know each other, victims are often hesitant to press official charges.

The homicide rate in the United States is particularly high in comparison with that of other industrialized nations, with assault rates lower than homicide rates and incidences of battered children relatively rare. The amount of violence in this country has been rising in the last ten years (partly because of better reporting). Violence rates are higher in the cities, and violent acts are committed slightly more often by young people (under 25) and most often by males. The high rates of violence among lower-class and minority people that the official statistics show are not supported by *victimization* studies. However, victims and attackers often have similar social backgrounds.

Many theories have been used to explain why people become violent. Perhaps the earliest *physiological* theory drew on studies of instinct in animals. It was thought that humans, like other animals, had an aggressive instinct. However, instinct theories could not account for variations in violence, and they underestimated the role of learning. More recently, some have claimed that the XYY chromosome in males contributes to violence, but men who have this chromosome do not consistently behave violently, so one cannot predict violent behavior in XYY males.

Psychological theories of violence focus on loss of control and learning. Loss of control can be caused by alcohol or can occur when efforts to attain one's goals are frustrated. This frustration then leads to aggression. However, it does not always result in aggression, and aggression often occurs without frustration. Learning theorists feel that violence is learned either through being rewarded or through simple *modeling*. Modeling theory—that people will copy the behavior of others—is behind much of the concern today over whether mass-media violence will encourage violence in children. There is little agreement on the role of mass media in producing violence in children.

Social-psychological theories focus on the impact of socialization on instilling *values* that support violence. The greatest force seems to be within peer-group associations: the more one interacts with one's peers, the more feedback one gets about norms of violence, such as toughness.

The *sociological middle-range* theories include the *violent subculture* perspective, which says that in some groups violence is the norm. Extreme violence, however, is said to occur totally outside any subculture or class group. *Strain theories* expand on this idea by claiming that people (lower-class people, for example) who are unable to achieve the goals of society (wealth, for example) through traditional means (saving money, for example) will use different means (violence, for example) to achieve them. However, evidence indicates that there is no association between violence and social class. *Control* theories, looking at the constraints on violence, claim that social bonds, such as ties to family or job, prevent violence.

A few *societal* causes of violence have been suggested. The "Frontier Spirit" theory says that the lawlessness of the West has been generalized to a modern day "violent mentality." The Australian and Canadian histories do not support this, however. The abundance of firearms in this country does seem to contribute to the homicide rate by making a murder weapon available in the heat of passion.

Society's response to violence reflects this concern over the ready availability of guns. Much effort has been put into passing gun-control legislation. In some areas, the response to immediate violence within the family setting (where most violence occurs) has been to use police who have some training to handle explosive family arguments and fights. Generally, however, our attempts to reduce violence have been ineffective because we do not know enough about the causes of violence.

229

SUGGESTED READINGS

Henry, Andrew F., and James F. Short Jr. *Suicide and Homicide: Some Economic, Sociological, and Psychological Aspects of Aggression.* New York: Free Press, 1954.

Mulvihill, Donald J., and Melvin Tumin. *Crimes of Violence. Staff Report to the National Commission on Causes and Prevention of Violence.* Vols. 11, 12, and 13. Washington, D.C.: U.S. Government Printing Office, 1969.

Newton, George, and Franklin Zimring. *Firearms and Violence in American Life: A Staff Report to the National Commission on the Causes and Prevention of Violence.* Washington, D.C.: U.S. Government Printing Office, 1969.

Surgeon General's Scientific Advisory Committee on Television and Social Behavior. *Television and Growing Up: The Impact of Televised Violence.* Washington, D.C.: U.S. Government Printing Office, 1972.

Wolfgang, Marvin E. *Patterns in Criminal Homicide.* Philadelphia: University of Pennsylvania Press, 1958.

"That Spring night I spent pillowed on your arm never really happened except in a dream. Unfortunately I am talked about anyway." Lady Suo

Bruce M Dean

8

Sexual Problems

Most other textbooks call the subject matter of this chapter "sexual deviance." This title can be seriously misleading, for sexual behavior is deviant only in relation to conventional modes of sexual expression. The line between conventional and deviant sexuality is, at best, hazy and controversial, and it has clearly been changing over the past twenty years. In fact, the similarities between conventional and deviant sexual expression are very great; people learn them in similar ways, and many people who engage in deviant behavior do not seem to view it differently from the way people who engage in conventional sex view their behavior. For example, many rapists appear to see little difference between what they do and conventional approaches to females; many prostitutes believe they are merely less hypocritical than housewives whom they accuse of also selling sex.

PART I: THE PROBLEM
SEXUAL PROBLEMS

Perhaps the most compelling reason for including conventional sex in our discussion is that many important and widespread problems beset conventional sexuality today. The extraordinary sales of books such as *The Joy of Sex,* and *Everything You Always Wanted to Know About Sex (But Were Afraid to Ask)* reflect the problems, anxieties, and frustrations over conventional sexual expression. Furthermore, problems sometimes attributed to "careless love," such as illegitimacy, are mainly problems of conventional sexuality.

To limit this chapter to sexual deviance would make it difficult to discuss these problems intelligently. Indeed, unless we understand the problems people typically find in expressing conventional sexual desires and in achieving competence, we miss the critical opportunity to see how deviant sexual expression can emerge from this conventional developmental process.

WHAT IS SEXUALLY DEVIANT?

All societies maintain norms about what kind of sexual behavior is permissible and when and with whom. But the substance of these norms often differs considerably. Some societies prohibit any sexual activity other than that between husband and wife. In traditional Irish society, for example, all manifestations of sexuality are considered shameful, and despite the fact that marriage occurs at a relatively late age, the only acceptable form of sexual behavior is marital intercourse for the purpose of procreation (Messenger, 1971). In Java, infidelity is abhored to such an extent that even slight deviations from norms governing conduct with a member of the opposite sex may arouse anger and suspicion. Hildred Geertz (1961) reports that among the Javanese there is "an almost paranoid watchfulness between spouses."

Perhaps more typical is the double standard governing sexual behavior. Men are permitted some latitude with regard to premarital and extramarital sex, but "nice" women are severely prohibited from such behavior. For example, in Puerto Rico, men typically resort to prostitutes and "unrespectable" women "but seem concerned about the fidelity of their wives and the chastity of their daughters to an almost phobic extent" (Stycos and

Hill, 1953). Such patterns are common, and until very recently, Americans followed a very marked sexual double standard.

Many other societies, however, give considerable sexual license to both sexes. In many Polynesian groups, for example, people freely engage in sex from an early age, and achieving sexual gratification for both males and females is a dominant theme in the culture. Upon marriage, fidelity is expected, but extramarital sex seems to occur with some regularity (Marshall, 1971).

No society places a high value on homosexual behavior, but some societies encourage it among adolescents and the unmarried. However, such homosexual activity is seen as a normal part of sexual maturation, and it in no way contradicts or substitutes for eventual heterosexuality and marriage (Davenport, 1965).

Incest—sexual relations among relatives—is everywhere taboo, but the definition of what counts as a relative varies considerably. In general, the incest taboo is intended to exclude sexual competition and conflict within the family, so what constitutes incest varies according to which per-

sons count as family members. However, all societies virtually require sexual intercourse between married couples (Davis, 1971a), and all societies prohibit the use of violence in gaining sexual compliance—rape, for example, is a very serious offense everywhere.

Although societies maintain rules about sexual conduct and although such rules seem always to prohibit incest and rape, the picture of conventional human sexuality across cultures shows more differences than similarities. Such variations challenge our notions about a universal sexual "instinct" or about "natural" sexual behavior. Obviously, the human body sets limits on the kinds of sexual expression that are physically possible or pleasurable, but considerable creativity exists within these restraints. Unlike the poor fish, who is born "knowing" its sexual destiny, humans possess considerable choice in the matter. As we shall see, this is perhaps both a blessing and a burden.

Sexual deviance, then, depends on social, not "natural," considerations. Deviant sexual behavior is what a particular society defines as impermissible or repugnant. Conventional sexual behavior is what society says is acceptable or even required. Before we can analyze sexual problems in the United States, we must determine what is and what is not sexually deviant or conventional in our society today.

THE SEXUAL REVOLUTION

We are in the midst of a widespread revolution in sexual conduct. Understanding where we are today requires studying where we once were. So in order to define the sexual norms that prevail in contemporary American society, we must turn back the clock. Until recent times, the dominant code of sexual morality in American society was decidedly puritanical. All sexuality outside of marriage or engaged in primarily for pleasure rather than for procreation was denounced as sinful. Sexual behavior other than coitus conducted in the male-facing-female position was considered wanton and perverse. Sex was regarded as a somewhat dirty business, not to be openly discussed by decent folks, and certainly no fit subject for literature or fine art. Polite people spoke of limbs, not legs, and

Figure 8.1 The question of conventional and deviant sex is a matter of relative social norms, not of absolute natural laws. Social norms vary over time and from culture to culture. (Left) The two men kissing at a French village wedding would be considered deviant in the United States.

Figure 8.2 (Right) The increased sale of books dealing with sex are part of the "sexual revolution." However, the fact that very explicit books on sex, such as David Reuben's Everything You Always Wanted To Know About Sex, *became best-sellers makes it clear that a major part of the revolution is the public desire to learn to be sexually adequate.*

233

if such a matter had to be mentioned at all, women had a bosom, not breasts.

An underground element of this strict sexual code was the double standard. Certain evasions of the letter of the code were to be expected of men so long as they kept up the appearance of moral compliance. It was understood that young men would "sow wild oats" and that married men would patronize prostitutes and so-called loose women. The warrant for such a double standard came from the widespread notion that sexuality was primarily a male trait—only men were thought to have lusts of the flesh. Because men had a sexual appetite, some provision was made for them to seek satisfaction; women, on the other hand, had no reason to violate the code because they lacked such needs (indeed, women who did experience lust and sexual pleasure were considered abnormal or corrupt).

Undoubtedly, many women found pleasure in and out of the marriage bed, despite the efforts that had been made to stifle their sensuality. Infidelity was not wholly restricted to males. Nonetheless, transgressions of the code had severe consequences, and illicit activities were therefore carried on in secret and with considerable guilt. Furthermore, the official, puritanical sexual code was enshrined in laws prohibiting adultery, fornication, lewdness, sodomy, perversions against nature, pornography, abortion, indecent exposure, and other diverse abominations. Many of these laws are still with us, although few are enforced.

From about the turn of the century, the gap between the official moral code and what people actually did began to grow. Women's ankles came into view. Bathing suits slowly ceased to resemble long winter underwear. Yet many held vigorously to the old code, and most people at least paid it public lip service. In the aftermath of World War II, the gap became acute. At that time, some people began to speak out against puritanical sexual standards. It was in this context that a scientific study struck a deathblow to the old morality. In 1948, Alfred Kinsey and his colleagues published the first volume of their monumental survey of human sexual behavior. Although it was a dry, expensive book filled with statistics and graphs, the first Kinsey Report on the sexual behavior of American males became a runaway bestseller.

(The second volume on females appeared in 1953 and had nearly as great an impact on the public's sexual attitudes.)

What the Kinsey studies revealed was that public attitudes about sex bore little resemblance to the behavior of the average American. Premarital sexual activity was widespread, especially among the better educated. The female orgasm was neither rare nor restricted to so-called lewd women, for the majority of American women reported at least sometimes experiencing orgasms. During adolescence, masturbation was virtually the rule among males and was not considered a dangerous perversion. Married couples commonly engaged in acts that were legally and morally categorized as abominable and perverse.

The Kinsey studies opened the floodgate to a new public view of conventional sexual expression. The norms began to readjust to what people were commonly doing. Nudity and sex became acceptable in movies and magazines. Novels no longer inserted asterisks (* * *) to indicate an unmentionable sexual passage; explicit sexual scenes became an ordinary part of fiction.

Although for the past few years people have described these changes as a sexual revolution, they have remained uncertain about the actual extent and character of changes in sexual behavior. Some have argued that the changes were more apparent than real—that the new sexual standards were restricted mainly to highly visible groups such as celebrities, students at elite colleges, and intellectuals. Others have argued that all classes and regions were affected.

In 1974, the first reliable nationwide data since those systematically collected by Kinsey between 1938 and 1947 became available. In *Sexual Behavior in the 1970s*, Morton Hunt (1974) compared these new data with the Kinsey findings and concluded that major changes had, in fact, occurred in sexual standards and sexual behavior. Today, most Americans approve of sexual practices, such as cunnilingus, that the older morality condemned. Furthermore, such practices are common between heterosexual couples, both married and unmarried. Perhaps one comparison is sufficient to indicate the extent of the revolution in American sexual behavior. Kinsey found that of all the single women he interviewed between the ages of eighteen and twenty-five, two-thirds were virgins. Thirty years later, Hunt found that three-fourths of the single women in this age bracket were not virgins.

As will be taken up in subsequent parts of this chapter, the sexual revolution has *not* meant unlimited acceptance of all forms of sexuality. Fetishism, group sex, and homosexuality have not become any more common since Kinsey's day, and contact with prostitutes has declined markedly (Hunt, 1974). Nevertheless, it is clear that Americans are engaging in more frequent and more varied sexual activity than they did thirty years ago.

Not everyone has hailed these changes. Many have denounced the new morality as moral decay that is bound to destroy the family and other American institutions. And many have warned that sexual liberation is a major cause of sex crimes. Concerted efforts have been made to restore censorship of "obscenity." Concerns like these cannot be dismissed out of hand. Such sweeping changes in sexual behavior are bound to have wide social consequences. We now consider some of these.

PROBLEMS WITH CONVENTIONAL SEX

The most obvious consequence of the recent sexual revolution has been a change in our expectations about sex, which has, in turn, created a new order of conventional sexual problems. Foremost among these is that adults, both male and female, are now expected to be sexually competent—to be able to both give and receive sexual pleasure. This expectation is altogether new in our society, and we are only beginning to grope with means for aiding individuals to achieve these sexual capacities. For many, the new sexual standards are a source of pressure, anxiety, and frustration.

With the double standard and the puritanical moral code, most people were able to avoid these problems. There was no such thing as a frigid woman because women were alleged to be incapable of sexual pleasure (unless they were abnormal). Consequently, there was no such thing as a man who was an inadequate lover—because sex was enjoyable only for men, any man capable of intercourse was sexually adequate. Obviously, this is no longer true. Today, sexuality is one of the

most dominant themes in women's magazines. Most women who are unable to respond sexually or whose husbands are inadequate lovers are aware that things are not supposed to be this way and that change is both possible and desirable. Furthermore, persons who find they are undesirable sexual partners are likely to suffer pangs of rejection and frustration they might once have escaped.

Indeed, many who have joined the sexual revolution and who seemingly are capable of performing in adequate ways still find the new sexual norms burdensome. A recent study by Lillian Rubin (forthcoming) offers many insights into this problem. In research intended to examine male and female sex roles in a sample of working-class couples, Rubin found that efforts to steer interviews to the subject of marriage almost inevitably were taken as invitations to discuss sexual relations. Her first discovery was that the widely hailed sexual revolution was not restricted to the educated or to the middle and upper classes (a finding also confirmed by Hunt's 1974 national study). Couples in her sample of young blue-collar families were full participants in the new sexual patterns. For example, 70 percent reported engaging in oral-genital stimulation. However, although these couples were *acting* liberated, they did not *feel* entirely liberated. Many of the women reported mixed emotions and guilt about their sexual behavior. Some said they could only let go sexually after a few drinks. Many often found their husbands' expecting them to achieve orgasm to be simply "another demand in a life already too full of demands" (Rubin, forthcoming). Indeed, one wife feared that her husband would read that some women achieve multiple orgasms: "It's hard enough to do it once! What'll happen if he finds out about all those women who have lots of climaxes?"

Husbands, too, reported problems with the new standard for conventional sexuality. Some found their wives too sexually demanding. Others developed problems with impotence. Rubin concluded that under present conditions there are enormous pressures felt by both men and women and that the transition to a new pattern of sexual relations will be painful and will probably depend on major changes in all aspects of sex roles (these matters are discussed further in Chapters 11 and 12).

235

Rubin's working-class couples were not atypical. It is estimated that 40 million Americans have read *Everything You Always Wanted To Know About Sex (But Were Afraid to Ask)*. Sexual behavior is changing rapidly, and many people feel they are not adequately prepared. This is not surprising, for human sexual behavior is not instinctual; it must be learned. But a society that used to prohibit the discussion of sex and to restrict sex to marriage is not a society that has developed institutions and resources for teaching people how to be competent lovers. In such a society, rapid change in conventional sexuality must occur without the benefit of effective means for sexual socialization. In our own society, the revolution in conventional sexual standards has produced more than these psychological problems of inadequate sexual socialization. Perhaps surprisingly, it has worsened the problems of illegitimacy and venereal disease.

Illegitimacy

Many people assume that a central factor in the sexual revolution was the availability of more effective and more suitable methods of birth control. Obviously, there is some truth in this assumption. Removal of fears of pregnancy has undoubtedly made it possible for many to evaluate sex on purely sensual grounds. However, despite the ready availability of birth-control devices, recent years have seen a profound increase in the proportion of infants born to unwed mothers. In 1940, there were 7.1 births per 1000 unmarried women, but in 1965, the rate rose to 23.5 (Davis, 1971a). And these figures clearly underestimate the number of illegitimate pregnancies. The illegitimate-birth rate does not take into account miscarriages, and it does not reflect "forced" marriages. Kingsley Davis (1971a) estimated that one-fourth or more of pregnancies in 1965 involved unmarried women.

The rising illegitimacy rate does not reflect a new trend toward bachelor motherhood. Recently, some women have chosen to become pregnant with no intention of marriage, but their number, so far, is small. Indeed, data indicate that most illegitimate births involve women under twenty.

The consequences of illegitimacy are often unfortunate. Illegitimacy often means a child adopted or raised by foster parents—or a young woman forced to live on welfare in order to keep and support her child. Sometimes, this process is only temporarily delayed by a forced marriage, for marriages involving a young and pregnant bride are the least stable of American marriages (Davis, 1971a); following divorce or desertion, the woman and child (or several children) are forced to rely on welfare. So far, the availability of legal abortion has not been much more effective than birth control in curtailing this problem.

Why should unwanted pregnancies be rising? The answer seems to be that premarital and extramarital sexual relations have increased greatly in recent decades. However, the changes in behavior have not been fully matched by changes in self-conception. Rubin (forthcoming) found that the overwhelming majority of working-class couples in her sample had regularly engaged in premarital intercourse. However, most had not used birth-control measures before marriage (and consequently, 44 percent of the women became pregnant before marriage). The reason they gave was that although they were engaging in sex, they were unwilling to surrender a "nice girl" self-conception. Securing birth-control devices means advance planning, and that struck them as an admission that they had become "bad girls." So long as they could regard sex as something that happened when they lost their heads or got carried away, they could maintain their self-respect.

Ignorance and poverty also play a major role in the continuing illegitimacy problem. Young people often do not understand birth control, cannot secure birth-control information and devices without their parents' knowledge, or cannot afford to do so. In a study of 4611 teenage girls, Melvin Zelnick and John Kantner (1972) found that of those who engaged in sexual intercourse, more than 75 percent never or rarely used contraceptive methods. The reason, they found, was mainly ignorance and mistaken notions about the chances of becoming pregnant.

Venereal Disease

Like illegitimacy, venereal disease (VD) has been rising rapidly during the sexual revolution. Present rates, expecially among young people, have been characterized as epidemic. Indeed, as Morton Hunt

236

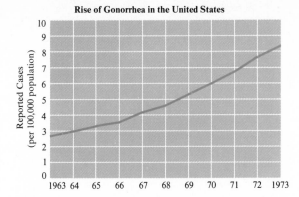

Rise of Gonorrhea in the United States

Figure 8.3   The significant increase in reported cases of gonorrhea has become of great concern to public health officials, who view the present level of venereal disease as epidemic.
(Center for Disease Control, 1972.)

(1974) put it, "Gonorrhea is now the second most common infectious ailment among teenagers, being surpassed only by the common cold."

Figure 8.3 shows that the reported cases of gonorrhea have more than doubled since 1963. These grim statistics undoubtedly underestimate the problem. For one thing, much treated venereal disease is not reported by physicians. For another, many cases go untreated. What is tragic about the upward trend in venereal disease is that modern medical methods of prevention and treatment could, for the most part, eliminate the problem. Thus, death, sterility, deformity, and other consequences of these diseases need not occur.

Unfortunately, the legacy of shame and ignorance about venereal disease, based on old puritanical views that VD is the just punishment of carnal sins, still plagues us at a time when the great increase in sexual activity makes the spread of these diseases much more common.

These facts make clear that sex problems in our society are not merely, or perhaps even mainly, problems associated with sexual deviance. Many Americans with wholly conventional sexual preferences confront considerable difficulties.

PROBLEMS OF SEXUAL DEVIANCE

Not so long ago, a discussion of sexual deviance would have likely begun with a section on premar-

ital and extramarital heterosexual relations. Such relations were contrary to the publicly supported norms, and a considerable stigma was often attached to people who were detected in such activities—especially women. But words such as adulterer and fornicator are not much in use any more. In fact, Hunt found that most Americans under fifty now agree that intercourse among unmarried persons is acceptable behavior, even when no strong bond of affection exists betweeen them. (The recency of this outlook is demonstrated by Roper polls, which found in 1937 and again in 1959 that well over half of the American public condemned premarital sex.) Furthermore, 1974 data show that 93 percent of married men and 70 percent of married women under thirty-five engaged in sexual intercourse before marriage (Hunt, 1974).

Obviously, it no longer makes sense to call such behavior sexual deviance, regardless of the attendant problems. But what does constitute sexual deviance in contemporary American society? There is no simple answer. It seems that deviance or conformity in sexual behavior is a question of degree. For example, virtually no one opposes sexual intercourse between married people. Some oppose sexual intercourse between people who are engaged, although most do not. More oppose intercourse between people who are not romantically linked, although the majority do not. Most Americans, however, disapprove of mate swapping and group sex. Although a near majority of Americans think homosexuality ought to be legal, the overwhelming majority consider it unnatural. A slight majority favor the legalization of prostitution, but the prostitute remains a social outcast. There is widespread support for tougher laws against rape and sexual molestation of children—deviant acts that are clearly at the far end of the conventional-deviant continuum.

One way to locate the point at which the conventional ends and the deviant begins is simply to adopt a standard of majority approval or disapproval: what the majority condemns is deviant. By itself, this criterion is inadequate. The majority may disapprove of some kind of behavior but may care little or lack sufficient power to do anything about it. In the case of sexual behavior, however,

237

majority approval is withheld precisely at the point that other proofs of deviance also begin. Sexual behavior of which most Americans disapprove is frequently punished in some way. To offer an example, there frequently are considerable social costs—loss of friends, loss of jobs, and even occasional prosecution—caused by public exposure as a swapping couple or as a homosexual. Although such sexual behavior is much less stigmatized than it was a few years ago, it still represents a significant violation of strongly held social norms. It is not the intent of this chapter to argue that homosexuality, for example, ought to be considered deviant behavior. It is so classified in this discussion because it is so considered in our society.

Why is sexual deviance a social problem? Mainly because there is a significant concern that something should be done to stop it, or at least to minimize its impact on others. Thus, even though most Americans are now willing to tolerate homosexual behavior among consenting adults, most parents do not want their children to become homosexuals and would like to know how to prevent it. And it is obviously unnecessary to argue why rape and child molestation arouse fear and anger.

In the remainder of Part I, we will attempt to assess the extent of sexual deviance in America. How much is there? Is it increasing? Who is involved? The answers to these questions depend, it turns out, on the particular variety of sexual deviance under consideration. We shall discuss four specific types of sexual deviance: mate swapping, homosexuality, prostitution, and rape.

Mate Swapping

Despite all the attention given it recently, mate swapping, or swinging, is a relatively rare occurrence. Hunt (1974) found that only 2 percent of the married persons in his sample had ever swapped with another couple, and most of these had done so only once. In addition, some of these persons had swapped only in previous, not present, marriages. The best estimate is that only a tiny fraction of 1 percent of Americans engage in such behavior with any frequency (Hunt, 1974). Advocates claim that mate swapping is common and that swingers are a highly uninhibited, unconventional, avant-garde group, but investigations of the swinging scene

reveal quite the reverse (Hunt, 1974; Walshok, 1971). Swinging is primarily restricted to a few lower-middle-class and middle-class couples who are very conventional in most other ways. They live ordinary lives, often in suburbia, and tend to be indistinguishable, generally, from middle Americans in terms of their political views, dress, and interests (other than sex).

Furthermore, what typically goes on at mate-swapping parties is hardly uninhibited. Often, couples are paired off by lottery, rotation, or some other technique that prevents open choice. Typically, there are many restrictions on acceptable behavior, and private liaisons away from the party are explicitly prohibited. Many regular participants, males and females alike, report considerable difficulty achieving orgasm in this setting, although they do not let others know about their trouble. Several observers have concluded that mate swapping does not really reflect sexual freedom; instead, it offers people who fear the consequences of infidelity a way of controlling and minimizing extramarital sexuality.

But whatever the cause of mate swapping, it seems too rare and too harmless (in the sense that only consenting adults are involved, and thus there are no victims) to be treated as a social problem.

Homosexuality

Perhaps nothing shocked public opinion more than Alfred Kinsey's report that one out of every three American males, and one out of every five females, had some homosexual experience during their lifetime. The figures, however, seemed to be unbelievable—and in fact they were. Although these figures have become an article of faith among homosexual activists and have undoubtedly played an important part in reshaping public attitudes toward homosexuality, these statistics have turned out to be the one significant instance of careless research that Kinsey was guilty of. His colleague Paul Gebhard has expressed dismay that these statistics ever got into print.

Kinsey's Report

Several errors led Kinsey astray. First, Kinsey did not select a random sample, and he was forced to seek volunteers to be interviewed. In an effort to

Betty and Sue are married. To each other.

Betty and Sue live like any other young married couple.

Betty pursues a successful career in publishing. Sue prefers to do the chores at home. Both will tell you they wouldn't have it any other way . . . except for one thing. Sometimes they feel very alone.

This week Eyewitness News explores the predicament of Betty, Sue and many others like them in a candid documentary entitled "Lesbians."

Hear lesbians talk openly about their philosophy and way of life. Learn about the social pressures that have forced them into hiding.

Watch "Lesbians." With Fred Anderson and the Eyewitness News team. This Monday through Friday. November 16-20 at 4:30 and 11:00 p.m.

Call the Eyewitness News team anything you like. Except indifferent.

**⑦ eyewitness news
kabc-tv/4:30 & 11:00pm**
bonds/lawrence/nahan/sloane

Figure 8.4   Although most people agree that there must be official efforts to control certain acts, such as murder and rape, controversy continues to surround laws that attempt to regulate such behavior as homosexuality. Some groups are fighting for the repeal of all laws that make crimes of activities that have no victims. Among their aims is the legalization of homosexual marriages.

be sure he secured as many life histories of homosexuals as he needed for detailed study, Kinsey frequently recruited interviewees in gay bars and other homosexual settings. Later, he lumped all his interviews of males together, without reflecting that his selection procedures were designed to greatly overselect homosexuals. In addition, he seemed willing to count virtually anything as homosexual behavior, including such behavior as mutual display of genitals among same-sex persons under the age of fifteen and any fleeting response to a "homosexual stimulus," even though no overt act occurred. Later researchers at Kinsey's Institute for Sex Research reanalyzed his data and concluded, even with his biased sample (which over-included active homosexuals), that no more than 10 percent of males (not 37 percent) had been to some degree homosexual for at least three years beyond the age of fifteen (Hunt, 1974). Even this number is exaggerated because of the sampling bias. Other researchers have concluded that 1 to 2 percent of American males are exclusively homosexual and that perhaps another 3 to 4 percent have relations with members of both sexes (Hunt, 1974).

Kinsey's data on females are similarly biased. For one thing, homosexuality is considerably higher among the unmarried, and his sample greatly overrepresented unmarried women. For another, he inflated his findings by using very broad, inclusive definitions of homosexual contact, as he had done with the male data (counting childhood incidents, for example). The best reappraisals of the Kinsey data suggest that homosexuality is about half as common among females as among males—0.5 to 1 percent of females are basically homosexual.

Hunt's Data

In light of the obvious revolution in sexual attitudes and behavior and the new visibility of militant homosexuals demanding their civil rights, many have supposed that homosexuality has been on the rise. But the 1974 data show nothing of the kind. Hunt reported that 1 percent of males and 0.5 percent of females in his nationwide sample rated themselves as "mainly" homosexual. An additional 1 percent of males and 0.5 percent of fe-

239

males saw themselves as bisexual. Hunt pointed out that even if these statistics were doubled in order to compensate for the possible under-representation of members of the overt homosexual community, homosexuality would still be a very uncommon sexual orientation in this country today. Hunt estimates that only 10 percent of males have had *any* homosexual experiences beyond age fifteen, and that about 4 percent of women have had such an experience. These data make it evident that what had changed about American homosexuality during the past twenty years is not its frequency but its visibility. With society's changing attitudes, many homosexuals are no longer hiding.

Who is homosexual? Given the relatively small proportion of people who are homosexual and the social stigma attached to this identity, it is no surprise that we do not know a great deal about who they are. But we do know a few facts. Not surprisingly, the majority are single (partly because homosexual marriages are not legally recognized). Homosexual women are often among the best-educated women, but homosexual men tend to be less educated than heterosexual men. The more committed males and females are to religious beliefs, the less likely they are to have had a homosexual experience. And as with all sexual activity, homosexual activity is more frequent among the young than among the old (Hunt, 1974; Athanasiou, Shaver, and Tavris, 1970; Weinberg, 1970; Schofield, 1965; Kinsey, 1948; 1953).

In addition, committed homosexuals tend to be clustered in large cities, probably because the anonymity of cities is important to persons who are socially stigmatized and because the presence of a number of homosexuals makes it possible to create and maintain a gay community.

In what sense can we speak of homosexuality as a social problem? One reason many may think it is a problem is its prevalence. Homosexuality, however, is much less common than it is generally thought to be. Perhaps the real reason homosexuality is a problem today is that, although it remains within the deviant category of sexual expression, homosexuals have organized to seek liberation from stigmatization and discrimination. Gay liberation is a social movement claiming a grievance

240

Figure 8.5   Homosexual behavior varies as much as heterosexual behavior does. The majority of homosexuals act and dress conventionally, but some male homosexuals prefer to dress as women (above).

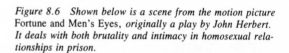

Figure 8.6   Shown below is a scene from the motion picture Fortune and Men's Eyes, *originally a play by John Herbert. It deals with both brutality and intimacy in homosexual relationships in prison.*

against social arrangements and demanding redress. Gays demand an end to laws classifying them as sexual perverts. Furthermore, they denounce as discriminatory hiring practices and civil-service codes that exclude them from employment (Sagarin, 1969). Thus, it is not the campaign *against* homosexuality that earns it the status of a social problem but the campaign to *legitimate* it that does so.

Homosexuality in Prisons

There is one setting where homosexuality continues to be regarded as a problem to be eliminated, however. A major complaint about jails and prisons is their high level of homosexuality, particularly of homosexual rape and assault. Considerable homosexuality is reported in both male and female prisons, but unlike the pattern found in the public at large, homosexuality seems to be more common among female than among male prisoners—about one-half of women and about one-fourth of men engage in homosexual acts during their confinement (Giallombardo, 1966; Ward and Kassebaum, 1965; Sykes, 1958). However, there appears to be none of the coercion that is often practiced by the aggressive male inmate against the recipient of his sexual attention. The women in prison emphasize affection in their involvements more than the male inmates do, just as female sexual behavior on the outside, both heterosexual and homosexual, is characterized by greater emotional attachments than is male sexual behavior.

Some who behave homosexually in prison did so before and will do so afterward, and others who started in prison will continue after release, but it appears that most do not continue beyond their confinement in the one-sex society of prison (Davis, 1970; Giallombardo, 1966; Ward and Kassebaum, 1965; Sykes, 1958).

Prostitution

In the past several years, prostitution has become much more visible. Every major city is filled with massage parlors, and streetwalkers openly solicit customers. However, for all the apparent boom in sex-for-sale, it is a declining industry. This downward trend was visible in Kinsey's time. Although

he found that younger men in his sample were as likely as older men to have had some experience with prostitutes (69 percent of all men had), the young men averaged only about half as many contacts with them as the older men did.

Hunt's 1974 survey revealed a sharp decrease since the 1940s. His data are restricted to premarital experiences with prostitutes. As Table 8.1 shows, there was a marked difference between older and younger men in 1974. More than half of those over thirty-five had sexual intercourse at least once with a prostitute during their days as single men. But only about a quarter of those under thirty-five had done so. Experience with prostitutes is even less common among males under twenty-five—only 3 percent said they had been with a prostitute in the past year. These findings match what observers of prostitution and prostitutes themselves report—that the main customers these days are older men.

Table 8.1 Percentage of Married Males Who Have Ever Had Premarital Intercourse with a Prostitute

EDUCATION	UNDER 35	35 AND OVER
High school or less	30	61
Some college or more	19	52

Source: Adapted from Morton Hunt, *Sexual Behavior in the 1970s* (Chicago, Ill.: Playboy Press, 1974) p. 144.

The main reason for this change is obvious. Young men today are having sexual relations with their girl friends and thus find much less need to resort to prostitutes. Older men are probably continuing a pattern established in their youth (when "nice" girls did not permit sexual liberties). Furthermore, older men probably find it more difficult than younger men to find willing sexual partners aside from prostitutes.

Do these downward trends mean that prostitution is likely to disappear in the foreseeable future? Probably not. Kingsley Davis (1971a) has argued that although the present trends are no doubt cutting down the size of the market for prostitution, the trend is unlikely to continue downward indefinitely: So long as there are men who, because of ugliness and deformity, timidity, or a desire to avoid emotional entanglements, cannot find voluntary sexual partners, there will be a market for

241

commercial sex and women to fill that market. We are unlikely to have a society in which men with such characteristics do not exist. Furthermore, the rapid growth of an elderly population made up mainly of widows creates the possibility of a market for male prostitutes—an idea that seems especially likely considering that today's sexually liberated younger women will become elderly women. Hunt's (1974) data show that very few widowed or divorced women over the age of fifty-five ever engage in sexual intercourse—a state of affairs that women are likely to find increasingly intolerable.

For the present, the best estimate is that about half a million prostitutes operate full time and entertain an average of 300,000 clients each day (Winick and Kinsie, 1971). Only a small proportion of prostitutes are ever arrested—in 1973, there were only about 35,000 arrests for prostitution. Prostitutes are now less likely to work in brothels, which reached their peak in the 1930s, and are more likely to be call girls or street walkers. Official data also indicate a decline in the average age of prostitutes, and there is evidence of a considerable number of teenage prostitutes, some of them only thirteen. Nonetheless, about 33 percent of the prostitutes are over thirty and 5 percent of the active prostitutes are over fifty.

The social organization of prostitution includes the prostitute and her customer and roles related to facilitating that commercial exchange, as well as the personal life of the prostitute and her relation to pimps, madams, and corrupted police. Prostitution is a *stratified* occupation. At the top are call girls, who work out of their apartments, have the most affluent clients, and make the most money. Some prostitutes continue to work in brothels maintained by madams and wait for customers to come to them. Others are bar girls, who solicit trade in taverns, bars, and night clubs. At the bottom are the streetwalkers, who roam a predetermined "stroll," soliciting pedestrian passersby or customers cruising in cars. Most prostitutes are streetwalkers, and their average income is estimated at around $10,000 a year (of which the prostitute is usually able to keep very little). Despite glamorization of the prostitute in autobiographies and in some magazines, most prostitutes are unattractive,

unhealthy, and poorly educated; they are disproportionately from lower-class groups and minority groups (Gray, 1973; Davis, 1971; Winick and Kinsie, 1971).

The prostitute's most important personal relationship is with her pimp—a relationship that comes as close to resembling an affectional or love relationship as most prostitutes ever have. The pimp usually has more than one prostitute, and he takes most or all of the money they earn. In exchange, he provides only acceptance, noncommercial male companionship, and sexual satisfaction. He acts as the prostitute's consort in public and squires her around in flashy clothes and cars, but he also often abuses her physically and attempts to keep her under his control. Thus, he is not just her boyfriend but her trainer, business manager, and status symbol within the "life" (Gray, 1973; Winick and Kinsie, 1971; Bryan, 1965; Murtagh and Harris, 1957).

Rape

The law recognizes two varieties of rape. *Statutory rape* applies when the female is below the legal age for consenting to sexual relations (usually sixteen or eighteen). *Forcible rape* applies to instances in which a woman is forced to submit to sexual advances (the law does not recognize the rape of males or the rape of wives by husbands). The statutory rape laws are rarely enforced these days. Forcible rape, on the other hand, is an extremely serious offense. In this chapter we restrict our attention to forcible rape.

Beliefs and Facts

According to the Uniform Crime Reports (UCR), 51,000 rapes were reported to the police in 1973. Since 1968, reported rapes have increased by 60 percent. It is very difficult to say what the actual number of rapes in the United States is. Obviously, many rapes go unreported. Sometimes the victim is ashamed to report it. Sometimes the victim fears callous treatment by police and prosecutors. And often the victim simply does not think reporting it is worthwhile. (Apparently for the same reason, most males do not report assaults.) Because rape, like homicide, is an uncommon crime, victimization studies do not find enough cases to provide a

Figure 8.7 *Although prostitution in the United States has declined for a number of years, it is safe to say that it probably will not disappear entirely. Economic conditions, women's liberation, and the sexual revolution have combined to change the form of prostitution in the United States. While many prostitutes in the United States now work in massage parlors, prostitutes in other countries, such as those in Spain (above), continue to solicit customers directly.*

Figure 8.8 *Women who have been raped complain often of being treated more like offenders than like victims, both by the police and in court. Women's groups have lobbied successfully in some states to reform legal procedures related to rape. (Below) The New York State Assembly voted unanimously to drop a controversial section from the New York Penal Code which had impeded convictions for rape.*

Assembly Votes to Drop Rape-Corroboration Rule

By DAVID A. ANDELMAN
Special to The New York Times

ALBANY, Jan. 14—The Assembly today unanimously voted to remove the requirement of corroboration in rape cases from the state's Penal Code—a move that for years has been urged by women's-liberation and civil-liberties groups and law-enforcement officials.

The surprise action, taken without debate, came on the opening business day of the Legislature, and the bill's sponsors predicted quick Senate approval as well.

"The gals did a lot of good, hard work," said the bill's chief sponsor, Assemblyman Alvin M. Suchin, Republican of Dobbs Ferry, attempting to explain the bill's quick passage by a vote of 130 to 0.

"It's a big day for women," said Sally McGee, coordinator of the rape committee of the Manhattan Women's Political caucus. She said at least two dozen women, starting tomorrow, would lobby for the bill in the Senate every Tuesday until the Senate approved the measure.

The bill removes all need for corroboration by a witness, except in cases of consensual sodomy or of so-called statutory rape, where the victim is under the age of consent—18—or has a mental defect.

In 1972, the Legislature removed the requirement that every material fact essential to constitute the crime be corroborated. However, most law-enforcement officials and women's and civil-liberties groups said a remaining requirement—the need for corroboration of the use of force and of actual sexual contact—still made conviction a virtual impossibility. The fact that rape convictions have not risen substantially in the last two years appeared to confirm this belief.

More than an hour after the Assembly approved the bill, Assemblyman Herbert J. Miller, Democrat of Queens, sought unsuccessfully to introduce an amendment to omit from the eased corroboration requirement

Continued on Page 27, Column 1

reliable basis for projecting a rate (although some projections have been published anyway). Assuming that about half of the rapes that occur are reported, about 100,000 American women are raped each year. That represents a substantial amount of suffering, humiliation, and fear.

Recently, rape has become a central theme in the women's liberation movement. In particular, the police have been condemned for insensitive and skeptical responses to women who report being raped, and the courts have been indicted for turning rape trials into trials of the victim. It is charged that the police often accuse women of leading the rapist on and that the courts permit the moral character of the victim to be challenged indecently. Unfortunately, these charges and their denials have occurred in a vacuum. Until very recently, we have lacked even the barest outline of facts about rape.

The first significant attempt to examine rape was made by Menachem Amir (1971), who analyzed data gathered from police files in Philadelphia for the years 1958 and 1960. Since 1970, Duncan Chappell and his associates have been gathering rape data from police files in New York, Boston, and Los Angeles, and they have now begun to publish their findings (Chappell and Singer, 1973; Chappell *et al.*, 1971).

These data make it possible to begin to get some realistic picture of what has previously been a crime shrouded in ignorance and fear and, therefore, subject to distortion and myth.

It is widely believed that the police are resistant to rape reports, question the validity of the charge, and discourage women from filing charges. This belief is not supported, at least by data for New York City—the only data available on the subject. Over a three-year period beginning in 1970, the New York police classified fewer than 10 percent of their rape complaints as unfounded. The usual reason for classifying a case as unfounded was the inability of officers to locate a victim after having been called or finding a victim too intoxicated to provide a coherent story (Chappell and Singer, 1973). Furthermore, the police dismissed *fewer* reported rapes as unfounded than they did cases of assaults or burglaries. This does not support the image of police unresponsiveness.

243

A second widely held belief about rape is that it often occurs among close friends and acquaintances. Amir's data gave some support to this view. He found that 48 percent of the rapes he studied in Philadelphia had involved a man who was the boyfriend, acquaintance, neighbor, family friend, or relative of the victim. However, Amir's data probably apply to a pattern of rape that once was common but has now become rare. Recent data show that the vast majority of rapes involve strangers (Chappell and Singer, 1973). It is possible that rapes may have grown out of an interpersonal dynamic in the past and that before the sexual revolution, rape may have been primarily rooted in an intimate relationship. Today, however, most rapists are strangers to their victims.

The data also suggest that rape typically does not involve the use of a weapon. In New York City, a knife was used as a threat in 20 percent of the cases, a gun in 8 percent. Physical force is the common threat. It would appear that rape-murder is relatively rare. Of 632 homicides in New York City in 1965, only 4 involved victims of rapes. Or put another way, of several thousand reported rapes, 4 led to homicide. However, in about 15 percent of New York City rapes, the victim suffered physical injuries.

In 61 percent of the rapes, the initial meeting between the rapist and the victim took place indoors. In four out of ten rapes the scene was the victim's own apartment, and another 13 percent occurred inside the victim's apartment building. Roofs and landings were the dangerous locations (Chappell and Singer, 1973).

Nationwide, the police make an arrest in about 55 percent of rape cases. Although this figure is lower than the arrest rate for homicide, it is much higher than the arrest rate police manage for most other crimes—only about 20 percent of burglaries and larcenies result in arrest.

Who Are the Rapists?

One important reason for the high arrest rate for rape calls attention to one of the most unusual features of rapists. Many rapists are caught because they reveal their identities to their victims. Frequently after the rape has occurred, the rapist acts as if he believes there are now grounds for

establishing a relationship with his victim. Many rapists seem to believe that the act of rape is a charade that women force men to go through to let women preserve the illusion of being "good girls." They seem to think that now that the victims know what great lovers the rapists are, they will want to see them again. Consequently, many rapists raise the question of future meetings, and some even phone their victims later and ask for a date (Chappell and Singer, 1973; Gebbhard *et al.*, 1965). This often leads to the rapist's arrest.

Rapists are young. Only 26 percent of rapists in New York City and only 14 percent in Philadelphia are over thirty (Chappell and Singer, 1973). Even though many are arrested, few rapists are *convicted* of their crime (a point we take up in Part III of this chapter). For this reason, it seems unlikely that rapists are young simply because older rapists are locked up. Rather, it seems that rape is a crime men stop committing when they get out of their twenties. One reason is that these men probably establish a more conventional sexual relationship and cease their criminal sexual activities.

Despite racist mythology, it would appear that until very recently interracial rape, and particularly the rape of white women by black men, was rare. However, the data suggest that rape of white women by black men is now becoming more common. In his study of Philadelphia in 1958 and 1960, Amir found that only 3 percent of the cases involved a black male and a white female and that 4 percent involved a white male and a black female. Data covering seventeen major cities for 1967 found that 10 percent of the cases involved black rapists and white victims, whereas less than half of a percent involved white rapists and black victims (Mulvihill *et al.*, 1969). Data for 1970 based on the District of Columbia found 21 percent of the rapes involved black males and white females (Hayman *et al.*, 1971). Data for Oakland, California, in 1971 found a third of the rape cases involved a black male and a white female (Agopian, Chappell, and Geis, 1974). Michael Agopian and his associates (1974) reported that many of the Oakland cases they studied had a distinct element of intended seduction—victims were often well treated both during and after the rape, and in a number of instances efforts to arrange future dates were made. Indeed, because inter-racial rape tends to be higher in those cities where interracial couples are more common, this change in the racial character of rape may reflect the strains on people trying to readjust to the lowering of barriers against interracial contact.

It must be pointed out, however, that most rape, like most other violence, is still intraracial, not interracial—it occurs within rather than between racial groups. But because black males are very disproportionately represented among rapists, black females face a much higher risk of rape than white females. Sixty percent of the rape cases studied in seventeen major cities involved the rape of a black female by a black male. Only 30 percent involved the rape of a white female by a white male (Mulvihill *et al.*, 1969).

Two final points should be made about rape. First, if, for whatever reason, women become in-creasingly willing to report rapes, the rape rate will obviously rise rapidly, despite the fact that the ac-tual number of rapes may not be increasing (and could even be going down). And it is possible that some of the recent rise in rape statistics only re-flects better reporting. The second point involves the number of rapists in the nation. If it is true that there are about 100,000 rapes a year in the United States, that does not mean there are 100,000 rap-ists. From what is known about rapists, they tend to be multiple offenders. Thus, 100,000 rapes could be the result of 10,000 rapists who strike less often than once a month. Or it could be the work of 1,000 rapists who strike every three or four days. There is no way to say how many rapists are loose in the country. But clearly, their numbers are much too few to justify the image of rapists lurking in every alley. However, it does not take a great many rapists to constitute a severe problem. For the woman who encounters him, even one rapist is far too many.

PART II: SOURCES
SEXUAL PROBLEMS

Our discussion of contemporary sexual problems has covered a wide range of conventional and criminal sexual patterns. In this section we ex-amine the way factors that determine sexual be-havior influence both conventional and deviant sexual patterns. By shifting our attention back and forth between conventional and deviant sexual problems, we can benefit by some striking com-parisons.

PHYSIOLOGICAL FACTORS

Whatever else it may be, sex is physical. But to say that is not to say much. Do humans possess a biological sex drive? How specific is such a drive? Do physiological differences influence sexual de-viance? How does biology interact with culture to influence human sexual patterns? These seem to be the significant questions.

The Sexual Drive
Sexual excitation and sexual desires seem a virtu-ally universal human characteristic (Kinsey, 1948; 1953). Social scientists are willing to accept the notion that there is some underlying biological urge involved in human sexuality. But, unlike other biological drives, such as thirst or hunger, sexual gratification is not required for individual survival. Furthermore, it is obvious that this drive is relatively nonspecific; that is, humans seem able to find sexual stimulation in and to attain sexual gratification from an amazing array of sources. In addition, humans, like the higher primates, have to be taught heterosexual pursuits. For example, Harry and Margaret Harlow's isolated monkeys failed to engage in sexual activities after being put among normal monkeys (see Chapter 2). In this sense, sex is not natural; our biology alone is in-sufficient to guide our sexual patterns.

Even with the knowledge of how learning and culture shape human sexual responses, some groups have tried to attribute some forms of sexual deviance, particularly homosexuality, to inherent biological differences. In particular, homosexual groups are inclined to attribute their preferences to inborn sexual traits. A very serious defect in this argument is that homosexuals (especially those who are exclusively homosexual) obviously have a low birth rate because they procreate less often. Thus, by natural selection, a genetic basis for homo-sexuality ought to have been bred out of the popu-

245

lation long ago (Davis, 1971a; Ollendorff, 1966).

A second problem is that twin studies—studies of genetically identical twins used to determine the role of inheritance for any trait—fail to reveal any tendency for the identical twin of a homosexual to also be homosexual (Akers, 1973).

Another approach ignores the question of inheritance and simply concentrates on searching for biological sources of sexual deviance. A wide range of factors have been studied:

Examinations of physical type, blood and urine samples, color blindness, taste threshold, and skin grafts have revealed no differences between the habitually homosexual person and the heterosexual person. Studies have found no connection between persons with deviant physiognomy and homosexual desires or behavior. Persons with abnormal, ambiguous, or contradictory sexual morphology, internal sex structure, and secondary sex characteristics show no disproportionate tendency toward homosexuality. Attempts to detect some anomaly of the chromosomal structure in homosexuals have failed. . . . No endocrinological differences between heterosexual and homosexual have been found. (Akers, 1973)

It may be that one day some significant hormonal or other biological difference will be found between homosexuals and heterosexuals. But such a discovery has not yet been made.

The Puberty Revolution

Recently it has been proposed that profound changes in human physical maturation over the past century may have played a major role in the contemporary sexual revolution. Virtually everyone knows that people in industrialized nations have been getting noticeably larger each generation in recent times. But an even more startling physical change has gone virtually unnoticed: People in industrial nations like ours have been *maturing* physically and sexually at progressively younger ages for more than a century. These changes can only be described as revolutionary.

A considerable body of data (see Figure 8.9) has been assembled to clearly demonstrate that the average age at which girls begin to menstruate has been declining rapidly since as far back as the mid-nineteenth century (Tanner, 1962; 1970). A little more than a century ago, girls began to men-

struate on the average at about age seventeen. (Females in some remote tribes such as those in New Guinea still mature this late.) Today, females are menstruating on the average nearly five years earlier—girls have been becoming women on the average four months earlier each decade since 1850. No similar data are available on the age of male puberty, but it is well established that males sexually mature later than females. Therefore, if the average seventeen-year-old girl was just beginning menstruation in the mid-nineteenth century, the average male was still prepubic. One thing we do know is that fifty years ago and more, males still did a considerable amount of growing after age eighteen; today the average male has completed his growth by that age (Tanner, 1970).

Changing nutrition and improved health (reflected in the rapid decline in mortality examined in Chapter 14) seem to be the primary causes of this extraordinary shift in the age of physical and sexual maturation (Tanner, 1970). Because Americans have long been the best-fed people on earth, it is no surprise to find that, as far back as the data go, American girls have menstruated somewhat earlier than girls in Europe. The decline in the age of maturity probably began earlier in the United States, but as is shown in Figure 8.9, it has followed the same downward trend as found in Europe.

Throughout this period of rapid decline in the age of physical and sexual maturity, the average age of marriage has changed little and has never dropped below twenty and a half for women or below twenty-three for men (Ryder, 1969; Davis, 1950). Thus, the gap between physical maturity and marriage has grown ever wider. Members of each new generation have been expected to wait longer between the time they become sexually capable and the time they become marriageable. In contrast to the prepubescent teenagers in times past, the modern American does not marry until about ten years after becoming sexually mature and thus passes through the peak years of sexuality outside the bonds of wedlock.

In the past, the norms confining sexual relations to marriage were facilitated by the fact that the marriage age was close to the age of puberty. Physical and sexual maturity no longer coincide

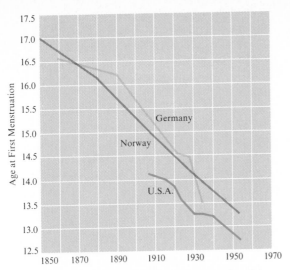

Figure 8.9 (Above) *An important biological stimulus of the sexual revolution can be seen in the rather spectacular drop in the age of puberty as indicated by the average age at which girls begin to menstruate. Since the middle of the last century, girls have begun to menstruate as much as four-and-a-half years earlier. Scientists believe improved health and nutrition caused this more rapid maturation of young people, which probably also accounts for the differences between American and European girls.*

(Adapted from J.M. Tanner, 1955.)

Figure 8.10   Views of what is deviant have changed with the sexual revolution. However, certain kinds of deviance, such as this man's kissing his doll, would be categorized as abnormal behavior by most people.

with social maturity. Put to such a test—when "shouldn't" was no longer backed up by "couldn't"—the norms against premarital sex collapsed. The puberty revolution was probably an important dynamic behind the sexual revolution.

PSYCHOLOGICAL THEORIES OF SEXUAL BEHAVIOR

Writing and research on sexuality have been dominated by psychological analysis, mainly because of the immense influence of the work of Sigmund Freud on twentieth-century psychological theory and on modern views of sexuality. A major thesis in Freud's work concerned the guilt and anxiety that commonly result from the *repression* of sexual urges or instincts. Such repression was a common source of neurosis, according to Freud, because the prevailing puritanical sexual code did not permit the free and natural expression of these urges (*libido*). Freud's psychoanalytic case studies are filled with an immense variety of clues to repressed sexuality that Freud detected in his patients.

Today, psychotherapists widely accept the Freudian view that repressed sexuality is a major source of psychological troubles. That view has provided an intellectual basis for regarding many puritanical sexual prohibitions as unnatural and harmful. However, as was pointed out earlier, at present we are in the midst of, rather than in the aftermath of, a revolution in our sexual practices and standards. Not only do some Americans remain firmly committed to the older moral standards but many who have adopted the new sexual practices have done so with feelings of ambivalence. Guilt remains a problem in conventional sexual behavior and, as will be taken up later, plays a major part in the sudden demand for sexual instruction and therapy.

However, the major focus of current psychological interest has not been directed so much toward understanding conventional sexuality as toward explaining sexual deviance—an effort that has led to bitter controversy.

Is the Sexual Deviant Sick?

Generally speaking, modern personality theorists regard deviant sexual behavior as symptomatic of

247

some fundamental psychological disorder; that is, they regard sexual deviants to be "sick" to some extent. Their behavior is rarely thought to reflect severe psychosis but is thought to stem from less severe, neurotic conditions:

It is generally agreed that most sexual deviates present psychological or psychiatric problems of one type or another. . . . A neurosis of some sort is by far the most frequently mentioned diagnosis of the sexual deviate by the majority of experts in this field. Often the sex offender may not have a generalized personality maladjustment but merely a pre-occupation with abnormal sexual impulses or desires. . . . Sexual deviation represents a symptom rather than a cause of underlying emotional difficulties and usually represents an outlet or relief from tensions. (Oliver, 1967)

This type of explanation has been applied to a variety of sexual deviations such as rape, child molestation, incest, prostitution, and exhibitionism (Oliver, 1967), but is most often applied to homosexuality (Ollendorff, 1966; Cappon, 1965; Ellis, 1965; Caprio, 1962). The homosexual is said to be suffering from repressed guilt, excessive anxiety, immature defense mechanisms, psychopathology, and other maladjustments that trace back to psychic trauma in early childhood, long before the onset of homosexual behavior.

There is much to criticize about the conception of homosexuals and other deviants as sick. First, it is based primarily on cases of people who come voluntarily to psychiatrists because they are troubled by their homosexuality. Those who come to see psychiatrists may be neurotic, but that says nothing at all about the mental health of the general population of people who engage in homosexual behavior. Similarly, the fact that some heterosexuals are treated by psychiatrists cannot lead to the conclusion that most heterosexuals are in need of similar treatment. Second, it seems plausible that sexual deviants may develop neurotic problems because of the psychic pressures they experience from being deviant. Finally, what valid evidence there is tends not to support the theory that persons who participate in homosexual behavior, even in exclusively homosexual contact, do so because they are emotionally disturbed (West, 1967; Schofield, 1965; Schur, 1965).

In the past few years, the view that homosexuality reflects psychological abnormality has been bit-

terly attacked by homosexuals and by many social scientists sympathetic to their cause. Calling homosexuals "sick" is a justification used to treat such people as perverts and make them change. In order to argue against this view, which implies that homosexuals should not object to being cured and which denies their claims that they are a wronged minority, homosexuals favor genetic explanations that justify their being the way they are. There have even been efforts to turn the psychological scales around in order to legitimate homosexuality. For example, some have claimed not only that homosexuals are well adjusted but that anyone who believes otherwise is "sick," afflicted with a neurotic disorder called homophobia, or fear of homosexuals (Weinberg, 1972).

In 1974, the American Psychiatric Association removed homosexuality from its list of pathological conditions, or diseases. At present, the trend is away from regarding homosexuals as sick.

Learning Theory

Explanations based on the idea of abnormality are not the only important psychological accounts of sexual deviance. Indeed, the notion that all forms of sexual behavior, whether conventional or deviant, are learned is rapidly becoming the dominant position. The *learning* approach argues that people engage in sexual deviance not because they are driven by abnormal psychological conditions or because they are biologically different but because they have learned such sexual behavior.

At least from the time of the Kinsey research, there has been a recognition that, aside from certain biological determinants of sexual arousal and orgasm, "human sexual behavior appear[s] to be the product of learning and conditioning."

Even some of the most extremely variant types of human sexual behavior may need no more explanation than is provided by our understanding of the processes of learning and conditioning. . . . Flagellation, masochism, transvestism, and the wide variety of fetishes appear to be products of conditioning. (Kinsey *et al.*, 1953)

A variety of evidence supports the notion that the process by which deviant sexual behavior is acquired (or by which a person is conditioned to respond to deviant stimuli) is the same as the process by which conforming sexual behavior is acquired and conditioned; the idea is that deviant sexual behavior differs only in that the predominant sexual morality of society disapproves of it.

Much of this evidence comes from reports of individuals deliberately or inadvertently socialized into deviant activities or from studies of the outcome of treatment methods that *decondition* (make one unlearn) sexual deviance (we discuss this method of treatment in Part III of this chapter). There is some experimental evidence that deviant patterns can be produced, extinguished, and reproduced by *conditioning*. For instance, in one experiment, adult, single, heterosexual male volunteers were induced (conditioned) to respond sexually to a fetish, an object that itself has no sexual content but that comes to arouse a sexual response (Rachman, 1966). (Some objects that psychologists know serve as fetishes are shoes and underwear.) The volunteers were shown color slides of attractive nude females and became sexually aroused (achieved an erection). Then they were shown pictures of women's boots, handbags, and other objects to which they did not respond sexually. But after several conditioning sessions in which the

Figure 8.11 Psychologists and psychiatrists have applied conditioning methods to homosexual behavior. The above photograph illustrates the procedure of visual desensitization, in which a subject who experiences anxiety in response to female stimuli is given relaxation training. When the subject is in a relaxed state, an image of a woman is projected onto a screen, and the subject is told to indicate the point at which he begins to feel anxious. After a time, the subject remains in a relaxed state for progressively longer periods, until he feels no anxiety in the presence of female stimuli.

slides of the nude women immediately preceded slides of black, knee-length women's boots, all of the men became sexually aroused just at the sight of the boots. The response to the boots continued over several trials, even in the absence of the original stimuli of the nude women, but eventually the men no longer responded to the boots as a sexual fetish. For some, the erotic response to the boots came back later, and simply by exposing them for a period of time to the boots without the accompaniment of other sexual stimuli, they again lost their attachment to the boots.

Such studies strongly support the hypothesis that sexual deviance *is learned and can be unlearned.* Simply by associating some formerly neutral object (boots, for example) with sexually stimulating images, one may learn to respond to a range of sights, smells, sounds, tastes, clothing, and physical surroundings, some of which are considered abhorent by society. There is, however, no difference in the learning process, only in what is learned.

249

SOCIAL-PSYCHOLOGICAL EXPLANATIONS

Thus far, our view has been restricted to the individual. But sex is preeminently social. Indeed, even when individuals masturbate they almost invariably fantasize the presence of a sexual partner (Hunt, 1974). Furthermore, although it seems certain that people learn their sexual preferences and practices, it is equally obvious that they learn them from (or with) others. We will now examine the part played by the immediate social environment in establishing patterns of sexual behavior.

Labeling Theory

As we have seen in previous discussions of labeling theory, it cannot account for a person's engaging in deviant behavior *before being labeled as a deviant.* In explaining sexual behavior, the importance of the theory is to show that labels, once attached to people, influence their future behavior: both deviant and conventional.

The label ''sexual deviant'' has enormous power to corrode social relationships. People so labeled are shunned: Heterosexual males are reluctant to be close friends with male homosexuals;

most women will not date men they suspect of homosexuality. Similarly, to be known as a prostitute, a rapist, or a child molester causes people to be shunned.

Sexual deviants are often restricted to associating with those most likely to maintain them in their deviant ways. Homosexuals find homosexual partners beckoning while women reject them. Prostitutes are accepted by other prostitutes, pimps, and customers but are rejected by others. Labeling has worse effects if it is officially recorded—the woman arrested for prostitution or the men and women with dishonorable military discharges for homosexuality can find it very difficult to escape their label, especially when it comes to finding legitimate employment. Nevertheless, the impact of social labels must not be overemphasized. The anonymity of modern urban life makes it fairly easy for many people to get a fresh start if they want one.

Perhaps the most frequent way that labeling reinforces sexual deviance is through one's self-conception. To an important extent, people can become the victims of self-labeling. Edward Sagarin (1973) has described the power of labels for homosexuals. He asserts that

emotions and actions are fluid and dynamic, learnable and unlearnable, exist to a given extent for a limited or longer period of time, but are constantly in a state of change. . . . However, people become entrapped in a false consciousness of identifying themselves as *being* homosexuals. They believe that they discover what they are (and by implication since this is a discovery, they must have been this all along).

People are very vulnerable to sexual self-labeling. Because we all must learn and evolve our sexuality with little benefit of open, public socialization, it is easy for us to feel perplexed and uncertain about ourselves. Most of us experience some anxiety about how we are going to turn out.

Indeed, the power of labels is as apparent in conventional as in deviant sexual behavior. Young men whom women find sexually attractive and competent probably become increasingly more successful (and more fixed into conventional sexuality) as they are labeled and label themselves "lovers." Similarly, women who come to regard themselves as sensual probably become more so.

Figure 8.12   Levels of Analysis and Issues Appropriate to Each Level. This summary chart does not cover all the important points raised in the chapter. Use it only to review what you have read. Page numbers are given for the full discussion of any topic.

Conversely, impotence and frigidity probably become more fixed conditions as failure leads people to think of themselves as being impotent or frigid.

Social Learning and Differential Association

The preceding discussion of labeling theory moves naturally to a discussion of learning, for labels are learned. As will be evident in a later discussion of subcultural deviance, some deviant sexual activity is reinforced by associates. The prostitute is immediately reinforced for her behavior by receiving money from her customer, and she is also reinforced by other prostitutes and pimps. Homosexuals are reinforced by their partners and by the gay subculture. For conventional sexual activities, most people are reinforced by others.

Some sexual deviance, however, is better explained by a simple conditioned-learning model than by social learning. Most voyeurs (peeping toms), exhibitionists, rapists, and child molesters are not reinforced by associates for engaging in such acts—they are solo operators. They continue such behavior without social reinforcement because the sexual behavior is *self-reinforcing*. By whatever accident of initial conditioning, it is the case that this is the way these people get their kicks. So long as that remains the case, their behavior will continue.

SOCIOLOGICAL EXPLANATIONS: MIDDLE RANGE

Most of us learn our sexual pursuits from others—and some of us learn deviant sexual behavior. We must now ask why some people learn deviant sexual behavior and others do not.

Strain Theory

What strain theory has to say about sexual behavior is in conjunction with personality theories on

Levels	Appropriate Questions	A Partial Synopsis of Present Conclusions
Physiological	Do humans possess a biological sexual drive? How specific is it?	There is a biological sexual drive, but it is not very specific; humans can be aroused by many things and have to be taught heterosexual behavior. (p. 245)
	Is sexual deviance caused by physiological differences?	Apparently not. For example, there seems to be no basis for the argument that homosexuals have inborn sexual traits. (pp. 245–246)
	Have recent biological changes influenced conventional sexual standards?	Changes in the average age of puberty probably have done so. (pp. 246–247)
Psychological	Is the sexual deviant mentally ill?	Psychoanalytic theories have explained sexual deviance in terms of psychiatric problems, but that view has received much criticism. (pp. 247–248)
	Is sexual behavior—both conventional and deviant—learned?	Yes. Both kinds of sexual behavior seem to be acquired and conditioned through the same kind of learning process. Deviance is learned and can be unlearned. (pp. 248–249)
Social-Psychological	Does labeling influence sexual behavior?	Self-labeling does. For example, a man may conclude that he must be a homosexual merely because he has engaged in one homosexual act. (pp. 249–250)
	Does differential association influence sexual behavior?	Yes. Because most sexual behavior involves a partner, sexual patterns tend to be formed and sustained by one's associates. (p. 250)
Sociological: Middle Range	Is sexual deviance a lower-class phenomenon?	Generally, no. However, prostitutes tend to come from poor families. (p. 252)
	Is most sexual deviance found in deviant subcultures?	Some is, for example, in the gay community and in the prostitute community. But most is not supported by a subculture, and little appears to be initially caused by subcultures. (pp. 252–253)
	Does sexual deviance reflect a low stake in conformity?	To some extent. If conventional sexual behavior is sustained through bonds to conventional persons (and through the high potential costs of deviance), then deviance is partly the result of the absence of these bonds and these stakes in conventional behavior. (p. 253)
Societal	Do American values conflict in the area of sexual behavior, thereby causing problems?	Traditional concerns about chastity and modesty conflict with values of romantic love and sexual fulfillment; such conflicts make it difficult to deal openly with sexual problems. (pp. 253–254)
	Does freely available pornography cause sex crimes?	No. It appears to reduce them. (pp. 254–256)

251

the one hand and class theories on the other. If our earlier conclusion is correct—that a mental-illness model does not adequately account for sexual deviance—then the application of strain theory to mental illness also fails to explain sexual deviance, for the theory simply says that psychological abnormality results from frustrated desires.

But strain theories can avoid the mental-illness model and concentrate on the *class differences* that are regarded as the fundamental source of strain. This line of analysis seems somewhat more fruitful. For example, the data we have suggest that prostitutes are predominantly from economically disadvantaged backgrounds. Despite the glamorous myths about prostitution recently fostered by such books as *The Happy Hooker*, prostitution is, for the most part, not very profitable; it is fundamentally an unskilled occupation. It is no more surprising that prostitutes do not tend to come from well-to-do backgrounds than it is that housemaids and ditch diggers do not come from such backgrounds. But, as we have seen in other discussions, strain theory cannot explain why all people who are frustrated by class differences do not deviate. Millions of women would seem to be frustrated (if strain theory is correct), but very few of them turn to prostitution.

Of late, it has become fashionable to discuss interracial rape in terms of strain theory. In *Soul On Ice* (1967), Eldridge Cleaver argued that his sexual assaults (when he was about twenty-two) on white women were a primitive form of revolutionary activity, that he was attempting to get even with his white oppressors through rape. Recent studies of interracial rape, however, suggest that this motive seldom exists (Agopian, Chappell, and Geis 1974). Most rapists, black and white, seem to be out only for sex. Furthermore, the fact remains that the overwhelming majority of black rapists victimize black women. How can this possibly be seen as getting even with whites?

Subcultural Deviance

Behind most of the social-learning and differential-association theories of sexual deviance is the notion that the sexual deviant conforms to the norms of some group within the society. This explanation is commonly applied to prostitutes and homosexuals.

252

A Prostitute

I was about fifteen, going on sixteen. I was sitting in a coffee shop . . . , and a friend of mine came by. She said, "I've got a cab waiting. Hurry up. You can make fifty dollars in twenty minutes." Looking back, I wonder why I was so willing to run out of the coffee shop, get in a cab, and turn a trick. It wasn't traumatic because my training had been in how to be a hustler anyway.

I learned it from the society around me, just as a woman. We're taught how to hustle, how to attract, hold a man, and give sexual favors in return. The language that you hear all the time, "Don't sell yourself cheap." "Hold out for the highest bidder." "Is it proper to kiss a man good night on the first date?" The implication is it may not be proper on the first date, but if he takes you out to dinner on the second date, it's proper. If he brings you a bottle of perfume on the third date, you should let him touch you above the waist. And go on from there. It's a market place transaction.

Somehow I managed to absorb that when I was quite young. So it wasn't even a moment of truth when this woman came into the coffee shop and said, "Come on." I was back in twenty-five minutes and I felt no guilt.

She was a virgin until she was fourteen. A jazz musician, with whom she had fallen in love, avoided her. *"So I went out to have sex with somebody to present him with an accomplished fact. I found it nonpleasurable. I did a lot of sleeping around before I ever took money."*

A precocious child, she was already attending a high school of demanding academic standards. *"I was very lonely. I didn't experience myself as being attractive. I had always felt I was too big, too fat, too awkward, didn't look like a Pepsi-Cola ad, was not anywhere near the American Dream. Guys were mostly scared of me. I was athletic, I was bright, and I didn't know how to keep my mouth shut. I didn't know how to play the games right.*

"I understood very clearly they were not attracted to me for what I was, but as a sexual object. I was attractive. The year before I started hustling there were a lot of guys that wanted to go to bed with me. They didn't want to get involved emotionally, but they did want to ball. For a while I was willing to accept that. It was feeling intimacy, feeling close, feeling warm.

"The time spent in bed wasn't unpleasant. It just wasn't terribly pleasant. It was a way of feeling somebody cared about me, at least for a moment. And it mattered that I was there, that I was important. I discovered that in bed it was possible. It was one skill that I had and I was proud of my reputation as an amateur."

Quote is from a former prostitute.
—Studs Terkel, *Working* (New York: Pantheon Books, 1974), pp. 57–58.

Because most sexual activity (both deviant and conventional) is inherently social, in the sense that it involves at least one other person, there is clearly some merit in the notion that it is supported by some degree of social approval. However, subcultural explanations imply more than social approval; they assume that some stable social environment exists within which people consider conventional the same behavior that outsiders regard as deviant. Most prostitutes associate with other prostitutes and their pimps, and this group constitutes a subculture within which prostitution is not deviant. It seems certain, too, that participation in this subculture increases the likelihood that a woman will remain a prostitute and will regard her behavior as legitimate. However, the main role of sexually deviant subcultures is to sustain deviance, not cause it to occur in the first place. Much writing that concentrates on how women are recruited into the subculture of prostitution seems to assume that joining the subculture is how women *become* prostitutes. However, Diana Gray's intensive study of teenage girls who were experimenting with prostitution found that becoming a member of the subculture did not typically *cause* women to become prostitutes. These girls began having intercourse for male attention and then moved on to money-for-sex transactions—all *before* encountering the subculture of prostitution. If they learned to be prostitutes, they learned primarily from men willing to buy sex, not from other women who were already selling sex. These girls began to associate with pimps and with other prostitutes after engaging in prostitution (Gray, 1973).

Similarly, it appears that homosexuals usually engage in homosexual behavior first and only later become participants in the gay subculture. Thus, the existence of a homosexual subculture tells us much about how homosexuals socially organize to sustain their deviance, but it tells us little about the source of deviance. Thus, the subculture reflects sexual preferences of individuals rather than causes them.

Control Theory

Diana Gray (1973) makes a strong case for control theory in accounting for prostitution. She found that her sample of teenage prostitutes had little to

lose and, from their point of view, much to gain by prostitution. Their occupational alternatives were not very attractive, for these girls overwhelmingly had poor school records and no valuable skills. Furthermore, they did not risk losing the respect of family and friends because they had few attachments to begin with. Indeed, the subsequent development of attachments (finding a boyfriend, for example) was the primary reason some of the girls in Gray's sample stopped being prostitutes.

Homosexuality, too, most often results from forming an attachment with a willing sex partner of the same sex. As was pointed out earlier, people tend to "discover" they are homosexuals when they find themselves engaging in homosexual acts. By the same token, so few people become committed to homosexuality probably because most people find they have too much to lose. Becoming a homosexual, in addition to risking attachments to persons with conventional sexual patterns, means foregoing many social rewards and relationships that are dependent upon marriage and family. The desire for children, for example, probably serves as a major inducement for most people to engage in conventional sexual behavior.

Control theory interprets rape the same way it interprets property crime. The rapist adopts illegal means to fulfill his desires for sexual gratification. Because rape convictions are seldom obtained, a rapist may accurately believe the rewards outweigh the risks.

SOCIETAL FACTORS

In Part I of this chapter, we saw that sexual behavior varies considerably from one culture to another. However, in addition to identifying which acts are conventional or deviant, cultural sexual standards may actually cause some deviant sexual acts to occur.

American Culture

It seems evident that the legacies of the puritanical sexual code in our society cause problems in conventional sexuality and also contribute to deviant sexuality. We have already seen that it is difficult for many people to fulfill their expectations concerning conventional sexual behavior. They are not sure how to have intercourse, for example, and find it difficult to learn. We have also seen that ignorance about the risks of pregnancy and about proper birth-control methods are a major cause of illegitimacy, and secrecy about sexual matters plays a major role in impeding effective treatment of venereal disease.

This same secrecy may also lead people into deviant sexual activity. For example, not knowing that many people have a homosexual experience without becoming committed homosexuals may cause some people to mistakenly label themselves as homosexuals and therefore to become homosexuals. Ignorance also seems to play a significant role in rape. Given that so many rapists seem to attempt to use rape as a means of establishing a sexual relationship with their victim (Chappell and Singer, 1973; Gebbhard *et al.*, 1965), they must badly misunderstand how such liaisons are achieved and know little about women's attitudes toward sex. Some men may take up rape or child molesting because they have failed to learn any successful way of obtaining legitimate sexual gratification. Studies of persons convicted of sexual offenses report them to be much more ignorant of sexual facts than are persons convicted of nonsexual offenses (The Report of the Commission on Obscenity and Pornography, 1970).

A second cultural factor that may give rise to sexual deviance is the definition of conventional sex roles. For example, if roles are defined so that males are extremely dominant, sexual patterns are likely to be very male oriented. Typically, sex-role definitions have meant the suppression of female sexuality and strict regulation of sexual access to females (female chastity and fidelity typically become extreme concerns). The usual by-product has been a very considerable amount of prostitution (Davis, 1971a), and many suspect that this view of sex roles also underlies rape. Clearly, for rape to provide sexual gratification, men must think of women as sexual objects that can be taken. Sex roles stressing male dominance and female sexual distance, or unattainability, may also contribute to homosexuality. For one thing, the opportunity for conventional heterosexual bonds is greatly reduced by the restrictions on female contacts with males. Thus, the opportunity to learn to respond sexually

to persons of the same sex is increased. For another thing, males who fall short of the highly masculinized notion of what men are supposed to be may be labeled as homosexuals and thereby may be made into homosexuals. Some further implications of sex and sex roles are taken up in Chapter 11.

The cultural standards of attractiveness also affect sexual patterns. What it means to be beautiful or handsome differs from one society to another. But every society has standards that specify who is and who is not attractive. In our society, attractiveness is associated with youthfulness. Thus, Americans become less and less sexually attractive to each other as they age. To the extent that lack of access to conventional sexual relations tends to lead to sexual deviance, sexual deviance may increase with age (taking into account that sexual desires also decrease somewhat with age). And the fact that the elderly are regarded as unattractive is a major source of business for prostitutes.

Pornography

Many Americans regard pornography as an urgent social problem. Indeed, a majority favor some censorship of sexual materials (Hunt, 1974). Most of the concern about pornography is based on the belief that it contributes to the moral decay of society and, specifically, that it causes sexual deviance. It is repeatedly charged that sex crimes result from reading smut or viewing pornographic pictures and films. In 1968, the outcry about the rapid trend toward nudity and about the depiction of explicit sex in movies, books, and magazines led to the appointment of a Presidential Commission on Obscenity and Pornography. The Commission spent two years gathering information on pornography. Leading experts did research on the effects of pornography on individual sexual behavior. In 1970, the Commission published its findings and recommendations. The report caused widespread consternation. The Commission found the evidence supported the following conclusions:

1. Less sexually explicit material aroused both male and female viewers more than did more sexually explicit material.
2. Experiments that made both pornographic and nonsexual magazines freely available to subjects found that within a short time the sexual material

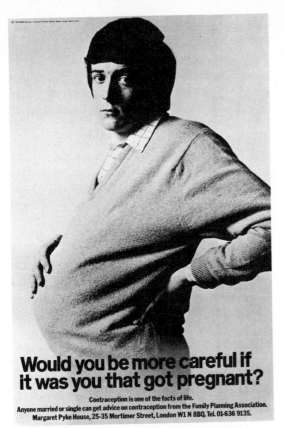

Would you be more careful if
it was you that got pregnant?

Contraception is one of the facts of life.
Anyone married or single can get advice on contraception from the Family Planning Association.
Margaret Pyke House, 25-35 Mortimer Street, London W1 N 8BQ. Tel. 01-636 9135.

Figure 8.13   Societal attitudes toward sex, sex education, birth control, and pornography appear to be related. Some societies permit little public discussion of these topics. Others are more open, as exemplified by this British poster advertising birth-control information.

Figure 8.14   Some people believe that topless bars and freely available pornography lead to the moral decay of society. Studies have shown, however, that liberal policies on pornography cause a decline, not an increase, in sexual deviance.

ceased to produce sexual arousal and subjects lost interest in it—humans quickly become satiated by pornography.

3. Juveniles' exposure to erotic or pornographic material had no effect on whether they committed sexual offenses.

4. Unwed pregnant teenagers were less likely to have been exposed to erotic material than were those who were not pregnant.

5. Sex offenders have substantially less exposure to pornographic materials than does the general population.

6. The Commission concluded that the present flood of pornographic material is more likely to reduce sex crimes and sexual deviance than to increase them.

This last conclusion was based in part on data from Denmark. Statistics on sexual offenses from 1958 through 1969 in Copenhagen are shown in Table 8.2. The Commission noted that increasingly liberal policies on pornography marked this period. The result was a very sharp decline in sexual offenses—for example, rape fell by about 48 percent. Indeed, the most rapid decline in sex crimes began in 1967 when the last significant restrictions on pornography were removed.

255

Table 8.2   Number and Percent Change in Sex Crimes Reported to Copenhagen Police, by Offense Category, 1958–1969

OFFENSE CATEGORY	1958	1969	PERCENT CHANGE
Rape (including attempts)	52	27	−48.1
Intercourse on threat of violence or by fraud, etc.	11	8	−37.5
Unlawful interference short of rape with adult women	100	52	−48.0
Unlawful interference short of rape with minor girls	249	87	−65.1
Coitus with minors	30	19	−57.9
Exhibitionism	264	104	−60.6
Peeping	87	20	−77.0
Verbal indecency	53	13	−32.5

Source: Adapted from R. Ben-Veniste, "Pornography and Sex Crime: the Danish Experience" (*Technical Reports of the Commission on Obscenity and Pornography*, Vol. 7).

The Commission's conclusion that people soon lose interest in pornography when it is easily available has been borne out by the declining fortunes of X-rated theaters in the United States. After a short boom, attendance and admission prices began to decline.

President Richard Nixon immediately disavowed the report of the Commission, even though he had chosen its members. Thus, like the belief that delinquency-treatment programs prevent delinquency, the belief that pornography causes sexual deviance continues to influence government policy.

PART III: RESPONSES SEXUAL PROBLEMS

Until very recently, the primary response to sexual problems was simply to outlaw them. Child molesting and rape are extremely serious crimes. Premarital and extramarital sexual relations are still prohibited by law in most states. So far, only two states (Illinois and Connecticut) have repealed laws against homosexual behavior between consenting adults. Prostitution is legal in only a few counties in this country. The Supreme Court recently reinstated obscenity statutes and gave authority for censorship to the local communities.

Backing up the law are public and private personnel policies aimed at "sexual misconduct." Homosexuals are barred from military service and excluded from hiring by many civil-service codes. College faculty members can have their tenure withdrawn and can be fired for "moral turpitude," which some schools interpret as including any sexual relations except with one's spouse.

Outlawing sexual problems has not proved very effective. Indeed, laws against most varieties of heterosexual relations are mainly unenforced today and obviously bear little relation to what people actually do. Furthermore, many of the problems discussed in this chapter can be helped little by laws—it would obviously be pointless to pass a law requiring married couples to achieve satisfactory sexual adjustment. In addition, the legal system has been relatively ineffective in suppressing even those forms of sexual deviance, such as rape, that nearly everyone abhors. Nevertheless, most responses to current sex problems have been legal ones. Efforts to deal with these problems through education or therapy—or even efforts to reappraise present policies in light of more accurate information—are in their infancy.

RESPONSES TO CONVENTIONAL SEX PROBLEMS

As was pointed out in Part I of this chapter, the main problem besetting conventional sexuality in the United States is the move from an era of sexual repression to an era of sexual expression, without a corresponding shift in people's ability to express themselves effectively.

Traditionally, sex education has been left to the family. But parents who lack knowledge about sex—and are themselves afflicted with problems of sexual adjustment—can hardly help their chil-

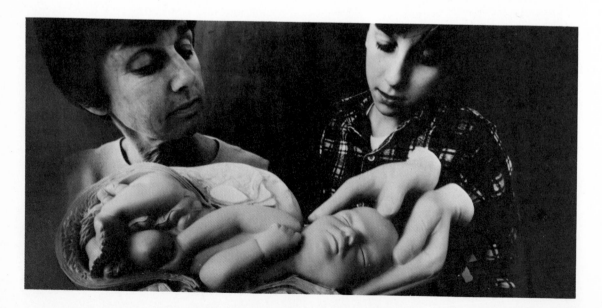

dren to adjust to the new era. A study conducted in 1967 found that 87 percent of parents dealt with sexual questions raised by their teenage children by issuing orders and by trying to restrict information rather than by discussion (Libby and Nass, 1971). Table 8.3 shows the main source of sexual information reported by Morton Hunt's (1974) national sample of American adults; few people reported receiving much sexual instruction from their parents.

Table 8.3   Main Source of Sexual Information: Total Sample by Percent*

SOURCE	MALES	FEMALES
Friends	59	46
Reading	20	22
Mother	3	16
Father	6	1
School program	3	5
Adults outside home	6	4
Brothers, sisters	4	6
Other, and No Answer	7	7

*Add to more than 100 because some respondents checked more than one answer.
Source: Adapted from Morton Hunt, *Sexual Behavior in the 1970s* (Chicago, Ill.: Playboy Press, 1974), p. 122.

Since World War II, there has been considerable effort to establish sex-education classes in the public schools. This has led to bitter community controversies because many parents committed to the older morality do not want their children to know about sex, and they object that such courses take

the position that sex is normal and beautiful. But Table 8.3 shows that few Americans report learning much about sex in school—the data for persons twenty-five and under are no different from these overall findings. One reason so few people reported learning much about sex in school is that sex courses concentrate on biology and physiology, use scientific terminology, and skirt most of the information that the students most urgently desire—"explicit information as to how the various sex acts are performed" (Hunt, 1974).

Friends are still the major reported source of sexual information. But expecting young people to find out everything from their friends seems a bit like asking each new generation of students to find out about arithmetic on their own and to instruct one another. Little wonder that the public response to explicit how-to-do-it sex books has recently produced a series of best sellers.

Such books obviously are meeting a great need, but sex books cannot solve everyone's problems. The recent proliferation of sexual therapists and sexual-therapy programs across the country indicate that book learning is not enough for many. Until about 1970, there was, for all practical purposes, no sexual therapy as such available in this country. The pioneering work of William H. Masters and Virginia E. Johnson in treating sexual maladjustment (usually treating married couples)

257

Figure 8.15 (Left) *Sex education in the public schools is still the subject of considerable controversy. While the battle over sex education rages between parents and school authorities, students are given little information about subjects of real concern to them.*

Figure 8.16 Sex therapy has become a thriving business stimulated by the successful treatment methods reported by the Masters and Johnson team. (Right) The young woman in the picture is practicing her sense of touch.

stimulated the new boom. Masters and Johnson reported sensational cures for impotence and frigidity from intensive-therapy sessions lasting only two weeks (Masters and Johnson, 1970). Since then, sex therapy has become an industry, and the field has drawn to it the usual number of quacks and con artists that rush into any new, profitable, and unregulated business. However, many of the new programs are reputable. All claim amazing results, and business is booming (Wolfe, 1974). For many people, it seems that talking about sex and sexual techniques is effective therapy.

Unlike solutions to some other social problems, the solutions for many problems of conventional sexuality are well known. Lack of a "cure" is not the reason why illegitimacy and venereal disease are growing problems. Pregnancy is easily preventable and is easily terminated. Venereal disease ought to have passed long ago into history, along with diphtheria, small pox, and polio. Clearly, these problems do not require massive changes in our institutions and policies. Collectively, we simply have to change our attitudes and get our heads straight.

RESPONSES TO SEXUAL DEVIANCE

A major conflict going on today is whether homosexuals ought to be changed or accepted. Homosexual groups deny they need any help, although many homosexuals seek it. Many social scientists argue that homosexuals ought to be helped—at least if they want help—to become heterosexuals.

Leaving aside the issue of whether such help ought to be available or whether homosexuals ought to be encouraged to accept it, we now ask, Is such help possible? Can homosexuality be "cured"?

Treating Homosexuality

The form of treatment most likely to be offered to the sexual deviant is some form or another of traditional psychotherapy, in which the person talks to a psychiatrist over several months or years.

Giving the patient insight into psychological causal factors for the development of his sexual deviation has proved to be of great value. Also, regarding sexual deviation as a symptom of deep underlying difficulties is an important concept of psychotherapy. Thus, the psychotherapist attempts to help the sex offender to a better personality integration and maturity which in turn leads the person to break away from his sexual deviation. (Oliver, 1967)

Daniel Cappon (1965) likewise argues that traditional psychotherapy is the best treatment for homosexuality and claims very high cure rates among his private patients. Another psychoanalyst, Adolf E. Meyer (1966), also judges that he has had great success with a group of homosexuals and bisexuals. However, such claims must be viewed with extreme caution. They are usually based on very little data about the characteristics of the patients or about what exactly was done to change them. Judgments of success are given with little follow-up data; for example, the assessment of cases cured is likely to be based on the fact that patients felt better about their deviancy, had a better attitude toward society, or were better psychologically adjusted—not necessarily on the fact that they changed their behavior. The evidence generally does not support traditional psychotherapy as a successful approach to treating sexual deviance (West, 1967; Schofield, 1965; Freund, 1960).

Behavior modification has had better success. The method is based on learning theory, and the strategy is to subject people to a series of conditioning experiences to change their behavior. There is no attempt to get to the "deeper" meaning of the problem; the problem is the behavior itself, and when that is changed, the problem no longer exists.

One common behavior-modification technique is aversion therapy, or *aversive conditioning,* in which willing individuals are presented with unpleasant stimuli in conjunction with stimuli associated with their deviant sexual patterns. Homosexual men see pictures of nude men or homosexual scenes; the male transvestite puts on women's clothes or cosmetics; the person with a sexual fetish is shown pictures of women's handbags, baby buggies, or whatever his fetish is.

Over a series of treatment sessions, these stimuli are paired with some aversive stimuli, such as an emetic drug to make the patient sick, electric shock, or a loud buzzing noise. The idea is to condition the person so that, later, the deviant

258

stimuli will elicit an unpleasant response rather than a sexual response. These and similar modification techniques have been used with some success—that is, they have produced changes in behavior after the treatment—for homosexuality, fetishism, transvestism, exhibitionism, and sexual impotence (McConaghy, 1971; Kushner, 1965; Lazarus, 1965; Blakemore, 1964; Bond and Hutchison, 1964; Glynn and Harper, 1964; Raymond, 1960).

There are, of course, serious ethical problems in subjecting people to such punishing treatment (Rachman and Teasdale, 1970; Bandura, 1969; West, 1967), but the ethical questions do not really apply if the treatment is used only for those patients who freely and voluntarily elect to undergo it with full knowledge of the nature of what they are undertaking.

Simple aversion therapy has not been entirely effective, mainly because it deals with only one aspect of the conditions that maintain the behavior; it attempts only to break the conditioned link between the deviant behavior and certain stimuli—it does nothing with conditioning toward nondeviant alternatives. Therefore, other more successful behavior-modification techniques have been developed: rewards are given for conforming sexual behavior at the same time that aversive consequences are given for deviant behavior (Feldman and MacCulloch, 1966, 1971; Thorpe *et al.*, 1964).

Merely increasing a person's aversion to homosexuality does not necessarily mean that he will turn to heterosexual outlets. Not only is the homosexual attracted to same-sex partners, he is also *not* attracted to opposite-sex partners; indeed, he may have a distaste for heterosexuality. Reducing his homosexual attractions while leaving his heterosexual inhibitions might only result in making him completely sexually inhibited. . . . The most effective way of changing behavior from homosexual to heterosexual patterns has been to combine aversive conditioning with positive reinforcement for heterosexual behavior. (Akers, 1973)

Whatever the particular technique, humans, unlike animals, can easily recognize the difference between the unnatural conditions of pain in the treatment environment and what happens to them in real life; therefore, whatever changes are produced by the therapy would probably not last outside that setting, and "the patients would revert to

homosexuality without the concomitant [therapy-induced] shock" (Sagarin, 1973). The learning process, of course, is subject to naturally occurring stimuli on the outside as well as to the made-up ones inside the treatment situation.

Success in the treatment setting will produce lasting results only if conditions after treatment sustain them. The treatment may be to no avail if the person has no available heterosexual alternatives [in the community]. Also, what happens in the relatively artificial therapeutic setting may not be strong enough to overcome years of reinforcement for homosexuality or lasting enough to withstand the sexual enticement and social reinforcement of homosexual friends if they are rejoined. For these reasons all the studies have found . . . the best prospects for therapy to be relatively young married or bisexual persons who have not established strong ties in the homosexual community. (Akers, 1973)

Behavior-modification techniques have been more effective than the usual talk therapy of psychoanalytic practice. When such procedures take into account the conditioning variables operating in the person's everyday life, they ought to become even more successful. Their achievements in this area ultimately depend on the willingness of the people who are troubled by their own sexual deviance to seek out new relationships in the outside world.

Rape Control

In Part I of this chapter, it was reported that the police make an arrest in more than half of the rape cases. One might suppose then that rapists are rapidly removed from society, and if not rehabilitated, at least kept off the streets for the term of their sentence. But this is not so. The fact is that arrest very rarely results in conviction. For example, Duncan Chappell found that of more than 400 men arrested for rape in New York City during the first half of 1972, only one was actually convicted of rape and only thirteen were convicted of any charge (Chappell and Singer, 1973). Chappell believes that it is the very seriousness the law attaches to rape that prevents conviction.

Because rape is a serious crime, the law requires a high standard of evidence for conviction. Such evidence is difficult to get in the case of rape because there are so seldom any witnesses to back up the testimony of the victim. Two consequences

259

follow, Chappell argues: First, district attorneys are reluctant to press rape charges because they know they lack the kind of evidence the law requires. Second, juries are reluctant to convict people for so serious an offense unless the evidence is good. Consequently, prosecutors lose many rape prosecutions, drop a great many more cases, and sometimes settle for letting the accused plead guilty to the lesser charge of assault.

Chappell believes that the legal system could more effectively help combat rape if it were made a much less serious offense—for example, if it were uniformly treated under the assault statutes. The reason is that simple assault is relatively easy to prove in court, and most arrested rapists would be subsequently convicted and sentenced instead of getting off. Such a change in the law would at least make it possible to try to treat rapists and would ensure their removal from society for a period of time.

260

We have also seen that rapists tend to be sexually uninformed and appear to misunderstand conventional sexual behavior. Therefore, the increase in public knowledge about sex may help reduce rape. Indeed, the experience of Denmark is that if sexual stimulation and expression are easily available (unrestricted pornography and legal prostitution), rape declines.

It seems utopian to suppose that any changes in society will eliminate all rape. We cannot expect that any more than we can expect to eliminate all homicide. However, many industrial nations presently have much less rape and homicide than does the United States, and it hardly seems utopian to strive to match them.

CHAPTER REVIEW

Definitions of what is sexually "deviant" change across societies and over time. A few generalizations can be made, however. Most societies maintain a *double standard* in sexual behavior—more restrictive rules for women than for men. "Mature sex" is generally equated with *heterosexual* behavior. *Incest* and *sexual violence* are almost universally condemned. Sexual norms have changed in our own society. Actions that were once defined as inappropriate have recently gained acceptance through a sexual revolution

that has led to increased approval of, for example, premarital or extramarital sex.

The greater sexual freedom in recent years has contributed to a few classic problems. Even with birth-control methods available, there has been an increase in the proportion of *illegitimate births* (mainly among less-educated and poor women under twenty); the resulting forced marriages have contributed to rising *divorce* rates. *Venereal disease* has reached epidemic proportions in this country as well, primarily because of the stigma attached to this disease and the consequent unwillingness to report it.

There are also unexpected problems associated with the new sexual freedom; these are affecting many more people than are illegitimacy and venereal disease. Society offers a person greater sexual freedom, but coping with that freedom without guilt is a problem. In addition, although we do not expect competence from someone untrained in any other behavior, we do expect competence from *everyone* in sexual matters. This expectation is a burden on the individual whose self-concept is threatened by sexual "failure."

The main problems with deviant behavior are the *stigma* we attach to such behavior. Homosexuality (involving small fractions of our population) has become a bigger problem today only because people see more *homosexuals*. Their greater visibility has been caused by gay liberation groups that want to achieve equal rights for homosexuals. Although *prostitution* is decreasing, it will not disappear because there will always be some demand for service of this kind. *Rapes* in recent years have increasingly been committed by strangers rather than by friends of the victim. Although rape reporting and apprehension rates have improved, *conviction* rates have not—and rapists tend to be multiple offenders.

We still face the question, however, of why sexual deviance occurs. Physiological theories stress the *time lag* that now exists between the onset of puberty and the age of acceptable sexual activity (about ten years on the average). Psychological theories consider sexual deviance either as a symptom of some other kind of "illness" or as a behavior that is learned through *conditioning*. Some social psychologists attribute the development of sexual deviance to the reinforcement given by one's associates. This occurs in a process of *social learning* and *differential association*. Other social psychologists claim that once people are publicly identified or *labeled* as deviant, they will associate only with those who accept them.

Sociological theories account for sexual deviance through strain theories, subcultural theories, and control theories. *Strain* theories say that sexual deviance is a result of the frustrations stemming from class and other differences. *Control* theorists claim that these very differences contribute to a freedom to deviate. *Subcultural* theories claim that sexual deviance such as homosexuality occurs within a stable and supportive social environment. Societal factors that contribute to the development of deviance include the *secrecy* and ignorance surrounding sex, definitions of *sex roles* that do not allow much latitude in behavior, a standard of *youthful attractiveness* that defines the elderly as undesirable, and finally, *beliefs* about the societal consequences of sexual deviance that do not always reflect objective reality (for example, the President's reaction to the findings of the President's Commission on Pornography).

Sex education is rare in the family, and in the schools it tends to be limited to *physiological* aspects. Other aspects, such as etiquette and technique, are provided by friends and books. An indication of the inadequacy of this approach is the recent success of *sexual-therapy* programs designed to help with conventional problems. Treatment programs for homosexuals have used *psychotherapy* (with little success) and *behavior-modification* techniques (with only moderate success among younger patients).

Perhaps the key to "controlling" sexual deviance lies less in treatment methods *after* the deviance has occurred and more in adequate and open sex education for *all* members of the society. Such knowledge may contribute to the solution of sexual problems by producing *both* individual conformity *and* increased societal tolerance.

SUGGESTED READINGS

Gagnon, John H., and William Simon (eds.). *Sexual Deviance.* New York: Harper & Row, 1967.

Gebbhard, Paul H., *et al. Sex Offenders.* New York: Harper & Row, 1965.

Hunt, Morton. *Sexual Behavior in the 1970s.* Chicago, Ill.: Playboy Press, 1974.

The Report of the Commission on Obscenity and Pornography. Washington, D.C.: Government Printing Office, 1970.

Winick, Charles, and Paul M. Kinsie. *The Lively Commerce: Prostitution in the United States.* New York: Signet, 1971.

261

Problems of Conflict and Inequality

Individual human behavior is a fundamental element in each of the problems of deviance studied in Unit II. However, the problems discussed in Unit III have much more to do with how societies operate than with how people act. Underlying each social problem is the fact that societies are so constructed that they produce inequality: some people have more power, property, and honor than others do. Much of the unit examines the extent and consequences of inequalities, especially in America today, but its major concern is to isolate and examine the rules and processes governing inequality, processes that determine who will be advantaged and who will be disadvantaged in this system.

Inequalities exist in all present-day societies and have existed in all past societies about which we know anything. As a result, human social life has always been prone to conflicts between those who receive more and those who receive less. Chapter 9 focuses on the general basis of economic inequalities and on the specific problems of poverty in the United States. It asks whether it would be possible to create a society in which all persons are equal in terms of power, property, and honor. Having explained why such a society probably would not be possible, the chapter then asks why some Americans are poor and whether poverty can be overcome.

Chapter 10 examines conflicts based on racial, religious, or cultural differences between groups within a society. It develops the argument that these conflicts are fundamentally over economic inequality and that they occur when a person's opportunity is substantially determined by his or her religious, racial, or cultural identity. Intergroup conflicts occur when the rules governing inequality in society are sensitive to differences between groups. Such conflicts cease when inequality is no longer along the lines of racial, religious, or cultural differences. Primary attention is given to past and present intergroup conflict and discrimination in the United States. Can present conflicts be resolved in the ways earlier ones were?

Finally, Chapter 11 examines how sex (gender) has operated as a basis for inequality. Having examined the subordinate position of women in society, the chapter examines how women came to be subordinate to men and how changing social conditions have made equality between the sexes desirable and possible.

"What a pretty kite the beggars children fly high above their hovel
— Issa

9
Poverty and Inequality

It is true that the poor have always been with us, but we have not always noticed them. For centuries, poverty was hardly noticed because it was so widespread and taken so much for granted. Ever since we began to believe that something could be done about poverty, we have alternated between periods of concern over poverty and periods of relative blindness to its continued existence as a social problem.

During the Great Depression of the 1930s, poverty was the dominating concern in American life, as it was in most other nations. Many who had never experienced poverty and never expected to were suddenly extremely poor. In response to the hunger and growing desperation of masses of Americans thrown out of work in the 1930s, the government put into effect its first significant poverty programs, including the welfare system that is still in operation today.

With the advent of World War II, the Great Depression ended. The emergency wartime economy had an almost insatiable need for labor, so wages rose rapidly. Following the war, the economic boom continued. Americans quickly achieved and as quickly took for granted a standard of living and a national affluence unparalleled in the history of the world.

PART I: THE PROBLEM
POVERTY AND INEQUALITY

For a time, hardly anyone seemed to notice that not all Americans were sharing in the national bounty. The poor seemed nearly invisible, for they were mainly hidden from the eyes of the affluent majority in depressed rural areas such as Appalachia; in racial and ethnic ghettos of the large cities; and in the rundown hotels and rooming houses that sheltered the aged. When the richest nation on earth looked again, it found millions of impoverished Americans in its midst.

THE REDISCOVERY OF POVERTY

A critical event in America's rediscovery of poverty was the West Virginia presidential primary of 1960. Ordinarily, success in this election is not considered to be a crucial step toward presidential nomination. But it was vital in 1960, for it presented John F. Kennedy with his most severe challenge: He had to win the primary election to prove that an overwhelmingly Protestant, rural border state would vote for a Roman Catholic candidate for President.

During Kennedy's all-out whistle-stop campaign in the heart of Appalachia, he came face to face with human conditions that stuck out like a crushed and soiled thumb on the clean hand of America.

The unemployment rate of West Virginia was about 10 percent, and one-sixth of the state's 2 million residents subsisted on welfare food. Among the coal-mining communities in the southern mountains, the unemployment rate was as high as 15 percent; over 50 percent of the families in some shabby towns had annual incomes below $3,000. The coal mines themselves were horrors. Safety regulations were largely unenforced, and the accident rate was four times that of British mines. Thousands of widows, crippled ex-coal miners, and victims of black lung—a disease caused by coal dust that usually results in slow death—were living in dilapidated mining camps, along with many miners who had been without work for as long as twelve years.

John F. Kennedy, the urbane and wealthy Bostonian, was brought face to face with desperate rural poverty. His visible reactions and his promises to push for federal programs to aid such depressed areas not only won him West Virginia's votes but helped the rest of the nation rediscover the poor. Throughout the remainder of the presidential campaign and during his brief term as President, John Kennedy attempted to transform poverty from a stark fact for some into a national awareness for all.

The time was ripe for a rediscovery of poverty. The civil rights movement had gained momentum during the late 1950s, and blacks had ceased to be invisible. The black population knew the harsh realities of poverty, for discrimination and the long legacies of racism had kept blacks from participating in postwar prosperity.

The controversies over civil rights and the condition of blacks soon brought other somewhat surprising facts regarding poverty to light. If it was true that blacks were disproportionately represented among the poor, it was not true that most poor people were black. By far, the majority of poor people were (and are) white. Furthermore, the welfare system, which had been intended originally as a temporary means for dealing with the effects of the Depression, did not wither away. Instead, throughout the postwar period of rapid economic growth, the welfare rolls continued to grow. What went wrong? Why were there still so many poor in this age of affluence? What could be done about it? In response to these conditions, Kennedy's successor, Lyndon Johnson, declared an all-out war on poverty. Unfortunately, he was soon also involved in a war on Vietnam, and the war on poverty came nowhere near its goal "to end poverty in this generation." Before we can decide how or whether a war on poverty can be won, we must define the concepts of poverty and inequality.

WHAT IS POVERTY?

Obviously, poverty is a relative concept. A welfare family from Mississippi (with a monthly income of about $50) would be unimaginably well-off on that income in Calcutta, India, where people literally live, raise their children, sleep, and die on the streets. Similarly, poor people in America today often live better lives than quite well-to-do people did in preindustrial times, when very few persons survived to old age.

Yet for all that, the plain fact is that we do not live in India. We live in a society that rightfully takes for granted many gains in the quality and security of life. We do not expect people to have to set up housekeeping on the street or to die of minor ailments in order to qualify as poor in this country. Nevertheless, the American poor are poor enough to suffer from hunger and cold and premature death. For purposes of discussion, it is necessary to formulate an adequate working definition of American poverty.

Income Sufficiency

The most widely used definition of poverty in America is *income sufficiency*—that amount of money needed to purchase the basic necessities of life. Although there are several standards that might be used to determine what level of income is sufficient, the measure used by the Social Security Administration has become the official government index of poverty.

The poverty index utilizes U.S. Department of Agriculture estimates of the costs of a minimal food budget, adjusted to the size of the family. The per person daily food budget is then multiplied by three to determine the approximate level of funds needed for all other living costs—housing, clothes, medical care, heat, lights, and other necessities. Thus, in 1973 the index classified as poor all nonfarm families of four with an income of less than $4,275. (Farm families must earn 15 percent less to count as poor, on the assumption that they can grow some of their own food.)

The arbitrary nature of any such measure is an obvious problem. For example, families with incomes even several dollars a year above the index are not officially defined as poor. Criticism that such a standard greatly underestimates poverty has led to efforts to classify certain families as "near poor." This added classification may be a step in the right direction, but it is a further demonstration of the arbitrariness of the poverty index. It shows that one could greatly increase or decrease the "extent of poverty" simply by raising or lowering the income standard in use.

Furthermore, many critics seriously challenge the suitability of the present poverty standard. They cite the U.S. Department of Agriculture estimates that only one out of four persons who live on the food budget declared sufficient in the index—from 81¢ to $1 a day—actually have adequate diets. As a result, many people with incomes *above* the poverty line also suffer from malnutrition—a condition that otherwise might justify their classification as poor.

An additional shortcoming of the index is that it does not reflect changes in the average standard of living. Even though it is readjusted annually, the index is absolute, not relative. Thus the index could show that the position of poor people was getting better even though the gap between how the poor live and how the average American lives could be rapidly widening. Because of this problem, many critics argue that any definition of poverty ought to reflect the *relative* disparity, or dif-

ference, between the positions of those on the top and those on the bottom of the economic system.

Poverty and Inequality

The late Richard Titmuss (1965), a leading British social-welfare expert, argued that poverty should not be defined as income insufficiency. He argued instead that the focus ought to be on the degree of *inequality* in the distribution of wealth in a society.

According to this conception, the extent of poverty is not gauged by the proportion of persons above or below a subsistence income level. Instead, it is gauged by the gap between the haves and the have-nots. Herman Miller (1964) assessed poverty in America by determining that in 1961 the top 5 percent of American families received 20 percent of the total national income of all families, while the bottom 20 percent of families received only 5 percent of that income. Since 1961, the share received by the top 5 percent has begun to decrease, yet this change has not helped the bottom 20 percent of families. Upper-middle-income families have gained instead. A recent economic study of family income reported that the inequality in actual buying power between the richest 20 percent of families and the poorest 20 percent almost doubled between 1947 and 1969 (Lally, 1973).

In Titmuss's view, this growing gap between the richest and the poorest families would indicate that poverty has increased in postwar America, even though no greater proportion of the population has fallen below the poverty line. Titmuss took the position that economic inequality, not an arbitrary level of income sufficiency, should be the measure, or defining factor, for poverty.

Clearly, income disparities must be considered, for if poverty is to be overcome, it is obvious that the money to make the poor no longer poor has to be taken away from those who have money. However, one's definition of poverty can determine the means one uses to attack the problem. In Titmuss's view, only strict income equalization can overcome poverty. But most other economists feel that the United States could reasonably afford to provide its citizens a decent standard of living without requiring the elimination of economic inequality. They feel that any solution to the problems of the poor in America must be consistent with what the majority of the population wants. And the majority is unlikely to want to greatly reduce its standard of living in order to achieve equality. Furthermore, it seems to be technically impossible to construct a society that could function without economic inequalities—a matter that we will discuss later.

For the moment, it is only necessary to recognize the difference between poverty defined as some substandard economic condition and poverty defined as inequality, that is, as the gap between those with the most and those with the least. Those whose primary concern is with inequality tend to dismiss programs to lift the poor above some arbitrary income standard as futile efforts to patch up an evil system. Those whose primary concern is with income insufficiency tend to dismiss arguments about inequality as impractical and unresponsive to the pressing needs of people whose suffering could be reduced now.

WHO ARE THE POOR?

In March 1973, 24.5 million Americans—12 percent of the population—lived at or below the official poverty line. In 1959, the first year in which comparable data were collected, 39 million people (22 percent of the population) were officially poor. The major decline in the numbers of officially defined poor people occurred during the middle 1960s when the government's poverty programs were in full-scale operation. Since 1968, however, when the Nixon Administration redirected some of the federal government's priorities, the extent of official poverty has remained constant.

WHO ARE AMERICA'S POOR?

Of the 24.5 million poor in 1973, about 67 percent were white. Although the incidence of poverty was greater among nonwhites, 33 percent of whom were officially poor, some 9 percent of the total white population were poor.

The poor were concentrated in fatherless homes. Nearly half of the poor consisted of families headed by a female; this was particularly true of the nonwhite poor (most of whom were black).

About 10 million of the poor in 1973, or 40 percent, were children. One out of every five persons under age eighteen in 1973 was officially classified as poor.

In 1973, approximately 15 percent of the poor were sixty-five or older. And of the elderly poor, a far higher proportion were white than nonwhite (19 percent of poor whites were over sixty-five, but only 8 percent of poor nonwhites were elderly). This difference reflected several factors. First, nonwhites have a shorter life expectancy than whites; they are thus less likely to survive to be classified as elderly poor people. Second, due to a higher birth rate, the nonwhite population is on the average younger than the white population.

Several million poor people, or about 12 percent, were blind, deaf, crippled, or otherwise seriously disabled (U.S. Bureau of the Census, 1973).

It is important to recognize that this profile of America's poor is *not* a portrait of welfare recipients. Whereas people must be poor to qualify for welfare, a very large number of the poor do not presently receive welfare payments (aside from their being qualified for food stamps). In fact, only 44 percent of those who are officially poor presently receive welfare—11 million persons. *Eight million of these welfare recipients are children.*

This profile of the American poor clearly shows that proposals to solve poverty by putting the poor to work fail to confront the whole problem. Job-training programs will not help raise the elderly, the disabled, or the children out of poverty. It is not clear that it would be either cheaper or advisable to send the mothers of fatherless young children out to work when the costs of child care are taken into consideration. Thus, whereas some people are poor for lack of employment, or because their employment does not pay a living wage, a great many poor people are unemployable rather than unemployed. In short, jobs cannot help poor people who are unable to take them.

BEING POOR IN AMERICA

So far, we have discussed poverty in abstract terms. But for people who are poor, there is nothing abstract about it. For them, poverty is not some arbitrarily selected level of income—it is a matter of struggling to feed hungry mouths and to keep a roof over their heads.

268

18 Part I—Sat., July 6, 1974   𝕃𝕠𝕤 𝔸𝕟𝕘𝕖𝕝𝕖𝕤 𝕋𝕚𝕞𝕖𝕤

Inflation Causing Nutrition Crisis Among U.S. Poor, Cranston Says

BY LEE HARRIS
Times Staff Writer

Inflation has caused a "nutrition crisis" among the nation's poor that could lead to illness or even the death of millions, Sen. Alan Cranston (D-Calif.) said Friday during a conference on inflation's impact on nutrition and health.

Cranston blamed the Nixon Administration for failure to prevent the crisis.

In fact, he said, the Administration had brought on the crisis.

Health and nutrition experts and directors of food programs in Los Angeles County testified for more than two hours, generally to the effect that governmental food programs had failed in most cases.

During the conference at the Federal Building in West Los Angeles there was talk of older people, unable to buy food, eating out of trash cans or eating cat and dog food.

"Many of our senior citizens are eating cat food or dog food. They are purchasing cat tuna because they cannot afford food," said Robert Forst, executive director of the National League of Senior Citizens.

Forst said a nutritional study in 1969 concluded that between 25 and 27% of the dog and cat food purchased was used for human consumption by poor people.

That figure has increased steadily, he said.

"People eat out of trash cans because they can't afford even the dog food," said Helen Boyd, director of the Episcopal City Mission Society and St. Barnabas Senior Service Center.

Mrs. Boyd, whose office is in the MacArthur Park area, said she often observed people searching the trash cans.

Cranston said the purpose of the two-day conference was to find out how the "nutrition crisis" related to California. He will meet with senior citizens today.

He wants suggestions from the experts and those who worked on food programs, said Cranston, who is a member of the Senate Select Committee on Nutrition and Human Needs.

He said a national nutrition policy study report of 26 food experts prepared for the committee concluded that federal food assistance programs "are failing to reach enormous numbers of impoverished persons."

"Slightly more than 15 million of an estimated 37 to 50 million persons eligible for food assistance are being helped by federal food programs," said Cranston.

"That means that between 22 and 35 million people are going hungry or are malnourished," he said.

His partial answer at this point, he said, is a balanced budget, a cutback in overseas spending and a stoppage in the overseas trips being taken by the Nixon Administration.

Cranston said money for these cutbacks could be used to finance food programs.

"Five years after President Nixon's promise to end hunger in America . . . the nation's needy are hungrier and poorer," he said.

Figure 9.1   These two women eating dog food are engaged in a meat boycott. However, inflation and rapidly rising meat prices have forced many poor people to eat dog food regularly just to maintain an "adequate" diet.

Perhaps the best way to make the circumstances of poor people understandable is to compare them with Americans of quite ordinary income who in no way think of themselves as well-off.

In 1974, the U.S. Department of Labor conducted a national study to determine how much income a family needed to maintain a "moderate standard of living." The Department based its budget on a hypothetical family of four: a thirty-eight-year-old father, his nonworking wife, their thirteen-year-old son and eight-year-old daughter. This family lives in rented housing (usually an apartment), travels by public transportation or buys a used car, and can rarely afford to eat at even inexpensive restaurants. A third of their income must be spent to feed the family adequately. To maintain this standard of living, the father must earn $12,600 a year—three times as much as this family could earn and still be classified as poor.

If this family wanted to buy their own home, eat out once in a while, and buy a new car every four years, $18,200 a year would be required—four-and-a-half times more than the poverty level.

In fact, the Labor Department computed that to keep this family going at an austere level of living—a level where they could barely meet their minimal needs—requires $8,200 a year. Yet to qualify as officially poor, a family can only earn half that amount.

Thus, when you read that more then 24 million Americans live below the poverty line, keep in mind that does not mean they simply have to be careful about what they spend. If you were to attempt to eat on 80¢ a day for the next week (the amount allotted in defining poverty), you would quickly discover it is not a matter of watching what you spend. It is a matter of trying to get enough food to keep going. You would quickly learn why many poor people have turned to buying dog and cat food even though they have no pets. It is the most nutritious food available in their price range.

PART II: SOURCES
POVERTY AND INEQUALITY

To understand what can or should be done about poverty, it is necessary to understand why it oc-

269

curs. We take up this inquiry next. But first we must explain why this chapter departs from the format used throughout Unit II.

You have become accustomed to assessing the causes of social problems by beginning with physiological factors and working up to societal factors. This chapter departs from that approach because poverty and other problems of inequality that are discussed in this unit require much more analysis at the societal level and are much less dependent on individual behavior. Acts of deviance require that individuals commit such actions, but people do not commit poverty. However, social inequalities, or class differences, can play a major role in producing or setting the stage for deviance.

We take up poverty first in this unit because it most directly confronts fundamental questions about inequality and the class system, questions that divide functionalist and conflict-theory explanations. Are class differences the root of all social problems? If so, can social inequalities be done away with? Can a process of revolution or evolution create a society in which all people have an equal amount of power, prestige, and material possession, a society in which deviance is either eliminated or greatly diminished? If so, then it is silly to deal with our problems piecemeal. Instead, we ought to get on with the process of creating the society that would be free of such problems. But if it is impossible to create a wholly equalitarian society, it would be wise to accept that fact and get on with the task of solving our problems as they currently exist.

Because of the overriding importance of these considerations, this chapter sketches the broad picture first then uses this background to discuss the detailed causes of poverty.

CAUSES OF INEQUALITY

In *The Communist Manifesto* of 1848, Karl Marx called for the creation of classless societies. Many have concluded that Marx anticipated a society in which there would be no inequalities, in which each person would have the same amount of material goods, power, and social prestige. It is not clear that Marx meant this at all. For as we shall see, a classless society in Marx's sense does *not*

Figure 9.2 Poverty is not always visible to most Americans. Migrant agricultural workers, like those shown above in the dormitory of a "model labor camp" in Florida, are rarely seen by most Americans. Nor are the more typical living conditions of most migrant workers, as shown in the photo below.

require a society without social inequalities. And while it may be possible to substantially eliminate classes, hopes for a society without inequalities are mainly supported by political doctrines, not by social science.

Recall from Chapter 2 what Marx meant by class: Classes are determined by the relationship to the means of production. Fundamentally, Marx believed industrial societies in the mid-nineteenth century were divided into two classes: the *bourgeoisie*, who owned the means of production, and the *proletariat*, or workers, who had to sell their labor power to the owners. The workers were exploited because the owners got more for what the workers produced than the workers were paid to produce it (the profits of capitalism). Marx also saw classes as primarily hereditary; that is, persons were typically born into either the owner class or the worker class, and a worker had little hope of ever becoming an owner.

In calling for the end of classes, Marx believed that these unequal class divisions would be destroyed if the means of production could be socialized—if land, factories, machines, and all other capital goods were taken over by the state, where they would be owned by all persons. Goods could then be sold without profit; the exploitation of the workers would thereby be ended. Furthermore, the basis for inherited class would be destroyed if three conditions were met: (1) if accumulations of capital could not be passed on (because they would no longer be individually owned), (2) if all people were given equal access to education and to good nutrition, and (3) if positions were assigned according to merit, not according to birth. Inherent in the phrase "from each according to his ability" is a factor that is fundamental to any question asked about social inequalities—that not everyone has the same ability. We will return to this question.

Unfortunately, Marx wrote very little about what the coming socialist society would be like. He concentrated on analyzing the defects of capitalism, not on determining alternative ways of organizing society. Considerable latitude was thus left to followers of Marx to advance a great variety of proposals and claims under their teacher's banner (near the end of his life, Marx once thundered,

"I am not a Marxist"). A major theme that developed in the political doctrine of Marxism (as distinct from Marxist social analysis) was that the revolution would produce not merely a classless society but one in which all persons would literally be equal. Following the Russian Revolution, the international communist movement proclaimed the fulfillment of this doctrine by claiming that Russia had become an equalitarian society.

In his satire of Soviet society, George Orwell responded to such claims of total equality by pointing out that some seemed to be "more equal than others" (Orwell, 1954). Clearly, the socializing of the means of production had not ended privilege in the Soviet Union. Privates were not the equals of generals in the Red Army. Nor were government clerks equal to Stalin and the top bureaucrats. Indeed, bitter charges were laid against Soviet Marxists by Leon Trotsky, who with Lenin was co-leader of the Revolution and who was exiled and later murdered on the orders of Josef Stalin. Writing in 1937, Trotsky pointed out that no sooner had the Revolution occurred than there arose a new basis for class in the Soviet Union: the bureaucracy.

The operations of the Soviet society still had to be managed after the Revolution. Efforts of workers still had to be coordinated. There was a pressing demand for expert knowledge and for management, which created positions that were inherently powerful. Trotsky asserted that the bureaucrats (or managers) in Soviet society had become a new ruling elite. He saw that it did not matter so much who *owned* the means of production (whether capitalists or the state) as who *controlled* the means of production. The people could not collectively control them; the managers could and did control the means of production. Thus, Trotsky argued that a bureaucracy inevitably tends to develop its own self-interests and is no less a source of social inequalites than is capitalism. The bureaucracy uses its power to enhance its own privileges and well-being and in all respects develops "the specific consciousness of a ruling 'class' " (Trotsky, 1937).

In all these ideas, Trotsky had been anticipated by many early critics of Marx. Max Weber, who recognized that there was more to class and thus to inequality than simply economic differences (recall Chapter 2), argued early in the twentieth century that the future was bureaucracy and that both capitalist and socialist nations would become increasingly bureaucratized and more similar (Weber, 1921). Even earlier, in 1896, an Italian political theorist, Gaetano Mosca, developed a devastating argument against the possibility of creating a society lacking social inequalities. In his book, *The Ruling Class*, Mosca developed an argument based on three main points: (1) Human societies cannot exist without political organization. People cannot run off in different directions; rather, the activities of individuals must be planned and coordinated. (2) Political organization inevitably requires inequalities in power because there must be leaders. (3) Because of the self-seeking nature of human beings, power will always be exploited to obtain other privileges, such as economic advantages. Mosca thus dismissed as naively utopian and idealistic the political claims of Marxists that socialism would produce a society cleansed of all inequalities. Twenty years before the Russian Revolution, Mosca correctly predicted that if the Communists ever came to power, they would clearly require political leaders—officials and bureaucrats—who would form a new ruling class.

All these arguments against the possibility of a society without social inequalities come together in modern functionalist analysis of the nature of societies (Lenski, 1966; Davis and Moore, 1945). The functionalist argument begins with the assertion that the positions in any society differ in their importance to the system as a whole. How can this assertion be demonstrated?

Assume that there exists a range of positions, all of which must be filled—someone must farm, someone must manufacture goods, someone must provide medical care. Assuming that all these positions must be competently filled, positions will differ according to how hard it is to fill them. Some positions require skills and abilities that, for several reasons, are in short supply.

First, the needed qualities may be scarce for genetic reasons. People seven feet tall, or with IQs of 190, or with perfect pitch, or with great manual dexterity are uncommon. To the extent that a position requires such qualities, it will be hard to fill. Second, some positions require a great deal of

training while others do not. Extensive training in particular tasks is always potentially in short supply. People must be motivated to undergo this training, and the time and money must be invested in training them. Third, other things being equal, some positions are by their nature more unpleasant than others. Some positions involve a high degree of stress, long hours, years of difficult training and study, and the like. (This point is often overlooked because many unpleasant positions demand qualifications that are in very great supply, and it is easy to find persons qualified to fill them. Yet, in one sense, persons to fill such positions are always in short supply because if all else were equal, people would avoid filling such positions.)

These considerations lead to a *supply-and-demand* analysis of social positions and to the conclusion that inequality is inevitable. *Society must differentially reward positions in proportion to the scarcity (real or potential) of the supply of persons qualified to fill a given position.* To guarantee that those positions requiring high-IQ persons, for example, are able to attract them, the reward system must be properly adjusted. Similarly, to ensure that persons undergo long and arduous training in order to qualify for positions requiring it, the reward system must be biased to attract them.

Thus, to Mosca's perception that some positions are inherently more powerful than others, modern functionalists add the proposition that some positions are more difficult than others to fill adequately. It follows that inequality is inherent in the structure of societies. In fact, systems that do not arrange to fill powerful positions with very competent persons will suffer from needless bungling. For example, for every famous general in history who snatched victory from a far superior enemy, there was an incompetent general who lost a victory that should easily have been won. Systems that place incompetents in command of their armies tend not to survive. The point is that if all positions carried similar power, prestige, and economic advantage, there would be little reason for anyone to seek the demanding positions and there would be no grounds to suppose that scarce talents would be placed where they are needed.

Few social scientists today reject this basic view of social inequalities, but many find it incomplete

(Lenski, 1966; Dahrendorf, 1959). They may agree that some degree of social inequality is inevitable (given the fundamental inequality of necessary social positions). However, they argue that *these inequalities tend to be exploited to make societies more unequal than they need to be.*

Those in powerful positions tend to exploit their power to get greater rewards than society would normally have to offer in order to attract qualified persons to those positions. One way of increasing their rewards is to control or artificially limit the available supply of qualified persons. For example, because they have a monopoly on medical skills and knowledge, physicians are able to limit the number of persons admitted to medical school and licensed to practice medicine. They are thus able to keep medical salaries far above the levels that would be needed to guarantee an adequate supply of talented people who want to become doctors. Similarly, a union can force wages up if it can limit the supply of workers who are permitted to perform certain work.

Thus, even if we assume that some inequality is inevitable, it does not follow that the extent of inequality in any given society is the minimum necessary amount. There is general agreement among social scientists that societies could function very efficiently with much less inequality than they now display. But how to prevent those in powerful positions from increasing their privileges beyond the required minimum is the subject of constant debate and fundamental uncertainty.

We may now return to Marx. Whatever else he hoped for, Marx hoped to end the inheritance of social inequalities. On this point there is widespread agreement between modern functionalists and conflict theorists as well. Indeed, making high social position depend on the accident of birth is incompatible both with the needs of society and with democratic ideals. Few now challenge the notion that society ought to provide all persons with an equal opportunity for achievement.

At issue is the *basis* of social inequalities. There is general agreement that social inequalities should not be based on such categories as race, religion, ethnicity, or sex. To the extent that these social categories result in economic and social inequalities, there is a defect in the organization and opera-

tion of the society that requires correction. There is also widespread agreement that the economic and social success of parents should not determine the fate of their offspring. The children of the lowliest members of society ought to have as good a chance for success as the children of the mightiest. Later in this chapter we assess the extent to which modern industrial societies have or have not overcome inherited social privilege. What is important to recognize is that none of the arguments that suggest the inevitability of inequality go on to suggest that inequality therefore need be inherited. Equality of opportunity and rewards for merit, not birth, are the official goals of both socialist systems and capitalist systems.

Furthermore, neither socialist nor capitalist systems any longer accept the premise that poverty is inevitable. In earlier times it seemed impossible to hope to feed and clothe everyone adequately. But the staggering gains in productivity that resulted from industrialization have made it feasible to provide a decent minimum standard of living for entire populations. Indeed, some industrial nations (the Scandinavian countries, for example) have virtually eliminated poverty in the absolute sense; that is, almost everyone has a decent standard of living even though some people have more money than others do. Demonstrably, then, it is possible to win a war against poverty. Yet the United States, the richest nation on earth, has failed to eliminate poverty of the kind that dooms people to hunger, cold, suffering, and hopelessness. Although it seems likely that we must accept continued social inequalities, we are not required to accept poverty. Why then does poverty remain a major American problem?

SOCIETAL CAUSES OF POVERTY IN AMERICA

In this section we first examine the extent to which America's successes and failures are the result of her devotion to a capitalist economic system. We then examine various aspects of American culture—especially the American ideology of individualism—to determine whether cultural factors are to blame for America's relative blindness to poverty. Then we examine how the overall success and affluence of our economic system and the relative lack of inherited privilege have supported this ideology of individualism and correspondingly shaped our views of poverty.

Capitalism or Americanism?

The most pervasive and enduring political conflict of modern times concerns the relative wonders of capitalism and socialism. Both are praised and damned, both are accused of repression, exploitation, and enslavement, and both are blessed as the road to utopia. Many observers blame all America's flaws on its capitalistic system. They claim that people remain poor in the midst of plenty because of capitalism and that we exploit poor nations because we are capitalistic.

Other observers maintain that we owe our economic success to capitalism and that our flaws stem not from capitalism per se but from peculiar features of our ideology and governmental structure that have little or nothing to do with capitalism. These conflicting claims must be considered. Before they are discussed, however, socialism and capitalism must be defined. Although there are not completely accepted definitions, some general characteristics of each can be outlined.

Capitalism as an economic system permits and protects *legal private ownership of the means of production.* In practice, the capital goods of society—its factories, machines, land—are owned by individuals who have the right to use this property for their own private gain. In additon, the distribution of resources and wealth is mainly determined by a *competitive market system.* What is produced, what it costs, and who will receive it are determined by competitive operations according to the costs of supply and the demands of consumers. Obviously, all capitalist economies impose some rules and limits on the market system—for example, the United States has outlawed price fixing and requires that many products must meet quality and safety standards. Nevertheless, most decisions are left to the market. As a result, decisions relating to production and to price are ordinarily left to the manufacturers and not set by government economic planners.

Socialism is in many ways the mirror image of capitalism. In principle, socialism denies the right

Figure 9.3 "Be Somebody." Everyone wants to be somebody, but the irony of that slogan in the midst of poverty and despair hardly escapes most slum dwellers (right). The desire to be somebody does not necessarily include fantasies of living the high life of millionaires (left), but it does mean finding a way out of grinding poverty. The amount of social mobility in the United States leads Americans to believe that people can climb out of poverty through hard work, yet many of the poor who want work cannot get it. Factory signs that once read, "Irish need not apply," today say to the poor, "the unskilled need not apply." How can you be somebody when so many doors seem closed?

of private ownership of the major means of production; capital equipment is owned in common, either by the government or by other public bodies (for example, communes and cooperatives). Instead of relying on a market system to determine production and distribution, socialism favors a *planned* economy.

To what extent are the accomplishments and the failures of the American economic system a result of capitalism?

It is not at all clear that America's economic power is the result of capitalism. Many socialist states have vigorous economies, and many capitalist nations do not. Raw materials, geography, and cultural tradition seem to have much more to do with economic power than does the fact that economic power is managed according to socialist or capitalist principles. China has made stunning economic progress since it shifted to socialism. Cuba has not. The Soviet Union became a superpower under socialism, America under capitalism.

The most fundamental charge laid against capitalism is that it is the reason for many of our social problems, and particularly for poverty. Some modern Marxists hold the view that social ills such as poverty can never be cured "by a government run by and for the rich, as every capitalist government is and must be" (Baran and Sweezy, 1966).

Can such a claim be substantiated? It depends on what one means by poverty. If poverty is defined as living in substandard conditions (judged against the standards of life possible within a society) then, as we shall see in the discussion of Norway, the claim against capitalism must be rejected. If poverty is defined as economic *inequality* as such, then admittedly it will not be eliminated under capitalism. But, as is discussed in a previous section, it seems unlikely that it could be entirely eliminated under socialism either—certainly all known socialist societies display a noticeable amount of inequality.

To gauge the possibility of poverty being solved under capitalism it is instructive to compare the United States and Norway. For when the basic social well-being of Norwegian and American citizens is compared, the American performance rates badly. For instance, infant mortality is 50 percent lower in Norway than in the United States.

275

Norway spends a larger proportion of its GNP on education and social security than America does. Norwegian cities are essentially slum-free. Although the average Norwegian citizen has a lower annual income than the average American does, the proportion of poor people in Norway is so small as to be insignificant. While more than one out of ten Americans lack the means to secure a basic diet, live in dilapidated housing, and cannot afford proper medical care, no significant number of Norwegians suffer under such circumstances (Heilbroner, 1972).

The accomplishments of the Norwegians against poverty should indicate gross differences in the economic structures of Norway and the United States. But both are capitalist countries. In both countries the means of production are privately owned. The income distributions of the two countries are very similar; that is, the relative income inequalities between the highest and lowest earning groups are much the same in both nations and are determined by a market economy rather than by a planned one. The differing accomplishments of the two nations, therefore, do not reflect differences in their economic structures; rather, they reflect differences in their policies of taxation and social welfare.

The point seems clear that a capitalist country can deal with poverty. For Norway redistributes enough income from its well-to-do citizens to those with low incomes to prevent poverty (Gruchy, 1966). Indeed, economists compute that American poverty could be similarly eliminated if between 1 and 1.5 percent of its GNP were diverted to the poor. Such a policy would bring all Americans to minimum levels of decent living within five years (Heilbroner, 1972). This redistribution of wealth would hardly dent the affluence of well-to-do Americans and would hardly imply any serious departure from capitalism.

Well then, why don't we get on with it? The answer seems to be elsewhere—in the defects of Americanism and American attitudes rather than in the defects of capitalism.

We must now sketch some of the peculiarities of the American ideology and how they are reinforced by the extraordinary affluence of America to find out just why the poor are poor. For until

Americans realize that poverty is primarily rooted in the operation of our social system, not in the individual defects of poor people, the situation is not likely to change.

The Ideology of Individualism

Chapter 2 discussed Alexis de Tocqueville's belief that America's social conscience and sense of community had been stifled by the sense of social equality of its inhabitants. Tocqueville and many other observers of the American scene have argued that America's liberation of the individual resulted in a highly self-centered and intensely competitive individualism, which in turn made it difficult for successful Americans to feel responsible for others who lost out in the race for success. What were the philosophical and social origins of this ideology of individualism?

The United States was born at the juncture of two profound and related European revolutions. One was the *egalitarian* revolution, which attacked the traditional privileges of aristocratic rank determined by birth. The other was the *industrial* revolution, which changed the nature of work and the character of the economy. The old aristocratic order in Europe had been based on the ownership of land—most people lived and worked on the large tracts of land that were owned by the aristocracy. The industrial revolution, however, encouraged these tenant farmers to leave the land and seek jobs in the new factories in the cities. In this process the traditional sources of the aristocracy's power were undercut. The factory owners and industrialists soon emerged as a new class with the wealth to demand political rights and power formerly accorded only the aristocracy. The battle cry of the new class, the middle class, was *egalitarianism*—belief in the equality of all persons regardless of social rank. Of course, to them egalitarianism did not mean *all persons*. Women were counted out, as were all others who did not own property. Still, the egalitarian claims of the new middle class were considered radical for seventeenth and eighteenth century Europe, and they were to lead to radical departures in the political structures of Western nations.

The American colonies were being settled at the height of these profound revolutions. Indeed, the colonies were overwhelmingly settled by antiaristocrats, egalitarian rebels, and poor people seeking to improve their lot. The War for Independence against England, the American Revolution, cut the thirteen American colonies off from Europe at the height of egalitarianism. And this political outlook became, in the wilderness of North America, the uncontested dominant view. The few vestiges of aristocracy that had been exported to America were swept away without taking root.

Egalitarianism stressed the fundamental equality of human beings. It also assumed that extensive individual freedom was a basic human right. People were to be permitted to seek their own destiny, unfettered by their social origins or by a repressive state. In addition the new nation was overwhelmingly Protestant, and Protestantism strongly reinforced the doctrines of individual responsiblity: Individuals were expected to be captains of their own soul and to behave so as to ensure their own salvation (Weber, 1948).

The virgin wilderness of America reinforced these beliefs. Land was easily available to anyone who wanted to take it, and it seemed that anyone could succeed beyond the wildest dreams of the European masses. Thus everyone *ought* to become successful, for it seemed that to be poor could not be blamed on the system but only on defects of personal character.

The beliefs in social equality and individual responsibility nurtured the creation of a nation of individualists, in which all persons looked out for themselves. Tocqueville offered this description of the competitive nature of American society:

It is strange to see with what feverish ardor the Americans pursue their own welfare, and to watch the vague dread that constantly torments them lest they should not have chosen the shortest path which may lead to it. . . . They have swept away the privileges of some of their fellow-creatures which stood in their way; but they have opened the door to *universal competition;* the barrier has changed its shape rather that its position. (Tocqueville, 1835)

Similarly, Francis J. Grund, a German who lived in the United States in the early nineteenth century, discussed the emphasis on material success in the American value system and the stigma associated with material failure and poverty.

Grund explained the addiction of Americans to ''business'' at the expense of leisure and other pursuits in life:

Active occupation is not only the principal source of their happiness and the foundation of their national greatness, but they are absolutely wretched without it, and instead the *dolce far niente* [pleasures of idleness], know but the horrors of idleness . . . the Americans pursue business with unabated vigor till the very hour of death. (Grund, 1837)

Gabriel Almond (1950) has summarized the consistent stream of observations about American values surrounding individual achievement and material success:

The American is primarily concerned with ''private'' values, as distinguished from social-group, political, or religious-moral values. His concern with private, worldly success is his most absorbing aim . . . The ''attachment'' of the American to his private values is characterized by an extreme degree of competitiveness. American culture tends to be atomistic rather that corporate, and the pressure of movement ''upward'' toward achievement is intense. (Almond, 1950)

Inherent in the American ideology of individualism, competition, and success is a basic reluctance to take responsibility for others. Because many Americans believe that both success and poverty are individual matters—that hard work will be rewarded and that poverty is the result of sinful laziness—it strikes them that welfare or guaranteed incomes, both provided by the taxes of hardworking citizens, are unfair rewards for laziness. Indeed, the incredible level of American success, as measured in terms of the wealth of the average person, furthers the belief that hard work leads *automatically* to success.

Affluence, Individualism, and the Poor

The fact that the American economy was amazingly successful from the earliest colonial times only served to confirm everyone's beliefs that motivated individuals can look after themselves and that others—who complain they are ''trapped'' in poverty—are merely unmotivated, or lazy.

America's rich farm land and natural resources have afforded her inhabitants an average standard of living previously undreamed of. In 1799 the

277

average personal income in the United States was over $400 a year (in dollars of 1968 purchasing power). That figure not only dwarfed the average incomes of Europeans at that time but was much larger than the average incomes in many nations today. For example, the average American colonist had a higher income in 1799 than does the average citizen of India, the United Arab Republic, Indonesia, or Nigeria today.

The United States has maintained its extraordinary economic performance from colonial times to the present. Since 1840 our economy has grown at a rate of about 1.6 percent per year (in real terms), which means that, holding prices constant, average personal income has doubled every forty-three years. Today the United States, with only 5 percent of the people on earth, accounts for 30 percent of the world's gross national product (GNP)—the total value of all goods and services produced in a year. The GNP of the United States is a bit less than $1 trillion a year, an amount equal to the *combined* GNP of *all* of the nations of Western Europe plus Japan and Canada. We not only produce a high percentage of the world's goods but also consume staggering amounts of the world's resources and commodities (see Figure 9.4).

To give more meaning to the wealth of the nation, we should consider our wealth at the individual level. Our GNP per capita (GNP divided by the total population) amounts to $5,500 per year for every man, woman, and child—as compared to $5,061 for the next highest nation, Sweden, and $4,101 for West Germany. In some Asian and African nations GNP per capita is less than $100 per year—less than many Americans spend annually on cigarettes. While Americans annually spend over $250 million (some estimate as much as $1 billion) on efforts to lose weight (Sherrill, 1971), many inhabitants of poor nations struggle to avoid starvation.

Because so large a proportion of Americans are so well-off and because they look back on a long-term and relatively rapid improvement in their circumstances, they find it difficult to comprehend poverty. Furthermore, even most of those Americans who are not very successful tend to blame themselves and not the economic system (Lane, 1962). They blame themselves because they do not

278

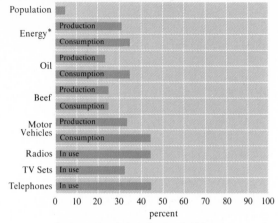

U.S. Production and Consumption of the World's Resources

*coal, natural gas, hydro and nuclear electricity

Figure 9.4 *While Americans make up only about 5 percent of the world's population, they consume a very large slice of the world's goods and resources. Americans consume about a third of the world's energy and possess close to half of the motor vehicles in existence. Such consumption patterns are characteristic of advanced industrial development. And therein lies a severe problem. Most of the people on earth live in underdeveloped nations. But today they are no longer content to do so. They, too, desire the high standard of living provided by industrialization. They, too, want cars, telephones, television sets. More urgently, they want food. Increasing the world's food supply depends on fertilizer, and that, in turn, depends on oil. But if the United States— merely one industrialized nation—requires so much of the planet's resources to sustain its present life style, it would seem impossible to raise the rest of the world to an equal level of life. It would appear that there simply are not enough resources to sustain such development. As Chapter 15 considers in detail, the natural limits on development threaten to increase the gap between the have and have-not nations and may lead to wars over resources.*

Percentage of Mobility by Country

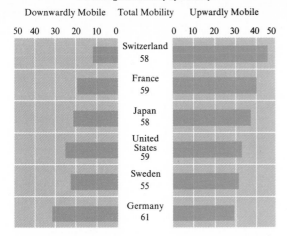

Figure 9.5   (Above) Chart of total intergenerational (father to child) mobility compared with upward and downward mobility for several nations. Note, however, that although the total intergenerational mobility for the United States and Switzerland is about the same, the two societies differ considerably in the percentages of people who are upwardly and downwardly mobile.

(Adapted from S.M. Lipset and R. Bendix, 1958.)

Figure 9.6   It is difficult for class consciousness to develop among working-class people in the United States because many workers earn as much money as people with higher-status occupations—and sometimes considerably more. Most American workers believe that they have a good chance to improve their status through upward mobility.

regard themselves as belonging to a class that is permanently locked into a low economic position; they believe (for reasons that will next be shown) that, despite their own lack of success, their children may achieve great success.

Social Mobility and Individualism

Marx hoped for a classless society. Insofar as that means wiping out hereditary social status, most Americans hold this hope today. Americans have long been inclined to think that theirs is a society in which success is primarily based on individual merit, rather than on advantages stemming from family background. To a considerable degree this belief has been confirmed by the findings of research—at least it has been found true for white America.

Social mobility is the process by which a society overcomes hereditary status. It is the process by which one ends up in a *different* economic position than that of one's parents. Upward mobility means rising above one's parents' position (a janitor's son or daughter who becomes a doctor); downward mobility means falling below one's parents' position (a doctor's son or daughter who becomes a janitor). Many studies of social mobility have found the process to be commonplace in all industrialized societies. For example, one recent study reported that 59 percent of American males end up in an occupation that is either of higher or lower status than their father's occupation; 58 percent do so in Japan, 55 percent in Sweden, and 61 percent in Germany (Lipset and Bendix, 1958). These data make it obvious that most sons are not inheriting the social positions of their fathers.

Another way of looking at mobility is to compute the correlation between the status of the family and the status achieved by the children when they become adults. Data on the United States show that family background accounts for only a relatively small part of occupational achievement (Blau and Duncan, 1967).

Although it is obviously an advantage in American society to be born a Rockefeller or a Ford, the system is relatively open. Most status is not inherited, and it shows no signs of becoming more so (Duncan, 1965). As a result, the rags-to-riches story thrives in the United States. Indeed Ameri-

279

cans sometimes exaggerate their lowly origins in order to bask in the glory of their achievement. President Lyndon Johnson once claimed the ruins of a chicken coop on his ranch as the humble house in which he was born.

Although a great deal of social mobility characterizes all industrial societies, research done by S. M. Miller (1960) and revised by Peter M. Blau and Otis Dudley Duncan (1967) established that there is a certain exclusively American claim to the rags-to-riches story. In a number of nations they examined the chances that sons of men in manual-labor occupations would rise into elite occupations. They found that this degree of social mobility was unusually high in the United States: 1 out of every 10 sons of manual workers was able to achieve an elite professional or managerial occupation in the United States. In Denmark only 1 out of 100 achieved such a dramatic rise in social standing; in Great Britain, only 1 out of 45; and in Sweden, only 1 out of 30. The data showed that rags-to-riches is more than a myth in America; the fact that it does occur so often reinforces the American faith in individualism and its rewards.

One very important condition must be attached to this view of American social mobility, however. Black Americans and other racial minorities do not share so readily these patterns of fluid social movement. Instead they are disproportionately locked into lower-income occupations. Yet, paradoxically, the very patterns of status by merit, not inheritance, that sustain white Americans make them insensitive to the plight of those excluded from these benefits.

SOCIOLOGICAL CAUSES OF POVERTY:
MIDDLE RANGE

We now move down a level in our analysis of poverty to examine how macro processes going on within American society produce poverty and to a considerable extent decide who will be poor. We begin with an examination of the way employment and anti-inflation policies contribute to the creation of poverty. Then we examine how urbanization and technological change have created groups of unemployable persons. We then briefly discuss how some of the major social problems taken up in

subsequent chapters influence poverty: racism, sexism, family problems, and aging.

Employment and Inflation Policies

Because politicians frequently pledge to reduce unemployment, many Americans believe that government policies are intended to produce full employment. They are not. Instead the economic policy of the government is to *prevent* unemployment from falling below 4.5 percent of the labor force. It is the intention of the government that at least 3.5 million Americans should be out of work. Why?

There are several reasons for this policy. First, a certain amount of unemployment is thought desirable to keep the labor force mobile enough to respond to shifting needs for workers. Second, and more important, economists believe that full employment inevitably causes inflation. Consider the following spiral. As the economy nears full employment, the ability of Americans to purchase goods (their purchasing power) increases beyond the amount of supplies available; the demand for steaks, television sets, and the like begins to force prices up. Furthermore, when full employment is nearly reached, workers are in a position to ask for higher wages. Wages thus increase faster than productivity. Because it now costs companies more in terms of labor costs to do the same amount of business, they increase their prices. Thus both increased demand for goods and increased wages drive up prices. But the end has not yet been reached. Because they must now pay higher prices for goods, workers demand even higher wages. The spiraling wage and price demands, the "wage-price spiral," have led to inflation, in which the value of the dollar, how much it will buy, has decreased. To avoid this inflationary spiral, the government tries to keep unemployment at a level that will exert less than maximum pressure on prices.

But why is inflation so bad? Is it so bad that it warrants keeping substantial numbers of people out of work to avoid it? The answer of most American economists is "yes." But many European governments have answered "no." We must examine inflation to see what effects it has.

Since the late 1960s, the rate of inflation has been rapid, and fear of inflation is especially wide-

Wage and Price Interactions Associated with Economic Inflations and Depressions

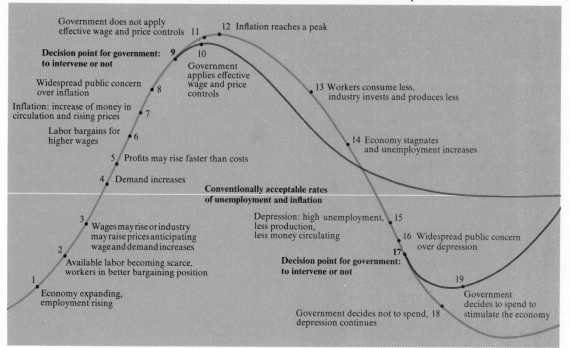

Figure 9.7   Wage and Price spiral. Beginning at the left of the curve, we assume a previous period in which (1) the economy is expanding and employment is rising. In an expanding economy, (2) labor may become scarce. If labor becomes scarce, workers are in a better position to negotiate for higher wages. Industry, of course, is aware of this trend. (3) Anticipation that higher wages may stimulate increased consumption as well as costs leads industry to raise prices, which, of course, contributes to the demand for those higher wages.

At this point we come to a horizontal line: the conventionally acceptable rates of unemployment and inflation, as determined from estimates made by economists and government authorities. (There is much controversy over which data and assumptions should be used to determine this line.) This is the rate—for example, it might be around 4 percent for either unemployment or inflation—beyond which, the authorities believe, the growing productivity of industry can no longer absorb inflation and at which unemployment is no longer composed largely of those unable, either permanently or temporarily, to work.

As wages climb, (4) demand for goods increases. Industry is able to justify rising prices on the basis of greater labor costs, but some industries may take advantage of the situation and raise prices more than what is reasonably justified by costs in order to (5) increase profits. Increasing prices and profits put pressures on labor (6) to bargain for higher wages.

We are now in the stage of (7) rapidly rising inflation where more and more money buys fewer and fewer goods and services. Such a situation leads to (8) widespread concern over inflation. Hardships are particularly great on per-

sons, such as pensioners, who live on fixed incomes.

(9) Government comes under pressure. In the United States, two powerful schools of economic thinking conflict: one school advocates a "hands off" policy to let the free market right itself; the other school, strong since the New Deal programs, advocates intervention by all the legal tools, such as control over interest rates, which are now at the government's disposal.

If the government (10) applies effective wage and price controls, under most situations the inflation cools down slowly to return to an acceptable rate. The drawbacks of such a policy might be the resentment of government interference, the chance that government might make mistakes in timing, extent, and fairness in the application of controls.

If the government (11) does not apply effective controls, it is likely that (12) inflation will continue to grow until profits and costs increase so much that demand and buying power are unable to keep up. As this situation occurs, (13) workers consume less, industry invests and produces less, (14) the economy stagnates, and unemployment increases—all leading to (15) economic depression.

Again, (16) widespread public concern pressures the government (17) to decide whether to intervene, this time to stimulate the economy by spending or by adjusting tax policies. If the government decides (19) to stimulate the economy, it is likely that the economy will begin to rise rapidly toward an acceptable rate of inflation and unemployment. If the government (18) decides not to stimulate the economy, it is likely that the economy will stagnate for a long period of time (unless an outside event such as war interrupts), with dangers of severe social dislocations and disruptions as were seen in the Great Depression of the 1930s.

spread now in the United States. For example, in 1973 the average prices paid for consumer goods rose by 8.8 percent for the year. Out of fear of inflation, the Nixon Administration experimented for a while with wage-price controls (which had little effect), maintained a relatively high level of unemployment, and justified massive cuts in government spending, especially in social services.

Contrary to popular belief, not everyone is affected adversely by inflation. Presumably, employed persons are not hurt because with a wage-price spiral, their wages tend to keep pace with prices. Nor are the wealthy and the industrialists hurt by inflation. When prices inflate, the returns on investments inflate with them. Indeed, investors are able to move their money to benefit from those prices that are inflating most rapidly (presently gold, fine art, and real estate).

Only one group in the population is hurt: those whose incomes do not rise with inflation. Persons with fixed retirement incomes, for example, are badly hurt by substantial inflation because as prices rise their income does not. Hence, they can afford to buy less and less. And persons living on welfare and other forms of public assistance usually are hurt because the government is very slow to grant them increases even when the cost of living has risen rapidly.

Persons with fixed incomes need not suffer from inflation, however. For example, in many European nations, people on fixed incomes receive a government subsidy to compensate them for lost buying power. Except for periods of extraordinary inflation—such as those caused by political instability or grave shortages, as during the Arab oil embargo—inflation is accompanied by real economic growth.

European nations have found that this growth in their economy offsets the costs of subsidizing those on fixed incomes, and everyone comes out ahead (Tobin and Ross, 1971). Put another way, full employment not only causes some inflation but also results in greater production of goods and services. Thus, despite paying subsidies to those on fixed incomes, many European nations have found that their welfare costs actually decreased during periods of full employment because of increased tax revenues.

As already indicated, however, not just any rate of inflation is acceptable. Obviously, when inflation becomes as rapid as it has been in most industrialized nations for the past several years, action must be taken to bring the rate of inflation down. However, such rapid inflation is not primarily caused by full employment and is not the kind of inflation we are discussing here. We are discussing mild inflation. The government's policy is to keep employment down in order to avoid mild inflation. But this policy is subject to criticism. For it means that the prosperity of the majority is paid for by the suffering of the poor. It is their unemployment that is used to keep the economy in tune.

We have pointed out that jobs are far from a total answer to poverty. But it must also be recognized that jobs would help a great many poor people. Many are poor for lack of work. Many more are poor because they can find only part time or very poorly paid work. Full employment and a tight labor supply would obviously cause a profound improvement in the economic circumstances of such persons. This becomes evident when we look past official unemployment figures to see the actual conditions that tend to be hidden by the method the government uses to estimate how many people are out of work.

The official unemployment figures exclude many people who might well be considered unemployed. First, only those persons without jobs who have actively looked for work during the previous week are counted as unemployed. Thus persons who have not actively sought a job because they know or believe there is no job presently available for them are not officially unemployed. Nor are persons with part-time jobs counted as unemployed even if they are actively seeking full-time employment. Persons attending high school or college are not counted as unemployed even if they are seeking work. Indeed, it has been said that college acts as a damper on unemployment by keeping large numbers of persons out of the labor market for a number of years.

It is also difficult to get data on certain groups that have high unemployment rates. Certain categories of Americans are badly underrepresented in both the United States Census and the Labor Department employment statistics because they lack a permanent address or are otherwise difficult for interviewers to find. Migrant workers and the floating population of single males in manual jobs are examples. It is estimated that nearly 20 percent of black men between the ages of twenty and thirty-five were not counted in the 1960 census (Gordon, 1972). Although they are underrepresented in the census data, it is known that these are the groups in the population with the highest unemployment rates; their absence causes the official unemployment rate to be incorrectly low.

A final source of bias in the unemployment rate is that persons working full time are considered to be employed regardless of their salary. A study by the U.S. Department of Labor in 1966 revealed that in ten selected slum areas 21 percent of those who were working full time were earning less than $60 a week. If such a person is the breadwinner for a family of three, he or she is below the official poverty line even though employed. In fact, in 1966 nearly 75 percent of the heads of officially poor families worked, and 40 percent were employed for the full year (President's Commission on Income Maintenance Programs, 1970).

The costs of less than full employment are obviously greater than official unemployment figures suggest. A tight labor market that would bring substantial proportions of those actually without work, or with only part-time work, into the work force and that would drive up wages for the fully employed poor would obviously have a major impact on poverty. But the cost of the effort to prevent inflation by maintaining high unemployment is still being borne by those least able to afford it.

Urbanization and Technological Change

Urbanization and technolgical change have served both as blessings for many Americans and as the causes of many new social problems. On the one hand, the immense productivity of advanced technology (and the urban life it has necessitated) has created a standard of living previously undreamed of. But these same factors have also produced poverty because our complex economy now demands a much higher skill level than in earlier times. Muscle power is simply no longer of market value. Persons without skills are condemned to poverty unless society chooses to find ways to prevent it.

Urbanization can also be linked to poverty. First, the move from farm to city left many remote rural communities behind. Changes in the rural economy have led these isolated groups to experience growing poverty. Having too little land to adopt modern machine farming methods and unable to compete with mass production methods, the owners of small farms have fared badly in recent decades.

A second poverty-producing consequence of urbanization is high geographic mobility. People and industries move frequently from place to place—nearly one out of every four American families moves in any given year. Only 5 percent of Americans now die in the community in which they were born (Eaton, 1971). People move mainly because of jobs, and those who find it difficult to move have an increased chance of poverty.

Poor people find it much harder to move than do the rest of Americans. They often lack reliable information about when to move (and where) to improve their chances of a job. They lack the funds as well as the marketable skills that would allow them to successfully relocate.

Despite all these barriers the poor have moved. In particular the poor have moved from impoverished rural areas (especially in the South) to the ghettos—both black and white—of large northern cities. White mountain folk from rural Appalachia have poured into Chicago, Cleveland, Detroit, and other industrial centers close to their home area. But with little education, no familiarity with the workings of urban life, and only manual skills to offer the labor market, they have mainly exchanged rural for urban poverty. Similar pressures have driven blacks to the North. They come equally unprepared to cope with urban life. During World War II, trainloads of blacks were recruited in the South and taken north to work in defense plants. They were crowded into temporary housing. Then the war ended, and with it the defense jobs. No one worried about what was going to happen to these new urban masses of unemployed blacks. They had nothing to go back to but hopeless rural poverty and the strict segregation of the South. So they stayed in northern urban poverty instead. And the black migration from the South continued. The poverty-stricken black urban ghettos continually had to make room for waves of newcomers. Since the late 1960s, when Watts and then dozens of northern ghettos exploded and burned, most people have been aware of the poverty and despair of the ghettos. But our society has not dealt successfully with racial problems.

Indeed, race plays a fundamental role in the one form of geographic mobility that has been reserved exclusively for the poor: that of migrant farm laborers. Drawn primarily from the border areas of the Southwest (mainly Chicanos) and from the poor of the Southeast (primarily blacks and poor whites), these migrant laborers and their families move from place to place, wherever it is the season of picking and harvesting different crops. Everywhere they stop, these families face harsh living conditions and low wages. Their movement is not in pursuit of a brighter future somewhere; it is simply a cycle of existence, difficult to escape. Frequently they return to where they started with no more money than when they left. Furthermore, because they are always on the move, the children of these migrant laborers are rarely able to obtain an education and poverty forces them to follow their parents into the fields.

Racism and Poverty

Americans have not been more responsive to white than to nonwhite poverty. For example, we have done little for poor whites in Appalachia—many of whom live in shabby mining towns with little hope of a brighter future. Yet it is obvious that racism does play a significant role in who is likely to be poor in America. Prejudice and discrimination have given most racial minorities in America a disproportionate share of poverty. In turn, the high proportion of poverty among nonwhites has undoubtedly stiffened public resistance to poverty programs.

The poverty of nonwhite racial minorities rests on two main conditions: (1) because of *past* discrimination and poverty, blacks, Chicanos, and Native Americans disproportionately lack the education and job skills that could pull them out of poverty; (2) because of *continuing* discrimination, even when minority members acquire the necessary education and skills, they do not receive the same financial rewards as whites.

Figure 9.8   Large urban areas are usually populated by a wide variety of ethnic and social groups, often living very different lives in adjacent or relatively close neighborhoods. Bilingual signs, ethnic restaurants and shops, and the customs, clothing, and language of the people will characterize a given ethnic neighborhood. But the social differences separating the middle class from the poor or the upper class are just as important to the social scientist. In the segment of the map of Chicago shown at right center, four very different areas are located within a few city blocks of each other: A middle-class ethnic area populated by Greek Americans (top left), a mixed, or nonethnic, middle-class area (top middle), a lower-class area inhabited primarily by poor people from Appalachia and Puerto Rico (top right), and finally, an upper-class area near Lake Michigan (bottom), which features expensive high-rise apartment buildings, yacht basins, parks, beaches, and other amenities within easy reach.

284

The competitive disadvantages of racial minorities are easy to demonstrate. Today the median level of education for white adults is 12.1 years; for blacks, only 10 years; and for Chicanos, 8.8 years. In a society where the major expansion of the job market is occurring in white-collar knowledge-work, a lack of education is becoming an insurmountable handicap. It is true that the education gap between blacks and whites has closed somewhat in the last few years. In 1973, according to the United States Office of Education, identical proportions of black and white eighteen-year-olds—54 percent—enrolled in college. However, it is also true that the black drop-out rate from college is higher than for whites, partly because of the inferior preparation provided by inner-city high schools. Furthermore, it is not at all clear that by achieving educational parity, or equality, with whites, nonwhites will achieve income parity.

Figure 9.9 shows that at every level of educational achievement blacks earn lower median incomes than whites do. Indeed the income gap between whites and blacks is greatest at the upper levels of education—that is, the income advantage of college educated whites over college educated blacks is considerably greater than the income advantages that whites with less than eight years of schooling hold over blacks with a similarly limited education. Furthermore, for the same occupations, blacks have lower incomes than whites (Blau and Duncan, 1967).

Some of these differences may stem from the fact that the quality of education received by blacks may be lower (because they are more likely to attend poorer schools) than that received by whites. For black professionals, such as doctors and lawyers, some of these differences stem from the fact that their black clients and patients are too poor to pay their bills or cannot pay as much for services. But Blau and Duncan (1967) conclude that even if these factors are taken into account, education still does not pay off as much for blacks as it does for whites.

This conclusion makes mockery of the widespread feelings among whites that blacks must earn equality by pulling themselves up by their own bootstraps and that giving special advantages to blacks is unfair. In fact, far from giving blacks

286

Figure 9.9   (Above) *Blacks have made many sacrifices to obtain equal educational opportunities. But, ironically, blacks reap smaller benefits than whites do for having an education.* (Below) *At every level of educational achievement, blacks have lower median incomes than whites. Furthermore, the higher the educational level, the greater the income gap between whites and blacks.* (U.S. Bureau of the Census, 1971.)

Income of Blacks and Whites by Educational Achievement

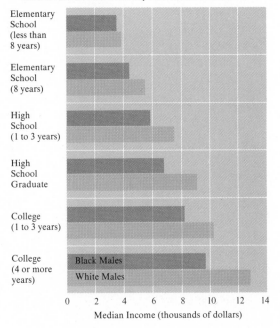

Median Income (thousands of dollars)

special advantages, we seem to be confronting them with special disadvantages. Even after paying his or her dues by sticking to the books and achieving advanced education and a high status occupation, a black, it seems, cannot *earn* full economic equality under present conditions.

The Family: Separation, Sexism, Fertility, and Poverty

It seems likely that poverty can create broken families. It is certain that broken families can cause poverty, for children usually remain with the mother and women have much lower earning capacities than men do. Another link between the family and poverty is fertility: large families are in much greater risk of poverty than are small ones. We now examine the role that these factors play in poverty.

Separation

Elliot Liebow (1967), Patrick Moynihan (1965), and a number of other social scientists claim that poverty can cause men to leave their families. These separations happen for several reasons. First, when a man finds he cannot support his family adequately, he responds in ways that may cause marital discord. He may suffer severe depression, he may begin to drink too much, or he may take his frustration out on his family. Any of these responses can produce conflict and result in marital separation. Or the man may simply flee the responsibilities of family life. He may also be driven out by a wife who finds him too great a liability. In addition, men often desert their families (or at least appear to) because it is usually difficult and often impossible for a family to receive welfare aid so long as the husband remains. Welfare programs have never shown much sympathy for unemployed men who appear able to work. And it is unusual for benefits to be granted a family with a working father no matter how meager and inadequate his earnings are.

Sexism

Welfare regulations strongly favor the female-headed family, and thus it should be no surprise that the overwhelming majority of welfare families are without a father. Furthermore, female-headed families are high poverty risks because of the disadvantaged economic position of women. To a much greater extent than men, women are likely to be unable to earn enough to support a family (in part because they must earn enough to pay for child care, a service men ordinarily obtain from their wives). The rising divorce rate, combined with welfare policies, is increasing the proportion of female-headed families in the United States and thus the risk of poverty.

Fertility

It is widely believed that some women have children in order to qualify for welfare or to extend their welfare benefits as their other children grow up. There is no evidence to support this belief. It is true that illegitimacy often results in a female-headed family and thus may force a woman to seek welfare. But it is not clear that women have children out of wedlock in order to get or stay on welfare. Given the small size of welfare payments, it is unlikely that many women would view welfare as an avenue to prosperity.

The widespread belief that women on welfare often have more children in order to extend their welfare benefits is also probably false. The fact is that poor families, whether on welfare or not, have a high fertility rate (President's Commission on Income Maintenance, 1970). Unfortunately, this higher fertility is directly implicated in their poverty. The reason is obvious. Given identical incomes, a family with five children will automatically be "poorer" than a family with one child (Exits from Poverty, HEW, 1968). Having large families is associated with downward mobility (having a lower social standing than one's parents), and having small families is associated with upward mobility (Blau and Duncan, 1967). There is considerable truth to the old saw, "the rich get richer and the poor get children." A major reason seems to be a lack of access to and effective use of birth-control information, for the poor desire smaller families than they have (President's Commission on Income Maintenance, 1970).

Aging

The fact that 15 percent of the official poor are persons over the age of sixty-five does not simply mean that some poor people live to become elderly; rather, it reflects the fact that many people become poor when they become old. Two-thirds of retired American households have an annual income below $2,500. Only 10 percent receive more than $5,000 a year. The unfortunate truth is that few people are covered by even minimally adequate pensions, and Social Security and old-age-assistance benefits are very meager. Think about living on $132.50 a month, which is the average Social Security benefit. All too frequently, getting old in America means becoming poor.

It is evident from the above discussions that social problems are intimately interconnected. Problems dealt with later in the book have already entered this chapter as causes of poverty. In subsequent chapters it will become evident how poverty in turn is a major cause of these other problems.

SOCIAL-PSYCHOLOGICAL SOURCES OF POVERTY

We now move to the immediate social environment of the poor. Here we examine how the social circumstances of the poor conspire to keep them poor. We examine the consequences of the stigma of poverty—of living in a social situation where those around you are poor and of how, to some extent, people learn to deal with poverty and, in so doing, learn to behave in ways that tend to keep them poor.

The Stigma of Disrepute

To be poor in an affluent society is to be discredited. After all, in an economy where the overwhelming majority of people are quite prosperous, what kind of person fails so woefully? The widespread American outlook of individualism, reinforced by the nation's extraordinary economic success, encourages the view that people are personally responsible for their own poverty. And the theme of personal responsibility runs through the thinking of the nonpoor as well as that of the poor.

Labeling theory argues that the stigma that is attached to being publicly identified as poor often has profound consequences for the self-conceptions of poor people and thus for their behavior. But not all poor people are equally stigma-

Figure 9.10   Although a pawn shop and a savings and loan company perform much the same function—both lend money—people generally regard them quite differently. The savings and loan establishment tends to be associated with the affluent, middle-class interests of its customers and is thus assumed by most people to be respectable, whereas pawn shops are associated with lower-class borrowers and are therefore not generally trusted by middle-class individuals. In this and many other ways, prejudices lead people automatically to evaluate differently places, behaviors, and people that may be objectively similar. Consequently, many poor people would not attempt to obtain a loan at a bank. But by patronizing a pawn shop, they are forced to pay a much higher interest rate.

tized. Some wear poverty with honor; some are condemned as slothful and shiftless. It is necessary to distinguish among types of poor people.

Recall from Chapter 7 that extreme forms of interpersonal violence, such as murder and child beating, are concentrated in a segment of the population that is virtually outside (below) the class structure. These people are not those with the lowest paying jobs, nor are they members of the ordinary labor force. They are virtually outside of normal society.

The recognition of a submerged underclass—persons sometimes identified as the "dregs"—is not new. For example, Harriet Martineau, a social critic of early nineteenth-century England, argued that it was vital to distinguish between the laboring poor and *paupers*—she characterized the latter as having accepted a life of abject poverty and uselessness (cited in Polanyi, 1944). Marx called them the *Lumpenproletariat* (the term was adapted from the German *Lump,* meaning ragamuffin), and he argued that it was critical to exclude such persons from any definition of the proletariat, or working class. Because these persons do not work, Marxists have long condemned them as apathetic, parasitic, and reactionary, and thus as potential enemies of the revolutionary working class. Indeed, Nikolai Bukharin (who, like Trotsky, was a brilliant Soviet Marxist subsequently killed by agents of Stalin) denounced the *Lumpenproletariat* as "shiftless," lacking "discipline," and given to actions "based only on foolish caprices" (1925). Both capitalists and Marxists have long drawn a sharp distinction between the deserving and the undeserving poor. It is the "undeserving" poor who are mainly subject to the unfortunate effects of the labeling process.

David Matza (1966) has used the term "disreputable poor" to identify the stigmatized portion of the poor. He argues that they are disreputable in the sense that other members of society, and especially the working or respectable poor, view them with resentment. Who are the people who bear this stigma?

Poverty that is associated with apparent idleness and indolence is a primary basis of disrepute, Matza argues. The stigma is given to persons who, although able-bodied, remain habitually unem-

ployed or who work only very irregularly. Poverty related to criminality (for example, families whose poverty is a result of the breadwinner being in prison), as well as poverty resulting from successive illegitimate births, is regarded as disreputable. In addition, considerable deviance attends poverty, and such deviance—alcoholism, addiction to drugs, violent behavior, and sexual promiscuity—also brings the poor into disrepute.

For the disreputable poor, all interactions with others, and especially with official agents and agencies, are likely to be a series of humiliations and degradations. For example, the social welfare system makes people reveal details about their private lives. If the caseworker asks about a recipient's sexual activities, an answer is required, on pain of losing welfare aid. Indeed, anything that is discrediting in the lives of the poor is apt to become public knowledge. For example, the family fights of the poor are disproportionately likely to become official police statistics.

The disreputable poor must confront a contemptuous world. But worse yet, they must face themselves. If, in so doing, they come to terms with their stigma, or label, by accepting it, they may seal their fate. They may come to accept themselves as moral lepers and may act accordingly. Indeed, the fact that they are deviance prone may only reflect the fact that they view themselves as the kind of people who do such things and, in any event, have very little to lose by doing them.

Poor Company

A major inducement to accepting (and obtaining) the stigma of disreputability is to be surrounded by others who are disreputable. In most cities there are areas where disreputable persons are concentrated (the worst slum is often called skid row). To be identified as living in such an area is almost an admission of disreputability. Matza (1966) has identified several types of persons found in these slum areas. First are the *dregs*—persons born in such areas but left behind when the other poor ethnic residents escaped upwards into society. Through successive waves of such upward movement, each leaving some group members behind, a population of hopeless, apathetic people builds up. In time they are joined by *skidders,* people who

289

have fallen into disreputable poverty and who have finally come to rest in the cheapest, least desirable place in the city. These people are the most degraded residents. They are often drunks or the mentally disturbed. Matza argues that skidders serve as a dramatic symbol for slum residents:

Skidders are important not because they are very numerous . . . but because they dramatically exemplify the worthlessness of effort . . . [many] take the skidders' fall as additional evidence of the meanness of social life and the whimsy of destiny.

Perhaps the most distressingly sad players in this scene are the *newcomers.* For very poor groups newly arrived in the city, the most disreputable neighborhood is often the only place they can find shelter. By living in such an area they are subject to being labeled as disreputable. Worse yet, by living in such an area, newcomers are subject to *becoming* disreputable. Everywhere around them is apathy and degradation. What chance do they have? Deviance is also all around them: Social-learning theory would anticipate that many newcomers would soon be engaged in deviant behavior. But newcomers not only learn to be deviant, they also learn to be poor.

Learned Poverty

The poor learn a number of responses to their circumstances, some of which serve to keep them poor. For example, poor people tend to live in the present because of the daily difficulties of trying to meet material needs. Young poor people may find it more attractive, in the short run, to hustle a living on the streets rather than to remain in school. They may accept menial jobs in order to ease their present circumstances. Only later do they find themselves as adults qualified to do only adolescent-level jobs. Young girls who flee a poverty-stricken home for early marriage often find themselves repeating the cycle of family poverty—low income, too many children, separation, and welfare. Escape from poverty often requires planning for the future and deferring present gratifications, that is, taking less now so that you can have more later. Many poor people have not learned to defer gratifications.

Perhaps the worst learned response to poverty is to accept it as inevitable. Many poor people feel

290

A Sharecropper Mother in Alabama
 . . . a mother has to teach her children some lessons, even if they are going to school.
  Once a while back, maybe two years it was, my girl came home and said the teacher made them say that everyone here in the country of America is born equal, and we're all the same. Well, I didn't say a word. I was preparing their supper, and I kept on thinking to myself, and I asked myself how I could let my children believe that, when that's not the way they're going to live. So, I called my girl over, and the other children, too; and I told them that there is the white man and the black man, and the rich man and the poor man, and the sheriff and the rest of us, and there's the ones who have got a say and the ones who don't. That's what I told them, and you know what, I had them repeat it to me, out loud, and they did; and I told them they should listen to what they just said, and they'd better keep repeating it to themselves, saying it, until the end of their lives, like we all do.

—Robert Coles, *Migrants, Sharecroppers, Mountaineers: Volume II of Children of Crisis* (Boston: Little, Brown, 1971), p. 149.

helpless, apathetic, and trapped. Once they learn such attitudes, they do not make either personal or political attempts to solve their problems or protest their "fate." Compared with the nonpoor, they are relatively unlikely to register to vote or to go to the polls, to take any interest in political events, or to otherwise make their existence felt politically (Campbell *et al.*, 1960). Although it is true that lately the poor have begun to display more political energy, as evidenced by such organizations as welfare-rights groups, only a small proportion of the poor have actually been involved. The greatest curse of poverty is that is saps the spirit.

PSYCHOLOGICAL FACTORS IN POVERTY

Most discussions of poverty focus on social and group attributes that make people poor. But not all members of these groups are poor. Whereas many blacks are poor, most are not. Whereas many female-headed families are poor, most are not. What determines which members of these groups will be poor? In this section we discuss aspects of the individual's personality that can influence economic success, beginning with the connection between motivation and poverty and concluding with the impact of mental illness on poverty.

Achievement Motivation

Americans widely believe that one's success is limited only by how hard one is willing to work. The analogy is frequently made with sports, where "being motivated" is offered as the explanation for nearly every success.

Social scientists have incorporated this commonsense explanation of success into their analysis of occupational and economic achievement (Featherman, 1972), with somewhat mysterious results. Consistently, social-science studies have found that measures, or tests, of *achievement motivation*—attitudes reflecting a strong desire to excel—are significantly related to success. Persons who score high on such measures tend to complete higher levels of education, to obtain higher status jobs, and to earn more money than do people who score low on such measures (Duncan, Featherman, and Duncan, 1972; Featherman, 1972; Elder, 1968). So far so good—although it is

extremely important to know that such studies have been limited mainly to white males living in major urban areas. Thus, we do not know the extent to which such motivation helps overcome the barriers to success that are imposed by race, sex, rural residence, or extreme poverty.

The mystery of achievement motivation is that we do not know where it comes from. For example, successful parents are not particularly successful in passing achievement motivation on to their children. Measures of achievement motivation are only very weakly related to a person's family background—for example, to father's occupation or income (Duncan, Featherman, and Duncan, 1972; Featherman, 1972; Elder, 1968). Thus, motivation does influence success, but it does not link the success of parents to that of their children.

Indeed, it seems that variations in individual motivation are a major factor in impeding the inheritance of social status and in creating social mobility. Because so many children of unsuccessful parents develop strong motivation to excel, and because so many children of successful parents do not, motivational differences stimulate social mobility—downward for those without it, upward for those who have it. It is important to realize, however, that the extent of the burden of being born into disreputable poverty is not yet known. Because the extremely poor, and especially extremly poor nonwhites, are underrepresented in the census and in survey studies of mobility, we do not yet know the extent to which extremely low status is likely to be inherited.

We know little about why some children develop high achievement motivation and others do not. Motivation does seem to be significantly related to the kind of encouragement children get from their parents (Rosen and D'Andrade, 1959). And it is also related to intelligence (Elder, 1968), which suggests that people may develop a need to excel from being rewarded for early successes that were produced by their exceptional talent. But whatever it is that motivates people to achieve, it plays an important role in determining their social status.

Deferred Gratification

An earlier discussion showed that people's adjustment to poverty may cause them to behave in ways

291

that will keep them poor. Many of their inappropriate responses can be characterized as failures to *defer gratification*—in effect, they favor the bird in hand and are unable to wait to gain the two in the bush. The ability to defer gratification has been studied in children by Walter Mischel (1961).

Mischel worked with school children, some of whom lived in fatherless homes. He gave each child the opportunity to take smaller rewards immediately or to wait a few days to receive much larger ones. For example, children could choose to take a small candy bar right then, or they could wait a week for a much larger one. Mischel found that children without fathers, in female-headed homes, were much more likely to choose the *immediate* rather than the delayed reward, whereas children in homes with fathers were more likely to choose the *delayed* reward. He reasoned that children with working fathers have more experience with obtaining pay-offs for waiting, with being told to "Wait 'til daddy gets home from work and we'll all go out for a treat." When there is no father around, no one to "wait for," Mischel suspects there is less occasion for experiences that reward the deferral of gratification. Children in fatherless homes may thus have a greater chance of growing up unprepared to invest in long-term goals. We do not know whether Mischel's explanation is correct or whether children in female-headed homes where the mother has a job do have more experience with delayed gratification. But if Mischel's explanation is correct, mothers who stay home and raise children alone should give the children more occasions to delay gratification.

Mental Illness and Poverty

Sociologists have long argued that the connection found between low social status and mental illness, especially schizophrenia, represents *social causation*—that people become mentally ill *because* of the stresses of being poor (see Chapter 5). However, recent evidence argues somewhat differently. It seems likely that schizophrenics are disproportionately *downwardly mobile,* so their mental disorder is probably more often a cause of their economic failure than an effect of it.

The evidence coincides with Matza's characterization of the skidders, who are the most degraded

Figure 9.11   Levels of Analysis and Issues Appropriate to Each Level. This summary chart does not cover all the important points raised in the chapter. Use it only to review what you have read. Page numbers are given for the full discussion of any topic.

of the disreputable poor. Skidders are so named because they skid downward in society until they reach the "lower depths." Among them are many of the mentally ill who can be observed wandering the streets and engaging in bizarre behavior.

We do not know yet what causes mental illness, but it is clear that stress plays an important role. If stress does trigger mental illness and if mental illness is a significant cause of poverty, that helps explain why some social groups have a higher risk of poverty. Migration from farm to city, broken families, and limited job opportunities are all obvious sources of stress.

PHYSIOLOGICAL SOURCES OF POVERTY

To conclude our search for the roots of poverty, we now consider the human body. First, we examine physical disabilities, then nutrition.

Physical Disabilities

Many people are so physically handicapped that they cannot support themselves. Unless society provides them with a decent living—a goal that welfare payments currently do not begin to approach—many of the blind, the crippled, the deaf, and those otherwise disabled are condemned to a life of poverty.

In addition, the high cost of medical care and the fact that many Americans lack adequate protection against the costs of serious, long-term illnesses are factors that can lead to poverty. Many well-to-do families have been reduced to subsistence levels of living because of continuing high medical costs.

There is another category of physical disability that is not immediately apparent but that seriously influences an individual's economic position. A variety of recent studies have found that physical

Levels	Appropriate Questions	A Partial Synopsis of Present Conclusions
Societal	Would it be possible to create a society in which there were no inequalities?	Apparently not. However, societies tend to be considerably more unequal than necessary. (pp. 270–273)
	Is capitalism the main cause of poverty in the United States?	Probably not. Some capitalist nations have eliminated many conditions of poverty. (pp. 273–276)
	Does the American belief in the doctrine of individualism influence our response to poverty?	Yes. Belief that each person is responsible for his or her fate encourages Americans to blame the poor for their poverty. (pp. 276–277)
	Does American affluence affect poverty?	Yes. Because the majority of Americans live so well, they lack a stake in antipoverty measures. (pp. 277–279)
	Does social mobility encourage negative attitudes toward the poor?	Yes, by encouraging the belief that all success is due to merit and by discouraging class consciousness among low-status persons. (pp. 279–280)
Sociological: Middle Range	Do government anti-inflation measures cause unemployment and underemployment?	Yes. Our monetary policies are meant to keep some unemployment. (pp. 280–283)
	Are urbanization and technological change causes of poverty?	Yes. Urbanization has forced migration from rural areas, bringing in many people untrained for urban occupations. Technological change has taken away the market for unskilled labor. (pp. 283–284)
	What other social factors are associated with poverty?	Racism, sexism, large families, and old age are causes of poverty. (pp. 284–288)
Social-Psychological	Does poverty cause some people to be labeled as disreputable?	Yes. A segment of the poor—Marx called them the *Lumpenproletariat*—are labeled as "shiftless" and "undeserving." This group is presumed to be very prone to deviant behavior, and their poverty is self-perpetuating. (pp. 288–290)
	Can poverty be learned?	Yes. Acceptance of poverty can be learned, and being raised in poverty may teach people to act in ways that are rewarded in the short run but self-defeating in the long run. (pp. 290–291)
Psychological	Does lack of achievement motivation cause people to be poor?	Perhaps. It appears that persons with high achievement motivation—a strong desire to excel—are more successful than those with low achievement motivation. However, children from poor families are about as likely as those from affluent families to have high achievement motivation. (p. 291)
	Does mental illness cause poverty?	To some extent it appears to. Persons who develop schizophrenia are very likely to be downwardly mobile. (p. 292)
Physiological	Do physical disabilities cause poverty?	They are a very important cause. Many people are poor because they are disabled, and disability payments are very low. Being short or unattractive also affects one's economic fate. (pp. 293–294)
	Does poor nutrition cause poverty?	It probably does. Many of the American poor suffer from inadequate diets, and research shows that poor diets can severely affect children's development. Thus, poor diet may play a major role in passing poverty from one generation to the next. (p. 294)

293

appearance, size, and body build influence success. Because studies have found that beauty often serves as a source of upward mobility for women, presumably extreme homeliness can serve as a source of downward mobility (Elder, 1969). There is also clear evidence that the obese are discriminated against in hiring and promotion and that taller males and females are more rewarded economically than are shorter ones (Deck, 1971; Tanner, 1970). The military has long rejected men for service on the basis of extreme ugliness. Clearly, physical shortcomings and deformities have been not simply a source of personal pain but also a source of poverty for some people.

Nutrition

There is ample evidence that substantial numbers of the American poor suffer from poor nutrition and that infants especially suffer from improper diets. Poor nutrition in infancy is extremely serious because it can damage physical and mental development. Lack of adequate protein, for example, may cause stunted and retarded children.

Birth weight is the best single measure of infant health and subsequent physical and intellectual development (Watson and Lowrey, 1967). When the data between black and white infants are compared, it is found that black infants are on the average smaller at birth and thus have a higher rate of infant mortality and birth defects than do white infants. It appears that a major cause of the interracial differences in birth weight is the difference in the diets of mothers. A serious consequence of inadequate diets, which are so widespread among the poor, may be that nutritionally based bodily damage is passed from one generation to the next.

Figure 9.12 Poverty damages people both mentally and physically. The diet of people in poverty areas such as Appalachia is often deficient in proteins and other essentials. One serious consequence is that pregnant women suffering from an inadequate diet give birth to underweight and nutritionally damaged children.

PART III: RESPONSES POVERTY AND INEQUALITY

In light of the many interrelated factors that combine to create poverty in the United States, we now attempt to assess the various policies, programs, and agencies that have been devised to deal with poverty. The underlying theme is why, and to what extent, these responses to poverty have failed or even worsened the problem. It seems useful to begin by sketching the historical development of present welfare institutions.

THE ORIGINS OF THE WELFARE SYSTEM

Our story begins nearly four centuries ago in England, where the problem of what to do with the unemployed, able-bodied worker first emerged. By the beginning of the seventeenth century hundreds of wandering, begging, and looting poor families in English towns and villages had become a nuisance and a threat. These families had been pushed off the feudal estates that they and their ancestors had farmed for centuries. Because of the increasing market for wool, the land they had farmed was needed for the grazing of sheep.

Seventeenth-century England was moving into an era of mercantilism, in which emphasis was increasingly placed on the manufacture and trading of goods, and these poor tenant farmers and their families now had unnecessary skills. Drawn to the villages, towns, and cities because there was literally nowhere else to go, many of these people were unable to find work, and the factory system, wage economy, and city life posed difficult adjustments for many who had been accustomed to receiving protection from the owners of the feudal estates.

The Poor Law, which was enacted in England in 1601 in response to these problems, became the basis for many of the policies toward the poor both in England and in the United States for centuries to come. One of the essential provisions of the Poor Law was the establishment of workhouses where the poor lived and worked. The law stipulated that the wages to be paid in these workhouses would be less than those received by the lowest-paid worker in the village or town. Such low pay, it was hoped, would keep the poor from seeking the workhouse and public support as a way of life. It was assumed that if wages paid in the workhouses were ample, there would be no incentive for the poor to leave them and become independent. In many of the workhouses, husbands and wives were separated, and in some places being poor was treated as a crime (Mencher, 1967).

Many of the persons who settled the American colonies brought with them the British view of the poor, to which they added some attitudes that grew out of the American experience. As we have already seen, America was perceived as the land of opportunity where all could succeed, given sufficient hard work, independence, thrift, and pride. Hard work meant both survival for the early settlers and esteem among their friends. Poverty in the face of such opportunity was incomprehensible and was interpreted as a sign of individual inadequacy and sloth.

The poor were systematically excluded from towns and told to move on, and when that failed, they were placed in the workhouses that were constructed early in the colonial settlements. In addition to the workhouses, the colonial settlements eventually developed a form of relief in which a poor person might remain at home and still receive the minimal necessities for survival. Colonial Americans stressed the difference between the worthy and the unworthy poor—the worthy being the widow, the crippled, the orphan, and the sick. The typical unworthy poor person was the able-bodied male who was unemployed because of laziness and lack of motivation.

Unemployment in early America tended to come in waves that corresponded with the fluctuations in trade and immigration. Many immigrants had difficulty finding work once they arrived in the port cities. Jobs were sometimes not readily available, because of the trade fluctuations of the developing economy. In addition, language barriers, illness, and poverty only increased the problems for newly arrived immigrants who had come to America in hope of finding a better life. Poverty had been almost taken for granted in countries where the laboring classes had always been poor. But in the New World, where it was assumed that economic opportunity existed everywhere for anyone who wanted to grasp it, poverty seemed to be a result of personal inadequacy. It is not surprising that efforts to help the poor generally emphasized the need to strengthen their character and to motivate them toward self-sufficiency.

During and after the Civil War, private charity organizations developed. These organizations operated in conjunction with local public-relief agencies. Accompanying the development of these organizations was an emerging belief in what was called "scientific philanthropy," or gift-giving with a purpose. The idea was that assistance should be given the poor not simply on the basis of their need but rather in such a way as to increase their self-sufficiency. This belief, and the charity societies that developed around it, attracted the support of a great variety of persons concerned with the problem, including rich philanthropists, lady bountifuls, evangelists, and social workers. These societies wanted alms to be given to the poor only after a careful investigation had been made to diagnose the cause of poverty in each case. Moreover, it was believed that if a successful person could help the poor person find his way to independence, that experience would be more valuable than charity alone. Thus, one slogan of this movement was ''Not alms, but a friend.'' This slogan represented the belief that the poor were needy because of poor socialization and inferior moral standards.

By 1900, relief through private agencies had all but replaced public relief in the United States. This voluntary relief system reinforced strong American views against government intervention in this area. Many critics blamed government intervention in England for the perpetuation of poverty in that country. Private relief was seen as the preferred alternative that would reduce the costs of poverty.

In the summer of 1928, however, private charity organizations reported that the number of impoverished individuals needing assistance was rising so fast that their resources to help the poor were insufficient. At that point government intervened in a substantial way. The deepening Depression of the 1930s put millions of people out of work, and the need for the federal government to provide protection against economic insecurity became even greater. But support for this idea did not come immediately. In the early depression years it was acceptable for government to provide food for livestock but not for unemployed persons. The American idea that an individual should look after his own welfare held on until 1935, when the Social Security Act was passed.

The Social Security Act established two separate systems for providing economic security. One system introduced the principle of social insurance, in which persons were required to contribute to the plan and thus had a ''right'' to receive benefits. This protection was extended only to the aged and the unemployed. Currently this social insurance program is known as the Old Age, Survivors, Disability, and Health Insurance (OASDHI).

The second system established under Social Security was public assistance, which required no contribution. Benefits were to be paid by the federal government according to the ability of the destitute to demonstrate need. The use of federal funds

Figure 9.13   Historically, American attitudes toward poverty have been ambivalent. Private charities carried the burden of relief until the Depression, but government efforts became predominant in the 1930s. Today, private efforts to combat poverty, particularly urban poverty, are not motivated entirely by charity. Big business and big banks recognize that urban poverty and decay also affect their interests. Restoring the inner city and making neighborhoods attractive and livable also maintains real estate values and aids banks and businesses.

Figure 9.14 Eliminating poverty seems less a problem of economics than of values and choices. America has the means to eliminate poverty—but does it have the will? The breakfast program organized by the Black Panthers is more than an economic response to poverty and undernourishment—it is a political act designed to call attention to the needs of the poor in our midst.

was a new practice, but public assistance was not a new concept; rather, it represented an evolution of the Poor Law of England and a shift of responsibility from private charities to public agencies. The public assistance program was intended to be only a residual measure to meet the temporary emergency needs of the poor (Wilensky and Lebeaux, 1965). It was assumed that in a reasonably short time, the need for this program would "wither away," as the nation recovered from the Depression and as the social insurance program grew to provide for those unable to work.

Welfare Today

One of the reasons for the recent dissatisfaction with public assistance is that the program, which was originally designed to be a temporary, stop-gap measure, has grown to a point that it currently represents one of the major social problems in the United States. With the soaring of public-assistance rolls, particularly in the 1960s, the welfare system has become widely disliked, by liberals as well as conservatives, and by the poor as well as the rich. One major problem with public assistance is that it was designed to provide aid according to need, and definitions of need have been influenced by political considerations (Piven and Cloward, 1971). Political influences on the system have created substantial inequities, including wide variation from state to state as to eligibility requirements and levels of benefits.

The public assistance system operates through five categorical programs: (1) Aid to Families with Dependent Children (AFDC), (2) Old Age Assistance (OAA), (3) Aid to the Blind (AB), (4) Aid to the Permanently and Totally Disabled (APTD), and (5) General Assistance (GA). In addition, twenty-five states have extended the eligibility standards for AFDC to include intact families with unemployed fathers (Marmor, 1973). In spite of this array of programs, including the insurance program described earlier, it is estimated that only 15 million of the 25 million poor in 1970 received any public assistance (Sampson, 1972).

Of these programs, the AFDC category has been the object of most attention, as a reflection of public concern about the growing number of female-headed families who receive assistance in this pro-

297

gram. However, families receiving AFDC tend to remain on the program for a relatively short time, as compared, for example, with Old Age Assistance recipients. Although a small proportion of AFDC recipients do remain on assistance for longer periods, the great majority appear to be drawn from the group of marginal poor—those who face irregular employment or financial crises that force them periodically to seek public assistance. The average monthly payment per AFDC recipient in January 1972 was $51.97. New York State paid the highest grants in the nation, amounting to $79.98 per AFDC recipient monthly, as compared, for example, with $14.73 per recipient paid in Mississippi. The current average monthly grant for a family of four on AFDC was approximately $197 monthly, or $2,400 per year.

AFDC recipients are allowed to work, but they can keep only the first $30 and only one-third of any additional income from work. The fact that they must give up such a large percentage of their earnings, or else lose all public support, serves to sap much initiative. This lack of incentive to work has been regarded as one of the key problems in the welfare system. In fact, only in recent years have recipients been allowed to retain any of their earnings; prior to that time all earnings were subtracted from the assistance grant. Many proposals for reforming the welfare system emphasize the need to find ways to make recipients want to become self-supporting. One of the problems with these proposals is that the use of incentives tends to increase the costs of welfare, at least in the short run, but theoretically these costs would be offset by increases in the number of welfare recipients who become self-supporting. A more fundamental problem is the lack of any programs to ensure that jobs paying an adequate wage are available to those recipients who are able to work. It seems that the availability of such programs would actually prevent unemployed persons from seeking welfare assistance. However, efforts to create such programs have not succeeded.

The Myth of the Welfare Cost Burden

In spite of the intensity of public concern, the costs of public welfare in the United States represent only a small proportion of government spending.

In fiscal year 1972, for example, only $10.6 billion was spent in all of these public assistance programs for cash payments that were made to recipients—exclusive of the cost of medical payments, social services, and administration and training, which amounted to another $10.8 billion (Dear, 1973). Considering that we spend approximately $14 billion a year to keep troops stationed in Europe, federal welfare costs seem rather low.

The burden on local and state governments has tended to be equally light. Since the 1960s, for example, costs of direct cash assistance to the poor have approximated about 4 percent of federal revenues, 8 percent of state revenues, and 3 percent of local government revenues (Sampson, 1972). Nevertheless, there remains a widespread belief among the public that substantially more is spent on assistance to the poor. Ronald Dear suggests some of the reasons why this belief persists:

Examination of social welfare data shows that remarkably little money—about $10.6 billion—is given directly to poor people. Our main income maintenance programs are our social insurance programs which cost $75 billion. These programs are self-supporting, paid for by employees or employer contributions into trust funds. This $75 billion doesn't cost the government a cent. Yet the amount taken in through OASDHI in tax is counted as government income, thereby helping to offset what would be a larger federal deficit. It is also counted as a government contribution to social welfare referred to in the federal budget as "human resources." The point I am making is that little money is actually given to poor people by the government. (Dear, 1973)

Alternatives to the Present Welfare System

Wilensky and Lebeaux (1965) have offered two useful concepts for analyzing social programs by distinguishing between *residual* programs and *institutional* ones. Residual programs are those that are intended to fulfill a temporary, emergency need of society when the normal means of meeting these needs break down, as in the case of severe economic fluctuations such as depressions. As a residual program, the present public assistance system was developed in response to the Depression, and it was assumed that the expected recovery of the economy would do away with the need to continue the program. There was a widespread public outcry when the nation recovered from the Depression and the public assistance programs continued to grow.

The second form of government-sponsored social programs are those that are intended to perform permanent functions for the society. Public education and social security are examples of institutional programs.

The argument has been made that as long as there is job insecurity, family disorganization, and illness in the society, public assistance programs will be needed and that, therefore, the present system of welfare should be converted into an institutional program. The suggestion is that a program that has previously been considered temporary, designed only to help in emergency situations, should be redesigned to serve a more permanent function. Accordingly, a variety of institutional programs to replace the present welfare system have recently been proposed.

Most of the recent proposals treat poverty as income insufficiency. One such proposal was the Family Assistance Plan (FAP), developed by Patrick Moynihan and advanced during the early years of the first Nixon administration. After obtaining some strong initial support, this plan was defeated in the Senate Finance Committee in 1970. FAP was designed to replace public assistance by providing a minimum annual income of $1,600 for a family of four ($2,400 including food stamp benefits). It proposed that these benefits cover not only the families of unemployed workers but that they be extended to cover families of working poor whose incomes fell below a specified level. This feature represented an effort to extend benefits to the near poor, a group that is neglected in the present welfare system. The proposal to include this group in the benefits was designed to prevent the near poor from sliding further into poverty.

A number of criticisms were leveled at FAP. First, unemployed individuals would be forced to take almost any job in order to become eligible for assistance payments. The criticism was valid in that the proposal did propose vigorous measures to encourage the unemployed to take any available work. A second criticism was that the payments were too low to move families above the poverty line. A third complaint, made by some members of Congress, was that the program would cost far more than the administration had estimated. When the proposal died in Congress, the administration made few efforts to revive it. Both the administration and Congress blamed each other for the failure of the Family Assistance Plan.

The Family Assistance Plan was based in part on the principle of the *negative income tax,* which had become increasingly popular, especially among economists, in the 1960s. It called for use of the income tax system to provide cash payments to individuals and families whose income fell below some designated level. The argument was that the current income tax system was currently being used to subsidize certain groups (homebuyers and oil companies, for example), in the form of deductions and tax rebates, and it could easily be extended to make payments to those whose incomes were below a certain level. The idea was attractive for its simplicity and for its use of an instrument, the income tax system, which reached the rich and poor alike. Furthermore, the negative income tax concept would allow for subsidy payments for the working poor as well as for the unemployed.

But the most serious weakness of the concept derived from its simplicity; namely, it would be difficult in such a system to respond to the financial crises that many poor families would experience between tax reporting periods. Low-income families tend to have few, if any, financial reserves, and they cannot afford to wait long periods before receiving emergency assistance.

Another proposal that has periodically been advanced is that of family or children's allowances, a plan that is followed in all Western industrialized societies except the United States. These plans represent an effort to make an investment in children; they recognize that a family's financial burden is a function of the number of children in the unit. Payments are made to all families, rich and poor alike. One of the advantages claimed for family allowances is that, by making payments to everyone, they reduce the stigma currently associated with welfare assistance. But even though a high proportion of government expenditures can then be recaptured through taxes (proposals usually call for family allowances to be taxed), the initial expenditure can be very substantial. Such programs have not been more seriously considered in the United States because of their initial expense.

In the debates about alternative proposals, several criteria have emerged for examining and evaluating income maintenance proposals:

1. Are the proposed benefit levels adequate?
2. Are the eligibility criteria and procedures demeaning and stigmatizing?
3. Is the proposed program administratively efficient and can it be administered equitably?
4. Does the program further separate the poor or promote their integration into the rest of society?
5. Does the proposal provide strong incentives for work and for maintaining family stability?

The proposals that have been considered in recent years have certain features in common. First, they call for a rearrangement of the current operating and financing responsibilities for welfare assistance. Most of them move toward federally established and controlled criteria for eligibility and toward consistent payment levels among the states. Second, the proposals move toward the concept of a guaranteed minimum income level for the poor, at least for those poor living in families. Third, the proposals address income insufficiency, not relative poverty. Thus, under all the proposals that have been considered, the poor would still be at the bottom of the socioeconomic ladder, but they would at least gain the right to a certain minimum level of income support with less stigma and shame than is now attached to welfare programs.

Government has also tried to reduce regional poverty through programs designed to promote social and economic development in high poverty areas. Similar efforts were made during the Depression of the 1930s—a prime example was the Tennessee Valley Authority, which provided funding for economic development and for the expansion of job opportunities for workers. In recent years, the Area Redevelopment Administration and the Economic Development Administration have been active in funding economic development programs for high poverty areas. Appalachia was a prime target for such programs in the early and mid-1960s, but similar, less publicized efforts were made elsewhere.

The government has also created training programs to give the poor skills so that they can get jobs. The Manpower Development and Training Act of 1962, for example, focused on retraining displaced workers and on providing basic skill training to persons detached from the labor force. However, these training programs have been severely criticized by those who say that jobs were often not available for the persons who had completed the training.

The Future

What the future holds for the poor in America is not clear. The widely held belief that the poor will always be with us has a long history. Certainly the persistence of poverty in the most affluent nation in the world tends to support that belief. However, the efforts to relieve poverty in the last decade or so—and the knowledge that has been accumulated about poverty as a result of those efforts—suggest that poverty in America is not a necessary condition but is rather the result of a series of societal choices and values. The cost of eliminating poverty, at least in the form of income insufficiency, was estimated to be somewhere between $10 and $20 billion in 1968. And that cost range appears to be within the nation's economic capacity. Thus, it would appear that what keeps us from eliminating economic poverty is not its cost but our beliefs about the poor and about helping them.

CHAPTER REVIEW

Americans have not consistently recognized poverty as a social problem. The latest "rediscovery" of the American poor began in the 1960s and spawned the War on Poverty. For most Americans, poverty has been defined in terms of income insufficiency, or lack of money for life's basic necessities. Most poor people are white and live in female-headed households; well over half are children, the aged, or disabled persons.

Karl Marx tried to determine the causes of poverty and attributed it to class-based oppression. He claimed that wealth and access to education could be equalized by taking the means of production from individual owners and putting it in the hands of workers themselves. Trotsky, however, felt that this would merely create a new basis for classes: bureaucracy. Others, in Weber's tradition, felt that inequalities were caused by more than economic factors. Functionalists, for example, have noted that positions in society differ according to the qualifications needed for the job and to the importance of the job. Positions are therefore differentially rewarded. Critics of functionalism claim that some people exploit these ''natural'' differences and thereby make inequalities worse.

While many have argued that capitalism somehow causes poverty, Norway's economic situation suggests that such is not the case. What probably is contributing to the problem is ''Americanism,'' a set of values and assumptions that emphasizes individual freedom and responsibility. Protestantism added a moral thrust to these values, and America's early frontier provided a means of relatively easy individual success through hard work. Implicit throughout this philosophy, however, is the reluctance to reward ''laziness'' by aiding the poor. And the amount of social mobility in America has only strengthened this philosophy.

Middle-range sociological theories explain poverty by referring to economic policies of the government that try to fight inflation by keeping unemployment rates at a minimum of 4.5 percent. Urbanization and technological dislocation have also contributed to the poverty of small-farm owners and of those unskilled persons who have moved out of the South or into the cities to seek employment. Racism has prevented minorities from acquiring adequate job skills and has contributed to lower salaries for those who are skilled. Within the family setting, poor people's inability to obtain adequate birth-control information contributes to high fertility rates and further poverty. Because Social Security benefits are inadequate, many of those who escaped poverty during their working years become poor as they grow old.

Social-psychological theories claim that once poverty occurs, a *labeling* process goes into effect. To the extent that they accept the label, the poor (especially the youth) become more prone to deviance. They tend to have associates who are also poor, and these friends teach them to live for the present by dropping out of school and taking low-level jobs. Often they will also marry early in an effort to escape the poverty of their parents' homes. All of this creates a vicious circle of poverty from one generation to the next.

Psychological problems, such as mental disorder or low achievement motivation, also contribute to poverty, but probably not as directly as do physical disabilities. Poor nutrition perpetuates these problems also into succeeding generations.

Society's response has reflected the long held beliefs in individual responsibility and the concern over the high costs of welfare (which, in reality, are not all that high). Benefits have been inadequate. Proposed alternatives to the present welfare system, such as the Family Assistance Program or child allowances, are all moving in the direction of guaranteed minimum income. No matter what system is adopted, however, it must have adequate benefits administered efficiently and equitably, without the stigmatizing effects of the present arrangements. Providing incentives for work and promoting social integration for the poor must be an integral part of any poverty program if it is to succeed.

SUGGESTED READINGS

Heilbroner, Robert. *The Economic Problem.* 3rd ed. Englewood Cliffs, N.J.: Prentice-Hall, 1972.

Liebow, Elliot. *Tally's Corner.* Boston: Little, Brown, 1967.

Lipset, Seymour M., and Reinhard Bendix. *Social Mobility in Industrial Society.* Berkeley: University of California Press, 1958.

Piven, Frances Fox, and Richard Cloward. *Regulating the Poor: The Functions of Public Welfare.* New York: Random House, 1971.

President's Commission on Income Maintenance Programs, Background Papers. Washington, D.C.: U.S. Government Printing Office, 1970.

301

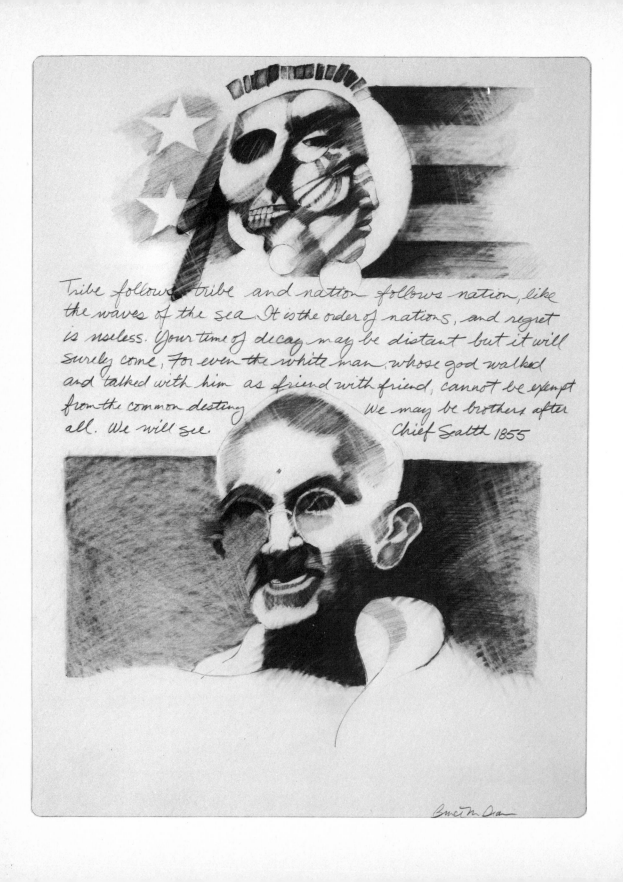

Tribe follows tribe and nation follows nation, like the waves of the sea. It is the order of nations, and regret is useless. Your time of decay may be distant but it will surely come, For even the white man, whose god walked and talked with him as friend with friend, cannot be exempt from the common destiny. We may be brothers after all. We will see. Chief Sealth 1855

10
Intergroup Conflict

Most of this chapter is devoted to the ways in which nonwhites in America today are victimized by the white majority. Yet, the chapter is not simply about race relations. Race is only one basis for conflicts between groups. It plays no part in conflicts between Catholics and Protestants in Northern Ireland (and played no role in conflicts between them in nineteenth-century America). Nor was race a factor in the 2,000 years of Christian persecution of Jews. And it is not a factor in the many bitter and bloody conflicts between tribes in new African nations.

In order to understand racial conflict, we must understand a broader phenomenon: *intergroup conflict based on noticeable physical or cultural differences between groups.* Religious, ethnic, tribal, linguistic, or other cultural differences have caused bitter conflict and have provided—as often as race has—the basis for the subordination and exploitation of one group by another. Such conflicts are common in all modern societies. And they may constitute the most serious internal problem of these societies today.

To explain intergroup conflict, we first discuss concepts that are commonly used to classify aspects of the problem; then we concentrate on the contemporary American situation and depict the subordination and exploitation of some nonwhite groups. Next we evaluate theories of intergroup conflict with a special concern to understand this social problem in the United States. Finally, we assess responses to racial injustice.

PART I: THE PROBLEM
INTERGROUP CONFLICT

Intergroup conflict can take a variety of forms. Although it always involves strains in relations between two or more groups within the same society, it may involve conflict between a dominant and a subordinate group or groups, or conflict between subordinate groups. For example, in addition to being in conflict with the dominant white population, a subordinate group, such as blacks in the United States, can be in conflict with another subordinate group, such as Puerto Ricans, especially in center-city neighborhoods.

The term *subordinate group* is preferable to the term *minority group,* and the term *dominant group* is preferable to the term *majority group.* Dominance does not necessarily result from superior numbers. A comparatively small group may dominate, repress, and exploit a very large group. For example, blacks in South Africa and Rhodesia outnumber whites by a large margin, but they are subordinate to whites. Similarly, persons of French ancestry greatly outnumber English-speaking Canadians in Quebec. The source of their present conflict, however, is the fact that the English-speaking minority has long economically dominated and exploited the French-speaking majority. Furthermore, a minority group may rise from a subordinate position without becoming a larger group. The Jews and the Japanese in the United States make up only small proportions of the population, but their influence is widely felt throughout our culture, and they are not dominated by the white Christian majority.

In the United States, subordinate groups are also minority groups—with the exception of women. Because we focus on intergroup conflict in the United States, we will often use these terms interchangeably. We defer to a later chapter our discussion of women as a subordinate group.

IDENTIFYING SUBORDINATE GROUPS

Subordinate groups have a number of essential characteristics. First, they must be culturally or physically different (to a noticeable degree) from the dominant group. Skin color, language, religion, or other distinctive differences must exist. Second, these differences must be seen as sufficiently important to give the dominant group a reason or excuse to discriminate against the subordinate group. *Discrimination* usually means specific acts against members of a group, whereas *prejudice* usually refers to attitudes held against members of a group. In either case, the dominant group treats members of the subordinate group on the basis of their group identity, without regard for their personal characteristics. Third, the dominant group's policies to exclude the subordinate group must work to limit or prevent intergroup relationships. The ingroup solidarity of the subordinate

Figure 10.1   When Columbus arrived in the New World (top left), *Native Americans were not only a numerical majority but were also dominant in terms of economic and military strength. In time, however, the Europeans increased greatly in both numbers and power. Native Americans won some battles, such as the battle at Little Big Horn in 1876* (top right), *where General Custer and his troops were defeated. (This painting was done by Red Horse, a survivor of the battle.) However, the Europeans and their descendants more often massacred large groups of Indians with their superior military power and weaponry. The massacre in 1890 of more than 200 Sioux at Wounded Knee, S.D. (bottom left)* was the last major military engagement between the two groups. Native Americans have since had subordinate status in terms of both power and size and, like these two Navajo children (bottom right), *have had to live on reservation lands.*

group usually serves to make such policies even more effective. Thus, *endogamy,* marriage within one's own group, is typical of both dominant and subordinate groups and helps keep them isolated. Endogamy is especially likely when racial differences are involved, because racial group membership is so visible. When race is not involved, members of subordinate groups often escape by passing, or appearing, as dominant-group members. Fourth, the subordinate group must have a sense of its grievances and act to resist or overcome subordination. Without this last factor, there will be no conflict.

When a subordinate group seeks to escape being exploited, it may adopt one of several strategies, or change from one strategy to another under the pressure of events (Wirth, 1945). The *pluralist* strategy uses the idea that different cultural groups can exist in the same society. It aims for peaceful coexistence with the dominant group. The subordinate group using this strategy wants to keep its cultural differences but have them tolerated by the dominant culture. For example, in the United States, Jews and Catholics have achieved social acceptance and economic equality without adopting the dominant Protestant religion. Consequently, America today is a religiously pluralistic society.

The *assimilationist* strategy is to give up cultural differences in return for absorption into the dominant culture. This pattern was typical for immigrants from Northern Europe who discarded their distinctive language and cultural patterns and soon became fully "Americanized." It was once thought that America was an ethnic melting pot where all immigrant groups would become assimilated. But later waves of immigrants after 1880—most were Southern Europeans and Eastern Europeans—found their culture less compatible with the White Anglo-Saxon Protestant (WASP) culture and have never fully assimilated.

The *secessionist* strategy is a more extreme version of pluralism. The group not only wishes to retain its cultural identity but also wants a certain degree of physical isolation and political and economic independence. The Amish are an example of an American group that has successfully achieved these goals—they remain apart from the rest of society with little contact or conflict.

Finally, the *militant* strategy seeks to turn the tables on the dominant group and make it subordinate. This is the goal of the more radical Catholics in Northern Ireland today. It was also the pattern adopted by European colonial powers who arrived as visitors in many underdeveloped countries and stayed on to rule. However, after winning their national freedom back from colonial powers, many African states today, such as Kenya and Uganda, have indeed turned the tables on the colonial powers. Where whites remain in these countries, they occupy a somewhat subordinate status.

In Part II we will consider the different strategies of various subordinate groups in the United States and evaluate both the causes and consequences of these choices. But before taking up these matters, we will examine the current position of subordinate minority groups in the United States.

THE SUBORDINATION OF NONWHITE MINORITIES

The primary basis of group subordination in the United States today is race. Religious minorities, such as Catholics and Jews, are no longer economically exploited. Only traces of earlier patterns of prejudice and discrimination against them remain. Even though overt racism, too, has also been declining in America, it remains a potent factor in determining social position. Our discussion focuses on three nonwhite minorities: blacks, persons of Spanish origin (Chicanos, or persons of Mexican descent, and Puerto Ricans), and Native Americans (American Indians). Although Asians long suffered from racist discrimination, they have recently achieved economic parity, or equality, with whites; anti-Asian beliefs and discrimination have greatly subsided.

The three major nonwhite minority groups in America today make up about 16 percent of the total population—together they number about 32 million people. Of these, blacks make up about 75 percent, or about 24 million. Nearly 9 million persons are identified as Spanish origin, including 5 million Chicanos, 626,000 Cubans, 1.5 million Puerto Ricans, and 1,356,000 persons of other Spanish origins. There are about 800,000 Native Americans.

All except the Native Americans are mainly urban groups; however, a substantial proportion of both the black and Chicano populations live in rural areas of the South and Southwest, respectively. Blacks are more evenly distributed throughout the United States and live in large numbers throughout the country, particularly in huge metropolitan communities. Chicanos reside mainly in the Southwest and far western states of Texas, Colorado, Arizona, New Mexico, California, Oregon, and Washington. The Puerto Ricans are concentrated in the East, mainly in Massachusetts, New York, Connecticut, and Rhode Island. Cubans are concentrated in Florida, Louisiana, and New York. Most Native Americans are scattered on more that 200 reservations within the continental United States, although some reside on the Alaskan reservations and in various urban communities throughout the nation.

Economic Discrimination

306

At present, minority groups in the United States experience many forms of economic discrimination. Discrimination occurs, for example, in trying to get a job, in wages received, in promotion on the job, in fringe benefits, and in keeping a job. Economic discrimination is so widespread that even today, after so many attempts to eliminate inequalities, minority groups are still the last to be hired and the first to be fired.

In comparison with the dominant white group, blacks, Native Americans, and Spanish-origin Americans disproportionately have the worst jobs and are underrepresented in the high-paying positions. Fifty percent of white Americans are employed in white-collar jobs, but less than 30 percent of employed blacks and less than 20 percent of the employed Spanish-origin population do white-collar work. In short, these groups are generally kept out of professional and technical positions, managerial and administrative jobs, and sales and clerical work (U.S. Department of Commerce, 1971, 1973). Four out of every 10 employed blacks are blue-collar workers. The comparable figures for Mexican Americans and Puerto Ricans are 6.2 out of 10 and 6 out of 10, respectively. In contrast, slightly more than 3 out of 10 employed whites are found in such blue-collar positions as craftsmen, transportation workers, and general laborers.

More than twice as many blacks and Chicanos and three times as many Puerto Ricans as whites are employed in service positions, including domestic work, household help, and other service roles. These are characteristically the lowest paying and the lowest status jobs in American society.

The unemployment and underemployment rates for blacks and other minorities are also high. Not only are thousands of minority persons unable to find jobs, but thousands more who are employed are underemployed (working only part of the time). Fully one-third of all black teenagers were unemployed in 1972, compared with about 14 percent of white teenagers. The unemployment rate of Native Americans is about ten times the national average and in many instances reaches as much as 40 percent of the potential labor force among that group (U.S. Department of Commerce, 1971, 1973).

High unemployment rates and underemployment combine to create a dismal economic picture for minorities. The median income of white families in 1970 was $10,236, whereas the figure for black Americans was only $6,279. But the median income of Spanish-origin families, $7,117, was considerably higher than that of blacks. Of this group, the Puerto Rican median income of $5,975 was slightly below that received by blacks, whereas the median income of Cubans, whose level of skill is generally higher than that of other Spanish speaking groups, was $9,546 in families whose head worked full time throughout the year (U.S. Department of Commerce, 1971).

Income data on men twenty-five years and older paint a grim portrait of the structure of poverty among minority groups. Slightly more than 28 percent of all blacks and 14 percent of all whites earned less than $3,000 in 1970. Slightly more than 19 percent of the Chicanos and about 15 percent of the Puerto Ricans also were in this category.

About 60 percent of both blacks and Chicanos and almost 75 percent of Puerto Ricans twenty-five years and older, in contrast to about 30 percent of whites in this age group, earned less than $6,000 in 1970. In the "$10,000 and over" category, white men—including Chicano men and Puerto Rican men—fared consistently better than black men (U.S. Department of Commerce, 1971).

Other data show that 50 percent of Native Americans have annual incomes below $2,000, and 75 percent of them receive less that $3,000 per year. Native Americans are clearly the most poverty stricken of all groups in the United States (Bahr *et al.*, 1971).

More than 30 percent of the 25.5 million Americans who were below the low income level in 1970 were members of the black, Chicano, and Puerto Rican minorities. More than 7.5 million of them were black, 2.2 million were Chicano, and another 424,000 were Puerto Rican. A refinement of these data shows that about 30 percent of all blacks were classified as below the low income level in 1970; 28 percent of the Chicanos and about 29 percent of the Puerto Ricans were similarly classified. The picture is even more disturbing for families headed by women. Almost one-third of white families headed by women are below the low-income classification. However, the black and Spanish-origin families in this category outnumber whites by a ratio of approximately two to one (U.S. Department of Commerce, 1971).

What are the reasons for these income disparities? To what extent are they the result of prejudice and discrimination and to what extent do they stem from the lower educational levels of minorities?

Education and Income

The median education attained by the dominant white population in the United States is 12.1 years; for blacks, it is 10.0; for Chicanos, it is 8.8; and for Puerto Ricans, it is 7.2. About 80 percent of all whites, 60 percent of all blacks, almost 50 percent of all Chicanos, and about 30 percent of all Puerto Ricans who are twenty-five years or older have completed four years of high school or more. These figures are important because a high correlation exists between income and education. Generally, the higher one's educational attainment, the higher is the income received. However, when we compare the level of education and median income of blacks and Spanish-origin Americans, we can begin to see that educational attainment is not the only factor; "color visibility" as we shall see, has played an important role.

Earlier in this chapter, we pointed out that blacks are better educated than are Americans of Spanish origin. Yet, in spite of these figures, the income structure is more favorable for Americans of Spanish origin than it is for black Americans. In almost every category, the Chicano and Puerto Rican groups fared better than blacks. The figures are even more exaggerated, of course, when one compares the income levels of blacks with those of the dominant white population. In 1974, the black male *college* graduate could expect to earn less than a white male *high-school* graduate, largely because of the wider employment opportunities open to the dominant white population. Although income is supposed to be generally related to education level, the evidence seems to suggest a close correlation between a group's income opportunities and its color proximity to the dominant group—the lower one's visibility, it seems, the greater is one's income opportunity.

Discrimination in the Schools

Discrimination within the educational structure, like discrimination in other areas, can be expressed in many ways. Even though the 1954 Supreme Court decision in the case of *Brown v. The Board of Education of Topeka* banned discrimination in public education, all minorities continue to experience educational discrimination in one form or another.

De facto (actually existing) discrimination is quite common in areas outside the South. Because of the concentration of disadvantaged groups in racial and ethnic ghettos and the failure of many cities to take action against segregation, the disadvantaged minorities of the United States still tend to be segregated in the school system. In almost every large American city, most blacks live in neighborhoods that are mainly black; Puerto Ricans and Chicanos live in similar neighborhoods; and the Native Americans are concentrated either in reservations or in urban communities.

Seemingly unaware of the effects of this racial isolation, the dominant white population continues to resist what is perhaps the best method of creating racial balance—busing to achieve integration in the schools. Opponents of busing generally fail to discuss the racial issues involved; instead, they argue that busing removes children from neighborhoods where they live and thereby may put the children's lives in danger. But busing in itself is certainly not an issue, for thousands of children are bused to school each day, perhaps as many as 50 percent of all school-aged children in the United States. Of this number, less than 3 percent are bused to desegregate the schools. Regardless of the pros and cons of busing, it is clear that the busing issue has brought much racial hostility to the surface, resulting in prejudice, fear, and violence. The issue has revealed how deeply rooted are racial prejudices against disadvantaged minorities. The busing issue has been used by politicians who have been able to turn people's prejudices and fears to their own political advantage.

The racial isolation in the public schools at the time of the 1954 Supreme Court decision still remains. Two decades after the desegregation order, nearly three-fifths of all black children in eleven Southern states are attending schools that are 80 percent or more black in enrollment. In Atlanta, for example, because of the white flight to the suburbs and the resulting concentration of blacks in the public school system, four-fifths of all Atlanta school children are black. This problem, however, is certainly not peculiar to the Deep South. Segregation has also been reestablished in cities outside the South, such as Newark, Baltimore, Boston, Philadelphia, Chicago, Denver, Los Angeles, Cleveland, St. Louis, and Oakland. And certain other Southern cities, such as New Orleans, that once resisted desegregation have made dramatic shifts toward creating a school system that is desegregated for the student body and the faculty alike.

Present-day segregated schools for nonwhites are often like segregated schools of the pre-1954 period. They are likely to be housed in substandard buildings; the schools are sometimes overcrowded, and children are often forced to attend schools on shifts; there are extreme shortages of books, laboratory equipment, and other educational facilities. Even worse, teachers assigned to these schools often carry with them notions that minority students are slow learners and are difficult to educate. Such attitudes among teachers are communicated, either directly or in subtle ways, to their

Figure 10.2   More than twenty years after the historic Supreme Court school desegregation decision (Brown v. Board of Education), *there is still resistance to racial integration of schools in both the South and the North. How much has really changed between the Little Rock situation in 1957* (above) *and the Boston school conflict of 1974* (below)?

students. These attitudes may seriously affect student performance.

This situation is demonstrated in the case of the Chicano population in the Southwest. Their enrollment of 2.5 million students is equivalent to one-fifth of all elementary and high-school students enrolled in Arizona, New Mexico, Texas, Colorado, and California. However, in many schools, Chicano children are excluded from advanced or upper-ability classes and are overrepresented in special classes for the mentally retarded. Teachers who are insensitive to problems generated by language barriers do not encourage Chicano students to remain in school. In addition, there are not enough Chicano teachers, so Chicano students do not encounter successful adults from their own minority group. All these factors speed up the drop-out rate and help account for Chicano underrepresentation in higher education.

Educational discrimination also occurs at the college level. Until 1970, black colleges and universities, staffed mainly by black faculties, were responsible for educating the overwhelming majority of all black college students. Beginning about 1970, more than half of the 532,000 black college students, representing about 6 percent of all college students, were attending white institutions in the United States. Many of these students began to feel discriminated against by white professors whom they found insensitive to their special needs. In addition, it seemed that the drive to increase minority-group enrollment on college campuses—an effort spurred by the enactment of the 1964 Civil Rights Act—was more talk than substance. Thus far, little progress has been made in raising the proportion of minority faculty members (Moore and Wagstaff, 1974).

These examples clearly show that patterns of discrimination persist in the educational system two decades after the nation was ordered to move forward "with all deliberate speed" to wipe out the educational inequities of the past.

Housing Discrimination

Discrimination in housing is one of the chronic problems facing American society. Residential segregation has wide-spread effects, for it follows almost naturally that within a segregated area all other institutions and most of the services are de facto segregated. Housing discrimination contributes greatly to intergroup conflict. Isolation by neighborhood prevents the intergroup understanding that might result from day-to-day interactions. Isolation thus heightens group visibility and strengthens boundaries between groups.

Today, most minority groups live in residentially segregated neighborhoods. Five-eighths of Native Americans in the United States live on about 200 reservations scattered throughout twenty-six states. Many of them live in sub-standard housing, generally without running water, electricity, or indoor toilets. The majority of Chicanos and Puerto Ricans live in *barrios* or *colonias*—segregated neighborhoods inhabited mainly by persons of Spanish origin. The dwellings are often deteriorating and overcrowded.

A glance at the housing patterns of blacks in almost any large city reveals the general pattern of housing discrimination. In the first place, the black population is largely an urban population. Almost 60 percent of all blacks live in the center city of large metropolises, in comparison with less than 30 percent of the dominant white population (U.S. Department of Commerce, 1971). Typically, houses in the center city are older and more likely to be run down. The plumbing in these houses is also more likely to be substandard. In 1960, for example, 21 percent of all center-city dwellings occupied by blacks lacked some or all plumbing, in comparison with 7 percent of white center-city dwellings. By 1970, these figures had been reduced for both groups. However, in the areas outside metropolitan communities, 49 percent of all dwellings occupied by blacks in 1970 and 9 percent of those occupied by whites lacked some or all plumbing facilities. Clearly, white Americans live in areas with more acceptable sanitation facilities than do black Americans (U.S. Department of Commerce, 1973). Homes owned by blacks also tend to be older than those owned by whites (U.S. Department of Commerce, 1973). Many of these older houses were already deteriorating when blacks moved in; the process continued because of too few repairs and excessive crowding.

Home-ownership rates tend to increase with high income. For example, only about 30 percent

309

of blacks who earn under $3,000 own their own homes. However, 70 percent of black families with an income in excess of $15,000 live in dwellings they own. Comparable figures for the white population are 53 percent (under $3,000) and 82 percent ($15,000 and over). Even in rental dwellings, minorities tend to receive considerably less for their money.

How does housing discrimination occur? First, realtors and zoning offices use various techniques to control the access of minority groups to the housing market. They include the following practices: restrictive covenants, or contractual agreements, between a real estate agent and a seller *not* to sell a given piece of property to certain groups; refusal of realtors to show or sell a house to a member of a minority group; overpricing a dwelling to discourage a prospective minority-group buyer; and zoning, a device whereby areas may not be built on or developed unless lots are of a specific size or dwellings are of a particular type (apartments or low-income housing may not be allowed).

Second, bankers and other money lenders may refuse to give mortages to minority-group members wishing to move into an all-white area. The required funds may, however, be available for buying homes within racial ghettos.

Third, agencies may refuse to enforce laws designed to prevent housing discrimination and intolerable living conditions. Dishonest landlords may also bribe inspectors not to report substandard conditions. Many people may refuse to comply with the law in order to purposefully slow down the enforcement of new laws. All of these factors conspire to keep most minority-group members confined to specific areas within the city or within rural communities.

Discrimination in the Administration of Justice

Minorities often complain that the structure of justice is unfair to them and that they are the victims of an undue amount of police brutality. Indeed, minority-group members are more likely to be suspected of a crime, apprehended, tried and convicted, and sentenced to longer terms than are members of the dominant group. In addition, they are more likely to serve the full term of their sen-

tence and less likely to be granted probation or parole after conviction of an offense.

This situation suggests defects throughout the criminal justice system (Wolfgang and Cohen, 1970). As Chapter 3 notes, policemen may hold prejudices they have learned in their own communities. Although police departments are aware of the problem and have made efforts to counteract it in their training programs, many police officers still react negatively in their contacts with minorities.

Partly as a consequence of discrimination in the criminal justice system, minority groups are overrepresented in criminal statistics and in the prison population. In some places, more than 50 percent of inmates in state prisons and city jails are black. In the Southwest, Chicanos are disproportionately represented in prisons. In New York City, the same applies to Puerto Ricans, and in states such as South Dakota, Native Americans are overrepresented in jails and prisons.

Such overrepresentation does not always directly reflect discrimination in the administration of justice, however. Most minority-group members are tried for crimes against other members of their own group. To argue against prosecution of the black burglar, for example, is to argue against giving police protection to blacks who are burglarized. Discrimination in the social structure causes some members of minority groups to resort to criminal behavior. As a control theorist would put it, because of the barriers of discrimination, too many minority-group members find they have little to lose—and a chance to gain much—by violating the law. However, the combination of discrimination within the criminal justice system and structural (institutionalized) discrimination, much larger in scope, accounts for a great measure of the overrepresentation of minority groups in prison.

PART II: SOURCES INTERGROUP CONFLICT

Because the United States was created by conquest and settled by extremely diverse immigrant groups, all the important bases for intergroup conflict have existed here—and all have produced

Figure 10.3   Asian Americans have been subject to much racial prejudice and discrimination. While Chinese and Japanese Americans have fared relatively better in recent years, few have forgotten the indignities and hardships of the past. (Top) The Alien Registration Act of 1940 is read to a group of Chinese Americans in New York's Chinatown; (below) Japanese Americans are tagged for identification purposes and sent to detention camps in 1942.

prejudice, discrimination, and violence. However, some intergroup conflicts have been more severe and persistent than others.

In earlier times, religion and culture were the main bases for conflict. In many of the original colonies, Catholicism was prohibited. Constitutional guarantees of religious freedom did not end Catholic-Protestant conflict. In the last quarter of the nineteenth century, an angry wave of anti-Catholicism swept the country. Some convents were burned and churches were defaced. Many employers openly refused to hire Catholics. In the United States today, however, conflict based on religion is not a social problem. We have come to terms with religious pluralism.

Closely related to religious conflict was hostility against certain ethnic groups, for example, against Poles, Italians, Greeks, and Jews. These conflicts, too, have for the most part dwindled, even though these groups have kept their cultural patterns. Another basis of conflict has been language. Throughout our history, groups without an English-speaking heritage have always had disadvantaged status. Spanish-speaking groups still do. There is no evidence that any society is at peace with language pluralism. Language continues to underlie French-English conflicts in Canada. Language minorities are discriminated against in India, the Soviet Union, and wherever else they are found.

Racial conflict is presently the main basis for intergroup conflict in the United States and most of the world. Because racial characteristics are biological and visible, racial minorities are not easily assimilated. Members of racial minorities cannot simply change their names or their church and pass as members of the majority. But racial differences do not mean that the pluralist strategy will ultimately fail. For decades, until after World War II, the Japanese were victims of harsh prejudice and discrimination. Indeed, during the war, most Japanese were imprisoned in detention camps, and most lost their possessions and property as a result. Yet, today, both the prejudice and the discrimination have greatly subsided, and Japanese Americans have attained economic parity with whites. The Chinese, also victims of racial prejudices, have also been moving rapidly into an equal position in our society. However, blacks, Chicanos, Puerto Ricans, and Native Americans are still victims of racial exclusion and economic disadvantage. What accounts for these differences?

In this section, we attempt to understand why some earlier intergroup conflicts subsided and why some remain. Only by examining these variations can we try to isolate the roots of intergroup conflict in our society.

SOCIETAL SOURCES

An individual's behavior has little bearing on whether he or she will suffer for belonging to a racial, religious, or cultural group that is the object of prejudice and discrimination. Furthermore, whether or not membership in a minority group will also make one a member of a subordinate group is an accident of time and place. Some societies (Brazil, for example) are relatively color blind. Others pay little attention to religious differences (for example, the United States today). For these reasons, the search for the causes of intergroup conflict is best begun by examining the features of societies as systems. Which features of American society contribute to the particular historical patterns of intergroup conflict we have just reviewed? In this section, we outline certain aspects of the American ideology and economy that have played a major role in shaping intergroup conflict. We then move to lower levels of analysis in order to say why certain conflicts have subsided and others have remained.

American Ideology and Bigotry

On July 4, 1776, the leaders of the American Revolution signed the Declaration of Independence, a philosophical document that has put a lasting mark on the American ideology. The second paragraph begins:

We hold these Truths to be self-evident, that all Men are created equal, that they are endowed by their Creator with certain unalienable Rights, that among these are Life, Liberty, and the Pursuit of Happiness.

These revolutionary lines defied aristocratic traditions and committed the United States to a noble experiment with democratic institutions based on individual liberty and equalitarianism. There is no doubt that the Founding Fathers seriously meant these sentiments. But there is also no doubt that Thomas Jefferson, who wrote them, and a substantial number of those who risked their lives and fortunes by signing them were slave owners.

This extraordinary contradiction was to haunt and deform American society for at least the next two centuries. In his monumental study of race relations in the United States, the Swedish economist Gunnar Myrdal (1944) identified the contradiction between our democratic ideals and the oppressed situation of blacks as the "American dilemma." How could a free people committed to individual liberty maintain a slave system and afterwards maintain a system of exploitation and discrimination that held another people in bondage? Indeed, how could such a system be squared with the doctrines of Christianity? Many believed they could not, and it was therefore no surprise that the strongest support for the abolition of slavery came from the same New England puritans who had formed the hotbed of early revolutionary and democratic sentiments. However, the majority of Americans found another way to "rationalize" these contradictions: The English and American legal and moral traditions could not accomodate *human* slavery. So Americans squared their religious and democratic ideals with the subjugation of blacks *by denying the humanity of blacks*. If the black race is inferior and something less than human, they reasoned, the blessings of equality need not include them.

Ironically, aristocratic ideals, such as those held by the Spanish, did *not* necessitate the dehumanization of blacks, for slavery was consistent with the aristocratic view. The Spanish could readily think of humans as slaves and thus felt no moral pressure to dehumanize and stigmatize blacks (indeed, the Spanish found no difficulty with the notion of white slaves). This is not to argue that slavery under the Spanish was less cruel than under the Americans or the English but that the results were importantly different. Once freed, black people in Spanish societies did not bear the burden of being regarded as biologically inferior. It is a sad irony of their democratic ideals that Americans had to dehumanize blacks in order to condone slavery

312

Figure 10.4   Ironically, the doctrine of individualism has made it harder, not easier, for blacks and other subordinate groups in the United States to get ahead. For the commitment to the belief that a person can succeed through individual merit makes people blind to social factors and conditions that hold the individual back and are beyond his or her control.

and that they could not regard the freed blacks as fully human (Tannenbaum, 1947).

Thus, prior to the Civil War, the condition of free blacks was almost as grim as that of slaves. In 1860, there were almost half a million free blacks in the United States, more than half of them in the North. But even there they were generally denied the right to vote. In some states they were not allowed to testify in court, and they were sometimes the victims of race riots (Litwack, 1961).

Following the Darwinian revolution in biology (and the idea of the survival of the fittest), a variety of outlandish biological doctrines of racial superiority came into vogue. These were eagerly seized upon by many white Americans to scientifically support their beliefs about black inferiority. It has required decades of suffering and persuasion to begin to undo these racist ideas. And, as will be discussed later in this chapter, biological notions of black inferiority still linger not only among the ignorant and intolerant but within seemingly respectable social-science circles.

313

A second irony of the American ideology is that the doctrine of individualism has also worsened the plight of subordinate groups in our society. As is discussed in Chapter 9, the belief that each person is responsible for his or her own destiny has made many Americans deaf to pleas to aid disadvantaged groups. Therefore, once blacks are free, or discriminatory barriers are removed, Americans tend to think nothing further needs to be or should be done to aid their progress. Instead, Americans are inclined to think that it is up to blacks to get ahead in life. As a Catholic housewife once told an interviewer before John F. Kennedy's death in 1963: "The Irish came to this country way after the Negro and had it just as tough. Today we have an Irish president of the United States. The difference is hard work and the blessings of religion" (Stark and Glock, 1969). Indeed, such views are not restricted to whites. Gary Marx (1967) found that about half of a national sample of black adults interviewed in 1964 agreed that "Before Negroes are given equal rights, they have to show that they deserve them"; two-thirds agreed that "Negroes who want to work hard can get ahead just as easily as anyone else." Unfortunately, wanting to work hard is not enough. Someone has to be willing to pay for your labor. Presently, there are few buyers for unskilled work. To the extent that social conditions prevent blacks, or other minorities, or poor people in general from obtaining marketable skills, these people cannot "get ahead." American commitment to individualism tends to blind us to social factors beyond the control of the individual and thus to the real causes of social inequalities.

However, not all aspects of the American ideology have worked against subordinate groups attempting to achieve equality. Our beliefs in fair play, in equality, and in Christian-Judeo or golden-rule ethics have been effectively used to justify the claims of subordinate groups. It is no accident that black pleas for justice have long been put in the language of religion. Common Christian beliefs serve as a major moral bond across the divide of race and as a legitimate basis for claims of brotherhood. The fact that a leader such as the Reverend Martin Luther King was invoking the name, not of *his* God but of *our* God, was of profound emotional significance for whites. By the same token, it would be futile to appeal for fairness to an oppressor who did not believe in fairness even for his own group. However, the fact that almost all Americans strongly believe that society ought to be fair gives weight to such appeals. It was precisely for these reasons that enslaving blacks put Americans in a moral dilemma. The treatment of blacks

did violate deeply held moral values, and the uneasy conscience of white America has played a large role in black liberation.

Functionalists have stressed the role of values in intergroup conflict and accommodation, whereas conflict theorists have emphasized the role of economic forces. Both lines of analysis shed light on different aspects of the same problems.

Economic Conflict

We pointed out earlier that a subordinate group is culturally or physically different from the dominant group. But we also noted that sometimes such differences cease to divide people. For example, Catholics remain significantly different from Protestants, but these religious differences no longer generate the conflict they once did. Similarly, the Japanese remain a noticeable nonwhite race, but they are no longer a subordinate racial minority. In fact, black, Chicano, and Native American spokesmen strongly protest the counting of the Japanese as minority-group members when it comes time to check and assess minority hiring practices. (However, many Japanese Americans, especially the younger generation, do not consider themselves members of the dominant group. Despite their higher degree of assimilation into mainstream America, many Japanese identify with the contemporaray problems of all Asian Americans.)

Noticeable cultural or physical differences identify a subordinate group only *if such differences are associated with economic inequalities.* For at least a century, the average American Catholic was economically inferior to the average American Protestant. This situation fueled Protestant-Catholic conflict: It provided Catholics with a grievance, and Protestants viewed Catholic economic gains as Protestant losses. Once Catholics achieved economic parity, this basis for conflict vanished. Many modern social scientists, following this line of reasoning, regard class conflict as the fundamental source of conflict between racially and culturally distinct groups (Hechter, 1974).

It seems likely that some degree of social inequality is inherent in human societies. However, such inequalities need not be based on classes, as Marx defined them. No matter how inequalities are determined, by a person's position at birth or by individual talent, there is always some conflict of interest between those on top and those on the bottom of the social hierarchy. However, such conflict is softened when all accept the fairness of the rules by which social position is gained and lost. Obviously, people are more likely to regard the rules as unfair when social position is *hereditary* than when position goes by *merit.* The issue, then, is the *basis* of inequalities in society, not whether they exist.

When social position is determined by membership in a racial or cultural group, it is determined by heredity. People—at least members of the subordinate group—will not regard such a system as fair unless they believe that membership in a given racial or cultural group is evidence of lack of merit. Often enough, subordinates do accept notions of their own inferiority. For example, for centuries the lower castes in India seem to have believed that they were born inferiors, meant by the gods to serve the upper castes (Lenski, 1966). However, when a subordinate group refuses to believe itself inferior, it becomes angry about being economically exploited. Thus, conflict theorists conclude that economic inequalities lie behind all racial and cultural intergroup conflict within a society; these disputes are about the use of cultural or racial characteristics to determine wealth.

It follows that conflicts will not subside until economic inequalities are overcome. Our commonsense notion is that the prejudiced beliefs of the majority must first be eliminated in order for subordinate groups to achieve economic parity. The conflict view sees this commonsense notion as getting things backwards. It argues that groups must achieve economic parity first and that the prejudice of the majority will subside afterward. They see the path to liberation, then, not as depending on changes in the hearts of the dominant

315

Figure 10.5 The "American Dilemma" involves affirmation of equality and justice but denial of equal rights to blacks. (Right) Martin Luther King, Jr. was put in jail after he was arrested on trespassing charges for trying to enter a "white" motel. The British faced a similar moral dilemma when Gandhi confronted the Government of England, demanding independence for India (far left). India's aspirations for independence had support from throngs of British people who saw the inconsistency of holding democratic values while denying Indian independence (left).

group but as depending on changes in the bank accounts of the subordinate group.

There is considerable evidence in American history that economic equality does in fact precede change in prejudiced beliefs and that changes in intergroup relations typically occur in this order. The last outbreak of American anti-Catholicism took place during the 1960 Presidential campaign. It was not until after John F. Kennedy was in the White House that many Protestants felt that in the future they could vote for a Catholic (Gallup, 1972). This change in the Protestants' attitude came long after Catholics had achieved economic parity with Protestants. Similarly, the decline in prejudice against the Jews and Japanese seems to have occurred after each group had already made it economically.

An additional source of support for this interpretation comes from studies showing that hostility toward disadvantaged racial minorities comes from those majority members who feel most threatened by the economic progress of the minority. For example, it is whites in the least skilled and poorest paying occupations who are most prejudiced against blacks and who most strongly support discrimination (Selznick and Steinberg, 1969). Furthermore, antagonism toward minorities tends to become most acute during "hard times," when economic competition is worst. As James Vander Zanden (1972) observed:

The major "anti-foreign" movements—the Native American Party in the 1830's, the Know-Nothing Party of the 1850's, the American Protective Association of the late nineteenth century, and the Post-World War I Ku Klux Klan—won their largest following in hard times. Various regional movements—against Chinese, Japanese, and Filipinos on the West Coast, Italians in Louisiana, and French-Canadians in New England—have similarly coincided with economic difficulties in these areas. At least two forces appear to operate in such settings. First, hard times have been associated with widespread unemployment that has intensified intergroup competition for jobs. Second, the frustrations associated with unemployment may breed hostile and aggressive impulses that are vented upon minority groups.

As Vander Zanden makes clear, economic troubles fuel the discontent of subordinate groups. But economic inequalities also motivate the dominant group: Economic exploitation of the subordinate group is a powerful motive for maintaining the status quo. Indeed, economic self-interest lies at the heart of racial and cultural suppression.

Colonialism

The *colony* offers the most obvious example of how the economic motive works in the subordination of one racial or cultural group by another. The British did not seize control of half the underdeveloped regions of the world for the honor of claiming that the sun never set on the empire. Nor did Spain suppress Central and South America for the sake of grandeur. Imperialism was motivated by profit. Under the colonial model, the subordinate group is exploited for cheap labor. The colony becomes a market for manufactured goods, and its natural resources are exported, all for the profit of the colonial power. In order to maintain their dominant position, colonialists typically erect a barrier of laws, customs, and institutions to keep the subordinate group in its place. For this reason, modern colonialism has always meant racism (Blauner, 1969). Many theorists have recently begun to use some elements of the colonial model to explain the situation of subordinate racial and cultural groups *within* societies.

Internal Colonialism

Because modern colonialism has mainly involved the subjugation of nonwhites by whites, nonwhite minorities in the United States have been able to identify with movements and spokesmen abroad that voice their anger with the foreign power. This identification has encouraged nonwhite Americans to apply much of the political theory from abroad to the American situation (Blauner, 1969). Thus, nonwhite groups have called themselves internal colonies. They have said that despite the lack of geographic separation between the colony and the colonizing nation, the relationship between dominant and nonwhite minorities is a relationship between the colonizer and the colonized. In other words, colonies can exist inside a country as well as outside it. Kenneth Clark (1965) pointed out that the politics, economy, and social structure of Harlem are controlled from outside the community. Blacks in Harlem buy in white-owned stores, work for white employers, are governed by white politicians and white laws, must live where whites permit them to live, and attend white-controlled schools. So their lot resembles that of exploited and controlled populations of traditional colonies.

The use of the colonial analogy, or comparison, has also influenced proposals for change. Colonies that won their freedom won it through *nationalist* movements—movements to establish national spirit, independence, and advancement. Thus, some minority leaders have become advocates of racial and cultural nationalism as the means for confronting the internal colonial situation. Racial and cultural nationalism has not only led to demands for separatism but has led a few to consider guerilla warfare and terrorism as useful tactics.

The internal colonial idea has been severely criticized as obscuring more than making clear the relationship between nonwhite subordinate groups and the rest of American society. Michael Hechter (1974) has found the internal-colony notion a powerful tool for understanding relations between England and the Celtic fringe (Wales, Scotland, and Ireland). But he suggests that it has several shortcomings in explaining black-white relations in the United States. For one thing, he argues, nonwhites are not an immense, exploited, numerical majority held under control by a tiny white majority. And whites are not foreigners; a slogan such as "Yankee, go home" has no meaning in the American context. Therefore, in Hechter's view, these differences make it unlikely that nationalism represents a realistic solution for internal colonies. Furthermore, in this context, freedom for nonwhites does not mean driving a handful of foreign oppressors out of a particular geographic area to which nonwhites have a prior claim.

Hechter's position seems to overlook arguments demonstrating that it is precisely because minority groups can document the facts of their economic, social, and political exploitation that many members of such groups perceive of themselves as a domestically colonized group (Blauner, 1969; Clark, 1965). For minorities in cities and Native Americans on reservations, the fundamental issue is their ability to resist continued attacks on their rights. Their rights are being overrun by absentee landlords or by dominant group members who live outside urban ghettos and reservations but who control the economic resources within such communities. They perceive those who control their resources much in the same manner as people who undergo international colonialism perceive the "foreigner" who takes over.

The failure of militant nationalist groups to enlist substantial support in nonwhite communities stems from their inability to deal effectively with the double identity of subordinates—they are members of both a minority group and of the American nation. For example, the great majority of blacks regard themselves as Americans and reject the idea of a new and separate black nation (Marx, 1967). "We built up this one," a black electrician told a survey interviewer. "This is my country. This is the only country I ever knew," was the way a heavy-equipment operator in Pittsburgh put it (Marx, 1967). Thus the majority of blacks want to be part of America, not apart from it, and this desire, too, greatly distinguishes them from colonial populations. Finally, blacks do not occupy a province or region that is attached to the United States. Instead, they are scattered throughout the nation. Thus, whether in conflict or harmony, it would seem that whites and nonwhites have no choice but to live together.

Despite its flaws, the internal-colony concept serves to make us aware that nonwhite minorities are being exploited. As will be argued later, disadvantaged minority groups in the past, such as the Irish, the Jews, and the Japanese, have overcome their circumstances primarily by possessing or creating a *strong community* able to seize control of its own economic and political fate. To the extent that nationalism and the insights of the internal-colony idea can aid blacks, Chicanos, and other nonwhite minorities in community building, they will importantly contribute to social changes.

SOCIOLOGICAL EXPLANATIONS: MIDDLE RANGE

So far, we have concentrated on very general features of the American value and economic systems. We now raise more specific questions. What accounts for the fact that some racial and cultural groups are presently in subordinate positions in our society and others are not? What social processes account for the present circumstances of groups such as blacks and Chicanos, on the one hand, and the Jews, Japanese, and Italians, on the other?

Immigration and Social Position

In order to understand the present situation of subordinate groups in the United States, it is necessary first to see how subordinate groups typically have gained equality in the past. Then we will be able to see whether the position of present minorities is similar to or different from that of earlier groups and whether the same patterns for achieving equality can be used.

The United States was founded through imperialism. The original English, French, and Spanish colonists used their superior technology to displace the Native Americans who, for thousands of years, had been the only inhabitants of the New World. Subsequent wars and land purchases established the United States as an English-speaking nation. However, new settlers soon began to arrive from other European nations. Few spoke English. And most, having come to escape poverty, were extremely poor. Each new nationality group found itself on the bottom of the economic and social ladder. But because the nation to be settled was large and because industrialization was rapidly growing, the new groups quickly found opportunities for economic advancement, and their children found it easy to feel they were Americans.

Later waves of immigrants found it harder to make their way in the United States. In the 1840s, millions of Irish arrived, fleeing the potato famine that ravaged the population of Ireland. The Irish found the going harder. They were unskilled, extremely poor, and Roman Catholic. They faced widespread hostility and intense discrimination (Duff, 1971).

Following the Irish, each new wave of immigrants posed more severe problems for the belief that newcomers would find their place in American society by assimilating. Like the Irish, the Italians, Poles, Greeks, Czechs, Hungarians, Russians, and Jews had no intention of changing their religion. Unlike the Irish, they were not English-speaking, and many of them had dark skins. Furthermore, among the newcomers were Asians who not only were of a different religion, culture, and language but also were members of a different race.

Extremely hostile sentiments were aroused in the dominant WASP society by the continued entry of these "different" people into the nation. On the West Coast, people were panicked by fears of the "Yellow Peril"—a vision of wave after wave of Asia's masses flooding the land and swamping the WASP culture. In the East, anger was directed against Jews, Italians, and Eastern Europeans.

Immediately following World War I, new immigration laws were enacted. These not only greatly reduced the total number of new immigrants permitted to enter each year but set quotas that all but eliminated entry of nonwhites and persons from Eastern Europe or the Mediterranean nations. Still, sizable numbers of these groups were already in the country. Most observers doubted that they would ever achieve economic parity or social acceptance. Yet most did.

Several factors appear to have played a critical role in the ability of these minority groups to escape their subordinate status. One important factor seems to have been geographic concentration. Partly because of discrimination in jobs and housing and partly out of a natural tendency to group together for self-help, most new immigrant groups lived in urban ghettos. As a result, they were able to maximize the political impact of their numbers. Indeed, they were often able to take control of, or at least become a major force in, the communities in which they lived. For example, had the Irish scattered across the nation, they would not have been a major voting bloc. But because they were concentrated in Eastern cities, they soon were able to take political control of many of these cities. Such control opened new opportunities, particularly for jobs on the city payroll. The stereotype of the Irish cop reflects the fact that the Irish long dominated civil-service positions in Eastern cities. Similarly, Jews did not scatter throughout the country but concentrated in major cities, especially in New York City. New York's three million Jewish voters are a small portion of the national vote, but they are a force to be reckoned with in New York elections. Even though minority concentration in the center city today fosters alienation and isolation, most new immigrant groups were able to find the political muscle to affect their social situation. They also were able to control institutions such as the local schools and adapt them to their special needs.

A second factor influencing the fate of a subordinate group is capital accumulation, and here again geographic concentration has played a major role. A group must develop sufficient economic independence from the dominant group in order to finance their own future. Fundamentally, economic independence means buying within the group (so that wealth can be retained) and reinvesting in operations beneficial to the economic position of the group. Physical concentration is important because a typical first step is to acquire the stores and shops serving the group. Without concentration, it would be difficult or impossible for the group to use its buying power to acquire the stores where they shop. A second step is to create their own financial institutions—banks, investment groups, and the like. This makes it possible to avoid discrimination by financial institutions controlled by the dominant group. At the turn of the century, a small neighborhood savings bank—the Bank of Italy—was vital to the economic progress of San Francisco's Italian community. By concentrating savings in its own bank, the San Francisco Italian community was able to fund its own members in aquiring and operating businesses. The ultimate success of this strategy is nicely told: After a few years this little bank changed its name to Bank of America, and under the control of its founder Amadeo P. Giannini, it became the largest privately owned bank in the world.

A third vital factor in the fate of a subordinate group is whether it develops (or has) a middle class. To progress, a group must have members trained in the professions, able to run businesses and financial institutions, and able to provide effective community leadership. Some groups arriving in America already had a sizable middle class, and their progress was relatively rapid (the Jews, Cubans, and Japanese, for example). Others (the Italians and Poles, for example) have progressed more slowly because they had to build a middle class after they arrived (Steinberg, 1974).

These factors have allowed many immigrant groups to achieve economic and social equality in America. The system is loose enough so that some groups, by building their own institutions based in the community, have prospered despite the antagonism of the dominant majority. But the question remains: Are such strategies possible and likely to prove effective for the subordinate minorities in America today?

Nonwhite Minorities As Immigrants

In recent years, there has been considerable opposition to making comparisons between the situation of nonwhite minorities and immigrant groups. One reason has been that such comparisons were often unfair—white ethnic groups have dismissed the plight of nonwhite minorities by saying "we had it tough too" and by implying that if blacks, Chicanos, and other minorities could not make it on their own "like we did," it must be due to laziness or lack of ability. Indeed, the fact that blacks in particular are not recent immigrants seems to challenge the idea that they can overcome their subordinate position in the same way that ethnics did. Many have concluded that race is a more severe basis than culture for intergroup conflict (race, as we have noted, involves differences that are visible).

It is true that blacks are not newcomers. As early as 1680, the majority of blacks in the United States were native born, and by the time of the American Revolution, 80 percent of blacks were native born. Many of them were fourth or fifth generation Americans (Fogel and Engerman, 1974). Unlike others arriving in the United States, blacks were not immigrants. They were slaves brought here against their will and held in bondage thereafter. In the process, they lost most of their original cultures. For decades following the Civil War, the conditions under which blacks lived changed little—they remained poverty-stricken farm laborers and tenant farmers in the American South. Indeed, the most recent evidence suggests that the position of blacks declined substantially after emancipation—that the diet, housing, and even income of the average black was worse in the late nineteenth century than it had been during slavery (Fogel and Engerman, 1974).

During World War I, blacks began to leave the remote rural South for the cities, and many began

319

to move north. They moved because wartime industry offered new employment opportunities and because the conditions of rural life were getting even worse. Black migration grew rapidly during the 1920s, dropped off during the Depression, and took on massive proportions following World War II. Between 1950 and 1969, about 2.3 million black Southerners moved north. Mechanization of Southern agriculture, a shift of the cotton industry from the South to the West and the Southwest, and strict segregation laws all played major roles in pushing blacks out of the rural South.

Today, more blacks live outside than inside the South. Furthermore, from having been an overwhelmingly rural population only a few years ago, blacks are now more urban than whites. The twelve largest American cities now contain over two-thirds of the black population living outside the South and one-third of all American blacks. Today more blacks live in New York City than in any single Southern state, and more live in Chicago than in the state of Mississippi. Like white migrants from the rural areas, blacks moving to the city tend to be poorly educated, not only in comparison with whites, but also in comparison with urban-born blacks (Lieberson, 1970). Like all rural migrants, they lack training for skilled jobs.

Stanley Lieberson (1970) has severely criticized research on blacks for failing to control for whether they were raised in rural or urban areas or in the North or the South. Lieberson pointed out that studies of white ethnic groups automatically take account of differences among first, second, and third generation Americans because these differences are often important. For example, the remarkable increase in the average education of Japanese American men between 1940 and 1960 (from 8.8 years to an average of 12.5 years of schooling) was almost wholly due to a great decline in the proportion of foreign-born Japanese. And the average education of those Japanese males who were born in the United States was already 12.2 in 1940. By the same token, the average income and education of urban blacks in the North is considerably lower because large numbers of rural-born blacks are counted. Lieberson suggests that black migration to cities be regarded in much the same way as immigration. (The same principle

may be applied to whites who migrate to the cities from rural areas.)

The point is that present-day nonwhite minorities are in many ways recent immigrants. To move to New York from rural Alabama may be more like moving there from rural Ireland or Italy than it is like moving there from Boston. Like many earlier immigrant groups, blacks moving out of rural areas are extremely poor. They lack education and marketable skills and must become familiar with a different culture. By the same token, Chicanos have recently moved from remote rural areas of the Southwest to the cities of the West and Southwest. In many ways, they, too, are immigrants rather than migrants. Indeed, many must learn English in the same way that most immigrant groups had to learn it. In addition, many Chicanos are recent immigrants from Mexico. Puerto Ricans, too, are recent immigrants.

It would be wrong to draw too many parallels between the success of earlier immigrants—in economic equality and acceptance—and the present circumstances of American minority groups. Nearly all successful immigrant groups were white. They did not have to deal with a society that, because of its involvement in slavery, had embraced vicious beliefs about the inferiority of nonwhite races. Indeed it is the historical legacy of slavery and the persistence of racism that puts blacks in the position of being poverty-stricken migrants to the city so many generations after their forebears first arrived on these shores.

Similarly, Native Americans owe their present subordinate position to racist elements in American culture that defined good Indians as dead Indians, that hunted them down and drove them onto reservations. As we have pointed out, racial differences present a more stubborn problem than do religious or ethnic and cultural differences. Catholics could claim to be Protestants or even become Protestants. Germans could learn English. But blacks, Chicanos, Puerto Ricans, and Native Americans cannot change their biology. Their easy identification as nonwhites makes it hard for them to seize opportunities that were open to white immigrants. Perhaps the best hope that race poses only a difficult problem, not an impossible one, is that the Japanese have so quickly overcome their

Figure 10.6   A society can, and usually does, transmit a great deal of prejudice to children. Children are seldom taught such overt racist dogma as that of the Ku Klux Klan (above). Usually children learn prejudices through various mechanisms of socialization—observing others, subtle rewards and punishments, and identification. In fact, these are the means by which children acquire any cultural norms, values, and attitudes.

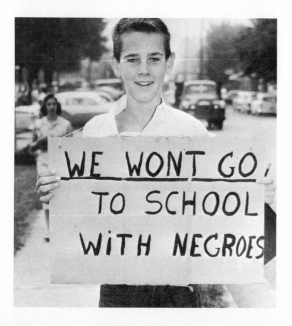

economic and social disadvantages, despite being nonwhites. But it is also important to keep in mind that the Japanese came here from an advanced industrial nation and never endured slavery.

Nevertheless, many recent efforts in the black community, loosely identified as the "black-power" movement, are directed at precisely those goals we have noted as basic to the progress of earlier successful groups. Blacks have recently found that their concentration in the large cities has made them a powerful local political force able to elect mayors and congressmen. Black parents are trying to make the schools responsive to the needs of their children, much as earlier ethnic groups did. Blacks recognize the need to develop their own financial institutions and to buy goods and services from black-owned businesses.

However, one problem faced by today's subordinate minorities was not faced by earlier immigrant groups—the lack of a market for unskilled labor. In earlier times the unskilled first generation of immigrants could find work. It was often dirty, hard work with bad pay. But it was work. Today, simple willingness to do hard work has little market value. As we have seen, unemployment and underemployment are so high among minority members they must resort to welfare for survival. But, the welfare system can contribute to family instability because usually families are excluded from welfare if there is an able-bodied man in the household, regardless of whether he can find work. Many fear that the black family has undergone severe damage as a result of these requirements of the welfare system and that the system continues to impede black liberation.

SOCIAL-PSYCHOLOGICAL SOURCES

We now examine human beings in their immediate social situations to see how prejudice and discrimination are both made and unmade. The underlying premise is that both bigotry and brotherhood are learned.

Intergroup Contact

At the beginning of this chapter, we pointed out that a critical factor in relations between dominate and subordinate groups is their lack of contact,

321

which creates a vacuum in which negative stereotypes and attitudes can flourish, unchallenged by experience. Such isolation easily creates negative attitudes, as Muzafer and Carolyn Sherif have demonstrated in a classic experiment (1953). The Sherifs worked with young boys attending summer camp. On a number of occasions they separated boys into groups, taking care to see that prior friendships were broken up by putting friends in different groups. These groups (the Bears, the Wolves, and so forth) made up the basic camp units for purposes of sports competition and the like. The Sherifs found that within only a few days, hostile stereotypes developed—"All Bears are liars," "All Wolves are cry-babies." However, they found that when activities requiring cooperation replaced competitive activities, these negative intergroup feelings and beliefs tended to dissolve. The Sherifs' experiment offers a basic insight into intergroup relations: Contact alone will not reduce intergroup conflicts; what is important is what kind of contact occurs.

In his classic study of prejudice (*The Nature of Prejudice,* 1954), Gordon W. Allport identified four critical features that influence whether contact between groups will decrease or increase prejudice: (1) Prejudice will decrease if contact occurs under conditions of equal status. But it will increase or remain high if contact follows a dominant-subordinate pattern. (2) Contact will be beneficial to the extent that members of both groups are pursuing common goals; (3) if they are dependent upon one another rather than in competition for goals; and (4) if the contact is given support by authorities, laws, or norms.

Hundreds of years of contact between whites and blacks in the South did not improve race relations because contact occurred under conditions of unequal status, because the economic situation created conflict, and because racism was upheld in law and local customs. On the other hand, race relations did improve when President Harry S. Truman ordered an end to segregation and discrimination on American merchant ships; whites became less prejudiced to the extent that they voyaged with black seamen holding equal rank (Brophy, 1945–1946). White policemen who work with black policemen also become more favorable

Figure 10.7   Various methods have been used to intimidate blacks (left) *or to discredit them; for example, labeling Martin Luther King a communist was one tactic used by white segregationists* (above). *Methods to improve race relations, on the other hand, must work to undo prejudices.* (Right) *Role playing is often an effective way to increase tolerance, understanding, and empathy between groups. In this interracial group, white policemen and black militants met with the ultimate goal of increasing cooperation and reducing tensions in the community; role playing was one technique used to achieve that end. The members of each group "exchanged races" by wearing a white or black mask and playing the role of a member of the other race. In this way, each person had the opportunity to directly experience the behavior, attitudes, and self-concept generated in members of the other group by the roles society assigns.*

to desegregation than do policemen who do not have such contact (Kephart, 1957). However, white policemen become more prejudiced against blacks if they are assigned to duty in black neighborhoods where contact is, of course, not on an equal basis and where goals are in conflict (Black and Reiss, 1967).

Differential Association and Social Learning

Studies of contact between groups show that you can change prejudiced attitudes if you can expose groups to one another in an appropriate situation. The technique is especially successful if a person is removed from a group where prejudice and discrimination are rewarded and placed in a new group where these are frowned upon. For example, many prejudiced whites quickly adjust when they must deal with blacks on equal terms in settings such as the army or college, where tolerant norms prevail. However, whether such changes will last depends on whether the person remains in such situations or returns to situations like the ones that created his or her initial prejudice. Thus, many Southern whites formed firm friendships with

blacks in the service, but they soon renewed racist views and practices after returning home (Stouffer *et al.,* 1949). Similarly, many whites with liberal racial views in college adopt more conservative ones later after living in suburbia for a time.

Attitudes toward others therefore depend not only on contact with those others but on the attitudes learned in one's social situation. A bigot is likely to be a person who has grown up in a prejudiced family, has prejudiced friends, lives in a community where discrimination is sustained by law or custom, and has experienced subordinate-group members only as social inferiors or competitors.

PSYCHOLOGICAL SOURCES

Perhaps most social-science efforts to understand intergroup conflict have been concentrated at the level of individual psychology. In keeping with the emphasis on individualism in the American outlook, for a long time our general reaction to prejudice was to search the individual human heart, or "conscience." And, to Americans, efforts aimed

323

at changing the human heart have seemed less socially disruptive than have efforts to change laws or economic institutions.

One drawback to the research done on the prejudiced personality is that studies have often shown that prejudiced attitudes often do not lead to discriminatory behavior, whereas tolerant attitudes are often held by persons who nonetheless engage in or condone discrimination (Merton, 1949a). The reason for this seeming paradox should be clear from the previous section: People often conform to the norms of the social setting in which they find themselves, regardless of what their personal preferences are.

Nevertheless, prejudiced attitudes and other personality factors do play some significant role in intergroup conflict. Thus, it seems worthwhile to review several of the more important lines of research into these factors.

Scapegoating

324

It is easily seen that individuals often use others as *scapegoats*—that people blame their own failures, troubles, and frustrations on others. For example, a chronically unemployed white may explain his troubles by claiming that "the niggers get all the good jobs these days." The underlying force behind scapegoating is believed to be the process of frustration-aggression. When frustration produces aggression, the argument goes, people do not just vent their aggression at any available target. Instead, they most often direct it toward those whose capacity to fight back is limited—toward weak victims. Subordinate-group members are attractive targets for aggression because they are less able to strike back (Dollard *et al.*, 1939).

The award-winning television play, *The Autobiography of Miss Jane Pittman* (CBS, 1974) shows the frustration-aggression-scapegoating process in a scene set during the Civil War. Young Jane and a younger black boy, walking toward Ohio to a new life after their emancipation from slavery, ask a distraught white woman for water. The white woman refuses to give them water and threatens to unleash her growling dog on them unless they leave immediately. Jane, a determined girl of about ten, stands her ground and says, "It is only water we want." The white woman, who has lost

her husband and her son at the hands of Yankee soldiers releases a tirade of verbal abuse on Jane and the young boy, screaming "I hate you! I hate all you Niggers! You are to blame for the death of my son and my man. I hate all you damn foul-mouthed niggers."

Clearly, Jane Pittman was not to blame for this woman's personal losses. But in the mind of the white woman, she was indeed to blame. Her emotional outburst was a form of scapegoating through which her hatred of Yankee soldiers—who would be untouched by her aggression—was vented on two black children.

It seems clear enough that scapegoating often plays an important role in prejudice. However, as an explanation of prejudice, it has several obvious weaknesses. First, frustration does not always lead to aggression. Second, people do not always displace their aggression onto scapegoats. Often enough, they vent their aggression on the real source of their frustration. Third, this theory only enters into intergroup conflict if subordinate racial or cultural groups exist. The theory does not say anything about why blacks or Jews or some other distinctive group constitutes an available source of scapegoats, that is, why such groups are in a subordinate status.

Authoritarianism

Perhaps the most famous single work on prejudice was done in Berkeley following World War II and was published as *The Authoritarian Personality* (Adorno *et al.*, 1950). The authors argued that prejudice satisfies deeply felt psychological needs of persons who have a rigid personality structure. Such persons are deeply fearful of and submissive to authority and have very low tolerance for ambiguity, or confusion. So, they value conventional behavior and become easily threatened and angered by any deviation from it. The prejudice of the *authoritarians* helps reduce the fear and threat they experience when they encounter persons who deviate from the religious, racial, or cultural standards that authoritarians think are normal. By holding such persons in contempt, authoritarians escape the need to question their own beliefs. The Berkeley group argued that this kind of authoritarian personality develops in early childhood, mainly

Fascism (*F*) Scale:
Obedience and respect for authority are the most important virtues children should learn.

Most of our social problems would be solved if we could somehow get rid of the immoral, crooked, and feebleminded people.

No sane, normal, decent person could ever think of hurting a close friend or relative.

Sex crimes, such as rape and attacks on children, deserve more than mere imprisonment; such criminals ought to be publicly whipped, or worse.

Ethnocentrism (*E*) Scale:
The many political parties tend to confuse national issues, add to the expense of elections, and raise unnecessary agitation. For this and other reasons, it would be best if all political parties except the two major ones were abolished.

There will always be wars because, for one thing, there will always be races who ruthlessly try to grab more than their share.

Anti-Semitism (*A-S*) Scale:
Jewish power and control in money matters is far out of proportion to the number of Jews in the total population.

Jews tend to remain a foreign element in American society, to preserve their old social standards and to resist the American way of life.

Politico-Economic Conservatism (*PEC*) Scale:
A child should learn early in life the value of a dollar and the importance of ambition, efficiency, and determination.

A political candidate, to be worth voting for, must first and foremost have a good character, one that will fight inefficiency, graft, and vice.

Figure 10.8 Sociologists have developed many scales to measure public beliefs and attitudes. Persons are asked to agree or disagree with a series of statements such as these shown above. Statistical analysis of the answers given to these questions makes it possible to assess the extent of beliefs such as anti-Semitism or political conservatism in the population. Frequently, one set of items (combined to form an attitude scale) is used to predict scores on another set in order to determine possible relationships between them. For example, many research studies have found a strong relationship between the Facism Scale and the Anti-Semitism Scale.

as a result of harsh, rigid parental discipline. The authors developed a scale—the *F* scale (or facist scale)—to identify those persons who have authoritarian personalities.

In the quarter century since Adorno's influential work was published, the *F* scale has been used in more than 1,000 research studies, many of them on prejudice. It is well established that persons scoring high on authoritarianism are especially likely to hold harsh prejudices against persons of different religions, races, and ethnic backgrounds. However, there is now considerable doubt that authoritarianism is a personality trait developed in childhood and that it is the factor that is responsible for producing prejudice.

A major blow to the theory was delivered by Gertrude Selznick and Stephen Steinberg (1969). Their research suggests that *both* authoritarianism and prejudice result from a lack of exposure to the cultural diversity of life and that lack of education is a key factor. Through education, people overcome the narrow view of life that comes from having experienced only the norms and styles of their own group—they become aware of the immense variation in customs and culture that characterizes the world. It is only through such experience that people overcome a natural tendency to think that their way of life is the only permissible and workable way. When an individual's education is taken into account, there appear to be no connections between his or her family background and authoritarianism (Selznick and Steinberg, 1969).

Table 10.1 Prejudice by Level of Education in the United States

EDUCATION COMPLETED	PERCENT WHO ARE PREJUDICED AGAINST BLACKS
Grade School	68
High School	49
Some College	32
College Graduate	23

Source: Adapted from Gertrude J. Selznick and Stephen Steinberg, *The Tenacity of Prejudice* (New York: Harper & Row, 1969).

Table 10.1 shows the powerful relationship between education and prejudiced attitudes against blacks. The overwhelming majority of white American adults with only grade-school educations are prejudiced. The overwhelming majority of college graduates are not. Of all factors that have been studied, education has by far the largest impact on prejudice.

PHYSIOLOGY AND INTERGROUP CONFLICT

Because race is presently the main basis for intergroup conflict in the United States, it is clear that

325

physiology plays an important role. Because of physiology, we can see racial differences. But such differences in themselves do not explain why conflict is generated. Race acts to divide our society because of the *cultural meanings* given to biological differences. Racism occurs when biological *differences* between races are interpreted as evidence of the biological *inferiority* of some race.

Earlier in this chapter, we pointed out that racism was used to make slavery and racial subordination acceptable, in spite of values of equality and freedom. By defining blacks as an inferior species, white Americans could justify their bondage (the same device was used to explain and excuse the conquest of the Native Americans). Notions that nonwhites were biologically inferior were held not only by Southerners or slave owners but also by abolitionists (Fogel and Engerman, 1974).

For generations, the battle against racism has focused on establishing the common humanity and biological equality of all races. Today, crude biological doctrines of racial inequality are quickly discredited—only a few disgruntled hate merchants still warn about tainting white blood with black or claim that nonwhites are lower on the ladder of ascent from the apes.

Nevertheless, during the past several years, a bitter and profound controversy has raged in social science over claims that blacks, as a group, are genetically endowed with less intelligence than whites. Because these claims have been made by respectable social scientists, not by kooks, their potential impact on racial attitudes is great. These claims of genetic inferiority have outraged blacks and have been seized upon gleefully by white racists. Thus, it is vital to examine the case.

For a long time, it has been known that blacks achieve a somewhat lower average score on IQ tests than whites do. For nearly as long a time, it was generally assumed by social scientists that these differences meant nothing more than that blacks had been the victims of many cultural deprivations—poor education, poverty, dull rural life, the miseries of slum life, and the like. And, in fact, studies showed that some of these factors, when taken into account, reduced the difference between black and white average IQ scores. For example, there is a smaller difference between

326

Figure 10.9 Levels of Analysis and Issues Appropriate to Each Level. This summary chart does not cover all the important points raised in the chapter. Use it only to review what you have read. Page numbers are given for the full discussion of any topic.

whites and blacks living in the North than between whites and Southern blacks. However, no study thus far has isolated enough environmental factors to eliminate all IQ differences between the races. But it is important to know that so far only a few crude measures of only some important environmental factors have been available in these studies. Thus, efforts to show that the relationship between IQ and race is spurious have only begun. A major block to research in this area is that very large samples are necessary. Satisfactory IQ tests are also expensive to administer. So, well-designed studies in this area would be extremely expensive and funding has not been available.

Nevertheless, despite the inadequacy of available data, in 1969 Arthur Jensen was asked by the *Harvard Educational Review* to assess the present state of knowledge on interracial IQ differences. Instead of concluding that appropriate controls for obvious environmental differences between blacks and whites had not yet been applied, Jensen turned to genetics to interpret the relationship. It is well established that some portion of IQ is inherited. It is also well established that some portion is the result of environment—identical twins reared apart have more similar IQs than do unrelated people, but their IQs are not as similar as those of identical twins raised together. Jensen was impressed by the fact that there is some genetic component in IQ and by the obvious fact that there are genetic differences between whites and blacks. He therefore argued that genetic differences cause the differences in average IQ that remain when these crude environmental controls are applied to the data. Hence, he predicted that even when all traces of racism and disadvantage are rooted out of society, blacks would, on the average, still lag a bit behind whites in terms of IQ.

Had Jensen been discussing some trivial difference between races such as height, most scholars

Levels	Appropriate Questions	A Partial Synopsis of Present Conclusions
Societal	Historically, did the American commitment to equality encourage racism?	Yes. In order to square the ideal that "all men are created equal" with the fact of continued slavery, it was necessary to deny the humanity of blacks. (pp. 312–314)
	Do values of individualism work against subordinate groups in America?	Probably. Americans are inclined to blame the unsuccessful for their lack of progress. (pp. 313–314)
	Is economic conflict at the heart of dominant-subordinate group relations?	Yes. Prejudice and conflict subside only after a subordinate group has achieved economic equality. (pp. 314–316)
	Do theories of colonialism apply to the situation of subordinate groups in America.	Yes and no. They do illuminate the fact that the basic institutions affecting subordinate groups are externally controlled but do not provide useful solutions where subordinate groups do not represent a numerical majority. (pp. 316–317)
Sociological: Middle Range	Do today's subordinate groups resemble recent immigrants?	To some extent. Moving to cities in the North or West from rural areas in the South or Southwest may be more like immigrating from another country than like migrating within the same country. (pp. 318–321)
	Does prejudice against nonwhites today make it more difficult for them than it was for earlier white subordinate groups to achieve equality?	Probably, in that nonwhites cannot escape their circumstances by passing as members of the majority. However, the Japanese have rapidly achieved economic equality despite being nonwhite and being the object of intense prejudice. Race may be a more severe obstacle for blacks than for other nonwhite groups, however, because of the historical legacies of slavery and racist beliefs. (pp. 310–312; 317–321)
Social-Psychological	Does contact between groups lead to improved relations?	Not necessarily. It depends upon the kind of contact that occurs. Contact lessens prejudice only if the groups are interacting as equals, are pursuing common goals, and are dependent upon one another. (pp. 321–323)
Psychological	Is scapegoating an important element in prejudice?	Only if groups already occupy a subordinate position. (p. 324)
	Is authoritarianism a cause of prejudice?	Authoritarianism and prejudice are probably not causally related; instead, both probably stem from lack of education and insufficient exposure to cultural diversity. (pp. 324–326)
Physiological	Do blacks score lower, on the average, than whites do on standard IQ tests?	At present this is the case. However, there is *no* support for the belief that this reflects a genetic difference between whites and blacks. It is likely that this difference is caused by the conditions under which American blacks live and not likely that it is a cause of the subordinate position of blacks. (pp. 326–328)

would have taken a wait-and-see attitude. While many would have pointed out that present evidence is not conclusive and others would no doubt have dismissed his claims as sheer guesswork, the question would have lacked urgency. But in a society struggling with a long legacy of racism, claims that blacks are genetically less intelligent than whites are bound to be inflammatory. Thus, Jensen's work has rightfully provoked a storm of angry criticism. Some of these attacks have been beside the point. For example, whether or not Jensen is a secret racist has no bearing on the truth or falsity of his case. However, it is urgent for everyone to realize that his case is based on many unproven and unlikely assumptions. For one, Jensen assumes that IQ tests developed with white populations are equally valid when used to test blacks. It is far from clear that these tests are valid measures of intelligence for blacks.

But Jensen's most glaring error was that he took the failure of a few inadequate attempts to find environmental sources for *all* the differences between the average IQ of blacks and whites and concluded that no future efforts would succeed. But many important environmental factors have not yet been assessed.

For example, we know that black infants display many signs of the fact that black mothers tend to have worse diets that white mothers. On the average, black infants have a lower birth weight than white infants. They also suffer higher infant mortality and a higher rate of birth defects (Watson and Lowrey, 1967). But when black and white infants who weighed the same at birth are compared, these differences disappear (Rush, 1972). The mother's diet is the major cause of these birth-weight differences and thus of higher black infant mortality and birth defects. This is clear evidence that the economic deprivations of blacks take a physical toll on their offspring. Yet, nutrition was not controlled in the studies Jensen relied on for his argument. Nor have such studies had any means for taking account of the damage racism can do to self-confidence and motivation. We cannot find American blacks who grew up in an environment free of racism to compare with whites in terms of IQ. By ignoring such untested environmental explanations and proclaiming his speculations about genetic dif-

ferences as scientific knowledge, Jensen wrongfully, and needlessly, rekindled the old racist beliefs that once permitted Americans to condone slavery.

PART III: RESPONSES INTERGROUP CONFLICT

We come now to the question of how our various social, economic, and government institutions have responded to prejudice and discrimination. What steps have these institutions taken toward correcting or alleviating these problems?

LEGISLATIVE AND COURT ACTION

At the state and local levels of government, some efforts have been made to reduce discrimination. For example, laws for fair employment practices have been passed to assure greater equality in access to jobs as well as in wages earned. However, in the United States, what happens at the local and state levels, to a large degree, depends on leadership—both moral and financial—from the federal government. The actions of Congress and the Supreme Court in the areas of education, employment, housing, and political freedom have played the major role in shaping policies that increase equality of opportunity for minority groups. Most Supreme Court decisions and congressional legislation on civil rights grew out of efforts to improve the status of America's black population. The following discussion thus focuses on the struggle of black Americans to destroy slavery and legalized racism. It is important to realize that in each case a change in the legal status of black Americans generally meant improved status for all disadvantaged minorities. Where discrimination was banned by the government, it was banned against all individuals, regardless of race, color, or national origin.

Reconstruction Legislation

Following the Civil War (1861–1865), there was a flurry of civil rights legislation that was designed to transform former slaves into free persons and to grant them all the rights and privileges of citizenship. The Thirteenth Amendment (1865) freed all slaves who were not freed under President Lincoln's Emancipation Proclamation of 1863. The Fourteenth Amendment (1868) declared that former slaves were citizens and thus had the right to equal protection and due process under the law. The Fifteenth Amendment (1870) granted the new citizens the right to vote. These amendments became known as the Reconstruction Amendments because they were designed to reorder American society and make it more egalitarian.

The Civil Rights Act of 1866 was the first federal law designed to protect the civil rights of American blacks. It not only declared that all persons born in the United States were citizens, with the exception of Native Americans, but also gave them certain basic rights: the right to make and enforce contracts; to sue in courts; to inherit, buy, and sell personal property; and to receive the legal protections normally granted all citizens. The law also called for equal punishment for crimes without regard to race or color.

The Civil Rights Act of 1875 was an extension of the 1866 Act. Whereas the 1866 Act stressed political equality, the 1875 Act emphasized social equality. It guaranteed "full and equal" access to public accommodations, such as inns, public transportation, theaters, and amusement places. It let blacks serve on juries. The law also outlined ways to enforce the Act and described the responsibilities of courts, district attorneys, and other officials. This Act was the only piece of civil rights legislation enacted by the American Congress for almost a full century. And it was destined to be set aside less than twenty-five years following its enactment.

The Reassertion of White Dominance

During those twenty-five years, a pattern of institutional racism grew up and became part of American life. The dominance of whites over blacks was written into the law and was supported by social custom. Those opposed to black rights enacted anticivil rights legislation in several states. They resorted to violence, through the Ku Klux Klan, in order to keep blacks from exercising their constitutional rights. They used political and economic clout wherever possible. The results of the great political crisis of 1876, the so-called Compromise

of 1877, showed that the federal government had not followed through with its responsibility to protect and safeguard the rights of black people.

By 1896, the widespread attack against the equality of blacks that had been partly realized during the Reconstruction period was in full force. In the case of *Plessy v. Ferguson* (1896), the United States Supreme Court upheld the principle of "separate but equal" as it applied to public transportation and facilities. There followed a rash of enactments of "Jim Crow," or "separate but equal," legislation, which quickly extended the principle to all aspects of social and political life. Jim Crowism, based on racial identification, became firmly established.

An Important Court Case

Not until 1954, in *Brown v. Board of Education,* did the Supreme Court declare that the principle of separate but equal was unconstitutional. Again, the specific case in this issue involved only one institution, education. However, the decision had broad impact on all aspects of social life. It dealt a death blow to Jim Crow laws in the United States and promised major changes in institutions as well as norms throughout the social system.

The sweeping changes suggested by the 1954 decision were not to be put into effect without a struggle. States responded with Ordinances of Nullification, anti-NAACP laws, laws that permitted schools to be closed and state funds to be diverted to private white schools. Federal troops had to be called out in some cases to protect the rights of black children to attend school. In September 1957, Central High School in Little Rock, Arkansas, was a case in point. In 1963, federal marshals had to order Alabama's Governor George Wallace, who had blocked an entrance to the University of Alabama, to step aside so that a black female student could enter. (Ironically, a decade later, Governor Wallace would crown a black female as the Homecoming Queen of the University of Alabama, indicating how customs can alter human behavior.) Federal marshals were also called to protect the right of James Meredith to attend law school at the University of Mississippi.

In 1959, after mounting pressure from civil rights groups and human rights groups, Congress

329

passed the first civil rights bill in 100 years. It was aimed at protecting voting rights, and it established the United States Commission on Civil Rights. The Act also provided for a jury trial in criminal contempt suits growing out of civil rights cases.

There were many loopholes in the 1959 law. Accordingly, the 1960 Civil Rights Act was passed to extend the powers of the Civil Rights Commission, to establish means to deal with people who tried to keep blacks from voting, and to guarantee desegregated education to children whose parents were in the armed forces.

The 1960s

The decade of the sixties saw the federal government assert itself in the area of human rights as it had never done before. Again, government action was a response to a large number of pressures, both internal and external. The civil rights movement—a coalition of reform-minded human rights groups—had focused people's attention on the income gap between blacks and whites. The bitter ideological quarrel with the Soviet Union at the same time pressed America to solve problems at home that marred her self-image of liberty and justice.

In reaction to these forces, President Kennedy took the lead by issuing a series of Executive Orders relating to civil rights. The first of these orders, issued in 1961, created the Committee on Equal Employment Opportunity. Steps were also taken toward ending job discrimination by firms that held government contracts. The second Executive Order (1962) announced an end to discrimination in federally financed housing and in the loan policies of federally insured lending institutions. The last of Kennedy's Executive Orders, issued about five months before his assassination in 1963, was meant to make even tougher restrictions against unfair hiring practices by firms that held government contracts.

However, it was under President Lyndon Johnson that the most significant social, political, and economic gains for nonwhite minorities were won. Johnson's call for a sweeping program of social legislation—his Great Society program—led to the enactment of two major civil rights bills. Undoubtedly, the death of President Kennedy in 1963

330

Figure 10.10   (Below) *Governor George Wallace of Alabama congratulates Terry Points, newly elected Homecoming Queen of the University of Alabama, on November 16, 1973. She was the first black to have been named Queen at the desegregated university. Ten years earlier, Governor Wallace had vowed, to the roars of the crowd, "Segregation today. Segregation tomorrow. Segregation forever!" Black students were kept out of the University of Alabama in 1963 by Governor Wallace, shown* (top) *confronting Deputy U.S. Attorney General Nicholas Katzenbach and an aide while reading a proclamation banning two black students from entering the university and* (above) *preventing blacks from entering the university.*

was a key factor in spurring the Congress to move forward in this direction.

The Civil Rights Act of 1964, which had been planned by the Kennedy Administration, provided better protection of citizens' voting rights. It forbade discrimination in hotels, theaters, restaurants, parks, libraries, hospitals, and other public places. It extended the life of the Commission on Civil Rights, and it established the Community Relations Service to help persons or communities attain their civil rights. This act was the most sweeping legislation in the field of civil rights since the Reconstruction Acts.

In 1965, the Voting Rights Act was passed by Congress. Just the year before, violence had erupted over the voter-registration drive in Selma, Alabama. Perhaps in response to the violence and to the fact that large numbers of blacks were kept from voting, this Act banned previously existing literacy tests and other discriminatory tests for voting and gave federal examiners the power to protect voters' rights. Dramatic increases in black voter registration, in black voting, and in the numbers of blacks elected to office followed the enactment of the Voting Rights Act.

The next major government response, the Civil Rights Act of 1968, followed on the heels of urban riots, civil disorders, and increasing pressure from civil rights organizations. In 1965, people had violently demonstrated their frustration over the slow pace of real change. In that year, people looted and burned along the major streets of Watts, the huge black ghetto in central Los Angeles. Watts was only the first of the violent urban explosions that would rock the country for several years. This rising note of militance and the spread of the civil rights movement to areas outside the South changed the direction of civil rights legislation.

For the first time, the civil rights movement was directly facing discrimination and de facto segregation in the North and West. Many white liberals who had been sympathetic to the movement—as long as it attacked institutional racism and segregation in the South—began to withdraw their support. This white backlash was applauded by many black militants who no longer saw a need for white involvement in the movement. Thus, the coalition that had once guided the movement was now

threatened. Efforts to enact civil rights legislation in 1966 and 1967 failed to win sufficient support in both houses of Congress. It was only the race riots that followed the assassination of the Reverend Martin Luther King on April 4, 1968, that persuaded Congress to approve civil rights legislation later in that year.

The most important part of the 1968 measure was its direct outlawing of discrimination in the sale of federally owned or insured housing and in the rental of apartments. Another provision gave additional protection for individuals attempting to integrate schools or housing units. As a result of this measure, a growing number of minorities have been able to get better housing. However, because of the inability of minorities in general to close the income gap between themselves and the white population, only members of the middle class have been able to take advantage of this legislation.

Many other pieces of legislation took effect under the banner of President Johnson's Great Society. Among these measures were the Head Start Programs for preschool children, the College Work Study Program, and the Upward Bound Project. They show the breadth of President Johnson's attempts to foster a more just society for those who are socially disadvantaged.

Other measures taken were those that created the Job Corps, Model Cities program, Manpower Development programs, the Neighborhood Youth Corps, Medicare and Medicaid, Urban Renewal programs, School Lunch programs, Child and Parent Centers programs, and the National Health Centers (Bardolph, 1970).

The election of Richard Nixon as President in 1968 effectively ended nearly a decade of government policy to improve the lot of the poor, deprived, and disadvantaged. Instead, a policy of "benign neglect" was put into effect. Enforcement of school desegregation was mixed and often confused. The President clearly stated his opposition to the busing of children to achieve integrated education. The new emphasis was on stimulating minority businesses and creating the impression that minorities were becoming less dependednt on the federal government.

Alienation of the masses of minorities from the federal government was apparent throughout the

331

five-and-a-half years of the Nixon Administration. Many minority-group members feared that Nixon would use repressive measures to prevent militant demonstrations for civil rights. Many minorities did indeed come to believe that the federal government was "the enemy."

MINORITY POWER MOVEMENTS

Because government institutions are generally slow in pushing for change, some minorities have taken the offensive within the system. The civil rights movement of the late 1950s and 1960s was a coalition of blacks, other minorities, and whites that aimed to improve the status of minority groups in American society. The coalition included the Congress of Racial Equality, the Southern Christian Leadership Conference, the National Urban League, the Anti-Defamation League, the American Jewish Congress, a variety of human rights councils, and representative organizations from other minority groups. The movement began with the Montgomery Bus Boycott of 1956 but received its greatest boost from the sit-ins of college students from North Carolina A & T College in Greensboro in 1960. The sit-ins showed a commitment to activism and a shift toward confrontation and militancy. As a result of the civil rights movement, all the civil rights legislation we have discussed was enacted. The coalition came to an end following the rise of the black power movement in 1968.

The black power movement owes it origins to Stokely Carmichael, who uttered the slogan "black power" while on a freedom march in Mississippi in 1966. The movement was both a call for unity among black people and a strategy that ultimately excluded many white liberals from the movement. Initially, the slogan was received with fear and anxiety by the dominant group because it represented the language of militant extremism. But after these fears had been laid to rest, black power came to be seen as an effort on the part of blacks to improve their economic, political, and social status. This movement led to a new emphasis on blackness and with it black pride and self-acceptance. Slogans such as "black is beautiful" and the use of symbols of blackness, such as

332

Figure 10.11 Dominant groups usually feel threatened by militant groups such as the Black Panthers (shown above is Bobby Rush of Chicago Black Panthers) and the Young Lords (below). Even though the Black Panthers are militant, they patrol their own neighborhoods to protect them from crime because they feel law-enforcement agencies are not doing the job adequately. Earlier white immigrants also found it necessary to organize ethnic protective associations similar to the Black Panthers, Young Lords, Brown Berets, Jewish Defense League, and others.

the wearing of Afro hair styles, dashikis, and African head dress, spread throughout the black community. Also, terms used to express racial identity changed. Thus "black" replaced "Negro" in many circles (although "Negro" was still preferred by some), and "colored" became passé.

New names appeared in the civil rights movement. Among these were Rap Brown, John Lewis, and Julian Bond of the Student Non-Violent Coordinating Committee (S.N.C.C.), and also Floyd McKissick and Roy Ennis of the Congress of Racial Equality (C.O.R.E.). These individuals were spokesmen for an increasingly radical group that aimed at confronting "the system."

Leaders changed among civil rights organizations, and new groups with new ideals emerged. The changes showed the diversity within the American black population (Blackwell, forthcoming). Malcolm X, for example, had influenced many black youths to accept their blackness and identity. After his death in 1965, the message of his speeches of the early 1960s was kept alive by followers in various activist groups. There were *cultural nationalists,* those committed to reestablishing a black cultural heritage; *revolutionary nationalists,* those committed to restructuring the American society in order to effect a redistribution of power; *black separatists,* who ranged from those who demanded a separate black nation-state in the American South to those who demanded community control by blacks; and *assimilationist integrationists,* those committed to the usual ways of entering into mainstream America but demanding a faster pace.

With the success experienced by blacks in the civil rights movement, other minorities began to assert themselves. The Chicano power movement and the resurgence of "red power" among Native Americans are notable examples.

The Chicanos made many inroads with Cesar Chavez, the persistent leader of the United Farm Workers, who improved the rights of Chicano farm workers. His fight against the lettuce and grape growers of the Southwest made other Chicano organizations step up their drive for equal rights.

The Alianza Federal de Mercedes and the Brown Berets, both organized during the 1960s, are the most militant Chicano groups. The Alianza's major goals have been to restore Spanish culture and to reclaim lands that were earlier lost to the dominant white (Anglo) culture. The Brown Berets, whose role is similar to that of the Black Panthers and the Jewish Defense League, have been called the "shock troops" of the Chicano movement. They are committed to self-defense, self-determination, and educational advancement.

In addition, several Chicano organizations were formed or already existed at the time that the civil rights movement was at its height. These organizations range from the militant Alianza to middle-class organizations such as the League of United Latin American Citizens. They focus on educational, social, economic, and political integration and advancement. Together, they are responsible for raising the sense of cultural identity among members of the Chicano movement.

The Native Americans have historically been opposed to the Bureau of Indian Affairs (B.I.A.), but it is only in recent years that they have actively protested against the agency's disregard of their rights. In 1973, their rage led to a violent attack against the Bureau's Washington, D.C., office and a seizure of property in Wounded Knee, South Dakota. Their goal is to achieve a greater share of power and resources for Native Americans. They seek rights to land lost through the breaking of some of the 400 treaties made between them and the federal government. They want better jobs and income; increased equality in educational opportunities; improved health and sanitation conditions; and a more positive response by the federal government after so many years of neglect.

The "red power" movement among Native Americans is relatively recent. But it is a movement that has many supporters among the dominant white population. And that support is likely to continue until their claim to justice is interpreted by white Americans as a threat to their own economic security and power.

THE FUTURE OF RACE RELATIONS

In no nation do minority groups acquire their rights at an even pace. In the United States, the pace has sometimes been quicker after crises, such as the

333

death of a highly respected leader. It may also speed up when the federal government uses force in response to the militant tactics of minority groups. The use of such force can be compared to Soviet methods of quelling political protest. Moreover, the rate at which power relations change largely depends on the government's willingness to enact favorable legislation and then to enforce it.

For the future, however, subordinate groups are not likely to remain placated or satisfied. They will keep insisting on broader participation in the nation's political, social, and economic institutions. They will demand equal protection under the law. They will insist on better housing and health care as well as equal access to quality education. And as the demands of subordinate groups increase, dominant groups are likely to feel endangered or threatened unless ways are found to reduce the tensions of intergroup relations.

334

CHAPTER REVIEW

In order for intergroup conflict to arise, noticeable cultural or physical differences must exist between groups. These differences, if important enough, will foster discriminatory practices on the part of the *dominant group* (those in power) and will ultimately limit intergroup relations. When members of the *subordinate group* (those not in power) recognize these limitations, conflict arises. In an effort to escape subordinate status, groups may work for *pluralism* (peaceful coexistence), *assimilation* (merger with the dominant group), *secession* (total physical isolation), or *militance* (a reversal of the dominant-subordinate positions). The subordination of nonwhite minorities in America involves 16 percent of the population—mostly black. Economically, these people tend to receive less prestigious jobs at lower pay than do members of the dominant group. Unemployment and underemployment rates also contribute to a disproportionately high poverty rate among subordinate groups. Part of this problem stems from the large proportion of minorities that fail to complete high school or college. This is not surprising, however, in view of the substandard school conditions that accompany de facto segregation. Poor housing conditions for minorities have also resulted from de facto segregation, and this, in turn, has reduced the amount of face-to-face interaction that could break down prejudice. These conditions have combined to make many minorities feel they have "little to lose," as control theorists would

Figure 10.12 *Native Americans have begun to assert themselves in recent years. The occupation of Wounded Knee, South Dakota, was as much a symbolic effort as a real action to draw attention to the dissatisfaction of Native Americans with the paternalistic rule of the Bureau of Indian Affairs. Shown above are Dennis Banks* (center), *Clyde Bellecourt* (right), *and an unidentified woman of the American Indian Movement (AIM) at Wounded Knee.*

say. They therefore deviate more often. Minority-group members also appear, more often than whites, to be suspected, apprehended, tried, convicted, and given long sentences.

To a great extent, American ideology has contributed to the problem. In order to resolve the conflict between their commitment to the slave system and their belief in liberty for all, American whites tended to dehumanize blacks, which, in turn, has shaped current views of blacks.

The belief in individualism has also made Americans reluctant to help minorities. Christian brotherhood, however, has helped cross racial lines. Economic conflicts have contributed to a rising hostility on the part of minority members, who are aware that heredity and racial characteristics are important criteria in the distribution of economic rewards. Many feel that they have, in effect, been "colonized" internally and that the first step in shedding subordinate status is to achieve economic independence and separatism. Others are less enthusiastic about ethnic separatism, primarily because they identify with the American system and have internalized the values of individualism that characterize it.

The process of losing subordinate status has been achieved by most of the minority groups who immigrated to this country. Each wave of immigrants faced low status and hostility. However, they were gradually able to improve their stations through their (1) geographic concentration; (2) accumulation of capital; and (3) development of a middle class. Lieberson has drawn a parallel between blacks and other immigrant minorities, but other social scientists claim that the experience of blacks is unique because of their loss of a unique culture and because of the persistence of racism.

How has America responded? During the Reconstruction, blacks were given all the rights of citizenship, but these were effectively removed during the succeeding years by custom as well as by law. Later, when Supreme Court decisions, such as *Brown v. The Board of Education,* tried to alter this pattern, many segregationists tried to obstruct justice. During the 1960s, however, a series of Civil Rights Acts and Executive Orders restored full citizenship to minorities, at least legally. Means of enforcement were provided, as were special improvement programs like Head Start and Upward Bound. Since 1968, emphasis has turned more toward stimulating minority business concerns than toward social legislation. Minority responses in recent years have taken the form mainly of increased awareness and pride on the part of individuals for their membership in a minority group. With this has come the strength to form organizations, to strike, and to demonstrate their desire and intent to reject subordinate status.

SUGGESTED READINGS

Blauner, Robert. *Racial Oppression in America.* New York: Harper & Row, 1972.

Marx, Gary T. *Racial Conflict: Tension and Change in American Society.* Boston: Little, Brown, 1971.

Mason, Philip. *Patterns of Dominance.* New York: Oxford University Press, 1971.

Myrdal, Gunnar. *American Dilemma.* New York: Harper & Row, 1944.

Newman, William N. *American Pluralism: A Study of Minority Groups and Social Theory.* New York: Harper & Row, 1973.

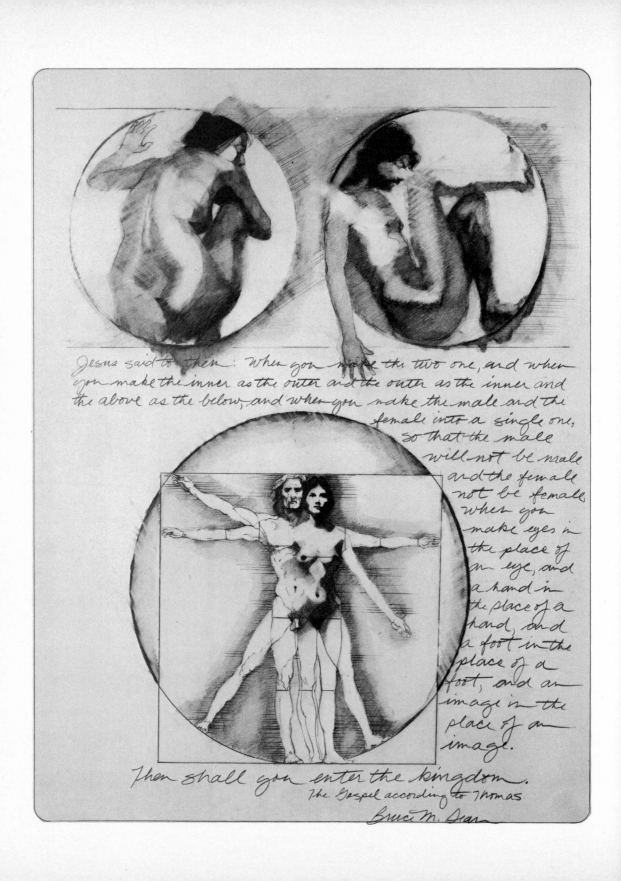

Jesus said to them: When you make the two one, and when you make the inner as the outer and the outer as the inner and the above as the below, and when you make the male and the female into a single one, so that the male will not be male and the female not be female, when you make eyes in the place of an eye, and a hand in the place of a hand, and a foot in the place of a foot, and an image in the place of an image.

Then shall you enter the kingdom.

The Gospel according to Thomas

Bruce M. Sear

11

Sex-Based Inequalities

Male dominance, inherited from our primate ancestors, is as old as the human species. From the beginning, male dominance among humans, like that among other mammals, was probably determined simply by brute strength. Human males are larger than females, and in all primate species, the degree of male dominance over females closely corresponds to the degree to which males are larger and heavier than females.

However, unlike other species, humans have an elaborate *culture*. Through culture we have radically altered the conditions of human existence. We are not limited to expressing our displeasure through growls, grimaces, and assaults. Indeed, brute strength has lost much of its original utility—muscle power is no longer a significant energy source in modern society. In fact, recent cultural changes, especially in technology, have altered and eroded the original conditions on which male dominance over females rested. Continuation of male dominance—now that it has become avoidable—has made women increasingly restive, and recently they have begun to demand equality. Sex-based discrimination and inequality have become our newest social problem.

In this chapter we attempt to develop the theme that *the changes in society that have made sexual equality possible are the same ones that have caused us to define sexual inequality as a social problem*. Thus, as you read the description of the present extent of sex-based inequalities in America, keep in mind that this picture is only a still photograph of a fluid and rapidly changing scene. Rapid change is the dynamic of the problem, of its causes, and of its solution.

PART I: THE PROBLEM
SEX-BASED INEQUALITIES

The problem of sex-based inequality in American society has two fundamental elements. First, there is a rapidly growing *social movement* dedicated to changing our basic conceptions of the terms male and female. Sexual inequality is a major social problem in our time because so many Americans believe it is a problem. Second, there are the actual *conditions* in society: In a great many important ways women are a subordinate group, denied equal status with men. In this section, we examine the development of the movement for women's liberation. Then we examine the changing conditions and grievances that gave rise to the movement. Such grievances reveal the main contemporary features of sexual dominance.

A BRIEF HISTORY
OF THE WOMEN'S MOVEMENT

This is not the first time in our history that women's rights have been a major social problem. To understand the present women's movement, it is instructive to study the rise and fall of an earlier feminist movement that began in the nineteenth century and ended following World War I. This earlier movement developed in both Great Britain and the United States and followed a rather similar pattern in both nations. We will restrict ourselves to the movement in the United States.

Feminist Forerunners

The earlier feminist movement began, in the United States at least, with women who either were active abolitionists, such as Elizabeth Cady Stanton (1815–1902), Lucretia Mott (1793–1880), and Lucy Stone (1818–1893), or were inspired by the abolition (antislavery) movement. The discrimination, both legal and social, that they experienced as women working in the abolition movement awakened them to the need for a women's movement. For example, in 1840 the women members of the American delegation to the World Anti-Slavery Conference in London had been refused seats—an occurrence that serves to remind us that social issues can be very narrowly defined. Such treatment led them to establish (at a conference held at Seneca Falls, New York, in 1848) a movement for the emancipation of women.

The issue of women's rights was not, of course, brand new. Well-to-do city women had been growing restive with their subordinate position for a number of years. For example, at the beginning of the nineteenth century, Mary Wollstonecraft wrote an eloquent essay on the subject of women's rights and their position in society. In 1776, Abigail Adams wrote a letter to her husband, John Adams, warning him that if women's rights was not a high-priority issue, women would make it one. According to sociologist Carol Andreas (1971), many women's clubs and educational groups sprang up among discontented women, chiefly among the wives of Midwestern businessmen in the 1830s. In some experimental communes of the 1830s and 1840s, equality of the sexes was often attempted in all spheres—socially, in work, intellectually, and sexually. During the Civil War, of course, women were important participants in the labor force, doing jobs in support of the war effort and the jobs left vacant by men.

After the war, the "woman question" was widely debated. Many adherents of the women's movement expected that when the right to vote was granted to blacks it would be extended to women as well. Their dismay at the lack of support even from their fellow abolitionists caused some of the spokeswomen to oppose passage of the Fourteenth Amendment to the Constitution, which gave black men the vote and other rights of citizenship.

In the early years of the movement, women's primary tactics were agitating and propagandizing to awaken attention to the injustices they suffered. At first, the feminists faced strong opposition and ridicule. Amelia Bloomer and others who tried to do away with the restrictive, steel-ribbed and whalebone corsets simply earned abuse and the lasting derogatory term "bloomers" for wearing more comfortable clothing. But as the ranks of the feminists steadily grew, their tactics became bolder. They held mass rallies and marches, engaged in civil disobedience, went to jail, and steadily gained support.

In the second half of the nineteenth century, when there was widespread concern about education, many women's colleges were founded. Despite much social opposition, even graduate education and training in professions like medicine and law were opened—although only to *exceptional* women.

From 1868 to 1870, the National Woman Suffrage Association published a weekly newspaper, *The Revolution,* with the motto: "Men, their rights and nothing more; women, their rights and nothing less!" Feminists turned their attention to a

338

great number of issues, including reforms in education, dress, industrial working conditions, religion, marriage, and divorce laws. By the turn of the twentieth century, they also concerned themselves with peace, prohibition of liquor, and economic legislation.

By the time the women's movement entered its second generation, toward the end of the nineteenth century, many of its leaders were educated and professional women, whereas formerly many had been housewives. Many of these new leaders had orthodox views on subjects other than suffrage. Questions of a "new morality," such as that championed by flamboyant Victoria Woodhull (1838–1927), and of a radical rethinking of the

family, such as that put forth by Elizabeth Stanton (who identified domestic slavery as the source of women's oppression), now tended to fade. The country had in the meantime changed from an agrarian society to an industrial one, and the change brought great concern with the evils and ills of city life. Great waves of immigrants reached America, only to suffer in the filth of the cities. Women such as Jane Adams (1860–1935), who might have concentrated their attention on feminist issues, were drawn instead into social work and efforts at social reform—for example, into the child-saving movement discussed in Chapter 6.

As the radicalism went out of the feminist movement the right to vote became the primary

Figure 11.1   The image of women as frivolous sex objects, portrayed in a Keystone Cops movie (top left), changed when women became a necessary part of the work force during World War II (bottom left). However, women's role in the labor force did not win them equal pay for equal work. More and more women are coming to realize that demands for equality cannot be won without concerted action, exemplified by this slogan displayed on the Statue of Liberty.

goal. The main emphasis was placed on the service that "feminine virtues" could provide for government. In the words of Waltraud Ireland (1970), "Women's emancipation had essentially been reduced to the right to vote." During World War I, much of the political rhetoric in America focused on "making the world safe for democracy," and as is usual in war, women also took on many new roles—yet they still were not entitled to a share in that democracy. Late in 1919, after lobbying, demonstrations, and picket lines that resulted in the jailing of militant women, and with the reluctant support of President Wilson, the vote was granted women by passage of the Nineteenth Amendment. But they failed to win broader social reforms.

Shortly thereafter, feminism disappeared as a mass-based social movement. But suddenly in the mid-1960s, the feminist movement was reborn.

The Women's Movement Today

Some commentators date the rebirth of the women's movement from the publication in 1963 of Betty Friedan's book *The Feminine Mystique,* which powerfully stated the grievances of contemporary middle-class women. Certainly this book was of great importance. But books do not create social movements. Indeed, all during the period beginning in 1920, when the women's movement lay dormant, important and eloquent books and articles stating the case for women continued to appear. Among the best were Suzanne La Follette's *Concerning Women* in 1926, Gunnar Myrdal's "A Parallel to the Negro Problem" in 1944, Ruth Hershberger's *Adam's Rib* in 1948, Edith M. Stern's "Women Are Household Slaves" in 1949, Helen Hacker's "Women as a Minority Group" in 1951, and Simone de Beauvoir's *Second Sex*, in 1953. But none of these writings started a social movement. Therefore, Friedan's book seems to have appeared just when conditions were ripe for a movement to occur. What were these conditions?

CONDITIONS OF INEQUALITY

Chapter 1 pointed out that social movements frequently arise when there is a growing discrepancy between the needs and aspirations of some group

and actual (or perceived) social conditions. Alice S. Rossi (1965) pointed out that women had not simply been standing still in terms of equality since the 1920s—they had actually been losing ground. Relative to men, the position of women in American society had been deteriorating. For example, a study by Jessie Bernard (1964) showed that the proportion of women, relative to that of men, in the higher-status professions had actually *decreased* since the turn of the century. There were proportionately fewer women doctors, lawyers, and professors than there had been in 1900. Since these early studies, considerable data have been gathered. These data show that the position of large numbers of American women, relative to the position of men, has been declining for a number of years.

As we shall see, a number of changes combined to bring about a crisis over sex-based inequalities during the 1960s. Four major factors must be considered: (1) changes in women's participation in the labor force; (2) changes in the duties of the wife-mother role; (3) changes in educational achievement accompanied by a widening of pay and status inequalities between men and women; and (4) the persistence of sexist stereotypes.

Women in the Labor Force

Since 1940 there has been a considerable increase in the proportion of women who do full-time or part-time work outside the home. The largest and most significant increases have been in the proportions of working wives and mothers. In 1940, 12.5 percent of white wives held jobs; in 1971, more than 39.7 percent were working. The proportion of working nonwhite wives almost doubled in the same period: 27.3 percent of them worked in 1940, whereas 52.5 percent held jobs in 1971.

Changes were even more marked for mothers (see Figure 11.2). In 1940, only 8.6 percent of mothers were members of the labor force, but by 1967, 38.2 percent of mothers worked (Bernard, 1971a). Some of this increase was accounted for by women entering the labor force after their children were grown, but there were also substantial changes among women with children still at home. Among women with children between the ages of six and seventeen, the proportion who worked rose

Percentage of Mothers in Labor Force

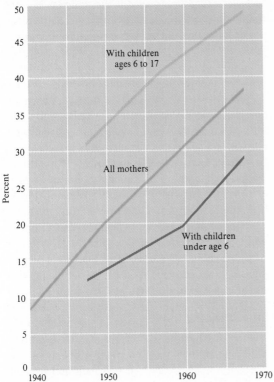

With children
ages 6 to 17

All mothers

With children
under age 6

Percent

1940   1950   1960   1970

Figure 11.2 (Above) *The working mother has become increasingly common in the United States. Although mothers with children under the age of six are still much less likely to work than are mothers with older children, their rate of entry into the labor market has risen as rapidly as the rate of women with older children. These trends are likely to continue (barring massive unemployment), and thus the demand for adequate child-care facilities is likely to grow. Indeed, willingness to demand their rights is a major feature of the new mood among women; (below)* a woman discusses women's rights with a man during a demonstration.

(U.S. Department of Labor, Women's Bureau, 1969.)

from 31 percent in 1947 to 49 percent in 1967. Mothers with children under the age of six more than doubled their participation in the labor force in the same period—their numbers increased from 13 percent working in 1947 to 29 percent working in 1967 (Bernard, 1971a).

The increased numbers of wives and mothers in the labor force created a number of strains. First, although increasing numbers of mothers with young children were working, child care was expensive and hard to find. Second, although many husbands of working women undoubtedly helped out with some domestic chores, such work was not defined as part of the role of husband and father, so most working women were also full-time "homemakers." Third, social disapproval of married women who worked continued to run relatively high. In 1936, 48 percent of the population disapproved, and in 1960, 46 percent disapproved, despite the great changes during this quarter century in the proportions of wives who did take jobs (Oppenheimer, 1969). The pressures on working wives and mothers came to be felt by more and more women who took jobs outside the home.

Perhaps the majority of women who entered the labor force did so out of economic necessity. For example, 32.8 percent of American families below the poverty line are families that have a woman as head of the household (United States Bureau of the Census, 1971). Obviously, such women do not have the choice of being supported by a man. And, to some extent, as we shall see shortly, the poverty of such families stems from the low wages paid women and the low-paying jobs open to them. But in addition to families without a male wage earner are families in which both the husband's and the wife's incomes are required to maintain a modestly comfortable life style. Women in such families must choose between working and having their families do without many of the things that they want and need.

During World War II, women reentered the work force in large numbers, with the active encouragement of spokesmen and propagandists from government and other social institutions, such as churches and schools. "Rosie the Riveter" became a popular symbol of women's capacity to fill traditionally male work roles. Child care was

341

made available, usually at places of work. After the war, official voices (echoed by the media) pressured women to give up their jobs to returning veterans and to resume their former roles, so that the men could find an America "just the way we left it." Child-care facilities closed down as the women left the factories.

Throughout the 1950s and 1960s opinion leaders decreed that the maintenance of the American home was a woman's highest calling and greatest fulfillment. For example, Dr. Benjamin Spock reinforced the newly developing idea that children could not be healthy or intelligent without full-time attention from their mothers.

Woman's role once again was defined almost solely in terms of service rather than productivity. There was concurrent emphasis on the definition of marriage as an institution with an emotional base—romantic love between husband and wife was the cement. Women who did not marry were increasingly branded as loveless or desexualized freaks. The question was posed: "Career or family?" with tacit agreement that a woman could not have both. But, as the Advisory Commission on the Status of Women (1969) has stated, fully 90 percent of women will work at some point in their lives—many, if not most, out of necessity. Cultural mythology and reality obviously are at odds.

Changes in the Role of Wife and Mother

Since the early 1930s, American women have tended to complete their families while they are quite young; the mean age of the American mother at the birth of her last child has been stable at about twenty-six or twenty-seven. Consequently, by the time the average mother is in her middle thirties, she no longer faces the demanding and time-consuming care of small children. Instead she faces the opportunity and perhaps the need to find something else to do with the time she once spent on infant care. In addition, the average life span has increased, so that most women have about forty years of life ahead of them by the time their youngest child begins school.

Labor-saving appliances, services, and products have reduced the time consumed by housekeeping duties. For example, before automatic washers and dryers became widely available after World War

II, and before the development of synthetic fabrics and permanently pressed clothing, wives often spent one full day washing clothes and another full day ironing them. The wife's role has historically included much more than simple child care. The reduction of this role to housecleaner and nurse, plus the possibility of having more leisure time, has led to growing unhappiness among many women, especially those isolated in "bedroom" suburbs. Despite the fact that the role of wife and mother is less time consuming than it used to be, there have been pressures on mothers to build their lives around this role, making it more elaborate and meaningful than it is. Many women naturally find this idea absurd. The reduced requirements of women's family roles has also given increasing numbers of them reason to reenter the labor force. And there they have found that the nature of their jobs and the amount of their pay magnify their frustration and discontent.

Education and Pay

The proportions of Americans completing high school and attending college have increased dramatically over the past few decades. These increases have occurred among both men and women, but men are still considerably more likely than women to obtain higher education. In 1956, 37.7 percent of female high-school graduates went on to college (Bernard, 1964), whereas 54 percent of them did so in 1967 (Harris, 1970). The corresponding percentages for men were 65.6 and 71.

But it is not so much the lag in achieving college educations that has produced discontent among women as the fact that such achievement is so much less rewarded for women than for men. (Chapter 10 pointed out that the same is true for blacks.) Several years ago, the median income of women with bachelor's degrees was approximately equal to that earned by men with eighth-grade educations! Indeed, the median income of women with college degrees is only 61.5 percent of that of men with degrees. This income gap is partly accounted for by the positions women achieve in the labor force. Bernard (1971b) concludes that clerical positions absorbed most of the increase in college-educated working women. These are low-paying, low-prestige, and dead-end occupations:

Earnings by Education for Men and Women

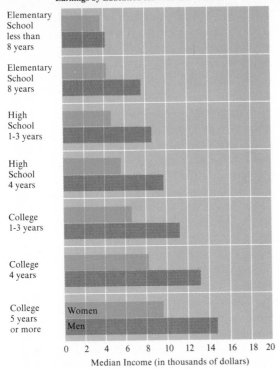

Elementary School less than 8 years

Elementary School 8 years

High School 1-3 years

High School 4 years

College 1-3 years

College 4 years

College 5 years or more

Women

Men

0 2 4 6 8 10 12 14 16 18 20

Median Income (in thousands of dollars)

Figure 11.3 (Above) *The educational level of workers usually determines not only the type of work they do but the level of pay they receive. However, women workers generally earn substantially less than do men who have the same amount of education.*
(U.S. Bureau of the Census, 1971.)

Figure 11.4   The graph below makes it clear that despite recent efforts to secure equal pay for equal work, the income gap between women and men has not been closing.
(U.S. Bureau of the Census, 1971.)

Income Gap Between Men and Women

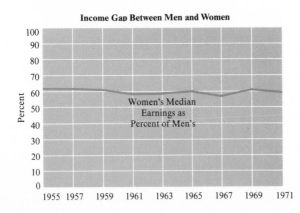

Percent

100
90
80
70
60
50
40
30
20
10
0

Women's Median Earnings as Percent of Men's

1955 1957 1959 1961 1963 1965 1967 1969 1971

typist, file clerk, receptionist. In 1968 more than 48 percent of employed women with from one to three years of college education were in clerical occupations.

It is true that women with degrees are generally employed in professional and technical occupations. However, they are heavily concentrated in the lowest-paying and lowest-status occupations in this group.

Women dominate such occupations as nurse, teacher, social worker, and medical and dental technician, but they are rare in the ranks of doctors, lawyers, and college professors. For example, Rossi (1969) pointed out that although women in 1969 made up 30 percent of doctoral candidates in sociology and 31 percent of sociology students who were also teaching undergraduates, they made up only 14 percent of full-time assistant professors, 9 percent of full-time associate professors, 4 percent of full-time professors, 1 percent of heads of graduate sociology departments, and 0 percent of the forty-four full professors in five elite departments (Berkeley, Chicago, Columbia, Harvard, and Michigan).

By the mid-1960s, then, there had developed a large and growing number of women whose status in terms of educational achievement was far higher than it was in terms of their income and occupational prestige. They were overqualified for the jobs they held. Women who had come, during the process of achieving college degrees, to see themselves as intelligent and socially valuable were assigned boring tasks, were denied authority, and were frequently expected to be office servants—to make the coffee, tidy up the office, run personal errands for the boss, and massage his ego. Worse yet, they often had to accept significantly lower pay than men, and sometimes lower job titles, for identical jobs. The proportion of women attending college continued to increase, and, therefore, so did the number of women caught in statuses that were inconsistent with their level of educational achievement.

Furthermore, as we noted earlier, the position of women relative to men has been getting *worse*. In 1940 working women were slightly more likely than working men to hold jobs in the two highest-status occupational categories—"professional-

343

technical'' and ''managers and officials.'' But as Dean D. Knudsen (1969) has pointed out, by 1969 working men were almost twice as likely as working women to hold these high-paying and high-status jobs (27.2 percent versus 16.4 percent). Thus, it is clear that the general rise in high-status positions and the decline in unskilled ones over past decades has benefited only men.

Moreover, the gap between the incomes of men and women *increased* by a stunning amount between 1945 and 1971. In 1945 the median income for women was $910 less than the median income for men. In 1971 the gap had widened to $3,806. For all their increases in schooling, and for all of their greater participation in the labor force, women were falling further behind men in job prestige and salaries.

Sexist Stereotypes

Sexual inequality is not simply a matter of jobs, pay, or the pains of housewifery. It also exists in our cultural definitions of the terms male and female. Male dominance has been supported by a complex set of values and beliefs that view true femininity as unsuited for taking on responsibility outside the home. Manly characteristics have been the ones considered necessary for holding such important positions.

These values and beliefs did not originate in American society. American settlers brought with them the legal, religious, and political expectations that had kept women subordinate in the Old World (Flexner, 1959). Under English common law, women suffered ''civil death'' upon marriage: They could not sign contracts, had no title to their own earnings or property (even when it was their own by inheritance or dower), and had no rights to their children in the case of legal separation. Furthermore, all religions, regardless of denominational differences, believed woman's place was determined by the limitations of mind and body that were punishment for the original sin of Eve—and as compensation, it was believed women were given the special virtues of modesty, meekness, compassion, and piety to fit them for their proper role of motherhood.

Today, the women's movement identifies such views as sexist. *Sexism* is the tendency to see

''sex'' (gender) as a factor of great importance in the organization of all aspects of society. As with racism, its counterpart, the dominant group sees its own orientation as the only right one. Just as racism in Western society results in white supremacy, sexism results in male supremacy. As Jessie Bernard (1971b) has pointed out, sexism amounts to the unconscious, unexamined, and unchallenged belief that the world as men see it is the only world, that the way of dealing with life that men have created is the only way to deal with it, and that what men think about women is the only way to think about women.

But sexism is not just a point of view restricted to men; women hold it as well. Women frequently are harsh judges of other women whose behavior deviates from role-prescribed behavior, and of course, it is mostly mothers who socialize their daughters into traditional feminine roles. Sexism permeates our culture. Adult women are frequently called ''girls''; this practice is analogous to calling an adult black man ''boy.'' Part II of this chapter discusses sexism in language in greater detail. Advertising, adult and children's literature, and most social institutions have actively promoted a view of women as narcissistic, silly, weak, headachy, emotionally unstable, and generally competent only to judge the whiteness of the wash. The titles ''Miss'' and ''Mrs.'' categorize women according to their marital status, but men are referred to as ''Mr.'' whether they are married or not. (Many women now prefer to use ''Ms.''—a title that does not indicate marital status.)

The pressure on women to be seen as attractive by men is both produced by and supportive of male dominance. The pressures to be attractive to men divide women by making them rivals and also make them dependent upon men: it is men who decide which women are attractive. Feminists identify this tendency to judge women by their appearances as treating women as *sex objects*. Consequently, they oppose such cultural forces as *Playboy*, which encourages men to treat a woman's body as a commodity. They also dislike women's sex magazines that foster the same preoccupation with men's bodies. And they deplore the ''counterculture's'' picture of women, such as that celebrated in the lyrics of many rock songs,

Career Woman

On first meeting, I'm frequently taken for the secretary, you know, traveling with the boss. I'm here to keep somebody happy. Then I'm introduced as the writer. . . .

I'm probably one of the ten highest paid people in the agency. It would cause tremendous hard feelings if, say, I work with a man who's paid less. If a remark is made at a bar—"You make so much money, you could buy and sell me"—I toss it off, right? He's trying to find out. He can't equate me as a rival. They wonder where to put me, they wonder what my salary is.

Buy and sell me—yeah, there are a lot of phrases that show the reversal of roles. What comes to mind is swearing at a meeting. New clients are often very uptight. They feel they can't make any innuendoes that might be suggestive. They don't know how to treat me. They don't know whether to acknowledge me as a woman or as another neuter person who's doing a job for them. . . .

I've developed a sixth sense about this. If a client will say, "Are you married?" I will often say yes, because that's the easiest way to deal with him if he needs that category for me. If it's more acceptable to him to have a young, attractive married woman in a business position comparable to his, terrific. . . .

Or there's the mistress thing: well, she's sleeping with the boss. That's acceptable to them. Or she's a frustrated, compulsive castrator. That's a category. Or lesbian. If I had short hair, wore suits, and talked in a gruff voice, that would be more acceptable than I am. It's when I transcend their labels, they don't quite know what to do. If someone wants a quick label and says, "I'll bet you're a big women's libber, aren't you?" I say, "Yeah, yeah." They have to place me. . . .

Housewife

How would I describe myself? It'll sound terrible—just a housewife. (Laughs.) It's true. What is a housewife? You don't have to have any special talents. I don't have any. . . .

I think Woman's Lib puts down a housewife. Even though they say if this is what a woman wants, it's perfectly all right. I feel it's said in such a snide way: "If this is all she can do and she's contented, leave her alone." It's patronizing. . . .

I don't look at housework as a drudgery. People will complain: "Why do I have to scrub floors?" To me, that isn't the same thing as a man standing there—it's his livelihood—putting two screws together day after day after day. It would drive anybody nuts. It would drive me wild. That poor man doesn't even get to see the finished product. I'll sit here and I'll cook a pie and I'll get to see everybody eat it. This is my offering. I think it's the greatest satisfaction in the world to know you've pleased somebody.

The career woman is a thirty-year-old single, script supervisor/producer and vice president of a large advertising agency. The housewife is a middle-class mother of three children.

—Studs Terkel, *Working* (New York: Pantheon Books, 1974): "Career Woman" from pp. 66–72; "Housewife" from pp. 299–303.

and the role of nurturing "Earth Mother" that women, are expected to play.

The essence of the traditional female role is widely held to be *service* to the emotional and physical needs of others—mainly those of children and husbands, and often of elderly parents as well. Indeed, the wishes and feelings of others must take priority over women's own. To the extent that women are sensitive to others' emotional needs, men can receive fulfillment of their demands upon women *without having to ask*. This has several important consequences. For one thing, men may exercise power over women without appearing to do so. Thus, both marriage partners and even outside observers may believe that unequal situations are situations of equality. The frequency of automatic service that men receive gives them the impression that women *ought* to please them, and it encourages anger and disdain toward women who do not. Such male expectations and reactions are central to sexist ideologies.

The persistence of this ideology has fueled female resentment. Women are now expected to hold jobs but not to excel at them. They must accept considerable responsibility but still defer to manly authority. However, to be "ladylike" is out of keeping with the actual lives of most American women today. Little wonder they resent the pressure on them to act like ladies.

345

PART II: SOURCES
SEX-BASED INEQUALITIES

This chapter began with the observation that male dominance is as old as the human species. But why? We now attempt to demonstrate that historic male dominance was based on specific social and physical conditions that only recently began to change. These changing conditions have made male dominance increasingly objectionable by making sexual equality possible and therefore desirable. Before attempting to explain how male dominance developed and finally became superfluous, it is necessary to discuss a general feature of human culture: *the division of labor*.

As far back as we have knowledge, human societies have to some degree displayed a division of labor, which simply means that not everyone performs the same set of tasks. Even among small wandering bands, who live by gathering wild berries and capturing small game, not every person regularly performs every task. Not everyone makes magic or performs religious rituals. Not everyone cares for infants. Not everyone prepares food. Not everyone hunts. And if the group is attacked, not everyone fights. As societies become more complex the division of labor reflects increasing *specialization*. More and more tasks become the special responsibility of a few members of society.

The reasons for the division of labor are obvious. Many tasks require special skills or training. Thus, through dividing tasks societies are more efficient, which means that those societies that develop specialization of tasks are more productive and enjoy a competitive advantage over those that do not. In the long history of human conflict, such advantages have determined which societies have survived.

The division of labor is fundamental to understanding the origins of male dominance and why it now seems so obviously unjustified. Therefore, throughout the discussion that follows, aspects of the division of labor provide the common theme.

PHYSIOLOGICAL FACTORS

Suppose you were suddenly put in charge of organizing a human society from scratch. Because it is your first assignment, you are only expected to design a relatively small and technologically unsophisticated society. First, you would have to determine which tasks are vital for the survival of that society and how people are to be assigned to fulfill these tasks.

You note right away that some of the most vital tasks require certain biological features that only some members of your society possess.

Women's Work

It is evident that the vital task of having babies could only be assigned to women. And because your society has not yet invented adequate baby formulas and bottles, you would also find that only women could be assigned the task of feeding in-

fants. Of course, once an infant is weaned it would be perfectly possible to turn it over to a man to raise. But this would not free the mother to become a hunter ranging far from home in pursuit of meat. Because of the very high mortality rates in premodern societies, once a woman has weaned one infant she must become pregnant again if your society is to maintain its population. (It is not uncommon for half of the children born in premodern societies to die before they are five.) Constant pregnancy undermines the health of the women, and although average life expectancy is short for all persons in your society, it is shorter for women. Few women live much beyond the end of their fertility.

Thus, in considering the division of labor, it is not even necessary to take account of the fact that men are larger and stronger than women in deciding who will be warriors or hunters. It is only necessary to recognize that most adult females will be pregnant, nursing an infant, or both, most of the time. In your premodern society, it is only sensible to divide tasks in light of this biological state of affairs. Women's work tends to be work that is compatible with pregnancy and child rearing. Thus, it will tend to be located in or near the home. Tasks requiring absence from home and freedom from caring for children will tend to be limited to males (D'Andrade, 1966; Murdock, 1949).

Male Dominance

But what has all of this to do with male dominance? Can't work be divided along sex lines without making women subordinate to males? Apparently not. In Chapter 9 we discuss the fundamental features of social inequality. The point is made that some positions in a society are inherently more powerful than others. One source of male dominance is that positions assigned to males, partly because of the limited tasks that could be assigned to females, tend disproportionately to be the positions with greater power. For example, throughout history military positions have been very powerful, both because of their importance in protecting the society from outside threats and because the military possesses the capacity to coerce other members of a society. Clearly, war making is not a household task, and those adults subject to repeated pregnancy and on whom infants are dependent for milk are not well suited to go off to fight (even if they were equally strong, which, of course, they are not).

Indeed, male dominance of the powerful positions in society becomes even greater as an economy shifts from subsistence agriculture to industry. As will be taken up in detail later in the chapter, when the family ceases to be the site of economic production—when people take up occupations—the more powerful social positions are all outside the family situation. But so long as women are unable to seek positions away from the family, they remain economic dependents and lack substantial power. Furthermore, so long as the social role of women is confined to the family—so long as a woman is economically dependent on a male and has no outside resources to sustain her—she is very exposed to physical domination as well. When challenged, men have simply been able to beat women into submission.

Thus, for centuries women have been captives of their biology: forced into a subordinate status by incessant pregnancy, child care, and their smaller size. Little wonder that women have had to resort to tactics of persuasion—demeaningly called feminine wiles—in order to escape total domination.

While certain biological differences seem to underlie the long history of male dominance, we must briefly note that a great many other biological differences (both real and imaginary) between the sexes have been used incorrectly to explain and often to justify male dominance. For example, it was long believed that because of their hormones and other biochemical features, women were naturally more emotional, more submissive, and otherwise less qualified than men to deal with responsible positions in life. It is now established that these "feminine" traits have nothing to do with female biology (Maccoby, 1966). Instead, they have to do with social facts—with the way boys and girls are raised and with the roles they are asked to perform.

THE SOCIAL PSYCHOLOGY OF SEX ROLES

You will notice that we have skipped the psychological level of analysis. This is not because we think psychological factors are unimportant in sex-

ual inequalities. Rather than simply describe psychological differences, we will try to explain the social context in which they are established.

The terms girl and boy invoke an extraordinary set of assumptions about what a human being will be like. Little girls will be nice, little boys will be active; little girls will be polite, little boys will be aggressive. The list could be expanded indefinitely. The main difference is that boys are supposed to grow up to be men, girls to be women. And those have been very different futures indeed.

The Evolution of Sex Roles

Let us go back to the division of labor and the dependent wife and mother role that has until lately been the inevitable fate of women. It is obvious that male and female roles required rather different skills, including different emotional and interpersonal styles. It is demonstrably better for the society as a whole if mothers, for example, are nurturant, or eager to provide for their children's needs. Women who feel little affection and concern for their infants will not raise children as well as women who have deep maternal feelings. Indeed, given the harsh conditions of life under which humans have typically lived, it taxes maternal skill simply to keep a reasonable proportion of infants alive. By the same token, it is better for a society as a whole if warriors are fierce. It is sad, but no less true, that gentle groups fare badly when they come in contact with warlike groups.

The traditional sexual division of labor is obviously enhanced by raising boys and girls who display quite different personality and behavior patterns. Furthermore, the whole system will work better *if people like being the way they are and doing what they do.* Through trial and error, human cultures evolved in ways that made it possible to develop distinctive sex roles and to socialize the young so that their particular roles seemed preferable and natural. A system operating on consent and preference is more efficient than a system that has to coerce its members into submission. Let us now see how such a system operates.

Childhood Socialization

The key is *childhood socialization.* From the day of birth, female and male infants are rewarded for

347

different kinds of behavior. Indeed, one of the most striking features of child development, and one found universally among human societies, is that at a very early age, children are able to correctly identify their gender. One of the very earliest things children know is whether they are girls or boys. Furthermore, knowledge of their own gender is the central organizing feature of children's views of themselves and of what behavior is and is not appropriate for them. For example, anyone who has spent much time around preschool children often hears them correct one another on the basis of proper sex-role behavior. Little boys who say they want to be mommys when they grow up are told they have to be daddys. Little girls are encouraged to become nurses, not doctors. Indeed, the whole pattern of childish play—including what toys are to be played with—has long been structured to develop attitudes and skills appropriate to adult sex roles.

348   Gender identity is not only established very early in childhood but, once established, it is virtually unchangeable. Studies of hermaphrodites (persons whose physical sexual identity is a mixture of both male and female sexual traits) have shown how difficult it is to change sex identity. In hermaphrodites, for example, secondary sexual characteristics may develop at puberty and raise questions whether a child brought up as a boy might be better suited physically to be a girl, or vice versa. One may raise the question, but considerable medical experience has shown that a person can very rarely change from one gender identity to another, even in late childhood, without great psychological trauma. Ordinarily, doctors treat hermaphrodites to make their physical sexual characteristics conform to the gender identity the child has already taken. They usually do not attempt to change hermaphrodites' sex identities to conform to their bodies (Stoller, 1968).

Even children whose sex is certain at birth may be misled about their gender, and this error often proves to be permanent. This can be seen among transsexuals—persons who are convinced they really are members of the opposite sex despite their physical sexual characteristics. Richard Green (1974) has studied a number of such persons who requested sex-change operations. He concluded

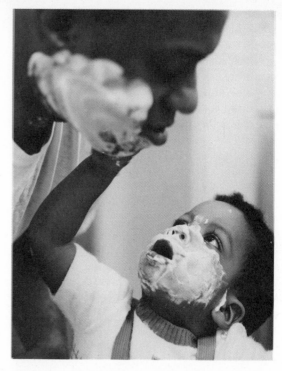

Figure 11.5   The learning of sex roles and sex stereotypes begins very early, practically from the moment of birth. Families generally attempt to socialize their children within roles they consider appropriate to the child's sex. The degree to which sex-role stereotyping is taken for granted may best be illustrated by an exception to the usual norms and customs. Shown here is Roosevelt Grier, one-time pro football star and bodyguard to Robert Kennedy, doing needlepoint as a hobby. Grier also wrote a book about needlepoint.

that transsexuals were fundamentally "tomboys" or "sissies" who failed to outgrow their tendencies to act like members of the opposite sex. He pointed out that it is much more stigmatizing for boys to be labeled as sissies than for girls to be regarded as tomboys in our society. Therefore, males are much more likely than females to be transsexuals as adults because they have been more deeply marked by their childhood deviance from sexual norms.

Green found no biological basis for transsexualism. Instead, he found that transsexual males have simply been socialized as females. Often they have been raised in the absence of adult males or male playmates, and many have been dressed as girls by a doting mother. Most transsexual adult males have long struggled to accept their masculinity but have found it incompatible with their inner convictions that they are really females, trapped somehow in the body of a male. Sex-change operations have now become relatively common at medical centers, such as those at Stanford and Johns Hopkins Universities. Furthermore, it is not uncommon for transsexuals to marry after undergoing such surgery.

It is probably a good thing that most children do recognize their true sexual identity early and that this identity is virtually irreversible. Considerable gender confusion would only aggravate problems of sexual behavior, which, as Chapter 8 points out, are already difficult enough. The problem is not in knowing that one is male or female but in thus being subjected to a culture that *defines appropriate sex role behavior in ways that produce the subordination of females.* What currently outrages supporters of the liberation of women are the multitude of ways in which our current institutions teach a female that she is "only a girl," and thus only suited for the subordinate role of wife and mother. Let us now examine how some of our institutions instill such beliefs in both males and females.

SEXISM AND SOCIAL INSTITUTIONS

Sex-role stereotypes of submissive women and dominant men are sustained in virtually every aspect of our culture. As we have seen, the family is a potent source of gender identity and early sex-role training, for the family in most instances remains the primary location of female subordination. It is the role of mother and wife that is the basic subordinate role in which women find themselves. And it is by observing the behavior of their parents that children gain their first, and most lasting, conceptions of how they are to act in adult sex roles. However, the family is not the only institution that sustains sexual domination. In this section we examine how the school and industry encourage and sustain the stereotyped sex roles that the family has instilled in children.

The Schools

If a little girl comes to school still thinking she is the equal of little boys, the textbooks she encounters in the first grade are likely to challenge her beliefs. In a recent assessment of first grade readers, Virginia Kidd (1970) reported that the books strongly stress sexual stereotypes of female inferiority. This excerpt from a leading first-grade reader illustrates the point clearly in a story about Janet and Mark. Janet tries on her new skates and falls down.

"Mark! Janet!" said Mother.
"What is going on here?"
"She cannot skate," said Mark.
"I can help her.
I want to help her.
Look at her, Mother.
Just look at her.
She is just like a girl.
She gives up."

Mother forces Janet to try again,

"Now you see," said Mark.
"Now you can skate.
But just with me to help you."

In another study, Marjorie U'Ren (1971) examined textbooks adopted for second through sixth grade use in California. She found that in 75 percent of the stories, the main characters were male. Stories about females were not as long as those about males. A page-by-page calculation revealed less than 20 percent of the story space was devoted to females. Only 15 percent of the illustrations depicted women or girls.

As she advances through the primary grades, a little girl soon learns that she in fact is excluded from a variety of activities. Perhaps foremost among these is sports. Although many girls play sports with boys during early school years, by about age ten or eleven they find their athletic careers are over. For at about that age boys begin to participate in organized sports programs. Today, rules prohibiting girls from these programs are being attacked in the courts. But for generations, the rules have been strictly enforced and in late grade school, girls have been forced into the role of onlookers while little boys developed their physical skills, their self confidence and ability to deal with stress, and especially their ability for highly cooperative activities by playing on teams. Not only have girls been excluded from boys' sports but they have not been offered any worthwhile women's sports programs in most school systems. Notable exceptions such as the hugely successful women's high-school basketball program in Iowa (see Figure 11.6) make it clear that women's sports programs have not languished because girls lack the talent or interest to play sports. Rather, women's sports have been opposed as unladylike and harmful to femininity.

Education for submission continues in college. College textbooks commonly use the word "man" to mean the human race (this book does not except when directly quoting other sources). Research has shown that although terms and phrases such as "Urban Man," "Man and Society," or "Economic Man" are meant to include women, both male and female students tend to take them literally to mean *man* (Schneider and Hacker, 1973). Little wonder that female students tend to feel excluded from significant activities suggested by such subjects as "the History of Man." As a subordinate group, they have been excluded from significant roles in that history, and even today women students seem fearful of trying to play important roles in society.

Matina Horner (1970) has demonstrated that female college students are handicapped by a fear of success in competitive situations. The majority of women she tested feared that high achievement by a woman would have threatening social consequences, including social rejection. Women students in Horner's study were asked to write a story based on the sentence "After the first-term finals, Anne finds herself at the top of her medical-school class." Men were given the same task, but "John" replaced "Anne" in the sentence they received. Over 65 percent of the women told stories that reflected strong fears of social rejection, fears about definitions of womanhood, and denial of the

350

Figure 11.6 In 1974 more than 25,000 girls in 443 Iowa high schools played interscholastic basketball. The five-day state tournament annually outdraws the boys' tournament and is shown on an eight-state TV hook-up reaching an estimated 3.5 million fans. In 1975, all but six of Iowa's 508 high schools will have girls' basketball teams. And how do Iowa boys feel about the success of girls' basketball? They fill the stands and cheer wildly. A major attraction of girls' basketball is that because it is played according to somewhat different rules, it is faster and permits more points to be scored than boys' basketball does. Iowa City fans still remember the tournament game in 1969, when Denise Long scored 93 points. The top stars often come to the tournament averaging more than 40 points a game for the season.

possibility that any mere woman could be so successful. These examples were handed in by three women students:

It was luck that Anne came out on top of her med class because she didn't want to go to med school anyway.

Anne is completely ecstatic but at the same time feels guilty. She wishes that she could stop studying so hard, but parental and personal pressures drive her. She will finally have a nervous breakdown and quit med school and marry a successful young doctor.

Anne cannot help but be pleased; yet she is unhappy. She had not wanted to be a doctor . . . she had half hoped her grades would be too poor to continue, but she had been too proud to allow that to happen. She had worked extraordinarily hard and her grades showed it. "It is not enough," Anne thinks. "I am not happy." She is not sure what she wants—only feels the pressure to achieve something, even if it's something she doesn't want. Anne says "To hell with the whole business" and goes into social work—not hardly as glamorous, prestigious, or lucrative; but she is happy.

In contrast, less than 10 percent of the men showed a tendency to avoid success. Rather, they expressed delight at John's success and predicted a successful career for him.

The degree to which college-age women have lost confidence in the ability of women has been repeatedly demonstrated by their rating men higher than women for the same performance. In one study, Philip Goldberg (1968) selected articles from the professional literature of six academic fields and combined them into two sets of booklets. The same articles were attributed to a male author in one set of booklets and to a female author in the other set. The different sets were then given to samples of college women to rate. Half the sample saw the male-authored set and half the female-authored set. In every case, the women rated the male-authored articles as more important and their author more competent. Thus are women educated by the schools to accept their subordinate status.

Industry

American culture is still permeated with the assumption that girls grow up to be wives and mothers, but we saw in the first section of this chapter that this assumption is no longer true, or is at least not the whole truth. The overwhelming majority of women hold jobs outside the home at some time during their lives. And a substantial minority of married women are regularly employed. However, even though women have entered the occupational structure in large numbers, they have not thereby overcome their subordinate status. We have already reviewed the present economic situation of working women. They earn substantially less than

351

Figure 11.7   Coos Bay, Oregon (pop. 13,500) ships more lumber than any other American port. It is also the home of Fran Sichting, a world class sprinter who has several times broken the American record for the 220 yard dash. Sichting not only trains with the men's track team of the local community college, but has competed in their meets, regularly beating male runners. Life in Coos Bay bears little resemblance to modern living. Sichting's husband hauls logs and often works an eleven-to-twelve-hour day. They hunt and fish for nearly all of the meat they eat. Sichting now does most of the deer and elk hunting by herself and claims she can cut up and wrap a deer and get the meat in her freezer in two hours. She dismisses women's liberation as irrelevant "around here. The men make a hard living and the wives have to help, even if it means staying home and keeping house." At the end of the 1973 track season, Sichting talked of giving up running because her husband objected to her absences. She returned to competition because he changed his mind. "He's very proud of me now, I think." Sichting's view of the female role is much more strongly shaped by the conditions of her frontier life than by her international athletic success. In the world of Coos Bay the conditions prompting and supporting sexual equality have not yet developed. (Quoted material from Women in Sports, *1974.)*

men and are very disproportionately employed in lower-status positions—especially in secretarial and clerical jobs—with little prospect for future advancement.

With respect to management jobs, women are in a double-bind situation. Men who manage our industrial and economic institutions believe that women are less seriously committed to careers than men are. In consequence, hiring and promotion policies are heavily biased in favor of men. These policies in turn give women little reason to be serious about their careers and reduce women's opportunity to get the necessary training for advancement to more responsible positions. Because women tend to behave in conformity to the stereotypes held by managers, they unwittingly reinforce men's belief that women are poor risks for promotion and training.

In a recent experiment in which 1,500 managers were asked to respond to a series of personnel decisions in which the sex of the employees was the only thing that varied, decisions differed greatly on the basis of sex (Rosen and Jerdee, 1974). Managers recommended actions that would result in much greater effort to retain males who were thinking of leaving the firm than to retain females with identical qualifications. They expected males would give top priority to jobs when there was a conflict between job and family obligations. But they expected females to give top priority to their families in identical situations. Their actions thus encourage women to put family first and to sacrifice career advancement. Then they penalize women for doing so.

An additional problem for women in jobs is that at present, the critical testing time in most careers comes during the first decade of work. By their early thirties, employees have been sorted out; the most promising males have been identified and have already been promoted to positions with bright prospects for the future. However, this age is precisely the period during which women are bearing children and are least able to devote themselves wholly to a career. When they get their children into school and try to resume or begin an occupational career, they find they are already thought to be too old for advancement. Ironically, women who defer childbearing to get started in a

Figure 11.8   Levels of Analysis and Issues Appropriate to Each Level. This summary chart does not cover all the important points raised in the chapter. Use it only to review what you have read. Page numbers are given for the full discussion of any topic.

career are often not promoted because employers think they will drop out later to have children.

At present, our society is structured in ways that make the subordinate status of women a self-fulfilling prophecy. The belief that women are unsuited for responsible jobs is sustained by treating women in ways that make them unsuited for such jobs or from demonstrating their suitability.

SOCIETAL SOURCES

We have seen how the needs of society have long conspired to keep women in domestic bondage. However, as was pointed out at the beginning of this chapter, rapid changes in society have eroded these conditions and have made the continuing subordination of women both undesirable and unnecessary. We now examine these changes in an effort to assess the future of relations between the sexes. Two extraordinary changes are discussed: changes in technology and reproduction.

The Reproduction Revolution

We have seen that a fundamental source of female subordination was biology. Until modern times, the fate of women was incessant pregnancy, child rearing, and early death. This is no longer true. In industrial nations women now have few pregnancies, and the average female has had all her children before she is thirty. There are several important reasons for this change. First of all, infant mortality has been so greatly reduced that, instead of half the infants dying, only a small percentage now die. Thus women do not need to have a great number of children in order to have a few reach adulthood. Second, children are now an economic burden rather than an asset. Until recently children were an important source of labor, especially for farm families. Indeed, as is taken up in Chapter 14, a large birth rate has become a major source of peril to society, and large families in industrialized nations are now regarded as undesirable. Third, contraception has made it possible to separate sexual behavior and reproduction so that women can

Levels	Appropriate Questions	A Partial Synopsis of Present Conclusions
Physiological	Did biological factors affect the traditional division of labor?	Yes. Until modern times, women were pregnant or nursing most of their adult lives, which undermined their health, limited their physical activity, and kept them close to home. This restriction, combined with the smaller stature of females, left the more powerful positions in society to be exclusively filled by males. Thus, biology trapped women in a subordinate status. (pp. 346–347)
Psychological*	Is gender identity established early in life?	Yes, often as early as age two. Once established, it tends to be very difficult to change. (pp. 348–349)
Social-Psychological*	Did sex roles develop in ways that further insured the subordination of women?	Yes. Males and females were long required to fill different roles vis-à-vis the division of labor, so it made sense to teach them to enjoy and take for granted their different roles. For its survival, a group living under harsh conditions requires nurturance from those who bear and care for children and aggressiveness from those who perform as warriors. Human societies have developed elaborate socialization mechanisms to raise boys and girls to display these different personality traits. (pp. 347–348)
Sociological: Middle Range	Is male dominance reinforced by the educational system?	Yes. Textbooks stress female submissiveness and male dominance. And until recently, girls were excluded from most competitive sports, through which boys developed physical skills, confidence, and the ability to deal with stress. Submissive attitudes that are taught early tend to persist. Research has shown that even women at the college level fear success and have little confidence. (pp. 349–351)
	Does industry tend to operate in terms of male dominance?	Yes. Much less interest is taken in preparing women for responsible positions. Many managers assume that most young women employees will drop out to become wives and mothers. (pp. 351–352)
Societal	Has the "reproduction revolution" eliminated a major cause of male dominance?	Yes. Women today have fewer pregnancies and live longer lives. For most of their adult lives, they are not pregnant and do not have young children. In addition, it is no longer necessary for women to nurse infants. Thus, women are no longer trapped by the biology of reproduction. (pp. 352–354)
	Has the "technological revolution" in work removed previous supports for male dominance?	Yes. Today, even in warfare, muscle power is of little importance. Very few jobs now require strength, so the larger stature of males is no longer a major advantage. Furthermore, with modern technology, homemaking no longer means endless drudgery. (pp. 354–355)

353

*In this chapter the Psychological and Social-Psychological levels are combined.

avoid incessant pregnancy. And when they do bear children, they do not have to stay at home to feed them. Bottles and nursing formulas make it possible for anyone to provide for an infant.

In consequence of many fewer pregnancies, adult female mortality has greatly decreased. Women now live longer than men, and both men and women can expect to live past seventy. Thus, women now have by far the majority of their adult lives left to live by the time their last child has entered school. For the first time in history, females have the possibility of a life not bounded by the biology of reproduction. Not only are women able to take part in activities away from home and hearth but they find they have a need to do so.

Technology

Changes in technology have liberated women from biological captivity by eliminating incessant pregnancy and early death. Similarly, technological change has eliminated other barriers to full participation of women in occupations.

Perhaps we can best illustrate those changes by examining the effects of technology on farm life. Because nearly all human beings, for several thousand years or more, lived on farms or in farming villages, the conditions of farm life provide an appropriate standard against which to judge the changes brought by modernization.

Farm life in America at the turn of the century was, as it had always been, a life of ceaseless toil. The men went out at dawn to feed and care for the livestock and to work the land all day. Meanwhile their wives also toiled all day long. Much of the time they were pregnant and the house was filled with young children to be looked after. Furthermore, with making their own soap, sewing their own clothes, canning their own food for winter, keeping wood in their stoves, washing clothes on a scrub board in a tub filled with water heated on the stove, and doing many other tasks, they had little time or energy to spend thinking about how life could be made different. Indeed, survival of the family required the full efforts of all family members. The notion of changing roles with their husbands would have struck women as senseless. There was nothing attractive about leaving the stove for the field. Besides, men could more easily perform the heavy outdoor work and were never pregnant.

Today few families live on farms. Even farm families have been greatly affected by technological change. Farmers still work hard, but they do most of their work with machines. Farm wives still have more work than do urban housewives, but they too now have many fewer children and many more household conveniences.

The changes in urban life—and the shift of our population to urban living—have profoundly changed the basis of traditional sex roles. As was

pointed out in previous chapters, very little work any longer depends greatly on muscle power. Work is now done with machines and with brains. The major shift in our economy presently is from industry based on production to industry based on knowledge work (see Chapter 2). There is no longer any objective basis for a sexual division of labor. Indeed, since the essential labor demand is for educated and intelligent workers, it is increasingly irrational to waste half of the available talent.

The problem is that we are still following cultural patterns that built up over thousands of years—ways of life that made the relative subordination of women seem necessary. It is diffcult to change our whole system of sex roles and the arrangements that sustain them, and it is especially difficult to change them without considerable trauma. That the problem is fundamentally in our heads—in how we think about sex roles rather than in social necessities—only makes change possible, not inevitable. Change must be won against the inertia of past traditions, and this, of course, is precisely what necessitates and motivates the contemporary women's movement.

In conclusion, we must make it clear that wiping out sex-based inequalities is not just a problem for women. We cannot change the female role without revising the male role to an equal extent, for male and female roles are inextricably linked. Thus, the hope of feminists is not simply to free women from sexist constraints but to free human beings, male and female, from these antiquated and dehumanizing bonds. This does not mean making men and women indistinguishable. It means keeping sexuality and marital relationships free from restrictions based on inequality between the partners.

PART III: RESPONSES
SEX-BASED INEQUALITIES

Sexual subordination is a problem that requires fundamental change in our society. We now examine present and past efforts to bring about such change. Unlike other subordinate groups in America, women are not a minority group. They therefore have much greater potential power to force social change. On the other hand, unlike minority racial and religious groups, women do not live apart from those who dominate them. Radical feminists who identify men as the enemy have not found many women responsive to such views. Thus, many strategies of group unity that subordinate minorities use to achieve their goals of equality are ill-suited to the liberation of women. For example, the separatist approach, which has sometimes been used to considerable advantage by racial and religious minorities, seems to miss the whole point of difficulties that presently exist between the sexes.

355

Figure 11.9   Technology and urbanization have been instrumental in changing the traditional roles of men and women. The development of labor-saving devices (contrasted to the old wood burning stove shown far left) has enabled many women to gain enough independence from household chores to hold jobs outside the home. And the addition of day-care centers for the children of working women has helped to free many women for tasks other than housekeeping.

Figure 11.10   The Equal Rights Amendment (ERA) to the Constitution of the United States seeks to bar any legal or governmental discrimination based on sex. Various women's organizations struggled to achieve congressional passage of the Act. With Senate action in 1972, the ERA was on its way toward ratification by the required two-thirds of the States. As this book goes to press, three more states need to ratify the ERA.

NEW YORK, THURSDAY, MARCH 23, 1972

Equal Rights Amendment Is Approved by Congress

WASHINGTON, March 22—The Senate passed the Equal Rights Amendment today, thus completing Congressional action on the amendment, which would prohibit discrimination based on sex by any law or action of any government—Federal, state or local.

The 49-year struggle of feminists to get the amendment through Congress ended at 4:38 P.M. when the 84-to-8 vote was announced.

Thirty-two minutes later, Hawaii became the first state to ratify the amendment when the state Senate and House of Representatives registered its approval at 12:10 P.M. Hawaiian standard time (5:10 P.M. Eastern standard time).

The Senate galleries, which were filled with women of all ages and more than a few men, mostly young, applauded, cheered and let out a few cowboy yells despite having been warned in advance by Senator William V. Roth Jr., Republican of Delaware, who was presiding, that such demonstrations were not permitted.

The next and final step before the amendment can go into effect is ratification by 37 more states, the three-quarters required by the Constitution.

What then are the relevant approaches? Our previous discussion established that sexual subordination is presently sustained by a sex-based division of labor, by socialization that prepares females for subordinate, not equal, status, and by arrangements and role relationships within the family. Equality between the sexes depends on changing these arrangements. In this section we discuss what kinds of changes are needed and what progress has been made in bringing them about.

CHANGING THE DIVISION OF LABOR

We have seen that women's subordination mainly resulted from a division of labor—based on unavoidable biological facts—that gave the more powerful positions to men. We have also seen that although the fundamental need for such a division of labor has subsided in modern societies, women are still disproportionately consigned to less powerful and lower-paying positions. Until sex no longer plays a role in the division of labor, women will not achieve equal status. Thus, an end to all hiring and promotion practices that foster a sexual division of labor is a central demand of those opposed to sex-based inequalities.

Legal Approaches

One word, little noticed at the time, in the Civil Rights Act of 1964 has recently affected the sexual division of labor. In Title VII of the Act, intended to prohibit job discrimination against nonwhites, the word "sex" appears. Thus, the act forbids employers to take account of "race, color, religion, sex, or national origin," when hiring or promoting workers. Subsequent court decisions have held that the Civil Rights Act makes it unlawful to bar women from such jobs as airline pilot or telephone installer, or to bar men from such jobs as airline steward or telephone operator.

Indicative of the changes forced by legal decisions is that newspaper want ads may no longer indicate sex restrictions on jobs or use sections called "Jobs For Men" and "Jobs For Women." Until recently, jobs such as secretary, receptionist, telephone operator, and the like appeared only in the women's job section. Such jobs as machinist, executive trainee, and the like appeared only in the

men's job section. This practice typically reflected strict hiring policies. Many ads even stated specifically that applicants had to be male or female.

Obviously, legal rulings do not cause immediate change. Instead, change comes slowly, along with scores of law suits brought against individual employers and unions. These suits result in the admission of a few women (or men) to a particular occupation, and only later can we expect to see any substantial sex balance achieved. Yet nearly every day new suits are being filed and won and fewer occupations remain restricted to only one sex. However, as we discuss later, simply ending sexual restrictions in employment practices will not by itself end a sexual division of labor—at least not rapidly.

In addition to legal decisions, government policies have played an increasingly formidable role in challenging discriminatory hiring practices. As was discussed in the previous chapter, some government agencies are now requiring firms receiving government contracts and universities receiving government grants to initiate *affirmative action* programs in hiring and promotion. Such programs must not simply be designed to end discrimination but must take positive steps to increase minority and female representation until it reflects representation of those groups in the general population. Government agencies will withhold or threaten to end the flow of government funds unless the employer initiates and adheres to an affirmative action program.

Recently, the Department of Health, Education and Welfare (HEW) held up millions in grant funds to the twenty universities scheduled to receive the largest amount of federal money. Funds remained frozen until these universities demonstrated that they were making progress in attracting minority and female faculty members. However, it was not expected that these universities could quickly restaff to the point that their faculties would reflect the racial and sexual make-up of the general population. For one thing, this would have required that many present faculty members be fired to create openings. Furthermore, substantial numbers of qualified minority and female Ph.D.s are not presently available to fill large numbers of positions. Women and nonwhite men have been

much less likely than white males to pursue graduate studies. The purpose of affirmative action is therefore to force maximum employment of available women and nonwhite scholars and to create an intense demand that will increase the enrollment of women and nonwhites in graduate school. Because the universities singled out for surveillance are the largest producers of new Ph.D.s, it is likely that pressure on them to begin affirmative action programs will be reflected most rapidly in graduate student recruitment and training.

The force of law and government policy is not present in all recent reform efforts, although it undoubtedly provides the basic push behind efforts to end a sex-based division of labor. Some businesses and organizations have initiated affirmative action programs on their own or in response to complaints made by their female employees. Thus, many corporations are actively seeking women members for their boards of directors and for executive positions. Several executive employment agencies now specialize in finding qualified women for management jobs in business and industry. So far, however, there has been more activity than achievement; few women have found their way into the executive suites.

357

Passed by Congress in March 1972, the Equal Rights Amendment—when it is ratified by thirty-eight states—will become the Twenty-Seventh Amendment to the U.S. Constitution. It portends massive changes toward the goal of sexual equality in employment and in all other areas in which women have encountered restrictions. The amendment is brief and inclusive:

Section 1.   Equality of rights under the law should not be denied or abridged by the United States or by any State on account of sex.

Section 2.   The Congress shall have the power to enforce by appropriate legislation the provisions of this article.

Section 3.   The amendment shall take effect two years after the date of ratification.

If finally ratified, it will nullify the hundreds of state laws that presently treat men and women differently. For example, not only will employers be required to hire and promote men and women on an equal basis, but they will not be permitted to

Figure 11.11   The women's liberation movement can be found in a variety of institutions. It seeks to correct stereotypes within the university (above) *as well as the home and the military.* (Below) *This type of ad to recruit women into the Army has been run for the last two years; the salary stated in the copy has increased.*

How to tell your parents you want to join the Army.

You're graduating from high school and not going on to college. You're not certain you know what you want to do. Or can do.

Tell your parents you can find out in today's Women's Army Corps. In one of over 400 good jobs, like communications, administrative procedures, data processing, medical, or personnel management.

Tell them we'll train you for your job, and pay you while you learn. $288 a month to start, plus free meals, housing, medical and dental care, and 30 days paid vacation every year.

Tell them you'll have a chance to see more of the world than just home. Places like Europe, Alaska, Hawaii, and the Far East. A chance to meet interesting people, make new friends and mature.

And tell them you can continue your education. Even go for your college degree. And that we'll pay for most of it.

If you need any more good reasons, see your Army Representative.

Today's Army wants to join you.

give women any benefits that are not for men too, including rest periods and maternity leaves, or in any other way make distinctions on the basis of sex. The amendment would also wipe out divorce laws that favor women. Many women, especially those who have chosen to fulfill traditional female roles, are threatened by these aspects of the amendment. Some of them may, in fact, suffer under a new legal status for women, for transitions from one set of rules to another often cause some inequities and abuses. Even though some women might prefer not having legal equality, it is hard to imagine how present trends toward full equality between the sexes can be long delayed.

Although the major change so far has been in increased opportunities, many women have not been able to take advantage of increased job equality. One thing that keeps women from seizing occupational opportunities is the lack of adequate, low-cost child care.

The Lack of Child Care

358

In March 1970, 6 million children under the age of six had working mothers, an increase of 2 million over 1960. Less than half of these children (45 percent) were in child-care centers. Typically, a child who is not in a child-care center is dropped off daily in a private home where a housewife acts as baby-sitter and provides only custodial care for a number of small children. Of these estimated 450,000 homes that take in the children of working mothers, fewer than 2 percent are licensed, and few offer any educational programs or activities (Roby, 1973). In comparison with other industrial nations, such as the Scandinavian countries, Japan, or Great Britain, child care in the United States is hard to find, of very poor quality, and expensive.

Lack of good child care constitutes discrimination against women in the job market. Of course, one can argue that men, too, cannot find acceptable, low-cost child care. That is fine in theory, but in practice it is mainly women who suffer. Because women typically earn considerably less than men do, the relatively high cost of child care is a greater burden—one that often makes it economically irrational for women to work until their children can enter public school. Unless a woman's earn-

ings are significantly more than the cost of child care, she might as well care for her own children. In addition, because women almost always receive custody of children in the case of divorce, women are much more likely than men to need child-care services. The lack of good child care at a reasonable price therefore serves to keep women out of jobs while their children are young and impedes their careers and job advancement during the critical young-adult years.

Child care is a major issue for women's groups. Some companies have responded by establishing their own child-care centers for the children of employees. Most have not. There have been efforts to coordinate, expand, and upgrade child-care programs through actions of the federal government, but these received a setback when President Richard Nixon vetoed the Comprehensive Child Development Program in 1971. It seems certain that adequate child-care programs will eventually be established in the United States. But until they are, women are the major losers.

But even with child care readily available and with sex discrimination in hiring and promotion made illegal, the sex-based division of labor will not end soon. It will continue as long as women are unprepared or unwilling to seize new occupational opportunities.

SOCIALIZATION AND RESOCIALIZATION

Earlier in this chapter we reported the results of Matina Horner's study (1970) showing that many college women feared success. With such attitudes, how can the majority of college women be psychologically prepared to compete for powerful and high-status occupational positions? They cannot. Thus, changes in rules and policies to make such positions available to women are not sufficient to bring substantial numbers of women into such positions. It is necessary to change women's self-conceptions so they are prepared to seek and accept such positions and the success that goes with them. We must find ways to change the *socialization* process.

Much of childhood socialization occurs in schools, so we must closely examine how girls and boys are treated and trained. Many school books transmit messages of subordination to girls by focusing on boys and depicting the lack of skill in little girls. Therefore, school books must be changed. And, if organized sports help boys build the self-competence and willingness to compete (and the ability to cooperate on teams), then the development of sports for girls is of critical importance. Childhood socialization must be changed to remove all the ways in which little girls are taught that they can't. Little girls must be taught that they can.

An additional problem is that women do not get enough information about many occupations that have been traditionally men's work in our society. For example, women know about the job of telephone operator; they have a general notion of what a phone operator does, how well the job is paid, and where to go to get it. But few women seem to have similar information about jobs such as telephone installer. Recently spokesmen for the telephone company have complained that they can find few women to train as installers, despite the fact that this job is much more highly paid than that of operator, for which the company has an excess of women applicants. Similarly, few women seem to know much about high-status positions in banking (although they know all about tellers' jobs), or about financial and business management positions in general. Lacking such knowledge, women cannot even consider whether they might like such work or be suited for it.

The past exclusion of women from many occupations in large part accounts for their lack of knowledge about many occupations as well as their fear of success. In the past, knowledge of such jobs was irrelevant to women. Furthermore, women have not had the example of other women to follow—they have not had any models to follow.

Role Models

Role models are a major element in the socialization process. We learn how to perform many roles by imitating the behavior of others. Traditionally, for example, little girls learned the wife and mother role by imitating their own mothers during play. Similarly, little boys have imitated their fathers. Role models outside the family also

strongly influence children's aspirations and expectations about the future. If little girls so often say they want to grow up to be mommys, nurses, teachers, or airline stewardesses, it is because they readily see these as women's roles—they see women successfully filling these roles. The tendency of little boys to say they plan to be firemen, policemen, baseball players, or president is similarly a response to observing men in such roles.

It is a lack of role models that so greatly limits women at present in what they hope to be and think it possible to be. They know women can be nurses. But until they see women successfully and happily running banks, driving firetrucks, or commanding troops, they will not know for certain that these are activities women can do—and therefore ones that they can hope to do.

The lack of female role models is a major element in affirmative action programs. It is all well and good for male college professors, for example, to encourage women to become scientists and scholars. But women will find such prospects easier to accept, and easier to evaluate, when they see a significant number of women on the faculties of famous universities.

It is important to recognize that ending a sex-based division of labor means more than changing the occupational distribution of women. It not only means bringing women into what have been men's jobs but also means bringing men into the traditionally female jobs. Most adults acknowledge that they were surprised the first time they dialed ''operator'' and a man answered. But until it is no longer surprising to find male phone operators or male nurses, we will retain many sex-based biases and stereotypes in our view of the world of work.

Consciousness Raising

Changes in patterns of socialization discussed so far are primarily aimed at changing the way future generations define male and female. If such changes are accomplished, little girls and little boys will grow up with a different conception of proper sex-role behavior. But most of the women in our society today have already been subjected to traditional sex-role socialization. It is too late to change the school books or to provide attractive role models for adult American women. For many women, the attempt to change traditional definitions has produced a crisis of identity. Their upbringing interferes with their ability to adjust to new circumstances. It is difficult to overcome ingrained submissiveness and conceptions of proper femininity. This problem is especially acute for many women who become divorced and find themselves unsuited for exchanging their dependent and subordinate wife and mother role for one of independence and self-reliance.

In response to this widely shared difficulty, many women have recently begun to band together in small groups to work through their difficulties. Such groups—often called consciousness-raising groups—provide a supportive social situation in which women can attempt their own *re*socialization. This self-help effort is modeled on other therapy groups such as those developed by addicts, alcoholics, and ex-convicts. The idea is to establish new behavior patterns and change one's self-conception. We have noted that male and female roles are inextricably interrelated. Recently, some men have also been meeting in consciousness-raising groups aimed at changing their views of women and to work out the basis for relations with them that are free of subordination.

THE FAMILY

The last major focus of efforts to overcome sexual inequalities is the family. It is the primary setting for male-female relations and thus for male dominance. Although the modern family is becoming increasingly unstable, most adult males and females spend most of their lives married. We have seen throughout this chapter that the reproductive role of the female partner in marriage and her immersion in housekeeping and child care has been a major basis for male dominance. We have also seen that present demands for sexual equality stem substantially from the fact that women are no longer required to devote their lives to these activities. Indeed, women are now nearly as likely to leave for work in the morning as they are to stay home and keep the house. Nevertheless, traditional submissive elements remain in many aspects of the role defined by the position of wife and mother. Thus, the family is the most important obstacle to

sexual liberation, and it is the institution most likely to undergo far-reaching changes as male dominance ends.

We have previously noted that traditional sex-role socialization presently occurs mainly in the family. By the time children arrive in kindergarten or first grade, they already display marked differences according to sex. For example, little girls are already nurturant and ladylike. Little boys are already aggressive and career oriented, and they regard girls as a subordinate group. As long as this model of sex roles is displayed by their parents, this pattern of socialization is likely to continue.

Furthermore, the family continues to encourage female subordination in adulthood. A recent national study of graduate students (Weiss, 1972) found that it was marriage, not discrimination by male faculty members against women students, that accounted for women's less distinguished performances. (For example, female graduate students were less likely to have published research articles or to be actively engaged in research projects than were male graduate students.) When age and marital status were controlled, the data showed that divorced women over thirty were as productive as any group of males, whereas younger married women were the least productive group. Married men, on the other hand, were more productive than were unmarried men. Clearly, marriage imposes burdens on women's career activities, but it facilitates men's careers. A married man has a wife to look after many of his needs, so he is free to concentrate more fully on career achievements. But for the married female graduate student, providing for the needs of a husband takes times and energy away from her career. In the modern family, many features of the traditional nurturant and submissive role of women remain, regardless of how unsuited they are to what women are actually doing with their lives. Probably the majority of working women are still expected to cook and take care of the home with little help from their husbands—indeed many working women still take this responsibility for granted.

Full participation of women in the world outside the home requires a substantial change in male participation within the home. And the emancipation of women from thousands of years of male dominance requires a massive readjustment of relations between husbands and wives.

The next chapter examines the changing family and the profound impact of changing sex roles on the maintenance and future form of family relations.

CHAPTER REVIEW

The early feminist movement was led by abolitionists and upper-middle-class women who felt they would receive the vote in the wake of the emancipation of blacks. When the Fourteenth Amendment gave the right to vote only to black *men,* the women's hopes were betrayed. In consequence, they formed a vigorous women's rights movement. After years of struggle, women secured the right to vote with the passage of the Nineteenth Amendment in 1919.

After the right to vote was granted, women's issues as such began to fade in importance. Most women settled into domestic roles in society until World War II, when the shortage of men required them to enter the labor force in great numbers. Women were urged to return to their homes when the war ended and the veterans came back. Many continued to work out of necessity, but they held less prestigious jobs at lower wages than equally qualified men enjoyed. But it was not until the 1960s that sex-based inequalities came to be recognized as a full-fledged social problem. Four basic factors contributed to social recognition of the problem: (1) A larger proportion of women were working and experiencing strains because child care was expensive and hard to find, because women had sole responsibility for the home, and because social disapproval of their working was strong; (2) women were completing their families earlier and living longer and therefore had more time to devote to working; (3) women became more aware of the increasing earnings gap between men's and women's salaries; and (4) sexist stereotypes were preventing the full utilization of women's skills.

The origins of sex-based inequalities are to be found in the historical *division of labor.* Physiological factors determined that such tasks as bearing and nursing children would be done by females. In combination with men's greater physical strength, these factors gave men a dominant position in society. Mothers *had* to nurture and protect their children; the socialization process therefore instilled gender identity early in children and fostered favorable attitudes toward maintaining that identity. That is, the girls were raised to be submissive and nurturant, and boys were raised to be dominant and aggressive. And both regarded this state of affairs as natural. Although the family is the primary source of learning appropriate sex roles, schools stress women's "inferiority" through language and illustrations in textbooks and through the general lack of emphasis on girl's sports programs after puberty. Industry, too, gets caught in a kind of labeling process in which employers define women as lacking commitment to their jobs, and women, seeing that commitment will not be rewarded, become alienated from their jobs. Finally, social changes have contributed to women's discontent. Lower infant mortality, technological changes, and the "reproductive revolution," with its improved methods of contraception, have largely freed women from continual pregnancy and child care. Moreover, physical strength is no longer necessary for most work. Traditional restrictions on women in the home and in industry thus now produce greater dissatisfaction among women than ever before.

Societal responses to sex-based inequalities have primarily taken the form of *legal* requirements for equality. Title VII of the Civil Rights Act of 1964 forbids sex discrimination, and *affirmative action* sees that positive steps are taken to increase the representation of women in various occupations until parity with men is reached. The Twenty-Seventh Amendment, if it passes, will assure women full and equal rights of citizenship. These legal rights cannot be fully implemented, however, until adequate child-care facilities are made available to working parents and until socialization of children no longer fosters beliefs in female inferiority. Consciousness-raising groups for adults may help alter sex stereotypes, as will changes in the delineation of male and female roles. Once these social and psychological changes have taken place, it is doubtful that the legal assurances of equality will be needed any longer.

SUGGESTED READINGS

Flexner, Eleanor. *Century of Struggle: The Women's Rights Movement in the United States.* Cambridge, Mass.: Harvard University Press, 1959.

Green, Richard. *Sexual Identity Conflict in Children and Adults.* New York: Basic Books, 1974.

Klein, Viola. *The Feminine Character: History of an Ideology.* London, England: Routledge & Kegan Paul, 1946.

Maccoby, Eleanor E. (ed.). *The Development of Sex Differences.* Stanford, Calif.: Stanford University Press, 1966.

Roby, Pamela (ed.). *Child Care—Who Cares? Foreign and Domestic Infant and Early Childhood Development Policies.* New York: Basic Books, 1973.

Sullerot, Evelyne. *Woman, Society and Change.* New York: McGraw-Hill World University Library, 1971.

361

Problems of Human Progress

The Book of Ecclesiastes claims "There is no new thing under the sun." This claim applies well to the social problems examined in Units II and III. Human societies have always been beset by problems of deviance and of conflict and inequality. But modern industrial societies are *a new thing under the sun*. Not surprisingly, a radically new kind of society has produced a novel set of social problems.

This unit examines four major problems that have arisen out of the conditions of modern life. We begin with the family and assess the painful ways in which it has been forced to readjust to new conditions. Then we examine the problem of old age. Because many people are now able to survive to old age, we must, for the first time, confront the question of how to provide for the care and comfort of a large number of elderly people. Chapter 14 moves on to problems of runaway population growth. These problems are also primarily the result of medical triumphs over the dread diseases that used to keep human populations in check. The last chapter examines the ultimate irony of our technological progress. We now possess the capacity not only to transform the planet but to destroy it.

It is a peculiarity of the modern age that nations and continents are no longer isolated. What goes on in one part of the globe may have profound consequences for all other parts. The new problems of modern times are international in scope. For this reason, we depart from the levels of analysis used in previous units. Instead, we concentrate almost entirely at the macro level— on how societies operate as a whole and on how they influence one another.

A second peculiarity of several of these new global problems is their extreme seriousness. Since human societies have always been troubled by problems such as crime, drunkenness, poverty, and intergroup conflict, it would appear that such problems can at least be endured if they cannot be cured. But it is certain that the developing population and ecological crises must be dealt with effectively and soon because we are unlikely to be able to endure them. What is at stake is nothing less than the survival of human life.

*Nobody's family can hang out a sign
"Nothing the matter here."* Chinese proverb

Bruce M. Deane

12
Family Problems

For at least fifty years, social problems textbooks have devoted a chapter to family *disorganization*. We break with this approach because we think it no longer suits the facts or offers the best interpretations of current trends. These trends are not in dispute. Clearly, the American family—and also the family in other advanced nations—is showing symptoms of change. And these symptoms could be interpreted as family disorganization. The divorce rate is rapidly rising. So are the rates of desertion, annulment, separation, illegitimacy, and extramarital sex. And the number of unmarried couples who live together is growing every year.

Many functionalists, seeing that people are violating norms governing family life, read these trends as an increase in family deviance. They interpret this deviance as a symptom of social disorganization—a breakdown in the effective operation of a major social institution, the family. Many conflict theorists draw similar conclusions. They argue that the growing instability of the family reflects the increasing decay of capitalist societies and that family problems will increase until capitalism is thrown out.

We put a less gloomy, but no less serious, interpretation on these deviant trends. We agree that family life today involves much stress, conflict, and misery. We also agree that many norms that sustain conventional family forms are breaking down. But we doubt that the breakdown either must lead to chaos (as many functionalists seem to think) or can be solved only by revolution (as many conflict theorists predict). Instead, we argue that problems facing the modern family reflect *change,* not collapse. We expect the trends to result in new social arrangements better suited to modern life. And once we have overcome some preconceived ideas about what a family is, we will easily recognize these new arrangements to be families.

This chapter concentrates on the American family. It does so not because the matters to be taken up are peculiar to the United States. They are not. Similar trends can be seen in all advanced industrial nations. However, because the United States is one of the most advanced of industrial nations, the process of change in family forms has gone further here than nearly anywhere else in the world. Therefore, by looking closely at what is going on in this country, we can most easily see what are probably the patterns of the future for families in all industrialized societies.

PART I: THE PROBLEM
FAMILY PROBLEMS

The major theme of this chapter is that the American family is changing. What we once meant by the term family, what we mean by it now, and what we might mean by it in the future may all be different. However, two aspects of the family in all societies always remain constant. It is only the details of these two aspects that change. First, the family has a certain *structure,* certain positions (for example, wife) and roles (behavior expected of persons who occupy the position) specified for the members. Second, the family has certain *functions,* duties to perform (for example, socialization of children). Of course, the structure and functions of families vary greatly over time and from place to place.

Indeed, rapid change in the American family's structure and functions is creating much of the American family's problems. The growing friction between family structure and the functions that the family is expected to fulfill puts pressure on the family to change both its structure and its functions in order to find a workable arrangement between the two. To understand how and why the American family is changing and the problems that result from these changes, we must first understand the structures and functions of families in general and how changes in them can cause problems.

FAMILY FUNCTIONS AND
FAMILY STRUCTURES

In every known human society, the basic unit of social organization has been the family. Obviously, the family consists of certain members and has a *structure.* But the family would not be universal unless it offered an efficient way to deal with important problems. Just what does the family do that makes it so important? Sociologists and anthro-

Figure 12.1   The large tracts of land available to the settlers of the American West affected both settlement patterns and the family structure of Americans. Unlike Europeans, whose extended families were clustered in villages or towns (below), American farmers generally had to live in relative isolation with their immediate nuclear families. (Above) Small towns developed in the American West, but they were primarily commercial centers serving farm families who were scattered over a wide area and who would periodically travel to such towns to buy needed supplies.

Figure 12.2 (Above) *The extended family was long portrayed as the ideal in America, but it has become increasingly obvious in recent years that this ideal is incompatible with the conditions of modern American life (and in fact has never been the typical American family form).* (Below) *In primitive societies, however, the extended family is not simply an ideal but a necessity. Mortality rates are so high that only a group of the extended family's size has the capacity to ensure the survival of future generations.*

pologists have drawn up various lists, which can be reduced to three main *functions*.

1. *Economic Support.* The family's productive members provide economic support for the less productive members—children, pregnant females, the elderly, and the disabled. Indeed, through the family, property rights are transmitted from one generation to the next.

2. *Reproduction and Child Rearing.* The family takes major and often sole responsibility for having and raising children until they mature. The long period of feeding, caring for, and socializing offspring requires a group.

3. *Emotional Support.* The family gives emotional support to its members throughout their lifetime. From the family, children receive love and a sense of security and belonging. Within the family, adults also find love, companionship, and identity. Married couples also find stable sexual relations. And the family offers continuity to the old. As friends and spouses of the aged die, the family remains to comfort them. And when the aged die, they do so with the satisfaction of knowing that the family survives them.

367

Given these three family functions, it is obvious why the family has been so central to the human experience. Indeed, throughout history the loss or breakup of one's family was a devastating blow. Because the functions that the family has traditionally fulfilled are so important, many Americans are showing a lot of concern over the family's increasing failure to serve these functions.

Families are characterized by their *structure* as well as by their functions. There are two basic family structures, the nuclear family and the extended family. The typical *nuclear* family is a household composed of one married couple and their minor children. This family structure is what ''family'' usually means to modern Americans. However, as we shall see, the nuclear family is a very new and unusual family structure. Typically, the nuclear family is centered on the bond between husband and wife—indeed, a childless couple constitutes one form of nuclear family. Because of this focus on the marriage bond, the typical nuclear family is sometimes called the *conjugal* family (''conjugal'' refers to the relationship between husband and wife). However, as will be discussed at length in this chapter, the marriage bond is often disrupted (by death, divorce, or separation). When this occurs, and when children are involved, the nuclear family typically becomes *matrifocal*, or focused on the mother, because the children ordinarily remain with their mother. This form of the nuclear family—made up of a mother and dependent children—is becoming increasingly common in our society and is a source of much concern about the ability of the family to survive and to fulfill its functions.

Unlike the nuclear family, which is limited to one adult couple and their children, the *extended*, or *traditional*, family contains several married couples and usually as many as three generations. Put another way, the extended family contains several nuclear families and includes not only parents and children but usually grandparents as well. Within the extended family, there is an important bond of dependence upon the older generation. For example, a group of brothers, their wives, and their children may live with their father and mother. Because the father owns the land and passes property on to his sons only at his death, he remains head of the family. The extended family has been the most common family structure in most societies, past and present.

The extended family can be organized in several ways. For example, in many societies a woman leaves her family at marriage to live with her husband's family, which often includes her husband's parents as well as the families of her husband's brothers. Extended families who live where the husband's parents reside are called *patrilocal* families; extended families who live where the wife's parents reside are called *matrilocal* families.

In the extended family, adults share responsibilities. For example, the elderly may take primary responsibility for child care and thus free more vigorous members of the family for economic production. When an adult is disabled, other adult family members pick up the slack by taking over his or her tasks. And when an adult dies, the surviving spouse and children receive support from the rest of the family. Indeed, perhaps the high mortality rates that were normal in human societies until very recently required the extended family form. In the past, frequently one marriage partner died while the children were still young. The fact

that the extended family contained more than one couple insured that children would be supported and cared for. The children, in turn, supported the surviving members in their old age.

The extended family provides a standard against which to examine how the American family has changed in modern times. But before we examine how and why the American family is changing and look at the consequent problems, we must see how problems arise in the family in any society.

POTENTIAL FAMILY PROBLEMS

At least four kinds of problems *could* afflict the family in any society. Our analysis of these problems provides the basis for the rest of the chapter.

One source of trouble is the *incompatibility between family structure and functions.* In some preliterate societies, for example, it is the mother's brother, not the biological father, who plays the primary male role in socializing children (an important function). If the family structure permits the mother's brother to carry out this function, there is no problem. For example, this function of socialization is carried out easily where children grow up in *extended, matrilocal* families. The uncles live close by and are able to fulfill such socializing functions as instructing male children about sexual behavior. However, if the family structure changes, it becomes difficult to continue certain patterns of socialization and other important functions of the family.

Incompatibility between family structure and functions means that family members cannot adequately perform the tasks assigned to the family in that society. We have mentioned that the mother's brother cannot readily fulfill his assigned role to his sister's children if he does not live nearby. A more contemporary American example can be seen in the matrifocal family. A single parent usually cannot provide both economic support for the family and adequate care for young children. Hence, either the child care must be delegated to others (baby sitters or child-care centers) to permit the parent to work, or the economic function must be assumed by an outside source such as a welfare agency in order for the child-rearing function to be fulfilled.

One reason the family undergoes change is that the conditions required for modern industrial societies are not suited to the extended family and its traditional functions. Thus, a second source of problems for the family is that its *structure and functions may be incompatible with other elements and conditions of society.* Industrialization puts severe pressures on the family to change its structure. Structural change, in turn, often makes it difficult for the family to continue to fulfill its essential functions without further structural change. It may also have to give up performing certain functions. Ceasing to perform certain functions may lead to further strains on family structures and functions.

For example, in the United States, the function of caring for young children is assigned to the family and has primarily been the responsibility of the mother. However, because of a change from farming to urban life that resulted from industrialization, it is no longer possible for women to do much productive work within the home while caring for children. Making soap, spinning wool, preserving food, and the many other ways in which wives contributed to the economic well-being of the family are no longer economically useful. To be economically useful, wives must now work outside the home, and many have begun to do so. Furthermore, new values and norms stemming mainly from outside the family now encourage women to want careers and to overcome their subordinate status. But women's new status tends to be incompatible with child care. Thus, there is increasing tension between the role of wife and mother and the role of liberated woman.

The conflict between social conditions, on the one hand, and family structure and functions, on the other, causes a great deal of unhappiness and discontent. People begin to demand that something be done. Obviously, there are two main ways in which relief could be sought. First, the family could be changed. The structure might be altered to reduce the burden of child care. For example, men might take on more child-care duties, or several nuclear families might share child-care duties. The child-care function of the family could also be reduced. The demands for inexpensive and adequate child-care programs propose to do just that.

A second possibility is that the society might be changed to be more compatible with present family structures and functions. For example, provision might be made to permit women to obtain leaves or defer their careers until children no longer require intensive care. The point is that when serious incompatibilities arise between the family and other parts of society, something has to give.

At present, what has been giving is the family. And this leads us to a third source of family problems, *deviance.* Within any society at any given moment there is a preferred or "normal" family with typical structure and functions. Families that seriously depart from this model are usually thought deviant, not simply because these families violate the norms but because people believe that deviance will be harmful for these families, for their members, and perhaps for society as a whole. As mentioned before, deviant families give rise to the notions of family disorganization. Something is going wrong with the families, either because individuals within the families fail or because certain outside factors, such as poverty or racial discrimination, especially affect these families.

When society is working well—when the incompatibilities that we have discussed are minimal—deviance as an explanation for family malfunctioning seems appropriate. For example, if personal failings of husbands or wives are the main cause of divorce, divorce can be seen as a problem of deviance, not as a problem of families in general. By the same token, if outside factors, such as poverty, overburden some families, divorce in these families can be seen as a limited problem, not a problem of the whole society. Even in the most stable society, there are always some deviant families. Thus, even if society is working well, deviance is always a source of family problems.

But it seems silly to speak of a given family form as deviant if that form has become the rule rather than the exception. Thus, if half of the adults in a society have been divorced, it is hard to regard divorce as unusual or deviant or as a limited problem. Nevertheless, if this change happens rapidly, people may continue to regard the outmoded form as an ideal until they have a chance to adjust to new circumstances. This process is what seems to be happening in the United States.

369

The fourth kind of family problem is *family forms that are harmful to their members.* For example, many persons believe that adopting a system in which children are raised in state nurseries rather than by their parents would be a harmful family form. They argue that children require more than just care and attention from adults, that children also require a stable and close relationship with at least one adult. If such a relationship is necessary, giving up newborn infants to nurseries and boarding schools may cause them severe emotional and developmental problems. It is known, for example, that children raised in orphanages fall behind in intellectual development (Dennis, 1938, 1960). Thus, a family stripped of child-care functions might have a very serious problem. But we cannot say this with absolute certainty. For one thing, the problem of children who are raised from infancy in state nurseries may stem mainly from the fact that the rest of society is not in harmony with this pattern of child rearing, not from the pattern itself. For another thing, no one would be able to study a society whose most prevalent family forms were seriously harmful to its members—either because the harmful forms would change as problems worsened or because the society itself would not last. For example, it may well be that many, even most, small groups in the distant past failed to develop the extended family form. We have no way of knowing, for only the groups that did discover that form seem to have survived long enough to leave a trace.

Having laid out the various ways in which the family in any society can develop troubles, we now examine problems of the American family.

THE AMERICAN FAMILY

Most American adolescents expect one day to fall in love, marry, and have children. The wife will then stay home and care for the children. And even if the wife does work, the husband will be the main breadwinner for the family.

Most people also realize that one day the children will leave home (to re-enact the cycle of love, marriage, and children). Although the wife may then take a full-time job, her major orientation in life will continue to be the home. One day the

The Total Cost of a Child, 1969*	
Cost of giving birth	$ 1,534
Cost of raising a child	32,830
Cost of a college education	5,560
Total direct cost	39,924
Opportunity costs for the average woman†	58,437
Total costs of a first child	$98,361

*These figures are based on simple accumulations of total costs without regard for the year in a child's life in which they must be made. Because of the considerable inflation that has occurred since 1969, the present cost of a child is considerably greater than is shown here.

†Depending on the educational background of the mother, the opportunity costs (earnings lost by not working) could be higher or lower.

Figure 12.3 (Top left) *This advertisement of a honeymoon resort caters to the American ideal of romantic love and sexual fulfillment in marriage.*

Figure 12.4 (Bottom left) *Careful family planning, birth control, and child spacing might become more widespread if the true costs of having a child were recognized by couples in their reproductive years.*
(From Commission on Population Growth and the American Future, 1972.)

Figure 12.5 *Child care often interferes with a woman's ability to work and earn an adequate income. However, there are exceptions, such as Illinois legislator Susan Catania, who manages to combine her job as state representative with caring for and feeding her infant daughter.*

husband will retire, and it is hoped that there will be grandchildren to dote on.

Behind this romantic image lie three fundamental beliefs that American married couples cherish. (These beliefs correspond to three family functions previously listed.) First, married couples expect to be economically self-sufficient throughout their lives. They do not plan to be supported for any substantial time by parents, children, or other relatives, nor by charity or welfare. Second, they expect to have children and to raise and care for them until they grow up. Third, they expect the family to provide the needed emotional support for each member.

Because most of us share these beliefs about the family, we do not readily see the problems they contain. The fact is that our present family structure has difficulty fulfilling these three functions. Furthermore, other parts of society have not been changed to allow for these family inabilities. We will see how the American family fares with these three functions.

371

ECONOMIC SUPPORT IN THE AMERICAN FAMILY

The first function that Americans expect the family to fulfill is to be economically self-sufficient. However, economic support for the family can come from either within the family or outside the family. Within the American family, either the husband or the wife or both can be the economic providers. Help from outside the family can take many forms in our society, but none of these provides economic security for most American families.

Husband As Provider

In the usual American nuclear family, the father is the sole income provider. Even today, most married women are not employed. As a result, the family is economically vulnerable. If the father dies or leaves, the family has financial hardship.

However, the same threat arises when the father remains in the family but his income declines because he loses his job, takes a pay cut, or becomes physically or mentally disabled. Similarly, the family is also threatened economically even when income does not decline but when the family incurs exceptional financial burdens, such as an unexpected child, or a disabled parent.

Ironically, the family may hinder the father's ability to cope with economic difficulties. The most common ways to increase income are to change jobs, to move to another place where opportunities are greater, and to obtain additional education or training. Each of these ways may involve a short-term loss of income. If the family is already financially hard-pressed, it often cannot withstand even short-term income losses. Thus, families most in need of more income are least able to take action to provide it. Indeed, the kind of pattern that a family follows may help sustain poverty. Compared with people who marry later, people who marry young have less education when they marry, have children at a younger age, and have more children. A family pattern such as marrying young limits how much the male can earn and at the same time increases the family's costs.

Perhaps the most severe stress on the family's economic independence occurs when the husband retires. By this time, most couples have not amassed enough wealth or accrued enough retirement benefits to avoid suffering economic hardships when they reach old age.

Wife As Provider

Wives are, of course, at least a potential source of family income. If the husband dies, deserts, becomes disabled, or loses his job, the wife is the only other source of income. However, because women usually earn less than men, when the wife replaces the husband as the family breadwinner, family income is usually cut in half. Female-headed families earn only half the median income of male-headed families (in 1972, $5,342 compared with $11,116). Furthermore, because the wife who works must hire someone else to perform her duties in the home, particularly to care for her children, it is often the case that little of what she earns remains for her family's own needs.

Once again, the families that most need additional income are least likely to benefit from the wife's employment. If the wife obtains a job that pays the minimum wage, she can hardly afford to pay another woman the minimum wage to care for her children. Indeed, the wife would lose money,

for her salary after withholding taxes would be less than the money she spends for child care. Middle-class wives qualify for better-paying jobs and thus can gain by paying another person the minimum wage. Moreover, because middle-class wives have fewer children, their child-care costs are lower and last a shorter time. These facts are a major reason why middle-class wives work more often than lower-class wives.

From the foregoing discussions, we see that many American families have great difficulty in being economically independent. The nuclear family lacks the resources of the extended family, where economic responsibilities are spread over many able adults.

Support from Outside the Family

The American family structure might be economically adequate if other parts of society helped out. Friends and relatives today feel less obligation to help and often cannot help other nuclear families with money problems except when they are short-term problems. And because friends and relatives of the poor are often also poor, even short-term aid usually goes to young middle-class and upper-class families, who have outside sources for financial help but who need it less than poor families do.

American society has only grudgingly provided public aid to families in financial difficulty, and then more often to female-headed families. Nevertheless, welfare programs, despite their defects, offer some economic safeguards. The same is true of retirement and pension plans. But perhaps the most common protection is insurance, especially life-insurance policies, which compensate the rest of the family for the earnings lost when the main income producer dies. Insurance companies widely advertise the need to insure the young father's life against an untimely death. Life insurance also protects the elderly wife against a poverty-stricken widowhood. This is a serious risk faced by older women because men have a shorter life expectancy than women and also because women are often younger than their husbands. In fact, the majority of men over sixty-five have wives, but the majority of women over sixty-five are widows.

The poor can seldom afford adequate life insurance, even through they are the ones who need

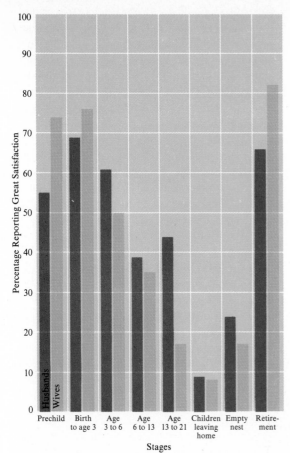

Figure 12.6 *Marital satisfaction declines after children are born. It continues to decline after children are past the infant and early childhood stages and does not rise again until after they have left home. It increases sharply with retirement.* (Adapted from B.C. Rollins and H. Feldman, 1967-1968.)

Figure 12.7 *On the average, women today devote much less of their lives to maternity than they did in 1900—both because their lifespan has increased and because they are having fewer children.* (Adapted from E. Sullerot, 1971.)

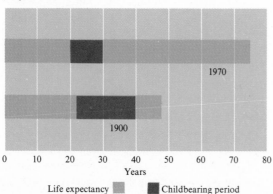

it most. The poor have a greater need for insurance protection because the poor family has a higher adult mortality rate. Compared with the husband in wealthier families, the low-income husband more often dies when his children are young. However, even the solidly middle-class family has economic weaknesses. Death, disability, many children, or retirement can easily destroy this family's financial independence.

When the American family has difficulty finding within itself the economic support it needs, the family also often cannot find that support outside itself. Therefore, the American family often fails to provide its members with the economic support that they require.

CHILD REARING IN THE AMERICAN FAMILY

The second function that Americans expect the family to fulfill is to have children and raise them to be competent adults. In a nuclear family, child-rearing responsibility falls mainly on the mother. The average family today has 2.3 children. In contrast with the large families of the past, the nuclear family's small number of children would seem to fit the American family's capacities. Nevertheless, caring for and socializing children still taxes the American family's resources.

Caring for Children

Because usually the age-span between children in a small American family is narrow, the older children are too young to help care for the still younger ones. More important, wives today have had little opportunity to learn how to care for the young. Siblings in the small nuclear family to which the wife was born were all young together, so when they grow up and become wives most of them cannot remember having lived with a pregnant woman or with an infant and hence have no experience in these matters. Furthermore, unlike the extended family, the nuclear family has no other experienced women to advise and aid young mothers in child care.

This lack of child-care knowledge creates obvious problems for new mothers in the United States. Most must depend on doctors and friends (who are no better informed) and on magazines and books to

373

discover the basics of infant care and child rearing. Little wonder that Dr. Benjamin Spock's book *The Common Sense Book of Baby and Child Care* has sold more than 23 million copies in 26 years. At the same time that the changed family structure has prevented women from learning to care for children, social scientists have made women intensely concerned about the pitfalls of raising children. Since the pioneering work of Sigmund Freud, Western society has come to believe that a child's emotional development can be easily damaged if he or she receives inadequate attention. This thought hardly comforts women who already lack assurance in coping with children. And this concern may explain why many women today are compelled to devote themselves far more totally to their children than their grandmothers did. However, the devotion of these new mothers seldom contributes to their happiness. Indeed, research shows that marital satisfaction declines for both men and women when children are born and does not rise again until retirement (see Figure 12.6).

Socializing Children

Families are expected to do more than simply care for their children. Families are also expected to socialize children—to teach them the same skills, facts, values, and attitudes required of the society's competent adult members. However, in the complex, industrial American society, these expectations are enormous. Hence, with other societal demands on the family, both the family and society are finding it hard to socialize children. Three important problem areas are education, sex roles, and multiple-mothering.

Education

Because our rapidly developing industrial society keeps demanding new knowledge and skills from the young, the family cannot keep up with the child's education. Consequently, we have created an elaborate educational system to help relieve the family of this burden. However, widespread criticism of the schools indicates that they are not effectively socializing the children. Indeed, research shows that student achievement depends more on a child's family than on the school (Coleman, 1966).

The schools do best with the students whose family best socializes them—children who already

know numbers and the alphabet when they begin school and are otherwise prepared to learn. The schools typically fail children whose families socialize them poorly. The poor and least educated parents, who most need aid to educate their children, find the schools less able to help their children than the children of affluent parents. The problem is not simply that schools are designed to favor the wealthier children. Despite immense efforts to enrich the schools to serve disadvantaged children, no effective method has been found (Jencks *et al.*, 1972). Thus, it is because we do not know how to prevent it that the schools turn out so many students who are nearly illiterate and thus doomed to face life without the skills needed to meet adult responsibilities. The school system has only very partially and imperfectly relieved the family from the duty of socializing the young.

Yet the family must find outside aid to raise children. For virtually no family can by itself adequately prepare its children for life today. Gone are the days when a girl could learn what she needed from her mother, or a boy from his father.

Sex Roles

Only in recent times have boys been raised so exclusively by women. In farming days, young boys soon left the house to trail into the fields after their fathers, uncles, and older brothers. In so doing, the boys constantly had models of adult male behavior. Today, few men work in locations where the young can observe them. Indeed, in the suburbs young boys are often almost exclusively in contact with mothers and female teachers. This has led some social scientists to worry about whether boys are being adequately socialized into appropriate sex-role behavior. On the other hand, many others worry that the family is too successful in teaching sex-role behavior that perpetuates patterns of male dominance. At present, we simply do not know whether the greatly reduced contact between young boys and adult males in our society is having important effects on sex roles.

Multiple-Mothering

Young children whose mothers work get much of their care from baby-sitters or from day-care centers. These children receive *multiple-mothering*; that is, they spend much of their time with a woman in addition to their own mother (Fein and Clarke-Stewart, 1973). The rapidly increasing proportion of mothers who take jobs is increasing the proportion of children who receive multiple-mothering. Today approximately 30 percent of women with children under age six are employed. (This figure does not include working mothers who are divorced, widowed, or separated.) Because multiple-mothering may have negative effects on a child's socialization, people have become alarmed at this increase.

Researchers have studied multiple-mothering to determine if it is harmful to children (Hoffman, 1963). The results suggest that preschool boys are often upset by multiple-mothering, whereas young girls may actually benefit from it. Preschool boys are more often withdrawn and overdependent when they have multiple-mothering than when they do not. However, preschool girls are more aggressive, dominant, and independent when they receive multiple-mothering than when they do not. Among older boys, multiple-mothering seems to have no impact except when the mother's working implies that the father cannot support the family. Older girls seem to have a more favorable image of themselves if their mothers work.

We have now shown that the nuclear family creates problems in the care and socialization of children. Furthermore, these problems affect not only the family but also other parts of society in at least two ways.

One way is that child-rearing practices rapidly change because mothers must now learn child care from books, magazines, and the news media and therefore quickly adopt new child-rearing ideas. Hence, mothers may put a mistaken child-rearing notion into widespread practice before its defects are spotted. When child-rearing practices were mainly passed from mother to daughter—and indeed when child-rearing occurred in view of grandmothers, aunts, and sisters-in-law—changes happened very slowly. Nevertheless, rapid adoption of new ideas can benefit society. For example, mothers will more readily accept new medical information and will not so quickly pass on old wive's tales.

The second way that family problems also affect other parts of society is that probably a higher proportion of children are poorly socialized today than in the days of the extended family. Today socialization is not the responsibility of several adults, but falls mainly on a wife who may have been little prepared for the task. Poor socialization can contribute to deviant behavior. Furthermore, shifting the socialization duties from the family to the schools has increasingly burdened the schools. And present needs for expanded, inexpensive, and dependable child care means that what families used to do is becoming something society must provide. The American family has difficulty in fulfilling its child-rearing function, and other social institutions have not taken up the slack.

EMOTIONAL SUPPORT IN THE AMERICAN FAMILY

The third function that the American family is expected to fulfill is to be the main source of emotional support—including love, affection, and companionship—for its members. Indeed, at a time when people move often, friends are repeatedly left behind and only family bonds offer long-term intimacy and affection. The main family bond is between the adult couple. Spouses hope to receive from each other both love and life-long companionship. The other important emotional bond is between parents and children. From their parents, children are expected to receive secure love and affection. And toward parents, children first develop the capacity for loving.

Today, these expectations are frequently not met. Couples may find that they do not provide each other with enough emotional support. Children also may not find enough warmth and affection between them and their parents. Indeed, these bonds are often broken. Divorce and separation remove one parent from the family and break the bonds between spouses and at least weaken the bonds between children and one parent. Also, after children mature and leave home, the bonds between them and their parents frequently wither.

Because today family bonds are often the only available source of deep relationships, the fact that they so commonly break down leaves many people at least temporarily without enough emotional support. This lack often does them great psychological

375

harm and rarely does them any good. We now discuss how divorce, isolation of parents from adult children, and death take this emotional toll.

Divorce

Divorce statistics are imperfect. At present in the United States, the data show that there is one divorce for every three marriages. However, these statistics do not mean that only a third of American adults divorce. The proportion is likely much higher than that because of at least four factors. The first is that many marriages involve persons previously divorced. About 75 percent of all divorced persons remarry within five years (Bernard, 1972). The second factor that makes the divorce rate look smaller is that separated couples are counted in the statistics as married. The third factor is that today couples may marry several times without bothering to seek a legal divorce. And the fourth factor is that many couples today live together as if married and then separate without adding to either the marriage or the divorce statistics.

376

Despite defects in the statistics, it seems clear that for a substantial proportion of Americans marriage is no longer usually a lifetime relationship. The average duration of a marriage as of 1967 was only *seven years* (U.S. Public Health Service, 1970). Because the divorce rate has been rising since 1967, and when more recent figures on marital duration become available, the data will most likely show the average American marriage to be even shorter.

Seven years is not a long time to be married, but it is long enough to have children. In fact, the majority of divorces involve children (62 percent of divorces in 1966 occurred between couples with children). With rare exception, women receive custody of the children following a divorce. Thus, the main result of divorce is that it creates female-headed families, at least until the woman remarries. At present, some 20 percent of white families and 30 percent of nonwhite families are female-headed. Some of these families were created by illegitimacy and some by death, but most were the result of divorce.

We have already mentioned that loss of the father from the family reduces family income by as much as half. Father loss also creates more intense

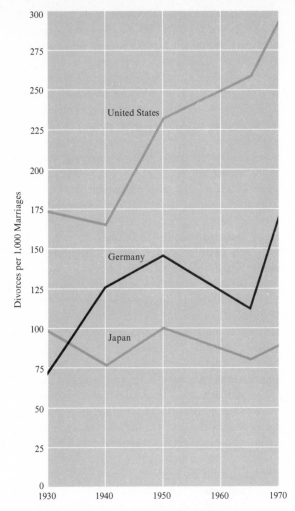

Figure 12.8   *Divorce rates in the United States have been climbing rapidly for over three decades. Other Western nations have experienced a similar but less spectacular increase in divorce rates; the more tradition- and family-oriented Japanese have experienced a much lower and somewhat fluctuating rate.*
(Adapted from United Nations *Demographic Yearbooks*, 1972.)

child-rearing problems. But perhaps the most serious divorce result is the loss of emotional support. However, between the adults, sometimes this emotional support was already missing before the divorce. For example, divorce may simply reflect the fact that there was no emotional support between the married couple. And at other times, divorce may mean that one marriage partner emotionally rejected the other. In any event, divorce usually weakens the exchange of love and affection between the father and the children. It is hard for the father to maintain emotional relations when he becomes a visitor in the home. In addition, relations often become more strained when the mother remarries and the children have to deal with both a father and a stepfather. And when the natural father remarries, his children must also cope with that. Also, when remarried parents each add more children to their respective families, the previous children may feel estranged from both their father's and mother's new families.

How severe are the effects of divorce on children? No uniform or marked effects have been found. However, divorce is more likely to upset the emotional stability of younger children than of older children, and of Catholic children and Jewish children than of Protestant children. And remarriage by the mother can cause great anxiety in children, especially older children (Rosenberg, 1965). Nevertheless, fear of hurting the children is not a good reason for an unhappy couple to remain married. Children of divorced parents are much better adjusted than children living in homes where the parents are together but unhappy (Landis, 1965; Burchinal, 1963; Nye, 1963).

Isolation of Parents from Children

Divorce separates many parents from their children while they are still quite young. The nuclear family ideal is that children will establish their own separate household upon marriage, and most children live away from their parents for a considerable period before they marry. Because the average American woman bears her last child by age twenty-eight, often by the time she is fifty her home is empty of children. Given that she can expect to live well into her seventies, if her marriage lasts, she will spend a longer period of her married life in a family consisting of only an adult couple than in a family of a larger size.

For many women who devote themselves to children and home, the children's departure causes serious despondency (Barth, 1970). Of course, men also feel the loss of the children.

Obviously, even if children move only a short distance from their parent's home, contact between parents and children is much less than when they lived together. But in fact, most children do not just move down the block. They often move to another city or even another part of the country. Americans are frequent movers. Only 5 percent of us now spend our lives in a single community. Indeed, nearly one out of every four American families moves in any given year. Because physical distance usually separates parents from adult children, relations between parents and children eventually diminish greatly.

Death

We have pointed out that the average American woman at a relatively young age finds herself once more in a two-person family, her nest empty. Worse yet, she is likely to spend her last years in a "family" consisting of only herself. Until this century, men outlived women because so many women died in childbirth or because often their health was weakened by childbirth complications. Women now rarely die in childbirth, and the average twenty-year-old woman will outlive the average twenty-year-old man by nearly seven years. Furthermore, women usually marry men several years older than themselves. This tendency is increased in remarriage. Men who remarry often choose women younger than their previous wife. Women, on the other hand, tend to marry men older than their first husband. As a result of all the factors we have mentioned, many American women are now widows. Of women over sixty-five, 62 percent do *not* have a husband living with them, and the great majority of these women are widows. On the other hand, 76 percent of men over sixty-five do have a wife living with them.

It is impossible for a "family" consisting of one person to give its member emotional support. Indeed, only an agency such as the U.S. Census Bureau, more interested in statistics than in in-

377

dividuals, would readily describe an elderly person living alone as a family.

Thus far, we have shown that today's American family is having great difficulty in fulfilling its three functions. We have said that a major reason for this trouble is the structure of the American family, that the nuclear family cannot fulfill these responsibilities, at least not without aid from other social institutions. Thus, we now take up two important questions. First, why has the nuclear family become the dominant family structure in the United States? Second, what incompatibilities between the family and society in America are pressuring the nuclear family?

PART II: SOURCES FAMILY PROBLEMS

Chapters in this unit depart from the format used in Units II and III because problems included in this unit are best understood at the macro level—the level where society works as a system of interrelated parts. For example, we argue in this section that social change in America has forced persons to adopt the nuclear family structure. Similarly, we argue that social change has also made the nuclear family unable to successfully cope with present social conditions.

Thus, we shall not seek to explain current family problems at the physiological, psychological, or social-psychological levels of analysis. Instead, we turn immediately to institutional and societal sources of family problems.

CREATION OF THE NUCLEAR FAMILY

The nuclear family structure has much to do with America's family problems. The extended family structure was well suited to fulfill the family functions that now threaten to overwhelm the nuclear family. Yet it would be futile to place blame on the nuclear family structure. For the nuclear family form was created—and the extended family form outmoded—by unavoidable social change. Unless we set the clock back several centuries and return nearly everyone to farming and village life, we cannot restore the extended family structure. And

378

Figure 12.9   The impact of grief and bereavement over the death of a family member may be somewhat softened through emotional support, a primary function of the family. If family bonds are broken and this emotional support is not available during a crisis in a person's life, great psychological harm may result.

short of a world-wide calamity that would wipe out billions of people, we can never return to simple rural living, for we could not support our present population without industry and complex technology. Thus, we must deal with the nuclear family structure. To do so, we must understand why the change to a nuclear family structure was necessary in the United States.

Immigration and Migration

Unlike in other, older nations, in the United States the extended family was probably never the most common family form, although at one time most American families may have thought it was. By immigrating to America, most settlers broke their extended-family ties. It was mainly young families and single people who came to the New World. Once the settlers arrived, the process continued. For as the American frontier continued to move westward, once again individuals and families pulled up stakes to migrate and left their relatives behind. In America, sons were not tied to their father's land and hence to their parents as had long been the case in Europe. Instead, the sons could easily find cheap or free land of their own. Furthermore, because American farms were extremely large compared with European standards or compared with peasant plots in today's underdeveloped nations, families could not cluster in a village from which men went out to the fields each day. Most families would have had to travel much too far from the village to their fields. The *family farm* was the only practical alternative, and it became the dominant mode of American rural life.

These large farms required a great deal of labor. But since land could be had almost for the asking, few persons would work as hired hands. Families responded to this labor problem with high fertility—children were the major source of farm labor. However, as the children became adults and desired families of their own, it did not make sense for all of them to try to live off their father's land. To do so would have required a marked decline in their standard of living. So they departed to settle their own farms and repeat the cycle. Often the eldest son did remain behind to eventually take over his father's farm. Thus, while the parents still lived, eldest sons often lived in an extended fami-

ly. But the majority of families (created by the children who left home) were nuclear families.

Urbanization and Industrialization

As the farmland became populated, something new happened. The United States began to massively industrialize, and factories offered wages far higher than could be made operating a marginal farm. Consequently, younger sons and daughters ceased to move to their own farms and, instead, moved to the cities. Thus began a great emptying of the rural areas. In 1820, 72 percent of the American population lived on farms. In 1969, only 5 percent lived on farms. The shift was equally dramatic in absolute numbers. As recently as 1917, more than 32 million Americans lived on farms. In 1969, only 10 million did so.

The move to the city was not only the result of the lure of industrial wages. Industrialization hit the farms too. New machines—the reaper, the threshing machine, and later, the tractor and the combine—greatly reduced the labor demands of farming. As one person with machines could farm more and more land, the farms began to grow in area. Smaller farms could not compete, and thus many farmers were, and continued to be, driven from the farm to the city.

If it was difficult to establish extended families in rural America, it was even more difficult to do so in the city. Cities do not at all resemble rural areas. If a family owns a farm, they live on it. And the farm remains in the same location year after year. But middle-class urban Americans constantly move to keep their jobs or to find better ones or to find a nicer place to live. Factories and offices move around, sometimes to other cities, and take their employees with them. Most nationwide companies assume that their employees are willing to move to another branch in another part of the country, as the company desires. Industry also assumes it can attract the workers it needs from other parts of the country.

All this movement makes it nearly impossible to keep several nuclear families joined together in an extended family structure. Although many American families often visit relatives, few related nuclear families actually share the same home any longer. In 1967, less than 2 percent of married

379

couples shared their household with relatives other than their own minor children.

The fact is that industrialization and urbanization are incompatible with the extended family form in *all industrialized nations.* Even in Japan, where family bonds seem very strong by Western standards, the nuclear family form has become widespread because of the processes of urbanization and industrialization.

Thus far, we have outlined why the nuclear family became the dominant form of American family life. We now examine how certain aspects of American society have greatly taxed the nuclear family structure. In so doing, we do not turn from the impact of the city and industry on the family—this continues to be an important underlying theme.

SOCIETAL PRESSURES ON
MARRIAGE PARTNERS

380

Earlier in the chapter, we painted a gloomy picture of the incapacity of the nuclear family structure to fulfill the three family functions. However, this inability does not mean that the American nuclear family is a complete failure. As long as most nu-

clear families are intact, they do manage to be economically self-sufficient, to rear children, and to provide members with emotional support. The trouble is that so many families do not remain intact. Therefore, we turn our attention to the husband-wife relationship, for it is here that present societal forces unfriendly to the family are focused. We will discuss four main forces that are pressuring the husband-wife relationship: romantic love, occupational segregation, the sexual revolution, and changing sex roles.

Romantic Love

One of the most characteristic features of modern American society is romantic love. A common belief in America is that people ought not to marry unless they are in love and that a marital relationship without love is unsatisfactory.

In the extended or traditional family of the past—and in many places throughout the world today—marriage was based on more practical considerations, such as property. Parents often selected the mate to insure that the match was practical. Because people married without expecting to find love, there was little basis for marital disappointment so long as the union was fertile, the

---

COMPATIBILITY'S PERSONALITY INVENTORY

Please give your first spontaneous reaction to each of the following questions. If you strongly agree with the statement, circle 1; if you agree, circle 2; if you neither agree nor disagree, circle 3; if you disagree, circle 4; if you strongly disagree with the statement, circle 5. Although it may be hard to decide on some questions, be sure to answer all of them.

	Agree		?	Disagree	
1. My parents were fairly religious and so am I.	1	2	3	4	5
2. Religious convictions help produce a home that is harmonious and stable.	1	2	3	4	5
3. I believe in God.	1	2	3	4	5
4. I attend church regularly and would prefer a mate who does the same.	1	2	3	4	5
5. Parents who do not provide religious training for their children are not fulfilling their responsibilities	1	2	3	4	5
6. I believe in the existence of a Supreme Being that controls the fate of mankind.	1	2	3	4	5
7. The breakdown of organized religion is a major problem in our society today.	1	2	3	4	5
8. My religious faith has helped me understand the difference between right and wrong.	1	2	3	4	5
9. A fine moral code can be a good substitute for a religious code.	1	2	3	4	5
10. A person can have high moral standards without being religious.	1	2	3	4	5
11. The portrayal of sex in the movies has gone too far.	1	2	3	4	5
12. I believe that married women who work desert their home for a career.	1	2	3	4	5
13. It is not appropriate to include sex education in the school program.	1	2	3	4	5
14. It is the parents' obligation and responsibility to tell their youth how to dress.	1	2	3	4	5
15. Long hair and beards are a sign of the breakdown in our society.	1	2	3	4	5
16. Current obscenity laws, covering magazines and books, are not strong enough.	1	2	3	4	5
17. Years ago people had more fun than they do today.	1	2	3	4	5
18. I frequently seek new and exciting experiences.	1	2	3	4	5
19. Children must learn when they are very young deep respect for law and order.	1	2	3	4	5

woman was a competent homemaker, and the man was an able provider. Neither husband nor wife expected to find his or her primary emotional support from the other. Instead, within the extended family, women gave each other understanding and companionship, and men's primary bonds were also to one another.

In America today property is not the economic basis of most family economies. In seeking a spouse, women do not look for husbands who own land, nor do men search for women with a dowry. Furthermore, in the nuclear family the mate is the sole adult source of emotional support. Indeed, because of the geographic mobility of modern society, the marital bond is perhaps the only permanent, close emotional bond with another adult that most people can have. For these reasons, Americans today are almost required to choose a mate on the basis of interpersonal attraction.

In principle, the husband-wife relationship should provide enough emotional support for adult couples. However, complete dependence on this single bond often makes it harder to maintain. Because it is the one vital emotional tie most people have with another adult, any discontent or threat to this relationship is difficult to tolerate. Hence, small disturbances in the relationship are easily magnified. Unfortunately, many aspects of modern life do cause tensions and disturbances in the marriage bond.

Occupational Segregation

Until recently, most men's and women's work was done in or relatively close to the home. The work setting was not a separate social world divorced from home and family. In contrast, today work generally segregates a person from the spouse. Most employed adults spend their working day involved with problems and duties that their spouses only know about through hearsay. Working adults are also involved with people whom the spouse never gets to know very well. Usually, only the man lives in this separate occupational world. Hence, the fact that the husband often develops interests and friends not shared by his wife causes an imbalance in the relationship between the husband and the wife.

The job setting may also offer emotional bonds that threaten the marriage. Because men usually bear the main financial burden for the family, their job often becomes their main concern. Unlike the wife at home, the women in the office are able to

381

Figure 12.10   The idea that similarity of attitudes breeds attraction and will ensure compatibility has long been popular and is one of the primary assumptions of computer-dating questionnaires, as suggested by this excerpt (left). The popularity and prevalence of computer-dating programs also indicate how many people have failed to find compatibility and happy relationships on their own.

Figure 12.11   (Right) Images of the happy American family are often portrayed in television series and advertisements. However, the ideal image does not correspond to the facts. Because of societal pressures, many American families do not remain intact.

relate to the man's main interests and activities. The office affair and the suspicions that wives have toward women at the office are common themes in humor and drama because the themes in fact reflect common occurrences.

Meanwhile, lacking the emotional support that men often find from fellow workers, the woman at home needs more support from her husband than he needs from her. The wife's need for more support gives rise to the frequent complaint of hardworking men that their wives demand too much attention. In turn, the wives correctly complain that their lives are dull because their husbands never want to do anything when they come home.

When women work, some of these problems are greatly reduced. Working women have office friendships, and they also come home ready to relax after a hard day at work. Thus, not surprisingly, women who work are more likely to report their marriage is a happy one than are women who do not work (Bernard, 1972; Dizard, 1968; Nye, 1963). Indeed, the evidence suggests that some women find enough personal satisfaction at work to permit them to continue in a marriage they find relatively unsatisfying (Bernard, 1972). Hence, when both husband and wife work, some of the imbalance is removed from their relationship.

However, having both the husband and wife work does not remove all job strains from the marriage. As the husband and wife spend their days in separate work settings, they may find that they have fewer common interests and friends. Furthermore, the likelihood that one marriage partner will form a strong romantic attachment outside the marital bond is increased because both partners are now exposed to temptations. In addition, when women work, they are less financially dependent on men, and this increases their freedom to end a marriage and increases men's freedom to do likewise. We mention this economic fact not to suggest that people ought to be financially trapped in a marriage they dislike but simply to point out that economic concerns once pressing against divorce no longer press so strongly.

The Sexual Revolution

The revolutionary changes in sexual norms and behavior that have recently occurred in our society provide new grounds for marital dissatisfaction. A major change is that female sexuality is now recognized. Clearly, when it was believed that women could not and should not enjoy sex, there were few grounds for sexual incompatibility. Today, married couples are expected to achieve an active and mutually satisfying sex life. Furthermore, the sexual revolution has increased the proportion of people who have premarital sexual relations. Thus, more people who enter marriage have some previous experience against which to assess their marital sexual relations. Also, the increased proportion of people who have extramarital sexual relations increases the risk that married people will find a more compatible sexual partner outside their marriage. Finally, a major sexual problem in American society is that many people have great difficulty learning to be sexually adequate.

All these sexual changes increase the pressure on the husband-wife relationship. Studies reveal that sexual dissatisfaction is common among married couples today. Furthermore, sexual satisfaction usually *declines* as the marriage gets older (Pineo, 1961).

At present, society assumes that the bond between husband and wife is a permanent, main source of emotional satisfaction. However, the high divorce rate testifies that this assumption is often wrong and that couples are increasingly calling it quits once the emotional intensity of their relationship declines. Many social scientists now claim that romantic love and sexual attraction are so fragile they often wear off as two people live together longer. Because so many people desire a romantic and sexually stimulating relationship, the spouses become dissatisfied as these aspects of the marriage cool off. Because most of us live in cities, we have the opportunity to privately pursue new relationships to replace or supplement a declining marital relationship.

Changing Sex Roles

A final change that is having a profound impact on the husband-wife relationship is the emancipation of women from subservience to men. Until recently, women have been almost the property of their fathers or husbands. In fact, under traditional English common law, rape was a property crime,

committed by one man against another man's property. By legal definition, it was impossible to rape a woman who did not belong to anyone. Thus, women were totally dependent on men.

Today, however, the recent and rapid entry of women into full-time occupations outside the home has given them greater freedom and reduced their economic dependence on their husbands. So the economic barriers to divorce have come down. The liberation of women also puts strain on the marriage because liberation requires altering male and female roles—hence, the roles of husband and wife, father and mother, son and daughter, and brother and sister. Trouble often arises if men refuse to assist in housekeeping and child-rearing duties when their wives work.

Furthermore, many men cannot deal with job competition from their wives. Our norms have not yet adjusted to women who are more successful, higher paid, or more famous than their husbands. Yet, as more women take up high-status career lines, the likelihood increases that the wife will outachieve her husband. At present, however, when the wife outachieves her husband, the couple runs a risk of divorce.

Of course, the problem is not simply male vanity. Women also have been raised to want to look up to their husbands. So long as that remains the case, women who are more successful than their husbands are likely to desire a divorce. Indeed, until women are fully liberated and society has adjusted to that fact, the family will continue to be unstable.

Changes in society are the main cause of the difficulties the contemporary family is having. But we do not see any reason to suppose that the family is helpless to adapt to these changes. On the contrary, the family seems to be changing rapidly to a form more in harmony with new social conditions and more able to fulfill its functions. We now examine some of the responses to family problems that indicate what the new family may be like.

PART III: RESPONSES FAMILY PROBLEMS

This section deals with family and societal responses to mutual friction as well as the family's future. More attention is given to the emotional-support function of the family than to the child-rearing and economic-support functions.

The child-rearing and the economic-support functions receive less attention because they have been treated in Part I of this chapter and in other chapters. For example, Chapters 11 and 14 treat child-rearing responses: Chapter 11 discusses child-care programs as a response to child-rearing burdens; Chapter 14 discusses birth control as a response to child-care burdens. Having fewer children is the main response of the nuclear family in industrialized nations to child-care problems, and this response has eased the burden. This trend will likely continue.

Reduced child-care problems also affect the family's ability to be economically self-sufficient. In industrialized societies, children are an economic burden rather than an asset. Having fewer children means less strain on family finances. Having fewer children and shifting some responsibility for them to child-care centers and to the schools also permit women to work. In turn, having two earners increases family income and makes the family less financially vulnerable: Self-sufficiency no longer rests on only one wage earner who may leave, die, or become unemployed. Furthermore, we have seen that a basic economic protection for the family lies in social programs such as those of health care, retirement, unemployment insurance, and welfare. Although American programs provide only minimal protection against poverty, the cost of more adequate programs is reasonable and many other industrial nations have successful antipoverty programs. It seems reasonable to suppose that the United States will eventually protect citizens from outright poverty.

Economic-support and child-rearing aspects now put aside, what requires attention here is the emotional-support function: the family's capacity to be the main source of love, affection, and companionship. At present, the capacity of the family to provide this emotional support for the great majority of adults is in question. Clearly, it does so for many. A substantial number of Americans do not get divorced, and many of them report their marriages to be happy and satisfying. But a substantial number of Americans do get divorced. When a marriage breaks up, it is evident that at least one spouse found too little emotional satisfaction in the relationship. Furthermore, it is certain that a broken marriage no longer serves the emotional needs of either spouse and that the bond between one

parent and the children is made more difficult. Thus, although the marriage bond does provide lasting emotional support for many families, it presently fails to do so for many others. We now examine the ironic fact that divorce evolved as a *response* to the emotional incapacities of many marriages.

DIVORCE AS A RESPONSE

Until very recently, divorce was not a common occurrence. Our laws made it very difficult for couples to obtain a divorce, and public opinion held divorce to be a disgrace. Indeed, divorce was strongly condemned by most major religious groups. Slowly, these attitudes became more permissive, and the laws were liberalized. As Americans put more importance on romantic love as the basis for marriage, critics of strict divorce laws charged that such laws needlessly forced many couples to live in misery and forced many blameless individuals to endure marriage to an intolerable spouse. Indeed, many champions of liberalized divorce laws argued primarily on behalf of women who were without recourse because they found themselves married to a drunken, brutal, deranged, or otherwise impossible man. Until recently, most women were wholly economically dependent on their husbands, so a woman not only faced tough legal restrictions against leaving her husband but found herself without means of support if she did. Legal reforms not only made divorce less difficult to obtain but gave women alimony to support them if they could show good reason for divorcing their husbands.

The hope of divorce reforms was to create better marriages by permitting intolerable marriages to be terminated. This goal was partly accomplished. However, liberalized divorce laws and greater social approval of divorce may also have caused more couples to be discontented with their marriages by encouraging them to expect more from marriage. Many couples who divorce today might have thought their marriage a good one fifty years ago, when most unsuitable marriages did not end in divorce. For the same reason, marriages that endure today may be much more satisfactory than were most marriages in the past.

Figure 12.12   The economic burden of child care can be reduced by tax-supported or privately financed child-care centers, which also enable many women to work outside the home and to avoid being on welfare.

Figure 12.13   A couple undergoing marriage counseling. Despite the general availability of counseling services, marital and family problems continue to increase.

In any event, liberal divorce laws have not solved our marriage problems. So many couples now get divorced that the major concern today is how people can find lasting happiness. Can marriage be made more secure and satisfying?

Many answers have been proposed to this question. We will consider four of these. The first answer is to *restore* marriage to a more durable state. The second is to adapt the family to a *serial marriage*—a pattern of divorce and remarriage. The third answer—the *open marriage*—is to shift the basis of the marital bond from romantic love to companionship. And the fourth answer is to form *group marriages,* which are something akin to the extended family.

THE RESTORED MARRIAGE

As the divorce rate has risen, many efforts have been made to restore marriage to a more durable state—for example, to restore the divorce rate to that of 1900, when there were only eight divorces for every one hundred marriages. These efforts assume that a permanent marriage is a healthy state that people need help to achieve. The efforts take two basic forms. The first form is to better prepare people for marriage. The second form is to help married people resolve their conflicts and renew their relationships.

Better Marriage Preparation

Various ways have been proposed to prepare people for stronger marriages. One way is to provide educational programs in high schools and colleges. The programs would help people enter marriage with more realistic expectations and with an understanding of how to deal with marital problems. ''How-to'' marriage and family courses have been popular among college students for the past forty years. These efforts may have aided many couples in achieving more satisfactory marriages. Nevertheless, such educational programs have not checked the the rising divorce rate.

Another suggested way to prepare people for marriage is to delay marriage or children until a couple know they are mutually compatible and mature. As early as 1927, Judge Ben B. Linsey proposed a ''companionate marriage.'' This plan

385

was elaborated by the philosopher Bertrand Russell in his book *Marriage and Morals* (1929). Under the plan, couples live together (without having children) for several years before they marry. Thus, prior to a marriage contract, the couple would either solve incompatibilities or break off the relationship. This plan still finds advocates. In 1966, the anthropologist Margaret Mead proposed in *Redbook* magazine that marriage should consist of two steps. The first step is *individual* marriage, which would be less legally binding than marriage today and thus would be easier to form and dissolve. The second step, *parental* marriage, would be more legally binding than individual marriage and would be taken only when the couple decided to have children.

To a considerable extent, Mead's proposals are already in widespread use (albeit without being embodied in formal legal distinctions). Today, young couples often live together for some period of time prior to marriage. Indeed, many young people today have already lived with several different persons before entering into marriage. Furthermore, many young couples delay having children for several years after marriage. Because divorce is relatively easy today, young couples who delay having children have nearly the equivalent of Mead's individual marriage. And many of these couples do divorce before having children (as Mead's plan anticipates). But despite these prechild divorces, about two-thirds of couples who divorce today do not do so until after they have children (thus, they have established the equivalent of Mead's parental marriage). It therefore seems doubtful that Mead's proposal would have its desired result: to prevent parents from becoming divorced. Although trial marriages are now widely practiced informally, they have not halted the rise in divorce nor reduced the tendency for divorce to involve children.

Marriage Repair

In an attempt to repair problem marriages, some states require that a couple seeking divorce undergo marriage counseling. And most states require a waiting period between divorce and remarriage to permit the divorced couple to reconcile their differences. Marriage counseling has become

an established profession, and sexual therapy is also rapidly becoming a boom industry. It is difficult to say how much effect these treatment programs will have on restoring marital stability. It is likely that in time we will complete the sexual revolution and that almost everyone will be sexually competent. If so, this present source of marital discontent may almost vanish. Indeed, having confidence in our sexual competence may cause us to be much more matter of fact about sex and thus reduce its importance in the romantic marital bond. However, there is little reason to hope that marriage counseling will have much impact on preventing marriage partners from becoming estranged from each other.

The therapeutic approach has so far shown little capacity to solve other problems such as alcoholism, drug addiction, juvenile delinquency, crime, mental illness, and sexual deviance. Why should we expect therapy to solve marital problems? Indeed, some of these other problems of deviance often play a major role in marital problems. In any event, marriage counseling has been widely used by unhappy couples for the past several decades. A great many say they found counseling helped to solve their marriage problems. But the divorce rate has continued to soar.

Some advocates of family counseling argue that present marital problems stem from society's permissiveness. These advocates say that people have lost their commitment to the old ethic of self-sacrifice, which made it unthinkable to put happiness before duties to children or before one's marriage vows. But what should we do to restore old virtues? Clearly, this line of thought proposes a massive cultural shift back to more traditional (even puritanical) beliefs and norms. When such shifts occur, they are usually caused by the rise of a totalitarian regime. If such should be the fate of the United States and other industrial nations, perhaps marriage will once again be a life-time bond for nearly every couple living under such regimes. Short of that, however, there is no evidence to suggest that we are likely to undergo a major change that will result in more restrictive views of marriage and divorce.

Clearly, some efforts to help couples establish durable marriages or resolve the problems that troubled a marriage have helped many. Yet it is equally clear that many other couples have not been helped and that further solutions are required.

SERIAL MARRIAGE

The present pattern of divorce and remarriage suggests that many people now find emotional support within the family by ending a relationship that no longer satisfies them and beginning a new relationship that does. This process is rapidly being aided by no-fault divorce laws that permit easy, friendly divorce and an end to the harsh alimony judgments that once made divorce economically ruinous for many men. These laws are possible because of female employment. And as women achieve equality, the financial constraints against divorce are likely to disappear entirely. Furthermore, it has become apparent, in recent years, that divorce is much less often a hostile breakup. Many divorced couples remain warm friends, often keeping in close contact through their mutual relations with children. For all these reasons, divorce is becoming a much less disruptive and upsetting occurrence. Should all these trends continue, many people may one day marry without expecting their relationship to last until death. Instead, people may assume that their emotional relationships during their lives will depend on several partners.

Serial marriage would help meet the romantic love ideal—for if and when love fades, people would seek a new love relationship. But what effects will serial marriage have on children? It was pointed out earlier that children suffer less from divorce than they do from an unhappy home, even though children seem best adjusted when both divorce is absent and their home is happy. Some of the negative effects divorce has on children may be related to the trauma that often still affects parents in a divorce. As yet, no studies have compared the children of parents who divorced as friends and who still maintain a firm friendship with the children of happily married couples. It may well be that children whose parents respect one another suffer little when the parents divorce or remarry.

Indeed, it has been suggested that children might be better off when parents remarry while remaining warm friends than they would be in even a happy, intact family. For serial marriage without bitterness restores some aspects of the extended family. Children are not dependent on only two parents; they have the equivalent of doting uncles and aunts in their lives. The children can enjoy warm relations with the new father in the home and also enjoy warm and lasting relations with their biological father and his new wife. Indeed, through their half-brothers and their half-sisters, new children in the home may enjoy relationships with the divorced father and with his new family. Thus, some people feel that a series of interlocking serial marriages offers a possibility to redefine family membership and restore a sense of family beyond the one-couple structure.

THE OPEN MARRIAGE

Open marriage is an attempt to restore marriage durability by shifting some of the emotional-support function to outside the family and by basing relations between spouses on long-term mutual interest and companionship. This marital form has been strongly advocated by George and Nena O'Neill in their book *Open Marriage* (1972). The O'Neills propose marriage based on complete equality between spouses and considerable flexibility in assigning family responsibilities, such as economic support, household tasks, and child care. The authors advocate an end to the possessive aspect of marriage—couples would retain many individual freedoms. Among these is the freedom to work out mutually acceptable patterns of sexual and emotional expression, including such relationships with persons other than the spouse.

The hope of open marriage is to preserve a stable, long-term relationship within marriage and still permit the wives and husbands to have extramarital relationships. This would mean that people would not have to sacrifice the rewards of a long-term relationship to find more intense emotional experiences. Whether people could learn to handle an open marriage without pangs of jealousy and rejection is hard to say. However, if the frequency of extramarital sexual relations continues to rise, many people may later discard the notion of infidelity, just as they have rejected the notion that a bride must be a virgin and that divorce is

387

shameful. It is very hard to say what kinds of relationships are possible until they have been tried.

THE GROUP MARRIAGE

In the group marriage, couples form something akin to an extended family with many emotional bonds. Group marriages of various kinds have appeared recently, especially in the counterculture that sprang up during the 1960s. One aspect of group marriage is that child care is shared among the members of the group. So child care may be much less burdensome in group marriages than it is in normal marriages.

In practice, group marriages are generally very unstable. Although some group marriages seem to persist, most of the members do not remain indefinitely—instead, people join, try participating for a while, and then leave.

Studies of utopian religious communes in the nineteenth century reveal one problem faced by group marriages. Many of the groups attempted free love within the group—any man and woman were permitted to have sexual relations. But the groups soon found that unregulated sexual activity put unbearable internal pressures on the group. The group was riddled with constant sexual competition and courtship. The groups that survived did so either by abandoning free love for stable pair relationships, by altogether banning sex, or by adopting rigid rules for rotating sexual partners and by prohibiting other sexual activity (Kanter, 1972). However, when these rules are adopted, people have to sacrifice the initial goal of greatly supplementing the emotional bond between spouses. Having an assigned sexual partner according to a rotating schedule is little different from the operations of mate-swapping groups.

Another problem is that the group marriage, like the extended family, is incompatible with the demands of modern life. Most adults must be free to move where job opportunities dictate. This is probably why most present group marriages have adopted the rural commune form. This places the group in the same economic conditions that fostered the extended family. However, few modern Americans hope to live in rural communes. For them, group marriage does not seem a workable response to family problems.

THE FUTURE

In this chapter, we have seen that the American family has been changing rapidly under the pressure of social conditions. We have also considered a number of ways in which the family has responded to present problems. What will emerge from all of this? What will the family be like if present trends continue? We expect that the future holds no single outcome. Instead, we think several forms of the family will exist side by side.

First of all, we expect that in the future fewer people will choose to have children. Indeed, this choice is already becoming more common, and this trend is likely to continue because of population pressures. Childless people will probably select several kinds of relationships. Others will perhaps have a series of relationships: some will be legal marriages; some will not. Still others may form permanent relationships.

However, most people will still probably choose to have children. And many of them will probably continue to form successful and permanent nuclear families. Others will probably continue to follow the emerging pattern of serial marriage (hopefully with less-traumatic divorces). And some others may continue to experiment with various group living arrangements.

Today, most divorced families are *matrifocal,* because children usually remain with the mother after divorce. Thus, most children experience only one mother and multiple fathers. As women become emancipated, this fact is likely to change. Children may stay with the father as often as with the mother.

However patterns later work out, there is no reason to see a chaotic future. Children are not going to be dumped in the streets while adults run hither and yon in pursuit of love. Parents who divorce do not love their children less than did the old-fashioned, life-long family. And even though they often get divorced, spouses do not necessarily divorce because they no longer love each other or are no longer concerned about each other's welfare. Indeed, their behavior could reflect the fact that they care very deeply and consider the marital bond important and for these reasons cannot endure a bad marriage.

If we recognize that families are not limited to a particular structure, then we can recognize as families any groups that people form to provide mutual economic benefits, to bear and care for children, and to provide emotional support. Thus defined, the family certainly will survive. Lest we seem too optimistic, we may add that readjusting the family to modern times is causing much suffering. Thus, it is vital to make social policies more compatible with family realities.

CHAPTER REVIEW

In recent years many changes have taken place in the structure of the family and in its functions. The shift from the *extended* structure to the *nuclear* structure weakened the family's ability to provide economic and emotional support. Changes in reproductive patterns and child-rearing practices have also placed a strain on the traditional marriage. Many of the current problems in the family stem from traditional expectations about marriage that are no longer fulfilled. Couples expect to be *financially independent,* for example, and feel a strain on the marriage when they are not. The financial hardship that results from a husband's not working, a wife's inadequate salary, or the family's acceptance of public assistance detracts from marital satisfaction. Child rearing has also become problematic because mothers in nuclear families lack experience and knowledge in this area. As a result of this and other factors, the *socialization* of children is increasingly being shifted to secondary groups such as schools and day-care centers. Finally, expectations regarding *emotional support* of the family are not being met because of divorce, high geographic mobility of children, and differences in life expectancy for men and women.

Some of these problems stem from the shift to the nuclear family, which resulted from industrialization as well as from migration and immigration patterns in the United States. Current societal pressures have also strained traditional marriage patterns. Because romantic love has replaced economic need as the main criterion for marriage, many marriages break up when romantic love fades. The occupational segregation of husbands and wives has increasingly led to their differing outside interests and to the opportunity for romantic attachments outside of the marriage. Further-

more, a wife who is no longer financially dependent on her husband is less hesitant to leave if the marriage becomes less attractive. The sexual revolution has also provided grounds for discontent from increased expectations of compatibility as well as from greater opportunities for premarital and extramarital activities. Finally, changes in traditional sex roles have caused marital dissatisfaction for husbands and wives who do not agree on definitions of those roles.

There have been several responses to these problems. The current tendency for couples to have fewer children than in the past has eased financial and child-care problems for many. The financial situation has further improved for those families in which both the husband and wife are employed. Filling the gap in emotional support of the family today has proven more difficult, however. Divorce was made easier in the hope that the quality of existing marriages could be improved. It is doubtful that that hope has been fulfilled. Attempts have been made to restore marriages through better preparation *before* marriage and through marital and sexual counselling *after* marriage. These efforts have not been successful in reducing the divorce rate, however.

Still other attempts have been made to redefine marriage and make *serial marriage* acceptable and less disruptive. Proponents of *open marriage* hope to redefine the bounds of acceptable behavior outside of marriage, thus maintaining an honest relationship within the marriage based on interests and companionship. *Group marriages* have turned out to be the least stable form. Which of these forms, if any, will become the norm in the future is still unknown. What is certain is that further attempts will be made to redefine marriage and find more successful forms.

389

SUGGESTED READINGS

Bernard, Jessie. *The Future of Marriage.* New York: World, 1972.

Goode, William J. *World Revolution and Family Patterns.* New York: Free Press, 1963.

O'Neill, Nena, and George O'Neill. *Open Marriage: A New Life Style for Couples.* New York: Evans, 1972.

Saxton, Lloyd. *The Individual, Marriage and Family.* 3rd ed. Belmont, Calif.: Wadsworth, 1975.

Spiro, Melford E., with the assistance of Audrey G. Spiro. *Children of the Kibbutz.* 2nd ed. New York: Schocken Books, 1967.

13
Aging

Why should college students be interested in the problems of aging? Of all the problems discussed in this book, the problems of old age in America are those you, personally, are least likely to escape. No one manages to get out of this world alive—and today most people do not die without becoming old.

For most of us, death does not come suddenly. Instead, we slowly wear down. Our looks, faculties, and health decline. Our hair and teeth begin to fall out. Sometimes our minds dim. And we gradually become unable to fully care for ourselves. We become dependent on others.

Old age is a fact of life in all human societies. All have some arrangements for dealing with it, but these differ greatly from one society to another. In some, the elderly are honored as sages and leaders. In others, the elderly are left along the trail to starve or die of exposure.

In modern industrial societies, the problem of what to do with the elderly has assumed critical importance. Because of recent advances in public health and medicine, life expectancy has greatly increased. Never before has any human society had so many aged people, because never before have so many people lived so long. In this sense, the problems of aging are modern problems.

As we shall see, the United States has substantially ignored the dramatic increase in its elderly population. Thus, a severe social problem has developed. The real problem is not simply that people get old but that our society neglects the elderly. Because of neglect, they become poor and lonely, which in turn weakens their physical and mental health. Thus, although people are living longer than ever before, the elderly in America are in fact dying before their time because of the effects of hardships that they experience after becoming old. If these conditions persist, the college students of today must look forward to a sudden fall into poverty when their working lives end.

PART I: THE PROBLEM AGING

Most people think of aging as a basically uncontrollable biological process. Aging *is* a biological process, but it is also influenced by social factors, including culture and social organization.

Three main social factors affect the lives of older Americans. The first is a confusing system for labeling people "old." The second is an economic system based on the notion that everyone can—and on the value assumption that everyone should—secure at least an adequate income through work. Our economic system also assumes that everyone is physically able to live in an independent household and to own and drive a car. Yet most older people are removed from the labor force or for some reason are unable to work and must live on pensions that are often inadequate. Many have no source of income beyond small welfare checks. Because many old people cannot meet the conditions for maintaining themselves, they become deprived. Our society does not provide adequately for its deprived groups. The third problem, which is an outgrowth of the second, is the way poverty and social deprivation work to speed up the aging process—both physical and mental. We will look at each of these areas of negative social effects on the life of the aged.

PROBLEMS OF DEFINITION

The classification of group members into various age categories is called *age grading*. Age grading affects both a person's opportunities and obligations. Industrial societies generally use age-grading systems, and age grades often determine which social roles a person can take on.

The criteria that societies use for age grading often relate to a specific organization or activity. For example, in many societies, one becomes an "elder" when one becomes the oldest member of a family. In other societies, a male becomes an elder when he is no longer able to hunt. In industrial societies, people are *arbitrarily* assigned to an age category; that is, there seem to be no specific criteria, such as social categories, function, or capability, used.

In the United States, we have several systems for age grading, and these systems frequently conflict. Age grading is sometimes done arbitrarily simply in terms of chronological age, or how old a person is, and at other times it is done in terms of

symptoms of aging, such as a decline in physical strength or prowess.

Even when age grading is done arbitrarily, there are variations from one social institution to another. For example, there are several different *legal* definitions of when an American becomes chronologically old. Sixty-five years is the most widely used and accepted definition. This age was arbitrarily selected in 1935 as the earliest date for retirement under the Social Security Act. However, under federal law, workers are classified as "older" after age forty-five. Widows are eligible for Social Security at sixty. The minimum retirement age under Social Security is now sixty-two. The federal civil service allows retirement after thirty years of service, regardless of a person's chronological age. Department of Labor employment projects for older workers start at age fifty-five. The Department of Housing and Urban Development uses sixty-two years old in determining whether people are eligible for "elderly housing."

When *holding a job* is the criterion, age is defined in terms of *ability to function*. At the age of thirty-five, one person's football career may be ending while another person's tenure as bank officer or politician has not yet begun. Thus, when the question is how well someone can function on a job or at what minimum age one can be expected to responsibly handle an important position, we are dealing with people's expectations and with age as a relative concept.

One of the most important definitions of "old" is the one determining the point at which the job *must* be given up. Mandatory retirement ages usually range between sixty-five and seventy. Accordingly, we will take "sixty-five and over" as a definition of "old people" that is related to the American occupational structure but is nevertheless arbitrary.

However, when most Americans think of age sixty-five, they think of *symptoms* of old age, such as declining health, energy, or mental capacities. Thus, a large part of the problem of the aged in American society relates to the injustices of an arbitrary system that implies that everyone over sixty-five is physically and mentally old.

People over sixty-five get angry when they are called "old." They also resent assumptions that

Figure 13.1 Four self-portraits by Rembrandt depict his own aging process. Age is a relative concept. The terms "young" and "old" have different meanings at different times in a given society. Also their definitions change from culture to culture.

Reproduced by courtesy of the Trustees, The National Gallery London
(top right, bottom right)

they are incompetent—for the same reason that other social groups, such as black Americans, Chicanos, and women, resent being stereotyped as incompetent, shiftless, or lazy. For individuals, chronological age is, in fact, a poor indicator of symptoms of aging. The older a group of adults born at the same time gets, the more *dissimilar* the individuals in the group become in terms of physical and mental abilities. This is not to say that aging does not finally take its toll, but it does not take its toll at the same chronological age for all people. Some people seem old at age fifty, whereas others do not begin to look or act old until they are in their late seventies.

ECONOMIC DIFFICULTIES

Apart from an image problem, older people suffer economic privation. Income (which here means any incoming funds from whatever source) is the single most important factor in the quality of life for all of us, including older people. Those with adequate incomes can afford adequate health services, housing, and nutrition, as well as recreation and transportation. Poverty-stricken older people must do without some or all of these benefits.

For 54 percent of older American families, income has fallen to less than half of what it was when the family head was between forty-five and fifty-four years of age. As people grow older, they not only fall below the poverty line but also fall well below their previous incomes and the national median income for all families. Two-thirds of retired Americans live below the poverty line.

Meeting Expenses

According to Robert Atchley and his co-workers (1972b), in 1969 the median income for American families with heads age sixty-five or over was $4,803, less than half the income ($10,085) for American families with heads between sixteen and sixty-four. Two-thirds of retired people are trying to live on incomes at or below the minimum required to provide a modest but adequate level of living. Only about 10 percent of retired American households have annual incomes of $5,000 or more, and 65 percent of them have annual incomes under $2,500.

393

Table 13.1 shows the percentage distribution in several types of expenditures for retired people at the two income levels in 1960. (Updated figures are not available for these two groups, but the gap between them remains fairly constant over the years.) For both income levels, the major expenses were food and housing. Although the percentage of income spent is almost the same for the two groups, in actual dollars the middle-income households spent over *four times* as much per year on food as did those with low incomes. Members of the low-income households suffer a shortage of the food energy necessary for an active life. A person cannot burn up calories in activity if the calories are not there to burn, and prolonged lack of food energy produces the look of wasting away in many of the older poor.

Table 13.1   Money Spent by Older Households by Annual Income, 1960*

TYPE OF ITEM	$1,000		$5,000	
	MONEY SPENT	PERCENTAGE OF INCOME	MONEY SPENT	PERCENTAGE OF INCOME
Food	389	38.9	1,615	32.3
Housing	316	31.6	750	15.0
Household Operation	54	5.4	235	4.7
Furnishings	26	2.6	295	5.9
Clothing	41	4.1	560	11.2
Transportation	38	3.8	565	11.3
Medical Care	73	7.3	370	7.4
Personal Care	17	1.7	100	2.0
Recreation	21	2.1	290	5.8
Miscellaneous	25	2.5	220	4.4

*More recent data are not available.
Source: Adapted from Robert C. Atchley, *The Social Forces in Later Life: An Introduction to Social Gerontology* (Belmont, Calif.: Wadsworth, 1972).

The low-income households spent just over 70 percent of their income on food and housing together, which left them somewhat less than $300 a year for expenses in the eight other categories. The greatest difference in spending between middle-income and low-income households occurred in the travel-and-recreation category, the "leisure arts" considered so necessary to a satisfying old age in our society. In that category of expenditure, the middle-income households spent fifteen times more money each year than did the low-income households. Thus, at a time in life when leisure

opportunities are expanding, resources to take advantage of these opportunities are declining for most older people.

Pension Income

A small but highly visible minority of retired Americans have ample incomes, but most are struggling to make ends meet. Social Security pensions are the main source of retirement income in America, yet the level of these pensions is generally inadequate. Private group pensions, public pensions, earnings, savings, and income from assets fill the gap for a few, but the vast majority are left to fend for themselves. Their only recourse is to accept charity, either cash gifts from the family or public assistance from the community, or to let things slowly run down.

Social Security Pensions

Social Security retirement pensions are the *only* source of income for nearly 80 percent of retired Americans. For these people, the average income is less than *one-quarter* of the average income of people their own age who are still working.

The Social Security system, as it now works, specifies that in order to qualify for a retirement pension, a person who entered the labor force in 1952 or later must work at least ten years at a job qualifying him or her for Social Security and must reach at least age sixty-two. Single women, widows, older retired people, and blacks are very likely to be drawing grossly inadequate pensions.

Most old Americans are eligible for Social Security pensions. As of 1967, nine out of ten couples or unrelated individuals of age sixty-five or over in the United States were receiving retirement pensions under Social Security. (The most recent data we have on *total* incomes of the elderly come from the 1968 Survey of the Aged, conducted by the Social Security Administration. For specific kinds of income, more recent data are given.) Most of those who were not receiving these pensions were entitled to them but were still at work.

The situation among women over sixty-five deserves a special look: Many older women who were drawing Social Security pensions were widows of workers, which means that they were drawing reduced pensions based on their dead hus-

SENIOR CITIZENS'
APARTMENTS
(NO PETS ALLOWED)

Figure 13.2   A political cartoon in the Los Angeles Times *calls attention to the nutrition crisis of the poor, many of whom are so impoverished they can only afford dog and cat food to eat.*

Figure 13.3   A person's occupation is an important part of his or her self-image and social status. When people are forcibly retired at age sixty-five, they lose more than income; they often lose the status and dignity associated with their former occupations. To help combat this loss, these military pensioners in Chelsea, London, are encouraged to wear their uniforms and medals for various occasions.

bands' incomes, and many single women over sixty-five were neither working nor entitled to Social Security pensions.

In 1971, Social Security pensions for the newly retired ranged from $845 annually to $3,545. Benefits for a retired worker plus a supplement for a spouse ranged from $1,161 to $5,317.

People who receive less than $160 per month ($1,920 per year) are below the poverty line defined by the Social Security Administration. Data on Social Security retirement pensions for 1971 show that no category of pensioners receives an *average* benefit at or above the poverty level. Of those who retire early, 91 percent of the women and 71 percent of the men receive incomes below the poverty level. Almost all widows of retired workers receive benefits below the poverty line; their average benefit is $121 per month. The average benefit to retired couples in 1971 was $200 per month, which means that the Social Security pensions of about half of the couples are also below the poverty line. Couples who retire early are especially likely to be below the poverty line (Social Security Bulletin, Annual Statistical Supplement, 1971).

It is clear that Social Security pensions do not provide adequate incomes for more than half of those receiving them. Despite recent increases in benefits, most recipients do not get enough money to cover even basic needs.

Minimum-Benefit Groups

The group receiving the minimum pension ($844.80 per year in 1971) is of particular interest. About 15 percent of all recipients are in this group. Half of the people in this group are retired single women, one-quarter are widows or retired single men, and one-quarter are retired married couples (Lauriat, 1970). Virginia Reno and Carol Zuckert (1971) have shown that people who draw the minimum pension from Social Security also tend to be those who have had little formal education, who had health problems that interfered with work, or who worked in service or unskilled blue-collar occupations. The same factors that caused many of these people to receive low Social Security pensions also prevented them from building up other kinds of resources that could be used in retirement,

395

as Patience Lauriat (1970) has pointed out. It should not be too surprising that many of those drawing the minimum Social Security pension have to work to supplement their pensions.

Single women, which includes unmarried, divorced, and widowed women, fare poorly in old age. As we have seen, there are many single women who receive no pensions at all, and single women who do receive pensions make up the bulk of pensioners who are far below the poverty line. Working women tend to earn little, and their careers are often interrupted by childbearing and child rearing. Widows do not qualify for the full value of their dead husbands' pensions, so their pensions are very low. Predictably, there are not many women with professional or technical occupations in the minimum-pension group.

Black workers also have Social Security pensions that reflect the effect of job discrimination. One-quarter of the men and one-fifth of the women who draw the minimum benefits are black. In 1970, the average pension for black workers, both men and women, was about $250 per year below the average for whites.

In general, the older a person is, the lower is his or her Social Security pension. Although there have been cost-of-living increases in the pensions to ease the impact of inflation, the fact that there has been an overall increase in real income since 1935 has not been taken into account. As a result, in 1970 the average pension of new recipients who were sixty-five years old was $1,772, but for those who were ninety-five or over it was $1,073. This problem is made worse by the fact that extreme old age drastically increases the need to buy services. Some elderly people cannot shop for their own groceries. Others can only get around by taxi.

Single women, black people, and older retired people, those with the lowest pensions, are also the people least likely to have income from earnings, assets, or gifts of money. These groups are most likely to receive public assistance in addition to a Social Security pension.

Other Pensions

Pensions other than Social Security that a person might receive are job-specific: They are either private group pensions from businesses or unions or they are public pensions from government employment, such as Railroad Retirement, military pensions, or other government pensions. Of the two categories of job-specific pensions, the public ones are considerably higher than Social Security pensions. Walter Kolodrubetz (1970) reported that in 1967 the median non-Social Security public pension was $2,720 for couples, $1,995 for single men, and $1,090 for single women.

Private pensions, in contrast, are often remarkably low. James Schulz (1970) quotes one source as saying:

In all too many cases, the pension promise shrinks to this: "If you remain in good health and stay with the same company until you are sixty-five years old, and if the company is still in business, and if your department has not been abolished, and if you haven't been laid off for too long a period, and there is enough money in the [pension] fund, and if that money has been prudently managed, you will get a pension."

Schulz concludes that the inequities of private pensions often outweigh their virtues. The Employee Retirement Income Security Act of 1974, which calls for substantial federal protection for those covered by private pensions, should be helpful. However, private group pensions are much less common than is generally thought and tend to be concentrated in high-paying industries and occupations that produce high Social Security pensions as well.

Job-specific pensions are not in themselves so impressive. However, most such pensions are *supplements* to a Social Security pension, and dual pensions yield modest but adequate incomes. In terms of *total* retirement income, those with dual pensions are indeed the elite. Their average pension income is twice as high as that of people drawing only Social Security (Kolodrubetz, 1970). Unfortunately, only about 20 percent of retired households in America receive dual pensions. It is interesting to note that among single retired women, only those with dual pensions have a pension income that, on the average, can provide the barest necessities of life (the average for single women is over $2,300).

People with high pension incomes are often the people who draw high incomes from assets. Incomes from assets and pensions are highly correlated with one another mainly because they both tend to be based on the same factor—income level during the working years.

Assets

Although saving money for your old age is an American social ideal, few people can actually manage to do it. About half of retired people draw income from assets, but the level of such income is generally low. In fact, most retired people have liquid assets of $2,000 or less. The yield depends on the form of investment, but $2,000 will usually yield no more than around $160 per year.

The most common financial asset of retired people is the ownership of a home. About 60 percent of retired couples and about 30 percent of retired single people own their homes free and clear. Owning a home is supposed to cut down drastically on income requirements, but Atchley (1972b) has estimated that home ownership can reduce income requirements by only $400 a year at best.

To summarize, most retired Americans, as we have seen, have low incomes. Moreover, Social Security pensions, the major source of income in retirement, are not adequate. The income picture for the retired is not improving, either. Millions of retired people have watched the buying power of their retirement incomes decline from ample to barely adequate. Retired people are on fixed incomes. As general levels of living increase and as inflation erodes purchasing power, those who have been in retirement for ten or fifteen years find their financial resources greatly reduced, even with the so-called cost-of-living increases in pensions.

America is rapidly approaching a crisis in retirement finance. David Peterson (1972) has reported that retired people increasingly see their incomes as inadequate and expect them to become more so in the future. Inadequate retirement income is likely to become an important political and economic issue in the next few years.

Employment

About a million and a half couples drawing Social Security pensions in 1967 also reported part-time employment. Median total incomes of working pensioners were almost as much as the income of fully retired people drawing dual pensions. The

primary reason people work while drawing Social Security appears to be that they need the money. Employment is not a major source of income for old people. Only about 20 percent of old people work. However, they earn nearly 30 percent of the aggregate income of all people sixty-five and over.

The Manpower Report

The *Manpower Report to the President,* put out by the Department of Labor (1971), reported several facts about participation in the labor force on the part of people sixty-five years or over, including the following data:

—The participation of older men in the labor force dropped from 47 percent in 1948 to 27 percent in 1970, but that of older women remained constant at around 10 percent between 1948 and 1970.

—From 1948 to 1970, participation in the labor force was slightly lower for older whites of both sexes than for older black people and people of other races.

—From 1948 to 1970, unemployment rates for older people tended to be lower than for twenty-five to thirty-four-year-olds among white women as well as among blacks and other races of both sexes.

—Older workers are much more prevalent among the long-term unemployed (people out of work twenty-seven weeks or more) than the total unemployed. For example, in 1970 men sixty-five and over constituted 2 percent of the total unemployed but 6 percent of the long-term unemployed.

—From 1970 to 1985, labor-force participation rates are expected to decline from 27 percent to 21 percent for older men and from 9 percent to 8 percent for older women.

—There is a very significant drop in labor-force participation rates after age seventy for both men and women.

Age Discrimination in Work

Statistics from the United States Department of Labor (1970) indicate that older persons remain unemployed longer than younger persons possessing the same skills, even though discrimination in employment on the basis of age is illegal. Official unemployment rates among older people are generally low, probably because they make up a disproportionately large share of the long-term unemployed rather than the total unemployed, and once their unemployment compensation runs out, they often become discouraged and withdraw from the labor force.

Discrimination on the basis of age is usually blamed on the older worker's ill health, lack of education, or technologically obsolete skills. However, unemployment studies of older workers conducted by the Department of Labor (1970) show that their attendance on the job is likely to be better than that of younger persons. Studies also show that they are less likely to change jobs and that their productivity compares favorably with that of younger workers in both blue-collar and white-collar occupations. Although it is true that some older people are slow to learn, the range of their learning speeds is wide, and many older people are quite capable of learning new skills.

Public Assistance

As we have seen, many retired people have no source of income other than their Social Security

Figure 13.4   The widespread neglect and resulting plight of our elderly has led to a number of reform efforts, including radio and television programs devoted to the problems of the aged. Such programs both reflect public concern and draw greater public attention to social problems.

398

NEGLECT OF THE AGED IS A BLIGHT ON AMERICA'S CONSCIENCE.

Broadcasters are concerned and are doing something about it.

When you become a "senior citizen," the road can get pretty bumpy and lonesome. And for many of the 20 million people in this country over 65 it's a trip they want to forget.

For them, the twilight years have turned into a nightmare of darkness. Financial darkness. Medical darkness. Housing darkness. And things aren't likely to get better soon. The over-65 group is growing twice as fast as the under-65 group. One quarter of them live below the poverty level. And almost two-thirds of those living alone or with non-relatives are poor or near-poor.

But America's broadcasters feel that life doesn't have to be downhill all the way just because you're on the far side of 65. The Storer TV and radio stations don't think so. And they're trying to convince their audiences.

In Detroit WJBK-TV and WDEE-Radio air problems of the elderly.
TV2 set up a live studio phone-in program entitled the "Senior Citizens Hotline". It gave the elderly a chance to phone in questions to a panel of experts on areas of concern to senior citizens. Results? Outstanding. More than 2,000 calls were received.

Among other specials produced by TV2 were hour-long discussion programs covering the fixed incomes, health costs and housing of today's elderly. And three reports throughout the year on a senior citizens' business venture in Oakland County.

WDEE-Radio on the other hand, devoted a 15-part series (which covered a 3-day span) to the elderly and welfare reform. On "Assignment: Detroit" it also conducted a number of interesting personal interviews on the cares and care of the aged with a Congregational minister and ladies of the Jewish Welfare Federation.

Atlanta's WAGA-TV pleads that aged's income is fixed but taxes aren't.
In a series of editorials, TV5 spoke out for property tax reform for elderly people. It pointed out that rising property taxes were putting the homes of old people on shaky ground.

The station also tried to get a freeze on school taxes for the elderly. (There are over 367,000 people over 65 in Georgia.) Things like homestead exemption, sales tax exemptions and reduced fares on public transit systems were covered.

When the American Association of Retired Persons and the National Retired Teachers Association were meeting in Atlanta, TV5 also aired an editorial entitled "Does life begin at 40 and end at ... 65?" Topics ranged from housing to medical expenses to retirement benefits.

Milwaukee's WITI-TV says to nursing homes: treat them right or don't treat them.
While TV6 applauded surveillance of nursing homes and an investigation into licensing abuses, it took state officials to task for too much talk and too little action. And for a reduced standard funding for nursing home operation.

At the same time, TV6 cautioned nursing home operators to work towards meeting state and federal standards. It pointed out that HEW threatened to remove funding for those operators who were negligent. In short, shape up or ship out.

As part of its concern for the financial plight of senior citizens, TV6 editorials also urged the Public Service Commission to allow the elderly to ride for half-fare during off-hours and weekends.

WSPD-TV and WSPD-Radio in Toledo push for money relief.
TV13 devoted no fewer than 24 editorials to "tax reform". Among the beneficiaries of this reform were to be senior citizens through a homestead exemption, plus a 10% property tax rollback. After 11 grueling months, the reform package was finally passed —the first substantial break for the elderly, budget-strapped homeowner in Ohio history.

To help make it easier for the aged to get around, the station also spoke out in support of ramps at curbs and stairways. And for tighter supervision of urban renewal projects which have a sizable bearing on adequate housing for the elderly. To stimulate understanding, TV13 also aired a report on the attitudes of the young toward the old. And vice versa. Then listened to reactions from local senior citizen organizations.

Meanwhile WSPD-Radio editorialized for more social security relief —the sooner the better. WSPD also took on the sky-rocketing cost of Old Folks Homes, and pointed out how increasing rates increased the likelihood of the elderly being forced out. A return visit by WSPD to an Old Folks Home showed that 15 occupants had moved in less than two months— apparently because of their inability to meet the rising rates.

Concerned stations—talking to concerned citizens.
All Storer stations get involved in the vital affairs of the communities they serve. It's a matter of policy with us, and a matter of pride for the people who staff our stations.

That's why our stations often do as routine, things that community leaders consider rather special.

We look at it this way. The more effective we are in our communities, the more effective we are for our advertisers, and the more effective we are for ourselves.

Broadcasting that serves.

STORER STATIONS
STORER BROADCASTING COMPANY

WAGA-TV Atlanta / WSBK-TV Boston / WJW-TV Cleveland / WJBK-TV Detroit / WITI-TV Milwaukee / WSPD-TV Toledo
WJW Cleveland / WDEE Detroit / KGBS Los Angeles / WGBS Miami / WHN New York / WSPD Toledo

pensions. We have also seen that these pensions are generally inadequate. Many people's pensions are so low that they need other income just to buy the bare necessities of life. Some retired people cope with this problem by working, but for one reason or another, only about 20 percent of them can do so. It is not surprising, then, that nearly 100,000 Social Security recipients, or about 8 percent, also receive public assistance. What is surprising is that more of them do not, especially the unmarried ones. About 3 percent are helped by relatives. That still leaves a sizable proportion with no way to supplement their pensions. Many of them do not seek public assistance because of pride. They consider such assistance charity and therefore unacceptable. A Social Security pension, in contrast, is seen as an earned right and therefore socially acceptable. Public-assistance programs are discussed in Part III of this chapter.

HOUSING AND TRANSPORTATION PROBLEMS

Our society makes assumptions about people's ability to get along by securing an adequate income, but old people have great difficulty doing so. What about the other assumptions—that people can maintain independent households and drive their own cars? Let us look at each of these areas in turn.

Living Space

For several reasons, housing is a key feature in the relationship between the person and his community. Where a person lives largely determines his or her opportunities for contact with other people. It also has a bearing on access to various community services. People often judge a community by whether it has housing that suits their needs. Finally, people, especially older people, lead much of their lives at home, and the quality of housing can either help or hinder their attempts to enjoy life.

Housing is a different sort of problem for older people than for the younger population. For older people, spiraling property taxes, maintenance costs, and rents often put adequate housing out of reach. Also, old people in generally poor health or with disabilities often need housing with special features, such as doorways and ramps for wheel-

chairs. If their houses cannot be adapted, they may have to move. Old friends may lose contact with one another, and ties to the community may be broken.

The living places of old people tend to be older than the average home and to have below-average values. They are more often dilapidated than younger people's houses. The households of elderly black people fall toward the bottom of the scale of housing values. Matilda Riley and Anne Foner (1968) have found that three-fourths of the elderly live in independent, detached houses. Only about 5 percent live in group housing, 1 percent in rooming houses, 2 percent in personal-care homes, 2 percent in nursing homes, 1 percent in mental institutions, and the rest with relatives.

Housing remains a problem primarily because of the relatively low incomes of older people. Constant increases in housing costs cannot be met on fixed retirement incomes. There is a desperate shortage of middle-income and low-income housing. As a result, most Americans experience an overall decline in the quality of housing they can get as they reach old age.

How To Get Around

There is scarcely any element in the distribution of goods and services in the United States today that is not built on the assumption that the consumer has a car. Shopping and service facilities, which fifty years ago had to be near housing or be easily accessible by public transportation, can now be located anywhere there is a major road and parking space. With a car, the average American makes use of many shopping or service facilities within a twenty-five-mile radius of home. Cars also allow for convenient long-distance travel. The rise of the automobile has brought reductions in service by many other forms of transportation.

For the average American, the automobile provides the answer to the transportation problem. But automobile transportation has two major features that limit its practicality for older people. The first is its expense: Buying, keeping, and insuring cars is beyond the means of most older people. The second is its physical requirements: Driving requires satisfactory vision, good coordination, and fast reflexes. The failing physical capacities of the old take their toll. Riley and Foner (1968) report that for the number of miles they drive, older people are involved in more than their share of accidents. In addition, more than two-thirds of drivers over seventy were at fault when they were involved in accidents. As Frances Carp (1971) has indicated, many older drivers restrict their driving to familiar routes and avoid night driving, and others give up driving completely.

Just over half of American households with heads over sixty-five owned automobiles in 1970. Income is a chief factor in owning a car for older Americans. Only 45 percent of older households with annual incomes under $5,000 own cars, but the figure for older households with annual incomes of $15,000 or more is 95 percent.

Income is not the only factor in owning cars among older people. Sex and marital status are also important. Three-quarters of old men are licensed drivers, but only one-fifth of old women are. Unfortunately, the older the woman is, the more important the ability to drive is, because only 20 percent of women age seventy or over have husbands who might do the driving. Thus, for most older people, auto driving is either too costly or too dangerous to be a practical answer to many of their transportation problems.

Automobiles and airplanes have become the primary means of passenger travel in the United States, and other passenger transport systems have cut back service. Intercity rail transportation used to be common but has been drastically cut down. Intercity buses use the interstate highway system and thus bypass rural communities, small towns, and even some medium-sized cities. Reduced population density in cities has caused the replacement of streetcars by the more profitable buses, but bus service outside rush hours and in small and medium-sized cities has been reduced in the past decades.

Public transportation was not the only system affected by the rise of the automobile. In employment, the highway system has allowed the labor force and employers to move into outlying metropolitan areas. In shopping facilities, most growth in the past twenty years has taken place in shopping centers that assume the use of cars. And small neighborhood stores have all but disappeared, as

has delivery service. In health care, the car has made it fairly simple for patients to get medical care outside the home, and doctors' house calls have virtually ceased. Drive-ins have taken the business from moderate-priced restaurants in many places. And churches have followed their congregations to the suburbs.

People without some access to cars cannot take full advantage of the distribution system. Old people make up a very large proportion of this group. The White House Conference on Aging ranked the problems of transportation near the top of its list of priorities.

SOCIAL EFFECTS ON THE AGING PROCESS

The third problem we pointed to as affecting old people in American society is that the workings of the social system have an actual effect on the physical and mental processes of aging themselves and, of course, on old people's general health and psychological well-being.

Effects of Dependency

Because of the decline in income, old age creates a progressive loss of independence for many Americans. Americans are taught to prize independence and guard it. No matter that the demands of job and family often reduce independence to an illusion, people still crave the illusion. Objectively, social independence means having enough money to get by, having a household of one's own, and having good enough health to be able to get around. Money generally goes first, usually as a result of retirement but sometimes as a result of illness in the family. Health goes next, and with it the ability to keep up a household and to get around.

Americans look down on adults who are dependent. Adults who cannot take care of themselves are considered moochers or parasites. In order to receive monetary support, the dependent person is often forced to show gratitude, to accept a subservient and inferior position, and to relinquish the rights of self-determination. For example, welfare recipients are expected to disclose many intimate details about their private lives. All this creates psychological injury, and it should be no surprise that some old people would rather die than become dependent. For American men, suicide rates are 30 percent higher at eighty, an age of high dependency, than they are at age seventy. Although suicide at that age may have any of several causes, a fear of dependency is surely important among them.

It is particularly trying in modern America for parents to become dependent on their children. If the older person can remain autonomous, or independent, then the parent-child relationship remains a good one. But to accept financial support from one's children is often seen as a role reversal that requires submission and loss of dignity.

Social Factors in Premature Aging

The social world affects the processes of physical and mental aging indirectly through its effects on health and directly through physical stress on the organism. Many people assume that ill health is brought on by aging. It is true that old age increases one's vulnerability to disease and disability, but it is equally true that prolonged illness or physical stress speeds up the aging process.

Premature aging is most common among the poor. The poor suffer physical effects from poor nutrition, from lack of *preventive* medical care, from alcoholism and drug addiction, from physically demanding jobs, and from living conditions that result in unusual physical stress. It can be said that millions of Americans are ''older'' than they would be if they were not poor—and over half the elderly in America are below the poverty line. Even among the advantaged, the stress that comes with high-pressure jobs, divorces, widowhood, moving to new homes, and so forth probably takes its toll in speeding up the process of aging.

Health

Health is important to everyone, but most Americans are lucky enough to be able to take reasonably good health for granted. Health affects people's ability to take part in most social roles. It also affects people's satisfaction with life and how they are treated by others. In later life, declining health cuts across all social and economic lines, becoming a major factor in determining whether older people participate in the family, on the job, in the community, and in their leisure pursuits. As people grow older, health needs require more and more of their income. A large number of medical facilities and services are geared toward the diseases and ailments that largely affect older people.

Many physiological functions tend to decline with age. Although the aged may function fairly well under conditions of rest, they have little reserve capacity. For example, they may falter under an increased physical load such as an extra suitcase, whereas younger people could easily adjust and be able to carry the extra weight. These changes make the older person more likely to suffer ill health and impairment of activity. Atchley (1972a) reports that a survey done in 1968 of the aging in the United States confirms this fact in regard to both *acute* and *chronic* conditions.

A chronic condition suggests some measure of long-term incapacity. The percentage of people with chronic disabilities is a rough indicator of the need for community care—nursing services, physical therapy, drugs, and home services. In 1968, 85 percent of the older population had one or more chronic conditions, compared with 38 percent of the population under age forty-five.

401

Acute conditions, in contrast, generally do not cause permanent disability. An older person is much less likely than a younger person to contract an acute disease. However, according to Atchley and his colleagues (1972a), when older people do suffer acute illnesses, their average recuperation time is over twice as long (thirty-five days) as that of the population as a whole (fifteen days).

Older people face more and more health-care needs with less and less money to pay for services. Medical costs in general are very high. Unlike working people, who usually have health insurance provided by their employers, retired people generally must buy their own coverage or services. Health-care costs for older people are much higher than those for other people. From 1967 to 1970, expenditures increased much more sharply for older people than for people of younger ages. Although the amount of public funds available for the medical care of the aged has increased dramatically, older people still have to pay, out of their personal resources, more for health care than younger people do.

Barbara Cooper and Mary McGee (1971) found that in 1970:

—After adjustment for population and price increases, personal health care expenditures for the aged from fiscal year 1967 to fiscal year 1970 show a growth of 9.2 percent a year—three times the annual rate for the youth and eight times that for the intermediate age group [ages 19–64].

—The average medical bill for an aged person ($791) was more than six times that for a youth ($123) and almost three times that for a person in the intermediate age group.

—Although third-party payments cover a substantial portion of the individual's medical bill, the average aged person paid $226 directly and the person under age 65 paid $100.

—Differences in the amounts spent for medical care for the three age groups vary considerably with type of expenditure: per capita hospital care expenditures for the aged were more than eleven times those for the young and more than twice those for the intermediate age group; for physicians' services, the aged's per capita expenditure was triple that for a young person and twice that for a person aged 19–64.

In spite of Medicare and other programs, many old people still cannot get adequate health care. They do not have the money, or they cannot get transportation, or there are inadequate services in small towns and rural areas, or the program does not cover the items they need, such as preventive medicine, eyeglasses, and dental care. American society still has a great distance to go in meeting the health-care needs of its old people.

Many psychological problems, such as those that result from dependency, are associated with old age. Psychological problems that are caused by the workings of the social system are often related to the loss of long-term roles. Children generally grow up and leave home while people are still middle-aged, so psychological difficulties caused by the loss of parental roles have usually occurred before old age. This leaves retirement, or the giving up, whether voluntary or forced, of one's job and full earning capacity, as the major societal source of possible stress in old age.

PROBLEMS OF RETIREMENT

A great many people, including many sociologists, see retirement as a social problem, at least for men. Giving up one's job is seen as causing a major identity crisis for the individual. Those who subscribe to this view say that the job is the major source of identity in American society. They also say that retirement prevents the individual from performing his or her most highly prized role. Thus the older person's identity breaks down and the person is less able to cope with life.

A contrasting view holds that retirement seldom triggers an identity breakdown because most people have several different identities. Atchley (1972b) has pointed out that in many cases people keep their job *identities* after retirement. Fred Cottrell and Robert Atchley (1969) found that retirement has no effect on self-esteem. Gordon Streib and Clement Schneider (1971) have found that retirement has little effect on physical health. If anything, removing job demands tends to *improve* health. Retirement may also make life easier for the mentally ill by allowing them to stay away from demanding, highly structured situations.

How do retired people themselves see their problems? Research from a wide variety of sources has shown that about 30 percent of the population reported difficulty in adjusting to retirement. However, closer inspection shows that of this 30 percent, 12 percent listed money problems as the worst aspect of retirement, and only about 7 percent reported difficulties associated with missing their jobs. The other 11 percent had difficulties that are basically unrelated to retirement, such as health problems or the loss of a spouse.

Americans, in fact, are increasingly looking toward retirement as a time to enjoy a well-earned independence. Most people retire *before* the mandatory age. Many other working people take the mandatory retirement age as welcome social permission to retire.

Consequences of Retirement

Retirement has a slight tendency to *increase* social participation for most people. But a small minority experience loneliness or social isolation. The extent to which retired people take part in activities outside their families depends on their work histories before retiring. Stable and orderly work careers allow people to build community ties. Retirement results in greater participation in leisure

Figure 13.5   Many older people experience loneliness and isolation as well as poverty. In addition to adequate retirement income, programs designed to involve the elderly in social and recreational activities are sorely needed.

pursuits for those who can afford them. This increase in leisure-time activities is gaining more social approval from both retired people and the general public (Atchley, 1974).

However, to the extent that retirement results in poverty, it restricts the individual's options: Poverty means not having enough to eat, which reduces a person's energy. Poverty also drastically limits the amount of recreation and travel a person can afford. As we noted earlier, retirement itself is seldom associated with moving to a new community, but it may cause a move to more suitable housing within the same community. Only about 2 percent of people who retire move to another state, but the increase in the general educational level of the retired population will probably bring about an increase in that percentage. People with higher levels of education tend to have higher geographic mobility.

Sometimes people use their involvement with their jobs to help them get over difficult periods during their lives. For example, the death of a spouse or the moving away of children is easier to bear when one is involved with one's work. About 40 percent of working women are already widows by the time they retire. Most children have grown up and left home long before their parents retire. People who do use their jobs to soften such losses may experience a crisis of adjustment later when they retire. Retirement generally has a positive impact on married couples, except among working-class couples for whom retirement often produces conflict. In working-class families, a more traditional conception of male and female roles means that upon retirement from work, the man suddenly intrudes into the "woman's world" of the daytime household.

Certain types of jobs do cause problems for their holders when they retire. Jobs that demand a great deal of personal involvement, such as many professional and managerial jobs, may leave a person little time to develop other activities that might lend meaning and structure to life. People who struggle all their lives to make a living also cannot develop the wide range of activities and leisure skills that give meaning and pleasure to retirement.

Some jobs produce poverty in retirement. Many of these are the same jobs that do not pay enough

403

to raise the worker above the poverty line before retirement. Other jobs carry no pensions with them or have pension systems with so many loopholes that many workers lose their pensions. Among all workers, as we saw, income drops, on the average, 50 percent after retirement, and for many retired households it drops a lot further than that.

Mandatory Retirement

Some jobs have mandatory retirement provisions attached to them. Such provisions create a problem for the capable older worker who wants to stay on the job. Mandatory retirement provisions state that when a person reaches a certain age, he or she must retire. These policies are usually formulated by employers. Occupations with mandatory retirement policies tend to be those in which there is a need to phase older workers out of a complex production process in an orderly way. However, it is by no means clear that mandatory retirement policies are the best means of accomplishing this.

Most of the arguments often used to justify retirement are not especially convincing. It is held that having workers retire when they reach a certain age makes retirement processing easy for employers. But many people have retired at various points before the mandatory retirement age. Thus, retirement at unpredictable times must also be reasonably easy for employers to administer. Another argument holds that mandatory retirement eliminates bias or discrimination in the phase-out process. However, employers consistently keep people on after the mandatory retirement age if it suits their purposes. Thus, mandatory retirement policies are not a foolproof way to get rid of discrimination. The most telling of the arguments concerns making room for younger workers. This is the argument that older workers are most sensitive to. Given that there are currently more people than jobs, a good case might be made for the idea that an individual is entitled to hold one only so long. However, the factual basis of this line of reasoning has yet to be demonstrated.

What can be said in favor of mandatory retirement? One thing is that it allows individuals a graceful exit from a job without having to admit to themselves or others that they can no longer do the job. Another is that it makes retirement a sure thing for people who might otherwise have stayed on the job simply out of habit. However, both of these arguments have been eroded by the fact that in recent years the trend has increasingly been toward retirement as soon as possible. People no longer need an excuse to retire.

What are some arguments against mandatory retirement? First, no one today can seriously argue that at age sixty-five or seventy people in general are so feeble, sick, or otherwise disabled that they should be excluded in wholesale fashion from the labor force. It is questionable whether this was true even forty years ago, when many mandatory retirement policies were being formulated. Whereas the overwhelming majority of people who retire do so because they want to and can afford it, there is a small but important minority who either do not want to or cannot afford to retire. Thus, it is true that mandatory retirement by definition discriminates against an age category, and this violates the principle of equal employment opportunity. Since chronological age alone is a poor predictor of the ability to perform on the job, it is an inappropriate criterion to use in a mandatory retirement policy. Second, as Erdman Palmore (1972) argues, mandatory retirement policies waste talent and productive potential.

Another argument against mandatory retirement is that it forces poverty on the retirer. Jobs carrying mandatory retirement provisions, however, are almost always jobs that provide pensions. So the charge that mandatory retirement brings poverty is true mainly for the small minority of people not covered by pensions or for those whose irregular work histories deprive them of adequate pensions. There are indeed thousands of older people working at jobs with adequate pension plans but who will reach the mandatory retirement age without having worked long enough with the same company to be entitled to a pension.

On balance, there seems to be little in favor of mandatory retirement policies. As retirement becomes an increasingly accepted part of life, these policies will become even more unnecessary. But there are two reasons why mandatory retirement policies probably will not change. First, the group that is currently being hurt by such policies is too small to be politically effective. The majority who

404

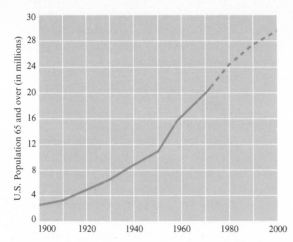

Figure 13.6   The proportion of persons over sixty-five has been growing in the United States since the turn of the century. Projections indicate that by the year 2000 almost 29 million Americans will be over sixty-five. A large population of the elderly will therefore be dependent upon a small working population for support. This may cause changes in mandatory retirement rules to permit persons over sixty-five to continue to perform their jobs.

(U.S. Bureau of the Census and U.S. Bureau of Labor Statistics.)

Figure 13.7   The marital status of men and women over sixty-five differs greatly. While the majority of men over sixty-five have wives, the majority of women over sixty-five are widows. The data show that since 1965 these differences have increased. One reason why older men are married and older women are not is that men have a shorter life expectancy than women do. Thus, if a couple is the same age, the odds are that the woman will become a widow. The odds are even greater that women will be widows because men tend to be older than their wives.

(From Commission on Population Growth and the American Future, 1972.)

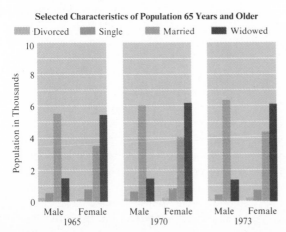

Selected Characteristics of Population 65 Years and Older

want to retire may see the "right to remain working" faction as a threat. Second, the mandatory retirement age is a deeply ingrained aspect of the institution of retirement, which means that change would not be easy.

PART II: SOURCES
AGING

This section is brief. We are not concerned with explaining why people get old. Instead, we want to understand why the elderly suffer in ways that are not a necessary result of the physical process of aging. The answers to this question are found in Chapters 9 through 12 and Chapter 14. The problems of the aged stem from a combination of the social problems we discuss in those chapters. Problems of poverty, racial and sexual discrimination, changes in the family, and changes in the age structure of the population combine to lay an especially heavy burden on the elderly. How does each of these problems affect the elderly?

 405

POPULATION

The most obvious feature of the aging problem in the United States is the immense change in the proportion of the population that is surviving to old age. In 1900, only 4 percent of Americans were sixty-five or older. Today, 10 percent of our population is sixty-five or older. These changes have been caused by the same factor that has produced the population explosion: a sharp *decline in mortality rates*. Not only has infant mortality fallen greatly in response to modern disease prevention but adult mortality has also declined. The life expectancy of the average person has been skyrocketing upward over the past fifty years. There is no way of knowing how high it will go. Fifty years ago people would have thought it absurd to predict that one day the average person could expect to live to be over seventy. Today that is what the average person can expect. Fifty years from now it is not impossible that people may expect to live to be a hundred. If so, and if retirement still occurs at sixty-five or under, then the average person will have nearly half of his or her adult life left to live *after* retirement. It is difficult to believe that people will accept living so long in the deprived circumstances now typical of life after sixty-five.

Even if average life expectancy does not continue to rise, the proportion of elderly persons will rise for a considerable time. Because of the post World War II baby boom, if our birth rate remains at the present level of replacement of deaths by births, the proportion of the population that is elderly will increase dramatically over the next fifty years. As is shown in Figure 14.2, those born during the baby boom will be passing through the post-retirement ages between the years 2005 and 2030. The task of supporting and caring for these people will fall upon a relatively small group of adults born after 1965. The child- and youth-oriented economy and culture created by the baby-boom kids during the 1950s and 1960s is likely to be repeated in magnitude by an elderly-oriented economy in the early decades of the twenty-first century.

If changes in the age make-up of the population are the primary cause of the problem of aging, these changes also offer a potential basis for change. As the size of the elderly population increases, its political impact also increases. Thus, each year the elderly population acquires more political power simply by becoming a larger voting bloc. Already this potential political clout is having political effects and could be sufficient to eventually bring about major social changes in pensions and social services for the aged.

FAMILY DISORGANIZATION

Chapter 12 details the rapid changes and the growing strains in American family life. These changes have worsened the plight of the elderly. At the very time when there are so many more elderly people, their problems have been shifting from a family affair to personal and public responsibility.

Historically, the elderly were looked after by their families. The extended family included not just parents and children but also grandparents. In the extended family, the elderly could do useful things. For example, grandparents could lavish care and attention on grandchildren, care that parents often could not provide. Thus, the elderly were an important part of the family. The extended family system supported the elderly and gave them roles to fulfill. It also sheltered the elderly from the loneliness and anguish caused by the death of spouses and friends. The elderly remained a part of an ongoing family.

The modern nuclear family is having enough difficulty maintaining itself, let alone providing for

406

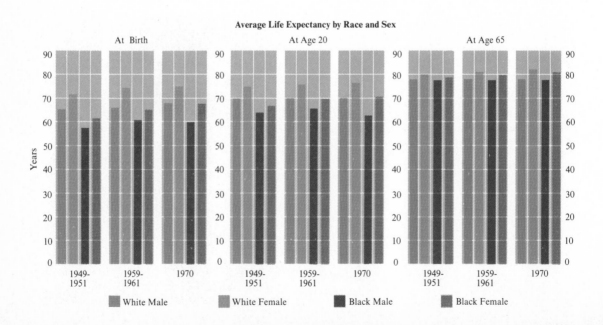

Average Life Expectancy by Race and Sex

At Birth   At Age 20   At Age 65

■ White Male   ■ White Female   ■ Black Male   ■ Black Female

the elderly. Typically, Americans today do not live with their parents, in-laws, or other relatives. Like the young family, the elderly family is on its own. Worse yet, in time the elderly family usually consists of a single member. One of the couple dies, leaving the other alone; usually it is the male who dies first. Thus, to be elderly in America typically means to be an impoverished widow.

POVERTY AND DISCRIMINATION

Chapter 9 attempts to explain the causes of poverty in the United States. The conclusion drawn is that poverty in America is unnecessary. Poverty does not reflect a lack of resources to ensure everyone a tolerable standard of living but reflects instead a choice not to adopt the policies necessary to do so. The poverty of the elderly clearly reveals the role of policy choices. Our national policy is to provide retirement benefits for nearly everyone through Social Security. But, as we have seen, policy fixes the level of benefits well below the official poverty line. If the majority of old people are poor, it is because their retirement incomes make them poor. Many other modern nations have diverted a sufficient portion of their national wealth into old-age benefits. In these nations, getting old does not mean getting poor. So long as the United States

continues to keep the old poor, the average American will complete a productive working life only to enter a life of poverty.

The situation of the aged is made worse by two other major social problems: discrimination based on race and that based on sex. The elderly tend to be women because in modern times women live longer than men. Because in the past most women did not work outside the home, most elderly women are covered by Social Security or private pensions only through their husbands. When they become widowed, their benefits drop substantially. Furthermore, women who did work, and who therefore now qualify for pensions or for Social Security, had lower salaries on the average than did men. The size of Social Security and private pension benefits is based on past earnings, so elderly women receive smaller payments on the average than do elderly men. Thus sex-based inequalities continue to burden women all the way to the grave.

A similar pattern afflicts elderly members of disadvantaged racial minorities. High rates of unemployment, and employment in marginal occupations, such as migrant farm laborer, has resulted in disproportionate numbers of minority members facing old age without being eligible for Social Security or a private pension. Furthermore,

407

Figure 13.8   At every age, the average life expectancy of the American female is higher than that of the American male. However, both male and female blacks have a significantly lower average life expectancy than whites do.

(U.S. National Center for Health Statistics.)

Figure 13.9   Three generations of a Lithuanian-American family. The modern trend away from the traditional extended family often means loneliness and hardship for surviving elderly spouses. For the young nuclear family, it means less access to the skills and the wisdom of grandparents.

because those who do qualify for Social Security or pensions received considerably lower average wages than did white workers, their benefits are lower. Another problem is that people who were less well-off prior to retirement have fewer resources to compensate for low retirement benefits. Americans who earned average wages before retirement are likely to have managed to pay off the mortgage on a home before retirement. Owning their homes outright makes it somewhat less costly for them to live, affords them a better place in which to live, and gives them an emergency financial asset. Also, some of these persons often enter retirement with modest savings. Minority-group members more frequently enter retirement not only with lower incomes but without these other resources. Finally, because economic discrimination continues against people of all ages in nonwhite minority groups, minority-group children are less likely than children from advantaged groups to be able to help their parents financially.

408   In all these ways, the problems of the elderly are a product of their special vulnerability to many of the most acute problems of American society. But it is clear that this vulnerability is mainly rooted in social policies. Thus, the best way to comprehend the problems of the aged is to assess present programs dealing with the problems of the elderly.

PART III: RESPONSES
AGING

National, state, and local governments, as well as private organizations, have developed numerous programs to meet the diverse needs of the elderly. Despite the programs to provide income, health-care financing, housing, and nutrition, most older Americans have a low standard of living. In less obvious areas, such as education, employment, recreation, and transportation, the institutional responses to the needs of old people are even more inadequate and poorly planned.

INCOME AND HOUSING

Nearly all the programs designed to provide financial support for the aged are governmental. In re-

cent years, the government has replaced general welfare programs with more specific ones. The program aimed at older people, called Aid for the Aged, was for years the major source of supplementary income for older Americans. People who were not eligible for Social Security or who had inadequate pensions relied heavily for support on Aid for the Aged. This program, which was replaced in 1974, was administered at the local level with both state and federal funds, but the benefit amounts varied from state to state.

At the beginning of 1974, the Supplemental Security Income (SSI) program replaced Aid for the Aged. SSI, which is a federal program administered at the local level, guarantees *every* older American at least $130 per month regardless of his or her prior work history. SSI is an improved system of support for older people whose home states provided grossly inadequate payments under Aid for the Aged. But income under SSI is still below the bare minimum. Under SSI, a couple receives $2,340 per year, a figure that is below the poverty level set before our recent rapidly climbing inflation. Neither Social Security nor Supplemental Security Income provides an adequate income for the aged. Obviously, we do not yet have means to ensure adequate incomes for the aged.

Supplemental income is a problem of government, but meeting the housing needs of the elderly is both a public and a private problem at this time. Public housing programs address themselves to the housing needs of the elderly poor. The private sector mainly serves the upper-income older population. The middle-income older population is served by neither.

The federal government has several programs to increase the number of public housing units for the elderly poor. About a third of all public housing is devoted entirely to the elderly. Old people also benefit from federally financed but privately developed low-income housing. Old people have fared somewhat better than the general population in securing public housing, yet—just to keep up with the growth in the population of needy old people—most cities need much more housing for the elderly than they now have.

At the other end of the spectrum, for old people with sizable incomes, private developers offer a wide range of choices, from apartments to condominiums to cottage communities to retirement hotels. Developers often offer full housekeeping, medical services, planned recreational programs, and prepared meals. Many offer a variety of living arrangements that range from full independence to skilled nursing care.

A typical whole-life program requires a sizable initial investment (as much as $30,000 for an efficiency apartment) plus a sizable monthly fee ($400 to $700, depending on services). Clearly, only a tiny percentage of the older population can afford these facilities. And it is still unclear whether such facilities are sufficiently profitable in the long run for the developers to continue to build and maintain them.

The two most neglected categories are the middle-income retired and those who need personal or nursing care. Middle-income retired couples very often live in their own homes, which are often expensive to keep up and too big to take care of. These people are too well-off to get into public housing or low-income housing for the elderly but not well-off enough to afford a retirement community. They offer little incentive to developers. These are the people who tend to be left behind as neighborhoods change. If they sell their homes, they can afford to rent for a few years, but after those funds are used up they face an uncertain future.

There is also a growing number of middle- and low-income old people who need personal or nursing care. Personal-care homes offer housekeeping and meal services, but the costs are high. Nursing care is even more costly. There is a great need for group housing for older people on a tight budget. At present, we have neither income nor health nor housing programs that can solve this problem.

HEALTH

There are both private and government programs to provide health care for the elderly. Volunteer services provided by such private organizations as the Arthritis Foundation, the American Cancer Society, and the American Heart Association have only a small effect on health care for the elderly. Some governmental programs exist specifically to help provide health services for the older population. Others are general health programs that result in improved health care for everyone, including the aged. Among the general programs are the Hill-Burton State Plan, a federal program that since 1946 has been the major force behind hospital construction in the United States; the comprehensive health planning agencies created in 1966 to integrate the health needs of local areas; state and local health departments; and the Medicaid program, which provides comprehensive hospital and medical services to the poor.

Medicare

Among the numerous programs aimed specifically at older people, the most far-reaching is Medicare, a Social Security-linked program. Nearly all older Americans are eligible for coverage under Medicare Hospital Insurance. Medicare Supplementary Medical Insurance is a voluntary program for which the older person pays a monthly fee. It covers some of the many types of non-hospital medical services not covered by Medicare Hospital Insurance. Medical checkups, prescription drugs, eyeglasses, and hearing aids are *not* covered by either part of Medicare.

Although the Medicare program has revolutionized health care for the elderly, particularly for those with short-run health-care needs, the picture is not so bright for those with disabling chronic diseases. Permanent nursing-home patients quickly run through their Medicare coverage, and there is no other program that will pay the bills. Such long-term health problems are probably the biggest single unmet health-care need of the older population. Prescription drugs, eyeglasses, and hearing aids are also relatively high-cost items that pinch the low incomes of the elderly.

Homes for the Aged

The most glaring example of the inadequacy of our institutions for handling the long-term care needs of the elderly is the county home for the aged. Most county homes do not even meet the licensing requirements for coverage under Medicare or Medicaid because they are old, dilapidated, understaffed, and grossly underfinanced. The cost of care in a modestly priced private nursing home is

409

about $500 per month. Most county homes must care for their residents for less than $200 per month. That the care they give is often substandard should not be surprising. Staff salaries are generally quite low, and although the few who are dedicated alleviate the problem somewhat, in many homes the patients are treated like so many objects to be fed, clothed, washed, and given medicine, without regard to modesty, privacy, or dignity. There is an almost complete lack of public concern about nursing-home care. The sad reality is that people in the county homes are out of sight and therefore out of the mind of the public.

A great deal of effort has been expended on health-care programs for the elderly. But people in this age category have high needs for medical care, and the results are still far short of adequate, especially with respect to long-term health care. This will become an increasingly severe problem because the population over age seventy-five is expected to double in the next thirty years.

Nutrition

Poor nutrition is a great problem among older people. Low income, poor health, and inadequate transportation make it difficult to buy and prepare food. Lack of motivation to cook for only one person and lack of appetite are also frequent problems among the elderly. Each year hundreds of deaths due to vitamin deficiencies and other nutritional problems are recorded among the older population. Malnutrition also kills people indirectly by making them more vulnerable to disease.

The elderly poor are often eligible for the Federal Food Stamp program, which covers the general population, but the program bears the stigma of charity. In 1973, the federal government instituted a $100 million program to provide low-cost hot meals at least five days a week for people sixty years or older and their spouses. The program gives priority to elderly people from minority groups and to those with low incomes. However, it also includes those who lack the skills and knowledge to select and prepare meals, those who have limited mobility (making it difficult for them to shop and cook for themselves), and those who do not prepare and eat well-balanced meals alone because they feel rejected and lonely.

Participants can pay for the meals they receive, but no one is turned away because of the inability to pay. The program provides transportation to the dining areas for people who need it and "outreach services" to find people in need of the program. It also provides a network of support services, including information and referral, health and welfare counseling, consumer and nutrition education, and a variety of opportunities for both recreation and volunteer services.

The program was handled in a fashion typical of government programs for the elderly. Guidelines were lacking, and President Nixon vetoed the funding twice. When funds were finally made available, program directors were given only a month to hire and train staffs and begin serving meals. Needless to say, although some meal programs are doing an admirable job, many of the operations are not very efficiently staffed or very efficiently run. As it stands, the nutrition program is ambitious, but it remains to be seen whether it can meet its objectives.

RECREATION, LEISURE, AND INVOLVEMENT

Leisure is a vaguely defined concept in our society. It generally refers to time free from work or other obligatory activities. Old age provides an increase in leisure time. When people retire, the problem is to find leisure activities that can give the same satisfaction as former activities did. Failing health and physical capacities may restrict leisure pursuits. And reduced income most often closes leisure activities to older people. Movies, concerts, and travel, although thoroughly enjoyable, are often luxuries that older people cannot afford. Even free activities, such as visiting parks and museums, require transportation, which is often unavailable or too expensive.

There are Senior Centers, Golden Age clubs, and other organizations for old people, but they seem to be important in the lives of only a very few old people. Senior Centers usually offer a variety of services and activities, such as handicrafts, music programs, sports, lectures, educational programs, games, and general socializing. Some also provide counseling services, hot meals, information and referral services, and other supportive

410

The Eskimos used to freeze their old people to death. We bury ours alive.

Maybe the Eskimos were more merciful than we are. Ask the old people in nursing homes across the country. A fast death is a blessing we deny them. Yet we deny them a human life, too. For these people, life is an endless succession of deprivations. The food is poor and there is not enough of it. A typical dinner at one Medicare-approved home consisted of one chicken wing and a scoop of dried-up mashed potatoes. Insanitary conditions, lack of medical care, uncaring, sometimes deliberately cruel attendants, lack of even the barest safety precautions against fire or accident, are all facts of life for these patients. Perhaps worst of all, there is nothing to do — day in and day out — but wait for death to come.

Who's to blame? That's what Medical World News set out to explore in an article on nursing homes. The answer? There are, of course, many reasons — not the least of which is the indifference of the medical profession. They shunt responsibility for health care to the institution administration.

That's how we saw it — and that's how we reported it. It's what doctors have come to expect from Medical World News — truth about the important issues they have to face every day, truth reported quickly and accurately. It's what makes us the best-read weekly news publication in the medical field.

If you want to reach the doctor, you need Medical World News.

MEDICAL WORLD NEWS

The Newsweekly of Medicine

A McGraw-Hill Magazine

Figure 13.10   In some societies, such as Japan, the aged are treated with respect and are considered a source of wisdom. By contrast, the American elderly are typically pushed aside. Advertisements like the one reproduced here call attention to the many elderly who are isolated in nursing homes and retirement communities, often called "storage bins" or "ghettos for the aged," where they sit idle and eventually die.

411

Practical Nurse, Old People's Home

In America, people doesn't keep their old people at home. At a certain age they put them away in America. In my country, the old people stay in the home until they die. But here, not like that. It's surprising to me. They put them away. The first thing they think of is a nursing home. Some of these people don't need a nursing home. If they have their own bedroom at home, look at television or listen to the radio or they have themselves busy knitting . . . We all, us foreigners, think about it.

Right now there's a lady here, nothing wrong with her, but they put her away. They don't come to see her. The only time they see her is when she say, "I can't breathe." She wants some attention. And that way she's just aging. When I come here, she was a beautiful woman. She was looking very nice. Now she is going down. If they would come and take her out sometimes. . . .

Things that go on here. I've seen many of these patients, they need help, but they don't have enough help. Sometimes they eat and sometimes they don't. Sometimes there's eight hours' wait. Those that can have private nurse, fine. Those that can't suffer. And this is a high-class place. Where poor old people . . . (She shakes her head.) . . .

Things so bad for old people today—if I could afford to buy a few buildings, I would have that to fall on. You got to be independent. So you don't have to run there and there and there in your old age. They don't have enough income. I don't want to be like that.

Quote is from a practical nurse from the West Indies, who works at a nursing home for upper-middle-class elderly. —From Studs Terkel, *Working* (New York: Pantheon Books, 1974), pp. 502–504.

programs. A few centers have professional staff members for such purposes. Most Senior Centers also attempt to participate in activities of the larger community by engaging in community-service projects, which are most often unpaid volunteer services. Many older people wish to be of use to the community and are willing to contribute their time and effort.

There are a few employment projects designed specifically to provide employment for older workers. The Foster Grandparent Program is perhaps the best known of these programs. Foster Grandparents work twenty hours a week at the minimum wage in various child-care institutions. The program gives the older person both the satisfaction of providing a needed service and a needed income supplement. Despite the success of the program, it generally has a low priority for local funds and is kept going only by federal support.

The Senior Aides program is a federal program designed to show the usefulness of older workers to social agencies through a federally funded forty-week training period. They learn new skills in the training program. For example, some learn to be teachers' aids in schools. This is a popular program among older people, and most of its training programs have long waiting lists.

Golden Age or senior-citizen clubs promote many of the same types of activities that Senior Centers provide. However, clubs without center facilities are generally more limited in the activities they can provide. Senior Centers are usually run as private, nonprofit corporations, often supported with United Fund money. At one time or another, Senior Centers have been supported by federal funds from a variety of departments.

Only a tiny proportion (1 to 5 percent) of the older population frequents Senior Centers in most communities. Of course, many old people cannot attend because of transportation difficulties, disability, poor health, and so on. Yet even in those communities where an all-out effort to bring people in has been made, only a small percentage (usually less than 15 percent) of the older population has even set foot in Senior Centers, much less taken an active part in the program.

For some older people, the Senior Center is a valuable place, providing involvement, friends,

Figure 13.11   Foster Grandparents is one of the few plans designed to use the time and skills of the elderly and apply them to important programs and services in society. One of the participants is shown above at a children's day-care center in Chicago.

Figure 13.12   Adult-education programs, including community schools that serve all age groups, are important in helping elderly people cope with our rapidly changing culture. The aged, whose children no longer live with them and whose life expectancy is still rising, often desire further education and have time to pursue it.

and a sense of self-renewal. For most, however, it is a continued reminder that older people are isolated and treated like outcasts. The Senior Center, however, seems destined to play an increasingly important role in the lives of older people, despite its present negative image.

Recreation and leisure are related to other factors, such as health and income. Leisure time for the older person is no longer a vague catch-all category of hours not spent at work. It is the central fact of life, and our institutions should therefore provide the opportunity for older people to engage in activities that can give them emotional and psychological satisfaction. For most older people, the main obstacles to enjoying leisure time are posed by inadequate income, health care, and transportation.

EDUCATION

Our society is one in which perhaps the greatest constant is change. Although old people's years of experience are valuable, they also must continue to learn new things or they will not be able to deal with change. The educational institutions in America fail miserably in providing adult education, especially education for the elderly.

Adult education is aimed primarily at basic reading and writing skills and at vocational education, yet most older Americans do not need or want either of these programs. Public-school education in the United States almost completely neglects older people. A countertrend is provided by the community school movement, which promotes the concept that public schools should serve the entire community at various times of the day. In many communities, programs for older people have become an integral part of the total educational program. Senior Centers and meal programs often make use of public-school facilities. Public libraries, too, offer information and recreation services to a great many older people.

There are few programs to help people prepare for retirement. Only about 10 percent of employees have a retirement-preparation program of any kind (Schulz, 1970). Mark Green and his colleagues (1969) found that where such programs exist the most common topics were financial planning, the use of leisure time, preventive health care, housing, and consumer education. They also found that such programs reduce anxiety and dissatisfaction with retirement, reduce health worries, and increase social participation during retirement.

Executives, professional people, and government officials generally do not need or want such programs. People in these upper-status jobs are accustomed to planning and manipulating their environment to achieve their goals. People in middle-status categories, such as clerks, salesmen, skilled workers, and foremen, are more likely to have programs available to them because they generally favor retirement, want to plan for it, and work for an organization that offers a formal program. Semiskilled workers are less likely to be exposed to formal programs, and their marginal literacy, their somewhat fatalistic attitude, and their history of many job changes make them unlikely to volunteer for such programs, even if they are available (Simpson, Back, and McKinney, 1966).

So far, we have discussed only those institutional responses that are national in scope or common to many communities. All these institutional responses show varying degrees of responsibility and cooperation among federal, state, and local government. Services usually are provided at the local level. In most communities there are dozens of unconnected government, private, and voluntary programs. Lack of coordination considerably reduces their effectiveness. The most common feature of local services, including services to the elderly, is the lack of responsibility within local government for the coordination of these services.

THE FUTURE FOR THE AGED

The proportion of older Americans in the population is going to increase rapidly, and the number of extremely old people is probably going to show a particularly large increase. From 1990 on, it is likely that comparatively small groups of young adults will be entering the labor force, and at the same time, people born during the baby boom after World War II will be approaching retirement. The future elderly baby-boom group will probably strain the financing of the Social Security system

413

unless a more adequate system, financed by employee, employer, and general tax-revenue contributions, is developed. Social Security financing at present puts the greatest burden on those at the lowest income levels. Changing that system is a major prerequisite for the development of adequate income for retired people.

Schulz (1970) maintains that private pensions cannot be expected to broaden coverage to include much more than 20 percent of the population because the easy-to-cover segment of the work force is already covered. Securing private-pension coverage for people who work for small-scale employers will be difficult. For those who are covered, the private-pension system must be reformed. For example, pension credit systems must be standardized so that people can change jobs without losing coverage. And pension funds must become reliable.

As we saw earlier, many of the federal programs for the elderly are designed to help offset poverty. If income in retirement does not improve, already inadequate programs in health-care financing, housing, nutrition, and transportation will undoubtedly be taxed beyond the breaking point. The rapidly growing number of old people will also overload existing health-care facilities. The greatly increased need for nursing homes and other nursing and homemaker services may significantly outstrip the ability to provide such services. Euthanasia, or mercy killing, especially at the request of patients, may also become a public issue.

Increases in average age will also bring changes in family structure, which is already under stress. Currently, the children of most older people are still middle aged, but about one in ten has a child who is over sixty-five. This proportion will increase in the future. Many older people now rely on their children to help them get around and deal with various problems. The effects of the increased reliance of the very old on already retired children cannot be predicted.

On the brighter side, the future will probably bring improved social status to those old Americans who escape being poor. Recent research by Donald Cowgill (1972) indicates that the status of the aged has risen slightly as industrial societies have matured. (The status of the aged lowers as societies begin to industrialize, probably in part because such societies are uncertain about where the aged fit after institutions such as the family rapidly change and no longer have the means to take care of the elderly.)

In recent years, the public image of a retirement without debt or poverty has improved considerably. In addition, the future will bring an older population with a much higher average level of education, a much smaller proportion of foreign born, and a much small proportion who were reared on farms. These changes should reduce a good bit of the current social distance between old people and people reared in different eras. Tomorrow's older person may also be more skillful at dealing with change than today's.

The prospects also look good for a more flexible definition of retirement. By 1990, some segments of the labor force, especially the service sector, will experience a labor shortage. The reason for this shortage is the decline in the birth rate at this time, which will result in fewer people to fill the jobs. The problem will no doubt be partly solved by allowing capable workers to stay on after the mandatory retirement age. Eventually, the mandatory retirement age may even be dropped.

It is also very likely that older people will become more politically active, particularly the older poor. Their numbers will increase greatly unless reform in the retirement income system occurs, and this should encourage more political groups such as the Gray Panthers and win a broader base of support for old-age political movements. The older generation's power will also be enhanced by its increased educational achievements and by the greater cultural similarity of its members.

There may well be a shifting upward of the age at which people technically and legally become old. By 1990, age sixty-five will probably be even more inappropriate than it is today. Based on today's average level of functioning, age seventy-five is a more realistic point of demarcation. Yet sixty-five is so ingrained in our legal system and way of thinking that change can be expected to come only slowly.

The most signigicant change the future holds is probably in the public image of what it means to be an older adult. In the future, the older population is

414

going to be more active and more obvious. Such changes should soften considerably the harsh image most people hold of aging as a totally negative experience. If we can solve the economic problems, we may find that the social image will take care of itself.

CHAPTER REVIEW

Old age affects almost everyone eventually, but many of the problems that accompany old age, in the United States at least, stem from society's reaction to it rather than from age itself. *Chronological age grading* in America affects the opportunities as well as the responsibilities given to older people. Most older Americans face economic hardships resulting from drastic declines in income after retirement. Although some receive both private pensions and Social Security, the majority (80 percent) live on Social Security benefits alone, which are generally inadequate and which put many older Americans under the poverty line. Savings accumulated for old age rarely fill the financial void because they average under $2,000. Those older people who are able to work despite legal restrictions on age most often do so out of necessity. It is not surprising to find that about two-thirds of the retired persons in America live at or below a "modest" living level. Many older people who qualify for public assistance do not accept it because of pride. Older people's economic difficulties affect the quality of their housing, too. Their houses become run down over time because many older Americans cannot afford to make repairs. Finally, in a culture based on individual mobility, the elderly find themselves without adequate transportation either because they cannot afford to own or are physically unable to drive a car or because public transportation is not conveniently located.

This economic or physical dependence on others casts most older Americans into a subordinate social position and robs them of self-dignity. Many of these people undergo premature aging as a result of stress, illness, or poverty. Far more have had chronic health problems. But nearly all Americans are labeled "old," at least initially, on the sole criterion of chronological age. Many problems result from retirement—often mandatory retirement at age sixty-two or sixty-five. As a result of retirement, most older people initially increase their social participation. But, because their income drops an average of 50 percent after retirement, many older Americans have to curtail their leisure activities because they can no longer afford them. Besides forcing many people into poverty, mandatory retirement also wastes valuable talent and experience.

The problems of the aged are related to other social problems in our society. Because of changes in public health many Americans live longer, which means that they have even longer periods of unemployment and poverty *after* retirement. Furthermore, the problems of the elderly are no longer private matters; because families are less able to care for their older members, support of the elderly is becoming a public responsibility. Finally, the poverty and discrimination experienced by people in the early years of employment affects the Social Security and pension benefits available to them later in life.

How has the country responded to the concerns of older Americans? In 1974, the government responded to their growing financial needs by establishing the Supplemental Security Income, which guarantees everyone an income of at least $130 a month. This income alone, however, is simply not adequate. Besides county nursing homes, most of which do not meet even minimum health standards, the government has helped establish decent, inexpensive public housing for the lower-income elderly. Private facilities are also available for those who are relatively well-off. The middle-income retired person, however, has virtually no outside help available. Health-care plans like Medicare are a step in the right direction because they help with major medical expenses, but they do not cover prescriptions, glasses, or hearing aids. Nutritional needs are being only partly met through food-stamp plans and programs offering low-cost hot meals. It has been difficult to establish successful recreation and leisure activities for older Americans, partly because large numbers of older people do not participate in programs such as Senior Citizens. However, more meaningful activities like Foster Grandparents and Senior Aids are flourishing.

There is a need for educational programs for retired Americans. There will be a large elderly population when the baby-boom youth reach retirement age. Perhaps this group will become politically active and will be able to bring about a change in the social and economic status of the elderly and also achieve other needed reforms.

415

SUGGESTED READINGS

Atchley, Robert C. *The Social Forces in Later Life: An Introduction to Social Gerontology.* Belmont, Calif.: Wadsworth, 1972.

Lopata, Helena Z. *Widowhood in an American City.* Cambridge, Mass.: Schenkman, 1973.

Riley, Matilda W., and Anne E. Foner. *Aging and Society: Volume 1, An Inventory of Research Findings.* New York: Russell Sage Foundation, 1968.

Streib, Gordon F., and Clement J. Schneider. *Retirement in American Society,* Itaca, N.Y.: Cornell University Press, 1971.

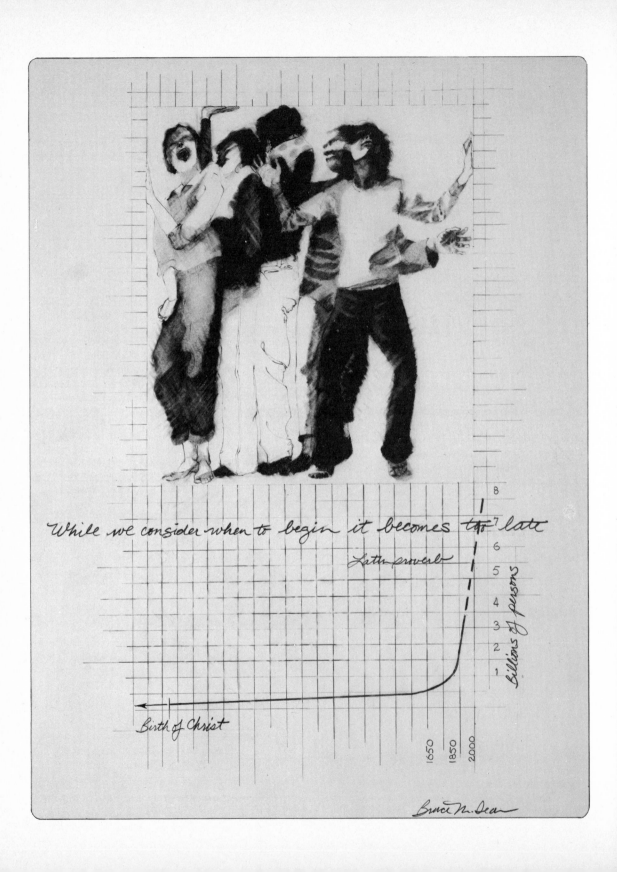

While we consider when to begin it becomes too late

Latin proverb

Birth of Christ

1650 1850 2000

8
7
6
5
4
3
2
1

Billions of persons

Bruce M. Dean

14
Population

Population growth is undoubtedly the most serious social problem facing humankind. It has already strained the social and material resources of many nations. Should present trends go unchecked for even a few decades longer, human fertility will have consequences almost too grim to imagine.

For most of human history, population grew so slowly that it hardly appeared to grow at all. Kingsley Davis (1971b) estimates that about 10,000 years ago, the whole human population totalled only about 5 million people. Growth was so slow that the population would have doubled only about once every 60,000 years. As recently as 1750, population growth was still so slow that it would have taken 1,250 years to double. Today, the world population is doubling once every 37 years, and there are more than 3.7 billion people.

When we project such rates into the immediate future, the results surpass comprehension. For example, if the present growth rate held, there would be 157 *billion* people on earth 200 years from now. Or, to offer an equally incredible example, at its present rate of growth, the population of Mexico will climb from 51 million people today to 2.2 *billion* people in 100 years (Davis, 1971b). Can you imagine Mexico with a population over half the size of today's world population, with more people than now live in India and China combined?

Obviously such populations are not simply inconceivable—they are impossible. Long before any such numbers could be reached, calamity would overtake us. Such projections merely show how close calamity is. That is why Paul Ehrlich (1970) speaks of "the population bomb" quietly ticking away and threatening soon to blow us up.

In this chapter, we outline the dimensions of the population peril and explain why it has occurred. Why, after thousands of years of infinitesimal increase, did human population explode? Finally, we explore means of averting population growth.

PART I: THE PROBLEM
POPULATION

Most of you have grown up with warnings about the dangers of the population explosion. You are also perhaps aware that in the last few years the American birth rate has been falling rapidly and that our population will probably soon cease to grow. Indeed, most industrial nations of the world, and perhaps China as well, seem to have headed off the potential crisis of unchecked population growth. Important as such success may be, it offers no reason to regard the danger as past because most of the world is not industrialized.

In the underdeveloped countries, population growth continues unabated, and there are no prospects in sight that it will be halted. In the long run, growth in these nations may be as serious a problem for Americans as would be a continuation of our own population explosion. We are all inhabitants of a single planet. If starvation, plague, political chaos, and ecological ruin occur on a massive scale in many parts of the world, they will cause severe problems for persons everywhere.

THE POPULATION EXPLOSION

Two factors enter into population growth. First is the *growth rate,* which is the net difference between the annual number of births and deaths divided by the total population. When we say a population is growing at a rate of 3.7 percent a year (Venezuela's present rate), that means that there are more births than deaths each year—enough to make the total population 3.7 percent larger at the end of a year than it was at the beginning of the year. Perhaps that does not sound like a great deal of growth; however, at that rate, the population will double in about nineteen years.

The second factor in population growth is the *absolute size* of the population that is growing at a particular rate. If the population is small, doubling it does not mean adding a large number of people to the world population. Obviously, doubling a population of a million only results in a population of 2 million, but doubling a population of 100 million adds another 100 million to the total. Remember, however, that doubling results in *exponential growth.* When even a tiny population continues at a rate of growth that causes it to double every few years, it will rapidly become a hugh population. For example, if a nation of 4 million people began to grow at 3.5 percent per year (thus

doubling every 20 years), in 20 years its population would be 8 million, after 40 years it would be 16 million, after 60 years it would be 32 million, after 80 years, 64 million, and, after a century of that rate of growth, the nation would have a population of 128 million people—thirty-two times more than when the growth began. Human populations have recently undergone this kind of explosive growth. The speed with which such redoubling produces astronomical totals has caused social scientists to speak of a population explosion, for such change is more like an explosion than like simple expansion. The arithmetic is inescapable, and the future it promises threatens to come upon us very rapidly.

As we have already pointed out, the population problem must be examined separately for developed and underdeveloped nations. Furthermore, the problem needs to be viewed from two different perspectives. First, rapid population growth means relatively *large families.* Such growth has serious implications for families and for family members, especially in modern times, regardless of what other effects population growth may have. Second, the size of populations and the rate of population growth have profound consequences for the operations of societies as systems—indeed, for the world ecological and social system. These consequences also require careful consideration.

THE POPULATION PROBLEM
IN DEVELOPED NATIONS

The population explosion occurred much earlier in the developed nations. The acceleration began sometime in the seventeenth century. Europeans consequently became an increasingly larger proportion of the world's population. Kingsley Davis (1971b) reports that in 1650, northwestern Europeans, living in Europe and overseas, made up 18 percent of the world's population. By 1920, they made up 35 percent. Recently, however, the growth of European and other industrialized populations has slowed, while growth in underdeveloped, non-European countries has become rapid. The decline in birth rates in industrial nations was briefly reversed during the post-World War II "baby boom" but has since declined (see

Figure 14.1   Every hour over 370 babies are born in the United States, which has a relatively low fertility rate compared with that of many underdeveloped countries.

Figure 14.2   The long decline in the United States birth rate was reversed during the baby boom, the period between 1940 and 1950 when a large number of couples who had postponed having children during the Depression began to have them again after the economy recovered and soldiers returned from the war. Today, the baby-boom children are causing the population to grow as they in turn have families (despite their relatively low fertility rate). After the turn of the century, the baby-boom children will cause a rapid increase in the elderly population.

(Adapted from National Bureau of Economic Research, 1968.)

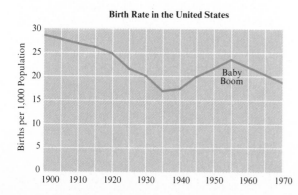

Birth Rate in the United States

Figure 14.2). In fact, the birth rate in the United States has recently reached a level described as *zero population growth.*

Two Parents, Two Children

If each generation produced only the number of offspring equal to their own number, a population would be stable; it would neither grow nor diminish. Advocates of zero population growth therefore propose that families limit themselves to only two children to prevent increased numbers of people. Actually, if this goal were achieved, the population would decline because adults who had no children would not be replaced in the population.

Another basis for achieving a stable birth rate is to permit each female to bear two children. Taking into account infant mortality and females who have no offspring, our population would be stable if the average female bore 2.1 children. At present, the average American female is bearing 1.9 children, slightly below the rate needed for replacement.

Even if this rate holds, our population will continue growing for forty to fifty years because our present population is relatively young—a consequence of the postwar baby boom. The babies born in the 1940s and early 1950s are just now entering their peak childbearing years. Even if they restrict themselves to only two children per couple, the population will grow to about 275 million by the year 2020. (It is 212 million today.) To state the matter coldly, despite the fact that the older population is increasing in size because of increased life expectancy, there are simply not yet enough older Americans to produce the number of deaths sufficient to balance the births. And there will not be a sufficient number until the baby boom children themselves become elderly after the turn of the century. But by then, many millions of people will have been added to the population. At that time, if the present birth rate holds, our population will stop growing. Assuming that our population does level off in this fashion, let us explore the impact of these population patterns. The American prospect resembles that of other industrial nations.

Fertility and the American Family

Large families are an economic burden in modern society. An income that affords average comforts

419

to a family of four may leave a family of eight in dire poverty. Indeed, as was pointed out in Chapter 12, the fact that children have become an economic liability rather than an economic asset has greatly changed the circumstances of the American family. The economic burden of children has been a major factor in the long-term decline in birth rates of industrial nations since before the turn of the century. Thus, for the modern family, a high birth rate is a problem.

However, given the low and still declining American birth rate, high fertility probably is not a major threat to the average family. Although too many children still burden the poor, large families are no longer the trend. Instead, it is *low fertility* that has major implications for the future of the American family.

Marriages in modern America have become increasingly short. The average marriage now lasts only seven years. In seeking explanations for this divorce trend, it is important to remember that the role of wife and mother (and therefore that of husband and father) has changed considerably because women now bear few children and are still young when they stop bearing children. Women can therefore be less dependent upon their husbands because they now are able to take a job outside the home and because divorce does not leave them with a houseful of children to support. For men, by the same token, divorce does not mean the financial difficulty it once meant.

The major functions of the family unit (aside from affection and companionship) have always been economic and reproductive. However, because wealth now primarily comes from jobs rather than from property, the family is no longer vital for the transmission of wealth. And because women are now able to earn their living, they are no longer economically bound to the family. In such circumstances, a massive decline in fertility greatly reduces another support for continuation of family units. Little wonder that the family is showing signs of fragility and that there is widespread concern whether the family unit will survive and, if so, in what fashion. As we shall see, this is quite different from the impact of the great increases in family size that presently characterize families in underdeveloped nations. High fertility may also

420

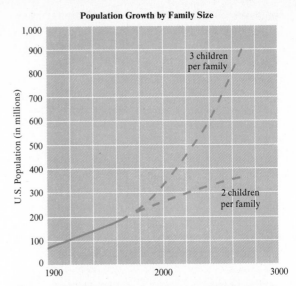

Population Growth by Family Size

Figure 14.3   The difference between a two-child family and a three-child family is the difference between population stability and exponential, or extremely rapid, growth.
(U.S. Bureau of the Census.)

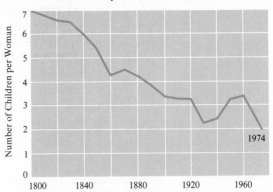

Fertility Rate in the United States

Figure 14.4   Since 1800 the fertility rate in the United States has dropped dramatically (except for the brief baby boom following World War II). This long-term downward trend reflects the demographic transition: In response to conditions of industrial society, especially the decline in infant mortality, families began to curtail their fertility. In contrast, death rates in today's underdeveloped nations have suddenly dropped to levels close to that of industrial nations but fertility remains at preindustrial levels.

Figure 14.5   (Far right) On the bottom right-hand corner of succeeding pages, you will see this same world map. The dots represent the approximate distribution of the world's population during different time periods, with a final map projecting population distribution in the year 2,000. With each succeeding time period, growth and density increase alarmingly.
(Adapted from Commission on Population Growth and the American Future, 1972.)

spell the end of families by imposing too great rather than too light a burden.

Fertility and American Society

In many respects, the population explosion has already delivered its major blows to American society. In the 200 years since 1776 our population has increased 100 times. Chapter 2 considered many consequences of the massive change in scale caused by immense population growth. We are a nation of large cities and large organizations, and we urgently need to learn how to manage and humanize life on such a scale. Furthermore, many of our social problems arise from the size, complexity, and impersonality of our society, especially of our cities. Troubles that once could be dealt with by friends or family are now often transformed into public problems because so many people do not have family and friends who are able to help them. To be neighborly today often means contributing to fund drives.

For American society as a whole, perhaps the major impact of a large population is the burden it places on the ecological life-support systems (see Chapter 15). More people require more food, use more mineral resouces, consume more water and air, and in other ways make more and more demands on the physical environment. Even if our population does increase to 275 million before it stabilizes, we will probably find ways to support such numbers. We may well have to stop consuming so much and reduce the material level of our lives, but our growth has not guaranteed disaster for us. If disaster comes, it seems more likely that it will stem from the calamitous consequences of population growth in underdeveloped nations.

POPULATION
AND THE UNDERDEVELOPED NATIONS

It is difficult, and probably dishonest, to avoid doomsday rhetoric when describing population trends in the underdeveloped world—a world encompassing most of Africa, Latin America, and Asia. For population growth not only means future prospects of horrid dimensions but has already caused great hardships, suffering, and social chaos. Consider but a few examples.

In the great cities in the underdeveloped world today live huge multitudes of squatters. These are the destitute, homeless people who have been driven from the rural regions by the sheer press of their numbers. They have erected huts and shacks in the parks, on playgrounds, and on vacant lots. In Calcutta, India, thousands of squatter families live (and die) without shelter on the sidewalks. In Caracas, Venezuela, more than 35 percent of the population are squatters. And squatters in Manila exceed half a million persons. In the inhabitable areas of Egypt today, an average of 2,424 persons reside on every square mile—and most of this area is considered rural! We need not project imaginary future catastrophes to warn of the population peril in the underdeveloped world. It is already at hand.

We now examine the present burdens that runaway population growth has imposed on the family and society in the underdeveloped world.

Fertility and the Family

The population explosion in underdeveloped nations is radically changing the organization of the family as well as pressing the family ever deeper into poverty.

Until recently, underdeveloped nations were still fundamentally rural societies, so the extended family was the norm. Population pressure has changed all that. Underdeveloped societies are rapidly becoming urban. And, uprooted from its rural surroundings, the *extended family* system is being replaced by *nuclear family* life (see Chapter 12). It is important to recognize that this move to the cities is not a true kind of urbanization. Unlike urbanization in industrialized societies, it is not the

421

World Population, 1850: 1,131 Million

result of mechanization and increased productivity of the farms, which creates a surplus rural population, or of industrialization, which creates a compelling need for urban labor. Instead, the move to the cities in underdeveloped nations is primarily a function of *rapid population growth* far beyond what the farms and plantations can support or use for labor. People in underdeveloped countries today are driven to the cities in search of some means of livelihood. There, most of them swell the ranks of the squatter population.

Consider the case of Venezuela. Venezuela's population is presently growing at a rate of 3.7 percent per year. At that rate, it must double every nineteen years. That rate is not countrywide, however. The rural population has been stationary, but city population is growing by 6 percent a year and therefore doubling every twelve years. All of Venezuela's growth is urban growth because migration from the farms balances the high rural birth rate.

In consequence of these shifts, the poorest Venezuelans are uprooted from their extended-family ties—and from all the support and protection that such families afford—and thrust into the city to live in extreme privation within the fragile capsule of the nuclear family. Furthermore, because of poverty, they lack many of the resources that nuclear families have in industrialized countries. For example, they cannot afford life and disability insurance to replace the protection once provided by their extended families against death or disability of the breadwinner. And because of the poverty of their societies, nuclear families in underdeveloped nations cannot rely on the state to provide for their old age or for the education of their children as can nuclear families in most industrialized nations.

Furthermore, unlike nuclear families in industrialized nations, those in the underdeveloped world have *high fertility*. Consequently, the family must support large numbers of children. Yet, because women are so burdened with incessant pregnancy and child rearing, they cannot enter the labor force to increase the family income. Thus, whereas the modern American family frequently has few children and two employed adult members, the nuclear family in countries like Venezuela has many children and only one adult able to work (and often he is unable to find work). As a result, many families

422

Figure 14.6   The consequences of unmanageable population growth in Calcutta, India. Humans die on the streets, and vultures feed on their remains.

Figure 14.7   A large family, like the Ugandan clan pictured below, was necessary for economic survival in agricultural societies of the past. Unfortunately, the tradition of having large families keeps fertility rates high in many underdeveloped countries, even after children become an economic burden.

send their children out to work at an early age to help support the family. Unlike child labor on un-mechanized farms, however, child labor in the city has low productive value, so children earn very little. Furthermore, child labor tends to impede long-range economic development because it interferes with education. So the new generation has no higher level of skills to offer an industrializing economy than did their forebears from the farm.

Under such conditions, as one might expect, the family displays signs of breakdown. The cities become filled with abandoned children and orphans. Illegitimacy, dissertion, and divorce become the norm as families collapse under the strains of privation and hopelessness.

Fertility and Society

Societies may also collapse under the burden of an exploding population. Earlier we mentioned that at its present rate of population growth, Mexico will have 2.2 *billion* people 100 years from now. However, that population size will never occur, for life in Mexico would become impossible long before that number could be reached. If the population is not checked by lowered fertility, it will be checked by death through famine, disease, and perhaps internal strife. That is the hideous prospect contained in the arithmetic of population growth.

We now examine two ways in which fertility threatens underdeveloped societies: by overtaking economic limits and by causing political chaos.

Economic Limits

The goal of all underdeveloped nations is *development.* Like the industrialized nations, they too would like the fruits of modern life—relief from arduous manual labor, good housing, education, abundant food and clothing, and all the goods that represent an improved quality of life. Among the cruelest ironies for developing nations is that the very aspects of modern technology most easily adopted by underdeveloped nations are the ones that have caused their populations to explode. And this rapid population growth in turn has cancelled out their efforts for economic development.

It is not the case that most underdeveloped nations have stagnant economies. Most of them are undergoing economic development at a rapid rate—in fact, their economies are presently growing more rapidly than those of the industrialized nations. However, their population growth literally consumes these gains about as rapidly as they occur. To illustrate the point, suppose a nation is increasing the value of the goods and services it produces by 3.5 percent per year. At that rate, the economy would double its productivity in twenty years. But if its population is also growing by 3.5 percent a year, there will be absolutely no increase in the goods and services available per person. Thus, although the economy would grow, the lives of individuals would not improve at all. Obviously, should economic growth slip *below* population growth, the standard of living would deteriorate despite development. This state of affairs is what underdeveloped nations now face. Most of their economic growth is used to keep their already dismal standard of living from getting worse.

Exponential population growth is not simply a treadmill that prevents poor nations from achieving greater economic development. The situation is even worse than that: The constant expansion of their economies, which is necessary simply to sustain their present population growth, cannot continue indefinitely. Productive capacities are not endlessly expandable; land, air, water, minerals, food, and other vital resources are limited. Considering these limited productive capacities, we see only calamity in the near future for underdeveloped nations. Very soon their economic expansion will encounter these limits. And with no gains in production to be eaten up by the expanding population, there will be progressively less for people who already live on the edge of survival.

423

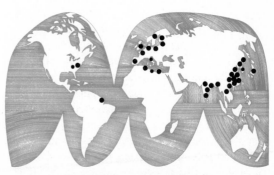

World Population, 1900: 1,590 Million

Indeed, it is estimated that already 60 percent of the people in the underdeveloped world suffer from malnutrition with the consequent widespread physical and mental retardation, and one person in five is eating so little as to be slowly starving to death (Heilbroner, 1974). Yet several decades from now, these same nations will have twice as many mouths to feed. As you read this chapter, it is *already too late* to prevent millions of people from starving to death. So the question now is how many millions and whether it will ever stop.

Political Chaos

Rapidly growing populations are also young populations. Families have large numbers of children and thus at any give moment children tend to outnumber adults. In such societies, there are also disproportionately high numbers of young adults. Hence the economies must grow very rapidly in order to provide an increasing number of jobs to absorb these waves of young people, and since rural populations tend to remain stable, these must be urban jobs. But rarely can economies expand rapidly enough to create enough jobs; therefore, there is growing unemployment, especially among young adults. As this process continues, there is increasing danger that these unemployed masses will be easily incited to riot and political unrest. As Kingsley Davis (1971b) put it:

Possessed of youthful energy and idealism, having no stake in the existing situation, being extremely numerous in relation to the adult population, these youths are politically explosive, often ready to follow any leader who promises the quickest and most violent solution. Their role in making and breaking dictators has often been demonstrated in backward countries, whether in Latin America or the Middle East.

Political unrest creates another irony for the underdeveloped nations: A volatile political situation makes it difficult for governments to force the changes and sacrifices necessary to halt the very processes that drive the people to pull down the governments. Regimes change, but the problems worsen. The economist Robert Heilbroner (1974) therefore predicts the rise of "iron governments" in most underdeveloped nations, for only powerful and repressive states will be able to "ram many needed changes, including birth control itself,

424

Figure 14.8   The development of authoritarian or "iron" governments like that of China may be the only way in which countries with large peasant populations can be forced to adopt needed changes such as birth-control.

Figure 14.9   The rapidly growing populations of underdeveloped countries can create political unrest, which can have world-wide consequences, especially if it affects the political stability of nations, such as Egypt (below), that have control over basic natural resources, such as oil.

down the throats of an uncomprehending and perhaps restive peasantry.''

It is possible that the rise of such regimes will be able to bring internal political stability to developing nations that are nearing political chaos because of population growth. However, the world population explosion equally threatens *international* political stability. As the conditions worsen in underdeveloped countries, the continued relative well-being of the developed nations is likely to increase the antagonisms between rich and poor nations. At present, poverty also means military weakness. But with the present spread of nuclear weapons to underdeveloped nations (India exploded a nuclear bomb in 1974), this situation may change. Therefore, the population explosion may imperil life not merely in poor nations but in all nations. The starving masses that crowd underdeveloped nations may one day find they have nothing to lose by risking nuclear war.

In Chapter 15 these themes are combined with questions about the ecological capacity of the earth. Plausible scenarios of global ruin are discussed. Behind each are the inexorable numbers of population explosion: 2, 4, 8, 16, 32, etc. But there is no comparable mathematics to show how we shall prevail against excessive fertility.

PART II: SOURCES
POPULATION

How did the population explosion occur? At the beginning of this chapter we pointed out that for most of human history, populations grew very slowly. Then suddenly, in the mid-seventeenth century, northern European populations began rapid growth. In the twentieth century, population growth began to soar in the rest of the world. And in a relatively short time, human populations have grown so large that we tremble at the consequences only a few years hence. What happened? What makes populations grow or decline?

THE MALTHUSIAN THEORY OF POPULATION

Thomas Malthus (1766–1834) was one of the first social scientists and is regarded as the father of

modern population studies. Malthus clearly saw that human populations could easily increase exponentially—that is, he recognized the arithmetic of population explosions. He observed that human populations did not (in his time or earlier) seem to follow an exponential pattern of growth, and he wondered why. In his famous book, *Essay on the Principle of Population,* first published in 1798, he argued that population growth followed a cyclical pattern. Malthus pointed out that every so often populations do begin to grow exponentially, in geometric increases (2, 4, 8, 16, 32, etc.). However, the supply of resources, principally food, that are necessary to sustain life do not increase exponentially. Resources increase arithmetically (2, 4, 6, 8, 10, etc.). Thus, populations quickly outstrip the supply of resources. At this point, positive checks on population growth occur. Growth is cut off, Malthus claimed, by certain checks, including starvation, disease, and war.

According to Malthus, death periodically intervened to halt exploding populations. His theory focused on three main elements—production, fertility, and mortality. He argued that when *production* increases and there are more goods (such as food and clothing) per person, *mortality* declines (people are healthier), and thus a population grows. Malthus pessimistically believed that humans are incapable of restraining their *fertility* and thus would *always* reproduce up to the limits of production. When this occurs, goods per capita decline past the danger point and mortality rises rapidly to halt population growth. In this process, obviously, the weakest and poorest members of society are those most likely to die. (A century

425

World Population, 1950: 2,509 Million

later, Charles Darwin found in Malthus' theory of human population cycles the general mechanism for the survival of the fittest, a concept that permitted him to form his general theory of biological evolution.)

At the time Malthus wrote, his theory seemed to fit the facts of population changes. For example, the population of England seemed to have followed this cyclical pattern for some centuries. Improvements in agricultural production were invariably followed by rapid population growth and, then, as these gains were eaten away by growth, inevitably *Malthusian checks* such as famine and plague appeared and cut back the population. Shortly after Malthus' theory was published, however, this vicious population cycle appeared to have been broken.

DEMOGRAPHIC-TRANSITION THEORY

426

Malthus' theory depended on fertility remaining high while fluctuations in mortality periodically permitted population increases or population decreases. But as the industrial revolution gathered headway, several unexpected things happened. Industrialization permitted a previously undreamed of rate of growth in productivity. Industrial nations were able to support vast populations in comparison with populations of medieval times. Industrialization revolutionized agriculture. Farm production rose incredibly. And the wealth generated by manufacturing permitted importation of large amounts of food and raw materials. But something else happened; productivity increases alone did not break the Malthusian cycle. In time, exponential population growth would overtake even the rapid production gains of industrialization. However, industrialization also began to influence fertility. People began having fewer children.

This change in fertility is called the *demographic transition* (demography is the study of human populations). In 1945, Kingsley Davis was the first to formulate a theory about why fertility was declining in industrialized nations. In his demographic-transition theory, Davis did not fundamentally dispute Malthus but merely pointed out that Malthus' theory seemed applicable only to *preindustrial* (underdeveloped) societies. Davis

proposed that in industrial societies, fertility will be curtailed by factors inherent in industrialization.

As we have seen, industrialization causes urbanization, and urbanization has much to do with curtailing fertility. In cities, children increase household expenses but do not contribute to the support of the family, as they do in farming families. However, family size initially increases in industrial societies *because economic growth causes a decline in mortality;* fewer children die in infancy and early childhood. Eventually, however, the pressure of too many children is relieved because couples begin to control their fertility. Thus, with the exception of the 1945–1955 "baby boom," the birth rate in industrial nations has been falling since before the turn of the century (Wrong, 1958). It is true that the populations of industrialized nations grew immensely over the past several centuries as mortality declined, but despite the problems created by this extraordinary growth, it would appear that controlled fertility will soon halt growth in industrialized nations.

Health Can Be Harmful

What accounts for population patterns in underdeveloped nations? We have seen that populations grew rapidly in some nations because of their rapid economic growth. The Malthusian checks were held in abeyance because agricultural and industrial productivity kept up with population growth. Eventually, declines in fertility also helped break the vicious cycle that afflicted preindustrial times. However, this explanation cannot account for present population explosions in the underdeveloped nations. These nations have *not* industrialized, and their population growth has *not* been caused by changing economic conditions.

What has caused the population explosion in underdeveloped nations has been a *massive decline in mortality*. It is a sad irony of our times that the future of these nations, and perhaps of all nations, has been imperiled by one of our noblest achievements—the ability to reduce the heavy and persistent early death and infant mortality that has long afflicted human societies. Through the application of a few cheap, easily exported medical and scientific discoveries and practices, such as vaccines for diseases and insecticides, death rates in underdeveloped nations have dropped miraculously in recent decades.

These scientific innovations developed slowly in the industrial world and only gradually lowered death rates. Meanwhile, productivity rose and family fertility adjusted to changed conditions. But in the underdeveloped nations, scientific and medical technology has sometimes literally fallen from the sky, changing mortality rates almost overnight. Kingsley Davis (1971b) reports the incredible case of Ceylon. The death rate there was cut almost in half in one year (from 1946 to 1947). What happened? The countryside was sprayed with DDT to kill mosquitos and other insects. In consequence, malaria and several other serious diseases declined greatly. The DDT was imported, as were the experts who ran the operation. The Ceylonese played no part in this program that changed their mortality. Nor did this program have any impact on their fertility. Thus, large numbers of infants and children who would ordinarily have perished survived, adding to the population and accelerating its growth further by producing even more offspring.

Until recent times, women were incessantly pregnant because only high fertility could ensure that sufficient children would survive to adulthood. Until modern times, widespread death of infants and children was an accepted part of human life. For example, a trip to any graveyard more than 100 years old will quickly reveal the very high ratio of children's to adult's graves. In preindustrial times, it was normal for half of the children to die before the age of six.

At the start of the century, infant and child mortality had declined greatly in developed nations but remained high enough in underdeveloped nations to require relatively high fertility. Then came a revolution in the underdeveloped nations' mortality that was not their doing. The change came from contact with industrial nations. Imported technology reduced mortality so rapidly that there was little time for traditional cultures, designed to encourage high fertility, to be modified. With the natural Malthusian check on mortality suspended and with food production rising simultaneously, population explosion has been the result.

In order to clarify this discussion, let us concentrate on a single case, the Latin American nation of Guyana (until 1966 know as British Guiana), to see how mortality was reduced.

Transforming Guyana's Environment

Environmental conditions were responsible for a high mortality rate in Guyana. Swamps and marshes supported malaria-bearing mosquitos, impure water supplies caused diarrhea and stomach disorders, and lack of sanitation in homes and towns promoted tuberculosis and other diseases. Even when these conditions are not fatal, they weaken people, reduce their resistance to infections, and generally increase their risk of death.

Figure 14.10 shows mortality rates from five major causes of death in Guyana from 1911 to 1960 (Mandle, 1970). These five causes accounted for about one-half of the deaths in that country from 1911 to 1936, but in the late 1950s, these five causes accounted for only one-fourth of the deaths. Such diseases as nephritis, pneumonia, and bronchitis, for example, are directly related to environmental conditions. These infectious diseases often accompany a disease, such as diarrhea, that is actually one of the environmental group. In fact, the incidence of infectious diseases increases as the environmental diseases become prevalent, especially in unhealthy bodies that have little resistance to infection. A population in poor health supports infectious diseases. The decline of these diseases contributes strongly to lower death rates.

As Figure 14.10 indicates, malaria was the most serious cause of death in Guyana until the early 1940s. At this point it began to decline sharply, and by the late 1950s it had virtually disappeared as a cause of death. The related infectious disease

427

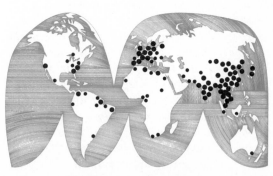

World Population, 1970: 3,630 Million

nephritis also declined sharply over this period. Getting rid of malaria was a central factor in the fall in the death rates not only in Guyana but also in numerous other countries in Asia, Africa, and Latin America (Davis, 1956). The key to the eradication of malaria is the elimination of the mosquito that carries the disease. The elimination of malaria was accomplished not by using hospitals and doctors or treating the population but by operating on the environment in which the population lives.

Two general methods were used: One was the tedious draining and filling of the swamps and stagnant waters in which the mosquito develops. These procedures were initiated in Guyana in the 1920s and contributed to the decline of the disease from that time until the end of World War II. In the postwar period, DDT became available, and its use is responsible for the subsequent rapid disappearance of the disease. The dangers of DDT are current concerns of everyone, but it is necessary to realize that for people who must choose between high infant mortality rates and the possible dangers of DDT, the choice will be to spray with DDT.

The high death rates from diarrhea and enteritis in Guyana and many other nations of Latin America, Asia, and Africa are a result of water supplies severely polluted with human waste. The more careful disposal of waste and the gradual improvement of water supplies contributed to a 50 percent decline in the death rates from diarrhea and enteritis. The general improvements in sanitation also had the effect of lowering the death rates from tuberculosis and other diseases. By 1960, mortality had fallen to one-third the level of 1920.

The major diseases in Guyana were essentially controlled by environmental intervention. It should be noted, however, that infant mortality was strongly reduced through educational programs directed at mothers (Mandle, 1970). Similarly, the targets in developing areas of the world in the postwar period were the water supplies and the minds of young mothers. In most regions the mosquito, too, was a target. As Figure 14.10 demonstrates, the effects on the mortality rates were spectacular.

However, death in nations like Guyana has only taken a holiday. Had the population stabilized in these nations, their reduced mortality rates might have been permanent. But as their population

428

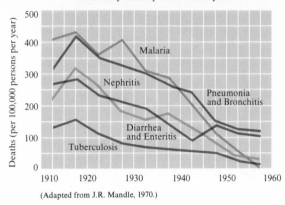

Mortality Rates by Disease in Guyana

(Adapted from J.R. Mandle, 1970.)

Figure 14.10 (Top) *Widespread communicable diseases accounted for most of the deaths in preindustrial societies. The world-wide impact of modern medical practices is shown in the sharp decline in death rates from five major causes of death in Guyana from 1911 to 1960. For example, malaria was a widespread killer in 1911, but by the late 1950s it had virtually disappeared. (Bottom) By 1959, three and a half million children in Thailand had been vaccinated for tuberculosis, one of the country's major health problems. The vaccination campaign was first carried out in urban areas, where the disease was most prevalent.*

growth soars it is obvious that low mortality is temporary. Hence, the next economic reverse they encounter—from drought, crop blight, raw material shortage, or civil strife—may produce considerable mortality in many underdeveloped nations. The Malthusian checks lurk offstage.

Culture and Fertility

The population explosion is caused by the maintenance of high fertility at a time of decreased mortality. It is not that families in underdeveloped nations have begun to have more children, rather it is that so many more of their children live to reproduce. Why has the birth rate remained high despite the hardships it is causing? The values and traditions of developing nations underlie the high fertility of their populations. In many areas, early sexual unions are viewed as natural and appropriate and are expected of all members of society. These societies offer women no means of support except through the family. A woman's alternatives are either to burden parents and siblings (who view the support of unmarried adult females as an imposition) or to marry. The latter course is almost invariable chosen, if indeed, it can be considered a choice.

The large-family ideal derives from the long experience of high rates of infant and child mortality. To be assured that one son would survive to continue the family line, to take over the father's land or trade, and to care for parents in their old age, parents had to have two or three sons. Because only about one-half of the infants born are male, rather heavy fertility was required to achieve these objectives. Although the abrupt decline in mortality levels in the underdeveloped nations has made it possible to achieve these objectives with smaller families, the time-honored ideal of a large family persists.

The traditional agricultural economies of underdeveloped nations are also frequently supportive of the large-family ideal. Because children are able to perform useful, productive agricultural work, they contribute to the household income from an early age. However, as the children grow into adulthood, problems arise. If more than one son should survive, the family plot must be divided, or some of the sons must seek employment

elsewhere. With levels of mortality low, as they are today, surplus population results from high fertility levels in underdeveloped nations.

The consequences of high fertility are evidently not yet understood by many people in the developing countries. Couples persist in bearing many children despite the fact that this behavior no longer involves social or economic gain. In fact, high fertility is even exhibited by couples who report a preference for small families. Several factors account for this persistence of high fertility. First, contraceptives are not readily available in some areas of Latin America, Asia, and Africa. Second, even when contraceptives are available, it is frequently the case that many people are unaware of their availability. Third, even when contraception is available and its availability is known, there is all too often a pervasive pessimism regarding it effectiveness. People view the claims of contraception, like those of magic, with suspicion. Traditional societies never had effective means of controlling natural events of any sort, and the belief that such control is beyond human capacity is rather strong (Stycos, 1968).

Finally, birth control is typically used only *after* a very large family has already been created. A recent study done in Caracas, Venezuela (Bamburger and Earle, 1971), found that only 13.4 percent of women of child-bearing age who regularly engaged in sexual intercourse were making any attempt to avoid pregnancy. But those women who were attempting to prevent pregnancy had already *been* pregnant an average of 6.6 times. Similarly, a recent campaign to encourage men in India to obtain vasectomies—a simple procedure that makes

World Population, 2000: 7,522 Million

429

men sterile but does not diminish their sexual capacity—seemed fairly successful in terms of the number of men treated. Then it was discovered that their average age was above fifty.

The crux of the problem is that the rapid changes in the conditions governing mortality have occurred without significant changes in the cultural traditions of these societies. For thousands of years, human culture has developed to insure sufficient fertility. Suddenly, these customs, values, marriage patterns, and sexual practices have become *dysfunctional.* The population explosion has occurred so rapidly that traditional cultures have not been able to adjust to it. It is important to recognize that the developed nations never had to cope with the demands for such rapid change. Mortality changes in the industrial nations occurred gradually as medical discoveries and practices were introduced. Indeed, declining mortality was simply one aspect of wholesale social change. The whole culture of industrializing nations gradually became modern. Thus, there was time for the family to change with the changing times. By contrast, the arithmetic of population explosion (unleashed by imported medical technology) overtook underdeveloped nations before they could hope to respond. Indeed, even if underdeveloped nations could somehow change their fertility patterns im-

mediately, it would already be too late for many of them to avert serious consequences. No immediate change can be expected. Indeed, many seriously imperiled nations are making no effort to change.

PART III: RESPONSES
POPULATION

Before we assess what is being done and what should be done to avert the population explosion, we must briefly examine what *can* be done.

Some suggest that we ought to concentrate on ways to support huge populations—that science must find ways to supply enough food and new technologies to avert Malthusian checks of famine and disease. It is easy to see why that solution is unrealistic. Returning to the arithmetic of population growth, we can quickly compute that in thirty more generations human density would be so great that each human being would have only 1/32 of a square inch of the earth's surface on which to stand. To make such a computation is, of course, more than a bit silly. But clearly it demonstrates that our faith in finding ways to take care of endless waves of babies is equally silly. Indeed, as we have pointed out, more than half the people on earth today are already underfed.

Others have suggested migration as a solution. People should leave overcrowded nations to settle in sparsely inhabited places. But, as Chapter 15 makes clear, the whole planet is reaching the saturation point in terms of supporting human life. And no one with the slightest technical sense supposes we can ship our excess billions off in spaceships.

So we are left with only two possible means to head off population growth. We can *increase mortality* or we can *reduce fertility*. No nation is likely to adopt a policy based on raising the death rate. Mortality may in fact take its toll of the population through nuclear wars, famine, or rampant disease. But death can be no government's policy. Thus, a reduction in fertility is really the only course available to nations. It is the course followed by industrial nations. But does this policy work in underdeveloped nations? That depends on two major factors: (1) on official recognition of the existence of a population problem and (2) on the capacity of governments to impose adequate controls on fertility. We now assess these factors.

RECOGNITION OF THE POPULATION PERIL

It may strike you as odd that space in this book is devoted to recognition of the most frightening problem in human history. Yet the fact remains that many of the nations most severely imperiled by runaway population growth ignore the problem. Some even deny that it exists. For example, in 1974 the government of Argentina—where population growth is not only eating up gains in economic growth but is actually outpacing economic growth—announced an official policy to encourage and stimulate fertility in hopes of rapidly increasing its population. Equating population numbers with political power, Argentina hopes to "catch up" to nations such as the United States. Clearly, if Argentina must enter a population race, that nation would be better advised to promote immigration from nearby nations that are already overcrowded. Sad to say, Argentina is not an isolated case. Many underdeveloped nations have long denied that they face a population problem.

Until the mid-1960s, such views were encouraged in underdeveloped nations by Marxist spokesmen, especially those from the Soviet Union. Frequently, United Nations policies in support of family-planning programs were attacked on the grounds that population problems are merely a propaganda tool of capitalist societies. The argument was made that capitalism, not overpopulation, was the cause of the economic woes of underdeveloped nations and that population problems, like all social problems, would disappear un-

Figure 14.11   One way for a society to approach the population problem is to calculate its optimal population level and, through rational family planning, maintain the population at that level. India, with the most urgent population problem of any country, has introduced a number of family-planning services in an attempt to reduce the high birth rate. Outdoor advertising in support of the two-child family can be seen in the picture on the left. Despite such efforts, the growing population of India has outstripped food production. The result has been periodic famines. (Right) Indians in Baroda receive food during a famine, but countless more starve.

der authentic socialist rule (Davis, 1971b; Brackett, 1968). Soviets have often been proponents of the idea that science can always provide for the growing masses. For example, one Soviet economist proposed at the World Population Conference in 1965 that the earth could support a population of 933 billion people (or 26,000 per square mile) by harnessing solar energy (Malin, 1965).

Meanwhile Communist China was quietly making massive efforts to curtail its own population growth and has recently claimed it will stabilize its population by the year 2000 (Heilbroner, 1974). The Soviet government has also shifted its view. The government now supports family-planning programs for underdeveloped nations that desire them (Davis, 1971b; Brackett, 1968).

An additional barrier to recognition of the population problem has been religious opposition, especially in predominantly Roman Catholic countries. Because the Catholic Church has long opposed artificial means of birth control, there has been a tendency for Church spokesmen to ignore or deemphasize the consequences of explosive population increases. However, Church doctrine has had much less influence on Catholics in industrial nations. For example, recent studies find that American Catholic couples widely practice con-

traception and that the average size of the American Catholic family is declining (Westoff and Ryder, 1969). However, the Church has more firmly opposed birth control in Latin America, probably with greater success because the majority of persons in those nations are suspicious of birth control anyway. During the 1960s, intense debate took place among Catholic prelates over birth control, and many Catholics hoped the Church would reconsider its position. But Pope Paul's official pronouncement, published in *Humanae Vitae,* July 1968, disappointed many devout Catholics. It reaffirmed opposition to artificial contraception.

CONTROL OF FERTILITY

Let us suppose that nations recognize the peril of rampant population growth. Let us also suppose that they conclude that their only option is rapid reduction of fertility to the level of zero population growth. How can they proceed?

The usual response has been to initiate family-planning programs. Typically, the government attempts to make contraceptives widely available, to instruct people in their use, and to encourage them to control their fertility. The first nation to initiate a family-planning program was India, in 1952. We

now have more than twenty years of experience with a variety of such efforts in a number of nations throughout the world.

As many population experts have pointed out and as continuing high fertility in these nations demonstrates, the programs have been unsuccessful. The reason for this failure is easily understood. The programs are voluntary. Contraception merely permits a couple to limit their family to the number of children they want. But families in underdeveloped nations want more children than the society can tolerate. Thus, if the average couple wants two or fewer children, the society might achieve population control if people were given the means to limit their family to the desired number. But if the average couple wants more than two children, the population will grow no matter how widespread the use of contraception. We have already seen that birth control in Venezuela, when it is used at all, tends to be used only after the average Venezuelan couple has already had close to six children. Therein lies the failure of voluntary family-planning programs.

It follows that such nations can only check their populations if they can convince people that they should *want* fewer children (and then show them how to have fewer children) or if they can *force*

couples to limit family size. So far, public-relations campaigns encouraging people to desire fewer children have failed. They have proved how difficult it is to rapidly change ingrained customs and values. That leaves force as the only means.

It would be easy to formulate a compulsory birth-control program. For example, each woman could be licensed to have a certain number of children. She could be permitted to yield her quota to another woman who wanted more children if the first woman did not wish to use it. Compliance to the rule could be enforced by abortion or sterilization. The problem is not in devising such a program but in the kind of government that it would take to impose legal controls in fertility.

Obviously, such a program could most easily be established in nations where most people did not want more children than they would be permitted. But in such nations there is no need for imposing compulsory birth control. Where the need for a compulsory birth-control program most urgently exists, it is likely to meet intense public resistance. Therefore, in order for nations to turn to force to lower fertility, they will need great powers of repression. We are describing here what Robert Heilbroner (1974) has called "iron governments," briefly mentioned earlier in this chapter. Such gov-

433

Figure 14.12 (Left) *Because of the government's ability to mobilize massive public support, China has made great progress in controlling its population growth and in raising agricultural production to feed its people.*

Figure 14.13 Famines, such as those in Sub-Saharan Africa (right), *India, and Bangladesh are likely to spread to other areas in the coming years as worldwide food shortages become more severe.*

ernments will be dictatorships based on miltary power. Heilbroner doubts that anything short of force can check "the descent into hell" caused by overpopulation. He therefore anticipates that as the crisis worsens and present governments become unable to cope with the problems, totalitarian governments are likely to emerge. Heilbroner also predicts that iron governments would be much more belligerent toward industrialized nations than are present-day weaker regimes and that the danger of wars over resources would likely increase.

These gloomy prospects make it obvious that the population explosion is not just someone else's problem. It threatens every nation and every person. There will surely be global famines and mass starvation. Today the sub-Saharan region of Africa is the scene of terrible suffering caused by drought.

As this book goes to press, the crops have failed in Bangladesh and the Philippines. World-wide appeals have already begun for food to avert starvation in these teeming nations. But these appeals come at a time when surplus grain supplies in other nations are almost depleted—drought caused the 1974 American corn crop to fall well below expectations. Even if food is found to avert these particular crises, it is clear that nations capable of producing surplus food cannot long meet the shortages that must continue to arise in many underdeveloped nations. For the fact is that many of these nations are developing food shortages so great they cannot be fed for any extended period. In such circumstances it may be more cruel to continue to send food than to deny their appeals for help. For more food from elsewhere will simple insure that there will be even more mouths to be fed and thus more people will die when the aid runs out. Therefore, we have come to a time when very painful decisions must be made about which nations to send supplies to and which ones to deny. We do not have the option of feeding them all. For the rest of your life, you will be hearing of terrible famines.

It is impossible to end this discussion on an optimistic note. We can say only that there are reasonable prospects that human society might ultimately survive the population explosion. But survival is not certain. It is only certain that there will be immense suffering.

Figure 14.14 Famines caused by drought or other weather-related catastrophies are likely to increase as world food surpluses become depleted and developed nations can no longer send relief to crisis areas.

CHAPTER REVIEW

Present population growth threatens to bury the earth in people. Rapid population growth occurred first in the industrial nations. Recently, however, growth in these nations has been brought under control. Not so in the underdeveloped nations, where consequences of runaway population growth not only threaten their future but possibly the future of the developed nations as well.

If the average couple has only two children, the population does not grow, for one generation simply replaces its own numbers. This is called *zero population growth*. Because fertility has slowly declined during industrialization (except for a brief baby-boom following World War II), industrial nations can expect to have populations in the future not much larger than they have today. It seems reasonable to suppose that these nations can support populations of this size. But in the underdeveloped nations, fertility remains high and populations are doubling in size every few years. For example, at its present rate of growth, Mexico will have 2.2 billion people to feed and clothe a hundred years from now. Such staggering growth overwhelms economic development. Even though these countries develop greater industrial and agricultural capacities each year, the gains must be divided among so many more people each year that each citizen receives less. Today, about 60 percent of the people in underdeveloped nations are so malnourished that they suffer chronic disease and early death. And even if population growth were immediately controlled, many people would still starve. Worse, there are no prospects that population growth will be halted soon. Thus, much death and suffering are certain. Faced with such critical conditions, governments in underdeveloped nations may prove politically unstable. "Iron governments" may rise to cope with the problems, and wars over resources may occur.

The first theory of population growth was developed by Thomas Malthus in the late eighteenth century. *Malthusian theory* argued that population growth would always outstrip economic growth and population would be cut back by famine, disease, and war. The *demographic transition* theory, on the other hand, dealt with the decline in population growth that stemmed from industrialization. It argued that families themselves control fertility as soon as children cease to be an economic asset. The problem in nonindustrialized, underdeveloped countries stems from the fact that modern medical discoveries almost miraculously lowered their death rates but did so without lowering fertility. Human culture has evolved to encourage large families because the high rates of mortality required large numbers of children to insure that some lived to adulthood. Rapid declines in mortality have not given the culture time to readjust. Thus, population growth has been rapid.

Attempts to halt population growth through family-planning programs have failed because too many people in underdeveloped nations desire large families. And birth-control devices are not used until after a large number of children have already been born. An alternative is compulsory birth-control programs in nations with excessive birth rates. Mandatory programs would require governments capable of great coercion, which is not an attractive prospect. However, it is more attractive than letting population be limited by starvation, plague, chaos, and war.

SUGGESTED READINGS

Ehrlich, Paul R. *The Population Bomb.* New York: Ballantine, 1968.

Heilbroner, Robert. *An Inquiry into the Human Prospect.* New York: Norton, 1974.

Malthus, Thomas, Julian Huxley, and Frederick Osborn. *Three Essays on Population.* New York: New American Library, 1960.

Scientific American. Vol. 231 (September 1974). (Entire issue devoted to major population problems.)

435

And there arose a smoke
out of the pit, as the
smoke of a great furnace
and the sun and moon
were darkened by reason
of the smoke of the pit.

revelation 9:2

15
Ecology

The social issues we associate with the words environment and ecology go far beyond the troubles of any particular population group. What is at stake is nothing less than the survival of the human species itself.

Ultimately, the problem of the environment is the problem of human evolution on earth. But the evolution of human beings is not merely a matter of genetic mutation and natural selection. The secret of human evolution lies in the shared knowledge (culture) and social institutions (society) that each generation contributes and passes down to the next. If we go the way of other species and become extinct, it will be because we were unable to make the necessary adjustments in our technology, social institutions, and patterns of thought.

PART I: THE PROBLEM
ECOLOGY

The challenge of the environment is that we become better human beings: We must become aware that the message of Genesis—that humankind would have "dominion over the fish of the sea, and over the birds of the air, and over every living thing that moves upon the earth"—does not give us license to plunder and degrade the earth's natural order.

Genesis is also the story of the expulsion of Adam and Eve from the Garden of Eden, a land in which the first man and woman lived in harmony with nature. God exiled them for violating his law. There is perhaps a warning in that story for us, that we might very well be expelled from our own land, from the planet Earth, if we continue to abuse the laws of nature. In spite of the fact that we realize increasingly that the earth itself has little more of life's necessities than it originally included, we are rapidly exhausting or poisoning these life supports because our social systems have failed to anticipate and control the harmful effects of our technologies. We have failed to consider the relationship between humans and their environment.

However, in contrast to the fact that Adam and Eve had somewhere to go after they could no longer remain in the Garden, we realize, since we have taken our first steps beyond this planet and have sifted moon dust through the mechanical fingers of instruments, that at least for some time to come there is nowhere else we can go. The nearest hospitable planet is within the realm of our imaginings but beyond the grasp of our limited technologies.

DEPLETION AND POISONING OF LIFE-SUPPORT SYSTEMS

The earth's biosphere—the surface layer of the planet and the surrounding atmosphere—sustains all life. Land, air, water, and energy are fundamental to the existence of living organisms. Questions of maintaining nature's beauty must therefore take a back seat to questions about the preservation of the life-sustaining capacities of the biosphere.

With the exception of certain microorganisms that derive their oxygen from other organisms, all life forms take oxygen directly from the air or from quantities of air dissolved in water. Water, too, is directly absorbed and converted by living things, and its availability and purity set limits on the possibility for life, as we know it, to exist. The availability of energy required to sustain life depends on the complex set of relationships and exchanges of energy among living organisms themselves.

The primary source of all energy that is consumed by organisms or transferred from one organism to another is, of course, the radiant energy of the sun—an insignificant dot among the giant energy furnaces of the Milky Way. Most plants can convert solar energy directly into food by using water and chlorophyll. Animals cannot directly use the sun's energy, as can plants, but must obtain this energy either by eating the food that plants manufacture or by eating other animals.

These simple facts are the origin of most ecological relationships among living organisms. The basic ecological relationships that make up the balance of nature are (1) *competition* among organisms for available light, water, or climatic conditions; (2) *cooperation* among organisms that are mutually dependent; and (3) *food chains* in which more highly differentiated organisms feed on the energy stored by organisms that are lower in the evolutionary order. Human beings have followed an evolutionary course in which their cultures and technologies have continually strained these natu-

438

ral relationships to the limit. In a mere twenty or thirty thousand years, little more than a pulse beat on the geological time scale, human cultures have so drastically depleted and poisoned the basic life-support systems of the planet that they now threaten the future of the human species and perhaps all of life itself.

Because societies need energy sources, they have had to alter their environments. If they had not done so, the natural environment would have set limits on their growth. Earlier technologies made it possible to domesticate animals and plants. Then human beings learned to raise food in controlled situations requiring large investments of energy for each increase in supply. They developed mechanical extensions of their bodies, such as the train and the automobile, and controlled harsh effects of the environment by heating or cooling their shelters. All these techniques are extremely costly of energy and of the mineral wealth of the earth's crust. Yet we have not made the major technological strides toward developing sources of energy other than those stored in the earth. The earth gives us fossil fuels—decayed plant and animal matter that slowly turns into coal and petroleum. And the fossil fuels we burn in immense quantities contribute mightily to the depletion and poisoning of available air and water in the biosphere.

Before the rise of modern science, people recognized that air, water, and energy were essential life-sustaining elements. Yet our discussion of the frailties of these life-support systems will demonstrate that, as a species, we have not yet fully understood that the atmosphere, the oceans, the rivers, and the earth's mineral resources are limited and may not be able to meet the severe demands we are placing on them.

Air

We inhabit the bottom of a vast ocean of air. More than 5 quadrillion (5,000,000 million) tons of nitrogen, oxygen, and carbon dioxide circulate in the skies above us. Even though this is almost an unimaginable quantity, it is seriously endangered by our excessive burning of oxygen and atmospheric pollution. Into this precious atmosphere, the United States, by far the world's leading air polluter, pours from 200 to 300 million tons of poisonous gases and particles each year. About 42 percent of these pollutants come from modern forms of transportation, another 21 percent from stationary fuel consumption (such as that by home furnaces), and about 14 percent from industrial production.

It would seem that with such vast quantities of air, our use of the skies as industrial dumping grounds would have little immediate effect. However, the circulatory systems of the skies do not necessarily distribute pollutants uniformly. Atmospheric pollution is primarily the problem of industrial and industrializing areas of the world, and its effects are felt most severely in regions that do the polluting. However, few scientists are willing to discount its long-range effects on other areas of the globe (Nobile and Deedy, 1972).

As all interns and student nurses know, they must clear an air passage for a patient in distress. A human can live for about five weeks without food, about five days without water, but only five minutes, at the most, without air. The same immediacy applies to air resources on the societal scale. Emphysema, lung cancer, and other respiratory disorders are the most rapidly growing diseases in industrialized countries, and in terms of direct damage to ourselves and our environment, pollution takes its most devastating toll when the air surrounding a city or town becomes poisoned with dust and gases. A tragic example is the deadly smog that covered London in December 1952.

Londoners had little advance warning, for the air that winter had been generally crisp and cool and city residents had enjoyed strolls in the winter sun. Suddenly an anticyclone eased over the city, bringing a dense, two-tiered cloud cover, high barometric pressure, and slow, clockwise winds around the edges of a two-hundred-mile radius. Within this sluggish weather mass, the air stagnated as the wind meters over London registered zero. Fumes and dust from factories, buildings, and cars mixed with the dead air, turning a light fog into a thick, yellowish layer of smog. Motorists found it impossible to drive in the streets, and pedestrians had to grope along the edges of buildings to find their way. For five days, there was no relief from the poisonous air that curled under door sills and took on more dust and pollutants from home heating systems. Finally, over a two-day

 439

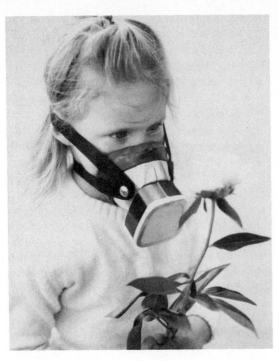

Figure 15.1   Air is essential to sustain life. Industrialization has brought with it a vast increase in air pollution, which can become severe enough to cause death—as it did in London in 1952—and can cause respiratory disorders even when it is less severe. To dramatize such effects of air pollution, a child wears an air pollution mask, which is said to filter out 90 percent of the contaminants in the air we breathe.

440

period, the wind picked up and the air cleared slowly, but not before more than 5,000 people had died from the poisoned air (Battan, 1966).

All the heavily industrialized and densely populated areas of North America experience moderate to severe air-pollution problems. Although the atmosphere above Los Angeles county is somewhat less polluted on the average than that of New York or Chicago, that area has severe pollution problems with smog—a mixture of fog and automobile and industrial fumes. Los Angeles has a severe smog problem because frequently the air above it does not circulate, so pollution builds up. Ironically, most of the people who originally populated Southern California went there to escape the difficult climates of the Eastern and Mid-Western industrial cities. In a mere generation, as the population of the area more than tripled between 1940 and 1970, Los Angeles became the prime North American example of the automobile city, a settlement composed of hundreds of suburban centers connected by a complex system of auto routes. It had no well-developed central city where dense areas of population could support the development of large-scale mass transit. Los Angeles, like suburban America in general, favors the private automobile as the common form of transportation. Unfortunately, this dependency on auto transport has seriously endangered the skies above Los Angeles and other rapidly growing American cities, to say nothing at this point of the energy demands of automobile transportation.

Air pollution creates hazards for plant as well as for human and other animal life. Agronomists have estimated, for example, that the crop damage from polluted air in Southern California amounts to over $100 million a year. Although people throughout the United States purchase more than 7 million cars per year, the automobile emissions are particularly serious in Southern California, where the climate and the topography combine to produce frequent *temperature inversions* (Battan, 1966).

Temperature inversions occur most often in warm climates where the sun heats the upper layers of the atmosphere. Normally, air heated by the warmer temperatures of the earth will rise above the colder air masses at higher altitudes. This upward movement of air carries pollutants in the surface air into the upper atmosphere where winds disperse them over wider areas. In a temperature inversion, the upper air is warmer than the lower air and the pollutants therefore stay in the surface air, often increasing to intolerable concentrations. Winds sweeping across flatlands or oceans will usually mix the air even where temperature inversions exist. But mountains that surround cities built in valleys (such as Los Angeles and other cities in Southern California) trap the layered air within the valleys and prevent winds from entering the valleys.

Environmental scientists have been aware of these problems since the first studies of air pollution and temperature inversions in Southern California appeared in 1944. Unfortunately, large-scale efforts to cope with the problem have only recently appeared. The situation was not con-

Figure 15.2 *Although many other cities outrank Los Angeles in air pollution, Los Angeles has become known as the smog capital of America. The air inversions of the mountain-ringed Los Angeles air basin (and of neighboring cities) periodically trap both fog and the exhaust emissions from industry and from the ever-present automobile. The result is eye-stinging, unsightly smog. When Los Angeles is free from smog* (left), *Mount Baldy, forty miles away, can be seen clearly, but during smog conditions* (far left), *the mountain is invisible and even downtown buildings are obscured.* (Right) *The air in New York City is even more polluted than that in Los Angeles. Air pollution—along with the ugly proliferation of television antennas—spoils the view of the Statue of Liberty.*

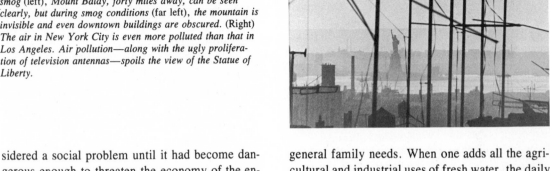

sidered a social problem until it had become dangerous enough to threaten the economy of the entire region—for example, by making it necessary to close factories during very smoggy periods.

So far in the history of human society, scientific knowledge of environmental problems has not been sufficient to prevent our cultures from exceeding the environmental carrying capacity of large regions of the earth. This point applies equally to the earth's supplies of pure water.

Water

Thus far in the brief history of human exploration in outer space, scientists have failed to discover any significant sources of free water—water that is not bonded to other substances. For example, water contained in the cells of living organisms or in chemical substances such as coal is not free. Free water is the vehicle for life, as we know it, on earth. The moon is as dry as a lump of baked pumice, and Mars is apparently equally arid. Perhaps water exists as a gas in the turbulant atmospheres of Venus and Jupiter, but few scientists expect those great planets to one day offer cool streams for thirsty interplanetary explorers. All the available water we know of exists on this planet in an abundance second only to that of atmospheric air. There are more than 354 quintillion (354,000,000,000 billion) gallons of water in the earth's seas, and the annual rainfall over the United States provides over 5,000 billion gallons of fresh, pure water. We each consume approximately 100 gallons daily for our drinking, washing, sanitary, and general family needs. When one adds all the agricultural and industrial uses of fresh water, the daily consumption per person increases to about 5,500 gallons in the United States and Canada. Yet, far from living in a period of superabundance of water, we are rapidly exhausting and polluting water sources in many areas of the country.

The availability of water has always established the limits of human population density. Many ancient civilizations in the Middle East, in Africa, and in Central America flourished and declined in accordance with their supplies of water. Millions of people have faced death from drought in the sub-Saharan region of Africa. The *carrying capacity* of world regions—that is, the ability of the environment to support a human population of a given size and at a particular level of cultural development—still depends in large part on the abundance of water.

Even in the United States there have been water shortages. For example, New York City in 1965 experienced a serious water shortage after two years of relatively light rainfall had left the reservoirs of that metropolitan region dangerously low. In the city and in surrounding counties, New Yorkers were warned to make light use of their air conditioners, to avoid taking wasteful baths, and to forget entirely about their baked lawns, because lawn sprinkling was banned during the water emergency. Since this crisis in water supply passed, the New York region has had a sufficient water supply, but other areas of the country are now experiencing dangerous depletions of their

441

supply. Two regions quite seriously affected by increasing demands for water consumption are the settlements of the Great Lakes and the arid states of the Southwest.

In *The Coming Water Famine* (1966), a dismal but well-documented assessment of America's water resources, Representative James Wright reports that the water level of Lake Huron and Lake Erie dropped more than five feet from 1953 to 1965. The lowered water left mud flats for hundreds of feet between the lakes and cottages that once bordered the water. Lakes Michigan and Superior are larger bodies of water, so the situation is not as serious; however, the level of these lakes is also dropping as this largest area of fresh water in the world strains to meet the demands of an ever increasing population in the Great Lakes Basin.

Along with the tremendous demand for drinking water goes the heavy demand for industrial uses of the water. The bulk of North America's steel tonnage is produced along the Great Lakes in cities such as Buffalo, Toronto, Erie, Cleveland, Chicago, Hammond, and Gary, where more than 1,300 tons of water are used for each ton of steel produced. Much of this water is pumped back into the lakes and has seriously polluted the waters, particularly in the Cleveland area of Lake Erie, with chemical wastes.

Even with the best of modern water-treatment systems in industry, there is still the problem of *thermal pollution*—or returning water that is too warm into the lakes and feeder rivers. Because warm water dissolves less atmospheric oxygen, raising the water temperature seriously endangers the lake's oxygen supply and kills many forms of aquatic life.

Eutrophication—the depletion of a water system's oxygen supply and the subsequent choking of other aquatic life by algae—is the key process in understanding the effects of human population on natural water systems. The balance of life in a lake, river, or ocean depends above all on the supply of oxygen dissolved in the water and the proper levels of available nitrogen and phosporous. When industry pours water heated by the excess energy of production into a natural waterway, the oxygen-carrying capacity of the water system decreases. Fish such as pike, which inhabit the deep-

er and less oxygen-rich reaches of Lake Erie, are the first to feel the effects of a decreasing oxygen supply. Pike have been dying in great numbers, and their decaying mass, washed to the shores, has sent people away from recreational areas of the lake's edges. Thermal pollution is a by-product not only of the steel industry but also of the most advanced modes of industrial production, especially the production of energy through nuclear fission.

Another problem is the insufficient water resources for the future, especially for our most rapidly growing population region, the Southwestern states of Texas, Arizona, and New Mexico. In this area of the country, ground water is pumped from wells that may extend hundreds of feet into the earth to the water-bearing layers of soil and rock known as the *aquifer*. Houston, Tucson, and Phoenix, cities whose populations have increased by more than 100 percent in the previous two decades, are almost entirely dependent on ground water. In these and similar cities, the all-important *water table*—the subterranean level at which well water is found—has been decreasing alarmingly in recent years.

In such areas, the aquifer is depleted after a period of time and the settlements decline, as has already occurred in the high-plains region of Northern Texas. Farming communities that thrived during the 1950s and 1960s, as federal grants made it possible to develop well-fed irrigation systems, have seen the water-table levels go below the point at which it is economically feasible to pump water. Where farming families and agricultural towns once prospered, there are now ghost towns, depressing testimonials to nature's limits and the lack of human foresight (Eckstein, 1961).

Environmental optimists frequently argue that more than two-thirds of the earth's surface is covered by water and that intensive exploration of the oceans' resources, after all, is still in a relatively early phase. The food and mineral resources of the seas are vast, they say, and desalination (removing the salt from sea water) could well be the means to acquire water supplies for future generations.

Such optimism about future environmental resources reflects careless thinking in people who are otherwise intelligent. They are struck by the seemingly inexhaustible quantities of available re-

442

443

After C. F. Powers and A. Robertson, *Scientific American*, November 1966, p. 100. All rights reserved.

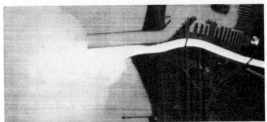

Figure 15.3   Pollution from technology speeds up the eutrophication (biological enrichment) of lake waters. The top three cross sections show the progression of this aging to its final result—the obliteration of a lake. (Top) (A) Phosphorous-bearing detergents and nitrogenous fertilizers from agricultural lands and (B) heated water by excess energy of production from industry are deposited into the lake. The pollutants (middle) increase the fertility of the lake, which in turn increase the demands on the oxygen supply, and the heated water decreases the water system's ability to carry oxygen, resulting in the (above) destruction of the lake. (Above right) The thermograph of the San Gabriel River shows the thermal outflow from the generating plants of the Southern California Edison Company and the Los Angeles Department of Water and Power. Where the river enters the bay, the water temperature was increased by more than 5 degrees Celsius. Because of our careless polluting, our fresh-water supply is decreased and (bottom right) fish and other aquatic organisms die.

sources but fail to consider the delicate ecological processes that maintain these vast systems. Desalination is at this time extremely costly and requires large amounts of scarce energy resources. Harvesting the seas for huge quantities of new vegetable and animal proteins is a noble thought, but we are already endangering the oceans' available food species. Our pollution of territorial waters in the industrial countries ignores and abuses all our knowledge of how life in the seas is sustained (Ehrenfeld, 1970).

Although 70 percent of the earth's surface is ocean water, the vital resources of energy and oxygen, which make those seas come alive with plant and fish life, are concentrated in thin bands along the major continental shorelines and at the polar regions of the planet. All sea life depends ultimately on the diatomes, one-celled algae that can thrive only in well-lighted waters to a depth of about 250 feet from the surface. The simple marine organisms that feed on the diatomes, and others that depend on more complex sea vegetation, thrive in shallow waters, particularly in the bays, marshlands, and other saltwater estuaries that are the biological breeding grounds for the open seas. These waters, however, are the most accessible to human use and abuse. The industrialized nations of the earth are rapidly destroying the oceans' breeding grounds by indiscriminately dumping industrial wastes and human sewage in them.

In its study, *Ocean Dumping,* the Council on Environmental Quality (1970b) told the President that in 1968 , 48.2 million tons of waste were dumped into off-shore waters at over 240 sites along the coastal fringes of the United States. Now, in the mid-1970s, the amount has gone up to more than 64 million tons, a rate of increase that, if kept constant, will result in 200 million tons by the end of the century. About 54 percent of this waste was polluted to begin with by heavy metals from industrial production, by bacterial growth from harbor dredging (removing sand, silt, mud,. and the like from the bottom of a body of water), and by raw sewage.

In consequence of these high levels of ocean dumping, the amount of the metal mercury found in Pacific halibut has increased to such poisonous levels that the largest of these fish must be elimi-

nated from the catches. Because of the ocean dumping, people have also become sick. For example, an epidemic of typhoid fever from contaminated shellfish struck Naples, Italy, in the summer of 1973. The dumping also threatens recreational use of the oceans. For example, the bays of Long Island—playgrounds for millions of New Yorkers—are now threatened by the spread of a ten-mile area of toxic sludge, a "dead sea" caused by ocean dumping off the coast of Long Island.

These are not isolated incidents but only a few of the endless examples of how the once bountiful marine breeding grounds have already been polluted with human waste. Progress is being made on some fronts in the struggle against water pollution; however, advances in environmental protection are now threatened throughout the world by the severe demands being placed on the earth's available energy resources.

Energy

Failure to comprehend the complex interrelationships between human beings and the biosphere often leads to hopelessly piecemeal solutions. Leaders react to environmental crises only when the public starts demanding immediate solutions to problems. Even though such problems have been developing for decades, few people have been prepared to understand them or look for effective strategies to cope with them. A case in point is the energy crisis, which became headline news in the summer of 1973 and received new urgency with the Arab oil embargo that followed.

However, if we mean by "energy" only the availability of fossil fuels and electrical power, we are forgetting the essential food energy that sustains human life. For the sad fact is that we are experiencing an energy crisis much more profound than the simple inability to obtain gasoline for our cars or to maintain the normal high levels of industrial production in North America. For example, an estimated 12,000 humans die each day throughout the world from malnutrition. This too is an energy crisis of enormous proportions.

The energy required to sustain human life on earth is primarily in the form of foods for individuals. Additional energy is required in the form of fuels to produce the artifacts of our cultures and to

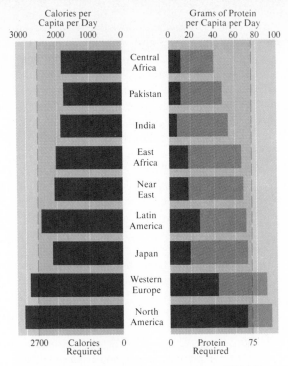

Calories per
Capita per Day

Grams of Protein
per Capita per Day

3000   2000   1000   0   0   20   40   60   80   100

Central
Africa

Pakistan

India

East
Africa

Near
East

Latin
America

Japan

Western
Europe

North
America

2700   Calories   0   0   Protein   75
          Required   Required

(Adapted from D.H. Meadows, D.L. Meadows, J. Randers, and W.W. Behrens, 1972.)

Figure 15.4   In most regions of the world, daily protein and calorie requirements are not being met. The main protein source (lighter portion of bar) is plants rather than animals (darker portion of bar).

Figure 15.5   For a person to gain 1 pound, the sea must produce a half ton of living matter. About 1,000 pounds of plankton feed and sustain 100 pounds of crustaceans, which in turn sustain 10 pounds of fish, which are needed for a human to gain 1 pound.

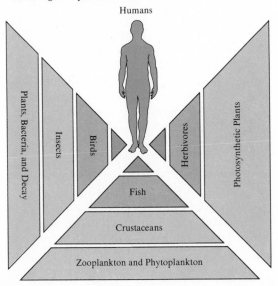

Humans

Plants, Bacteria, and Decay

Insects

Birds

Herbivores

Photosynthetic Plants

Fish

Crustaceans

Zooplankton and Phytoplankton

extend the sphere of our activities into regions that would not otherwise support our species. Whether it is used internally as food, or consumed externally as fuel, the energy is obtained by burning organic matter with oxygen in the air. The basic chemical equation for energy consumption is

organic matter + oxygen = carbon dioxide + energy

In the human body and in every living cell, food is burned to yield the energy necessary for life processes. Nutritionists estimate that from 2,500 to 4,500 calories of energy per day are required for an active person, depending on body weight and types of activities performed. Most of this energy can be supplied by carbohydrates, but unless the diet also contains adequate amounts of proteins and minerals, cell growth cannot proceed normally. Vegetable protein can supply most of the protein needed, but it lacks certain kinds of protein that are found only in animals. However, industrialized countries import much more animal protein than they need. And much of this comes from areas of the world populated by people whose diets are deficient in animal protein.

In *Diet for a Small Planet* (1971), an impassioned critique of the North American diet, Frances Moore Lappe argues that

Fully one-half of the harvested agricultural land in the U.S. is planted with feed crops. We feed 78 percent of all our grain to animals. This is the largest percentage of any country in the world. In Russia, 28 percent of grains are fed to animals, while in developing countries, the percentage ranges from 10 to 0.

In addition, Lappe observes that the amount of nutrients an animal takes in is far greater than the amount the animal produces for human consumption. "For example, the protein production ratio for beef and veal in North America is 21 to 1." Other livestock are more efficient protein converters, but Lappe and other nutritionists estimate that roughly 20 million tons of protein that could be fed directly to human beings are fed each year to livestock.

We annually import millions of tons of high quality animal proteins, such as South American beef, for direct consumption, and we use fish meal (700,000 tons yearly from Peru and Chile) for

445

Energy Options for the Future*

Kind of Energy, Extent of Use, and Sources	How the Energy Is Released	Advantages	Drawbacks
Fossil fuels In widespread use. Coal, petroleum, or natural gas. Found in certain portions of the earth where animal and plant remains have decayed into fossil fuels.	The fuel is burned to boil water and produce steam. The steam is then used to generate electricity.	The technology is well developed and can easily be improved by new techniques. Likely to provide three-fourths of all electricity even in the twenty-first century.	Considerable thermal and air pollution. All fossil fuels will run out in the next few hundred years. Coal mining is very damaging to the environment.
Nuclear (fission) Used in industrialized countries and only occasionally. Uranium and other radio-active metals. Found in certain areas of the earth. Metals that are more abundant may be used if breeder reactors are perfected. †	The atoms of the fuel are split (which releases energy) in a chain reaction. The heat produced by the reaction is used to boil water and produce electricity in the same manner in which the heat from fossil fuels is used.	Essentially no air pollution and in improved models, perhaps slightly less thermal pollution than present power generation produces. *If* breeder reactors prove practical, fuel supply is nearly unlimited.	How to dispose of radioactive wastes is a problem. Conventional nuclear reactors will run out of fuel early in the twenty-first century. Breeder reactors may not be practical. They can also be used to manu-facture nuclear weapons.
Theromonuclear (fusion) Method of power use is hypothetical. Hydrogen or lithium. Hydrogen is found in seawater, and lithium in certain rocks.	The atoms of the fuel are fused (which releases energy) into pairs. To begin this reaction requires great heat and energy (usually a small fission "bomb"). The heat produced by the reaction is used to boil water and produce electricity in the same manner in which the heat from fossil fuels is used.	In one version, the fuel supply (a form of hydrogen) is almost limitless. Air pollution is absent, radio-active waste is essentially absent, and thermal pollution is probably minimal.	No one knows whether fusion power can be made to work. If it can, the only limiting factor is possible thermal pollution of the earth's atmosphere.
Geothermal Used occasionally. Masses of very hot rock that can extend from several hundred feet to several miles beneath the earth's surface.	Holes from the earth's surface to the hot rock underneath allow water occurring naturally underground that is heated by the hot rock to rise to the surface in the form of very hot water or steam. Holes can also be drilled from the surface to the hot rock, and water can then be forced down to be heated and rise as steam. The steam is used to produce electricity in the same manner as when fossil fuels are used.	The energy is free. No air pollution.	Suitable sites may be scarce, and drilling and site preparation costs may be high. If deep-lying salt water is used as a heat source, saline pollution may be a problem. Thermal pollution probably would be severe.
Solar power Used occasionally. Sunlight (due to thermo-nuclear reactions in the sun).	Sunlight is focused upon a molten salt or some other medium. The medium transfers the heat to boil water to produce electricity in the same manner as when fossil fuels are used.	The energy is free and very abundant. No air pollution. Even today, solar house heating might be cheaper then electric heating in the United States.	Even though desert, very large areas of land would be required to absorb enough sunlight to be practical for large-scale use. Solar power is impractical in climates that are not sunny. It may affect climate adversely and create thermal water pollution.

*We have omitted some sources of power that are unlikely to have a major impact, such as windmills, tidal generators, and hydroelectric power.

†Using uranium as a raw material, breeder reactors make more fuel than they consume.

446

Figure 15.6   The energy crisis and resulting price increases of petroleum products have focused interest on developing practical solar-energy and fusion-power processes. (Top) A house designed to be heated largely by the sun's energy. Solar heat is absorbed by the water-filled panel and drums. The heated water circulates throughout the house, providing warmth and hot water. Thermonuclear fusion, seen by many as the best solution to the energy problem, presents great technological problems and challenges. (Above) Dr. Leonard M. Goldman is studying ways to use high-powered lasers to produce thermonuclear fusion. Many scientists are trying to develop methods to control the fusion process for electrical energy generation.

feed. The diets for people in underdeveloped countries decline as a function of their integration into a world economy dominated by the United States and other countries that consume large amounts of protein (Lappe, 1971).

The issue of food availability and protein nutrition is directly related to the fuel crisis of the 1970s. To make up for world-wide nutritional deficiences, the United States and other industrialized nations have attempted to create a "green revolution" in Asian and African economies. We have introduced new strains of high-yield wheat and "miracle rice" to boost agricultural output. These new plant strains do increase yields by as much as 40 to 50 percent, but they also demand large increases in the use of nitrogen fertilizers. The production of these chemicals requires larger amounts of fossil fuel. Due to the energy crisis, the cost of fuel has become prohibitive to many of these African and Asian economies, and they therefore cannot afford either to produce or to buy the chemical fertilizers needed. The Philippines alone are now suffering a shortage of about 800,000 tons of chemical fertilizers.

447

The shortages of gasoline, fuel oil, and electrical power, which have become a pressing issue in the United States and Europe since 1973, were predicted by ecology-minded scientists decades ago. Of course, students of population have long been aware that increases in population soon outstrip increases in resources, particularly the food resources from farm production. But the consequences of our reliance on fossil fuel to satisfy the ever increasing energy demands of modern society generally did not become apparent until the 1950s, when books such as Harrison Brown's *The Challenge of Man's Future* were published.

Writing in 1954, Brown, a geophysicist, outlined the problems facing the world community due to population pressure, industrial pollution, and potential shortages of food and raw materials. Perhaps his most significant findings related to the depletion of the earth's energy resources. "Consumption of the earth's stores of fossil fuels has barely started," he wrote, "yet already we can see the end. In a length of time which is extremely short when compared with the span of human history, and insignificant when compared with the length of time during which man has inhabited the earth, fossil fuels will have been discovered, utilized, and completely consumed.'' At current rates of consumption, which can only *underestimate* the worldwide demand for energy, deposits of petroleum and natural gas will be exhausted by the year 2200. Deposits of coal and lignite will remain until after the year 3000 and, with the promised development of safe nuclear reactors, these deposits could be converted into petroleum products to provide the transition between fossil fuels and new sources of inexpensive and readily available energy, from either the direct conversion of sunlight or the control of the nuclear fusion reaction.

The great hope of science in the industrialized nations is to eventually use the almost limitless release of energy in the process called fusion, when two hydrogen atoms are ''fused'' (hence the term ''fusion'') under great heat and pressure to form one atom of helium. In the hydrogen bomb, this reaction is triggered by the enormous furnace created by a nuclear fission reaction—a small ''atomic bomb.'' (''Fission'' means splitting; in this process, atoms are split rather than ''fused,'' and energy is released.) Fusion is the same kind of process by which our sun provides us with energy (heat and light). Atomic fusion offers many advantages over present atomic power plants that use fission. For one thing, they do not produce the dangerous atomic wastes that present plants do. For another, fusion does not require costly fuels. However, control and use of nuclear fusion is still beyond the capabilities of the world's scientists and engineers. This is a technology that, like the development of cancer preventives, promises to require immense investments of scientific talent, money, and time before the ends are achieved. Our experiences with technology since the turn of the century have prepared us to await the results of this research with great optimism, but there are indications that the breakthroughs required may not occur in time to save human societies from a period of agonizing belt tightening. If, on the other hand, the technologies are developed to provide cheap and plentiful new sources of energy, there are even more ominous indications that the ecological systems of the planet could not tolerate the widespread overheating this would produce.

Overheating our planet may prove to be the great environmental issue of the twenty-first century. The economist Robert Heilbroner estimates that at current rates of growth in energy consumption, the average temperature of the earth will have increased by approximately 50 degrees by the year 2070, an increase that would spell disaster for human life (Heilbroner, 1974). In their report on this issue, the Council on Environmental Quality presents comparative figures for energy consumption as societies advance and industrialize.

In primitive society, energy utilization consists mostly of the food consumed by the individual. This corresponds to a power output of about 100 thermal watts per person. The world average—including primitive and technologically advanced regions—is somewhat more than 1,000 thermal watts per person. In the highly industrialized United States, energy consumption is equivalent to 10,000 watts for each individual. If world population grows to 5 billion and if the worldwide average of energy use increases to 10,000 watts per person, man-made energy input into the atmosphere would reach almost one-hundredth that of the natural net radiation balance over land areas. (Council on Environmental Quality, 1970a)

The report concludes that an increase of only 1 percent in the radiation balance of the earth would, if it continues over time, cause severe melting in the polar ice cap and a concomitant rise in the sea level, plus serious disruption of the oceans' currents. In the long run, then, the solutions to the various energy crises we are experiencing today, as well as the solutions to our impact on other life support systems, will depend on a view of man in nature that can track the environmental consequences of all our plans and actions. Among ecologists, this perspective might be called the ''ecosystem view.''

THE ECOSYSTEM

In her memorable speech to the United Nations World Conference on Environmental Problems, India's Indira Gandhi summed up the fundamental concept of the ecosystem: ''Life is one and the world is one and all these questions are interlinked.'' Barry Commoner further develops the ecosystem concept in his book *The Closing Circle* (1971):

The environment makes up a huge, enormously complex living machine that forms a thin dynamic layer on the earth's surface, and every human activity depends on the integrity and proper functioning of this machine. Without the photosynthetic activity of green plants, there would be no oxygen for our engines, smelters, and furnaces, let alone support for human and animal life. Without the action of the plants, animals, and microorganisms that live in them, we could have no pure water in our lakes and rivers. Without the biological processes that have gone on in the soil for thousands of years, we would have neither food crops, oil, nor coal. This machine is our biological capital, the basic apparatus on which our total productivity depends. If we destroy it, our most advanced technology will become useless and any economic and political system that depends on it will founder. The environmental crisis is a signal of this approaching catastrophe.

Commoner's essential point is that human beings inhabit a world of ecological relationships in which each part of the environment is intimately linked to all others. When any natural element in the complex equation of natural balances is disrupted, many others will also be modified with potentially tragic consequences. The very basic life-support systems that we have briefly discussed are not independent entities, so we cannot study these systems by reducing them to their constituent elements and properties. Rather, we must always study the relationships among these elements—the complex ways in which changes in one element may have far-reaching effects on other elements.

Similarly, *quantitative* changes in some part of an ecological system may result in *qualitative* changes—often destructive ones—in the system itself. A case in point is the ecology of the area in and around a fresh water lake such as Lake Erie. Part of the vast inland ocean in America's Great Lakes Basin, Lake Erie and its surrounding countryside support a population of over 13 million people clustered in six major cities and hundreds of smaller towns and villages.

The human ecology of the region depends primarily on the combination of highly fertile farmland and a diversified base of industrial production that can capitalize on the central location of this waterway system for the shipment of raw and finished materials. Industry depends heavily on the ample water resources of the region for production

and industrial cooling, and the lake has also supported much of the leisure and recreational needs of the area's population. According to the best-informed economic thought, such as Edgar Hoover's *The Location of Economic Activity* (1948), the cities and towns of this region are ideally situated. Now, however, after more than a century of almost unbridled economic growth, it appears that the ecological systems of the lake are imperiled and that large areas of the deep central basin may be biologically dead. Lake Erie's problems do not stem from a single cause—such as population pressure, or industry, or even human greed—they result from the combined weight of several direct assaults made on the life-support systems of the lake itself.

Thermal pollution in this area is only one problem. Another is the pollution of such waterways with phosphorus-bearing detergents. These pollutants vastly increase the population of some types of algae, which die and decay, using up much of the oxygen needed for fish and other aquatic animals. In this way the vicious cycle of oxygen depletion continues. For Lake Erie and other environmental sore spots of the earth, the eventual result of the cycle can only be called an eco-catastrophe. Still another problem is the runoff from nitrogeneous fertilizers from farming lands; it is poisonous to all forms of aquatic life.

None of the damage that human societies have inflicted on ecological systems is easy to correct. Among scientists and environmental activists who are concerned with problems such as that of Lake Erie, there are grounds for serious differences. Some believe that Lake Erie's restoration would require massive scouring of the lake bottom at a cost of untold millions or billions of dollars. Others cite successful restoration projects as examples and argue that proper environmental policies and the strict enforcement of those policies can restore the lake.

For example, until very recently, the Hudson River was in danger of becoming a dismal slough of human excrement and waste. Now, through the investment of billions of dollars in sewage treatment plants along the length of the river, fish are returning to the Hudson. There is hope that within the next decade the river will once again become a

449

leisure and recreation site for the more than 26 million inhabitants of the Hudson basin.

For every ecological disaster, such as the pollution of Lake Erie or the strip mining in the Cumberlands (a region including parts of Kentucky, Tennessee, and the Virginias), there are success stories such as that of the Hudson River or of the once fearfully polluted air of Pittsburgh, which recent programs have vastly improved. Critics of the environmental movement can claim these cases as evidence against the dire predictions of earth activists. But we cannot understand these controversies until we have discussed the more general debate over the relationships between human social organization and the natural environment.

PART II: SOURCES
ECOLOGY

Faced with visions of our doom through ecological disaster, we understandably search for the guilty culprits. Who has done this to our land, our water, our air, our beautiful and fragile spaceship earth? Many rich fantasies have been offered that fix blame on a variety of evil-doers. However, the search for villains is itself as absurd as the most intricate of these fantasies. *We* are to blame. Each of us and all of us.

But in what ways are we to blame? What are the major causes of the ecological problems we face? In this section we will consider the answers to these questions. Four main features of societies often claimed to be sources of trouble will be assessed: growth, capitalism, urbanism, and technology. Only by unravelling the underlying sources of our environmental peril can we evaluate present and proposed responses to the problem.

IS GROWTH THE PROBLEM?

Many chapters in this book have stressed the fact that modern societies dwarf all previous human experience. Suddenly, societies have become huge, and their immensity has created many new problems and made old ones worse. Nowhere are the consequences of growth so profoundly felt as in the ecological system. Through their sheer numbers, humans are having an unprecedented impact on the life-support systems. Furthermore, the economic growth required to sustain such numbers has greatly amplified this impact. Hundreds of millions more people are now acting upon nature with previously undreamed-of powers. These have been the consequences of past growth. The peril we face is continued rapid growth.

Of the many social scientists concerned with the ecological problems of continued economic and

Figure 15.7   Many people believe that food shortages could be overcome by clearing the jungles of the Amazon for agriculture. However, such attempts have shown that the soils in these areas quickly turn to infertile, bricklike or stony layers of laterite. (Left to right) The process of laterization. (1) Sediment is washed down from the mountains by heavy rains. This process creates silica-rich soil. (2) Vegetation starts to grow, fed by more rain, but the silica-rich soil is leached by continuous runoff of water. (3) The emerging tropical rain forest is sustained not by the original rich soil but by organic nutrients from its own decomposing vegetation. (4) Clearing the jungle leaves only the leached silica-barren soil, which is now mostly composed of oxides of aluminum and iron—an infertile and hardened layer of laterite that is impossible to cultivate for crop production.

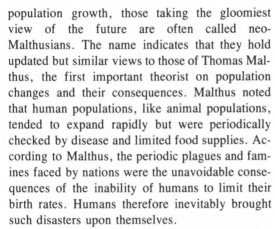

Figure 15.8   (Right) This aerial photo shows some of the widespread damage to vegetation and topography caused by strip mining in West Virginia.

population growth, those taking the gloomiest view of the future are often called neo-Malthusians. The name indicates that they hold updated but similar views to those of Thomas Malthus, the first important theorist on population changes and their consequences. Malthus noted that human populations, like animal populations, tended to expand rapidly but were periodically checked by disease and limited food supplies. According to Malthus, the periodic plagues and famines faced by nations were the unavoidable consequences of the inability of humans to limit their birth rates. Humans therefore inevitably brought such disasters upon themselves.

In more modern times, the human race seemed to have found the means to overcome this brutal fate—not by limiting growth but by overcoming the harsh checks upon it. We conquered plagues and greatly reduced mortality. And we developed the means to produce food in incredible amounts. The neo-Malthusians argue, however, that the age-old checks of famine and disease still await us. Rather than removing these natural checks on growth, we merely raised them to a much higher level or postponed them for a longer time.

The most prominent group of neo-Malthusian scientists is the Club of Rome, under the direction of Dr. Aurelio Pecci, an Italian industrial manager and scientist. The Club of Rome is devoted to

studying the interplay of economic, political, natural, and social factors on a global scale. A major and controversial achievement of the club was the recent creation of a "World Model." Constructed under the direction of Donella and Dennis Meadows and their colleagues at the Massachusetts Institute of Technology, the World Model is actually a computer program designed to project into the future the present rates of change in population growth, industrialization, urbanization, agricultural production, and pollution. Such projections make it possible to estimate what life will be like if present trends persist unchecked. The results of work with the model were published in *The Limits to Growth* (1972). The future seen through the World Model is very grim:

If the present growth trends in world population, industrialization, pollution, food production, and resource depletion continue unchanged, the limits of growth on this planet will be reached sometime within the next hundred years. *The most probable result will be a rather sudden and uncontrollable decline in both population and industrial capacity.* [italics added]

The model shows that if present rates continue, resources will soon become inadequate to maintain industrial output; pollution will increase, further eroding our resources; and food production will decline for lack of fertilizers and other essential resources. These changes, the Club of Rome predicts, will gravely decrease the earth's capacity to support human life and will result in catastrophic famines and increases in disease. These effects will prompt the outbreak of social disorders. Thus, the population will be sharply reduced through the old brutal Malthusian checks. Furthermore, *both* industrial and population growth must be cut back considerably if this grim future is to be averted. Unchecked, either form of growth will produce the predicted collapse of the world system.

On the other hand, the World Model predicts a rosy future if present population and industrialization levels are stabilized. For example, if the world's population could be held at the 1975 level (an impossible assumption) and if high levels of capital growth could be channeled into increased food production, then in the year 1990 one would be able to say: There is now

more than twice as much food per person as the average value in 1970, and world lifetime is nearly 70 years. The average industrial output is well above today's level, and services per capita have tripled. Total average income per capita . . . is about $1800. This value is about half the present average U.S. income, equal to the present average European income, and three times the present average world income. Resources are still being gradually depleted, as they must be under any realistic assumption, but the rate of depletion is so slow that there is time for technology and industry to adjust to changes in resource availability. (Meadows, Meadows, *et al.,* 1972)

Not everyone agrees with the Club of Rome predictions. A group of British scientists challenged its gloomy projections in a collection of essays, *Models of Doom* (Cole *et al.,* 1973). They pointed out that the main reason the World Model projects a collapse of the world system is that it assumes resources will be depleted. But, the British group argues, past history has shown that new exploitable resources are continually being discovered and that usable resources have for a long time been growing faster than the population. Thus, there is no reason to assume, as the World Model does, that resources will soon be depleted. It seems more likely, the British group argues, that exploration and scientific discovery will continue to keep resources growing faster than the population, thereby preventing the Malthusian catastrophe.

452

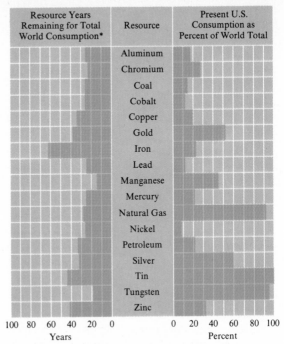

Resource Years Remaining for Total World Consumption*	Resource	Present U.S. Consumption as Percent of World Total
	Aluminum	
	Chromium	
	Coal	
	Cobalt	
	Copper	
	Gold	
	Iron	
	Lead	
	Manganese	
	Mercury	
	Natural Gas	
	Nickel	
	Petroleum	
	Silver	
	Tin	
	Tungsten	
	Zinc	

100 80 60 40 20 0   0 20 40 60 80 100
      Years   Percent

*Based on the number of years known global reserves will last with consumption growing exponentially at the average annual rate of growth.

(Adapted from D.H. Meadows, D.L. Meadows, J. Randers, and W.W. Behrens, 1972.)

Figure 15.9   Listed above are some essential resources for industrial societies. As mineral reserves become depleted and more expensive to recover, either replacements must be found or the minerals must be recycled. The time remaining before we run out of these major resources is based on projected rates of consumption and on profitable recovery of deposits. The United States consumes large amounts of the world's resources, and much consumption results in waste (below).

The vast amount of junk that Americans toss away every year includes:
214 million tons of carbon monoxide, sulfur oxides, hydrocarbons, particulates, and nitrous oxides (over a ton per American)
55 billion tin cans (275 for each of us)
20 billion bottles (100 apiece)
65 billion metal and plastic bottle caps (325 each)
  7 million cars (our annual output has to go *somewhere* after 100,000 miles or so)
10 million tons of steel and iron scrap (an average of 1,000 pounds each)
150 million tons of garbage and trash (4.1 pounds per person daily)
3 billion tons of tailings, mine debris, and waste (4 tons for each of us each day)

(list from Heilbroner, 1972)

This challenge to the assumption that resources will not continue to outstrip population growth was written before the recent world-wide energy crisis occurred. Thus, it demonstrates the difficulty of assuming that the future will simply resemble a continuation of the past. The fact that for the past 100 years we have been able to develop new resources faster than we have depleted the old ones does not prove that we will continue to be able to do so. Any lag in new scientific breakthroughs or a decline in new natural resource discoveries would justify the Club of Rome's projection of a decline in resources.

The rosy future predicted by the World Model—if industrial and population growth are held at present levels—has also drawn severe criticism, and with seemingly more justification. The problem is the major differences in industrial development that presently exist among the world's nations. For even if industrial growth could be stabilized at present levels—which the World Model indicates is a step needed to avoid a catastrophe—the underdeveloped nations of the earth would be locked in poverty and suffering. At present, there is not the slightest prospect that the underdeveloped nations would accept such a state of affairs. Their governments would find it politically impossible to sacrifice all hopes of emerging from such misery. For example, even if the present per capita GNP of India were tripled, it would only amount to $300 per person per year, compared with the current U.S. per capita GNP of nearly $4,000 per person. Stabilizing industrial growth throughout the world would require the people of nations like India to accept a standard of living far below that of industrialized nations.

For such nations, the only hope of catching up is to *continue industrial growth.* For this reason, the most rapid industrial growth going on in the world today is that occurring in underdeveloped nations. Thus, the efforts of these nations to catch up are likely to cause a world-wide catastrophe. The only alternative to offset their growth is to find the means to limit or even cut back the level of living in industrialized nations. But how could a government of an industrialized nation find it politically possible to intentionally lower the average standard of living of its population? It seems very unlikely that such self-sacrifices would be made willingly. And that raises an even grimmer prospect.

As Chapter 14 explains in detail, the industrialized nations are not only islands of affluence and modern technology but are also islands of controlled population growth. Thus, even though populations in the United States, Canada, Europe, Japan, and probably China will continue to grow somewhat over the next two generations, they are expected to stabilize after that time at a size that will be possible to support. This is not the case for societies in the underdeveloped world. There is not the slightest sign of slowdown in their present population growth. This portends a grotesque vision for 100 years from today. The industrialized nations will be supporting roughly 1.4 to 1.7 billion people, but the underdeveloped nations—which today struggle to support about 2.5 billion people—will be inhabited by *40 billion* people if the birth rate holds and if catastrophic waves of disease and starvation do not occur. Thus, there is every prospect for the gap between the developed and the underdeveloped nations to grow into a chasm. A small proportion of the world's population will inhabit islands of comfort, but they will be surrounded on all sides by the worst horrors in human history.

The situation of the underdeveloped nations also presents a danger for industrialized nations. Can we expect people living in such dire straits to accept their fates quietly? Might they not attempt to take what they need by force? Today, atomic weapons are spreading among the less industrialized nations. India exploded a nuclear weapon in the spring of 1974. Many nations are currently receiving atomic power plants from the United States—plants that could be used to produce fissionable materials for nuclear weapons (as India did from the power plant given it by Canada). Can or would a government resist using nuclear blackmail if millions of its citizens were dying of starvation? Indeed, if the position of the Third World worsens, as present projections would lead us to expect, would they have anything to lose from an atomic war?

It is possible that in underdeveloped nations new governments may arise with the totalitarian power to halt population growth quickly. In fact, China

453

seems to have taken successful steps in this regard. The Chinese government claims that it will achieve zero population growth within the next twenty-five years. If other governments of underdeveloped countries take similar action, total disaster may be averted. But there is no guarantee that such political transformations will take place.

Even if world population is checked, however, we still face the question of how to provide sufficient industrial development to raise conditions in underdeveloped nations. No government of an industrialized nation is likely to voluntarily cut back its standard of living in the interest of the underdeveloped nations, but it is possible that such cuts could occur in industrial nations in response to pressures less drastic than nuclear blackmail. For example, we have recently seen the oil-producing nations band together to force much higher oil prices upon industrial nations. The effect has been to force industrialized nations to cut into their affluence and transfer wealth to certain underdeveloped, oil-rich nations. Other developing nations that presently supply needed raw materials are making similar moves to force a more favorable exchange from the industrialized nations. Such pressures may help equalize living conditions. However, many underdeveloped nations do not possess resources vital to the industrial nations. They therefore cannot use embargos and other economic weapons to improve their circumstances.

The future dilemma is clear: Growth must be checked, or else. But somehow the economic inequities among nations throughout the world must also be overcome, or else.

IS CAPITALISM THE PROBLEM?

Many critics argue that solutions to the world environmental crisis must await the elimination of capitalistic economic systems and the private ownership of property. Marxist social scientists such as Paul Sweezy and Gabriel Kolko argue that the failure of a nation as rich as the United States to solve its major social problems, including the devastation of the life support system, is due to the fact that capitalism is a system rooted in human greed. It is therefore a system with no capacity for social actions that do not directly contribute to increased profits. In short, American factories pollute because their profits depend on the industrial processes that create pollution. Americans use too much energy and consume too much of the earth's wealth because such consumption is profitable to the capitalists who sell the goods. Thus, the Marxists conclude, the profit motive must be done away with, and people must be reeducated to work for the collective good of humankind rather than for their own selfish pleasures—if the planet is to be saved.

In his recent prophesy of social catastrophe, *An Inquiry into the Human Prospect* (1974), Robert Heilbroner argues that the same factors that have produced the stunning economic achievements of capitalism may in the end be its fatal flaws. These factors are "the stress on personal achievement, the relentless pressure for advancement, the acquisitive drive that is touted as the Good Life."

Despite these indictments against capitalism, the environmental record of most existing socialist countries is not noticeably better than that of the United States (Heilbroner, 1974). Whatever their ideological rhetoric or their economic organization, all nations, as they undergo industrialization, seem to impose the same blight upon the life support systems. Thus rivers in the Soviet Union such as the Volga, the Ural, the Ob, and the Northern Dvina are terribly polluted by wastes from factories along their banks. Eastern European industrial cities are plagued by smoke and dust in their air, and oil on the Caspian and Black seas has seriously threatened the fishing and tourism industries there. Of course, one might argue that none of the contemporary socialist countries lives up to the ideal of socialism, but that argument would equally apply to contemporary capitalist nations. Although in theory the ideal socialist society is supposed to inflict less damage on the environment than one run on the principles of capitalism, the actual problems encountered in both types of societies are quite similar. As Heilbroner (1974) observes:

Industrial civilization achieves its economic success by imposing common values on both its capitalist and socialist varients. There is the value of the self-evident importance of efficiency, with its tendency to subordinate the optimum human scale of things to the optimum technical scale. There is the value of the need to "tame"

454

the environment, with its consequence of an unthinking pillage of nature. There is the value of the priority of production itself, visible in the care both systems lavish on technical virtuosity and the indifference with which both look upon the aesthetic aspects of life. All these values manifest themselves throughout bourgeois and ''socialist'' styles of life. . . . styles of life that, in contrast with nonindustrial civilizations seem dazzlingly rich in every dimension except the cultivation of the human person.

ARE CITIES THE PROBLEM?

Many with deep concerns about the ecology of earth are inclined to place the blame for present problems upon city life. However, there are two quite distinctly different schools of thought on the alternatives to city life, and these differences reflect quite different beliefs about what is wrong with cities. The first of these might be called the nostalgia view. It pines for a return to a simple life style patterned after the ways of simple horticultural peoples such as American Indian tribes. According to this view, humans went wrong when they lost personal touch with nature and the natural life, and they must once again learn to live in close harmony with nature. The second school might be called the humane-city approach. It takes for granted the necessity for large-scale technical societies and is concerned to structure modern cities to make them more habitable and less ecologically harmful. It will be clear that only the second view has any serious merit. However, the romantic attractions of the first give it considerable claim on public attention, so we will evaluate it.

Nostalgia for the Simple Life

The problems of modern society have led many people to hold romantic recollections of the past. This nostalgic view is especially pronounced in the comparisons some people make between environmental problems of contemporary life and the more natural relationship of simple societies to their environments. It is thus to condemn modern ways that Dorothy Lee quotes from the observations of a wise Wintu Indian:

The White people never cared for the land or deer or bear. When we Indians kill meat, we eat it all up. When we dig roots, we make little holes. When we build houses, we make little holes. When we burn grass for grasshoppers, we don't ruin things. We shake down acorns and pinenuts. We don't chop down trees. We only use dead wood. But the White people plow up the ground, pull up the trees, kill everything. . . . How can the spirit of the earth like the White man? . . . Everywhere the White man has touched it, it is sore. (Lee, 1959)

It is true that horticultural societies and hunting-and-gathering bands always lived at the top of an elementary natural food chain, subsisting on animal and plant life. Thus, the natural order of things influenced their way of life more than they influenced the plant and animal world. However, it is not at all clear that such groups had less profound environmental impact because they were ''in tune'' with nature and more respectful of it. It seems more to the point to say that simple societies merely lacked the capacity to damage nature more than they did.

In fact, anthropological and archeological evidence suggests that agricultural methods used by inhabitants of simpler societies were often destructive of the natural environment. Centuries ago, primitive tribes in New Zealand and Africa slashed and burned to make fields and then moved on when the land fell unproductive after several growing seasons (Burch, 1971). The huge denuded tracts of land eroded; the forests never returned. Indeed, it was not modern society that in Biblical times chopped down the forests of the Middle East and turned that area into an arid waste.

The point is not to blame simpler societies for being sometimes hard on the environment but to realize that *human culture is not natural* (in the sense that animal life is). Human culture involves the ability to act upon nature, to shape and modify it in ways that enhance the prospects of human existence. An elephant can snap off trees that would resist the puny shoves of the strongest man. But a human with an axe can easily cut down trees that would dwarf the strength of elephants. The nostalgia for simpler life styles is actually a rejection of human culture. From the day the first human used a club to increase the power of his blows, humans were no longer natural. A true return to nature would necessitate giving up all inventions, including fire and digging sticks, and returning to a life like that of the wild chimpanzee.

455

For anything short of that is only a question of degree—how much and what kind of culture—for all culture is unnatural.

Some versions of the nostalgia for simpler times advocate a return to rural subsistence farming, for example, to rural communes. But such a way of life offers no sensible alternative to or guidance for the problems of modern times. Returning to a simple life in tune with nature is either fantasy or nightmare. It is a fantasy to think a simple agricultural life is possible, given huge present populations. Even if it were possible, the return to such a life would be a nightmare; it could be purchased only at the cost of billions of lives—for only a fragment of the population could be supported by a nonindustrial economy. We cannot learn how to preserve our environment by taking lessons from simple societies. Their people know less about the problem than we do. Modern people must solve this modern ecological crisis for themselves. That means finding modern solutions.

456

Humanizing the Cities

If rural communes or other attempts to return to the simple life are no solution to our present problems, it is nonetheless clear that modern urban life creates social problems. Something is wrong with our cities and with the quality of life they provide. It is the concentrated heat of cities that dangerously overwarms the atmosphere. It is human waste from the city, sewage and garbage, that fouls the waterways and oceans. It is the masses of city people who litter and clog the highways and overload the national parks and beaches. Worst of all, in some ways the culture and pace of the city isolates people from nature and blinds them to the wonders of the natural environment. Cities are a problem. Yet, to paraphrase the great architect Frank Lloyd Wright, if the salvation of civilization requires that we raze the cities, then the prospects for civilization are dim indeed. We cannot abandon city life. Our only alternative is to modify it.

Changing the cities is the primary aim of modern urban architects and planners. Recall from Chapter 2 that large cities are fundamentally a new thing in human experience. We built them badly because we did not understand how to build them better. Only now have we gained enough experi-

Figure 15.10   The nostalgia for the ''simpler'' life of the past has motivated some people to escape the city and seek alternative ways of living in rural areas.

Figure 15.11   To what extent does a society's efficiency take precedence over the satisfaction of its members? According to philosopher and architect Paolo Soleri, productivity and satisfaction need not be incompatible. (Below) His design for an experimental community that will preserve the ecology of an area and enrich the human environment. Built on ten acres of Arizona desert, Soleri's prototype urban environment will be surrounded by parks, farmlands, and wilderness. The city itself will be so compact that none of the 3,000 inhabitants will have more than a fifteen- or twenty-minute walk from their homes to the areas set aside for work, school, and entertainment. The design offers the vitality of city life without the current problems of urban sprawl, transportation, and pollution.

ence with cities to begin to recognize ways to make them more habitable. Urban ecologists have therefore begun a battle to bring nature back into the cities on a grand scale, through the preservation, creation, and effective use of open space. Other social engineers and planners are trying to design cities in ways that make them less vulnerable to congestion and decay. It seems fair to say that the conditions of future human existence depend greatly on the success of such efforts. However, whether the cities remain hideous or are made humane, more and more people are going to become city dwellers.

A 1969 United Nations study—*Growth of the World's Urban and Rural Population, 1920–2000*—clearly demonstrates that the rate of world urbanization has been rising steadily since the turn of the century. In 1920, 14 percent of the world's people lived in cities of 20,000 or more; by 1960, the proportion had increased to 25 percent.

Countries throughout Latin America, Africa, and Asia are experiencing a technological revolution in agriculture. Technology has increased the efficiency of farm production but has also driven untold numbers of technologically "obsolete" farm workers to the cities. In these rapidly urbanizing areas of the earth, people have not yet dealt with the need to bring nature into the cities. For them, the more basic questions are how the new urbanites will find the jobs and housing and survive in the new and difficult city environment. True, the newer cities of the world still have the opportunities to avoid ecologically disastrous and totally artificial environments for their people. But unless the Third World nations attain the capital necessary for city planning and economic and social development, their urban dwellers will one day be forced to live in the desperate urban squalor of cities like Calcutta.

It is important to remember that the needs of large numbers of people crowded together into cities has not only led to pollution of the city environment but has also led to pollution outside that environment. This is because the city is dependent on other sections of the country to provide the goods and services that cannot be provided in the city. For example, the power-generating installations of the Four Corners area of Colorado that supply

electricity to the rapidly urbanizing Southwestern United States and that belch tons of pollutants into the area's air are hundreds of miles away from the nearest metropolis.

Also, as ecologists such as Barry Commoner (1971) point out, although the cities spawned technology, and hence pollution, technology has become a force independent of urban needs. This is implied by the fact that since 1945 the rate of urbanization in the United States has not kept up with increases in pollution levels.

IS TECHNOLOGY THE PROBLEM?

The Mirimichi River in New Brunswick, Canada, had always been one of the finest salmon spawning rivers in North America. Although the East Coast salmon industry had become depressed through generations of overfishing, the Mirimichi continued to nourish hundreds of thousands of salmon in its insect-rich Northwestern reaches. Then, in 1953, a thin mist of DDT, sprayed from planes at the rate of one pound per acre, settled over millions of acres of the North Woods. Salmon were almost entirely eliminated from the quiet tributary streams of the Mirimichi, for the DDT—designed to get rid of the bud worms in the balsam forests—killed the water insects on which the young salmon depended for their food. The paper industry requires huge cuttings of balsam for its pulp supply, and the DDT could be expected to save millions of trees from the budworm parasite. The salmon were innocent victims of this indiscriminate spraying.

It would be more accurate to say that the salmon were victims of ignorance—human ignorance of the complexity of ecological systems. Back in the 1950s, there was much less awareness of the potential dangers of insecticides and other new ecological technologies. Rachel Carson, whose book *Silent Spring* (1962) documented the destruction of the Mirimichi salmon and other ecocatastrophes, was one of the first contemporary writers to alert the public to the dangers of runaway technology. Before the appearance of *Silent Spring*, even the literate public had little knowledge of the dangers of insecticides, and agricultural policy makers were free to use and abuse

457

these dangerous chemicals as they pleased. Soon to fall victim of cancer, Rachel Carson carefully reviewed the known evidence linking the deposit of chlorinated hydrocarbons (essential components of insecticides) in human tissue to the incidence of cancer and other degenerative diseases. She pointed out that for the first time in recorded medical history, cancer had become the single most important cause of death in children. Although the causal links are still not known, the children born since 1945 have generally received their first doses of insecticide residues in the fetal stage of growth. Although her critics attacked her as a prophet of gloom and doom, Rachel Carson's contribution became a model for all who wished to see human technology harnessed for humane and ecologically sound purposes. She did not warn against technological change per se but attacked its indiscriminate use.

In the years since *Silent Spring,* ecologists have increasingly turned their attention to the unanticipated consequences of new technologies. It is generally accepted today that rapid population growth, urbanization, and the "overheated," affluent economies of the industrialized countries all threaten the natural tolerances of the ecosphere. However, it is particularly the indiscriminate application of new production technologies that causes the most severe environmental pollution. In *The Closing Circle* (1971), Barry Commoner notes that

while production for most basic needs—food, clothing, housing—has just about kept up with the 40 to 50 per cent or so increase in population (that is, production *per capita* has been essentially constant), the *kinds* of goods produced to meet these needs have changed drastically. New production technologies have displaced old ones. Soap powder has been displaced by synthetic detergents; natural fibres (cotton and wool) have been displaced by synthetic ones; steel and lumber have been displaced by aluminum, plastics, and concrete; railroad freight has been displaced by truck freight; returnable bottles have been displaced by nonreturnable ones. On the road, the low-powered automobile engines of the 1920's and 1930's have been displaced by high-powered ones. On the farm while per capita production has remained about constant, the amount of harvested acreage has decreased; in effect, fertilizer has displaced land. Older methods of insect control have been displaced by synthetic insecticides, such as DDT, and for controlling

weeds the cultivator has been displaced by herbicide spray. Range-feeding of livestock has been displaced by feedlots.

Each of the technologies that Commoner reviews has contributed to the affluence of the American population, and many have come to be considered necessities of the American life style. But feedlots for the increased production of beef also greatly concentrate animal waste, and thus the nitrate runoff, in local streams. Synthetics such as nylon and plastic require large investments of energy and do not degrade back into the ecosphere. An entire continent has been bulldozed and graded to allow for comfortable travel in private automobiles, which creates pollution.

Do these relationships prove that technological change in human society is the primary cause of our contemporary environmental problems? Again, the answer is not to be found in embracing "naturalism." If technology itself is the villain then let us do away with fire and agriculture and all the artifices of our species that modify our environment. Clearly, such a sacrifice is neither possible nor desirable. The problem of technology is not so much in its products or its methods as in the *cultural process* whereby they are applied. Economists and ecologists have come to call this process *suboptimization.* The term refers to the nearsighted application of a solution for one problem without regard for its effects outside a narrow set of goals.

Kenneth Boulding (1970), whose essays in economics have become contemporary classics of the environmental literature, sees the problem of suboptimization as the central issue of the human impact on the environment. "Obviously," he writes,

the deep, crucial problem of social organization is how to prevent people from doing their best when the best in the particular, in the small, is not the best in the large. The answer to this problem lies mainly in the ecological point of view, which is perhaps the most fundamental thing we can teach anybody. I am quite sure it has to become the basis of our educational system.

The logical extension of Boulding's argument would be to change social institutions to permit social organization to better cope with environmental crises.

In summary, analysis of each of the primary causes of environmental problems leads to this

458

conclusion: Political decisions must play the central role in helping humans adapt to the natural environment. The social responses to ecological peril and to resource scarcities will depend largely on the outcome of political struggles and on changes in human life styles. Of course, the politics of environmental control will focus on different issues. In the cities the struggle for new open spaces and a more viable human environment must dominate the political stage; in the remaining coal and oil fields of the earth, many of the crucial issues will concern repair of mined-over lands and the just allocation of precious energy resources; on the seas the issues will hinge around control of ocean dumping, fishing rights, and the preservation of the earth's remaining estuaries. The list could be expanded indefinitely. The real issue is whether humans will develop enough awareness of ecological relationships to make the necessary

changes in their political institutions—where crucial decisions originate.

PART III: RESPONSES
ECOLOGY

As American troops began to withdraw from the devastated countryside and defoliated forests of Southeast Asia at the end of the 1960s, it seemed for a brief period that the momentum of mass demonstrations and campus protest would carry over to the organization of protest against environmental despoilation at home. Eco-catastrophes such as the massive "blow out" of oil in the Santa Barbara channel in 1969 brought more broadly based support for the environmental cause than it ever had before. Earth Day 1970, a nationwide observance of concern for the environment by university stu-

459

Figure 15.12   Large crowds gathered and walked together on 5th Avenue in New York City, and in many other cities across America, in observation of "Earth Day" on April 22, 1970. The ecology movement has developed its own symbols, such as the "ecology flag."

dents, environmental groups, the mass media, and political leaders throughout the nation, was another central event in the growth of the environmental movement in the United States and throughout the world. For the first time in its history, the Gallup Poll in 1970 recorded ''the environment'' among the country's major problems.

SOCIAL AND LEGISLATIVE RESPONSES TO THE ENVIRONMENTAL CRISIS

In response to intense political pressure from so many segments of the society, Congress passed a series of environmental measures including the Clean Air and Water Act (1968) and the National Environmental Protection Act (NEPA, 1970) which established the Council on Environmental Quality. NEPA also established the procedures for environmental review by requiring Environmental Impact Statements for all projects involving the use of federal lands and federal funds. Parallel legislation was passed in most states and some, such as Oregon and Vermont, passed even more stringent controls over the packaging industry to ensure the recycling of bottles and cans. Environmental law became firmly established in the nation's law schools, and the membership lists of the Sierra Club, the National Wildlife Federation, and the Audubon Society, and ecology action groups

460

swelled as never before. Through the efforts of these groups, and over the severe objections of President Nixon, the further development of the Super Sonic Transport plane was shelved.

Three years after the victories of Earth Day and its legislative aftermath, in the face of the energy crisis and concerted lobbying by industry, the momentum of the environmental movement seemed to ebb. *Environment Magazine* reported in its November 1973 issue that of the more than half a dozen environmentalist magazines begun during this period, none survived (Sills, forthcoming). As citizens struggled to find gasoline to commute to their jobs, legislators throughout the nation hurried to suspend environmental standards in recent legislation. Congress passed emergency legislation to construct the Alaska oil pipeline even though few congressmen were confident that the environmental impact of the project on the delicate tundra of the North Slope had been adequately assessed. President Nixon quietly stripped the Council of Environmental Quality of all its research funds and moved them over to his newly created Office of Energy Resources in order to persuade a dubious public that the nation would reach his goal of ''energy self-sufficiency by 1980.''

For all its youthful exuberance, the ecology movement of the early 1970s was not a fad. Its setbacks do not spell the end of organization to

save the earth's natural beauty and natural resources any more than the reversals of the American labor movement during the Great Depression in the 1930s prevented ultimate victories for oganized labor. New social institutions are not created easily; they require years of small victories by dedicated people. Setbacks require changes in strategy, and at all times the movement must continue to build as broad a base of support as possible. In this regard, three areas of analysis of the environmental movement are especially relevant. First, we must inquire into the social origins and ideologies of environmental activists; second, we must explore the extent to which environmental concerns are institutionalized in the actual structures of government and education; and third, we should speculate on the future directions the environmental movement will take in adapting to the changing concerns of contemporary society.

THE ENVIRONMENTAL MOVEMENT: ORIGINS AND IDEOLOGIES

Concern for the natural environment has always been a minority position in the United States. This is a culture in which the themes of mastery over nature and the transformation of the earth by an industrious citizenry have been extremely powerful values. For generations our people have reveled in the seemingly inexhaustable bounty of the land. Thus historians such as the late David Potter (*People of Plenty*, 1954) believe that the quest for economic abundance and ''the good life'' are the most commonly held values of the American people. The defenders of nature have always had tough going against this cultural grain. Nevertheless, the large scale destruction of the nation's forests and wildlife and the massive land-grabs of the industrial revolution were never without critics. The contemporary environmental movement in the United States has its origins in the preservationist philosophies and politics of early nineteenth-century intellectuals such as John James Audubon, James Fenimore Cooper, Thomas Cole, Francis Parkman, and John Muir. These advocates of the natural environment focused their attention particularly on the goal of preserving tracts of wilderness and thereby ensuring for future generations the experience of virgin forests and undeveloped natural vistas (Potter, 1954).

The nineteenth-century preservationist movement did achieve many of its goals. For example, the National Parks and many of the state park systems in the United States and Canada would probably not have been created without the intervention of these preservationists against the land developers and forest exploiters. In the period between the two World Wars, however, the movement

461

Figure 15.13   The ecology movement encompasses a variety of special concerns, including groups (far left) intent on stopping the commercial hunting of whales (center left) and groups that make periodic efforts to clean up our cities. (Left) A broom and bucket brigade works in Harlem and (right) a group of school children clean up Union Square Park in New York as part of Earth Day activities.

waned. Until the 1960s environmental-action groups tended to remain scattered and weak; their influence in the halls of government was generally uncertain. On the other hand, the Great Depression did bring new levels of awareness of environmental problems in rural America. The severe problems of erosion, drought, and dust-bowl formation in the late 1920s and early 1930s produced conservationist policies in the ''New Deal'' administrations of Franklin Roosevelt. In response to the grinding poverty of large sections of the nation, where decay of the environment was depriving millions of rural people of their livelihoods, the federal government created the Civilian Conservation Corps and instituted other land improvement measures on a scale that had never been attempted before in this country.

The culmination of the conservationist movement in the New Deal era was the creation of the Tennessee Valley Authority (TVA) in 1933. Originally designed to provide flood control and electrical power to the rural inhabitants of the Tennessee basin, the project became the model of the articulation of developmental and conservationist goals through federal intervention in regional planning. TVA, according to President Roosevelt,

envisioned in its entirety, transcends mere power development: it enters the wide fields of flood control, soil erosion, afforestation, elimination from agricultural use of marginal lands, and distribution and diversification of industry. In short, this power development of waterways leads logically to national planning for a complete river watershed involving many States and future lives of millions. (Selznick, 1966)

Although the project remains the nation's greatest experiment in regional development and grass roots planning, many of its lofty goals appear to have been subverted. By the 1960s the TVA was coming under increasing criticism for its strip-mining practices in Kentucky, and, contrary to the project's original aims, local communities seemingly were becoming less involved in project decisions. In his study, *TVA And The Grass Roots* (1966), Phillip Selznick pointed out at least 25 years ago the problems such regional authorities have in resisting vested interests:

In the exercise of discretion in agriculture, the TVA entered a situation charged with organizational and po-

litical conflict. The New Deal agricultural agencies, such as Farm Security Administration and Soil Conservation Service, came under attack of the powerful American Farm Bureau Federation, which thought of them as threats to its special avenue of access to the farm population, the extension services of the land-grant colleges. Under the pressure of its agriculturalists, the Authority did not recognize Farm Security Administration and sought to exclude Soil Conservation Service from operation within the Valley area. This resulted in the politically paradoxical situation that the eminently New Deal TVA failed to support agencies with which it shared a political communion, and aligned itself with the enemies of those agencies.

Reviewing his research with the TVA, Selznick warns, ''If there is a practical lesson for leadership here it is this: if you have to compromise, guard against organizational surrender.'' The contemporary environmental movement often places its faith in governmental commissions; it should heed this warning well.

From 1960 to 1970 the environmental movement in the United States experienced a period of marked growth and enthusiasm; it was stimulated by the increasing visibility of pollution and environmental decay in the cities, which gave the lie to the unprecedented affluence of the period. At the same time, the American public, more mobile than ever before after the steep increase in auto sales after World War II, set out in cars to experience for itself the grandeur of the continent. From 1950 to 1968 the annual visitation in state parks increased by 350 percent. In the National Parks the acceleration was even greater: there were 33.2 million park visitors in 1950 and 150.8 million in 1968, an increase of more than 450 percent. During this period, the amount of parkland also increased, by 30 percent for the National Parks and 75 percent for the state parks, an important increase but hardly enough to match increased demand. James McEvoy suggests that people who see parks for the first time now see ''a crowded and semiurbanized environment.'' They need little more than a frustrating visit to an overcrowded park to convince them that this country has little open space left—it is no wonder that the number of Americans who considered themselves active in the environmental movement in 1970 surveys was estimated at roughly 11 million (McEvoy, 1972).

Perhaps the greatest victories of the environmental movement have come in the new responses from institutional sectors of the society that have taken up the cause of environmental protection. Despite success with committees in industry, religious organizations, trade unions, and community organizations throughout the United States and Canada, the composition of the movement's activists remains primarily middle class and white. According to William Burch, a sociologist who for years has been an activist and student of the movement, environmental causes draw their greatest support from creative artists, economic conservatives, and the intellectual left: unfortunately, these particular groups in society are relatively powerless—although advantaged—segments of the population. In addition, the most powerful environmental groups, particularly the Wilderness Society, the Sierra Club, and the Audubon Society, are generally committed to preservationist goals. They seek the protection of wilderness and wildlife but often neglect the problems of the poor, the city bound, and those in underdeveloped nations, for whom economic development is the last saving hope.

THE POLITICS OF ENVIRONMENTAL DEFENSE

Leaders of the environmental movement in the United States and Canada are becoming quite sensitive to the charges of elitism that have been leveled against them in recent years. In consequence, they are attempting to broaden the movement's base of support by speaking out on issues that concern segments of society other than the middle class. The Sierra Club, for example, has become a strong advocate of urban mass transportation, and the membership of the Club in New York City, far from the Big Sky country of the West, has now exceeded 4,000 activists. At the same time, such groups are attempting to guide national and local policies toward more realistic economic goals. They seek to combine the necessities of material development with a concern for environmental protection. At present, and probably long into the future, the main arena of their political activities is the institutions of government that make critical environmental decisions.

The peak years of the environmental movement, the late 1960s and early 1970s, produced a wide range of regulatory legislation and commissions, including the Council on Environmental Quality and the Environmental Protection Agency. These agencies were created by the National Environmental Protection Act of 1970. On the eve of the presidential elections in 1972, Congress passed the Federal Water Pollution Control Act—over President Nixon's veto. This bill provided the strongest water-pollution control measures in the nation's history. The act called for strict regulation of industrial water pollution, requiring industry to use the "best practical" means of pollution control by 1977, and the "best available" means by 1981. In addition, the act authorized 24 billion dollars in funds to monitor water quality and to construct pollution-abatement projects. Prior legislation had only allowed federal money to account for 55 percent of the funds for municipal water treatment plants, but the new law increased the Federal government's share to a maximum of 75 percent.

In the case of air pollution, the existing laws and policies are not quite as generous with capital funds, but they do provide the potential for strict enforcement if an aroused citizenry forces its leaders to take firm action. The Air Quality Act of 1967 requires the Department of Health, Education and Welfare to establish air quality control regions within states to set standards limiting the levels of pollution according to criteria and control technologies that HEW has provided. "If the states fail to do this the Secretary of HEW is empowered to set the standards." With such legislation already secured, the future of environmental protection in the United States will depend on the continued and increased agitation by informed activists to ensure that the laws are enforced.

Concern for the problems of human beings in their natural environment is clearly passing now from a consensus stage to a conflict stage of development—everyone can agree on first principles up to a certain point, but people begin taking sides when their economic welfare is concerned. The issues we have outlined here are generating more and more partisanship as the ecosystem view challenges larger numbers of vested interests. It is important to remember that most of our present

463

environmental legislation was passed before the end of an unprecedented period of economic prosperity in North America. As the economy suffers recessions, as commodity shortages and inflation threaten the security of the American level of living, we begin to sacrifice hard-won environmental protection measures. Economic contraction, however, can result in some positive environmental change. A case in point is the massive conversion to smaller automobiles by Detroit auto manufacturers after 1974. But the pressure of public opinion for environmental quality controls also wanes, for environmental causes are less popular during hard times. However, even with unfavorable conditions, environmental activists know that the time is short, and they will continue to take their cases before the courts when they can.

ECOLOGY: THE WORLD VIEW

It matters very little that the inhabitants of North America and other highly modernized areas of the planet are comfortable in an improving natural environment if the majority of the world's people are suffering at our expense. The earth's life support systems know no international boundaries. People in the poor lands are tied by the tightest of ecological bonds to people in the rich lands. At least a million people will die of starvation in Africa and Asia between 1975 and 1976. And also by 1976 the rice lands of Vietnam and Cambodia will still not have been restored. Once these countries were the primary rice suppliers for Southeast Asia, but that was before the lands were poisoned by American chemicals, before the peasantry was crushed by a generation of wars against colonialism. Once we were confident that the agricultural riches of the United States alone could feed the world, but now we are faced with increasing food shortages at home. Farmers are sowing all the acreage they can afford to cultivate, given the current high prices for fertilizers. And we are reaching the limits of agricultural productivity with current technologies: increases in fertilization are not yet producing corresponding increases in crop yields. New discoveries are urgently needed in physics, biology, botany, and the social sciences—but will they arrive on time? The oceans are increasingly con-

taminated with chemicals that lower their capacity to produce oxygen, but in the United States we annually burn two-thirds more oxygen than can be produced by the plant life on our continent. These are gloomy facts certainly, but they are not intended to create a sense of doom. Rather, they

Figure 15.14   As finite resources become depleted, recycling will become essential, and probably very profitable. Recycling programs for steel and aluminum containers have begun to reduce material shortages as well as waste.

464

point out the most pressing needs and challenges of the future. We must have more people who understand the ecological view and who are willing to apply their abilities as technicians and political activists to world environmental problems. And we as citizens must be willing to give our support to effective government planning and to pay for programs that will lead to meaningful change. We must do this in the name of humanity throughout this small planet.

CHAPTER REVIEW

Modern society is rapidly using up and polluting natural resources. The effects of air pollution are worst in industrial areas, and efforts to control it are only recent. And water supplies, which always determine an area's carrying capacity, or ability to support life, are being depleted as well as polluted. Optimists believe that desalination of sea water will provide sufficient water supplies in the future and that harvesting the oceans will provide food supplies. But they fail to take into account the oceans' delicate *ecosystem.* Energy, whether in the form of food or fuel, is also becoming more scarce. The use of new, more productive strains of grain requires more nitrogen fertilizer, which, in turn, taxes energy resources. As the availability of fossil fuels declines, scientists look to the development of nuclear fusion. However, if the technology for its control becomes available, there will still be the danger of overheating the earth as a result of increased energy consumption. All these problems are interrelated because every part of the ecosystem is linked with every other part, and a change in one part will therefore have consequences in other parts.

In looking for the sources of the present ecological problems, many people examine the unprecedented *population growth* of recent years for the answers. Neo-Malthusians, for example, claim that instead of removing the natural checks (for example, famine and disease) on population growth, we have merely forestalled them or escalated their levels. The Club of Rome feels that resources will soon be inadequate if present population and consumption patterns keep growing and the kinds of resources available remain the same. If population growth can be stopped (which is doubtful), there is hope. Others predict that new energy sources will become available to support larger populations. Some social scientists feel that the *economic system* of capitalism, which they feel is based on greed, is responsible for the present ecological condition. However, the fact is that socialist societies face similar environmental problems. Because *urbanization*

has contributed to our ecological problems, there has been a desire on the part of some to return to the simpler agrarian societies of the past. However, these societies, too, had *culture,* and human culture itself always involves acting on nature to enhance human life. Simpler societies, in fact, did alter life-support systems but did not have the technology to destroy it on the *scale* that we do. Furthermore, it is simply unrealistic to think that an agrarian society could support a population the size of ours. A better alternative would be to make cities a better place to live. A final source of the problem is indiscriminate use of *modern technology* without regard for its effects outside the narrow range of its goals. The only way of dealing with all the sources of environmental problems is through politial decisions.

In the United States, responses have been primarily legal. Congress passed the Clean Air and Water Act (1968) and the National Environmental Protection Act (1970), which requires an Environmental Impact Statement for any project involving the use of federal lands or funds. The energy crisis has eroded some support for the environmental movement, but legal requirements are still effective in making people *think* about the ecosystem *before* the damage is done. Thinking about the environment is not a recent phenomenon, however. The environment movement had some strength as early as the nineteenth century, when intellectuals worked for preservation of wilderness areas. Interest in this declined until the 1960s and 1970s, when it was renewed again largely because of overcrowding and the increased *visibility* of pollution. The current movement is predominantly white and middle class, but its issues have broadened to include matters such as mass transit. Emphasis is placed on legislation and the courts. While there remains conflict in the movement over the means of protecting and restoring the environment, there is at least general agreement over the need for both.

465

SUGGESTED READINGS

Burch, William. *Daydreams and Nightmares.* New York: Harper & Row, 1971.

Commoner, Barry. *The Closing Circle.* New York: Alfred A. Knopf, 1971.

Heilbroner, Robert. "The Human Prospect," in *New York Review of Books.* Vol. 20, No. 21, 22 (supplement), January 24, 1974.

Lappe, Frances M. *Diet for a Small Planet.* New York: Friends of the Earth—Ballantine, 1971.

Meadows, Donella, *et al. The Limits to Growth.* New York: Signet, 1972.

Contributors

Ronald L. Akers holds a Ph.D. in sociology from the University of Kentucky. He has been a faculty member at the University of Washington and at Florida State University and is now at the University of Iowa. He has written numerous theoretical and research articles pertaining to his interest in criminology, juvenile delinquency, deviant behavior, law and society, and the sociology of occupations and professions. He is author of *Deviant Behavior: A Social Learning Approach* and co-editor of *Law and Control in Society* and *Crime Prevention and Social Control*. Professor Akers contributed to the chapter "Sexual Problems."

Robert C. Atchley received his B.A. from Miami University and his M.A. and Ph.D. from American University. Following two years of teaching at George Washington University, he returned to Miami University where he is currently an associate professor of sociology and director of the Scripps Foundation for Research in Population Problems. He was instrumental in setting up a Gerontology Center at Miami to serve as a focal point for Miami's efforts in research, public service, and training in the area of gerontology. Author of ten books and numerous articles, Professor Atchley's latest book is *A Sociology of Retirement*. He is responsible for the chapter "Aging."

James E. Blackwell is a professor of sociology and chairman of the department of sociology at the University of Massachusetts at Boston. He received his B.A. and M.A. from Western Reserve University and his Ph.D. from Washington State University. His teaching career includes positions at Case Western Reserve University, California State University at San Jose, and Grambling College. He has published primarily in the fields of intergroup behavior, community development, and deviant behavior. He is co-editor of *Black Sociologists: Historical and Contemporary Perspectives*, co-author of *Community Development Focus*, and author of the forthcoming *The Black Community: Diversity and Unity*. Professor Blackwell is responsible for the chapter "Intergroup Conflict."

Katharine Briar received her B.A. from Connecticut College, her M.A. in social work at Columbia University, and is a doctoral candidate in social welfare at the University of California, Berkeley. Formerly with the RAND N.Y.C. Institute, she is currently an instructor and program coordinator in Social Service Education at Edmonds Community College in Lynnwood, Washington. Professor Briar contributed to the chapter "Poverty and Inequality."

Scott Briar is Dean of the School of Social Work, University of Washington in Seattle. Formerly, he was on the faculty of the University of California, Berkeley. He received his B.A. from Washburn University, his M.A. in social work from Washington University in St. Louis, and his Ph.D. from Columbia University. He has published extensively on social welfare, social work, and delinquency and is Editor-in-Chief of the *Social Work Journal*. Dean Briar contributed to the chapter "Poverty and Inequality."

Archie Brodsky received his B.A. from the University of Pennsylvania and has worked as a rock critic and free-lance writer in the fields of psychology and medicine. He is currently serving as Creative Director of Fred's Firm, Inc., Brookline, Mass., where he has collaborated with Stanton Peele on a series of journal articles in the areas of addiction and organizational psychology. A co-author of *Love and Addiction*, Mr. Brodsky has written a manual on student volunteer administration for ACTION and is assisting a physician in writing a book on the doctor-patient relationship. His articles have appeared in *Rolling Stone, Psychology Today*, and other journals. Mr. Brodsky, along with Stanton Peele, is responsible for the chapter "Alcoholism and Drug Addiction."

Howard S. Erlanger received his B.A. and Ph.D. from the University of California, Berkeley. He is presently assistant professor of sociology at the University of Wisconsin, Madison. He is co-director of an NIMH-sponsored study of interpersonal violence and also co-director of a national study of the American Legal Profession, which focuses on non-traditional legal careers. His paper on social class and the use of corporal punishment recently appeared in the *American Sociological Review*. Professor Erlanger contributed to the chapter "Interpersonal Violence."

Michael J. Hindelang earned his doctorate in criminology from the University of California, Berkeley. Before his present position in the School of Criminal Justice at the State University of New York at Albany, he taught at California State University, Los Angeles. He has directed research projects in the areas of self-reported illegal behavior, the uses of criminal justice statistics, and shoplifting. Currently, he is analyzing results of a survey of criminal victimization conducted by the Bureau of the Census and the Law Enforcement Assistance Administration. He has published widely and is writing a textbook, *Juvenile Delinquency and Juvenile Justice*. Professor Hindelang is responsible for the chapter "Crime and Delinquency."

William Kornblum is an assistant professor of sociology at the Graduate School of the City University of New York. He received his Ph.D. in sociology from the University of Chicago and taught sociology at New York University and the University of Washington. A specialist in comparative urban sociology, he is presently conducting research on the ecology of urban leisure areas for the National Park Service, U.S. Department of the Interior. He is the author of *Blue Collar Community* and has published articles on human ecology and politics in *Urban Life and Culture, The Nation, Planning Magazine*, and other journals. Professor Kornblum is responsible for the chapter "Ecology."

Stanton Peele is assistant professor of organizational behavior at the Graduate School of Business Administration, Harvard University. He received a Ph.D. in social psychology from the University of Michigan and has worked as an organizational consultant with the National Institute for Personnel Research in Johannesburg, South Africa. He is also President of Fred's Firm, Inc., an editorial and consulting firm through which he consults with the Massachusetts Department of Correction. His major academic and political interest is in helping people achieve control over their lives in an institutionalized environment. His research, writing, and consulting are in such areas as addiction, prison reform, and blue-collar work. The major expression of his outlook is in his forthcoming book *Love and Addiction*. Professor Peele, along with Archie Brodsky, is responsible for the chapter "Alcoholism and Drug Addiction."

467

Lynne Roberts, assistant professor of sociology at the University of Washington, received her Ph.D. from Stanford University. She has published a number of articles utilizing mathematical models to account for interaction in three-person groups. She is co-author of *Utility in Choice in Social Interaction,* published in 1970. Professor Roberts recently completed a two-year term on the advisory board of the National Science Foundation for sociology and a three-year term as associate editor of the *American Sociological Review.* She is presently completing a book on the use of experimental methods in the social sciences. Professor Roberts contributed to the chapters "Sex-Based Inequalities" and "Family Problems."

Rodney Stark received his Ph.D. from the University of California, Berkeley, in 1971 and since that time has been professor of sociology at the University of Washington. He is the author of six books, including *Christian Beliefs and Anti-Semitism* (co-authored with Charles Y. Glock) and *Police Riots.* He has published many articles in scholarly journals and written for such magazines as *Harper's* and *Psychology Today.* As principle author of this book, Professor Stark designed its contents, wrote chapters 1, 2, 3, and 14, and was responsible for Part II of each chapter. In addition, he rewrote and revised other portions to create an integrated text.

Marijean Suelzle received her B.A. and M.A. from the University of Alberta, Edmonton, and is presently a Ph.D. candidate at the University of California, Berkeley. She has taught at the University of California, Berkeley, and at California State University, San Francisco, and has recently joined the Northwestern University faculty. Her primary teaching interests are in social research methodology, socialization and personality, family, and sex roles, and she has published numerous articles in this area. Professor Suelzle contributed to the chapter "Sex-Based Inequalities."

R. Jay Turner is presently associate professor of sociology at The University of Western Ontario. He received his B.A. in psychology from Sacramento State College and his Ph.D. in sociology from Syracuse University. Previously, he was a member of the faculties of psychiatry and sociology at Temple University, research associate at the Temple University Community Mental Health Center, director of the Research and Evaluation Unit of that Center, and senior research scientist at the New York State Mental Health Research Unit in Syracuse. Specializing in the area of psychiatric sociology, his research and writing have focused on the role of social factors in the occurrence and outcome of psychiatric disorder. Professor Turner is responsible for the chapter "Mental Illness."

Rita Roffers Weisbrod received a B.A. and an M.A. in sociology from the University of Minnesota and a Ph.D. in social psychology from Cornell University. She has taught at the University of Washington and Cornell University and has engaged in research studies at UCLA, the Bell Telephone Laboratories in New Jersey, and Cornell University. Her interests are in the development of social competence and the learning of social norms, cross-cultural studies of socialization, and the family. She is co-editor of *Comparative Perspectives on Social Psychology.* Dr. Weisbrod contributed to the chapter "Family Problems."

References

A

Adorno, Theodor, *et al*. *The Authoritarian Personality.* New York: Harper & Row, 1950.

Advisory Commission on the Status of Women. *California Women: Report of the Advisory Commission on the Status of Women.* Sacramento: State of California Documents Section, 1969.

Agel, Jerome. *The Radical Therapist.* New York: Ballantine, 1971.

Agopian, Michael, Duncan Chappell, and Gilbert Geis. "Intra-Racial Forcible Rape in a North American City: An Analysis of 63 Cases," in I. Drapkin and E. Viano (eds.), *Victimology: A Reader.* Lexington, Mass.: Lexington Books, 1974.

Akers, Ronald L. *Deviant Behavior: A Social Learning Approach.* Belmont, Calif.: Wadsworth, 1973.

Alexander, Franz G., and Sheldon T. Selesnick. *The History of Psychiatry.* New York: Harper & Row, 1966.

Allport, Gordon W. *The Nature of Prejudice.* Reading, Mass.: Addison-Wesley, 1954.

Almond, Gabriel A. *The American People and Foreign Policy.* New York: Harcourt Brace Jovanovich, 1950.

American Correctional Association. *Manual of Correctional Standards.* Washington, D.C.: American Correctional Association, 1966.

Amir, Menachem. *Patterns in Forcible Rape.* Chicago: University of Chicago Press, 1971.

Andreas, Carol. *Sex and Caste in America.* Englewood Cliffs, N.J.: Prentice-Hall, 1971.

Anttik, I., and R. Jaakkola. *Unrecorded Criminality in Finland.* Helsinki: Kriminologinen Tutkimuslaitos, 1966.

Ardrey, Robert. *African Genesis: A Personal Investigation into the Animal Origins and Nature of Man.* New York: Atheneum, 1961.

———. *The Territorial Imperative. A Personal Inquiry into the Animal Origins of Property and Nations.* New York: Atheneum, 1966.

Asch, Solomon. "Effects of Group Pressure Upon the Modification and Distortion of Judgments," in Guy Swanson, Theodore M. Newcomb, and Eugene L. Hartley (eds.), *Readings in Social Psychology.* New York: Holt, 1952, pp. 2–11.

Atchley, Robert C. *The Social Forces in Later Life: An Introduction to Social Gerontology.* Belmont, Calif.: Wadsworth, 1972.

———. *The Sociology of Retirement.* Cambridge, Mass.: Schenkman, 1974.

Atchley, Robert C., *et al. Ohio's Older People.* Oxford, Ohio: Scripps Foundation for Research in Population Problems, 1972.

Athanasiou, Robert, Phillip Shaver, and Carol Tavris. "Sex," *Psychology Today,* 4 (July 1970), 39–52.

B

Babigian, Hardutun M., *et al.* "Diagnostic Consistency and Change in a Follow-up Study of 1215 Patients," *American Journal of Psychiatry,* 121 (1965), 895–901.

Bahr, Howard, *et al.* **(eds.).** *Native Americans Today: Sociological Perspectives.* New York: Harper & Row, 1971.

Bales, Robert F. "Attitudes Toward Drinking in the Irish Culture," in David J. Pittman and Charles R. Snyder, *Society, Culture, and Drinking Patterns.* New York: Wiley, 1962, pp. 157–187.

Ball-Rokeach, Sandra. "Violence and Values: A Test of the Subculture of Violence Thesis," *American Sociological Review,* 38 (1973), 736–749.

Bamburger, Michael, and Margaret Earle. "Factors Affecting Family Planning in a Low Income Caracas Neighborhood," *Studies in Family Planning,* 2 (1971), 175–178.

Bandura, Albert. *Principles of Behavior Modification.* New York: Holt, Rinehart and Winston, 1969.

———. *Aggression: A Social Learning Analysis.* Englewood Cliffs, N.J.: Prentice-Hall, 1973.

Bandura, Albert, and Richard H. Walters. *Adolescent Aggression.* New York: Ronald Press, 1959.

———. *Social Learning and Personality Development.* New York: Holt, Rinehart and Winston, 1963.

Baran, Paul A., and Paul M. Sweezy. *Monopoly Capital.* New York: Monthly Review Press, 1966.

Bardolph, Richard (ed.). *The Civil Rights Record: Black Americans and the Law 1849–1970.* New York: T. Y. Crowell, 1970.

Barnes, Harry E., and Negley Teeters. *New Horizons in Criminology.* 3rd ed. Englewood Cliffs, N.J.: Prentice-Hall, 1959.

Barnett, Arnold, Daniel J. Kleitman, and Richard C. Larson. "On Urban Homicide," (Working Paper). *Innovative Resource Planning in Urban Public Safety Systems.* Cambridge, Mass.: M.I.T. Operations Research Center, March 1974.

Battan, Louis J. *The Unclean Sky.* Garden City, N.Y.: Doubleday, 1966.

Bean, Lee L., *et al.* "Social Class and Schizophrenia: A Ten Year Follow-up," in Arthur B. Shostak and William Gomberg (eds.), *Blue-Collar World: Studies of the American Worker.* Englewood Cliffs, N.J.: Prentice-Hall, 1964, pp. 381–391.

Beauvoir, Simone de. *The Second Sex.* H. M. Parshley (ed. and tr.). New York: Knopf, 1953.

Beccaria, Cesare B. *Dei Delitti e Delle Pene.* Florence: F. Le Monnier, 1945 (orig. pub. 1764).

Becker, Howard S. *The Outsiders.* New York: Free Press, 1963.

———. *Social Problems: A Modern Approach.* New York: Wiley, 1966.

Belson, William. "The Extent of Stealing by London Boys and Some of Its Origins." Survey Research Center, London School of Economics, 1969.

Berkowitz, Leonard. *Aggression: A Social Psychological Analysis.* New York: McGraw-Hill, 1962.

———. *Roots of Aggression: A Re-Examination of the Frustration-Aggression Hypothesis.* New York: Atherton Press, 1969.

———. "Simple Views of Aggression," in Ashley Montagu (ed.), *Man and Aggression.* New York: Oxford University Press, 1973, pp. 39–52.

Bernard, Jessie. *Academic Women.* Cleveland: World Publishing, 1964.

———. "Changing Family Lifestyles: One Role, Two Roles, Shared Roles," *Issues in Industrial Society,* 2 (1971a), 21–28.

———. *Women and the Public Interest: An Essay On Policy and Protest.* Chicago: Aldine-Atherton, 1971b.

———. *The Future of Marriage.* New York: World Publishing, 1972.

Black, Donald J., and Albert Reiss. *Studies in Crime and Law Enforcement in Major Metropolitan Areas.* Washington, D.C.: Government Printing Office, 1967.

Blackwell, James E. *The Black Community: Diversity and Unity.* New York: Dodd, Mead, forthcoming.

Blakemore, C. B. "The Application of Behavior Therapy to a Sexual Disorder," in H. J. Eysenck (ed.), *Experiments in Behavior Therapy.* New York: Macmillan, 1964, pp. 165–175.

Blau, Peter M., and Otis Dudley Duncan. *The American Occupational Structure.* New York: Wiley, 1967.

Blauner, Robert. "Internal Colonialism and Ghetto Revolt," *Social Problems,* 16 (1969), 393–408.

Blum, Richard H. "Mind-Altering Drugs and Dangerous Behavior: Narcotics," in the President's Commission on Law Enforcement and the Administration of Justice, *Task Force Report: Narcotics and Drug Abuse.* Washington, D.C.: Government Printing Office, 1967, pp. 40–63.

Blum, Richard H., *et al. Drugs I: Society and Drugs.* San Francisco: Jossey-Bass, 1969.

Blumer, Herbert. "Social Problems as Collective Behavior," *Social Problems,* 18 (1971), 298–306.

Bond, Ian K., and Harry Hutchison. "Application of Reciprocal Inhibition Therapy to Exhibitionism," in H. J. Eysenck (ed.), *Experiments in Behavior Therapy.* New York: Macmillan, 1964, pp. 80–86.

Boulding, Kenneth. "Fun and Games With the Gross National Product—The Role of Misleading Indicators in Social Policy," in Harold W. Helfrich (ed.), *The Environmental Crisis.* New Haven: Yale University Press, 1970.

Brackett, James W. "The Evolution of Marxist Theories of Population: Marxism Recognizes the Population Problem," *Demography,* 5 (1968), 158–173.

Bradburn, Norman M., and David Caplovitz. *Reports on Happiness.* Chicago: Aldine, 1965.

Brecher, Edward M., and the Editors of *Consumer Reports. Licit and Illicit Drugs: The Consumers Union Report on Narcotics, Stimulants, Depressants, Inhalants, Hallucinogens, and Marijuana—Including Caffeine, Nicotine, and Alcohol.* Boston: Little, Brown, 1972.

Briar, Scott. "Welfare from Below," in Jacobus Ten Brock (ed.), *The Law of the Poor.* San Francisco: Chandler, 1966.

Brophy, I. N. "The Luxury of Anti-Negro Prejudice," *Public Opinion Quarterly,* 9 (1945–1946), 456–466.

Brown, Bertram S. "A National View of Mental Health," *American Journal of Orthopsychiatry,* 43 (1973), 700–705.

Brown, Harrison. *The Challenge of Man's Future.* New York: Viking, 1954.

Bryan, James H. "Apprenticeships in Prostitution," *Social Problems,* 12 (1965), 287–297.

Bukharin, Nikolai. *Historical Materialism.* New York: International Publishers, 1925.

Burch, William. *Daydreams and Nightmares.* New York: Harper & Row, 1971.

Burchinal, Lee G. "Personality Characteristics of Children," in F. Ivan Nye and Lois Wladis Hoffman (eds.), *The Employed Mother in America.* Chicago: Rand McNally, 1963, pp. 106–121.

Burgess, Robert L., and Robert L. Akers. "A Differential Association-Reinforcement Theory of Criminal Behavior," *Social Problems,* 14 (1966), 128–147.

Burnham, David, and Sophy Burnham. "El Barrio's Worst Block Is Not All Bad," in Daniel Glaser (ed.), *Crime in the City.* New York: Harper & Row, 1970, pp. 154–162.

Buss, Arnold H. *Psychopathology.* New York: Wiley, 1966.

C

Cahalan, Don. "A Multivariate Analysis of the Correlates of Drinking-Related Problems in a Community Study," *Social Problems,* 17 (1969), 234–247.

Cahalan, Don, and Ira Cisin. "American Drinking Practices: Summary of Findings from a National Probability Sample," *Quarterly Journal of Studies on Alcohol,* 29 (1968), 130–151.

California Department of Corrections. *California Prisoners.* Sacramento: Department of Corrections, 1967.

Campbell, Angus, Philip E. Converse, Warren Miller, and Donald E. Stokes. *The American Voter.* New York: Wiley, 1960.

Cappon, Daniel. *Toward an Understanding of Homosexuality.* Englewood Cliffs, N.J.: Prentice-Hall, 1965.

Caprio, Frank S. *Female Homosexuality.* New York: Grove Press, 1962.

Carp, Frances. "On Becoming an Ex-Driver," *Gerontologist,* 11 (1971), 101–103.

Carson, Rachel. *Silent Spring.* Greenwich, Conn.: Crest, 1962.

Cason, Hulsey, and M. J. Pescor. "A Comparative Study of Recidivists and Non-Recidivists Among Psychopathic Federal Offenders," *Journal of Criminal Law and Criminology,* 37 (1946a), 236–238.

———. "A Statistical Study of 500 Psychopathic Prisoners," *Public Health Reports,* 61 (April 19, 1946b), 557–574.

Cavan, Ruth, and Jordan Cavan. *Delinquency and Crime: Cross Cultural Perspectives.* Philadelphia: Lippincott, 1968.

Chambliss, William. "A Sociological Analysis of the Law of Vagrancy," *Social Problems,* 12 (1964), 67–77.

Chappell, Duncan, et al. "Forcible Rape: A Comparative Study of Offenses Known to the Police in Boston and Los Angeles," in James M. Henslin (ed.), *Studies in the Sociology of Sex.* New York: Appleton-Century-Crofts, 1971, pp. 169–190.

Chappell, Duncan, and S. Singer. *Rape in New York City: A Study of the Data in Police Files and Its Meaning.* Seattle: Battelle Institute, 1973 (mimeo).

Chein, Isidor. "Psychological Functions of Drug Use," in Hannah Steinberg (ed.), *Scientific Basis of Drug Dependence: A Symposium.* London: Churchill, 1969, pp. 13–30.

Chein, Isidor, et al. *The Road to H: Narcotics, Delinquency, and Social Policy.* New York: Basic Books, 1964.

Clark, John P., and Larry L. Tifft. "Polygraph and Interview Validation of Self-Reported Deviant Behavior," *American Sociological Review,* 31 (1966), 516–523.

Clark, John P., and Eugene P. Wenninger. "Socio-economic Class and Area as Correlates of Illegal Behavior Among Juveniles," *American Sociological Review,* 27 (1962), 826–834.

Clark, Kenneth. *Dark Ghetto.* New York: Harper & Row, 1965.

Clark, William, and William Marshall. *A Treatise on the Law of Crimes.* Chicago: Callaghan, 1967.

Clausen, John A. "Drug Addiction" in Robert Merton and Robert Nisbet (eds.), *Contemporary Social Problems.* New York: Harcourt Brace Jovanovich, 1966a.

———. "Family Structure, Socialization and Personality," in Martin L.Hoffman and Lois W. Hoffman (eds.), *Review of Child Development Research.* New York: Russell Sage Foundation, 1966b, Vol. 2, pp. 1–53.

———. "Mental Disorders," in Robert K. Merton and Robert Nisbet (eds.), *Contemporary Social Problems.* 3rd ed. New York: Harcourt Brace Jovanovich, 1971.

Clausen, John A., and Melvin L. Kohn. "The Ecological Approach in Social Psychiatry," *American Journal of Sociology,* 60 (1954), 140–151.

———. "Relation of Schizophrenia to the Social Structure of a Small City," in Benjamin Pasamanick (ed.), *Epidemiology of Mental Disorders.* Washington, D.C.: American Psychiatric Association, 1959, pp. 69–86.

Cleaver, Eldridge. *Soul on Ice.* New York: Random House, 1967.

Clinard, Marshall B. *Sociology of Deviant Behavior.* New York: Holt, Rinehart and Winston, 1968.

Clinard, Marshall B., and Richard Quinney (eds.). *Criminal Behavior Systems: A Typology.* New York: Holt, Rinehart and Winston, 1973.

Cohen, Lawrence E., and Rodney Stark. "Discriminatory Labeling and the Five-Finger Discount," *Journal of Research in Crime and Delinquency,* 11 (1974), 25–39.

Cole, H. S. D., et al. (eds.). *Models of Doom: A Critique of the Limits to Growth.* New York: Universe Books, 1973.

Cole, Nyla, et al. "Some Relationships Between Social Class and the Practice of Dynamic Psychotherapy," *American Journal of Psychiatry,* 118 (1962), 1004–1012.

Coleman, James S. *Equality of Educational Opportunity.* U.S. Department of Health, Education, and Welfare. Washington, D.C.: Government Printing Office, 1966.

Commoner, Barry. *The Closing Circle.* New York: Knopf, 1971.

Conover, Donald. "Psychiatric Distinctions: New and Old Approaches," *Journal of Health and Social Behavior,* 13 (1972), 167–180.

Cooley, Charles Horton. *Social Organization.* New York: Scribner, 1909.

Cooper, Barbara, and Mary McGee. "Medical Care Outlays for Three Age Groups," *Social Security Bulletin,* 34 (May 1971), 3.

Cottrell, Fred, and Robert C. Atchley. *Women in Retirement: A Preliminary Report.* Oxford, Ohio: Scripps Foundation for Research in Population Problems, 1969.

Council on Environmental Quality. *First Annual Report.* Washington, D.C.: Government Printing Office, 1970a.

———. *Ocean Dumping: A National Policy.* Washington, D.C.: Government Printing Office, 1970b.

Cowgill, Donald O., and Lowell D. Holmes. *Aging and Modernization.* New York: Appleton-Century-Crofts, 1972.

Cumming, Elaine. "Primary Prevention—More Cost Than Benefit," in Harry Gottesfeld (ed.), *The Critical Issues of Community Mental Health.* New York: Behavioral Publications, 1972, pp. 161–174.

Cumming, Elaine, Ian Cumming, and Laura Edell. "The Policeman as Philosopher, Guide, and Friend," *Social Problems,* 12 (1964), 276–286.

Cumming, John H. "Some Criteria for Evaluation," in Leigh M. Roberts et al. (eds.), *Comprehensive Mental Health.* Madison: University of Wisconsin Press, 1968, pp. 29–39.

471

D

Dahrendorf, Ralf. *Class and Class Conflict in an Industrial Society.* Stanford, Calif.: Stanford University Press, 1959.

D'Andrade, Roy G. "Sex Differences and Cultural Institutions," in Eleanor E. Maccoby (ed.), *The Development of Sex Differences.* Stanford, Calif.: Stanford University Press, 1966.

Darwin, Charles. *On the Origin of Species.* Cambridge, Mass.: Harvard University Press, 1964 (orig. pub. 1859).

———. *The Descent of Man and Selection in Relation to Sex.* 2nd ed. (rev. enl.) New York: Appleton-Century-Crofts, 1930 (orig. pub. 1871).

Davenport, William. "Sexual Patterns and Their Regulation in a Society of the Southwest Pacific," in Frank A. Beach (ed.), *Sex and Behavior.* New York: Wiley, 1965, pp. 164–207.

Davies, D. L. "Stabilized Addiction and Normal Drinking in Recovered Alcohol Addicts," in Hannah Steinberg (ed.), *The Scientific Basis of Drug Dependence.* London: Churchill, 1969, pp. 363–373.

Davies, D. L., Michael Shepherd, and Edgar Myers. "The Two-Years' Prognosis of 50 Alcohol Addicts After Treatment in Hospital," *Quarterly Journal of Studies on Alcohol,* 17 (1956), 485–502.

Davis, Alan J. "Sexual Assaults in the Philadelphia Prison System," in John H. Gagnon and William Simon (eds.), *The Sexual Scene.* Chicago: Aldine, 1970, pp. 107–124.

Davis, James A. *Education for Positive Mental Health.* Chicago: Aldine, 1965.

Davis, Kingsley. "The World Demographic Transition," *Annals of the American Academy of Political and Social Science,* 237 (1945), 1–11.

———. "Statistical Perspectives on Marriage and Divorce," *Annals of the American Academy of Political and Social Science,* 272 (1950), 14.

———. "The Amazing Decline of Mortality in Underdeveloped Areas," *American Economic Review,* 46 (1956), 305–318.

———. "Sexual Behavior," in Robert K. Merton and Robert Nisbet (eds.), *Contemporary Social Problems.* 3rd ed. New York: Harcourt Brace Jovanovich, 1971a, pp. 313–363.

———. "The World's Population Crisis," in Robert K. Merton and Robert Nisbet (eds.), *Contemporary Social Problems.* 3rd ed. New York: Harcourt Brace Jovanovich, 1971b, pp. 363–407.

Davis, Kingsley, and Wilbert Moore. "Some Principles of Stratification," *American Sociological Review,* 10 (1945), 242–249.

Dear, Ronald B. "What Does America Spend on Social Welfare?" in Ronald B. Dear and Donald G. Douglas (eds.), *Poverty in Perspective.* Skokie, Ill.: National Textbook, 1973.

Deck, Leland. "Short Workers of the World, Unite!" *Psychology Today,* 5 (August 1971), 102.

Dennis, Wayne. "Infant Development Under Conditions of Restricted Practice and of Minimal Social Stimulation: A Preliminary Report," *Journal of Genetic Psychology,* 53 (1938), 149–158.

———. "Causes of Retardation Among Institutional Children: Iran," *Journal of Genetic Psychology,* 96 (1960), 47–59.

Dentler, Robert A., and Lawrence J. Monroe. "Social Correlates of Early Adolescent Theft," *American Sociological Review,* 26 (1961), 733–743.

Dion, Karen K. "Physical Attractiveness and Evaluation of Children's Transgressions," *Journal of Personality and Social Psychology,* 24 (1972), 207–213.

Dizard, Jan. *Social Change in the Family.* Chicago: University of Chicago Press, 1968, Chap. 2.

Dohrenwend, Bruce P., and Barbara S. Dohrenwend. "The Problem of Validity in Field Studies of Psychological Disorder," *Journal of Abnormal Psychology,* 70 (1965), 52–69.

———. *Social Status and Psychological Disorder: A Causal Inquiry.* New York: Wiley, 1969.

———. "Class and Race as Status Related Sources of Stress," in Sol Levine and Norman A. Scotch (eds.), *Social Stress.* Chicago: Aldine, 1970, pp. 111–140.

Dollard, John. "Drinking Mores of the Social Classes," in *Alcohol, Science, and Society.* New Haven, Conn.: Quarterly Journal of Studies on Alcohol, 1945, pp. 95–104.

Dollard, John, *et al.* *Frustration and Aggression.* New Haven, Conn.: Yale University Press, 1961 (orig. pub. 1939).

Drucker, Peter F. *The Age of Discontinuity: Guidelines to Our Changing Society.* New York: Harper & Row, 1969.

Duff, John. *The Irish in the United States.* Belmont, Calif.: Wadsworth, 1971.

Duncan, Otis Dudley. "The Trend of Occupational Mobility in the United States," *American Sociological Review,* 30 (1965), 491–498.

Duncan, Otis Dudley, David L. Featherman, and Beverly Duncan. *Socioeconomic Background and Achievement.* New York: Seminar Press, 1972.

Dunham, H. Warren. "The Schizophrene and Criminal Behavior," *American Sociological Review,* 4 (1939), 352–361.

———. *Community and Schizophrenia: An Epidemiological Analysis.* Detroit: Wayne State University Press, 1965.

E

Eaton, Joseph W. (ed.). *Migration and Social Welfare.* New York: National Association of Social Workers, 1971.

Eaton, Joseph W., and Robert J. Weil. *Culture and Mental Disorders.* New York: Free Press, 1955.

Eckstein, Otto. *Water Resource Development.* Cambridge, Mass.: Harvard University Press, 1961.

Efron, Vera, Mark Keller, and Carol Gurioli. *Statistics on Consumption of Alcohol and on Alcoholism.* New Brunswick, N.J.: Publications Division, Rutgers Center of Alcohol Studies, 1972.

Ehrenfeld, David W. *Biological Conservation.* New York: Holt, Rinehart and Winston, 1970.

Ehrlich, Paul R. *The Population Bomb.* New York: Ballantine, 1968.

Elder, Glen H., Jr. "Achievement Motivation in Occupational Mobility: A Longitudinal Analysis," *Sociometry,* 31 (1968), 327–354.

———. "Appearance and Education in Marriage Mobility," *American Sociological Review,* 34 (1969), 519–533.

Ellis, Albert. *Homosexuality: Its Causes and Cures.* New York: Lyle Stuart, 1965.

Elmhorn, Kerstin. "Study in Self-Reported Delinquency Among School Children in Stockholm," in Karl Christiansen (ed.), *Scandinavian Studies in Criminology.* Vol. 1. London: Tavistock, 1965, pp. 117–146.

Empey, LaMar T., and Maynard Erickson. "Hidden Delinquency and Social Status," *Social Forces,* 44 (1966), 546–554.

Empey, LaMar T., and Steven G. Lubeck. *The Silverlake Experiment: Testing Delinquency Theory and Community Intervention.* Chicago: Aldine, 1971.

Ennis, Philip H. *Criminal Victimization in the United States: A Report of a NORC Survey to the President's Commission on Law Enforcement and Administration of Justice.* Washington, D.C.: Government Printing Office, 1967.

Erickson, Kai T. "Notes on the Sociology of Deviance," in Howard S. Becker (ed.), *The Other Side: Perspectives on Deviance.* New York: Free Press, 1964, pp. 9–21.

Erickson, Milton H. "Criminality in a Group of Male Psychiatric Patients," *Mental Hygiene,* 22 (1938), 459–476.

Erlanger, Howard S. "The Anatomy of Violence: An Empirical Examination of Sociological Theories of Interpersonal Aggression." Unpublished Ph.D. dissertation, University of California, Berkeley, 1971.

———. "Social Class and the Use of Corporal Punishment in Childrearing: A Reassessment," *American Sociological Review,* 39 (1974), 68–85.

Erskine, Hazel. "The Polls: Gun Control," *Public Opinion Quarterly* (Fall 1972), 455.

Eysenck, Hans J. *Crime and Personality.* Boston: Houghton Mifflin, 1964.

F

Faris, Robert E., and Henry W. Dunham. *Mental Disorders in Urban Areas.* Chicago: University of Chicago Press, 1939.

Featherman, David L. "Achievement Orientations and Socioeconomic Career Attainments," *American Sociological Review,* 37 (1972), 131–142.

Federal Bureau of Prisons. *Prisoners in State and Federal Institutions for Adult Felons.* Washington, D.C.: Government Printing Office, 1970.

Fein, Greta G., and Alison Clarke-Stewart. *Day Care in Context.* New York: Wiley, 1973.

Feinberg, Irwin. "A Comparison of the Visual Hallucination in Schizophrenia with Those Induced by Mescaline and LSD-25," in Louis J. West (ed.), *Hallucinations.* New York: Grune & Stratton, 1962, pp. 64–76.

Feldman, Maurice P., and Malcolm J. McCulloch. *Homosexual Behavior: Therapy and Assessment.* Elmsford, N.Y.: Pergamon Press, 1971.

Feldman, Maurice P., and Malcolm J. MacCulloch, *et al.* "The Application of Anticipatory Avoidance Learning to the Treatment of Homosexuality," *Behavior Research and Therapy,* 4 (1966), 289–299.

Feshbach, Seymour, and Robert D. Singer. *Television and Aggression: An Experimental Field Study.* San Francisco: Jossey-Bass, 1971.

Fleming, Joyce D. "Field Report: The State of the Apes," *Psychology Today,* 7 (January 1974), 31–46.

Flexner, Eleanor. *Century of Struggle: The Women's Rights Movement in the United States.* Cambridge, Mass.: Harvard University Press, 1959.

Fogel, Robert W., and Stanley L. Engerman. *Time on the Cross.* Boston: Little, Brown, 1974. 2 vols.

Fort, Joel. *The Pleasure Seekers: The Drug Crisis, Youth, and Society.* Indianapolis: Bobbs-Merrill, 1969.

France, Anatole. *Crainqueville.* Winifred Stephens (tr.). Freeport, N.Y.: Books For Libraries, 1922.

Freeman, Howard E., and Ozzie G. Simmons. *The Mental Patient Comes Home.* New York: Wiley, 1963.

Freund, Kurt. "Some Problems in the Treatment of Homosexuality," in H. J. Eysenck (ed.), *Behavior Therapy and the Neuroses.* Elmsford, N.Y.: Pergamon Press, 1960, pp. 312–325.

Friedan, Betty. *The Feminine Mystique.* New York: Norton, 1963.

Fromm, Erich. *Escape From Freedom.* New York: Holt, Rinehart and Winston, 1941.

Fuller, Richard, and Richard Myers. "The Natural History of a Social Problem," *American Sociological Review,* 3 (1941), 320–328.

G

Gagnon, John H., and William Simon (eds.). *Sexual Deviance.* New York: Harper & Row, 1967.

Galbraith, John Kenneth. *The New Industrial State.* Boston: Houghton Mifflin, 1967.

Gallup, George H. *The Gallup Poll: Public Opinion 1935–1971.* Vol. 1. New York: Random House, 1972.

Gardner, Elmer A., *et al.* "A Cumulative Register of Psychiatric Services in a Community," *American Journal*

473

of Public Health, 53 (1963), 1269–1277.

Gebbhard, Paul H., *et al*. *Sex Offenders*. New York: Harper & Row, 1965.

Geertz, Hildred. *The Javanese Family*. New York: Free Press, 1961.

Geiger, Lawrence H. "Age, Reported Marijuana Use, and Belief in Some Assumed Negative Effects of the Drug." Paper presented at the 26th Annual Conference of the American Association for Public Opinion Research, Pasadena, California, May, 1971.

Giallombardo, Rose. *Society of Women: A Study of a Women's Prison*. New York: Wiley, 1966.

Gil, David. *Violence Against Children*. Cambridge, Mass.: Harvard University Press, 1970.

Glasscote, Raymond M., *et al*. *The Treatment of Drug Abuse*. Washington, D.C.: Joint Information Service of the American Psychiatric Association and the National Association for Mental Health, 1972.

Glock, Charles Y., and Rodney Stark. *Religion and Society in Tension*. Chicago: Rand McNally, 1965.

Glynn, J. D., and P. Harper. "Behavior Therapy in Transvestism," in H. J. Eysenck (ed.), *Experiments in Behavior Therapy*. New York: Macmillan, 1964, p. 164.

Gold, Martin. *Delinquent Behavior in an American City*. Belmont, Calif.: Brooks/Cole, 1970.

Goldberg, E. M., and S. L. Morrison. "Schizophrenia and Social Class," *British Journal of Psychiatry*, 109 (1963), 785–802.

Goldberg, Philip. "Are Women Prejudiced Against Women?" *Transaction*, 5 (April 1968), 28–30.

Goldberg, Steven R. "Relapse to Opioid Dependence: The Role of Conditioning," in R. T. Harris *et al.* (eds.), *Drug Dependence*. Austin: University of Texas Press, 1970.

Goldhamer, Herbert, and Andrew W. Marshall. *Psychosis and Civilization*. New York: Free Press, 1953.

Goldings, Herbert J. "On the Avowal and Projection of Happiness," *Journal of Personality*, 23 (1954), 30–47.

Goode, Erich. *Drugs in American Society*. New York: Knopf, 1972.

———. **(ed.).** *Marijuana*. Chicago: Aldine, 1969.

Gordon, David M. *Theories of Poverty and Underemployment*. Lexington, Mass.: Lexington Books, 1972.

Gordon, Michael. "The Social Survey Movement and Sociology in the United States," *Social Problems*, 21 (1973), 284–298.

Gouldner, Alvin W. "Cosmopolitans and Locals: Towards an Analysis of Latent Social Roles," *Administrative Science Quarterly*, 2 (1957), 281–292.

———. "Reciprocity and Autonomy in Functional Theory," in Llewellyn Gross (ed.), *Symposium on Sociological Theory*. New York: Harper & Row, 1959, pp. 241–270.

Gove, W. R. "Societal Reactions as an Explanation of Mental Illness: An Evaluation," *American Sociological Review*, 35 (1970a), 873–883.

———. "Who Is Hospitalized? A Critical Review of Some Sociological Studies of Mental Illness," *Journal of Health and Social Behavior*, 11 (1970b), 294–304.

Gove, W. R., and P. Howell. "Individual Resources and Mental Hospitalization: A Comparison and Evaluation of the Societal Reaction and Psychiatric Perspectives," *American Sociological Review*, 39 (1974), 86–100.

Graham, Hugh Davis, and Ted Robert Gurr. *History of Violence in America: Historical and Comparative Perspectives*. New York: Praeger, 1969.

Gray, Diana. "Turning-Out: A Study of Teenage Prostitution," *Urban Life and Culture*, 1 (1973), 401–424.

Green, Mark, *et al*. *Pre-Retirement Counseling, Retirement Adjustment, and the Older Employee*. Eugene: University of Oregon Graduate School of Management, 1969.

Green, Richard. *Sexual Identity Conflict in Children and Adults*. New York: Basic Books, 1974.

Groves, W. E., *et al*. *Study of Life Styles and Campus Communities: Preliminary Report*. Baltimore: Johns Hopkins University, 1970.

Gruchy, Alan. *Comparative Economic Systems*. Boston: Houghton Mifflin, 1966.

Grund, Francis J. *The Americans*. New York: Johnson Reprint Corporation, 1968 (first American printing, 1837).

Guerry, Andre M. *Essai sur la Statistique Morale de la France*. Paris: J. B. Bailliere and Sons, 1860.

Gurin, Gerald, Joseph Veroff, and Sheila Feld. *Americans View Their Mental Health*. New York: Basic Books, 1960.

H

Hacker, Helen Mayer. "Women as a Minority Group," *Social Forces*, 30 (1951), 60–69.

Haney, C., C. Banks, and P. G. Zimbardo. "Interpersonal Dynamics in a Simulated Prison," *International Journal of Crime and Penology*, 1 (1973), 69–97.

Hardt, Robert, and George Bodine. *Development of Self-Report Instruments in Delinquency Research*. Youth Development Center. Syracuse, N.Y.: Syracuse University Press, 1965.

Harlow, Eleanor. "Diversion from the Criminal Justice System," *Crime and Delinquency Literature*, 2 (1970), 136–171.

Harlow, Harry F., and Margaret K. Harlow. "The Affectional Systems," in Allan Schrier, Harry Harlow, and Fred Stollnitz (eds.), *Behavior of Nonhuman Primates: Modern Research Trends*. Vol. 2. New York: Academic Press, 1965, pp. 287–333.

Harris, Ann Sutherland. "The Second Sex in Academe," *American Association of University Professors Bulletin*, 56 (September 1970), 283–295.

Hartmann, George W. "Personality Traits Associated with Variations in Happiness," *Journal of Abnormal and*

Social Psychology, 29 (1934), 202–212.

Hayman, Charles R., *et al.* "Rape in the District of Columbia." Paper presented to the American Public Health Association, October 12, 1971.

Hechter, Michael. *Internal Colonialism: The Celtic Fringe in British National Development.* Berkeley: University of California Press, 1974.

Heilbroner, Robert. *The Economic Problem.* 3rd ed. Englewood Cliffs, N.J.: Prentice-Hall, 1972.

———. *An Inquiry into the Human Prospect.* New York: Norton, 1974.

Henry, Andrew F., and James F. Short Jr. *Suicide and Homicide: Some Economic, Sociological, and Psychological Aspects of Aggression.* New York: Free Press, 1954.

Hershberger, Ruth. *Adam's Rib.* New York: Pellegrini & Cudahy, 1948.

Heston, Leonard L. "Psychiatric Disorders in Foster Home Reared Children of Schizophrenic Mothers," *British Journal of Psychiatry,* 112 (1966), 819–825.

Hindelang, Michael. "Age, Sex, and the Versatility of Delinquent Involvements," *Social Problems,* 18 (1971), 522–535.

Hirschi, Travis. *Causes of Delinquency.* Berkeley: University of California Press, 1969.

Hirschi, Travis, and Rodney Stark. "Hell-fire and Delinquency," *Social Problems,* 17 (1969), 202–213.

Hoffman, Lois Wladis. "Mothers' Enjoyment of Work and Effects on the Child," in F. Ivan Nye and Lois Wladis Hoffman (eds.), *The Employed Mother in America.* Chicago: Rand McNally, 1963, pp. 95–105.

Hollingshead, August B., and Fredrick C. Redlich. *Social Class and Mental Illness: A Community Study.* New York: Wiley, 1958.

Hook, Ernest B. "Behavioral Implications of the Human XYY Genotype," *Science,* 179 (1973), 139–150.

Hoover, Edgar M. *The Location of Economic Activity.* New York: McGraw-Hill, 1948.

Horner, Matina. "Femininity and Successful Achievement: A Basic Inconsistency," in Judith M. Bardwick *et al., Feminine Personality and Conflict.* Belmont, Calif.: Brooks/Cole, 1970, pp. 45–74.

Hunt, Morton. *Sexual Behavior in the 1970s.* Chicago: Playboy Press, 1974.

I

Ireland, Waltraud. "The Rise and Fall of the Suffrage Movement," *Leviathan,* vol. 2, no. 1 (May 1970), 4–7.

Isbell, Harris. "Clinical Research on Addiction in the United States," in Robert B. Livingston (ed.), *Narcotic Drug Addiction Problems.* Bethesda, Md.: Public Health Service, National Institute of Mental Health, 1958, pp. 114–130.

J

Jaco, E. Gartly. *The Social Epidemiology of Mental Disorders.* New York: Russell Sage Foundation, 1960.

Jaffe, Jerome H. "Drug Addiction and Drug Abuse," in Louis S. Goodman and Alfred Gilman (eds.), *The Pharmacological Basis of Therapeutics.* 4th ed. New York: Macmillan, 1970a, pp. 276–313.

———. "Narcotic Analgesics," in Louis S. Goodman and Alfred Gilman (eds.), *The Pharmacological Basis of Therapeutics.* 4th ed. New York: Macmillan, 1970b, pp. 237–275.

Jahoda, Marie. "The Meaning of Psychological Health," *Sociology Casework,* 34 (1953), 349–354.

Jencks, Christopher, *et al. Inequality: A Reassessment of the Effect of Family and Schooling in America.* New York: Basic Books, 1972.

Jensen, Arthur R. "How Much Can We Boost IQ and Scholastic Achievement?" *Harvard Educational Review,* 39 (1969), 1–123.

Johnson, Lloyd. *Drugs and American Youth.* Ann Arbor: University of Michigan Institute for Social Research, 1973.

Jones, Ernest. *The Life and Work of Sigmund Freud.* New York: Basic Books, 1953.

Jones, Reese T., and George Stone. "Psychological Studies of Marijuana and Alcohol in Man," *Psychopharmacologia,* 18 (1970), 108–117.

Joreen. "The 51 Percent Minority Group: A Statistical Essay," in Robin Morgan (ed.), *Sisterhood Is Powerful.* New York: Random House, 1970, pp. 37–46.

475

K

Kallmann, Franz J. *The Genetics of Schizophrenia: A Study of Heredity and Reproduction in the Families of 1,087 Schizophrenics.* New York: J. J. Augustin, 1938.

Kantor, Rosabeth Moss. *Commitment and Community: Communes and Utopias in Sociological Perspective.* Cambridge, Mass.: Harvard University Press, 1972.

Kelley, Clarence. *Crime in the United States, 1972: Uniform Crime Reports.* Washington, D.C.: Government Printing Office, 1972.

Kephart, William. *Racial Factors and Urban Law Enforcement.* Philadelphia: University of Pennsylvania Press, 1957.

Kidd, Virginia. "'Now You See,' said Mark," *The New York Review of Books,* vol. 15, no. 4 (September 3, 1970), 35–36.

King, Rufus. "Narcotic Drug Laws and Enforcement Policies," *Law and Contemporary Problems,* 22 (1957), 113–131.

Kinsey, Alfred C., Wardell B. Pomeroy, and Clyde E. Martin. *Sexual Behavior in the Human Male.* Philadelphia: Saunders, 1948.

Kinsey, Alfred C., Wardell B. Pomeroy, Clyde E. Martin, and Paul H. Gebhard. *Sexual Behavior in the Human Female.* Philadelphia: Saunders, 1953.

Kitsuse, John I., and Malcolm Spector. "Toward a Sociology of Social Problems: Social Conditions, Value-Judgments, and Social Problems," *Social Problems,* 20 (1973), 407–419.

Kittrie, Nicholas. *The Right to be Different.* Baltimore: Johns Hopkins Press, 1971.

Knight, Robert P. "The Psychodynamics of Chronic Alcoholism," *Journal of Nervous and Mental Disease,* 86 (1937), 538–548.

Knudsen, Dean D. "The Declining Status of Women: Popular Myths and the Failure of Functionalist Thought," *Social Forces,* 48 (1969), 183–193.

Kohn, Melvin. "Social Class and Schizophrenia: A Critical Review," *Journal of Psychiatric Research,* 6 (1968), 155–173.

———. *Class and Conformity: A Study in Values.* Homewood, Ill.: Dorsey Press, 1969.

———. "Class, Family and Schizophrenia: A Reformulation," *Social Forces,* 50 (1972), 295–313.

Kolb, Lawrence. "Factors That Have Influenced the Management and Treatment of Drug Addicts," in Robert B. Livingston (ed.), *Narcotic Drug Addiction Problems.* Bethesda, Md.: Public Health Service, National Institute of Mental Health, 1958, pp. 23–33.

Kolodrubetz, Walter. "Private and Public Retirement Pensions: Findings from the 1968 Survey of the Aged," *Social Security Bulletin,* 33 (September 1970), 3–22.

Korn, Richard, and Lloyd McCorkle. *Criminology and Penology.* New York: Holt, Rinehart and Winston, 1959.

Kramer, Morton. "Statistics of Mental Disorders in the United States: Current Status, Some Urgent Needs, and Suggested Solutions." Paper presented before the Royal Statistical Society on March 19, 1969.

Kushner, Malcolm. "The Reduction of a Long-Standing Fetish by Means of Aversive Conditioning," in Leonard Ullman and Leonard Krasner (eds.), *Case Studies in Behavior Modification.* New York: Holt, Rinehart and Winston, 1965.

L

Labreche, Gary, *et al.* "Social Class and Participation in Outpatient Care by Schizophrenics," *Community Mental Health Journal,* 5 (1969), 394–402.

La Follette, Suzanne. *Concerning Women.* New York: Albert and Charles Boni, 1926.

Lally, Maureen A. "The Quest for Economic Justice," *Colloquy,* vol. 6, no. 8 (October 1973).

Landis, Paul H. *Making the Most of Marriage.* New York: Appleton-Century-Crofts, 1965.

Lane, Robert E. *Political Ideology.* New York: Free Press, 1962.

Langner, T. S., and S. T. Michael. *Life Stress and Mental Health.* New York: Free Press, 1963.

Lappe, Frances M. *Diet For a Small Planet.* New York: Ballantine, 1971.

Lasagna, Louis, *et al.* "A Study of the Placebo Response," *American Journal of Medicine,* 16 (1954), 770–779.

Lauriat, Patience. "Benefit Levels and Socio-economic Characteristics: Findings from the 1968 Survey of the Aged," *Social Security Bulletin,* 33 (August 1970), 3–20.

Law Enforcement Assistance Administration. *National Jail Census.* Washington, D.C.: Government Printing Office, 1971.

———. *Expenditures and Employment Data for the Criminal Justice System, 1970–71.* Washington, D.C.: Government Printing Office, 1973a.

———. *Corrections.* National Advisory Commission on Criminal Justice Standards and Goals. Washington, D.C.: Government Printing Office, 1973b.

Lazarus, Arnold A. "The Treatment of Sexually Inadequate Man," in Leonard Ullman and Leonard Krasner (eds.), *Case Studies in Behavior Modification.* New York: Holt, Rinehart and Winston, 1965.

Lee, Dorothy. *Freedom and Culture.* Englewood Cliffs, N.J.: Prentice-Hall, 1959.

Leighton, Dorothea C., *et al. The Character of Danger: Psychiatric Symptoms in Selected Communities.* New York: Basic Books, 1964.

Lennard, Henry, *et al. Mystification and Drug Misuse.* San Francisco: Jossey-Bass, 1971.

———. "The Methadone Illusion," *Science,* 176 (1972), 881–884.

Lenski, Gerhard. *Power and Privilege: The Theory of Social Stratification.* New York: McGraw-Hill, 1966.

Lewis, Walter D. *From Newgate to Dannemora: The Rise of the Penitentiary in New York, 1796–1848.* Ithaca, N.Y.: Cornell University Press, 1965.

Libby, Roger W., and Gilbert D. Nass. "Parental Views on Teenage Sexual Behavior," *Journal of Sex Research,* 7 (1971), 79.

Lieberson, Stanley. *Ethnic Patterns in American Cities.* New York: Free Press, 1970.

Liebow, Elliot. *Talley's Corner: A Study of Negro Streetcorner Men.* Boston: Little, Brown, 1967.

Lilly, John C. *Mind of the Dolphin.* New York: Avon Books, 1969.

Lindesmith, Alfred R. *Addiction and Opiates.* Chicago: Aldine, 1968.

Lipset, Seymour M., and Reinhard Bendix. *Social Mobility in Industrial Society.* Berkeley: University of California Press, 1958.

Litwack, Leon F. *North of Slavery: The Negro in the Free States, 1790–1860.* Chicago: University of Chicago Press, 1961.

Lofland, Lyn H. *A World of Strangers.* New York: Basic Books, 1973.

Lombroso-Ferrero, Gina. *Criminal Man.* Reprint ed. Montclair, N.J.: Patterson-Smith (orig. pub. 1911).

Lorenz, Konrad. *On Aggression.* Marjorie Kerr Wilson (tr.). New York: Harcourt Brace Jovanovich, 1966.

Lukoff, Irving, *et al. Some Aspects of the Epidemiology of Heroin Use in a Ghetto Community.* No. 514–410/159 1-3. Washington, D.C.: Government Printing Office, 1972.

M

Maccoby, Eleanor E. (ed.). *The Development of Sex Differences.* Stanford, Calif.: Stanford University Press, 1966.

McClelland, David, *et al. The Drinking Man.* New York: Free Press, 1972.

McConaghy, Nathaniel. "Aversive Therapy of Homosexuality: Measures of Efficacy," *American Journal of Psychiatry,* 127 (1971), 1221–1224.

McCord, William, and Joan McCord. *Psychopathy and Delinquency.* New York: Grune & Stratton, 1956.

———. *Origins of Crime: A New Evaluation of the Cambridge-Somerville Youth Study.* New York: Columbia University Press, 1959.

McEvoy, James. "The American Concern with Environment," in William Burch (ed.), *Social Behavior, Natural Resources, and the Environment.* New York: Harper & Row, 1972.

McKelvey, Blake. *American Prisons: A Study in American Social History Prior to 1915.* Reprint ed. Montclair, N.J.: Patterson-Smith, 1968 (orig. pub. 1936).

Malcolm, Andrew H. "V.A. Drug Clinics Seek Solutions After 14 Months of Drive Against Addiction," *The New York Times,* March 6, 1972, p. 27.

Malin, K. "Food Resources of the Earth," *Proceedings of the World Population Conference,* 3 (1965), 385–387.

Malthus, Thomas Robert. *Essay on the Principle of Population.* Anthony Flew (ed.). Baltimore, Md.: Penguin, 1971 (orig. pub. 1798).

Mandle, Jay R. "The Decline in Mortality in British Guiana, 1911–1960," *Demography,* 7 (1970), 301–315.

Mann, Marty. *Marty Mann Answers Your Questions About Drinking and Alcoholism.* New York: Holt, Rinehart and Winston, 1970.

Markham, James M. "What's All This Talk of Heroin Maintenance?" *New York Times Magazine,* (July 2, 1972), 6–9+.

Marmor, Theodore. "On Comparing Income Maintenance Alternatives," in Ronald B. Dear and Donald G. Douglas (eds.), *Poverty in Perspective.* Skokie, Ill.: National Textbook, 1973.

Marshall, Donald S. "Sexual Behavior on Mangaia," in Donald Marshall and Robert Suggs (eds.), *Human Sexual Behavior.* New York: Basic Books, 1971, pp. 103–162.

Marx, Gary. *Protest and Prejudice: A Study of Belief in the Black Community.* New York: Harper & Row, 1967.

Marx, Karl, and Friedrich Engels. *The Communist Manifesto.* Eden Paul and Cedar Paul (trs.). New York: Russell and Russell, 1963 (orig. pub. 1848).

Masters, William, and Virginia Johnson. *Human Sexual Inadequacy.* Boston: Little, Brown, 1970.

Matza, David. *Delinquency and Drift.* New York: Wiley, 1964.

———. "Poverty and Disrepute," in Robert K. Merton and Robert A. Nisbet (eds.), *Contemporary Social Problems.* 2nd ed. New York: Harcourt Brace Jovanovich, 1966.

Maxwell, Milton A. "Alcoholics Anonymous: An Interpretation," in David J. Pittman (ed.), *Alcoholism.* New York: Harper & Row, 1967.

Mazer, Allan, and Leon S. Robertson. *Biology and Social Behavior.* New York: Free Press, 1972.

Mead, Margaret. "Marriage in Two Steps," *Redbook,* 127 (July 1966), 48–49.

Meadows, Donella, Dennis Meadows, *et al. The Limits to Growth.* New York: New American Library, Signet, 1972.

Mechanic, David. "Problems and Prospects in Psychiatric Epidemiology," in Edward H. Hare (ed.), *Psychiatric Epidemiology.* New York: Oxford University Press, 1970, pp. 3–22.

Mencher, Samuel. *Poor Law to Poverty Program.* Pittsburgh: University of Pittsburgh Press, 1967.

Merton, Robert K. "Social Structure and Anomie," *American Sociological Review,* 3 (1938), 672–682.

———. "Discrimination and the American Creed," in R. M. MacIver (ed.), *Discrimination and National Welfare.* New York: Institute for Religious and Social Studies, 1949a.

———. *Social Theory and Social Structure: Toward the Codification of Theory and Research.* New York: Free Press, 1949b.

———. "Social Problems and Sociological Theory," in Robert K. Merton and Robert A. Nisbet, *Contemporary Social Problems.* 3rd ed. New York: Harcourt Brace Jovanovich, 1971, pp. 793–845.

Merton, Robert K., and Robert A. Nisbet. *Contemporary Social Problems.* 3rd ed. New York: Harcourt Brace Jovanovich, 1971.

Messenger, John C. "Sex and Repression in an Irish Folk Community," in Donald S. Marshall and Robert C. Suggs (eds.), *Human Sexual Behavior.* New York: Basic Books, 1971, pp. 3–37.

Meyer, Adolf E. "Psychoanalytic Versus Behavior Therapy of Male Homosexuals: A Statistical Evaluation of Clinical Outcome," *Comprehensive Psychiatry,* 7 (1966), 110–117.

Meyer, Alan S. (ed.). *Social and Psychological Factors in Opiate Addiction: A Review of Research Findings, Together with an Annotated Bibliography.* New York: Bureau of Applied Social Research, Columbia University, 1952.

477

Middendorff, Wolf. *The Effectiveness of Punishment, Especially in Relation to Traffic Offenses.* South Hackensack, N.J.: Fred B. Rothman, 1968.

Miller, Herman P. *Rich Man, Poor Man.* New York: T. Y. Crowell, 1964.

Miller, S. M. "Comparative Social Mobility," *Current Sociology,* vol. 9, no. 1 (1960).

Miller, Walter B., *et al.* "Aggression in a Boys' Street-Corner Group," *Psychiatry,* 24 (1961), 283–298.

Minturn, Leigh, and William W. Lambert. *Mothers of Six Cultures.* New York: Wiley, 1964.

Mischel, Walter. "Father Absence and Delay of Gratification: Cross-Cultural Comparisons," *Journal of Abnormal and Social Psychology,* 63 (1961), 116–124.

Montagu, Ashley (ed.). *Man and Aggression.* 2nd ed. New York: Oxford University Press, 1973.

Moore, William, Jr., and Lonnie Wagstaff. *Black Educators in White Colleges.* San Francisco: Jossey-Bass, 1974.

Morris, Norval, and Gordon Hawkins. *The Honest Politician's Guide to Crime Control.* Chicago: University of Chicago Press, 1970.

Mosca, Gaetano. *The Ruling Class.* Hannah D. Kahn (tr.). New York: McGraw-Hill, 1939 (orig. pub. 1896).

Mosher, Loren R., and David Feinsilver. "Special Report: Schizophrenia." National Institute of Mental Health, Center for Studies of Schizophrenia. Washington, D.C.: U.S. Department of Health, Education, and Welfare, 1970.

Moynihan, Daniel Patrick. *The Negro Family: The Case for National Action.* Washington, D.C.: Government Printing Office, 1965.

Mueller, John E. *War, Presidents and Public Opinion.* New York: Wiley, 1973.

Mulvihill, Donald J., and Melvin Tumin. *Crimes of Violence.* Staff Report to the National Commission on Causes and Prevention of Violence. Vols. 11, 12, and 13. Washington, D.C.: Government Printing Office, 1969.

Murdock, George P. *Social Structure.* New York: Macmillan, 1949.

Murtagh, John M., and Sara Harris. *Cast the First Stone.* New York: McGraw-Hill, 1957.

Myers, Jerome K., and Lee L. Bean. *A Decade Later: A Follow-Up of Social Class and Mental Illness.* New York: Wiley, 1968.

Myers, Jerome K., and Leslie Schaffer. "Social Stratification and Psychiatric Practice: A Study of an Outpatient Clinic," *American Sociological Review,* 19 (1954), 307–310.

Myerson, Abraham. "Alcohol: A Study of Social Ambivalence," *Quarterly Journal of Studies on Alcohol,* 1 (1940), 13–20.

Myrdal, Gunnar. *An American Dilemma: The Negro Problem and Modern Democracy.* New York: Harper & Row, 1944.

———. "A Parellel to the Negro Problem," (Appendix 5) in *An American Dilemma: The Negro Problem and*

Modern Democracy. New York: Harper & Row, 1944, pp. 1073–1078.

N

Nader, Ralph. *Unsafe at Any Speed: The Designed-In Dangers of the American Automobile.* New York: Grossman, 1965.

National Advisory Commission on Criminal Justice Standards and Goals. *A National Strategy to Reduce Crime.* Washington, D.C.: Government Printing Office, 1973.

National Council on Crime and Delinquency. *Uniform Parole Reports Newsletters.* Washington, D.C.: Government Printing Office, January 1972.

National Institute of Mental Health. *Alcohol and Alcoholism.* Public Health Service Publication No. 1640. Washington, D.C.: U.S. Department of Health, Education, and Welfare, 1967.

Newton, George, and Franklin Zimring. *Firearms and Violence in American Life: A Staff Report to the National Commission on the Causes and Prevention of Violence.* Washington, D.C.: Government Printing Office, 1969.

Nisbet, Robert A. "Introduction: The Study of Social Problems," in Robert K. Merton and Robert A. Nisbet, *Contemporary Social Problems.* 3rd ed. New York: Harcourt Brace Jovanovich, 1971, pp. 1–25.

Nobile, Philip, and John Deedy (eds.). *The Complete Ecology Fact Book.* Garden City, N.Y.: Doubleday, 1972.

Nye, F. Ivan. *Family Relationships and Delinquent Behavior.* New York: Wiley, 1958.

———. "The Adjustment of Adolescent Children" in F. Ivan Nye and Lois Wladis Hoffman (eds.), *The Employed Mother in America.* Chicago: Rand McNally, 1963, pp.133–141.

Nye, F. Ivan, and James F. Short Jr. "Reported Behavior as a Criterion of Deviant Behavior," *Social Problems,* 5 (1957), 207–213.

O

Ødegaard, Ørnulv. "Pattern of Discharge and Readmission in Psychiatric Hospitals in Norway, 1926–1955," *Mental Hygiene,* 45 (1961), 185–193.

O'Donnell, John A. *Narcotic Addicts in Kentucky.* Chevy Chase, Md.: National Institute of Mental Health, 1969.

Oelsner, Leslie. "Scales of Justice," New York Times News Service, printed in *The Daily Enterprise,* September 28, 1972.

Offer, Daniel, and Melvin Sabshin. *Normality.* New York: Basic Books, 1966.

O'Leary, Vincent, and Joan Nuffield. *The Organization of Parole in the United States.* 2nd ed. Washington, D.C.:

National Council on Crime and Delinquency, 1972.

Oliver, Bernard J. *Sexual Deviation in American Society.* New Haven, Conn.: College and University Press, 1967.

Ollendorff, Robert H. *The Juvenile Homosexual Experience and Its Effect on Adult Sexuality.* New York: Julian Press, 1966.

O'Neill, Nena, and George O'Neill. *Open Marriage: A New Life Style for Couples.* New York: Evans, 1972.

Oppenheimer, Valerie Kincade. *The Female Labor Force in the United States: Demographic and Economic Factors Governing Its Growth and Changing Composition.* Population Monograph Series No. 5. Institute of International Studies. Berkeley: University of California Press, 1969.

Orwell, George. *Animal Farm.* New York: Harcourt Brace Jovanovich, 1954.

P

Packer, Herbert. *The Limits of the Criminal Sanction.* Stanford, Calif.: Stanford University Press, 1968.

Palmore, Erdman. "Compulsory Versus Flexible Retirement: Issues and Facts," *Gerontologist,* 12 (1972), 343–348.

Patterson, G. R., *et al.* "Assertive Behavior in Children: A Step Toward a Theory of Aggression," *Monographs of the Society for Research in Child Development,* vol. 32, no. 5 (1967).

Peele, Stanton, with Archie Brodsky. *Love and Addiction.* New York: Taplinger, 1975.

Peterson, David A. *The Crisis In Retirement Finance: The Views of Older Americans.* Ann Arbor: University of Michigan—Wayne State University Institute of Gerontology, 1972.

Piliavin, Irvin, and Scott Briar. "Police Encounters with Juveniles," *American Journal of Sociology,* 70 (1964), 206–214.

Pineo, Peter C. "Disenchantment in the Later Years of Marriage," *Marriage and Family Living,* 23 (February 1961), 4.

Pittman, David J. (ed.). *Alcoholism.* New York: Harper & Row, 1967.

Piven, Frances Fox, and Richard Cloward. *Regulating the Poor: The Functions of Public Welfare.* New York: Random House, 1971.

Platt, Anthony. *The Child Savers: The Invention of Delinquency.* Chicago: University of Chicago Press, 1969.

Polanyi, Karl. *The Great Transformation.* New York: Holt, Rinehart and Winston, 1944.

Porterfield, Austin L. *Youth in Trouble.* Fort Worth, Texas: Leo Potishman Foundation, 1946.

Potter, David. *People of Plenty.* Chicago: University of Chicago Press, 1954.

Powers, Edwin, and Helen Witmer. *An Experiment in the Prevention of Delinquency: The*

Cambridge — Somerville Youth Study. New York: Columbia University Press, 1951.

President's Commission on Law Enforcement and the Administration of Justice. *Task Force Report: Corrections.* Washington, D.C.: Government Printing Office, 1967a.

————. *Task Force Report: Juvenile Delinquency and Youth Crime.* Washington, D.C.: Government Printing Office, 1967b.

President's Commission on Income Maintenance Programs. *Background Papers.* Washington, D.C.: Government Printing Office, 1970.

Q

Quetelet, Adolphe. *A Treatise on Man.* Edinburgh: William and Robert Chambers, 1842.

Quinney, Richard (ed.). *Crime and Justice in Society.* Boston: Little, Brown, 1969.

R

Rachman, Stanley. "Sexual Fetishism: An Experimental Analogue," *Psychological Record,* 16 (1966), 293–296.

Rachman, Stanley, and John Teasdale. *Aversion Therapy and Behavior Disorders.* Coral Gables, Fla.: University of Miami Press, 1970.

Ray, Marsh B. "The Cycle of Abstinence and Relapse Among Heroin Addicts," in Howard S. Becker (ed.), *The Other Side: Perspectives on Deviance.* New York: Free Press, 1964, pp. 163–177.

Raymond, M. J. "Case of Fetishism Treated by Aversion Therapy," in H. J. Eysenck (ed.), *Behavior Therapy and the Neuroses.* Elmsford, N.Y.: Pergamon Press, 1960, pp. 303–311.

Reiss, Albert J., Jr. *Studies in Crime and Law Enforcement in Major Metropolitan Areas.* Washington, D.C.: Government Printing Office, 1967.

————. *The Police and the Public.* New Haven: Yale University Press, 1971.

Remington, Frank, Donald Newman, and Marygold Melli. *Criminal Justice Administration.* Indianapolis: Bobbs-Merrill, 1969.

Reno, Virginia, and Carol Zuckert. "Benefit Levels of Newly Retired Workers: Findings from the Survey of New Beneficiaries," *Social Security Bulletin,* 34 (July 1971), 3–31.

The Report of the Commission on Obscenity and Pornography. Washington, D.C.: Government Printing Office, 1970.

Rieff, Robert. "Mental Health Manpower and Institutional Change," in Emory Cowen, Elmer A. Gardner, and Melvin Zax (eds.), *Emergent*

Approaches to Mental Health Problems. New York: Appleton-Century-Crofts, 1967, pp. 74–91.

Riley, Matilda W., and Anne E. Foner. *Aging and Society: Volume 1, An Inventory of Research Findings.* New York: Russell Sage Foundation, 1968.

Rimland, Bernard. "Psychogenesis Versus Biogenesis: The Issues and the Evidence," in Stanley C. Plog and Robert B. Edgerton (eds.), *Changing Perspectives in Mental Illness.* New York: Holt, Rinehart and Winston, 1969, pp. 702–735.

Roby, Pamela (ed.). *Child Care—Who Cares? Foreign and Domestic Infant and Early Childhood Development Policies.* New York: Basic Books, 1973.

Room, Robin. "Drinking Patterns in Large U.S. Cities," *Quarterly Journal of Studies on Alcohol,* Supplement No. 6 (May 1972), 28–57.

Rosen, Benson, and Thomas H. Jerdee. "Sex Stereotyping in the Executive Suite," *Harvard Business Review,* 52 (March–April 1974), 45–58.

Rosen, Bernard C., and Roy D'Andrade. "The Psychological Origins of Achievement Motivation," *Sociometry,* 22 (1959), 185–218.

Rosen, George. *Madness in Society.* Chicago: University of Chicago Press, 1968.

Rosenberg, Morris. *Society and the Adolescent Self-Image.* Princeton, N.J.: Princeton University Press, 1965.

Rosenthal, David. *Genetic Theory and Abnormal Behavior.* New York: McGraw-Hill, 1970.

Rosenthal, David, and Seymour S. Kety (eds.). *The Transmission of Schizophrenia.* Elmsford, N.Y.: Pergamon Press, 1968.

Rossi, Alice S. "Equality Between the Sexes: An Immodest Proposal," in Robert Jay Lifton (ed.), *The Woman in America.* Boston, Mass.: Houghton Mifflin, 1965, pp. 98–143.

———. "Sex Equality: The Beginning of Ideology," in Betty Roszak and Theodore Roszak (eds.), *Masculine/Feminine: Readings in Sexual Mythology and the Liberation of Women.* New York: Harper & Row, 1969, pp. 173–186.

Rossi, Peter H., Emily Waite, Christine E. Bose, and Richard E. Berk. "The Seriousness of Crimes: Normative Structure and Individual Differences," *American Sociological Review,* 39 (1974), 224–237.

Rothman, David. *The Discovery of the Asylum: Social Order and Disorder in the New Republic.* Boston: Little, Brown, 1971.

Rubin, Lillian. *A Study in Progress of Blue-Collar Family Life.* (Forthcoming.)

Rubington, Earl. "The Hidden Alcoholic," *Quarterly Journal of Studies on Alcohol,* 33 (1972), 667–683.

Rush, David. "Perinatal Mortality, Race, Social Status, and Hospital of Birth: The Association with Birth Weight," in *The Proceedings of Birth Defects Symposium, III.* Albany, N.Y.: New York State Department of Health, Birth Defects Institute, 1972.

Russell, Bertrand. *Marriage and Morals.* New York: Liveright, 1929.

Ryan, William. *Blaming the Victim.* New York: Random House, Pantheon Books, 1971.

Ryan, William (ed.). *Distress in the City.* Cleveland, Ohio: Case Western Reserve University Press, 1969.

Ryder, Norman B. "The Emergence of a Modern Fertility Pattern: United States 1917–66," in S. J. Behrman *et al.* (eds.), *Fertility and Family Planning: A World View.* Ann Arbor: University of Michigan Press, 1969.

S

Sagarin, Edward. *Odd Man In: Societies of Deviants in America.* New York: New York Times Book Co., Quadrangle Books, 1969.

———. "The Good Guys, Bad Guys, and the Gay Guys," *Contemporary Sociology,* 2 (January 1973), 3–13.

Sampson, Timothy J. *Welfare: A Handbook for Friend and Foe.* Philadelphia: United Church Press, 1972.

Sanders, Wiley B. (ed.) *Juvenile Offenders for a Thousand Years: Selected Readings from Anglo-Saxon Times to 1900.* Chapel Hill: University of North Carolina Press, 1970.

Sanua, Victor D. "Sociocultural Aspects of Psychotherapy and Treatment: A Review of the Literature," in Lawrence E. Aft (ed.), *Progress in Clinical Psychology. Vol. 8.* New York: Grune & Stratton, 1966, pp. 151–190.

Schachter, Stanley, and Jerome Singer. "Cognitive, Social and Physiological Determinants of Emotional State," *Psychological Review,* 69 (1962), 379–399.

Scheff, Thomas J. "The Role of the Mentally Ill and the Dynamics of Mental Disorder: A Research Framework," *Sociometry,* 26 (1963), 436–453.

———. *Being Mentally Ill: A Sociological Theory.* Chicago: Aldine, 1966.

Schneider, Joseph W., and Sally L. Hacker. "Sex Role Imagery and Use of the Generic 'Man' in Introductory Texts: A Case in the Sociology of Sociology," *American Sociologist,* 8 (1973), 12–18.

Schofield, Michael. *Sociological Aspects of Homosexuality.* Boston: Little, Brown, 1965.

Schulz, James H. *Pension Aspects of the Economics of Aging: Present and Future Roles of Private Pensions.* Washington, D.C.: Government Printing Office, 1970.

Schur, Edwin M. *Narcotic Addiction in Britain and America: The Impact of Public Policy.* Bloomington: Indiana University Press, 1962.

———. *Crimes Without Victims: Deviant Behavior and Public Policy.* Englewood Cliffs, N.J.: Prentice-Hall, 1965.

———. *Radical Non-Intervention: Rethinking the Delinquency Problem.* Englewood Cliffs, N.J.: Prentice-Hall, 1973.

Scott, William A. "Research Definitions of Mental Health

480

and Mental Illness," *Psychology Bulletin,* 55 (1958a), 29–45.

————. "Social Psychological Correlates of Mental Illness and Mental Health," *Psychology Bulletin,* 55 (1958b), 65–87.

Scrimshaw, Nevin S., and John E. Gordon (eds.). *Malnutrition, Learning, and Behavior; Proceedings.* Cambridge, Mass.: M.I.T. Press, 1968.

Seevers, Maurice H., and Gerald A. Deneau. "Physiological Aspects of Tolerance and Physical Dependence," in W. S. Roof and F. G. Hofmann (eds.), *Physiological Pharmacology.* Vol.1. *The Nervous System—Part A.* New York: Academic Press, 1963, pp. 565–640.

Selznick, Philip. *T.V.A. and the Grass Roots.* New York: Harper & Row, Torchbooks, 1966.

Selznick, Gertrude J., and Stephen Steinberg. *Tenacity of Prejudice.* New York: Harper & Row, 1969.

Shaw, David. "Legal Scholars Wage Debate on Sentencing," *Los Angeles Times,* July 21, 1974, p.1.

Sherif, Muzafer, and Carolyn W. Sherif. *Groups in Harmony and Tension: An Integration of Studies on Intergroup Relations.* New York: Harper & Row, 1953.

Sherman, Lewis J., *et al.* "Prognosis in Schizophrenia," *Archives of General Psychiatry,* 10 (1964), 123–130.

Sherrill, Robert. "Before You Believe Those Exercise and Diet Ads Read the Following Report," *Today's Health,* 49 (August 1971), 34–36+.

Shibutani, Tamotsu. "Reference Groups as Perspectives," *American Journal of Sociology,* 60 (1955), 562–569.

Short, James F., Jr., and F. Ivan Nye. "Reported Behavior as a Criterion of Deviant Behavior," *Social Problems,* 5 (1957), 207–213.

Short, James F., Jr., and Fred L. Strodtbeck. *Group Process and Gang Delinquency.* Chicago: University of Chicago Press, 1965.

Sills, David. *The Volunteers.* New York: Free Press, 1957.

————. "The Environmental Movement and Its Critics," *Human Ecology,* forthcoming.

Silverman, Daniel. "Psychoses in Criminals: A Study of 500 Psychotic Prisoners," *Journal of Criminal Psychopathology,* 4 (1943), 703–730.

————. "The Psychotic Criminals: A Study of 500 Cases," *Journal of Clinical Psychopathology,* 8 (1946), 301–327.

Simpson, Ida H., Kurt W. Back, and John C. McKinney. "Exposure to Information on, Preparation for, and Self-evaluation in Retirement," in Ida Simpson *et al.* (eds.) *Social Aspects of Aging.* Durham, N.C.: Duke University Press, 1966.

Smith, M. Brewster. "'Mental Health' Reconsidered: A Special Case of the Problem of Values in Psychology," *American Psychologist,* 16 (1961), 299–306.

Smith, M. B., and N. Hobbs. "The Community and the Community Mental Health Center," *American Psychologist,* 21 (1966), 499–509.

Snyder, Solomon H. *Madness and the Brain.* New York: McGraw-Hill, 1974.

Social Security Bulletin. Annual Statistical Supplement. Washington, D.C.: Government Printing Office, 1971.

Sonnedecker, Glenn. "Emergence and Concept of the Addiction Problem," in Robert B. Livingston (ed.), *Narcotic Drug Addiction Problems.* Bethesda, Md.: Public Health Service, National Institute of Mental Health, 1958, pp. 14–22.

Spector, Malcolm, and John I. Kitsuse. "Social Problems: A Re- Formulation," *Social Problems,* 21 (1973), 145–159.

Spergel, Irving. "An Exploratory Research in Delinquent Subcultures," in Rose Giallombardo (ed.), *Juvenile Delinquency: A Book of Readings.* New York: Wiley, 1966, pp. 233–246.

Spitzer, Stephan P., and Norman K. Denzin. *The Mental Patient: Studies in the Sociology of Deviance.* New York: McGraw-Hill, 1968.

Stark, Rodney. *Police Riots.* Belmont, Calif.: Wadsworth, Focus Books, 1972.

Stark, Rodney, and Charles Y. Glock. "Prejudice and the Churches," in Charles Y. Glock and Ellen Siegelman (eds.), *Prejudice U.S.A.* New York: Praeger, 1969.

Stark, Rodney, and James McEvoy III. "Middle Class Violence," *Psychology Today,* 4 (November 1970), 52–54+.

Steen, Edith M. "Women Are Household Slaves," *American Mercury,* 68 (1949), 71–76.

Steinberg, Hannah (ed.). *Scientific Basis of Drug Dependence: A Symposium.* London: Churchill, 1969.

Steinberg, Stephen. *The Academic Melting Pot.* New York: McGraw-Hill, 1974.

Stinchcombe, Arthur L. *Constructing Social Theory.* New York: Harcourt Brace Jovanovich, 1968.

Stoller, Robert J. *Sex and Gender: On the Development of Masculinity and Femininity.* New York: Science House, 1968.

Stouffer, Samuel, *et al.* *The American Soldier.* Princeton, N.J.: Princeton University Press, 1949.

Streib, Gordon F., and Clement J. Schneider. *Retirement in American Society.* Ithaca, N.Y.: Cornell University Press, 1971.

Stycos, J. Mayone. *Human Fertility in Latin America: Sociological Perspectives.* Ithaca, N.Y.: Cornell University Press, 1968.

Stycos, J. Mayone, and Reuben Hill. "The Prospects of Birth Control in Puerto Rico," *Annals of the American Academy of Political and Social Science,* 285 (January 1953), 141.

Surgeon General's Scientific Advisory Committee on Television and Social Behavior. *Television and Growing Up: The Impact of Televised Violence.* Washington, D.C.: Government Printing Office, 1972.

Sutherland, Edwin H. *Principles of Criminology.* 4th ed. Chicago: Lippincott, 1947.

481

Sutherland, Edwin H., and Donald R. Cressey. *Principles of Criminology.* 7th ed. New York: Lippincott, 1970.

Suttles, Gerald. *Social Order of the Slum.* Rev. ed. Chicago: University of Chicago Press, 1968.

Sykes, Gresham H. *The Society of Captives.* Princeton, N.J.: Princeton University Press, 1958.

T

Tannenbaum, Frank. *Slave and Citizen: The Negro in America.* New York: Knopf, 1947.

Tanner, James M. *Growth at Adolescence.* 2nd ed. Philadelphia: F. A. Davis, 1962.

———. "Physical Growth," in Paul H. Mussen (ed.), *Carmichael's Manual of Child Psychology.* 3rd ed. New York: Wiley, 1970, pp. 77–155.

Tappan, Paul. *Crime, Justice, and Correction.* New York: McGraw-Hill, 1960.

Thorpe, J. G., *et al.* "A Comparison of Positive and Negative (Aversive) Conditioning in the Treatment of Homosexuality," *Behavior Research and Therapy,* 1 (1964), 357–362.

Titmuss, Richard. "Poverty vs. Inequality: Diagnosis," *The Nation,* 200 (February 8, 1965), 130–133.

Tobin, James, and Leonard Ross. "Living with Inflation," *The New York Review of Books,* vol.16, no.8 (May 6, 1971), 23–26.

Tocqueville, Alexis de. *Democracy in America.* Vol 2. Phillips Bradley (tr.). New York: Knopf, 1960 (first English ed. 1835).

Trotsky, Leon. *The Revolution Betrayed.* New York: Pathfinder Press, 1937.

Turner, Anthony G. *San Jose Methods Test of Known Crime Victims.* LEAA Statistics Division Technical Series, Report No. 1. Washington D.C.: Government Printing Office, 1972.

Turner, R. Jay. "Social Mobility and Schizophrenia," *Journal of Health and Social Behavior,* 9 (1968), 194–203.

———. "The Epidemiological Study of Schizophrenia: A Current Appraisal," *Journal of Health and Social Behavior,* 13 (1972), 360–369.

Turner, R. Jay, *et al.* "Marital Status and Schizophrenia: A Study of Incidence and Outcome," *Journal of Abnormal Psychology,* 76 (1970), 110–116.

Turner, R. Jay, and M. O. Wagenfeld. "Occupational Mobility and Schizophrenia: An Assessment of the Social Causation and Social Selection Hypothesis," *American Sociological Review,* 32 (1967), 104–113.

Tylor, Edward Burnett. *The Origins of Culture.* Vol. 1 of *Primitive Culture.* Gloucester, Mass.: Peter Smith, 1970 (orig. pub. 1871).

U

Ullmann, Leonard P., and Leonard Krasner. *A Psychological Approach to Abnormal Behavior.* Englewood Cliffs, N.J.: Prentice-Hall, 1969.

United Nations. *Growth of the World's Urban and Rural Population, 1920–2000.* New York: United Nations, 1969.

U'Ren, Marjorie. "The Image of Woman in Textbooks," in Vivian Gornick and Barbara K. Moran (eds.), *Woman in Sexist Society: Studies in Power and Powerlessness.* New York: Basic Books, 1971.

U.S. Bureau of the Census. "Illustrative Projections of Money Income Size Distributions for Families and Unrelated Individuals," *Current Population Reports,* Series P–23/47. Washington, D.C.: Government Printing Office, 1971.

———. *Selected Characteristics of Persons and Families of Mexican, Puerto Rican, and Other Spanish Origin: March 1971.* Series P–20, No. 224. U.S. Department of Commerce. Washington, D.C.: Government Printing Office, 1971.

———. *The Social and Economic Status of Negroes in the United States, 1970.* Series P–23. U.S. Department of Commerce. Washington, D.C.: Government Printing Office, 1971.

———. "Characteristics of the Low Income Population: 1972," *Current Population Reports.* Series P–60, No.88. U.S. Department of Commerce. Washington, D.C.: Government Printing Office, 1973.

———. "The Social and Economic Status of the Black Population in the United States, 1972," *Current Population Reports,* Series P–23, No. 46. Washington, D.C.: Government Printing Office, 1973.

U.S. Department of Health, Education, and Welfare. *Juvenile Court Statistics.* DHEW Pub. No. (SRS) 72–03452. Washington, D.C.: Government Printing Office, 1970.

U.S. Department of Labor. *The Law Against Age Discrimination in Employment.* Washington, D.C.: Government Printing Office, 1970.

———. *Manpower Report to the President.* Washington, D.C.: Government Printing Office, 1971.

U.S. Department of Labor: Women's Bureau. "Fact Sheet on the Earnings Gap." Stock number 2916–0004. Washington, D.C.: Government Printing Office, December 1971 (revised).

———. "Facts on Women Workers of Minority Races." Stock number 2916–0001. Washington, D.C.: Government Printing Office, June 1972 (revised).

———. "Women Workers Today." No. 0–543–758 (28). Washington, D.C.: Government Printing Office, 1973 (revised).

U.S. Public Health Service. "Increase in Divorce: U.S. 1967." PHS Pub. 1000, Series 21, no. 21. Washington, D.C.: Government Printing Office, 1970.

V

Vaillant, George E. "A Twelve-Year Follow-up of New York Narcotic Addicts: 1. The Relationship of Treatment to Outcome," *American Journal of Psychiatry,* 122 (1966), 727–737.

Vander Zanden, James. *American Minority Relations.* New York: Ronald Press, 1972.

Vaz, Edmund (ed.). *Middle Class Juvenile Delinquency.* New York: Harper & Row, 1967.

Vorenberg, Elizabeth, and James Vorenberg. "Early Diversion from the Criminal Justice System: Practice in Search of a Theory," in Lloyd Ohlin (ed.), *Prisoners in America.* Englewood Cliffs, N.J.: Prentice-Hall, 1973.

Voss, Harwin L. "Socio-economic Status and Reported Delinquent Behavior," *Social Problems,* 13 (1966), 314–324.

W

Waldo, Gordon, and Simon Dinitz. "Personality Attributes of the Criminal: An Analysis of Research Studies 1950–1965," *Journal of Research in Crime and Delinquency,* 4 (1967), 185–202.

Waller, Willard. "Social Problems and the Mores," *American Sociological Review,* 1 (1936), 922–934.

Wallerstein, James S., and Clement J. Wyle. "Our Law-abiding Law Breakers," *Federal Probation,* 25 (1947), 107–112.

Walshok, Mary Lindenstein. "The Emergence of Middle-Class Deviant Subcultures: The Case of Swingers," *Social Problems,* 18 (1971), 4.

Ward, David A., and Gene G. Kassebaum. *Women's Prison: Sex and Social Structure.* Chicago: Aldine, 1965.

Watson, Ernest H., and George H. Lowery. *Growth and Development of Children.* 5th ed. Chicago: Year Book Medical Publishers, 1967.

Watson, J. B., and R. Rayner. "Conditional Emotional Reactions," *Journal of Experimental Psychology,* 65 (1968), 251–260.

Weber, Max. *The Protestant Ethic and The Spirit of Capitalism.* New York: Scribner's, 1930 (orig. pub. 1921).

Weil, Andrew T., *et al.* "Clinical and Psychological Effects of Marihuana in Man," *Science,* 162 (1968), 1234–1242.

Weinberg, George. *Society and the Healthy Homosexual.* New York: St. Martin's Press, 1972.

Weinberg, Martin S. "The Male Homosexual: Age-Related Variations in Social and Psychological Characteristics," *Social Problems,* 17 (1970), 527–537.

Weiss, Carin. "The Development of Professional Role Commitments Among Graduate Students." Unpublished M.A. Thesis, University of Washington, 1972.

West, Donald J. *Homosexuality.* Chicago: Aldine, 1967.

Westoff, Charles F., and Norman B. Ryder. "Recent Trends in Attitudes Toward Fertility Control and in the Practice of Contraception in the United States," in Ronald Freeman *et al.* (eds.), *Fertility and Family Planning: A World View.* Ann Arbor: University of Michigan Press, 1969, pp. 388–412.

Whyte, William F. *Street Corner Society: The Social Structure of an Italian Slum.* 2nd ed. Chicago: University of Chicago Press, 1955.

Wikler, Abraham. "On the Nature of Addiction and Habituation," *British Journal of Addiction,* 57 (1961), 73–79.

———. "Some Implications of Conditioning Theory for Problems of Drug Abuse," in Paul Blachly (ed.), *Drug Abuse: Data and Debate.* Springfield, Ill.: Charles C Thomas, 1970.

Wilensky, Harold, and Charles Lebeaux. *Industrial Society and Social Welfare.* New York: Free Press, 1965.

Williams, Jay R., and Martin Gold. "From Delinquent Behavior to Official Delinquency," *Social Problems,* 20 (1972), 209–229.

Wilson, Cedric W. M. "An Analysis of the Mechanisms Involved in the Taste for Drink," in Hannah Steinberg (ed.), *Scientific Basis of Drug Dependence.* London: Churchill, 1969.

Wilson, James Q. *Varieties of Police Behavior: The Management of Law and Order in Eight Communities.* Cambridge, Mass.: Harvard University Press, 1968.

Wilson, Warner R. "Correlates of Avowed Happiness," *Psychological Bulletin,* 67 (1967), 294–306.

Winick, Charles. "Physician Narcotic Addicts," *Social Problems,* 9 (1961), 174–186.

———. "Maturing Out of Narcotic Addiction," *Bulletin on Narcotics,* 14 (January 1962), 1–7.

Winick, Charles, and Paul M. Kinsie. *The Lively Commerce: Prostitution in the United States.* New York: New American Library, Signet, 1971.

Wirth, Louis. "The Problems of Minority Groups," in Ralph Linton (ed.), *The Science of Man in the World Crisis.* New York: Columbia University Press, 1945, pp. 347–373.

Wolfe, Linda. "Take Two Aspirins and Masturbate," *Playboy,* 21 (June 1974), 114–116+.

Wolfgang, Marvin E. *Patterns in Criminal Homicide.* Philadelphia: University of Pennsylvania Press, 1958.

Wolfgang, Marvin E., and Bernard Cohen. *Crime and Race.* New York: Institute of Human Relations Press, 1970.

Wolfgang, Marvin E., and Franco Ferracuti. *The Subculture of Violence: Towards an Integrated Theory in Criminology.* London: Tavistock, 1967.

Wright, James. *The Coming Water Famine.* New York: Coward-McCann, 1966.

Wrong, Dennis H. "Trends in Class Fertility in Western Nations," *Canadian Journal of Economics and Political Science,* 24 (1958), 216–229.

Y

Yablonsky, Lewis. *The Violent Gang.* New York: Macmillan, 1962.

Yarrow, Marian R., *et al. Child Rearing: An Inquiry into Research and Methods.* San Francisco: Jossey-Bass, 1968.

Z

Zelnik, Melvin, and John F. Kantner. "Sexuality, Contraception and Pregnancy Among Young Unwed Females in the United States," in U.S. Commission on Population Growth and the American Future, *Demographic and Social Aspects of Population Growth.* Washington, D.C.: Government Printing Office, 1972, pp. 355–374.

Zigler, Edward, and Irvin L. Child. *Socialization and Personality Development.* Reading, Mass.: Addison-Wesley, 1973.

Zilboorg, Gregory, and G. W. Henry. *A History of Medical Psychology.* New York: Norton, 1941.

Zinberg, Norman E. "The Truth Is that Heroin Is Not a Drug of Pleasure," *Boston Globe, February 6, 1973, p. 20.*

Zinberg, Norman E., and David C. Lewis. "Narcotic Usage I: A Spectrum of a Difficult Medical Problem," *New England Journal of Medicine,* 270 (1964), 989–993.

Zinberg, Norman E., and John A. Robertson, *Drugs and the Public.* New York: Simon and Schuster, 1972.

Zubin, Joseph, *et al.* "Cross-National Study of Diagnosis of the Mental Disorders," *American Journal of Psychiatry* (Supplement), 125 (1969).

Name Index

A

Adams, Abigail, 338
Adams, Jane, 339
Adams, John, 338
Adorno, Theodor, 324, 325
Agel, Jerome, 148
Agopian, Michael, 244, 252
Akers, Ronald, 107, 222, 246, 259
Alexander, Franz G., 149
Allport, Gordon, 322
Almond, Gabriel, 277
Amir, Menachem, 243, 244
Andreas, Carol, 338
Anttik, I., 169
Ardrey, Robert, 209, 210
Aristotle, 171
Asch, Solomon, 33
Atchley, Robert, 393, 397, 401, 402, 403
Athanasiou, Robert, 240
Audubon, John James, 461

B

Babigian, Hardutun, 132
Back, Kurt, 413
Bahr, Howard, 307
Bales, Robert Freed, 103
Ball-Rokeach, Sandra, 217
Bamburger, Michael, 429
Bandura, Albert, 212, 213, 259
Baran, Paul, 275
Bardolph, Richard, 331
Barnes, Harry E., 191
Barnett, Arnold, 203
Battan, Louis J., 440
Bean, Lee, 151
Beauvoir, Simone de, 340
Beccaria, Cesare, 172, 191
Becker, Howard S., 4, 5, 6, 105, 106
Beecher, Henry K., 94
Belson, William, 169
Bendix, Reinhard, 279
Bentham, Jeremy, 172, 191
Berkowitz, Leonard, 210, 211
Bernard, Jesse, 340, 341, 342, 344, 376, 382
Black, Donald, 323
Blackwell, James E., 333
Blakemore, C. B., 259
Blau, Peter M., 279, 286, 287
Blauner, Robert, 316, 317

Bloomer, Amelia, 338
Blum, Richard, 88, 89, 90, 103, 110
Blumer, Herbert, 4, 5, 23
Bodine, George, 163
Bond, Ian K., 259
Bond, Julian, 333
Boulding, Kenneth, 458
Brackett, James W., 432
Bradburn, Norman M., 133
Brecker, Edward M., 88
Briar, Scott, 62, 63, 64, 66, 71, 73, 74, 75, 79, 81, 198
Brophy, I. N., 322
Brown, Bertram S., 134
Brown, Harrison, 447
Bryan, James H., 242
Bukharin, Nikolai, 289
Burch, William, 455, 463
Burchinal, Lee G., 377
Burgess, Robert, 107
Burnham, David, 110
Burnham, Sophy, 110
Buss, Arnold H., 126, 127

C

Cabot, P. Sidney de Q, 68, 80
Cabot, Richard Clarke, 67, 68, 70, 71, 184
Cahalan, Don, 91, 92
Campbell, Angus, 291
Caplovitz, David, 133
Capone, Al, 115
Cappon, Daniel, 248, 258
Caprio, Frank S., 248
Carmichael, Stokely, 332
Carp, Frances, 400
Carson, Rachel, 457, 458
Cason, Hulsey, 179
Cavan, Ruth, 158
Chambliss, William
Chappell, Duncan, 243, 244, 254, 259, 260
Chavez, Cesar, 333
Chein, Isidor, 100, 103, 107, 111
Child, Irvin L., 212
Cisin, Ira, 91, 92
Clark, John, 157, 163, 169, 170, 202
Clark, Kenneth, 316, 317
Clarke-Stewart, Alison, 375
Clausen, John A., 29, 90, 91, 114,

125, 131, 136
Cleaver, Eldridge, 252
Clinard, Marshall B., 34, 202
Cloward, Richard, 297
Cohen, Lawrence E., 178
Cole, H. S. D., 150, 151
Cole, Thomas, 461
Coleman, James S., 374
Commoner, Barry, 449, 457, 458
Conover, Donald, 132
Cooley, Charles Horton, 31, 32
Cooper, Barbara, 402
Cooper, James Fenimore, 461
Cottrell, Fred, 402
Cowgill, Donald, 414
Cressey, Donald, 176, 177
Cronkite, Walter, 9, 48
Cumming, Elaine, 127, 154, 227

D

D'Andrade, Roy G., 27, 291, 346
Darwin, Charles, 174, 426
Davenport, William, 232
Davies, D. L., 100
Davis, Alan J., 233, 236, 241, 247, 254
Davis, James A., 133
Davis, Kingsley, 241, 242, 245, 272, 417, 418, 424, 426, 427, 428, 432
Dear, Ronald B., 298
Deck, Leland, 27, 292
Deedy, Wayne, 439
Deneau, Gerald A., 101
Dennis, Wayne, 29, 370
Dentler, Robert A., 169, 170
Denzin, Norman K., 142
Dinitz, Simon, 177
Dion, Karen, 27
Dizard, Jan, 382
Dohrenwend, Barbara S., 131, 132, 135, 136, 147
Dohrenwend, Bruce P., 131, 132, 135, 136, 147
Dollard, John, 92, 211, 324
Drucker, Peter F., 15, 52
Duff, John, 318
Duncan, Otis Dudley, 279, 286, 287, 291
Dunham, Henry, 131, 144, 176

Glossary and Index

A

abolitionists. *Members of the antislavery movement during the several decades preceding the Civil War. Women in the abolitionist movement were instrumental in founding the women's movement in the United States,* 338.
See also women's liberation movement.

achievement motivation. *Attitudes reflecting a desire to accomplish or attain goals,* 291.

acute disability. *A short-term incapacity,* 401.
See also chronic disability.

addiction. *A physiological or psychological dependence on alcohol, drugs, or other substances.*
alcoholism and drug addiction compared, 85, 88–90
behavior modification therapy and, 102
as disease, 90
historical and cultural variations, 88–90, 103, 104, 105
indicators of, 87–88
physicians and, 98–99, 114
power needs and, 104
prevalence of, 90–93
rate of cure, 116
responses to, 113–120
social ambivalence and, 89
sociological variables and, 92, 99, 102, 109, 110, 113, 114, 116, 119
sources of, 93–113
theories of, 101–113
treatment of, 116–120

affirmative action. *The hiring policy of actively recruiting and promoting members of subordinate groups with the goal of increasing their representation to the proportion they represent in society,* 356–357.
See also discrimination in hiring; subordinate group.

age grading. *The division of the people of a society into different status levels and social roles based on age groupings,* 392.

aggregate. *A temporary gathering of people who do not have any organized or lasting interrelationship,* 32.
See also group; interaction.

aggressive instinct. *A biological predisposition toward aggressive behavior found by Lorenz and other scientists in animals and assumed by some to exist in humans,* 209–210.

aggravated assault. *Assault in which the actions of the victim contribute to the crime,* 167, 168.
victim participation and, 209
See also assault; interpersonal violence; symbolic violence.

aging. *The process of growing old, including its social, emotional, and biological aspects,* 22.
discrimination and, 407–408
economic problems of, 287–288, 393–399
education and, 413

effect of industrialization on, 414
extended family and, 406
family disorganization and, 406–407
future problems of, 413–415
health and, 409–410
health services and, 401–402
housing and transportation problems of, 399–400
population and, 405–406
poverty and, 407–408, 414
problems of definition, 392–393
responses to problems of, 408–415
sexual deviance and, 254
sexual attractiveness and, 254
social class and, 408–409
social effects on, 400–405
sources of, 405–408

agitation. *Attempts to create and arouse public interest in a social or political problem,* 6–11.

agronomy. *The applied science of the production of field crops and soil management,* 440.

alcoholism. *See* addiction.

alienation. *Estrangement from other people, from one's work, or from one's society or culture.*
as problem of urbanization, 50–51

American dilemma. *The problem of the contradiction between the democratic ideals of the United States and its oppression of subordinate groups,* 312.
See also subordinate group.

appeasement gesture. *A gesture of submission made by an animal to ward off aggression by another animal of the same species,* 210.

assault. *A physical attack on a person,* 203.
alcohol and, 211
race and, 217
regional variations, 207
social class and, 217
See also aggravated assault; interpersonal violence.

assimilationist integrationists. *Members of subordinate groups committed to speeding up the pace of integration,* 333.
See also black separatists; cultural nationalists; revolutionary nationalists.

489

chronic disability. *A long-term or recurring incapacity*, 401. *See also* acute disability.

chronic unemployment. *A state of being out of work continually and for extended periods of time.* interpersonal violence and, 220

civil disobedience. *Purposeful violation of laws on grounds of conscience*, 9–10, 317. feminism and, 338

class consciousness. *The awareness of one's social-class position, of the relationships between one's own class and the other classes in society, and of the dependence of one's personal interests on the position and attainments of one's social class as a whole*, 38. *See also* false consciousness; objective class; social class; subjective class.

Classical conditioning. *An experimental procedure in which a stimulus that normally evokes a given response is repeatedly presented with a stimulus that does not usually evoke that response, with the result that the latter stimulus will eventually evoke the response when presented by itself. Also known as Pavlovian conditioning*, 140–141. *See also* learning theory; operant conditioning; reinforcement theory; social-learning theory.

Classical School of criminology. *A school of thought that developed in Europe during the eighteenth and nineteenth centuries whose views still influence modern criminology. The main tenets of the school were that society has the right to punish wrongdoing but must grant certain safeguards to freedom; that people are rational beings who can choose how to act; that, therefore, the way to prevent crime is to make sure that the consequences (punishment) of committing a crime exceed the pleasures or benefits gained; and that, for these reasons, offenses and their punishments had to be written out in advance and known by people*, 172. *See also* Positive School of criminology.

colonialism. *The control and administration of the internal affairs of one nation by another nation that wishes to enhance its international position, secure cheap sources of labor and raw materials, and gain another market*, 316–317. *See also* imperialism; internal colony.

community treatment programs. *Programs whose philosophy is that the chances of recovery by mental patients are improved if they are treated in the community rather than institutionalized and if their environment is disrupted as little as possible*, 149–154.

companionate marriage. *An arrangement whereby, for a period of time, an unmarried couple lives together as a preparation for, or a trial period of, marriage*, 385–386. *See also* group marriage; individual marriage; open marriage; parental marriage; serial marriage.

competitive market system. *An economic system in which the value of goods, services, and wages is determined by the market principle of supply and demand*, 274.

concept. *An expression of a general idea about the nature of or relations between phenomena, usually constituting a category for their classification*, passim.

conditioning. *See* classical conditioning; operant conditioning.

conflict theory. *Theories of society that view social phenomena of the past, present, and future as a result of conflict. One school views society as a collection of groups and institutions with antagonistic values (value-conflict approach); another school, as groups with antagonistic class interests (class-conflict approach)*, 41–45. of crime and delinquency, 184, 185, 190 of intergroup conflict, 314–315 of poverty and inequality, 272–273 radical therapy and, 147–148 *See also* functionalism.

consciousness-raising groups. *Small, voluntary groups organized by members of a subordinate group for the purpose of resocializing themselves in order to gain greater awareness of their condition and establish new behavior patterns*, 359–360. *See also* resocialization; subordinate group.

491

control. *A process of holding constant factors other than the independent variable and chance in order to see whether a relationship between the independent and dependent variable holds when all else is equal. In experiments, control is accomplished through randomization of subjects; in nonexperimental analyses, by statistical manipulation of the data*, passim. *See also* dependent variable; experiment; independent variable; randomization; spuriousness.

control group. *In an experiment, a group of subjects who have the same characteristics as the experimental group but who do not undergo the experimental manipulation.* *See also* experiment; experimental group.

controlled use. *The use of regular daily doses of drugs or alcohol within the context of a normal productive life*, 98–100.

co-optation. *The process through which an organization maintains and stabilizes itself by absorbing new and critical segments into its structure*, 11–14, 15–20.

correlation. *The mutual relationship between two or more variables.* *See also* relationship; variable.

cortical inhibitions. *Fatigue and insensitivity of the brain due to overstimulation*, 175.

D

493

E

M

machismo. *An exaggerated notion of masculinity, toughness, manly self-assurance, and virility,* 216.

majority group. *See* dominant group.

male dominance. *The practice of keeping women subordinate to men,* 337–361.
    division of labor and, 346–347
    historical view of, 337
    responses to, 355–360
    sources of, 345–355

Malthusian theory. *The view that while food supplies increase arithmetically, populations increase geometrically, and only through certain positive checks (war, famine, disease) and preventive checks (delayed marriage, celibacy) do populations remain at a manageable size,* 425–426, 451.
    Malthusians, 451–453
    See also demographic transition theory.

mandatory retirement. *A policy whereby the age of retirement from an occupation is fixed and compulsory,* 392, 404–405, 414.

marginal poor. *Those who are irregularly employed and are periodically forced to seek public financial assistance,* 298.
    See also disreputable poor; *Lumpenproletariat.*

marriage. *See* companionate marriage; group marriage; individual marriage; open marriage; parental marriage; serial marriage.

marriage counseling. *Professional therapy designed to help married couples cope with their marital problems,* 386.

mate swapping. *The practice of married persons exchanging mates with other couples for sexual purposes,* 238.

maturing out. *The tendency of drug addicts and alcoholics to outgrow a drug or alcohol habit,* 99–100.

mean. *A measure of central tendency or an average computed by dividing the sum of a set of items by the number of items in the set. For example, the average height of a group is the total height of all the members divided by the total number of members.*
    See also median.

median. *In a set of items ranked from low to high, the item that has half the items above it and half below. For example, if the median family income in the United States is $11,200 a year, half the families in the United States receive more than $11,200 a year and half receive less than $11,200 a year.*
    See also mean.

Medicare. *A Social Security-linked program that tries to take care of the medical needs of the aged,* 402, 409.

mental illness. *A serious failure to adapt mentally to external conditions that incapacitates a person in some ways.*
    biochemistry and, 34
    categories of, 127–130
    deviant behavior and, 130
    extent of, 133–136
    historical and cross-cultural variations, 123–125
    interpersonal violence and, 211
    marital status and, 135
    measurement of, 130–133
    poverty and, 292
    problems of defining, 125–127
    psychoactive drugs and, 137–138
    responses to, 149–154
    rural-urban variations, 146–147
    selection interpretation of, 135–136, 144–146
    social-causation interpretation of, 135–136, 144–146
    social class and, 135–136, 143–144
    social mobility and, 144
    stress and, 144
    See also social disability.

methadone maintenance. *A program by which methadone, a drug cross-dependent with but less debilitating than heroin, is used to withdraw users from dependency on heroin,* 117–118.
    See also heroin maintenance.

migrant farm laborers. *A group of persons who rely on seasonal employment as crop harvesters and who move from place to place in search of employment,* 15, 283–284.

migration. *Movement from one country, region, or geographical area (emmigration) to another country, region, or geographical area (immigration),* 36–37.
    family and, 379
    immigration and poverty, 295
    immigration and social position, 318–319
    nonwhite minorities as immigrants, 319–321
    solution to population problems, 431

militant strategy. *A strategy of a subordinate group to escape exploitation by making the dominant group subordinate,* 305.
    See also assimilationist strategy; dominant group; pluralist strategy; secessionist strategy; subordinate group.

minority group. *See* subordinate group.

misfit theory. *The view that those who commit the most violent crimes are social misfits, outside the class system,* 218–220.

missocialization. *Improper or inadequate socialization,* 28.
    See also resocialization; socialization.

model psychoses. *Artificial disorders induced by drugs that produce symptoms resembling those of functional disorders,* 137–138.

499

modeling. *In social-learning theory, a form of learning in which a person learns how to perform an act by watching another person do it.*
addiction and, 97–98
aggressive behavior and, 213–215

mortality.
aging and, 405
DDT and, 427
decline of, 426–427
economic growth and, 426
effects of increasing, 431
in Guyana, 427–429
Malthusian theory and, 425
rate, 53
reduction of, 47
See also infant mortality.

muckraking. *The search for and exposure of real or alleged corruption, scandal, or the like, especially in politics,* 10.

N

nationalist movements. *Social movements to establish national identity, independence, and advancement. Sociopolitical movements, generally of colonized peoples, to establish a national identity; to gain independence from the colonizing nation, state, or power; and to achieve economic and political advancement,* 317.
See also black separatists; cultural nationalists; revolutionary nationalists.

negative income tax. *A proposal to use the income-tax system to fund a program to provide cash payments to individuals and families whose income falls below a designated level,* 299.

neurosis. *A mental disorder that prevents the victim from dealing effectively with reality, although there is no clear break with reality as in psychosis; it is characterized by anxiety and partial impairment of functioning, although the neurotic individual can still carry on in most areas of his or her life,* 127–128.
sexual deviance and, 247–248
sexual repression and, 247
stress and, 128
See also psychosis.

no-fault divorce. *A dissolution of a marriage by the common agreement of wife and husband. A no-fault divorce does not involve a law suit, and the former spouses often separate amicably,* 387.
See also divorce.

norms. *Prescriptions for correct or acceptable behavior,* passim.
commitment to, 182–183
of deviant groups, 109
governing sexual behavior, 231–232
rate of interaction and conformity to, 215
values and, 42
See also deviance; expectation; values.

nuclear family. *A household composed of one married couple and their children,* 367.
care of children and, 373
creation of, 378–380
social change and, 378
societal pressures on, 380–383
in underdeveloped countries, 421–422
See also extended family.

O

objective social conditions. *States of society that exist whether or not they are socially recognized.*
in Appalachia, 265–266
sex-based inequalities and, 337–338
social problems and, 3–5

open marriage. *A marriage based on companionship and mutual interests that allows the partners to explore extramarital relationships,* 387–388.
See also companionate marriage; group marriage; individual marriage; parental marriage; restored marriage; serial marriage.

operant conditioning. *A form of training in which certain of an organism's spontaneous activities are reinforced or punished,* 140–141.
See also classical conditioning; learning theory; reinforcement theory; social-learning theory.

opiates. *Drugs that either contain or are derived from opium and that have a soothing or dulling effect on the user. The term "opiate" is also used as a generic term for anything that has such an effect,* 89–91.

organized crime. *Crime committed by members of a formal organization devoted to activities that are in violation of the law,* 171.
psychoactive drugs and, 115
See also crime.

outpatient clinic. *A clinic where patients come to receive treatment rather than enter a hospital for treatment,* 131.

outreach services. *A policy by which the staff of a social program go out into the community in search of those in need of the program,* 410.

P

parental marriage. *Proposed by Margaret Mead, a long-term marriage for the purpose of having children,* 386.
See also companionate marriage, group marriage, individual marriage, open marriage, restored marriage, serial marriage.

501

503

S

504

505

507

temperature inversion. *An atmospheric condition in which the upper air is warmer than the lower air so that the lower, cooler air, which is heavier, cannot rise, thus trapping pollutants near the surface of the earth,* 440-441.
See also pollutant.

territoriality. *The tendency of animals to stake out and defend particular geographical areas,* 210.

theory. *A group of general propositions used as principles of explanation for a class of phenomena.*
See also demographic-transition theory; differential-association theory; instinct theory; personality theory; psychoanalytic theory; reinforcement theory; social-control theory; social-learning theory; strain theory; subcultural-deviance theory.

therapy. *See* aversive therapy; behavior-modification therapy; reinforcement therapy; radical therapy.

tolerance, drug. *The bodily adaptation to a drug (or alcohol) necessitating larger amounts of that drug to produce the same effect,* 87.
See also addiction; cross-tolerance; cross-dependence.

transsexual. *A person who feels he or she is a member of the opposite sex despite his or her physical sexual characteristics,* 348–349.

U

Uniform Crime Reports (UCR). *See* index offenses.

urbanization. *The process of changing from a rural to an urban way of life, including industrialization, population increases, and complex division of labor,* 50–52.
in developing countries, 421–422
family and, 379–380
geographic mobility and, 283
heroin use and, 90
industrialization and, 47, 50
population and, 426
poverty and, 283–284
rate of, 457
See also population.

V

values. *General societal standards about what is desirable, how things should be, and what ultimate goals are to be pursued,* 42–44.
diagnosis of mental illness and, 133
reference groups and, 32
social science and, 56
See also norms.

variable. *Anything that can have more than one value or is capable of change,* 69.
See also dependent variable; independent variable.

vice crime. *Activities that are illegal because they are considered personally, morally, or socially harmful. Prostitution and gambling are vice crimes in most states in the United States,* 158.
See also crime; delinquency; street crime.

victimization survey. *A survey that asks subjects about crimes of which they were victims. These surveys are used to check the reliability of data gathered from official sources and self-report studies,* 163, 168–169.
of interpersonal violence, 202, 209–226
See also self-report study; survey research; index offenses.

W

War on Poverty. *A series of social service programs established under the Johnson Administration during the middle and late 1960s whose stated goal was to eliminate poverty in the United States,* 15, 266.

WASP. *A commonly used term derived from the initials for the words "white Anglo-Saxon Protestant" that refers to a member of the dominant and privileged group in the United States,* 305.
resistance to immigration by, 318.
See also dominant group.

welfare system. *A system of public assistance created by the Social Security Act of 1935 intended to provide for the temporary emergency economic needs of those hard hit by the Depression of the 1930s. It was assumed that as the nation recovered from the Depression, the welfare system would be phased out. Instead, it has grown to enormous proportions but in a patchy, disorganized fashion that does not really meet the needs of the poor. Many critics of the present welfare system have suggested that because the problems of job insecurity, family disorganization, and illness are likely to be with us for a long time, permanent, well-planned, government-sponsored social programs intended to aid all those who need help should be established,* 294–300.
black families and, 321
functions of, 16–17
See also poverty programs.

Credits and Acknowledgments

Special thanks are extended to the following persons for their help in providing and developing graphics: Bruce M. Dean, artist, for his creative contribution; Kitty Anderson, for her role as production artist in preparing camera-ready art; Laurie Wermuth, for her help as graphics researcher; E. Paul Slick and Kitty Anderson, for doing most of the production art on charts, graphs, and diagrams; Robert Bruegel, for his help in developing preliminary graphic concepts; Pat Campbell, for her editorial contributions; and Richard Tewes, for proofreading.

Chapter 1

2—Bruce Dean, excerpt from "Gandhi and the One-Eyed Giant," by Thomas Merton, *Gandhi on Non Violence,* Copyright © 1964, 1965, New Directions Publishing Corporation. Reprinted by permission of New Directions Publishing Corporation; 5—(top) Library of Congress, (bottom) UPI-Compix; 7—(top) Copyright © New York Times, Jan. 15, 1967, (bottom) Burt Glinn/Magnum Photos; 8—(right) Ken Regan/Camera 5; 10—Provincial Archives, Victoria, British Columbia; 16—Everett Peck; 18—(top left) Dennis Brack/Black Star, (bottom left) Paul Sequeira, (right) George Gardner; 19—(left) Laurence Laurie & Associates, Courtesy UPI-Compix, (right) Eve Arnold/Magnum Photos; 20—(top) Jan Lukas/Rapho-Guillumette, (center left) Arthur Sirdofsky, (center right) Yvonne Freund/Rapho-Guillumette, (bottom) Ray Ellis/Rapho-Guillumette.

Chapter 2

24—Bruce Dean, quote from Thomas E. Gaddis and James O. Long, *Killer: A Journal of Murder,* Copyright © 1970, MacMillan Publishing Company; 26—UPI-Compix; 27—Yerkes Regional Primate Center, courtesy of Dr. Duane M. Rumbaugh; 28—John Oldenkamp; 30—(left) courtesy of Harry Harlow, (right) *The Wild Child,* Copyright © 1973 by F. Truffaut; 33—(top right) from Solomon Asch, (bottom) from *Twelve Angry Men,* United Artists, 1957; 36—(top) Sanford H. Ruth/Rapho-Guillumette, (center) Hillelson/Magnum Photos, (bottom) Ken Heyman/Magnum Photos; 42—(bottom) Alan Mercer; 51—Bruce Davidson/Magnum Photos; 54—(top left, top center) UPI-Compix, (top right) Charles Gatewood, (center left) Bill Owens/BBM Associates, (center center) UPI-Compix, (center right) Doug Armstrong, (bottom left) George Rodger/Magnum Photos, (bottom center and right) UPI-Compix; 55—(top left) Chicago Aerial Survey, (top center) Georg Gerster/Rapho-Guillumette, (top right) Kitty Anderson, (center left) Bay Area Rapid Transit, (center center) UPI-Compix, (center right) Elihu Blotnick/BBM Associates, (bottom left) Lorenzo Gunn, (bottom center) Bay Area Rapid Transit, (bottom right) Lorenzo Gunn.

Chapter 3

58—Bruce Dean; 61—Michael Lowy; 63—(top) Charles Bellin/Photophile, (bottom) Doyle Dane Bernbach Advertising for General Telephone & Electronics, Art Director: Domenick Marino; 65—Courtesy of Piliavin and Briar; 69— Copyright © New York Times, March 29, 1973; 74—American Institute of Public Opinion (The Gallup Poll); 77—(top left) Elihu Blotnick/BBM Associates, (top center, top right, center left) Payson Stevens, (center center) Aerial Photographers, Inc., New York, (center right, bottom left, bottom right) Payson Stevens.

Chapter 4

84—Bruce Dean; 86—(top) Copyright ® New York Times, Jan. 19, 1968, (bottom) Hecht, Vidmer Inc. for Narcotics & Drug Abuse Center; 88—Reprinted by permission of Grove Press, Inc. Copyright ® 1959 by William S. Burroughs; 89—(left) National Audiovisual Center, (right) Culver Pictures; 91—(top) Culver Pictures, (bottom) adapted from U.S. Bureau of Narcotics and Dangerous Drugs, *Drug Abuse and Law Enforcement Statistics;* 94—Rosenfeld, Sirowitz & Lawson for WABC-TV, Art Director: Stan Block, Writer: Adam Hanft, Director of Advertising and Press Information at WABC-TV: Jon Olken; 98–99—adapted from J. Fort, M.D., *The Pleasure Seekers,* Bobbs-Merrill, 1969, pp. 236–243; 103—Fred Bauman; 104—Universal Television; 106—County of Los Angeles Health Department Alcoholic Rehabilitation Center; 112—The Advertising Council; 118—(top) Curt Gunther/Camera 5, Schick Center, courtesy of Arnold Carr Public Relations.

Chapter 5

122—Bruce Dean; 124—(top) The Bettmann Archive, (bottom left and right) Culver Pictures; 126—(top) Associated Press; 128—(top) Bill Bridges; 129—adapted from U.S. Department of Health, Education and Welfare, National Institute of Mental Health, *Statistical Note 81;* 131—Karl Nicholason; 132—adapted from Norman Bradburn and David Caplovitz, *Reports on Happiness,* Aldine, 1965, p. 9; 134—adapted from U.S. Department of Health Education and Welfare, National Institute of Mental Health, *Utilization of Mental Health Facilities 1971,* 1973; 136—(bottom) Doyle Dane Bernback, Inc. for Mobile Corporation; 140—Steve McCarroll; 141—UPI-Compix; 146—Alan Mercer; 147—Charles Gatewood; 150—Eric Aerts; 151—Bill Bridges; 152—Ron Thal; 153—John Oldenkamp/IBOL.

Chapter 6

156—Bruce Dean, poem # 57 by Lao Tsu, from *Tao te Ching,* translation by Feng & English, published by Vintage Press, reprinted with the permission of Random House, Inc.; 158—(top) Copyright ® New York Times, Nov. 23, 1972, (bottom) adapted from Federal Bureau of Investigation, *Crime in the U.S. 1972,* UNIFORM CRIME REPORTS; 160—Wally Arrington/Black Star; 161—Hays/Monkmeyer Press Photo Service; 164—adapted from Federal Bureau of Investigation, *Crime in the U.S. 1972,* p. 115, UNIFORM CRIME REPORTS; 171—(top) Steve Rose/Nancy Palmer Photo Agency, (center) Arthur Sirdofsky, (bottom) Sugi/BBM Associates; 177—Philip Zimbardo; 182—(left) *Zorba the Greek,* 20th Century Fox; 185—UPI-Compix; 186—Young & Rubicam for the Legal Aid Society, New York; 188–189—Copyright ® 1974, Los Angeles Times, reprinted with permission; 192—adapted from Keith Melville, "Prisons Are For People," *The Sciences,* Vol. 13, No. 9, November 1973, p. 15, Copyright ® The New York Academy of Sciences. Reprinted with permission; 193—Danny Lyon/Magnum Photos; 195—Danny Lyon/Magnum Photos.

Chapter 7

200—Bruce Dean; 205—(top) adapted from United Nations, *Demographic Yearbook,* 1955–1967, (bottom) adapted from Federal Bureau of Investigation, UNITED CRIME REPORTS, 1968; 206—(left) adapted from Law Enforcement Assistance Administration, (right) Paul Sequeira; 208—(top) adapted from the Task Force Victim-Offender survey; (bottom) Marc & Evelyne Bernheim/ Woodfin Camp and Associates; 212—(left) Charles Harbutt/ Magnum Photos, (top right) Homer Page, New York, (bottom right) UPI-Compix; 213—Gaynor & Ducas Inc., for Storer Broadcasting Company; 216—Michael Abramson; 217—The Bettmann Archive; 218–219—(bottom) Copyright ® by Jules Feiffer. Reprinted with permission of Publishers-Hall Syndicate; 221—(top) UPI-Compix, (bottom) Department of Justice, LEAA Newsletter; 224—Bernice Abbott; 225—George Gardner.

Chapter 8

230—Bruce Dean, poem LXXIII by Lady Suo from Kenneth Rexroth, *One Hundred Poems From the Japanese.* All rights reserved. Reprinted by permission of New Directions Publishing Corporation; 232—Dorka Raynor/Rapho-Guillumette; 233—Newsweek Inc.; 237—adapted from Department of Health, Education and Welfare, Center for Disease Control, *Morbidity and Mortality: Annual Supplement. Summary 1972,* Vol. 21, No. 53, p. 4; 239—(top) Richter & Mracky-Bates, Inc. for KABC-TV, Art Director: Stanley Davis, Copywriter: Carol Corbett, Account Supervisor: Robert M. Klosterman, Director of Advertising and Public Relations for KABC-TV: Jack Brembeck, (bottom) Curt Gunther/Camera 5; 240—(top) Sherry Suris/ Rapho-Guillumette, (bottom) *Fortune and Mens Eyes,* Twentieth Century Fox; 243—(top) Henri Cartier-Bresson/ Magnum Photos, (bottom) Copyright ® New York Times Jan. 15, 1974; 247—(top) adapted from J. M. Tanner, *Growth at Adolescence, Copyright ®* 1955 by Blackwell Scientific Pub. Ltd., (bottom) Alan Mercer; 249—Bernie Cleff; 255—(top) Family Planning Association, London, (bottom) Charles Gatewood; 256—Charles Moore/Black Star; 257—Carole Graham/BBM Associates.

Chapter 9

264—Bruce Dean, quote from *Haiku Harvest, Japanese Haiku Series IV* translation by Peter Beilenson and Harry Behn, 1962, p. 45, Copyright ® Peter Pauper Press; Copyright ® 1974, Los Angeles Times. Reprinted with permission; 269—(bottom) UPI-Compix; 270—Nancy Hamilton; 274—Henri Cartier-Bresson/Magnum Photos; 275—Dennis Brack/Black Star; 279—(top) adapted from Seymour Lipsit & Richard Bendix, *Social Mobility in Industrial Society,* University of California Press, 1958, (bottom) Doyle Dane & Bernback for Volkswagen of America, Inc.; 281—created by Harlan Lewin, 1974; 285—(top) Paul Sequeira, (center) Chicago Aerial Survey, (bottom) Paul Sequeira; 286—(top) adapted from U.S. Bureau of the Census, *Current Population Reports: Consumer Income,*—Series P-60, No. 80., Oct. 1971, p. 105, (bottom) UPI-Compix; 288—(top) Home Savings and Loan Association, Los Angeles, (bottom) Sepp Seitz/ Magnum Photos; 290—(top) William J. Warren, Los Angeles, for OEO; 294—Ken Heyman; 296—The Chase Manhattan Bank, New York; 297—Paul Sequeira.

Chapter 10

302—Bruce Dean; 304—(top left) from a Letter to Sanchez, 1493, Rare Book Division, New York Public Library; (top right) National Anthropological Archives, Smithsonian Institution, (bottom left) National Archives

(#111–SC–82385), (bottom right) Office of Economic Opportunity; 308–UPI-Compix; 311–(top) National Archives (#210–GC–160), (bottom) UPI-Compix; 313–Henri Cartier-Bresson/Magnum Photos; 314–(left) Brown Brothers, (right) BBC Radio Times Hulton Picture Library; 315–UPI-Compix; 321–(top) Brown Brothers, (bottom) UPI-Compix; 322–UPI-Compix; 323–Columbia Broadcasting Company; 325–adapted from T. W. Adorno, E. Frenkel-Brunswick, D. J. Levinson, and R. N. Sandford (eds), *The Authoritarian Personality,* Harper & Brothers, 1950, pp. 225, 110–111, 68–69, and 158; 330–(top and center) UPI-Compix, (bottom) Wide World Photos, Inc.; 332–(top) Paul Sequeira, (bottom) Michael Abramson.

Chapter 11
336–Bruce Dean; 339–UPI-Compix; 341–(top) adapted from Department of Labor Women's Bureau, *Handbook of Women Workers,* Bulletin 294, pp. 24, 26, 41, 1969, (bottom) Sid Sattler/Nancy Palmer Photo Agency; 343–adapted from U.S. Department of Commerce, Bureau of the Census, *Current Population Reports,* P–60, No. 80, 1971; 348–(top) Burk Uzzle/Magnum Photos, (bottom) UPI-Compix; 349–Reprinted from pp. 45–46 of *Around the Corner* by Mabel O'Donnell. Copyright © 1966 by Harper & Row Publishers, Inc. Reprinted with permission; 351–(left) Dave Snazuk, courtesy of *Womensports,* (right) Bud Lee, courtesy of *Womensports;* 354–(left) UPI-Compix, (right) Department of Housing & Urban Development; 355–Copyright © New York Times, March 23, 1972; 357–(top) Bettye Lane, (bottom) N.W. Ayer & Son, Inc. for U.S. Department of the Army.

Chapter 12
364–Bruce Dean; 366–(top) The Bettmann Archive, (bottom) Geahard Julius/Photophile; 367–(top) Bill Owens/BBM Associates, (bottom) N. R. Farbman, *Life* Magazine, Copyright © Time, Inc.; 370–(top) courtesy of Cove Haven Resort, (bottom) adapted from *Population and the American Future,* The Report of the Commission on Population Growth and the American Future, p. 81, Table 9.1, from Ritchie H. Reed and Susan McIntosh, Cost of Children, 1972; 371–UPI-Compix; 373–(top) adapted from B. C. Rollins and H. Feldman, "Marital Satisfaction Over the Family Life Cycle"; (bottom) adapted from E. Sullerot, *Women, Society and Change,* Copyright © 1971, McGraw-Hill Company. Used with permission; 376–adapted United Nations, *Demographic Yearbook 1972;* 378–(top) Courtesy of Dr. Robert Reed, Fort Scott, Kansas, (bottom) Photophile; 380–Copyright © 1969 by International Compatibility, Inc.; 381–Gordon Menzie/Photophile, 383–Copyright © by Jules Feiffer, reprinted with permission of Publishers-Hall Syndicate; 385–(top) Peter Goodman/BBM Associates, (bottom) Bruce Roberts/Rapho-Guillumette.

Chapter 13
390–Bruce Dean, poem from *Zen Poems of China and Japan,* translation Copyright © 1973 by Lucien Stryk, Takashi Ikemoto, and Taigan Takayama. Reprinted by permission of Doubleday & Company, Inc.; 393–(top left) Copyright © Johan Maurits Van Nassau, Mauritshuis, The Hague, (top right) *Rembrandt Self-Portrait, 1640,*

reproduced by courtesy of the Trustees, The National Gallery, London, (bottom left) Duke of Sutherland Collection on loan to the National Gallery of Scotland, (bottom right) *Rembrandt Self-Portrait 1669,* reproduced by courtesy of the Trustees, The National Gallery, London; 395–(top) Copyright © 1974, The Los Angeles Times. Reprinted with permission, (bottom) BBC Radio Times Hulton Picture Library; 398–(top) Alan Mercer; Courtesy of Gaynor & Ducas, New York, for Storer Broadcasting Company; 403–(top) Alan Mercer, (bottom) Courtesy of Vacations for the Aging, New York; 405–(top) adapted from *Population and the American Future,* The Report of the Commission on Population Growth and the American Future, p. 65, Figure 7.2, from the U.S. Bureau of the Census, (bottom) adapted from U.S. Department of Commerce, Bureau of the Census, *Current Population,* series P–20, P–57, P–60, and unpublished data. Labor force, beginning 1960, U.S. Bureau of Labor Statistics, *Employment and Earnings,* monthly; 406–adapted from Health, Education and Welfare, U.S. National Center for Health Statistics, *U.S. Life Tables & Actuarial Tables, 1939–41, 1949–51, 1959–61,* and *Vital Statistics of the U.S.,* annual; 407–Paul Sequeira; 411–(top) World Medical News, (bottom left) Rita Freed/Nancy Palmer Photo Agency; 412–(top) Paul Sequeira, (bottom) UPI-Compix.

Chapter 14
416–Bruce Dean; 419–(top) Jim Jowers/Nancy Palmer Photo Agency, (bottom) adapted from Richard A. Easterlin, "The American Baby Boom in Historical Perspective," *Population, Labor Force and Long Swings in Economic Growth,* National Bureau of Economic Research, 1968; 420–(top) adapted from (prior to 1900) U.S. Department of Commerce, Bureau of the Census, *Historical Statistics of the U.S. Colonial Times to 1957, 1961, (1900 to 2020) Current Population Reports,* series P–25, (2021 to 2050) unpublished Census Bureau projections, (beyond 2050) extrapolation; (bottom) adapted from (prior to 1917) a selection from Figure 10 in Ansley Coale and Melvin Zelnik, *New Estimates of Fertility and Population in the United States,* Copyright © 1963 by Princeton University Press, p. 38. Reprinted with permission of Princeton University Press. (1917 to 1968) U.S. Department of Health Education and Welfare, National Center for Health Statistics, *Natality Statistics Analysis,* series 21, no. 19, 1970. (1969–1971), U.S. Department of Commerce, Bureau of the Census, *Current Population Reports,* series P–23, No. 36, "Fertility Indicators: 1970," 1971. The figure for 1971 is based on an unpublished Census staff estimate; 421–adapted from United Nations and U.S. State Department; 422–(top) Margaret Bourke-White/Time-Life Picture Agency, (bottom) Charles Harbutt/Magnum Photos; 423–adapted from United Nations and U.S. State Department; 424–(top) Marc Riboud/Magnum Photos, (bottom) Bruno Barcey/Magnum Photos; 425 and 427–adapted from United Nations and U.S. State Department; 428–(top) adapted from Jay R. Mandle, "The Decline of Mortality in British Guinea, 1911–1960," *Demography,* 1970; (bottom) UNICEF, photo by Jack Liwg; 429–adapted from United Nations and U.S. State Department; 430–UNICEF; 431–Henri Cartier-Bresson/Magnum Photos; 432–Caio Mario Garrubba/Rapho-Guillumette; 433–UNICEF; 434–Georg Gerster/Rapho-Guillumette.

513

Chapter 15
436—Bruce Dean; 439—UPI-Compix; 440—UPI-Compix; 441—Bruce Davidson/Magnum Photos; 443—(top) John Dawson after Charles F. Powers and Andrew Robertson, Copyright ©, *Scientific American,* November 1966, p. 100. All rights reserved, (center) Mike Murphy, U.S. Army Corps of Engineers, San Francisco, (bottom) Richard Carter; 445—(top) adapted from Donnella H. Meadows, Dennis L. Meadows, Jorgen Randers, William W. Behrens III, *The Limits of Growth:* A Report for the Club of Rome's Project on the Predicament of Mankind. A Potomac Associates book published by Universe Books, 1972; 446—from *The World of Biology* by P. William Davis and Eldra Pearl Solomon, Table 24–1, Copyright © 1974 by McGraw-Hill, Inc. Used with permission of McGraw-Hill Book company; 447—UPI-Compix; 450—John Dawson; 451—Kenneth Murray/Nancy Palmer Photo Agency; 452—(top) adapted from Donnella H. Meadows, Dennis L. Meadows, Jorgen Randers, William W. Behrens III, *The Limits of Growth:* A Report for the Club of Rome's Project on the Predicament of Mankind, Table 4, A Potomac Associates book published by Universe Books, 1972; 456—(top) Danny Lyon/Magnum Photos, (bottom) from Paolo Soleri, *Arcology: City in the Image of Man,* Copyright © 1969 by MIT Press, used with permission of the publisher; 459—(bottom) UPI-Compix; 460—(left) Asahi Shimbum, (center) Syndication International/Photo Trends, (right) UPI-Compix; 461—UPI-Compix; 464—American Can Company, Annual Report 1970.

Social Problems Book Team

Roger G. Emblen, *Publisher*
Rose Fujimoto, *Publishing Coordinator*
Cynthia A. Farden, *Project Editor*
Elaine B. Kleiss, *Associate Editor*
Michael Mendelsohn, *Designer*
Richard N. Carter, *Associate Designer*
Linda Rill, *Graphics Research Editor*
Chris Sawyer, *Production Supervisor*
Howard Smith, *Marketing Development Manager, Social Sciences*